Unravelled Dreams

One of the greatest hopes and expectations that accompanied American colonialism – from its earliest incarnation – was that Atlantic settlers would be able to locate new sources of raw silk with which to satiate the boundless desire for luxurious fabrics in European markets. However, in spite of the great upheavals and achievements of Atlantic plantation, this ambition would never be fulfilled. By taking the commercial failure of silk seriously and examining numerous experiments across New Spain, New France, British North America, and the early United States, Ben Marsh reveals new insights into aspiration, labour, environment, and economy in these societies. Each devised its own dreams and plans of cultivation, framed by the particularities of cultures and landscapes. Writ large, these dreams would unravel one by one: the attempts to introduce silkworms across the Atlantic world ultimately constituted a step too far, marking out the limits of Europeans' seemingly unbounded power.

Ben Marsh is Reader in History at the University of Kent. He is the author of the award-winning *Georgia's Frontier Women: Female Fortunes in a Southern Colony* (2007) and *Understanding and Teaching the Age of Revolutions* (2017), and has published widely on early and revolutionary American history. His research on silk has featured in several exhibitions, including *Enlightened Princesses: Britain and Europe, 1700–1820* (Yale Center for British Art and Historic Royal Palaces, 2017), and he won the UK Textile Society's Natalie Rothstein Memorial Prize in 2013.

Unravelled Dreams

Silk and the Atlantic World, 1500–1840

Ben Marsh

University of Kent

CAMBRIDGE
UNIVERSITY PRESS

CAMBRIDGE
UNIVERSITY PRESS

University Printing House, Cambridge CB2 8BS, United Kingdom

One Liberty Plaza, 20th Floor, New York, NY 10006, USA

477 Williamstown Road, Port Melbourne, VIC 3207, Australia

314 321, 3rd Floor, Plot 3, Splendor Forum, Jasola District Centre, New Delhi – 110025, India

79 Anson Road, #06–04/06, Singapore 079906

Cambridge University Press is part of the University of Cambridge.

It furthers the University's mission by disseminating knowledge in the pursuit of education, learning, and research at the highest international levels of excellence.

www.cambridge.org
Information on this title: www.cambridge.org/9781108418287
DOI: 10.1017/9781108289672

© Ben Marsh 2020

First published 2020

Printed in the United Kingdom by TJ International Ltd, Padstow Cornwall

A catalogue record for this publication is available from the British Library.

Library of Congress Cataloging-in-Publication Data
Names: Marsh, Ben, 1976– author.
Title: Unravelled dreams : silk and the Atlantic world, 1500–1840 / Ben Marsh.
Description: Cambridge, United Kingdom ; New York, NY : Cambridge University Press, 2020. | Includes bibliographical references and index.
Identifiers: LCCN 2019048995 (print) | LCCN 2019048996 (ebook) | ISBN 9781108418287 (hardback) | ISBN 9781108289672 (epub)
Subjects: LCSH: Silk industry – Atlantic Ocean Region – History. | Atlantic Ocean Region – Commerce – History.
Classification: LCC HD9928.A787 M37 2020 (print) | LCC HD9928.A787 (ebook) | DDC 338.4/7677390918210903–dc23
LC record available at https://lccn.loc.gov/2019048995
LC ebook record available at https://lccn.loc.gov/2019048996

ISBN 978-1-108-41828-7 Hardback

For Lils, who is my glorious silk, and for Alfie, Thomas, Ella, and Tess, who are my industrious, marvellous worms.

Contents

The plate section can be found between pp. 274 and 275.

Colour Plates

Figures

Maps

Tables

Acknowledgements

This book and the fragmented subject matter that it deals with have required considerable support, advice, and patience to reach a satisfactory terminal point. At times over the years, I have felt much like my silkworm subjects – scrabbling around for sustenance and consuming incessantly (in libraries and archives), shedding skin (from chapters), pausing seemingly inexplicably (over teaching terms), fluttering majestically (during research leave and fellowships), and attempting to transform these leaves into something that hangs together. It has been a deep and abiding pleasure to have been involved in the many seminars, panels, conferences, collaborations, symposia, forums, and venues great and small, all of which have helped to shape my thinking and vastly improved my yield, for what it is. I am hugely thankful to all the many friends and colleagues amongst overlapping scholarly communities who have encouraged me, guided me, picked me up, inspected and inspired me, checked my temperature, defended me from predators, and allowed me to spin ideas in one form or another.

You will know who you are, and if you are not here, you should be: Lesley, Clare, Brenda, Mary, Giorgio, Luca, Dagmar, John, José, Claudio, Roberto, Maxine, Daryl, Amanda, Donald, Rudi, Vijaya, Angela, Robert, Karolina, William, Martin, Beverly, Hanna, Lauren, Gordon, Annie, Andy, Bartolomé, Lauric, Suzanne, Evan, Trevor, Nicholas, Hermann, Claudia, Tim, Allan, Elodie, Naomi, Owen, Bertrand, Phil, Colin, Emma, Phia, Robin, Mike, Alasdair, Alastair, Richard, Michael, Stuart, George, Ruben, Ambrogio, Karen, Charlotte, Becky, Noah, Jasmine, James, Sheila, Hugh, Kenneth, Aske, Nuala, Frank, Emma, Simon, Marina, other Simon, Natalie, Brad, Tom, Rachel, Sophie, Inge, Betty, Perry, Ken, Jonathan, Jane, Chris, Geoff, Will, Peter, Steve, Sarah, Zara, Jo, Kate, Lynn, Marise, Cindy, Catherine, Erika, Jennifer, Lori, Karin, Chris, Ron, Sally, Michael, Paul, Fredrika, Josh, Allison, Sara, Catherine, David, other Chris, Janice, Sharla, Shaun, Sarah, other Hugh, Jack, Laura, Meg, Beau, Kimberly. Thanks for the eyes, ears, references, and suggestions.

I would like to extend particular thanks to the funding bodies and organisations who have invested in my historical pursuit of failed endeavours, for I have been the glad recipient of research support from the Arts and Humanities Research Council, the Pasold Research Fund, the Royal Society of Edinburgh, the Carnegie Trust, and the Library Company of Philadelphia, as well as the beneficiary of research time, resources, and expertise from the University of Stirling, where this project began, and the University of Kent, where it ended. In between, I have also benefited from the wisdom, bibliographic recommendations, and warmth and camaraderie of curators, archivists, and librarians at a host of repositories; particular thanks are owed to the American Antiquarian Society, the Beinecke Library, the Library Company of Philadelphia, the Royal Society of Arts, the Archivo de Indias, the Archives Nationales d'Outre-Mer, the John D. Rockefeller Library, the Textile Society, and the kind people who put me up or who put up with me while away at these and other locations. I have aired some of my research as journal articles and a chapter in an edited volume, so I would like to extend my thanks not only for permission to draw from them in this fuller form, but to the editors and their readers for offering heartening enthusiasm and valuable suggestions during the process. Portions of Chapters 6, 9, and 11 were respectively published as 'Silk Hopes in Colonial South Carolina' in *The Journal of Southern History* (Nov. 2012); '"The Honour of the Thing": Silk Culture in Eighteenth-Century Pennsylvania' in *Threads of Global Desire: Silk in the Pre-Modern World*, edited by Dagmar Schäfer, Giorgio Riello and Luca Molà (Boydell and Brewer, 2018); and 'The Republic's New Clothes: Making Silk in the Antebellum United States', in *Agricultural History* (Fall 2012).

Huge thanks also to Michael Watson, Emily Sharp, the insightful and judicious reviewers of various drafts of the manuscript, copy-editor Frances Tye, and the production team at Cambridge University Press (particularly Raghavi Govindane and Ruth Boyes), all of whose patience and stamina I have tested in different ways. This project ended up situated on the vertices where numerous subfields meet – including the histories of textiles, trade, labour, environment, technology, animal studies, and Atlantic imperialism – and it ended up surveying unwieldy chunks of time and space, looking for very small things from a high altitude. Considering that I dislike sharp points and am wary of heights, this has often taken me beyond my comfort zone, and I am mindful that there remain numerous imperfections, many features overlooked and several likely failures of interpretation or translation, which are my own, and for which I apologise. But we have to start and end somewhere.

1 Prologue

An article now cultivated in each of the four quarters of the globe: this is silk! The work of that little worm which clothes mankind with the leaves of trees digested in its entrails. Silk! That double prodigy of nature and of art.

Abbé Raynal, 1770[1]

Spontaneous Generation and Marvellous Transformations

Under magnification, the fibres of cotton, linen, and wool appear twisted, hatched, knobbly or scaled. In contrast, silk strands were described in 1665 by the first English micrographer as 'small, round, hard, transparent, and to their bigness proportionably stiff, so as each filament preserves its proper Figure, and consequently its vivid reflection intire'. So Robert Hooke, a man hardly renowned for his emotional or descriptive eloquence, could not help marvelling at the fibres of silk, which 'above those of hairy Stuffs, or Linnen', appeared as if translucent cylinders of coloured gemstones. The same year, across the English Channel, French agronomist Christophle Isnard determined 'that nature worked to make silkworms incomparably more admirable than all the other animals on the earth', going so far as to compare the silkworm and its output to the glorious transformations and resurrection of Jesus Christ. His fascination was mirrored by that of a gifted teenage artist and naturalist in Frankfurt, Maria Sibylla Merian, for whom the life cycle of the silkworm had already inspired the beginning of a long and distinguished transatlantic career in entomology and the study of metamorphoses.[2] These observations,

---

[1] Abbé Raynal, *A Philosophical and Political History of the British Settlements and Trade in North America, from the French of Abbé Raynal, in Two Volumes* (Aberdeen: J. Boyle, 1779), 1: 282–3.

[2] Robert Hooke, *Micrographia: Or, Some Physiological Descriptions of Minute Bodies Made by Magnifying Glasses. With Observations and Inquiries Thereupon* (London: Printed by J. Martyn and J. Allestry, 1665), 6, 7, 159; Christophle Isnard, *Mémoires et instructions pour le plant des meuriers, nourriture des vers à soye & l'art de filer* ... (Paris: Chez l'auteur et

bouncing around northern Europe in the 1660s, reflected the growing reach of the humble silkworm into European societies, publications, and imaginations – and above all, into European materiality. By the end of the seventeenth century, silkworms and their prized product were positioned at the cutting edge of fashion, and increasingly at the cutting edge of science and technology. They were already instrumental to Europe's burgeoning transoceanic commercial activity in Asia, and were becoming the subjects of increasing literary attention at home, since first finding their mouthpiece in the Latin poetry of Italian humanist Marco Girolamo Vida in 1527. Vida had begun his tribute by bemoaning how, for the earliest silkworms, 'No honours to their fruitless works were paid', their threads hanging unused and unnoticed.[3]

This book sets out to show that silkworms were also at the cutting edge of Atlantic imperialism between the sixteenth and nineteenth centuries. Though their traces often hang unnoticed, they are meaningful not because raw silk became a successful American commercial product, but because, in spite of almost every conceivable encouragement across different European powers and within the fledgling United States, it ultimately did not. It is fitting, of course, that the fields of commodity history and Atlantic trade have concentrated on the 'winners': the long list of transformative raw materials extracted and exported from the Americas – the silver, sugar, tobacco, rice, and cotton. The object of this work is not to repackage silk as a successful Atlantic product, but rather to offer a deep and wide-ranging interrogation of its failure.

The history of failure is something of an inbuilt blind spot for historians, whose eyes naturally gravitate to development-oriented narratives. Economic history, no less than political history, has been written by the winners – and the Atlantic world in particular has tended to succumb to the tyranny of supply and demand. But by taking the commercial failure of silk seriously, historicising it, and examining the numerous experiments (large and small) across New Spain, New France, many small corners of northern Europe, and especially British North America and the early United States, we can locate new insights into the determinative matrix of aspiration, labour, environment, and economy in these societies. Each devised its own dreams and plans of cultivation, framed by the compound particularities of cultures and landscapes. Writ large, these dreams would unravel one by one: the attempts to introduce silkworms to new regions around the Atlantic world – powered by

chez Georges Soly, 1665), 284, 287, 292, 300; Elisabeth Rücker and William T. Stearn, *Maria Sibylla Merian in Surinam* (London: Pion, 1982), xi, 8, 10, 85.
[3] Marcus Hieronymus Vida and Samuel Pullein, *The Silkworm: A Poem, in Two Books*, trans. Samuel Pullein (Dublin, 1750), 17.

Europeans' consuming appetite for their fibre – ultimately constituted a step too far, marking out the limits of Europeans' seemingly unbounded power. That they were bewildered by this failure, and for over 300 years sought to counter environmental and demographic odds stacked against them, turning from one site to another, and mobilising every theory and workforce that they could muster, was a profoundly energising force. It opened up creative models of colonialism, exchange, domestic production, and regional interconnection – some of which would disappear altogether, some fall into myths that would be recycled, and others which would become spurs to more commercially successful projects as people, policies, and ideas were recycled from silk to other more competitive and achievable products. Raw silk was the nearly cochineal in New Spain, the nearly tobacco in Virginia, the nearly rice, the nearly indigo, the nearly cotton; it left as its tombstones neglected non-native mulberry trees scattered across multiple continents.

To pause and assess how they got there is firstly to recognise that the Atlantic world had some defining features – its vast distance, its spread, its cultural hybridisation, and in large parts of the post-contact Americas, its societies' existential fragility and manufacturing deficits. Yet at the same time, the mulberries, transplanted by dreams of silk production, bear witness to how the Atlantic world and its evolution was always bound up inescapably with global developments. That raw silk did not become one of the iconic products of the Americas had global implications. Whether the dying of this 'butterfly' in the New World had the power to help generate floods of trade around the Indian Ocean, to consolidate silk production around the Mediterranean, or to cause the revisiting of European beliefs and technologies, is impossible to prove empirically. But even without far-flung counterfactuals, this chaotic history of successive episodes in the Americas underscores how each of them was enmeshed in transnational and extra-Atlantic circuits: Native American uptake was compromised by Eurasian disease, Spanish attempts were interrupted by Pacific supplies, French efforts were trumped by domestic production, English opportunities were undercut by East Indian trade, American hopes were compromised by international manufactures.

The unravelled dreams of silk therefore help us to see the Atlantic past as fractal – even if its history tends towards the linear, or triangular. Fractals, such as snowflakes or crystals, are objects in which the same patterns occur over and again at different scales and sizes. In the Atlantic world patterns repeated themselves, with subtle variations, defined above all by questions of environment, labour, and imperial demand. Commodity projection and successful production appeared natural and progressive, a fixed feature which served from the earliest encounters as a foundation stone for claims to European sovereignty. But beneath the appearance were variables of huge complexity and dynamism, which helped shape the particularities of the Atlantic world itself, and instructed its tendency to be self-similar across different scales. My larger hope is that this exposition of one commodity's prolonged transoceanic ordeals will encourage others to do likewise: to root around the middens of the past, the archives of failed endeavours, and use them to get closer to the sense of contingency that contemporaries felt about the places, people, clothes, creatures, and forests around them.[4]

Published works proposing the introduction of sericulture (silk cultivation) in the Spanish, French, and British empires would often stress the miraculous effect that silk raising promised to have on the political economy of states that were dependent on imports. Authors and poets naturally enjoyed the opportunity to play on the silkworms' personal metamorphoses (from larvae to caterpillars to cocoons to moths) and to compare them to the hoped-for metamorphosis of the state, through domestication or colonialism. Silkworms were an influential entomological analogy invoked in the service of European national promotion and self-critique, especially in the century after 1650, as naturalists came to better understand and share their insights about the functioning of the insect world.[5]

To take one example, silkworms were directly involved in the debunking of the archaic theory of spontaneous generation (the long-standing idea that organisms could emerge from non-living matter), when the Italian naturalist and court physician to the Medici grand dukes of Tuscany, Francesco Redi, spent a heroic amount of time watching flies lay eggs and observing caterpillars' activities on trees. Redi's 1668 work explicitly repudiated the claim that 'the mulberry tree produces the silkworm, on being impregnated with the seed of any chance animal', which had been advanced by the eccentric German Jesuit scholar Athanasius Kircher amongst others (and had featured in many publications trying to

---

[4] For selected considerations: Bethany Aram and Bartolomé Yun Casalilla, *Global Goods and the Spanish Empire, 1492–1824: Circulation, Resistance and Diversity* (London: Palgrave Macmillan, 2014); E. D. Melillo, 'Global Entomologies: Insects, Empires, and the 'Synthetic Age' in World History', *Past & Present* 223, no. 1 (1 May 2014): 233–70; Scott A. Sandage, *Born Losers: A History of Failure in America* (Cambridge, MA: Harvard University Press, 2005). For an excellent review essay on approaches to Atlantic history and its distinctive features: Cécile Vidal, 'Pour une histoire globale du monde atlantique ou des histoires connectées dans et au-delà du monde atlantique?' *Annales. Histoire, Sciences Sociales* 67, no. 2 (2012): 279–300.

[5] Janice Neri, *The Insect and the Image: Visualizing Nature in Early Modern Europe, 1500–1700* (Minneapolis: University of Minnesota Press, 2011).

advance silk cultivation). Redi described the suggestion that silkworms could spontaneously emerge from the decayed carcasses of mules or calves as a 'fabulous belief' ascribable to an elegant passage in Girolamo Vida's poem, but with no foundation in fact. Redi proved by experiment that his mulberry-crammed rotting flesh produced nothing but maggots, which became flies![6] 'Do not marvel at all these strange births and transformations', he warned in a moment of existential relativity amidst the Medici and the maggots, 'for we ourselves, are nothing more than caterpillars and worms'.[7] But between 1500 and 1840, political econo-mists and consumers showed little of the humility that he advocated, as silk became an increasingly visible part of how states and individuals dressed themselves up.

No experienced silk raisers can have lent credence to the theory of spontaneous generation, for it can never have worked, but it was nonetheless recirculated and repurposed. A New Spanish planter, Gonzalo de Las Casas, in late-sixteenth-century Oaxaca (Mexico) cast doubt on the theory, but used it to make a point by suggesting it may have been propounded by ignorant or devious Moors.[8] For their part, the French in the early eighteenth century attributed the suggestion to the Spanish.[9] Indeed, such theories of spontaneous generation or directions for 'abiogenesis' had surprising longevity, with the method of overfeeding a young cow mulberry leaves being recommended in Pennsylvania as late as 1770.[10] Only with the nineteenth-century experiments of microbiologist Louis Pasteur did those remaining believers in spontaneous generation relent (by which stage nobody was slaughtering leaf-satiated calves).[11]

The early spread of international scientific research into the organism was actually intimately connected to wider ambitions of growing silk around the Atlantic basin – of spontaneously generating strange births

[6] Francesco Redi, *Experiments on the Generation of Insects*, ed. Mab Bigelow (Chicago: Open Court, 1909), 109, 123. The original was published as *Esperienze intorno alla generazione degl'insetti* (Florence, 1668).

[7] Redi, *Experiments*, 103.

[8] Gonzalo De las Casas, *Arte nuevo para criar seda*, ed. Antonio Garrido Aranda (Granada: Servicio de Publicaciones de la Universidad de Granada, 1996), 210, 229v–230.

[9] Noël Chomel, *Dictionnaire oeconomique* (Lyons: Printed by the author & Pierre Thened, 1709), 71. Spanish culpability was repeated by the English author Henry Barham in 1719 but with the theory dismissed with the phrase 'Credat Judaeus'. Henry Barham, *An Essay upon the Silk-Worm: Containing Many Improvements upon This Curious Subject; Together with Large Collections from the Most Approved Authors* (London: Printed for J. Betterham and T. Bickerton, 1719), 161.

[10] *Pennsylvania Gazette*, 12 April 1770, p. 1.

[11] Agnes Ullmann, 'Pasteur-Koch: Distinctive Ways of Thinking about Infectious Diseases', *Microbe (American Society for Microbiology)* 2, no. 8 (2007): 383–7.

and transformations in silk industries themselves. In the late 1660s, the secretary of the Royal Society (comprising leading intellectual figures in England) reached out to Italian specialists to ask them to contribute to the frontiers of biological and colonial knowledge, inviting them to reflect on new or notable features of 'especially the *silkworm* and its productions'. The upshot was Marcello Malpighi's remarkable 60,000 word treatise, *Dissertatio epistolica de bombyce*, the first systematic dissection of an insect, which offered a foundation for many of the descriptive and illustrative conventions of modern biology and scientific illustration (see Plate 1). Upon its production, the Royal Society immediately conferred the status of Fellow upon Malpighi, while rivals such as Jan Swammerdam (another debunker of spontaneous generation) queried several of the specific claims. While such pioneering and celebrated moments in European scientific production have rightly been judged significant, seldom has their timing or content been linked to the plantation of mulberries in the American colony of Virginia or to bizarre questions about the impact of feeding silkworms on lettuce (that had been thrown up by English experimentation).[12] Yet contemporaries such as the diarist and horticulturist John Evelyn had little doubt about the interconnections: he had drawn on Virginian insights for the chapter on mulberry trees in his major survey of forestry, had welcomed Malpighi's 'incomparable History of the Silkworme' in 1669, and went on to record in February 1672 (as a member of the Council of Foreign Plantations) that 'we enter'd on enquiries about improving the Plantations by silks'.[13] His comments reflected a wider appreciation that timeworn theories, like decaying old silk centres, stood ready to be eclipsed in the dynamic crucible of a New World.

In the long run of course, silkworms failed to effect a marvellous transformation upon the Atlantic economy. But they paid testament to the experimental spirit, profound adaptability, and indomitable conviction of early American communities. By placing transatlantic efforts to generate silk under the microscope, we see how they were differently constructed as the Atlantic world evolved, and begin to understand why

---

[12] Matthew Cobb, 'Malpighi, Swammerdam and the Colourful Silkworm: Replication and Visual Representation in Early Modern Science', *Annals of Science* 59, no. 2 (January 2002): 111–47; Marcello Malpighi, *Dissertatio epistolica de bombyce* (London: Martyn & Allestry, 1669).

[13] John Evelyn, *Diary and Correspondence of John Evelyn, F. R. S.*, ed. William Bray, 4 vols. (London: Henry Colburn, 1882), 309, 357; John Evelyn, *Sylva: Or a Discourse of Forest Trees*, 4th ed. (London: Arthur Doubleday & Co., 1706). For a consideration of Evelyn's own mulberry trees at Sayes Court Park in Deptford, Karen Liljenberg, 'In Search of John Evelyn's Mulberry', 3 August 2016 at www.moruslondinium.org/research/john-evelyns-mulberry.

they were so frequently flawed and yet frequently resurrected. Attempts to generate raw silk in the face of environmental and logistical handicaps revealed features common to Spanish, French, British, and early US efforts, with their distinctive triangulation of race, space, and empire, and their intensive drawing on Atlantic networks of knowledge, materials, and people. Yet they also exposed a gap between the Atlantic powers with Mediterranean borders, who had longer familiarity with sericulture and nearby access to supplies, and those in northern Europe (including Britain) farther removed from sources, for whom the challenge was more pronounced for reasons of deficits in both their climate and their human capital. These equations would change somewhat as developments occurred that reoriented East Indies trade and European manufacturing centres, and as commercial conflicts ebbed and flowed. Silkworms and their trials, in macro terms, therefore exposed both the extent and the limits of commodity projection in the Early Modern Atlantic.

The intertwining of the international and the local was no less pronounced when it came to the people involved in forwarding silk production across the Atlantic. Several illustrious names lent their patronage and capital to ventures – from Hernán Cortes to James I and later British monarchs, to a range of American luminaries (such as Benjamin Franklin), who were keen initially to impress imperial patrons, and subsequently to secure a New World of textile independence after the American Revolution, as silk raising took a nationalistic and republican turn. Less familiar names, but arguably more important people to sericulture's prospects, were the regional entrepreneurs, botanists, planters, and a host of opportunistic or desperate workers at the local and household levels. These were the men and women (whether of European, Indian, or African origin) who laid out thousands of mulberry orchards, who reconfigured their domestic spaces to accommodate the peculiarities of the seasonal hatchings of helpless caterpillars, and who demonstrated innovation and developed expertise in spite of the profound difficulties of colonial environments, and the shortcomings of much of their advice literature. This history serves to expose this array of often nameless actors, who sought to put in motion the grander ambitions at the heart of colonial projects, responding to the assortments of bounties, land grants, rewards and assistance framed by imperial bodies and institutions. One of its central and recurring claims is that the shadowy gaps left around the successful commodity flows – through which American colonialism has been understood – help us to expose how much labour adaptation, improvisation, and creative agency derived from marginalised groups, especially women.

The nature of efforts at silk production in the Americas – episodic, opportunistic, and dependent upon the intermittent provision of materials and expertise – does not naturally lend itself to a systematic overview. Failure, after all, is typically something we look to downplay or forget. As in the process of reeling raw silk from cocoons (outlined below), threads need to be teased out, often break, and require attention to detail, so this account offers an interpretation based on a regional dissection of the attempts at sericulture. Its chapters are clustered within three parts, following this prologue which is designed to offer a global assessment of the spread of sericulture (up to the Atlantic barrier in 1500), and to explain the general processes and practices of production, which may be as unfamiliar to readers as they were to denizens of northern Europe and America. Part I addresses the 'Emergence' of sericulture (for the fibre under Hooke's microscope was unknown in the Americas prior to Columbian contact), and considers various European initiatives to transplant mulberries and silkworms with varying degrees of success. The regions treated in this part are New Spain in the sixteenth century, English Virginia in the seventeenth, and French possessions around the Caribbean (particularly Louisiana).

Part II, 'Persistence', begins with a survey of the changing patterns and ambitions of silk production in Europe, before looking closely at the particularities of Britain and its colonial ambitions in North America. The competition between nations, merchants, and manufacturers in Europe and Asia, driven by high consumption of silk goods, prompted a host of efforts to domesticate silkworms – even in unlikely places. While first Spain and then France had largely retreated from transatlantic projects in sericulture, relying instead on deepening their domestic output, Britain's distinctive circumstances encouraged it to persist in new ways. These chapters go on to explain how proponents generated significant investment and activity in the Lower South (South Carolina and Georgia) and New England, each region manifesting its own peculiar features and facing its own drawbacks during the eighteenth century. Although several of the early challenges had now been overcome, and metropolitan support was better coordinated, organisational and environmental factors continued to compromise sustainability. Individual colonies, townships, and households made extraordinary adjustments to try to accommodate silkworms into their regimens, though there was little sense of synchronicity.

Part III, 'Convergence', explores the ways that attempts to grow American silk became increasingly integrated, mutually informed, and developmental in the final third of the eighteenth century. The efforts in Pennsylvania were taken forward even as the British American imperial crisis threw into question many long-standing ideas about silk and its worth. Ultimately, the onset of the American Revolution forced a reconfiguration of the arguments in favour of raw silk production, and the areas in which it was pursued. The commercial and political fallout of the revolutions at the end of the eighteenth century disrupted silk's place, closing off some productive possibilities and opening or reopening others. In the United States, silk was eventually repackaged to assume a nationalistic bent: making American silk now depended upon making silk American, which was accomplished by some sleight of argumentation and a growing interest in textile manufacturing. The epilogue explores the last great fling with American sericulture in the United States – the mulberry mania of the 1820s and 1830s – noting the common resonances with earlier Atlantic colonialism, and the distinctive twists provided by new methods, materials, and media in the early nineteenth century.

Lighting the Globe

Since the most marvellous transformation in the silkworm's life cycle involved the moth's breaking out from its cocoon to the light, it is fitting for us to begin in the dark. Picture if you will, a map of the world, arrayed as if in deep shadow, the continents barely perceptible, edged against the blacker oceans. This imaginary shadow world represents the globe before human beings alighted on the possibility of unravelling the kilometre-long protein filament (composed of fibroin glued with gummy sericin) that the silkworm, *Bombyx mori*, secretes in constructing its cocoon. People had long twisted plant fibres to create rudimentary textiles, and domesticated many animals (amongst them sheep, pigs, and cattle) whose hides proved invaluable to clothing. But at some mythic moment of realisation, their attention alights upon the horned caterpillars that nestle amidst springtime forests, exclusively eating mulberry leaves from the *Morus* plant (which had originated around the Himalayas). Let us imagine at this juncture – perhaps the point at which a handful of the thin single filaments were first drawn off the cocoons, and plied with one another by twisting slightly to make a crude yarn (raw silk) of manageable texture and unparalleled fibrous strength – that a tiny light appears that punctures the darkness. This miniature LED represents the first time that humans intentionally usurp the silkworm's cocoon, ending its life prematurely, to steal the product of its labour. Raw silk first came to light in this way, sometime around 5000 BCE, amongst the wild mulberry trees of Neolithic eastern China, for by that date basic tools (such as spindle whorls and primitive backstrap looms) appear in the river valleys and lowlands.[14]

Chinese legend has long lent added cultural weight to this moment, attributing the discovery to Empress Leizu, the wife of the Yellow Emperor, Huángdì, who ruled in the twenty-seventh century BCE. Around the sixth century CE, in the Northern Chou dynasty, the mythic character of Leizu was elaborated to knit existing state ceremonies together with aspects of popular culture that had long personified silk-worm goddesses. Leizu supposedly chanced on the idea of using silkworm cocoons when one dropped into her hot green tea, and the fibrous protein thread began to unravel as she looked on. Many legendary attributions to her have since followed, including the invention of the silk reel (a wooden device to pull off and intertwine the cocoon filaments), the invention of the loom (to form the yarns into textiles by cross-binding warp and weft), and the spiritual title of 'Silkworm Mother' (*Cangu nainai*) or 'First Sericulturalist'. This famed origin story immortalised Leizu as a sericultural patron saint, emphasising her femininity, ingenuity, and maternalism, and proved not only to be important to the Chinese rituals and sacrifices that marked each silk-raising season, but to be culturally transmissible. The story had made its way by 1763, for instance, to a small house in the colonial town of Newport, Rhode Island, where one American family named individual silkworms after the legendary Yellow Emperor and his fellow founding sovereigns. As silkworm cultivation spread, so too would its core associations with female labour and prestige.[15]

If we tracked each cocoon unravelling as a light, then between the first-ever reeling of raw silk and the reign of the Yellow Emperor around 2750 BCE, when carbon-dated archaeological fragments from Huzhou (on the edge of Lake Tai, Zhejiang province – see Map 1) tell us that silk was being grown, we would witness raw silk's luminosity expand across the Yangtze and Yellow River basins and their growing numbers of mulberry. The glow of sericulture was brightest around the strongholds of the Shang

[14] Peng Hao, 'Sericulture and Silk Weaving from Antiquity to the Zhou Dynasty', in *Chinese Silks*, ed. Dieter Kuhn (New Haven: Yale University Press, 2012), 66, 73; Dieter Kuhn, *Textile Technology: Spinning and Reeling, Science and Civilisation in China*, ed. Joseph Needham and Ling Wang (Cambridge: Cambridge University Press, 1988), 137–41. For the earliest evidence of non *Bombyx* sericulture outside of China, using the wild silk moth *Antheraea* in the Indus Civilisation (*c.*2500 BCE), see I. L. Good, J. M. Kenoyer, and R. H. Meadow, 'New Evidence for Early Silk in the Indus Civilization', *Archaeometry* 51 (2009): 457–66.
[15] Fan Lizhu, 'The Cult of the Silkworm Mother as a Core of Local Community Religion in a North China Village: Field Study in Zhiwuying, Boading, Hebei', *The China Quarterly* 174 (21 July 2003): 359–72; Dieter Kuhn, 'Tracing a Chinese Legend: In Search of the Identity of the "First Sericulturalist"', *T'oung Pao* 70, no. 4/5 (1984): 213–45.

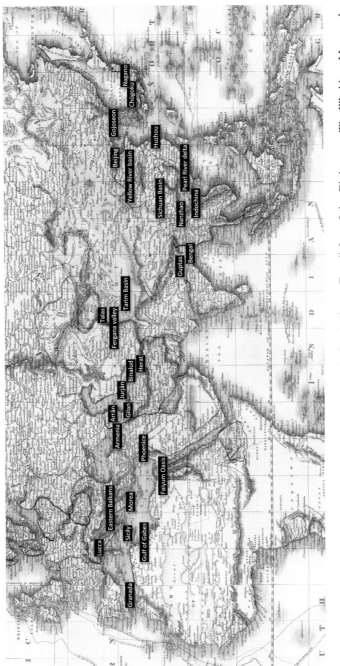

Map 1 World map showing places cited in spread of sericulture. Detail from John Pinkerton, *The World on Mercator's Projection* (London: Cadell and Davies, 1812). Image No. 0732064

dynasty (*c.*1500–1050 BCE) when it probably became a specialised state monopoly, and the Western Zhou dynasty (*c.*1050–775 BCE), in whose royal tombs have been found numerous silk garments and embroidery, the improving quality of their fibres indicating that domesticated silk-worms were being selectively bred. The *Shih chi* (the oldest collection of Chinese poetry, dating from this era) recorded mulberry groves being inspected, leaves being plucked on the banks of the Yellow River, and 'young women, with their baskets high' bearing the softest fodder 'to feed their silk-worms, newly hatched and weak'.[16] The glow intensified and spread into south-central China during the next half millennium with the Eastern Zhou dynasty, when taxes on acreage first mentioned silk, and Confucian philosophers such as Mengzi advised rulers to 'let mulberry trees be planted about the homesteads'.[17]

During the closing centuries of the Zhou period, known as 'the Warring States Period' on account of political fragmentation (475–221 BCE), we begin to see lights flick on in neighbouring regions as sericulture began its long global journey: first in Indochina, where small concentrations of the lights settle in parts of Vietnam and Thailand; next, to the north-east of China, where the borders of the Yellow Sea are lit up when raw silk production reaches the Korean peninsula. In both cases of transmission, political conflict likely encouraged sericulture's spread: internal weakness fostered workforce migration and neighbourly state competition, while consolidation (as when the Han dynasty administered the Gojoseon territory in Korea in the first century BCE) brought the intentional trans-plant of resources and workers to enlighten marginal zones.[18]

That the *Bombyx* silkworm was held to be an agent of civilisation who occupied the minds of Chinese intellectual luminaries more than any other owed to the growing cultural and trade value of silk.[19] The pulsing light in the heart of China became a defining feature of the imperial Han dynasty (206 BCE to 220 CE), which carefully regulated silk production while popularising it through taxation, standardisation, and advances in technology and trade.[20] Beyond the heartland, what had once radiated as occasional diplomatic gifts of finished silks, or wartime tributes, became

---

[16] James Legge, *The She King; or, the Book of Ancient Poetry, Translated in English Verse* (London: Trubner & co., 1876), 97, 141, 143, 181, 185, 205, 277.

[17] A. C. Muller, 'Mencius (Selections)', 2014, 1A: 3, 7A: 21, 7B: 27, www.acmuller.net /con-dao/mencius.html; Kuhn, *Textile Technology*, 285; Hao, 'Sericulture and Silk Weaving from Antiquity to the Zhou Dynasty', 75–7.

[18] Mary Schoeser and Bruno Marcandalli, *Silk* (New Haven: Yale University Press, 2007), 20.

[19] Kuhn, *Textile Technology*, 247.

[20] Shelagh Vainker, *Chinese Silk: A Cultural History* (New Brunswick: Rutgers University Press, 2004), 47.

regular exports of surpluses of silks in all guises (as finished cloths, semi-processed yarns, or bolts of raw silk), bringing Asian merchants, markets, and elite consumers increasing exposure to the commodity. The high value-to-weight ratio of silk would ultimately make it the driving product of westward-bound trans-Eurasian trade – the famed 'Silk Road' – with mostly non-textile luxury goods and horses returning the other way.[21] By virtue of its physical qualities and cultural associations, silk was amongst the first commodities to break what Fernand Braudel famously described as 'the tyranny of distance' in global commerce, yet distance always remained troublesome enough to make it worth chasing production.[22]

Transmission to Central Asia depended on sericulture breaching the western boundaries of China. Another origin myth marked this moment, purportedly around the first half of the first century CE, when an envoy of the Buddhist kingdom of Khotan (modern-day Hotan, in the Xinjiang Uyghur Autonomous Region) persuaded a Chinese princess, the bride-to-be of King Vijaya Jaya, to smuggle silkworm eggs and mulberry seeds in her headdress and establish the culture in the fertile Tarim Basin on the fringe of the Taklamakan Desert. The claim, later made by a monk Hsüan Tsang, journeying eastwards home to China in c.645 CE, recounted that the princess's illicit transfer prefigured the spread of knowledge and materials from Khotan to India and beyond. The princess, in step with Buddhist sanctions on killing sentient creatures, reportedly prohibited 'the working up of the cocoons until the moths of the silkworms had escaped', inaugurating a variant of Ahimsa silk (or 'peace silk', whereby the silkworm is not harmed).[23] Slightly later archaeological finds of yellow cocoons in Maralbashi (just east of Kashgar), from which the moths had sortied, attest to this practice.[24] The breaching of cocoons, though, meant that the filament could not be reeled off in one piece. The life of the moth came at the price of the ease of reeling the raw silk, for the pierced fibroin cocoons had to be painstakingly hand-combed and spun to generate a useable yarn, and this calculus of animal life versus human labour rarely

[21] Richard von Glahn, *An Economic History of China: From Antiquity to the Nineteenth Century* (Cambridge: Cambridge University Press, 2016), 196–8.
[22] Fernand Braudel, *Civilization and Capitalism, 15th–18th Century*, rev. trans (Berkeley: University of California Press, 1992), 429; Debin Ma, 'The Great Silk Exchange: How the World Was Connected and Developed', in *Pacific Centuries: Pacific and Pacific Rim History since the Sixteenth Century*, ed. Dennis Owen Flynn, Lionel Frost, and A. J. H. Latham (London: Routledge, 1999), 38–65; Schoeser and Marcandalli, *Silk*, 23–5.
[23] J. E. Hill, 'Appendix A: "Introduction of Silk Cultivation to Khotan in the 1st Century CE"', in *Through the Jade Gate to Rome: A Study of the Silk Routes during the Later Han Dynasty, 1st to 2nd Centuries CE* (Charleston, SC: Booksurge, 2009), 466–7; Dieter Kuhn, ed., *Chinese Silks* (New Haven: Yale University Press, 2012), 207–8.
[24] Dated to Tang dynasty (618–907 CE). Kuhn, *Textile Technology*, 311–12.

stacked up well for introduced species such as the *Bombyx* silkworms, except where protected by religious precepts (as in Jainism).

By the fourth century CE, regular sericulture became established in Sogdiana (now Uzbekistan and Tajikistan), lighting up several important agricultural zones such as the Fergana valley and the hinterlands of westerly market cities such as Samarkand and Bukhara. The Silk Road thus created in its wake, as if ploughed by its caravans, a Mulberry Furrow, as the ambition to produce silk took root wherever trade and consumption of silk fabrics occurred. The hardiness, adaptability, and fast-growing properties of the *Morus* genus (mulberry) encouraged this process. So too did the fact that silk almost always arrived first into the hands, and therefore minds, of elites – individual or institutional actors (especially religious ones) with the political and economic clout to shape landscapes of production. The intention was almost always to bring sericulture closer to the state, often via the state-church, or in the case of the looser polities of Central Eurasia, the ruler and his *comitatus*.[25] State inducements usually targeted itinerant experts, such as the prominent members of the Hata clan who originated in China but migrated to Japan via Korea, bringing large numbers in the fourth century, where they were naturalised and ordered by Japanese imperial bodies to engage in silkworm rearing. Such mandates recurred in Japan, alongside decrees ordering the cultivation of mulberries, prompting a dull glimmer of sericulture in western territories, particularly in the rolling hills of the Chūgoku region. The likely diffusion point from Korea became bound up with gendered myth and poetry, one epic (the *Kojiki*) recording that Emperor Nintoku's Queen Consort Iwa No Hime took up residence with a Korean immigrant woman, Nurinomi, to better understand the novelty of silkworms, 'these marvellous insects', and how they could be nurtured.[26]

By the fourth and fifth centuries CE, though the luminescence in China remained dazzling, spines and clusters of light shuttled across the Persian

---

[25] Christopher Beckwith, *Empires of the Silk Road: A History of Central Eurasia from the Bronze Age to the Present* (Princeton, NJ: Princeton University Press, 2009), 21–3, 76–7; Thomas T. Allsen, *Commodity and Exchange in the Mongol Empire: A Cultural History of Islamic Textiles* (Cambridge: Cambridge University Press, 1997), 103–4; Xinru Liu, *Silk and Religion: An Exploration of Material Life and the Thought of People, AD 600–1200* (Delhi: Oxford University Press, 1996), 4.

[26] I. Honda, *The Silk Industry of Japan* (Tokyo: The Imperial Tokyo Sericultural Institute, 1909), 1–2. For examples of the imperial pronouncements, see the references to mulberry trees and silkworms in the *Nihon Shoki* ('Japanese Chronicles', completed in 720 CE), such as the orders of Emperor Yūryaku (scroll fourteen): http://nihonshoki .wikidot.com/scroll-14-yuryaku. On sericulture's colonising of Japanese cultic practices and understandings, see Michael Como, *Weaving and Binding: Immigrant Gods and Female Immortals in Ancient Japan* (Honolulu: University of Hawaii Press, 2009), 136–52.

Empire of the Sasanian dynasty (224 to 651) and began to flicker more earnestly in the Indian subcontinent, where *Bombyx* sericulture perhaps competed with the lower-grade wild silk (*kauśeya*) spinning production in the Gupta dynasty's (*c.*300–550) imperial territories. The brightest of the Sasanian regions beginning to produce raw silk were concentrated in Khorasan Province (today's north-eastern Iran), especially in fertile pied-monts and plains around the Binalud Mountains where mulberries thrived and could be serviced by settled populations in cities such as Nishapur and Sabzevar, and amidst the hills and plateaus that marked the north-western fringe of the Hindu Kush, near Herat (western Afghanistan). To what extent these earliest Persian *Bombyx* silkworms were fed upon imported white mulberries (*M. alba*) or, perhaps more likely initially, indigenous black mulberries (*M. nigra*) is hard to say.[27] By this time, silk fabrics themselves had already journeyed as far as the outer westward fringes of the Mediterranean world (to North Africa and Gaul), as products mostly made from Chinese-raised silk yarns, but increasingly woven by non-Chinese artisans. The Romans, most famously Pliny, may have been initially uncertain of the fibrous origins of the silk thread and piece goods they purchased – which is ironic given that they carried and planted black mulberries (for their fruit) as far as forsaken Britannia. But eastern silk quickly became one of a small collection of lightweight luxury goods that the Roman elite prioritised in their trading activities, with Egyptian merchants adding a direct seaborne route to markets in the Indian Ocean from *c.*250 to 450 CE.[28]

The eastern Mediterranean burst into light towards the end of the reign of the Byzantine Emperor Justinian (527–65), who sponsored a direct mission to bring sericulture to the Eastern Roman Empire – ostensibly borne out of frustration at failing to secure adequate raw silk, because of competition with Persia, and the faltering of alternative trade routes intended to bypass the Sasanians via Ethiopia or the Russian steppes. As the contemporary historian Procopius of Caesarea reported, the Levant had been dependent upon raw silk supplied from the East, 'from very early times', ever since Phoenicians had settled silk merchants and artisans in the cities of Beirut and Tyre. Procopius gave most of the credit to 'certain monks' who promised the emperor a solution to his

---

[27] A. H. Dani and V. M. Masson, *History of Civilizations of Central Asia: Development in Contrast* (Paris: UNESCO, 2003), 404; Rudolph P. Matthee, *The Politics of Trade in Safavid Iran Silk for Silver, 1600–1730* (Cambridge: Cambridge University Press, 1999), 15, 34. The earliest Persian agricultural manual, *Kitāb al-filāḥa*, suggests both types of mulberry were widely present before the tenth century CE.

[28] Liu, *Silk and Religion*, 21; Schoeser and Marcandalli, *Silk*, 22, 26; Vainker, *Chinese Silk: A Cultural History*, 59.

commercial dilemma. Based on their first-hand experience of a country they called 'Serinda' situated north of India, the monks revealed the animal origins of the raw silk, and explained how, while the silkworms themselves were not transferable, their 'innumerable eggs' might be. Justinian promised them rewards of 'large gifts' should they secure, repatriate, and hatch these silkworms in Byzantine territory, which they did by heating them in dung.[29] The later author Theophanes added extra layers of mystique to this exchange by reporting in the ninth century that the illicit eggs had been concealed in a hollowed staff, and that neither Eastern Romans nor Turks had appreciated 'the manner in which the worms were hatched'. Though scholars have debated quite who these sketchy figures may have been – most probably Nestorian Sogdians whose schismatic Christianity and mercantile reach proved connective – by the start of the seventh century, and almost certainly before, the symbiotic culture of mulberry trees and *Bombyx* silk moths had lit corridors in the provinces of Syria and Phoenice (centred on modern Lebanon), reaching the eastern shores of the Mediterranean.[30]

Where the environment permitted, the mulberry thrived, and the speed of initial uptake in Byzantine sericulture can only have been enhanced by the worsening of relations and outright conflict with the Sasanian Persians in the 610s, and the invasions of Avars and Slavs which compromised peaceful long-distance trade in raw silk. Enough production had been secured that, in spite of the definitive loss of the eastern provinces under the seventh-century Islamic Arab onslaught, new lights flickered into view and spread north and westward across Anatolia, settling in the most densely inhabited littoral regions of the shrinking Byzantine territories (particularly the Armenian zones of the Black Sea and the population centres on either side of the Aegean Sea). Expansion was encouraged by state support, the manufacturing and commercial exuberance of Constantinople, and officials such as the *kommerkiarios* who vouched for quality and controlled distribution via warehousing. While Byzantine armies retreated and lights went out in war-torn parts of Asia Minor, Byzantine sericulture advanced in the eighth century,

[29] Procopius and H. B. Dewing, *Procopius, with an English Translation* (London: W. Heinemann, 1914), 1: 193; 6: 227–31, 297–301.
[30] At least one Chinese source, the *Weilüe* (orig. *c.*250 CE; extant fragments republished in 429 CE), makes mention of Romans raising *sangcan* (usually 'silkworms'), inviting the possibility that sericulture had already arrived (logically, in Syria) long before Justinian's reign, though the likely site and meaning have been disputed. See for a supportive interpretation, Schoeser and Marcandalli, *Silk*, 24; Claudio Zanier, *Where the Roads Met. East and West in the Silk Production Processes (17th to 19th Centuries)* (Kyoto: Italian School of East Asian Studies, 1994). And for a sceptical one, John E. Hill, 'The Peoples of the West' (the *Weilüe*, trans. 2004), at http://depts.washington.edu/silkroad/texts/weilue/weilue.html, esp. note 16.

crossing to add a few lights in the Balkans to those now shimmering in the Peloponnese, and becoming more concentrated in the rural hinterlands of key cities. Southern Greece became known as *Morea* ('land of mulberries') from the ninth century, and further consolidation of sericulture – much freer from the early protectionism and guild restrictions – had occurred by the tenth, creating regional epicentres in locations such as Thebes and Southern Calabria (where 8,107 trees were counted in a survey *c*.1050). The entrenchment of moriculture (mulberry planting) in westerly Byzantine territories was encouraged by strong trading demand for raw and finished silks in Constantinople and, in turn, for Byzantine silks and mixed fabrics in Italian cities, Islamic states, Russia, and the Balkans. Naturally, the quality of the raw product and the technical consistency of the processing stages (reeling, throwing, dyeing, and so forth) varied, meaning certain regions' silk was suited to certain uses or grades of fabric. The resilience of the mulberries and vitality of sericulture ensured that the lights remained strong in southern Italy, in spite of the change of sovereignty and Norman occupation of Apulia and Calabria from the mid-eleventh century.[31]

Even as projectors within the Byzantine Empire ferried parcels of silk-worm seed across islands and systematised mulberry orchards along the northern flank of the Mediterranean, a more concerted vector of diffusion was arriving in parallel to the southward, shuttling lights westwards along the North African coast. By the mid-eighth century, the phenomenal Islamic conquests begun in Arabia had connected long-standing centres of silk production (like those in Khorasan and Syria) to new territories within a single caliphate (the Umayyad dynasty, 661–750), centred on Damascus. The economic and cultural value of silk largely eclipsed early Hadīth traditions that had ruled against its wearing, helped by the fact that the Quran did not expressly prohibit the fibre. Eventually an Islamic sumptuary consensus emerged that gave pride of place to part-silk textiles (with silk often used for the warp), and that limited human or animalistic figures on designs, but encouraged artistic inscriptions in ornate strips, fringes, or embroidery. Islamic consolidation thus supported rather than

[31] Heleanor B. Feltham, 'Justinian and the International Silk Trade', *Sino-Platonic Papers* 194 (2009); Anna Muthesius, 'The Byzantine Silk Industry: Lopez and Beyond', *Journal of Medieval History* 19, no. 1–2 (January 1993): 1–67; David Jacoby, 'Silk Economics and Cross-Cultural Artistic Interaction: Byzantium, the Muslim World, and the Christian West', *Dumbarton Oaks Papers* 58 (2004): 197–240; Roberto S. Lopez, 'The Silk Industry in the Byzantine Empire', *Speculum* 20 (1945): 1–42; Nicolas Oikonomidès, 'Silk Trade and Production in Byzantium from the Sixth to the Ninth Century: The Seals of Kommerkiarioi', *Dumbarton Oaks Papers* 40 (1986): 33–53; David Jacoby, 'Silk in Western Byzantium before the Fourth Crusade', *Byzantinische Zeitschrift* 84–5, no. 2 (1992): 452–500; George C. Maniatis, 'Organization, Market Structure, and Modus Operandi of the Private Silk Industry in Tenth-Century Byzantium', *Dumbarton Oaks Papers* 53 (1999): 326–7.

shrank the global spread of silk by opening it up to new consumers and standardising design and production through the *ṭirāz* system (issuing instructions to workshops to ensure they served the state), all assisted by the impressive communication network that eased transfers of goods, people, and technology across the Muslim world, and that persisted in spite of the erosion of the Abbasid Caliphate (750–1258).[32]

Sericulture correspondingly brightened and spread in the northern provinces bordering the Caspian Sea (from east to west: Jurjān, Tabaristān, Jilān, Azarbayjān, Arrān) and was rekindled in Armenia, from where it was poised to take root in neighbouring Turkic Khazaria along the foothills of the Caucasus. The combination of coastal moisture and warmth likewise fostered radiance in the western mountain ranges of Syria and Lebanon, where raw silk yields increased and fed vibrant industries in Aleppo, Antioch, Homs, and Damascus. Some of this Islamic raw silk, known as *ibrīsm*, had distinctive properties (texture and lustre), by virtue of the cocooned pupae being destroyed by baking them under the sun (rather than by steaming or salt-poisoning) before reeling off the filaments, though imports of Chinese raw silk and yarn persisted, meaning different permutations evolved as silk products diversified and industries specialised. Syrian experts in moriculture and sericulture brought mulberries to Egypt, and lights perhaps flickered for a time in the Faiyum Oasis, watered by a western channel of the Nile, but environmental conditions were most conducive farther west, and in due course a more pulsing light took hold around the Gulf of Gabès (then Ifrīqiya, now Tunisia). Around the middle of the eighth century, the first significant numbers of 'Syrian' mulberry trees used for silk raising were reported in al-Andalus, Islamic Spain, by Arab chroniclers. Little clusters of light, beginning in communities nestled around the mountainous south-eastern parts of the Iberian Peninsula soon became long, radiant pulses. They worked themselves, fittingly, into a crescent, an early secular symbol of authority for Muslim rulers, running eastwards from the south of Portugal around the burning white of Granada and Almería and up the coast beyond Valencia. The proximity of Ifrīqiya to Sicily meant that mulberries and silkworm seed easily accompanied this final point of Arabic penetration under the Aghlabid dynasty by 902, where production was concentrated in the western toe of the island.[33]

[32] Liu, *Silk and Religion*, 136–57; Jacoby, 'Silk Economics and Cross-Cultural Artistic Interaction: Byzantium, the Muslim World, and the Christian West'; Germán Navarro Espinach, *El despegue de la industria sedera en la Valencia del siglo xv* (Valencia: Generalitat Valenciana, 1992), 31.
[33] Liu, *Silk and Religion*, 159–60; D. Jacoby, 'Silk Crosses the Mediterranean', in *Le vie del mediterraneo: idee, uomini, oggetti (secoli xi–xvi)*, ed. G. Airaldi (Genoa: ECIG, 1997),

Sicily was a meeting point of the two systems of silk production –
Byzantine and Islamic – that had arrived in Western Europe independently of one another, and that would leave distinctive legacies in
the developing Italian and Spanish silk industries respectively. In
1147, the island bore testament to the growing efforts made by
Latin Christian polities to take ownership of the production and
diffusion of silk, when its Norman king Roger II sanctioned a raid
specifically on Byzantine silk zones in Greece, capturing experts
whom he then installed in Palermo to diversify and refine
production.[34] That same year, King Alfonso VII of Castile-León
and a Genoese force besieged Almería, occupying the wealthy silk
city (renowned for its imitation of Persian fabrics) and plundering its
wares and population.[35] These feats of silk crusading were less transformative, however, than the slow and steady mercantile strangula-
tion that brought silk production within the orbit of the trading cities
of northern Italy by the late twelfth century. First latching on, like
parasites, to the vibrant commercial exchange of raw silks, dyestuffs,
and finished silks around the eastern Mediterranean and Black Sea,
enterprising elements within Italian cities (initially Lucca and Venice)
next set up workshops to produce Byzantine-type silks. The westward
relocation of European centres of silk manufacture from Greek to
Italian cities, accelerated by the Fourth Crusade's destruction of
Constantinople in 1204, did not diminish the glow of raw silk production where it existed in the Peloponnese and the eastern Balkans,
but gave a new importance to controlling its quality and trade. The
mulberry seedlings and silkworm stocks available in Peloponnesian
ports such as Corinth, Patras, Koroni and Methoni, and on larger
Aegean islands such as Andros and Euboea, would in turn become
vectors for sericulture's transmission from the Byzantine to the Latin
worlds. For their part, the exiled silk manufacturers from
Constantinople set up operations in locales such as Smyrna (now

55–79; Jacoby, 'Silk Economics and Cross-Cultural Artistic Interaction: Byzantium, the
Muslim World, and the Christian West', 198 201; Paulino Iradiel Murugarren and
Germán Navarro Espinach, 'La seda en Valencia en la edad media', in *España
y Portugal en las rutas de la seda: Diez siglos de producción y comercio entre oriente
y occidente* (Barcelona: Universitat de Barcelona, 1996), 184; Espinach, *El despegue de
la industria sedera*, 31; A. Y. Al-Hassan, ed., *Science and Technology in Islam: Technology
and Applied Sciences* (UNESCO, 2001), 136–9; Schoeser and Marcandalli, *Silk*, 32.

[34] Lopez, 'The Silk Industry in the Byzantine Empire', 24; Jacoby, 'Silk in Western
Byzantium before the Fourth Crusade', 485.

[35] John Bryan Williams, 'The Making of a Crusade: The Genoese Anti-Muslim Attacks in
Spain, 1146–1148', *Journal of Medieval History* 23, no. 1 (January 1997): 29–53.

Izmir), Bursa, and Nicaea, sustaining the glow of Anatolian sericulture within Nicaean and Seljuk Turkish territories.[36]

Between around 1250 and 1500, the global vista of spreading *Bombyx*
sericulture showed constellations not so much leaping across distances
as edging, creeping and deepening in prominence, particularly in the Far
East, Transcaucasia, and Italian dominions. Chinese production had
continued apace under the Southern Song dynasty (1127–1279), especially in the populous Jiangnan region where the new court was relocated
(modern Hangzhou), the western Sichuan Basin, and the southerly
Pearl River Delta.[37] Increasing attention to coastal exchange somewhat
mitigated loss of control over the ancient overland silk trade, furnishing
raw silk to Korea, Japan, the Philippines, and India's Coromandel
Coast, as well as to markets in the Arab and Mediterranean worlds via
Muslim and Jewish traders.[38] Though subsequent Mongol conquests
across Eurasia were initially disruptive and locally damaging to silk
production, the Khans' unification of territory and restoration of peace-
able commercial circuitry, as well as their acute appreciation of silks as
tax, tribute, and portable signifiers of supremacy, ultimately encouraged
considerable expansion of raw silk output in existing centres.[39] The
Mongol Yuan dynasty (1271–1368) oversaw a widening of mulberry
acreage in China, the *Yuan Shih* chronicle recording government
decrees that insisted, for example, that where the land was suitable,
'each male adult is to plant twenty mulberry' and imposed collective
tending of orchards. Such measures generated an increase of over
50 per cent in raw silk weight furnished as taxation by 1328 (when 655
tons were yielded up).[40] Burgeoning demand from the state and the

---

[36] David Jacoby, 'Silk Production', in *The Oxford Handbook of Byzantine Studies*, ed.
Elizabeth Jeffreys, John F. Haldon, and Robin Cormack (Oxford: Oxford University
Press, n.d.), 426–7; Olimpia Urdea, 'Sericiculture in Romania between Tradition and an
Uncertain Future', *Analele Universităţii Din Oradea, Fascicula: Ecotoxicologie, Zootehnie Şi
Tehnologii de Industrie Alimentară* 10, no. B (2011): 387–91; Jacoby, 'Silk in Western
Byzantium before the Fourth Crusade.'

[37] Kuhn, *Chinese Silks*, 118, 169–71, 206–8, 260–1. The largest ever period of silk production before the 1930s probably occurred under the Tang dynasty around 710 CE when
over 370 million mulberry trees supported production of in excess of 1.3 million tons of
cocoons and generated 8,500 tons of silk thread. Ibid., 205–6.

[38] Liu, *Silk and Religion*, 184–6; Chuan-Hui Mau, 'A Preliminary Study of the Changes in
Textile Production under the Influence of Eurasian Exchanges during the Song-Yuan
Period', *Crossroads – Studies on the History of Exchange Relations in the East Asian World* 6
(September 2012): 145–204.

[39] Thomas Allsen, *Commodity and Exchange in the Mongol Empire: A Cultural History of
Islamic Textiles* (Cambridge: Cambridge University Press, 1997), 27–45. On the
Mongolian era as a distinctively integrative phase in the trade of textiles, especially
silks, see ibid., 101–6; Ma, 'The Great Silk Exchange: How the World Was Connected
and Developed', 40–6.

[40] Kuhn, *Textile Technology*, 286–8.

market, along with the large labour pool, prompted not only an expansion of output but also a high degree of specialisation and intensification. Developing techniques in moriculture (such as dwarf tree cultivation to allow easy pickings or grafting different varieties to one another to maximise leaf spread), silkworm breeding (such as warming the silkworm trays), and silk reeling, throwing, weaving, and design all left their mark in instructional literature such as the *Nong Shu* agricultural treatises of 1149–1313 and the *Nongsang Jiyao* manual, whose distribution ran beyond 15,000 copies in 1286–1329.[41] They also influenced the spatial reconfiguration of the silk industry, as mulberry plantations became somewhat separated from silkworm-raising operations, and high-grade yarn processing and weaving gravitated towards larger, central workshops and urban enterprises. Diffusion in sericulture depended above all on systematically selecting teaching experts or elders, from whom skills would cascade through the rural community (*she*), and on effective use of labour-intensive practices, such as piling up river sediment around the trunks of mulberries as fertiliser, or preventing overgrowth between them where harmful insects lurked.[42] These improvements contributed to a reliable, high-quality output of raw silk – known for its superior uniformity and whiteness, and, in effect, a brand leader for much of the world in the centuries to come. The Ming dynasty (1368–1644) would literally capitalise on this production, establishing a government-operated system of silk workshops of unparalleled complexity and scope that by the late sixteenth century was devoting around 10 per cent of the annual state revenue to the production of silks.[43]

In the late thirteenth century, Marco Polo reported on the imposing scale and infrastructure of this Chinese sericulture, having returned from his path-breaking tour of the world to northern Italy – the incipient European beacon of silk production. The Venetian's fanciful travelogue made a particular point of highlighting sericulture in 'Georgiania' (Georgia), 'the Sea of Ghel' (Gilan), and many parts of Yuan China such as 'Cambaluc' (Beijing), where mulberry trees were 'so numerous

---

[41] Kuhn, *Chinese Silks*, 328–32.

[42] Mau, 'A Preliminary Study of the Changes in Textile Production under the Influence of Eurasian Exchanges during the Song-Yuan Period'; Chuan-Hui Mau, 'Les progrès de la sériciculture sous les yuan (xiiie-xive siècles) d'après le Nongsang jiyao', *Revue de Synthèse* 131, no. 2 (2010): 193–217. The most common grafting combination was of *Morus alba* var. *multicaulis* (known as *Lu-sang*) onto the trunk of *Morus bombycis* (known as *ching-sang*). Kuhn, *Textile Technology*, 289–301.

[43] Kuhn, *Chinese Silks*; Dagmar Schäfer, 'Power and Silk: The Central State and Localities in State-Owned Manufacture during the Ming Reign (1368–1644)', in *Threads of Global Desire: Silk in the Pre-Modern World*, ed. Dagmar Schäfer, Giorgio Riello, and Luca Mola (Woodbridge: Boydell and Brewer, 2018), 21–47.

that whole districts are full of them'.[44] But a more material story was unfolding in the territories around his homeland, for between the twelfth and fifteenth centuries, Italian cities firstly developed and diffused silk manufacturing industries (starting with Lucca, Venice, Bologna and Genoa), and then successfully introduced mulberry trees and domesticated sericulture in their hinterlands. They gradually and proportionally weaned their improving manufactures off foreign supplies of raw silk. By 1500, lights had flashed on across the Italian peninsula, as market forces (particularly elite consumer demand for high- and medium-quality fabrics) rode roughshod over the frenzied webs of restrictions, proscriptions, and death threats to craftspeople that were thrown up by defensive merchants, guilds, and polities. A particularly energetic and competitive sericulture took root, along with thousands of mulberry trees, and diffused outwards in the Tuscan-Emilian Apennines and westwards along the Po Valley, shining particularly in northern Tuscany (Pescia and Pistoia), the Veneto (Vicenza), and eventually northern Lombardy and Piedmont (Milan). So prolific were these burgeoning industries in the Early Modern period that Italian-wrought silk products would become a pre-eminent target for European consumers, and in due course, Italian-raised raw silk a pre-eminent model for projectors and states seeking modernisation, prestige, and profit.[45]

In 1500 then, the long westward sweep of the light of sericulture remained poised on the edge of the shadowy Atlantic world. Over the next 350 years, like a faulty bulb, the Americas and parts of northern Europe would flicker and flame, glint and twinkle where silkworms were reeled off, but rarely catch light for long. In the grand view, the fragmentary American splutters in the mid-nineteenth century would be followed by a pattern of long global retraction, as sericulture's largely westward loop was rewound – the southern European glow beginning to flicker out under the onslaught of the silkworm disease, *pébrine*, from the late 1840s, followed by dimming of the robust radiance in the Middle East. At the start of the twentieth century, the brightest luminescence had retreated back to East Asia, where it was particularly intense in Japan. There, in spite of the small land mass, progress in technology and biological science had turned it into the primary provider of the world's largest market for raw silk, the teeming standardised factories of the United States, but

---

[44] Marco Polo and Henry Yule, *The Book of Ser Marco Polo the Venetian Concerning the Kingdoms and Marvels of the East*, 3rd ed. (2 vols., London: John Murray, 1903), 1: 50, 52, 415 (Beijing), 423; 2:13, 22, 31, 126, 132, 136, 141, 152, 157, 158, 176, 178, 181, 187, 219, 226.

[45] Luca Molà, *The Silk Industry of Renaissance Venice* (Baltimore, MD: Johns Hopkins University Press, 2000), 15–22.

synthetic fabrics and global conflicts would soon challenge production everywhere.[46] By the early 2010s, the bulk of the shrinking global annual production of 563,366 tons of reelable cocoons had withdrawn back to mainland China (66 per cent), the originator of sericulture, leaving a strong pulse in India (27 per cent), a dim glow in Uzbekistan (5 per cent), sparse specks in Thailand, Iran, Brazil, and Vietnam (each between 2,500 and 5,000 tonnes), and tiny flecks in Korea, Romania, Afghanistan, Japan, and Cambodia.[47] If the art of raising silk is a measure of civilisation itself, as the Abbé Raynal tellingly suggested in his popular survey of European colonialism in 1770, then the world has been going backwards for some time.[48]

The Preconditions of Transfer

The peoples, regions, and economies that successfully adapted to the cultivation of *Bombyx* silkworms over the space of some 2,000 years (before 1500) had several features in common, which might be viewed as prerequisites of the transfer of sericulture from one zone to another. One of the commonest of these features was that silkworm raising – though technically the first step in the convoluted process of manufacturing silk fabrics – was usually the last of those steps to be transferred from one economy to another. In what Giorgio Riello has usefully characterised as 'reverse engineering', it was the arrival of silk goods not silkworms into a virgin area that typically prefigured the establishment of silk-weaving and silk-finishing industries, as state-supported elites (such as the Sasanian shahs, Byzantine emperors, Muslim rulers, or Italian princes) stamped their authority upon competitors by domesticating and developing prized manufactures in their homelands, relying on imports of semi-processed or raw materials for their artisans to work up in dedicated workshops.[49]

Successfully relocating the component stages of silk production depended firstly upon the labour mobility of those with expertise.

---

[46] L. Cafagna and G. Federico, 'The World Silk Trade: A Long Period Overview', in *La seta in Europa. sec. xiii–xx*, ed. S. Cavaciocchi (Florence: Le Monnier, 1993), 683–98; Ma, 'The Great Silk Exchange: How the World Was Connected and Developed', 54–5.

[47] Data from Statistics Division of the Food and Agriculture Organization of the UN, averaged for 2010–2013: http://faostat3.fao.org/. For a recent prognosis, see R. K. Datta and Mahesh Nanavaty, *Global Silk Industry: A Complete Source Book* (New Delhi: S. B. Nangia, 2007).

[48] Raynal, *A Philosophical and Political History of the British Settlements and Trade in North America, from the French of Abbé Raynal, in Two Volumes*, 1: 21.

[49] Giorgio Riello, 'Textile Spheres: Silk in a Global and Comparative Context', in *Threads of Global Desire: Silk in the Pre-Modern World*, ed. Dagmar Schäfer, Giorgio Riello, and Luca Molà (Woodbridge: Boydell and Brewer, 2018), 327.

Southern provinces in China evolved into a primary site for sericulture after
a Tang military commissioner (Xue Jianxun) ordered several thousand
soldiers resettling there in c.765 'to marry women from the north who
were skilled', while the neighbouring Tibetan empire (peaceably) and
kingdom of Nanzhao (forcibly) advanced silk production by securing
craftspeople from western Sichuan.[50] Tang Chinese prisoners taken by
the Abbasids after the Battle of Talas in 751 proved instrumental in
spreading silk expertise throughout the Arab world.[51] Thereafter, Islamic
silk expansionism and imitationism relied upon incentives and moving
skilled workers from one zone to another, even across long distances as
when Syrians bridged Egypt, the Maghreb, and al-Andalus. Imperial silk
workshops in Constantinople, and probably private operations, used
enslaved Muslims whose silk skill sets and technical know-how stood to
benefit production, and Byzantine weavers were likewise co-opted in
Cairo. The Theban industry of the mid-eleventh century grew because of
either the spontaneous immigration or careful recruitment of well-qualified
artisans from across the Byzantine Empire, and a complement of Jewish
producers from the Muslim Levant. In turn, Roger II, the Norman conqueror of Sicily, specifically targeted the successors of these silk workers
whom he captured and deported from Corinth and Thebes in 1147 to
emulate the prized Greek silk manufacturing and dyeing industry in his
Italian lands.[52] Mongolian policy from 1219 was at pains to safeguard
textile artisans from slaughter, and often to forcibly relocate them across
cultural zones within subjugated territories – leading to clusters of foreign
craftspeople diversifying silk products in a number of cities.[53] And the
quick-fire growth of Italian industries in the fourteenth and fifteenth centuries depended upon the emigration of expertise: at times a drip-feed of
entrepreneurial individuals under contracts to neighbouring polities, and
where circumstances permitted, a surge of silk artisans (setaioli).[54]

In most of these cross-cultural instances, the value of the expert labour
depended upon a group's knowledge and mastery of technical stages in
silk manufacturing – experience in judging materials, implementing processes and practices, technological innovations, and design secrets. With
such expertise and demand in situ amongst pools of weavers, dyers, and
thread-processing artisans, it was usually a logical progression on

[50] Kuhn, *Chinese Silks*, 207.
[51] Ma, 'The Great Silk Exchange: How the World Was Connected and Developed', 44.
[52] Lopez, 'The Silk Industry in the Byzantine Empire', 24; Jacoby, 'Silk Economics and
Cross-Cultural Artistic Interaction: Byzantium, the Muslim World, and the Christian
West', 224–7; Jacoby, 'Silk in Western Byzantium before the Fourth Crusade', 485.
[53] Allsen, *Commodity and Exchange in the Mongol Empire: A Cultural History of Islamic
Textiles*, 30–7.
[54] Molà, *The Silk Industry of Renaissance Venice*, 20–51.

economic grounds to seek to add the regional production of the silk moth to the production of silk cloth. Local supplies of the right kinds of raw silk would allow manufacturers to economise, specialise, and mitigate their being at the mercy of risky external trade, especially since the raw materials always constituted the biggest slice of production costs for luxury products. The presence of expert silk raisers (such as the Tang soldiers' wives) in rural districts around new-found silk industries, especially early on, was a vital component of development, as was the effective diffusion of their particular skills: ecological anticipation, responsive nurturing of healthy crops of silkworms, visual inspection of cocoons, strict supervision of reeling, breed selection, and recycling of waste products (such as inferior or pierced cocoons). And even where direct substitution of local raw silk for distant imports was not feasible on the grounds of differences in quality or consistency of the yarns, such was the diversity of silk products and their offshoots that even crude local raw silk could be mobilised for low- to medium-grade fabrics (often in the weft), or otherwise co-opted into production and trade systems. As a rough rule of thumb, it took between 100 and 200 years from the establishment of silk manufacturing in a given locale to the definitive arrival of nearby sericulture, with the gap narrowing over time.[55]

As has already been intimated, agents within the pre-existent silk trade were usually the vectors by which the critical materials for establishing *Bombyx* sericulture – silkworm eggs (always) and mulberry seeds or saplings (often) – made their way to a new region. The transport of eggs was simplified by the fact that they were small and lightweight – carried carefully in papers and pouches more commonly than in illicit headdresses or bamboo staffs. But the transport of eggs was also complicated by the limited time span before they might hatch into larvae, which was temperature dependent, and by the fact that they were very fragile and vulnerable to spoilage and small predators. The most commonplace transfers were land-bound across nearby borders, for before 1500 silkworms had only traversed short marine intervals, such as the Korea Strait (120 miles) or the Strait of Sicily (90 miles). An initial supply of eggs was obviously necessary to launch sericulture, but proximity and exchange frequently remained important, for they offered the possibility of genetic replenishment when silkworm cohorts failed or deteriorated in output or quality, as they were prone to do. As a consequence, some subregions developed particular reputations for specialising not so much in raw silk but in robust stocks of eggs that would translate to hardy and healthy silkworm larvae.

---

[55] Timings estimated from Ma, 'The Great Silk Exchange: How the World Was Connected and Developed', 42.

The importance of healthy stocks lay in that – for all their wondrous qualities – *Bombyx* silkworms had been domesticated to the point of being a fairly inept and completely dependent species, virtually defenceless in the natural world (unless you count their smell) and only able to reproduce with substantial help. Silkworms are fragile creatures, physiologically and genetically, falling prey easily to diseases caused by protozoa (most notoriously *pébrine*), fungi, bacteria, and viruses – and doing so most commonly in areas where silkworm seed is produced by farming populations.[56] The flourishing advice literature that accompanied silkworms on their global adventures bore testament to this fragility. Across languages and centuries, authors from different cultures implored human hosts to be hygienic, observant, quiet, meticulous, and responsive. They sought to identify and explain the warning signals that could presage calamitous cocoon harvests, and to forewarn of the symptoms visible in caterpillars' bodies and in their peculiar behaviours – their chomping, pausing, shedding, growing, sleeping, fitting, wandering, climbing, and dying: always dying. This insect vulnerability served not only as a brake on sericulture's spread but also as an anthropological force in its own right – shaping human spiritualism, rituals, traditions, folk remedies, gender relations, and seasonal labour cycles, in the quest to keep silkworms healthy long enough to yield up their fibroin, before terminating them.

In contrast to the hapless *Bombyx* silkworms, the deciduous mulberry trees whose leaves they feed on are hardy evolutionary athletes, genetically dynamic and now divided into many different species and varieties that are highly inter-fertile, having adapted to a range of global environments.[57] Indeed, so effective has the *Morus* genus been at adapting and hybridising that its taxonomy has been long contested, not helped by confusion about colours: at times the 'black mulberry' has red fruit, the 'red mulberry' white fruit, and the 'white mulberry' can have purple or black fruit. This changeability was grafted into the literary canon when the Roman poet Ovid narrated the myth of Babylonian lovers Pyramus and Thisbe in his *Metamorphoses*, describing how water nymphs stained the mulberry's fruit from white to blood-red as a memorial to their tragic love.[58] More practical

[56] R. Govindan, T. K. Narayanaswamy, and M. C. Devaiah, *Pebrine Disease of Silkworm* (Bangalore: University of Agricultural Sciences, 1997).

[57] Ningjia He, Chi Zhang, Xiwu Qi et al., 'Draft Genome Sequence of the Mulberry Tree Morus Notabilis', *Nature Communications* 4 (19 January 2013): 2445; Kevin S. Burgess and Brian C. Husband, 'Habitat Differentiation and the Ecological Costs of Hybridization: The Effects of Introduced Mulberry (Morus Alba) on a Native Congener (M. Rubra)', *Journal of Ecology* 94, no. 6 (1 November 2006): 1061–9; Peter Coles, *Mulberry* (London: Reaktion Books, 2019).

[58] Ovid, *Metamorphoses*, trans. Arthur Golding (London: W. Seres, 1567), book 4, lines 50–4.

has been the mulberry's ready capacity for speedy growth and transplantation – whether grown from seed, planted from cuttings, or self-pollinated.
While initially requiring plentiful moisture, the trees are tolerant of poor soils
and periodic drought, though repeated pruning can bring risk of pathogen
infection and pest infestation. Mulberries' success or otherwise as fodder for
silkworms has depended much on the extent of their foliage and the timing
of its arrival – and several cultivars reflect these priorities in their low height
and spreading canopy (to ease leaf picking). The mulberries that work best
for sericulture display a range of interrelated characteristics: high absorption
of soil nutrients, constant and dense leaf growth, orderly growth of shoots,
high capacity for regrowth, leaves of good size, shape, and depth, and disease
resistance. The degree to which these characteristics are present depends
upon three environmental determinants: air temperature, humidity, and soil
fertility – meaning that tropical and subtropical zones ordinarily lend themselves to faster or stronger moriculture than temperate climates. In some
parts of the world, mulberry leaves can thus be harvested nearly throughout
the year, while in others (including much of northern Europe and America)
leafing occurs only in seasonal periods.

Rationalising moriculture, to render leaf collection more efficient and
shape orchards to environments was always a feature of successful regions
of silk raising.[59] In ideal environments, such as the Chinese regions where
sericulture thrived, more than one harvest of silkworms was possible per year
(known as bivoltine for two or multivoltine for more, the latter only practicable in tropical countries). But even then, the first harvest usually remained
by some margin the most profitable in terms of quality and quantity, and the
worth of any given harvest was closely tied to the weather.[60] The atmo-
spheric and environmental needs of the silkworms and cocoons were not
always compatible with those of the trees. For example, while high humidity
is an asset for mulberries' growth, warm and rainy days are more likely to
generate disease in silkworms and have repercussions for stored cocoons,
which become vulnerable to attack by fungus beyond 70 per cent
humidity.[61] Any given region adapted to sericulture had had to overcome
these difficulties, finding ways to offset variations in species, genetic hardiness, soils, and environments, and to survive the inevitable blips associated
with shorter-term weather patterns and diseases.

[59] Sandra Soria Re, 'La morera para la cria del gusano de seda', *Artesanías de América:
Revista del CIDAP* 58, no. 5: 8.
[60] Hao, 'Sericulture and Silk Weaving from Antiquity to the Zhou Dynasty', 107.
[61] Cassina Rizzardi, and Giulia Allara, 'Curso de formacion sericola', *Artesanías de América:
Revista del CIDAP* 58, no. 5: esp. 41, 45; V. K. Rahmathulla, 'Management of Climatic
Factors for Successful Silkworm (Bombyx mori L.) Crop and Higher Silk Production:
A Review', *Psyche: A Journal of Entomology* (2012), Article ID 121234.

Given that generating raw silk required the human-curated symbiosis of these two distinctive organisms, we can lastly identify prerequisites relating to demographic and labour configurations. A key component common to nearly all places in which sericulture took hold was the presence of a suitable reserve of labour: significant numbers of people whose work patterns were flexible enough that large chunks of time could be appropriated at certain times of year into intense and spatially challenging activity, before dropping back to baseline levels. This criterion was important across a host of regions and periods, and the seasonal work with silkworms was often an additional cash crop or supplementary income stream for peasant families (whether they sold mulberry leaves, silkworm-rearing labour, cocoons, or raw silk skeins having reeled them off). As proposed in the schema in Table 1, the intensity of labour participation and the spaces in which labour was mobilised could vary, with more likelihood of centralisation as sericultural zones became established and technologies standardised. Silk raising at the start of the period covered by this book was overwhelmingly confined to traditional, decentralised, small-scale, peasant households, and coexisted alongside agricultural staples: rice, tea, wheat, vines. It was labour-intensive, especially during the latter periods of feeding the worms in each cycle, and typically involved a substantial element of female and child labour, which carried through to the reeling of the cocoons, achievable with wonderfully simple hand-reeling machines.[62] Plentiful hands and households were needed for the exhausting but physically manageable leaf collecting, sorting, silkworm feeding, cleaning, safeguarding, pupae terminating, and cocoon reeling.

Some regions specialising in sericulture moved towards more centralised models that allowed for a higher degree of quality control and consistency of product, and the greatest pressure came at the critical point of reeling the raw silk from the cocoons. This moment defined the value and the possible uses of the silk yarn, meaning that successful silk zones found ways to enhance and diffuse competence in the skill of reeling. It was the point at which people, technology, materials, and environment all converged – a steaming, scalding, frenetic, anxious stripping of the silkworm's shelter. The pre-sorted cocoons bobbed in hot water, reelers teasing out their ends with rapid hands and eagle eyes, quickly replacing those cocoons that wound out, and drawing the same number of filaments up to join a collective yarn; the thread passed through a hook and was then wound onto a wooden reel with enough lateral movement and aeration to make sure the coils did not stick or knot. Ending up with

---

[62] Navarro Espinach, *Despegue de la industria sedera en la Valencia*, 155.

Table 1 *Variants in labour participation in silk production*

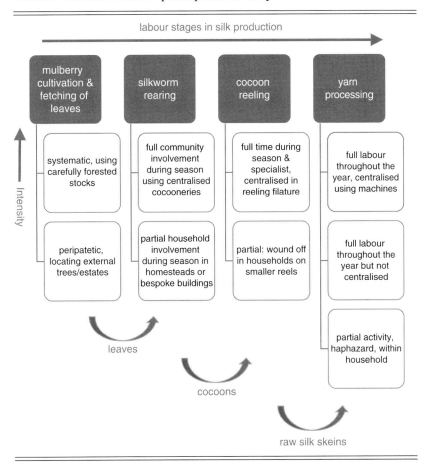

an even skein was paramount for quality, workability, and therefore value. Its significance was heralded in the scores of regulations and advice manuals that addressed the art of reeling, many of them prompted by frustrations further down the silk manufacturing line as vexed throwers (or throwsters), dyers, and weavers sought to redress shortcomings in their raw materials.

In summary then, the successful transfer of *Bombyx* sericulture has always required pre-existing demand from an established silk industry with state support, access to replenishable stocks of silkworm eggs and abundant proximate mulberry trees, environmental conditions (particularly temperature and humidity) that allowed the symbiosis of these two to occur effectively, a dense rural labour pool able to devote itself to seasonal bursts of activity, and access to expertise in the technical complexities associated with silkworm raising and especially silk reeling. These prerequisites and their consequences are neatly illustrated if we revisit silkworms' leap across the Korean Strait. State support was necessary but not sufficient in the first instance, for Japan's successful expansion in sericulture depended upon its environmental and labour assets: its ability to secure the raw materials and skills from continental Asia, and to nurture the Japanese populations of trees, silkworms, and people. Sericulture in the central and south-western districts of Heian Japan (794–1185) was vulnerable to cyclical downturns either when environmental conditions were challenging or when social factors imperilled labourers, as with the collapse of the court and militarisation of society from the late twelfth century. From the turn of the eighteenth century though, sericulture spread north-westward throughout the country, especially settling on the hillsides of central Nagano and Gunma provinces, with output more than doubling by 1715 and exceeding 1,300 tons by the 1820s. The increase in silk production in the later Tokugawa shogunate (c.1720–1867) owed much to the abundant labour pool of the Japanese peasantry and its experience in silviculture, as well as attention to selective breeding and improving productivity, including via handbooks (the first commissioned in 1701 in Tsugaru) and the relocation of experts from Kyoto. By the late eighteenth century this density had given rise to a distinctive trade in hybridised silkworm eggs, bred by specialist merchants in Shindatsu who came to dominate local economies and establish reputations much farther afield. Japanese sericulture's strength, widely recognised by admiring Europeans such as Matthieu Bonafous in the nineteenth century, lay in its 'wealth of empirical know-how' and attention to detail – derived and then adapted from the labour-intensive Chinese model. Technological development (especially the mechanisation of reeling) and the injection of European-style capital and infrastructure only became boosting forces from the late nineteenth century.[63] As the transfer to Japan showed, it was possible to domesticate and develop

---

[63] Mikael S. Adolphson, Edward Kamens, and Stacie Matsumoto, *Heian Japan: Centers and Peripheries* (Honolulu: University of Hawaii Press, 2007), 296, 312–16; Tessa Morris-Suzuki, 'Sericulture and the Origins of Japanese Industrialization', *Technology and Culture* 33, no. 1 (1992): 101–21 (quote on 111); Michael Como, 'Silkworms and Consorts in Nara Japan', *Asian Folklore Studies* 64 (2005): 111–31.

sericulture given access to stocks, opportunistic rulers, a compliant environment, and disposable labour.

The Atlantic Barrier

The Atlantic Ocean is more or less the farthest distance it is possible to travel around the planet from the regions of silk's origination: some 7,000 miles going westwards across the Eurasian land mass or some 8,500 going eastwards across the Pacific. As the Spanish agronomist Antonio de Elgueta y Vigil put it in his 1761 survey, 'this is the race that Silk has undertaken, from its origin in China, crossing all of Asia and Europe, until reaching America, from whence there was no more solid ground, and the joyous circumnavigation was complete'.[64] This had not stopped the march of mulberries, for, as Christopher Columbus himself remarked on the forests of the newly discovered Americas, according to his son, there was an 'abundance of mulberry trees for making silk, which bear leaves all the year'.[65] Silk had clearly been on Columbus's radar, for his annotations on his copy of Marco Polo's travels highlighted silk's abundance in eastern Asia as a major incentive for setting out to find an oceanic passage to Cathay; when his iconic voyage in 1492 became desperate, he promised his crew that he would add 'a silk jacket' to the reward for the shipmate who first sighted land.[66] Columbus and others' discovery of indigenous mulberry trees in the Americas was one of the environmental 'proofs' that anchored many silk dreams in the hemisphere over the coming centuries, marking these lands out from northern Europe's mulberry-light landscapes.

Central America possessed its own species of mulberry, the *Morus celtidifolia*, whose leaves were smaller and rougher than those of their Old World cousins, and whose distributional range reached on a longitudinal axis from northerly Mexican territories such as Chihuahua down to parts of Panama (though now naturalised farther). While now synonymous, *M. celtidifolia* was once distinguished from *Morus microphylla*, the stocky mulberry trees with smallish fruit found

[64] Antonio de Elgueta y Vigil, *Cartilla de la agricultura de moreras y arte para la cria de la seda* (Madrid: G. Ramirez, 1761), 59.
[65] Fernando Colón, *Historia del almirante Don Cristóbal Colón en la cual se da particular y verdadera relación de su vida y de sus hechos, y del descubrimiento de las indias occidentales, ilamadas Nuevomundo* (Madrid: T. Minnesa, 1892), 276. Columbus's own journal refers to how 'some of the trees bore some resemblance to those in Castile'. Julius Olson, *The Northmen, Columbus, and Cabot, 985–1503* (New York: Charles Scribner's Sons, 1906), 121.
[66] Miles H. Davidson, *Columbus Then and Now: A Life Reexamined* (Norman, OK: University of Oklahoma Press, 1997), 80–92; *The Diario of Christopher Columbus's First Voyage to America, 1492–1493* (Norman, OK: University of Oklahoma Press, 1991), 63.

along a more latitudinal belt running from the western part of today's state of Texas across to Arizona. The second distinct species of indigenous mulberry, which carpeted much of what is now the eastern United States, was the larger red mulberry, *Morus rubra*, which ranged across a sizeable rectagonal area cornered by the north-eastern Great Plains down to northern Florida. Phylogenetic research confirms that these distinct native species of North and Central America form a clade with the Asian mulberries within the *Morus* genus. In other words, like the humans who lived amongst them, at some point in the distant past there had likely been a 'single origin of native New World species' after which these American taxa had branched off, relocated, and evolved some distinctive characteristics, with the Texan and Mexican mulberries, as we might expect, remaining particularly similar.[67]

These trees played host to many species of lepidopterans (moths and butterflies), including wild silk moths, many from the family *Saturniidae*, which would enthuse and confuse American explorers and botanists, but none whose raw silk genuinely approached the fibrous quality and harvestable scale of that of the selectively bred *Bombyx mori*. Had such fellow insects' wild silk been included in our earlier sphere of illumination, not only India but also sub-Saharan Africa and parts of the Americas would have appeared less shady, for peoples on both continents had taken to harvesting and working up into textiles the silk bags of various species of caterpillars indigenous to their environments. Sacks or clumped cocoons were opportunistically gathered, combed out, and processed by spinning into coarse yarn, and put to use in weaving, sewing, and padding. Insofar as this involved the human appropriation of fibrous matter generated by metamorphosing insects, there was a shared baseline feature with *Bombyx* sericulture, but the activities were markedly different: neither in the productive processes, nor in the final product were there many similarities, except that the latter tended to be ascribed high value.[68]

---

[67] Madhav Nepal, 'Phylogenetics of Morus (Moraceae) Inferred from ITS and TrnL-TrnF Sequence Data', *Systematic Botany* 37, no. 2 (2012): 448; Madhav Nepal, Mark H. Mayfield, and Carolyn J. Ferguson, 'Identification of Eastern North American Morus (Moraceae): Taxonomic Status of M. Murrayana', *Phytoneuron* 26 (2012): 1–6; Qiwei Zeng, Hongyu Chen, Chao Zhang et al., 'Definition of Eight Mulberry Species in the Genus Morus by Internal Transcribed Spacer-Based Phylogeny', *PloS One* 10, no. 8 (12 January 2015): e0135411. Additional information on native distributional range taken from the United States Department for Agriculture Germplasm Resources Information Network (GRIN) at: www.ars-grin.gov/cgi-bin/npgs/html/taxon.pl?435175 #dist and the Biodiversity International New World Fruits Database, at http://nwfdb .bioversityinternational.org/detail/?uid_fruit=770.

[68] On the wild silkworms of the Americas: Néstor Kriscautzky and Elsa Gómez, 'Tecnologia Apropiada de Origen Precolombino', *Artesanias de America: Revista del CIDAP* 58 (2005): 91–7; Paul M. Tuskes, James P. Tuttle, and Michael M. Collins, *The Wild Silk*

Columbus's interest in the silk-raising potential of American mulberry trees in the 1490s, and his cajoling of his crew with the prospect of a silken doublet, were telling reminders that the fabric's desirability showed no signs of plateauing in spite of its familiarity. The spread of silk fabrics and silk workshops throughout Europe, facilitated by the leakage of Italian expertise, meant spiralling demand for ever-larger quantities of raw silk across countries from Portugal to Russia. It was a demand that could accommodate all shapes and sizes of raw silks, and work them up and weave them out for appropriate consumers – from the most lavish court dress and princely furnishings to the most economical country garb, mixed textiles, ribbons, trimmings, and crude thread. But one of the defining features in the expanding silk industries (that coincided with both the proliferation of East Indian trade and Atlantic colonialism) was their growing appetite for particular kinds of raw silk to fit to specialised centres of manufacturing. As Europeans developed familiarity and expertise in silk manufacturing, they brought new technologies to bear upon processes ranging from reeling cocoons to twisting yarns and to weaving and finishing. Northern Italy was a particular site of innovation and diffusion, playing host to a number of pioneering developments linked to avid consumer demand, diversification, and specialisation. Technological advances in silk-throwing machinery (which doubled and twisted the yarn) allowed better quality and standardisation of semi-finished materials, which in turn placed pressure on producers and traders to furnish manufacturers with raw silk yarns, skeins, and bales of suitable consistency. As this manufacturing technology spread northwards and westwards through Europe after the fifteenth century, more and more manufacturers sought out raw silk that had been subjected to advanced reeling techniques, which could later be processed in hydraulic silk mills into the very thin warp threads preferred by growing numbers of weavers for high-end products.[69]

Moths of North America: A Natural History of the Saturniidae of the United States and Canada (Ithaca, NY: Comstock Pub. Associates, 1996), 52–4, 96, 184, 227–30. On Africa: E. McKinney and J. B. Eicher, 'Unexpected Luxury: Wild Silk Textile Production among the Yoruba of Nigeria', *Textile – the Journal of Cloth & Culture* 7, no. 1 (2009): 40–55; Addis Teshome Kebede, 'Diversity in Structure, Composition and Properties of Silk from African Wild Silkmoths' (PhD thesis, University of Nairobi, 2012). For an overview, with particular attention to the Indian *muga* (*Antheraea assamensis*), *tussah* (*Antheraea paphia*), and *eri* (*Philosamia synthia*) silkworms which feed on different forest leaves or plants: Manjeet Jolly, Satyendra Chowdhury, and S. K. Sen, *Non-Mulberry Sericulture in India* (Bombay: Central Silk Board, 1975). On potential for new ways of harvesting wild silk, see Tom Gheysens, Andrew Collins, Suresh Raina, Fritz Vollrath, and David P. Knight, 'Demineralization Enables Reeling of Wild Silkmoth Cocoons', *Biomacromolecules* 12, no. 6 (13 June 2011): 2257–66.
[69] Molà, *The Silk Industry of Renaissance Venice*, 307; Espinach, *El despegue de la industria sedera*, 114–15.

The questions provoked by the high cost of finished silk goods and this collective craving for raw silk amongst the ambitious, competitive European states clustered around the eastern Atlantic seaboard were broadly similar, reflecting the infamous volatility of harvests and prices in raw silk from year to year, volatility that became more acute the further manufacturers were from production centres.[70] They boiled down to one target: how best to secure international supplies of high-quality raw silk for home industries? Beneath this overarching query followed a range of subsidiary considerations. Can it be grown domestically? If not adequately, can market share be expanded in existing trade routes at low cost? If not effectively, can crowded Mediterranean markets be bypassed to access or engineer new production overseas, while ensuring adequate quality of raw silk? These were questions which tied together the interests of powerful metropolitan forces within Early Modern states: the political elite consumer, the long-distance merchant, the luxury artisan. In addressing such questions, these agents and their capital ultimately became involved in the expansion of global exploration, Asian trade, European production, and Atlantic colonial experimentation.

It was no coincidence that silkworms and Atlantic colonialism featured prominently amongst the subjects artistically curated by Johannes Stradanus to represent the triumph of European civilisation in his *Nova Reperta* (new inventions of modern times) (see Fig. 1.1). Nor that Francis Bacon specifically invoked the silkworm in his *Novum Organum* (new logic in the interpretation of nature) as an exemplar of breaking from old conceits into new waters, as the figurative ship on Bacon's title page – itself largely borrowed from a Spanish publication – sailed through the Pillars of Hercules, departing the tired Mediterranean into the Atlantic Ocean. Reflecting on the transmission of knowledge, Bacon pointed out that in times of yore 'if any one had ventured to suggest the silkworm' as the animal origin of the fibre of such tenacity, beauty, and softness, 'he would have been laughed at as if dreaming'.[71]

---

[70] On this volatility in the early modern era, see for example: Niels Steensgaard, *The Asian Trade Revolution of the Seventeenth Century: The East India Companies and the Decline of the Caravan Trade* (Chicago: University of Chicago Press, 1974), 32–3; George Bryan Souza, *The Survival of Empire: Portuguese Trade and Society in China and the South China Sea, 1630–1754* (Cambridge: Cambridge University Press, 1986), 117–19.

[71] Johannes Stradanus, *Nova reperta* (Antwerp: Phillips Galle, 1590); Francis Bacon, *Novum organum*, ed. Joseph Devey (New York: P.F. Collier & Son, 1620), 85–6; Marília dos Santos Lopes, *Writing New Worlds: The Cultural Dynamics of Curiosity in Early Modern Europe* (Newcastle: Cambridge Scholars, 2016), 126–27; Jorge Cañizares-Esguerra, *Nature, Empire, and Nation: Explorations of the History of Science in the Iberian World* (Stanford: Stanford University Press, 2006), 14–27.

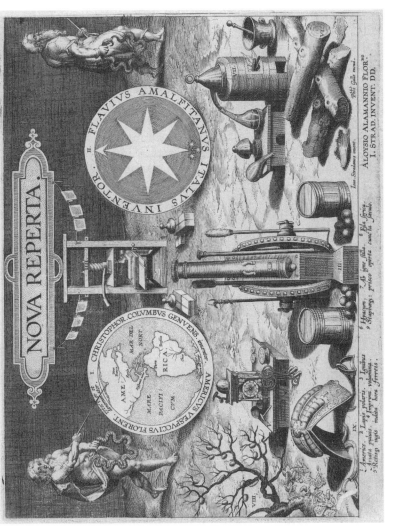

Figure 1.1 Title page to Johannes Stradanus (or Jan van der Straet), *Nova reperta* (Antwerp: Phillips Galle, *c*.1590). He depicts silkworms, cocoons, and mulberry leaves in the bottom left corner as amongst the most advanced acquisitions of European culture, reflecting the conquest of agricultural technology and constituting the only animal represented (besides humans and allegorical snakes); they sit adjacent to the onwards global march of Europeans into the Americas. Metropolitan Museum of Art

The efforts to bring silk culture to American colonies mirrored, in many ways, the patterns that had characterised silk's colonising of earlier peoples and nations. Rulers and governments have arguably interfered with silk more than with any other fibre, and Atlantic colonial powers, like Chinese imperial authorities, Byzantine rulers, and the princes and city councils of Renaissance Italy before them, drew up formal contracts with silk specialists, monitored their rivals' activities, and tried desperately to persuade skilled foreign artisans to migrate. They imposed duties, penalties, and prohibitions with one hand, and offered bounties, privileges, and patronage with the other.[72] Indeed, American projectors – whether Spanish, French, English, or later US citizens – were deeply conscious of earlier models of expansion, which shaped how they understood both the feasibility of introducing sericulture and the best methods for doing so.

In other important ways, the Atlantic world was a distinctive proposition for the expansion of silk cultivation. Given the costs and the distance, diffusion could not readily occur in a spontaneous way: it needed to be premeditated. The issue of migration across the ocean changed the relative weight of 'push' factors (such as a downturn in homeland conditions) and 'pull' factors (such as incentives to move), inflating the importance of the silk specialists' knowledge and adding weight to the role played by supporting authorities. A substantial part of the difficulty in replicating sericulture was that it necessitated not just expertise but also the speedy transfer of very fragile insect larvae, along with the large-scale reshaping of landscapes over a period of years to make space for high numbers of trees, and the complex emulation or adaptation of technology. Transatlantic sericulture therefore posed unprecedented challenges because of the varied environments and existing ecosystems into which Old World mulberry species and silkworms were to be transplanted, the fast-evolving demographic and labour configurations in Atlantic societies, and the breathless economic leaps being taken as the Columbian Exchange radicalised commodity production and gave further impetus to global trade.

In the grand view, and with the benefit of hindsight, perhaps one way to see Atlantic silkworms is as having lost a historical race of sorts. Oceanic trade and the expansion of production in older areas effectively eclipsed the need to persist with American sericulture, and, in overtaking, further exposed the credibility gap between the rationale offered by political economists and the realities experienced

---

[72] The claim about governmental intrusion is made in Dennis O' Flynn and Arturo Giráldez, 'Silk for Silver: Manila-Macao Trade in the 17th Century', *Philippine Studies* 44 (1996): 55. The welter of measures in Italy are explained in Mola, *The Silk Industry of Renaissance Venice*, 29–33.

during efforts at silk raising in the Americas. Between the sixteenth and eighteenth centuries, more and more silk goods would divert away from the land-based Eurasian silk routes towards the oceans, ferried increasingly by the great East India Companies from ports off Iran, Bengal, and later China back to warehouses (especially Dutch and British ones) in northern Europe. The oceanic acquisition of silk did not straightforwardly trump the older caravan routes: for one thing, animal-based portage of such lightweight luxury goods remained economically competitive for a long time, and for another, many trading regions and circuits involved producers or consumers who were fairly impervious to seaborne influence. But it was a logical solution for peripheral European powers who were at a geographical disadvantage but possessed technological and organisational advantages in relation to the financing of mercantile shipping. Increasing raw silk importation to Western Europe via the Cape between 1650 and 1800 was prefigured and abetted by European traders' muscling in on the vibrant pre-existent trade in silks in the Indian Ocean and Pacific. Before sericulture really took hold in Tokugawa Japan, for instance, the interloping Portuguese from Macau (until 1639) and the Dutch from Taiwan were profiting by furnishing Japanese weavers with Vietnamese and Chinese raw and semi-processed silk.[73] Only gradually, and erratically, did the vectors of global trade match European demand for raw silk up with Asiatic sericulture, balancing this with continuing reliance on smaller quantities of market-leading materials from northern Italy. And only after the mid-nineteenth century have scholars described 'a single, unified global market for raw silk'.[74] So if the result of the race between American sericulture and globally sourced alternatives seems to have a foregone conclusion to us now, it most certainly did not at the time.

Interpretations of efforts to introduce *Bombyx* sericulture to households, communities, and colonies in the Atlantic world have often

---

[73] The Chinese did not ship their silk directly due to anti-Japanese sentiment and a Ming government prohibition, partly flamed by the attacks of coastal *wakō* pirates. Michael Cooper, 'The Mechanics of the Macao-Nagasaki Silk Trade', *Monumenta Nipponica* 27, no. 1 (1972): 423–33; Souza, *The Survival of Empire: Portuguese Trade and Society in China and the South China Sea, 1630–1754*, 53, 214–18; Jonathan Israel, *Dutch Primacy in World Trade, 1585–1740* (Oxford: Clarendon Press, 1989), 186; Hoang Anh Tuan, *Silk for Silver: Dutch-Vietnamese Relations, 1637–1700* (Leiden: Brill, 2007).

[74] Ma, 'The Great Silk Exchange: How the World Was Connected and Developed', 49–50, 57–61 (quote on 61); G. Federico, *An Economic History of the Silk Industry, 1830–1930* (Cambridge: Cambridge University Press, 1997).

selectively tended to disparage and downgrade them, as when scholars have claimed that they were delusions that 'persisted for two centuries', or fantasies that 'were just that – dreams'.[75] Often this is a function of underestimating their extent. It bespeaks a sense that the culture of silk was somehow antithetical to the project of American settlement: 'The tending of silkworms and the winding of Silk were not calculated to nourish the qualities required to subdue the forests and cultivate the swamps of a new country', suggested John Bishop in 1866, drawing on tropes of deforestation and clearance that fit poorly with the reality of plantations of millions of mulberries.[76] Sometimes the interpretations reflect our tendency as historians, and particularly our archives' tendency, to give precedence to commercial criteria for what constituted 'success' and to overlook meanings and cultural and economic impact that could be local, fleeting, and have intense personal dimensions of value.

Several of the works which have engaged with struggles to introduce silk, because disconnected, have allowed writers to grind axes in their explanations, whether of a local, national, racial, or class variety. Nineteenth-century Americans blamed the poor dexterity of enslaved African Americans, Mexicans blamed the Spanish government, imperial Britons blamed 'the temperament of either the English or African race' for being incapable of patient attention and minute observation, corporations claimed to have been undone by 'the ignorance and awkwardness of the Irish peasantry', while early-twentieth-century French intellectuals blamed the impossible conservatism of peasant farmers and rural types, who evolved 'with a sloth that brings despair to all professors of agriculture'.[77] And many contain straightforward errors: one of the most influential surveys of American textiles, William Bagnall's seminal (and still hugely useful) work at the end of the nineteenth century, *The Textile Industries of the United States*, was wrong to assert that the culture of silk was not commenced until the 1730s in South Carolina and the 1760s in Connecticut, wrong to claim that 'from 1759 the production and exportation rapidly decreased till about the time of the American Revolution, when it had

---

[75] Louis B. Wright, *The Dream of Prosperity in Colonial America* (New York: New York University Press, 1965), 35; Karen Ordahl Kupperman, *The Atlantic in World History* (Oxford: Oxford University Press, 2012), 97.

[76] John Leander Bishop, Edwin Troxell Freedley, and Edward Young, *A History of American Manufactures, from 1608 to 1860: Comprising Annals of the Industry of the United States in Machinery, Manufactures and Useful Arts*, 3 vols. (Philadelphia: E. Young & Co., 1866), 1: 359.

[77] J. Henry Lefroy, *Memorials of the Discovery and Early Settlement of the Bermudas or Somers Islands, 1515–1685*, 2 vols. (London: Longmans Green and Co., 1877), 1:500n1; George Richardson Porter, *A Treatise on the Origin, Progressive Improvement, and Present State of the Silk Manufacture* (London: Longman, 1831), 45; A. Beauquis, *Histoire économique de la soie* (Grenoble: Imprimerie Generale, 1910), 54.

nearly ceased', and wrong to state that 'there is no record, that ... sewing-silk, silk-stockings, or silk-fabrics were made, to be sold, anywhere in the colonies'.[78]

Failed commodities, because they are less often scrutinised and therefore corrected, grow their own historical misperceptions that can prove surprisingly resilient.[79] Contrary to such interpretations, silk was much more than a mere fantasy: it brought sustained investment and activity across multiple peoples, centuries, and American sites; this activity was often profoundly meaningful to individuals and communities; and in the process of seeking to surmount local and structural challenges, these efforts left important legacies in relation to the shape of empires, economies, and environments. The different attempts would unravel, often for different reasons. But connecting these dreams of sericulture allows us to better understand three features at the heart of Atlantic imperialism: its unbounded cultural conviction, its environmental limitations, and its diverse human stories of encounter and adaptation.

[78] William R. Bagnall, *The Textile Industries of the United States* (Cambridge, MA: The Riverside Press, 1893), 61–2.

[79] Some still in evidence in: Melillo, 'Global Entomologies: Insects, Empires, and the "Synthetic Age" in World History', 250; Stephanie Green and Zoe Meyer, *Mulberry & Silk* (Rye: Sage Press, 2003), 3, 12, 13.

Part I

Emergence

> They will raise so much silk here that it will be one of the richest places in the world, and become the heart of the silk trade, because there are already many plantations of mulberries here. With these and the planting and raising in many other parts of New Spain, in a few years, more silk will be raised in New Spain than in all of Christendom.
>
> Fray Toribio de Benavente ('Motolinia'), 1540[1]

Introduction: East and West, *c*.1480–1560

The first silkworms known to have been subjected to an Atlantic crossing were procured by Doctor Sancho Ortiz de Matienzo from the kingdom of Granada. In 1503, this canon of the cathedral of Seville, in his capacity as treasurer of the Casa de Contratación (the brand-new royal agency created by Queen Isabella I of Castile to superintend Spanish-American colonisation), arranged for the eggs to be carefully packed, and loaded into the hold of one of two ships on the nearby dockyards.[2] Soon, they were dispatched down the Guadalquivir, the only great navigable river in Spain, from which they sailed out into the Gulf of Cadiz, and set a course for Hispaniola, the first island to have been settled by Columbus in 1492, after his flagship ran aground on Christmas Day. At some point in the intervening 3,000 miles of ocean, the silkworm eggs hatched, and, stifled for air and bereft of food, they died. It was a fate that would be shared by many thousands of their peers in the centuries to come, no matter how much care was lavished on their oceanic storage. The half an ounce of spoiled seed went virtually unnoticed amongst the heavier merchandise that was eagerly awaited

---

[1] Motolinia, 'Historia de Los Indios de La Nueva España', in *Colección de documentos para la historia de México*, ed. Joaquín García Icazbalceta, vol. 1 (Mexico City: Librería de J. M. Andrade, 1858), 239.

[2] Libro de cargo y data, Archivo General de Indias (hereinafter AGI), Contratación 4674, 19v.

by early colonists, valued at more than a million *maravedís* (Spanish currency).[3]

Despite this inauspicious first voyage, the sixteenth century would witness a remarkable rise of silk production in the Spanish Empire, as Iberian conquistadors and caterpillars converged upon Meso-American Indians and mountain forests. By the 1560s, amidst the brutal extraction of gold and silver, silk production blossomed into one of the Americas' first post-Columbian cash crops, and for a time it sustained a manufacturing industry that helped satiate the growing markets of a Latinising America. Perhaps strangely, this first colonial attempt at establishing silk cultivation across the Atlantic would prove unquestionably the most successful of all those in the Americas, linking the victims of the European *Reconquista* with those of the American *Conquista*: a Moorish speciality became a Mixtecan Indian opportunity. But it was a function of the dramatic pace of global interconnection in the sixteenth century that, within four decades of the first harvesting of American raw silk in the 1540s, the first Asian raw silk in bulk arrived in America from the other direction, across the Pacific. A commercial battle followed between the valuable fibrous proteins emitted by the silkworms of Granada (in Spain and New Spain), and those of their long-distant ancestors in China. Its result, the collapse of raw silk production in New Spain, was heavily influenced by the decline of Indian populations and the paranoia of the Spanish Crown in terms of protecting its peninsular interests.

It was no coincidence that the first Atlantic silkworms were procured from the kingdom of Granada. Lying in the far south-east of the Iberian Peninsula, the region was the first point at which Islam, and with it, sericulture had reached mainland Europe via North Africa. Protected by the Sierra Nevada Mountains, the Nasrid dynasty proved to be the last bastion of Muslim resistance to the Christian *Reconquista*, crumbling only in 1491 in the face of the concerted pressure of the united Catholic Monarchs. The capitulation of Granada, even at the time, was recognised as a major historical turning point, though the anticipated onwards surge of Christian European sovereignty into Islamic North Africa proved less significant than the subsequent unleashing of consolidated Iberian energy, capital, and militarism into the Atlantic and into mainland Europe. In 1492, at the stroke of a pen by the terms of the Treaty of

[3] Miguel Angel Ladero Quesada, *El primer oro de América: Los comienzos de la casa de la contratación de las Yndias, 1503–1511* (Madrid: Real Academia de la Historia, 2002), 25, 92. For comparison, a pig was worth approximately 400 and a cow 2,000 *maravedís*. David Satava, 'Columbus's First Voyage: Profit or Loss from a Historical Accountant's Perspective', *Journal of Applied Business Research* 23, no. 4 (16 January 2011).

Granada, the emirate's substantial population of silk producers and its flourishing urban silk industry were added to those already controlled by the Crowns of Castile and Aragon, in Andalusia and several eastern provinces. Castilian and foreign merchants were quick to arrive to try to secure a slice of the wealthy trade out of Granada's famous silk market (the *alcaicería*), joining the Genoese cabal that had been permitted to operate under the Nasrid sultans. Further up the Mediterranean coast, long-standing Islamic domination of the region's silk industries, once buttressed by Jewish trade networks, had already been eroded in the fifteenth century by the creeping infiltration of Italian trading and manufacturing interests, with Genoese influences spreading into north-eastern port cities, gaining traction by virtue of their commercial links and technical distinction in silk working. Once famed for its workshops and geometric designs, Granada had increasingly become a supplier of raw materials for manufacture in other cities – Genoa, Montpellier, Florence, and Lucca – and the number of weaving units in the major centres of Granada, Almería, and Malaga had fallen somewhat.[4]

Silk, then, was one of the most significant prizes secured in the capture of Granada, and one of the reasons Catholic victors were initially hesitant to pursue the kinds of repressive measures that would follow in later decades. The skills and materials associated with sericulture had been embedded for generations in the people and the landscape, dispersed amongst the rural Arabic-speaking peasantry with their hillside mulberry stocks. The mulberry harvesting took place from late March and early April, when the leaves were collectively stripped and then divided up amongst the workers, with the trees' owners receiving a large share. The least profitable and least centralised work of silkworm raising and cocoon reeling, in particular, fell disproportionately to Granadan women, though they were also involved in more advanced stages, and perhaps particularly so during the late Nasrid period. Firmly rooted in the countryside by the late fifteenth century, the silk industry then branched into networks of exchange, manufacture, and trade that generated extensive tax revenue which reflected both the commodity's value and its dominance in nearby

[4] Elizabeth Woodhead Nutting, 'Vivir por la seda: Morisca Women, Household Economies, and the Silk Industry in the Kingdom of Granada, 1400–1570' (MA thesis, University of Texas at Austin, 2010), 20–1; David Coleman, *Creating Christian Granada: Society & Religious Culture in an Old-World Frontier City, 1492–1600* (Ithaca, NY: Cornell University Press, 2003), 29–30; Paulino Iradiel Murugarren and Germán Navarro Espinach, 'La seda en Valencia en la edad media', in *España y Portugal en las rutas de la seda*, ed. Comisión Española de la Ruta de la Seda (Barcelona: Universitat de Barcelona, 1996), 190–3; Germán Navarro Espinach, *El despegue de la industria sedera en la Valencia del siglo XV* (Valencia: Generalitat Valenciana, 1992), 37–8, 63–85.

markets, especially in the western Mediterranean and the Maghreb.[5] The iconic success of silk production was such that when Nasrid Granada was finally taken, its Christian rulers sought to ensure as much continuity and as little disruption as possible – doing little more than rediverting tax revenue to Castile, and leaving in place the guild officers, commercial practices, and Arabic terminology of the silk industry.[6] Over the coming decades, they sought to manage the paradox of eradicating Islam while benefiting from the high efficiency and profitability of traditional Moorish silk production.

In 1501, the Catholic Monarchs issued orders in line with 'ancient practice and custom,' insisting that all silk business be conducted through the *alcaicerías* of Granada, Malaga, and Almería. Over the next decade, they rolled out Spanish legislation that encoded earlier Muslim practices – amongst them, claiming a 10 per cent levy on all silk sales, an extra tariff on exports, and reissuing instructions for the many charges and practices associated with the commodity's regulation.[7] The widespread availability of black mulberries (*morales*) throughout Granada, and especially in mountainous locales, meant that there was initially little need or will to engineer a replacement of one species with the other (white mulberries, usually *moreras*).[8] Indeed, such was the high esteem of established nurseries that in 1520 Granada prohibited the planting of imported white mulberries and demanded the felling of those that had been brought from Messina, Murcia, and Valencia, the ordinance bemoaning the tendency to 'respect that which has quantity and not quality' – and betraying a conservatism which has variously been imputed to either rural Morisco lobbyists, livestock farmers eager for pasture lands, or

[5] José Enrique López de Coca Castañer, 'La seda en el reino de Granada (siglos XV y XVI)', in *España y Portugal en las rutas de la seda*, 34–7; Nutting, 'Vivir por la seda', 32–4.
[6] Royal decree of May 1492, in Rafael Marín López, *Documentos para la historia de la seda en el reino de Granada (Siglos XV–XVIII)* (Granada: Universidad de Granada, 2008), 42–4. Arabic terms for silk-industry officers regulating weights and quality included the *geliz* (city government officer), *motalefe* (quality controller of raw silk skeins), and *hafiz* (master of seals). López de Coca Castañer, 'La seda en el reino de Granada', 44–5. For similar continuities in preserving the infrastructure of silk production earlier in the *Reconquista*, see Espinach, *El despegue de la industria sedera*, 29, 34–5, 121.
[7] The most comprehensive compilation of such measures was the 'Arancel de los derechos Moriscos de la seda del reino de Granada', 21 November 1505, alongside others showing continuity in Marín López, *Documentos para la historia de la seda*, 45–54 (quote on 46).
[8] Vincent Lagardère, 'Mûrier et culture de la soie en Andalus au moyen age (Xe–XIVe siècles)', *Mélanges de la Casa de Velázquez* 26, no. 1 (1990): 97–111; José Enrique López de Coca Castañer, 'Morales y moreras en la sericultura', in *La Andalucía medieval: Actas, I jornadas de historia rural y medio ambiente (Almonte, 23–25 Mayo 2000)*, ed. Javier Pérez-Embid Wamba (Huelva: Universidad de Huelva, 2002), 453–70.

Christian authorities keen not to disrupt profits.[9] While encouraging continuity in the internal aspects of silk production, Castilian rulers did, however, early signal their intent to change the external dimensions of the silk trade to maximise on their new asset. From 1500, Granada's access to foreign raw materials (in silk skein, thread, or cocoon form) was abruptly stopped, not just from North Africa but also southern Italy and the Levant.[10] Forced to subsist on local raw materials, the looms of the silk emirate that had long faced east found themselves reorientated, like the Catholic kingdoms that had finally conquered them, towards the west.[11]

As more and more 'Old Christian' immigrants (with many from Andalusia and Toledo, as well as Italians) filled the workshops and market stalls of departing Moors, Granada became the centrepiece of Castile's silk trade, and was soon shipping large quantities of finished goods throughout Spain and out across the Atlantic to hungry new colonial societies. Under Christian control, the *alcaicería* and the panoply of artisans linked to the silk trade fell under the oversight of officials appointed to the Casa del Arte de la Seda (1511). Acting as the customs house for the whole kingdom, and rendering taxation on all silk sales and exports (mostly via Malaga to Valencia and to Italian mercers), it would go on to contribute substantial sums to the Crown treasury, in the process helping to subsidise the lavish costumes of the court. In the middle of the sixteenth century, Pedro de Medina reported that almost all of the city of Granada's 'common people make their living by silk', with the harvest bringing some 50,000 ducats in taxation; only there was such municipalised vertical integration possible, culminating in the production especially of damasks, velvets, and taffetas.[12]

The demographics of sericulture in Granada were less transformed than those of silk manufacturing in the first half of the sixteenth century:

---

[9] Cited in Manuel Garzón Pareja, *La industria sedera en España: El arte de la seda de Granada* (Granada: Archivo de la Real Chancillería, 1972), 135–6. This understanding of the relative suitability of white and black mulberries would be reversed by the early nineteenth century. López de Coca Castañer, 'La seda en el reino de Granada', 52–3.

[10] 'Pragmática de los reyes católicos prohibiendo la entrada de seda en Madeja, Hilo, Capullo, pero si en Cedazos', 20 August 1500, Marín López, *Documentos para la historia de la seda*, 45.

[11] Eloy Martín Corrales, 'Comercio de la seda entre España y Mediterráneo', in *España y Portugal en las rutas de la seda*, 160–79 esp. 160, and see also ibid., 84–5, 122. Much silk trade continued to longstanding markets in North Africa (such as Oran, Tunis, and Fez) from Andalusia and Granada, some of it in return for slaves, horses, or ransomed captives, but increasingly carried by Italian interlopers.

[12] Pedro de Medina, *Libro de grandezas y cosas memorables de España* (Seville: Domenico de Robertis, 1548), cxlv. Using Pierre Marteau's historical currency conversion tool, this crudely translated to £20,000 sterling: www.pierre-marteau.com/currency/converter.html.

Morisco women continued to be enormously important, albeit their historical visibility declined substantially with the transition to Christian records.[13] One report in the summer of 1514 highlighted that silkworm seed was fetching a good price, but that as a consequence, the 'New Christians' were mixing fine eggs with defective ones – causing an estimated loss of a third of the silk that might otherwise have been raised.[14] Regional techniques, materials, and commercial practices changed comparatively little, though there were significant structural changes to sericulture's organisation. Licensed inspectors (*veedores*) prowled the reels that drew cocoon filaments into yarn from 1513, checking 'that all the silk that they reel is clean and in much perfection'. Silk workers were subject from the 1520s to tightening quality control, as Castilian authorities sought to calibrate their output to ensure that Castile's finished textiles could compete with the best European industry standards. From 1535, cocoon reelers (*hiladores*) had to pass an examination that monitored the consistency of their raw silk, hire trainee assistants, and receive a set rate of cash payment for their work. These measures followed earlier attempts to prevent unlicensed materials from circulating in the market: inconsistent raw silk, dyes that did not hold, yarn that did not last, and other flaws and frauds that ultimately cost manufacturers.[15] They bespoke a slight but perceptibly growing contrast between the more outward-looking and prescriptive world of city artisans (with a high Old Christian component) and the more inward-looking and flexible world of rural households (with a high Morisco component). By 1560, one official estimated that Granada's sericulture spanned 336 towns and places, involved 40,000 silk raisers, and generated 135,000 lb of raw silk per year.[16]

The turning of Granada's silk from east to west brought it ever higher repute amongst the aristocracy of the Iberian Peninsula, whose appreciation of silk fabrics (and failure to restrict their consumption) can be measured by the array of sumptuary laws issued and reissued across the sixteenth century.[17] Success also brought closer scrutiny by the Crown and an increasing tax burden – being one fifth, in 1505, of what it would

---

[13] Nutting, 'Vivir por la seda', 38–41, 50. For evidence that Christian immigrants were involved in sericulture from the 1520s, and allegedly given preferential treatment by officials, see: 'Real cédula de Carlos I ordenando que la tasación del capullo de seda sea igual para los cristianos nuevos y los viejos', 1526, in Marín López, *Documentos para la historia de la seda*.

[14] Registro General Sello, August 1514, cited in López de Coca Castañer, 'La seda en el reino de Granada', 47.

[15] Marín López, *Documentos para la historia de la seda*, 56–7, 71–3, 119–20.

[16] Contaduría Mayor de Cuentas, cited in López de Coca Castañer, 'La seda en el reino de Granada', 50.

[17] Juan Sempere y Guarinos, *Historia del luxo, y de las leyes suntuarias de España* (Madrid: Imprenta Real, 1788).

become in 1561, by which time the export of raw silk had also been prohibited.[18] The sense that sericulture was an industry that offered high yield to sovereign powers was doubtless one of its attractions as a 'New World' prospect in the same period. It was one of the lessons of the wider *Reconquista* of Al-Andalus, completed in 1492, that silk production was an undertaking that could bring wealth even to dusty and forbidding subtropical landscapes. Silk offered a way to morph the labour of non-Christian peoples into a vehicle of Christian glory, and to act as an engine of economic and technical development. It was associated with colonisation programmes, usually in a second wave as feudal landholders graduated from military appointees to agricultural consolidators and entrepreneurs – neatly captured in the phrase *señoríos de la seda* (lordships of silk).[19] And by the 1540s, even the growing quality and quantity of Granada's silk was not enough to meet spiralling demand, with raw silk being siphoned off to feed other Castilian silk industries, particularly through Genoese agents, and finished cloths being exported to Italy, Portugal, and Flanders and across the Atlantic. More capacity was required, which focused elite and commercial attention upon securing overseas sources of raw silk, and enlarging domestic supply – if needs be through experimentally and covertly introducing white mulberries, a practice which gathered momentum and controversy in Granada in the 1550s.[20]

Besides Granada, other neighbouring Spanish territories and islands expanded their silk production in the sixteenth century, often at the independent behest of the Aragonese nobility, though the quality and scale of Granada's raw silk set it apart, as shown in the province's prohibition in 1512 of the import of silks from Valencia and Murcia to avoid reputational contamination.[21] Andalusia and Valencia had long-standing traditions of silk production and extensive silk-raising regions,

---

[18] Kenneth Garrad, 'La industría sedera granadina en el siglo xvi y en conexión con el levantamiento de las alpujarras (1568–1571)', *Miscelanea de estudios Árabes y Hebraicos* 5 (1956): 91–2; Marín López, *Documentos para la historia de la seda*, 19. The annual Venetian *muda* (Mediterranean convoy of galleys) continued to bring away from Granada various kinds of semi-finished silks and non-filament silk waste known as *cadarzo*, which were traded in North Africa. López de Coca Castañer, 'La seda en el reino de Granada', 54–5.

[19] Teresa Pérez Picazo and Guy Lemeunier, 'El caso murciano', in *España y Portugal en las rutas de la seda*, 104.

[20] López de Coca Castañer, 'Morales y moreras en la sericultura', 456–65.

[21] Marín López, *Documentos para la historia de la seda*, 19–20. For proscriptions of importation of Levantine raw silk into the mainland and examples of expansionism to Mallorca, Carles Manera-Joana Escartín, 'La evolución de la manufactura de la seda en Mallorca', in *España y Portugal en las rutas de la seda*, 133, 173.

and the Italianised development of Valencia's silk industry benefited
from both Granadan raw silk imports and its own territorial upsurge
in the culture of white mulberry trees from the start of the fifteenth
century, particularly in well-watered hillside locations like those
around Xàtiva, in the districts of Safor and the Ribera Alta, and
the immediate environs (Huerta) of the city of Valencia.[22] Murcia
began later but enjoyed pronounced expansion in the sixteenth
century, bringing localised environmental and social change, especially along the water-rich areas of the Segura River valley, which
were to be planted out with white mulberry nurseries.[23] Murcia's
raw silk was commercially exported to other places for its processing, for there was little manufacturing to speak of *in situ*; this
exchange was famously captured by Miguel de Cervantes in the
scene in which his eponymous hero, Don Quixote, falls foul of his
hapless horse when trying to challenge six silk traders, who are on
the way from Toledo to buy up raw materials in Murcia.[24] Murcian
magnates successfully pioneered ways of deploying their control of
land to foster silk production amongst the peasantry – offering long
leaseholds using detailed contracts that specified labour duties and
favourable terms for sericulture, or re-landscaping zones in the aftermath of floods to position the workforce better amongst mulberry
nurseries.[25]

Such lessons across south-eastern Spain in how to synchronise political
sovereignty, environment, and labour had wider applicability at the dawn
of American colonialism. The opportunity to capitalise on high demand
for silk, made ever more urgent in light of the introduction of new
technology which allowed the manufacturers of Toledo and Seville to
improve capacity and quality in their spinning and twisting of silk, would
reach out across the Atlantic.[26]

---

[22] Murugarren and Espinach, 'La seda en Valencia en la edad media', 194–6; Espinach, *El despegue de la industria sedera*, 40–1, 92–4.

[23] Juan Fontes Torres, 'Produccion sedera murciana en la edad media', *Murgetana* 46 (1977): 29–37; Pedro Miralles Martínez, 'Seda, trabajo y sociedad en la Murcia del siglo XVII' (PhD thesis, Universidad de Murcia, 2000); Pedro Olivares Galvañ, *Historia de la seda en Murcia*, 2nd ed. (Murcia: Editora Regional de Murcia, 2005).

[24] Miguel de Cervantes Saavedra, *Don Quixote*, trans. James H. Montgomery, rev. ed. (Indianapolis: Hackett Pub. Co., 2009), 35.

[25] Teresa Pérez Picazo and Guy Lemeunier, 'El caso murciano', 102–7.

[26] Julián Montemayor, 'La seda en Toledo en la época moderna', in *España y Portugal en las rutas de la seda*, 123–4, 195–6; Miralles Martínez, 'Seda, trabajo y sociedad en la Murcia del siglo XVII', 61.

The New World of Silk, *c.*1520–1580

Silk accompanied the earliest voyagers who ventured across the Atlantic, both materially and metaphorically. Amidst the spectacular carnival of encounters that followed European discoveries of landmasses in the Americas, fragile explorers found themselves in desperate need of reassurance about the cultural superiority of their own civilisation. As the pre-eminent prestige Eurasian textile, silk played an important part in staking these claims to sophistication. So where early conquistadors admired the intricate textiles of the indigenous peoples they encountered, they often compared them to silks, as when Hernán Cortés described the cottons arrayed in the great plaza in the Aztec capital city Tenochtitlán in 1520 as having 'the appearance of the silk-market at Granada', or the fabric presents of Moctezuma as marvellous 'even though they were of cotton and not silk'.[27] But given that most straggling, improvisational bands of Iberian adventurers carried few luxuries with them (a fact often remarked upon by American 'Indians' unimpressed with their visitors' gifts), recognition of the value of silk in the Americas would find its most important early expression amidst the fledgling Spanish ports and towns. The organisation of half-conquered territories involved trying to bring order to isolated outcrops of plunder, dysfunctional communities that often degenerated into infighting, civil war, and bloody personal or costly legal reprisals. And as the Spanish impulse not just to claim but also to display civilisational order became more pressing in the early decades of the sixteenth century, likewise possessing the trappings of that order became more necessary. As one of the most identifiable hallmarks of a European ruling elite, and more particularly as a fibre then unknown in the Americas, silk therefore offered a unique signifier of power and respect for precarious colonial authority.[28]

---

[27] Hernán Cortés, *Letters from Mexico*, ed. John Huxtable Elliott and Anthony Pagden (New Haven: Yale University Press, 2001), 101, 104. See also R. H. Major, *Select Letters of Christopher Columbus* (London: Printed for the Hakluyt Society, 1847), 123; Bartolomé de Las Casas, *Historia de las Indias, escrita por Fray Bartolomé de las Casas* (Madrid: Impr. de M. Ginesta, 1876), 4: 485.

[28] Some writers have posited *Bombyx* silk culture in the Americas predating European arrival in the late fifteenth century, but these are highly dubious contentions given the overwhelming weight of textual, archaeological, and material evidence to the contrary. The counterfactual tenacity of some of this literature can be attributed to the mention of silk in the Book of Mormon. But this is a reflection more of the history of silk influencing the history of religion (Joseph Smith's rise overlapped with the period of serico-mania in the United States, which is discussed in the epilogue) than of religious works accounting for silk's origins. For an example of these stretched claims, proposing 'a cultivated Nephite species ... [that] could have perished from neglect in the post-Cumorah period', Maurice W. Connell, 'The Prophet Said Silk', *The Improvement Era* 65, no. 5 (1962): 324–45. Note: 'Indians' is hereinafter used to describe indigenous peoples of the Americas, though recognised as a colonial exonym and misnomer.

Silk was very early and very pointedly used to mark out status in the New World. Widely prohibited to regular colonists, a royal decree in 1501 gave express permission to Nicolás de Ovando (who as governor of the Indies represented the majesty of the monarchy) to dress in coloured brocades, silks, and fabrics with gold, jewels, and precious stones.[29] Ovando's brocaded silks bore testament to his indisputable cultural prestige, much like the Aztec Tlatoani (leader), whom Cortés described as 'dressed . . . very rich in their way and more so than the others', or the Sapa of Tawantinsuyu (emperor of the Incas), whom Guaman Poma explained was clad in specially wrought clothing 'out of material finer than taffeta or silk'.[30] In 1509 and 1513, the Spanish proscriptions were again issued, listing silk goods amongst other expensive apparel as prohibited from wear for ordinary colonists, and prescribing a range of penalties for transgressors.[31] But first on the islands, and then on the mainland, silk clothing began to be authorised to others marked out by royal authority or by economic status.[32] In 1513, a royal decree gave explicit permission to Pedrarias Dávila (the departing governor of Castilla de Oro – a province embracing much of modern-day Nicaragua, Costa Rica, Panama, and northern Colombia) and his wife Isabel de Bobadilla, to dress themselves in silk and gold brocades, so that the Indians would grasp what this rare alien fibre was, though one imagines it was his many years of militantly subduing Moors that proved the most imposing feature of Dávila's oft-maligned New World career.[33] Silk therefore helped to map Old World categories of display across the Atlantic, and its visibility was equally important to the other crucial prong of Spanish colonial activity, the Catholic Church, whose early spaces it soon adorned. As an agent of Christian majesty, silk had long been associated with heavenly spaces and bodies, and given its portability and novel exoticism for Indians (in stark contrast to its familiarity for Moorish aficionados), it served a distinctive

---

[29] 'Real Cédula a frey Nicolás de Ovando', 22 September 1501, AGI, Indiferente, 418, 1: 52v.

[30] Cortés, *Letters from Mexico*, 84; Guaman Poma, *El primer nueva corónica y buen gobierno* (1615), 302: online digital version of the Royal Library, Copenhagen's *Corónica*, at: www .kb.dk/permalink/2006/poma/info/en/project/project.htm.

[31] 'Prohibición de usar prendas de sedas en Indias', 12 November 1509, AGI, Indiferente, 418, 2: 87v–89v; 'Modo en que han de vestir los pobladores de Tierra Firme', 28 July 1513, AGI, Panama, 233, 1: 61r–64r.

[32] 'Real Cédula a Miguel Díaz [de Aux]', [San Juan/Puerto Rico] 22 July 1511, AGI, Indiferente, 418, 3: 141v–142v; 'Orden a Francisco de Garay', [Santiago/Jamaica] 20 July 1515, AGI, Indiferente, 419, 5: 445–447v. Antonio Herrera y Tordesillas, *Historia General de los hechos de los castellanos en las Islas i tierra firme del Mar oceano* (Madrid: Nicolas Rodriguez Franco [orig. pub. 1601–1615], 1730), 3: 151–2.

[33] 'Exención a Pedrarias en las normas sobre vestidos' and 'Preeminencias en el vestir para Pedrarias y su mujer', AGI, Panama, 233, 1: 82v–83r; 139v–140r.

role by veneering cultural claims through lavishly embroidered or bro-caded altar cloths, vestments, and furnishings.[34]

As wealth began to flow back from conquistador incursions and the extractive and productive operations that were organised in their wakes, the Spanish Americas developed a particular taste for silk consumption. We can measure it somewhat in the echoes of commercial grievances, as when merchants of Santo Domingo complained in 1545 that the island's authorities imposed unfair extra conditions on their trade in textiles, forcing them to sell silk, cloth, and linen goods (amongst others) at artificially low prices should they fail to dispose of their cargos within six days.[35] Or when Isabel Pérez, an inhabitant of Seville, demanded restitu-tion for 10 lb of silk that had been confiscated in error aboard the *Santiago* in 1558, as she and others were exporting silk goods in growing volume.[36] And as more complex social hierarchies developed in the new settlements spreading across the continent, silk was called upon to help demarcate them. Wealthy, middling, mixed-race, and Indian residents of Cuenca, a provisioning town established in the 1550s near the gold mines of Santa Barbara, soon showed discernment in their silk-trading and -purchasing habits, helping to spawn new sumptuary acts across the Viceroyalty of Peru in 1571 that banned free blacks and mulatto women from wearing silk mantles.[37]

The refinement of cargos and sea routes, and the explosion of traffic that was shuttling between Seville and the Americas, eventually increased the probabilities of getting *Bombyx* larvae successfully across the Atlantic. Sancho de Matienza had been asked in 1504 and again in 1505 to source and speedily package up silkworm eggs, finding them listed amongst the

---

[34] For examples of silk's use in sacristies in mission churches and chapels: 'Real disposición', 16 October 1595, AGI Indiferente, 426, 28: 224v; Alessia Frassani, 'The Church and Convento of Santo Domingo Yanhuitlan, Oaxaca: Art, Politics, and Religion in a Mixtec Village, Sixteenth through Eighteenth Centuries' (PhD thesis, City University of New York, 2009), 75–6.

[35] 'Real Cédula', 7 February 1545, AGI, Santo Domingo, 868, 2: 229v.

[36] 'Devolución de diez libras de seda a Isabel Pérez; 25 April 1558, AGI, Panama, 236, 9: 261r–262r; 'Devolución de un comiso a Hernando de Torres', 26 November 1573, AGI Panama, 236, 10: 352r–353r. On the few dozen merchants trading in silks for the American market out of Toledo in the sixteenth century, see Julián Montemayor, 'La seda en Toledo en la época moderna', in *España y Portugal en las rutas de la seda* (Barcelona: Universitat de Barcelona, 1996), 122.

[37] Royal Cédula of 11 February 1571, cited in Angel Rosenblat, *La población indígena y el mestizaje en América* (Buenos Aires: Editorial Nova, 1954), 2: 156; Diego Arteaga, 'Vestido y desnudo: La seda en Cuenca (Ecuador) durante los siglos XVI y XVII', *Artesanías de América: Revista Del CIDAP* 58 (2005): 189–205; Elena Phipps, 'Textiles as Cultural Memory: Andean Garments in the Colonial Period', in *Converging Cultures: Art and Identity in Spanish America*, ed. Diana Fane (New York: Harry N. Abrams, 1997), 152.

items requested by the governor – alongside more instrumental resources such as caravels, slaves, and gunpowder; but evidently no solution had yet been found to the problem of sustaining the seed through the voyage.[38] The silkworm eggs were intended for symbiosis with identified trees on Hispaniola, a fact underscored by the absence of requests for Spanish mulberry seed or saplings at this point. It is unclear quite what species the Caribbean target tree was: Ovando's instructions in 1503 reported that 'we are informed there are many mulberries in these islands for making silk', and fifteen years later, Bartolomé de Las Casas claimed there were as many as weeds in the Greater Antilles, and that their bark was used by the indigenous Taínos for cloth and paper. Natives called the trees *guacimas* and Las Casas described them as rougher and thicker versions of *moreras* (white mulberries), with hard black fruit that fattened local pigs. Unless Las Casas was badly mistaken, we may assume that since the fruits are often dispersed by birds, and the trees wind pollinated, either as a consequence of an eastward spread of *M. celtidifolia* from Mexico, or a south-eastward spread of *M. rubra* from what is now the US south-east, the plants appear to have made it to the Caribbean where they were available and recognisable.[39]

Plans to establish sericulture were given added momentum in the late 1510s by the efforts of Las Casas. Las Casas, originally amongst the settlers with Ovando, had returned from the West Indies where he had been disgusted at the barbarity of the treatment of Taíno Indians by the Spaniards under both that governor, and subsequently with new incursions into Cuba. Hoping that silk raising might operate to the benefit of the Indians whose welfare he now began to champion, in 1518 he ranked silk production amongst his earliest remedies for governmental policies under his so-called community scheme. His fifth formal proposition for the Greater Antilles – after measures to entice more white landholders, loosen taxes on gold, limit slavery, and subsidise Christian labour immigration – was to offer a scheme of rewards for the production of 'so many pounds of silk' in each region. He claimed 'it is believed that this is the best land in the world for it' and that taking advantage of the trees could

[38] 'Respuestas a cartas', 27 December 1504 and 27 December 1505, AGI, Indiferente, 418, 1: 142 and 144v.
[39] 'Instrucion secreta para el Gobernador Fray Niculas Dovando', 29 March 1503, in Joaquín Francisco Pacheco, Francisco de Cárdenas y Espejo, and Luis Torres de Mendoza, *Colección de documentos inéditos, relativos al descubrimiento, conquista y organización de las antiguas posesiones españolas de América y Oceanía: Sacados de Los archivos del reino, y muy especialmente del de Indias* (Madrid, 1864), 31: 178; Tao Orion, *Beyond the War on Invasive Species: A Permaculture Approach to Ecosystem Restoration* (White River Junction, VT: Chelsea Green Publishing, 2015), 139; Casas, *Historia de las Indias, Escrita Por Fray Bartolomé de Las Casas*, 4: 324.

effect 'miracles'.[40] The new young king Charles (soon Habsburg Emperor Charles V) and his regents duly advertised a bounty of 30,000 *maravedís* per year for whosoever should first raise 12 lb of silk in the Indies.[41] This proved to be the first state reward in a 300-year sequence of incentives that straddled European nations and American regions. Las Casas, now recruiting for his much larger vision for the social and economic improvement of the Indies, was expressly instructed to send experts in sericulture and in silk reeling – perhaps an emphasis on technical experience that reflected a perceived shortcoming a dozen years earlier, when such experience had not even been mentioned. But the scheme collapsed when Las Casas, a better writer than organiser, antagonised Castilian nobles and lost royal support, choosing to turn to missionary societies as an alternative vehicle for his aspirations.[42]

It has been assumed that Las Casas's scheme marked the end of Spanish silk projection in the Greater Antilles, but a few planters continued to pursue ambitions on Hispaniola. In 1538, Diego Caballero was embarking on a range of textile experiments on his extensive hacienda, which boasted a sugar mill and a large population of Spaniards, blacks and Indians spread throughout more than sixty houses of stone and straw. He had them tended to by a priest, and, in the lyrical way that Caballero described it, he offered a sort of progressive sanctuary that could lovingly recycle the labour of Spaniards fleeing from other parts of the New World. He expressly mentioned 'mulberries for silk' and dyestuffs in a letter begging an extended land grant from the Crown. Caballero was an arch-opportunist, and could afford to persist in investments where others left off, having already amassed a fortune by plundering Indians from the Nicaraguan coast and forcing them to dive for pearls. The move to prospective textile production, moreover, was a logical step since he had cemented his wealth by adapting to his changing environment, publicly reining in his exploitative slaving and making himself one of the main conduits of manufactured goods flowing into the Spanish Americas. Any material prospects of sericulture, however, dwindled when Caballero returned home to strut around Seville making ostentatious benefactions.[43]

[40] Las Casas, 'Remedios para las islas Española, Cuba, Sant Juan y Jamaica', in Pacheco et al., *Documentos Inéditos de Indias*, 7: 107–8.

[41] 'Real Cédula', 10 September 1518, AGI, Indiferente, 420, 8: 48v–50. See also J. Sarabia Viejo and Rio Moreno de Del, *Los inicios de la agricultura european en el nuevo mundo, 1492–1542* (Seville: Caja Rural de Huelva y Caja Rural de Sevilla, 1991), 273.

[42] Rolena Adorno, *Polemics of Possession in Spanish American Narrative* (New Haven: Yale University Press, 2014), 61–98; Woodrow Wilson Borah, *Silk Raising in Colonial Mexico* (Berkeley and Los Angeles: University of California Press, 1943), 2–3.

[43] 'Informe sobre la merced solicitada por Diego Caballero', 26 February 1538, AGI, Santo Domingo, 868, 1: 113r. On Caballero's remarkable career, see Enrique Otte, 'Diego

It was on the mainland of Central America that the problem of engineering symbiosis between silkworm larvae and mulberry leaf was first resolved. By this second wave of shipments, the Spanish imperial machinery was well attuned to the peculiar demands of transporting the miniature sacks or boxes which contained the ounces of seed from Granada, to the point where authorities issued explicit instructions requiring 'diligence and care' and pressed that silkworms be dispatched 'as urgently as possible' so that there would be no further losses.[44] It was probably not a coincidence that it was the *first* of many ships to leave Seville for Mexico in 1532 that carried a 'good quantity of silkworm seed' – the dormant larvae sharing what must have been a noisy voyage with thirty donkeys and a hundred rams hand-picked for breeding up a new continent's livestock.[45] For much of the remainder of the century, capacity for silk production would be measured and expressed not by numbers of workers or reels, but by the weight of silkworm seed a community could work up. This was both a throwback to the fragility of Atlantic transhipment and an adaptation of a long-standing Moorish tradition of counting outwards from the weight of initial seed.[46] It is probably fair to say that silkworm larvae ended up having one of the most comfortable and cosseted Atlantic voyages of any living creatures of the early modern era, in a process aiming at dryness and coolness. By one set of meticulous instructions, they were gently placed into lead vessels, each containing no more than 2 lb of seed, then nestled into a wide bag filled with bean flour (*harina de habas*), which in turn was wedged into a barrel filled with cleaned dried straw or bran, which in turn was fitted into a pipe or cask of salt, that was placed somewhere delicate on a part of the ship where it would avoid excess heat, moisture, or direct sunlight, such as the stern cabin, usually occupied by the captain.[47]

One of the salient indicators that silk production went on to become a commercial success in New Spain in the second half of the sixteenth century is that so many individuals sought to take credit for its initial introduction, somewhere between 1525 and 1540. The Crown's reward of 1518 may have retained some appeal, being claimable throughout the

Caballero, funcionario de la Casa de La Contratación', in *La Casa de La Contratación y La Navegación Entre España y Las Indias*, ed. Antonio Acosta Rodríguez, Adolfo González Rodríguez, and Enriqueta Vila Vilar (Seville: Universidad de Sevilla, 2003), 315–39.
[44] 'Carta de los oficiales de la Casa de la Contratación', 8 November 1537, AGI, Indiferente, 1092, 238: 2.
[45] 'Carta de la reina al presidente y oidores de México', 20 March 1532, AGI, Mexico, 1088, 2: 27r–30v.
[46] Lagardère, 'Mûrier et culture de la soie en Andalus au moyen age (xe–xive siècles)', 101–2.
[47] Las Casas, *Arte nuevo para criar seda*, 231v. Cf. Christopher M. Parsons and Kathleen S. Murphy, 'Ecosystems under Sail': Specimen Transport in the Eighteenth-Century French and British Atlantics', *Early American Studies* 10 (2012): 503–29.

Indies (and inheritable), and being more achievable given the discovery of native *M. celtidifolia* trees amongst the forests of Mexico. But it was far from the minds of Hernán Cortés and his followers in their initial frenetic quest for gold in 1520–1 which culminated in the destabilisation, plundering, and then quasi-assumption of the Aztec imperial infrastructure. Only once control was crudely established, with native populations still reeling from the catastrophic impact of smallpox, was attention turned to means of establishing sustainable profit in this richly settled part of the continent – its dense peopling itself reflecting its agricultural fecundity. By early 1524, with the onetime renegade Cortés now acknowledged as an instrument of imperial administration, the territory had been parcelled out into *encomiendas*, by which Spanish settlers and occasional others were 'entrusted' with Indian peoples (in practice an exploitative pool of labour and tribute), this legal system sitting awkwardly across traditional fiefdoms and ethnicities.

While this process was underway, around 1523, it seems that Cortés himself made an attempt at raising silk in the palace garden at Coyoacán, which served as the first capital of New Spain until the ruins of Tenochtitlán to its north had been built over. He had written to the king in 1522, emphasising 'the need for plants of every sort' to conduct trials, a letter with which he had enclosed copies of ordinances that he had issued, which he felt to be in step with royal power. They included, of course, sumptuary laws that regulated the wearing of velvets, silks, and brocades, or their use for saddles, shoes, and sword-belts.[48] The letter itself did not specify silkworms or mulberry trees, though this claim would be made by the great early-seventeenth-century archivist and historian Antonio Herrera, who wrote a magisterial multivolume history of the Spanish Americas, *Décadas*.[49] When precious silkworm seed arrived the next year from Spain, one writer recalled that Cortés's silk, however, 'was raised very loosely, and to no profit', a lack of knowledge meaning that only enough cocoons were yielded to sustain some leftover stock on the mainland for future trials. Since no *M. nigra* (black) or *M. alba* (white mulberry) trees had yet been planted, this must have been the first time in history that *Bombyx mori* caterpillars successfully fed and self-propagated on American foliage. Hernán Cortés persisted and, after securing a reprieve in Spain from the Crown for various misdemeanours, and newly ennobled as First Marquis of the Valley of Oaxaca, brought a female silk-reeling expert back to Mexico in 1530, who was paid thirty

---

[48] Cortés, *Letters from Mexico*, 336.
[49] Herrera y Tordesillas, *Historia General*, 3: 92, 93, 123. This first claimed that in 1522 'Castillians planted mulberries, and from these silk grew well.'

ducats (approximately fifteen English pounds) to bring fresh silkworm seed with her.[50] In her necessity and in her anonymity, this unnamed woman, like the first transport of eggs, prefigured much that was to come in Atlantic sericulture.

It was in step with Cortés's lifelong habits of womanising and picking fights, that his silk efforts should likewise end with a woman and be disputed by a rival, in this case Diego Delgadillo. Delgadillo was appointed with a handful of others to the first royal *Audiencia*, supposedly tasked with overhauling the disorderly situation in the colony. But upon his group's arrival in New Spain in 1528 they proceeded to dirty their own hands with the political and economic spoils of government, concentrating especially upon the Valley of Oaxaca, whose marquisate was even then being conferred upon Cortés on the other side of the Atlantic. Oaxaca is the Hispanic rendering of an earlier well-fitting Nahuatl phrase for the settlement, meaning 'amongst the trees', though it was renamed Nueva Antequera in 1529 under the first *Audiencia* and accorded the status of a city to protect against Cortés's intrigues upon his return. The Spanish had followed the Aztecs in selecting it as a valuable site from which to control and monitor the large Zapotec and Mixtec settlements in the Valley of Oaxaca, for it was situated across major trade routes, and, as the founding instructions put it, 'is the richest and most populated region' between Mexico City and Guatemala. Like many colonial towns in the Mexican highlands, once definitively refounded by Delgadillo's family, it would comprise of a miniature neat gridded nucleus of Spanish residents surrounded by a large number of Indian settlements.[51]

Delgadillo's indirect battle with Cortés extended beyond the jurisdictional, and in either 1529 or 1530 he too raised silkworms just outside Mexico City, in the garden of his hacienda on the road to Chapultepec. Delgadillo, whom Herrera pointedly notes, 'as a Man of Granada, knew how to raise silk' used a quarter of an ounce of silkworm eggs given to him by Francisco de Santa Cruz that had survived passage from Seville.[52] Delgadillo almost certainly had a better result than Cortés, but it is striking that he too decided not to reel off any silk but to retain all of the crop in the form of silkworm seed. Returning two ounces to Santa Cruz, which was insufficient in the opinion of a subsequent judicial tribunal, Delgadillo either retained or distributed the rest amongst peers keen to invest in sericulture. The overall picture in this chaotic and traumatic period,

---

[50] Las Casas, *Arte nuevo para criar seda*, 210r; Borah, *Silk Raising in Colonial Mexico*, 6.
[51] Cédula of October 1529, AGI, Justicia, 231, 463v; for a wider discussion of the settlement and region, see John K. Chance, *Race and Class in Colonial Oaxaca* (Stanford, CA: Stanford University Press, 1978), 30–4.
[52] Herrera y Tordesillas, *Historia general*, 3: 181.

then, is of competing powerbrokers, mindful of the tractable labour force and extensive mulberries 'amongst the trees', seeking to gain control over the critical resources for the pursuit: land, seed, and labour.[53]

The interest and patronage of such major figures was an important stimulus. But as it would prove throughout the Americas, in order to give silk production a fighting chance amongst other colonial priorities, and especially to move it from tentative silkworm feeding to effective cocoon reeling, more hands-on expertise and dissemination was needed. Unlike the pointed exaction of cacao, maize, cotton, and cochineal, cultures which had all been practised and formed a component of tribute in the pre-Hispanic period, raw silk had to be bolted on to the productive capacities of indigenous peoples, or at least that is how Spaniards viewed the matter. The *encomienda* system, with its focus on labour and its denial of inheritance (for the lands remained under the disposition of the Crown), was not necessarily a sound vehicle for encouraging long-term estate development or the pursuit of sustainable products. Fortunately for Spanish landholders, the Indians were quick to perceive the benefits for themselves of adapting to this peculiar culture, whose product was so highly valued by Europeans.

The secret of Spanish success in Central America in the sixteenth century lay in the distinctive convergence of three factors that would rarely align in other American zones in the years to come, even zones where indigenous or introduced mulberries seemed to thrive. These were firstly, a pool of available Old World experts able and willing to help surmount the initial difficulties with sericulture, especially in setting out adequate trees and teaching the art of reeling. Secondly, colonial authorities – at times both state and church bodies – reaching for tributary profit and committed to experimentation and diversification. And thirdly, a dense, adaptable, and ambitious labour force with considerable experience in rendering textiles and of seasonally harvesting insects.

The pool of middling Spanish sericultural experts revealed themselves less through vaunted mentions in great histories such as Herrera's, but rather in more mundane snippets of correspondence, contracts, or ruling decrees. In October 1537, a Murcian expert named Hernando Marín Cortés (no relation of the conquistador) formally undertook to plant 100,000 feet of mulberry trees in the space of 15 years in the districts of Huejotzingo, Cholula, and Tlaxcala, major sites just northwest of modern-day Puebla that he felt ideal for sericulture. In the partly torn contract, made in Tenochtitlán, he claimed to have already planted out many trees and to have been the first to raise silk in the kingdom after

---

[53] Borah, *Silk Raising in Colonial Mexico*, 7–8.

its conquest. He was granted the use of forest mulberries around Cholula, the labour of forty-five Indians along with their wives for reeling, and a dedicated adobe building in which to establish operations. He also requested a grant of *encomienda* for the pueblo of Tepeji (now Tepexi de Rodríguez, Puebla), a town whose population he planned to use to plant out thousands of the trees, the profits of which he would hold exclusively for five years and then divide for a farther fifteen years with the Crown.[54] By the early 1540s, one commentator noted that over half of the promised trees were growing at a rapid pace, five times faster than in Spain.[55] Though the Tlaxcalans, as ever, seem to have done their own thing, Indians at Huejotzingo initially embraced the project and secured good terms of their own to persist, while thousands of the saplings Marín Cortés cultivated in the Valley of Atlixco would go on to be transplanted to form new nurseries.[56] In a similar vein further south, other Murcians in the late 1530s including Juan Marín (and probably two brothers) applied for permission to grow silk in towns in the Mixteca Alta, including the promising pueblo of Texupa, using indigenous mulberries, and were so successful that the latter became something of a centre of diffusion.[57] Inevitably, the preferences of experts like Marín Cortés and the Maríns would shape Meso-American sericulture into a Spanish likeness, and over time there was a shift away from using the rougher indigenous *M. centidifolia* to using imported mulberries—such that those of Eurasian origin provided the major source of leaves by the 1570s. As Herrera put it, writing about the Bishopric of Oaxaca in 1601, 'they used to raise silk, by the industry of the Castilians, with the mulberries of the land [*morales de la tierra*] ... and the Castilians planted lots from Castile, which catch hold everywhere'. It is noteworthy, given the debates in Spain and gradual moves towards a preference for white mulberries, that there was little explicit identification or discussion of which Eurasian mulberry cultivars were preferred in New Spain. It may be that planters brought black mulberries when arriving from Granada and white mulberries if from Murcia or elsewhere. They were less likely in the New World to be wedded to cultural assumptions about the relative merits of either tree, though, partly because of the lesser influence of Morisco traditionalists in the Americas, and partly because of the need to experiment and adapt to American soils and climates – which, as in Spain, probably offered better

---

[54] 'Plantación de moreras: Huejotcingo, Cholula y Tlascala', 6 October 1537, AGI, Patronate, 180: 68r.
[55] Motolinía, 'Historia de los Indios', 239.
[56] Borah, *Silk Raising in Colonial Mexico*, 12–13.
[57] Las Casas, *Arte nuevo para criar seda*, xxv–xxvii.

prospects to the more cold-resistant black mulberry at higher altitudes.[58]

What many of these contracts had in common was that they were approved and licensed by Antonio de Mendoza, a shrewd appointment as first Viceroy of New Spain in 1535, whose fifteen years in office solidified Crown control of an unruly region. Unlike many of the early conquistadors, who came from the rugged terrain of Extremadura, Mendoza (like Delgadillo) was himself from southern Andalusia, a part of Castile where silk was a prominent feature of the economy. His oversight would see the culture of silk cemented as a major part of the economic world of Indians and *encomenderos*, and his main contribution was in securing the pool of Old World expertise and helping it to thrive.[59] Even as Murcians were rationalising mulberry nurseries in the uplands, foothills and valleys of Mexico and Oaxaca, Mendoza's proactive approach to hiring Granadan specialists left a bill to be resolved by the Casa de Contratacion, who were ordered to pay for the costs of the oceanic passage of 'the two sugar-makers and the two reelers of silk solicited by the viceroy' in 1537, the specialists having also spent six *ducados* on tools and equipment.[60] The original quest actually sought out 'two or three reelers' with the critical adjunct that they were not to be Moriscos and, if married, their wives could accompany them, another tacit recognition of the traditional importance of female labour and expertise.[61] A later letter instructed the Viceroy to keep up the good progress he had been making in planting out 'mulberries for raising silk', and in the accompanying trials.[62] Mendoza responded by licensing all *encomenderos* to deploy their Indian labourers in sericulture, with immediate effects, and at the same time, the Viceroy extended shrewd and well-intentioned protection to Indian communities, for instance in special grants to native silk-growers at Jaltepec and Camotlán, where local Spaniards were hindering uptake.[63]

As experts in moriculture and reeling sailed with their mulberry plants and silkworm seed for the entry port of Veracruz, encouraged by the

[58] Antonio Herrera y Tordesillas, *Descripción de las Indias Ocidentales* (Madrid: Nicolas Rodriguez Franco [orig. pub. 1601], 1730), 20. On the expansion of Old World mulberries in New Spain, see also Las Casas, *Arte nuevo para criar seda*, 210v. On developments in Spain, López de Coca Castañer, 'Morales y moreras en la sericultura', 468–9.
[59] Borah, *Silk Raising in Colonial Mexico*, 10.
[60] 'Armamento de la armada de Blasco Núñez Vela y otros asuntos', 30 April 1538, AGI, Indiferente, 1962, 6: 52–3.
[61] The ship master was to be paid upon delivery by officials in New Spain. 'Construcción de fortaleza en La Habana y otros asuntos', 20 March 1538, Indiferente, 1962, L.6, f.27v–28.
[62] 'Real Disposición', 13 May 1538, AGI, Mexico, 1088, 3: 77.
[63] Las Casas, *Arte nuevo para criar seda*, 210; Borah, *Silk Raising in Colonial Mexico*, 14, 42.

Viceroy, favourable winds also bore down on interior populations, in the form of the active encouragement of religious orders. The first bishop-elect of Mexico, the Franciscan Juan de Zumárraga, like las Casas before him, sought to use silk as a means of improving the economic and social conditions of the Indians, of whom he was styled 'Protector' from 1528. He commissioned the writing of a pamphlet (which has not survived) by a church Precentor, Alonso de Figuerola, intended to 'instruct the Indians from silk raising to dyeing'. Zumárraga also urged the Council of Indies early on to send Moriscos from Granada to acculturate Indians in silk techniques, though as noted this was expressly prohibited in 1538, in line with the policy of keeping a notional distinction between the pure-blood Spanish settlers and Indians of the Americas. Dominican friars, though ardently opposed to the *encomienda* system, also claimed agency in encouraging sericulture amongst indigenous communities, especially in places where they were able to concentrate activity, as at the town of Teposcolula (a hundred miles north-west of Oaxaca) in the early 1540s. Their net impact was undoubtedly positive, though some religious figures claimed that silkworm feeding caused Indians to neglect prayers and devotion during Lent, and at least one friar later ordered the destruction of a large number of mulberry trees in the valley of Meztitlán.[64]

With stocks of silkworm eggs regularly available, native mulberry trees and, increasingly, introduced species being planted, grafted, and relocated into accessible nurseries with adequate hydration, and experts spreading techniques and technologies from Murcia and Granada, several of the necessary prerequisites were in place to transfer sericulture to the New World. Nonetheless, had native communities shown either recalcitrance or ineptitude – qualities that Europeans were not slow to accuse them of – its potential might well have remained unrealised. Instead, the impressive speed with which harvests of raw silk grew from the early 1540s was a tribute to indigenous resilience, ingenuity, and adaptability in the face of astonishing and unprecedented cultural pressures. The race to find a single smoking gun – a Spaniard to claim the king's 30,000 *maravedís* – has too often detracted from attention to silk's thousands of real pioneers: the women, children, and men amongst

---

[64] Aranda suggests that the arrival of Murcian experts may have been prompted by a Dominican request, in Las Casas, *Arte nuevo para criar seda*, xvi–xvii. On mendicant support and the Flemish Augustinian, Fray Nicolás de San Pablo (Witte), Robert Ricard, *The Spiritual Conquest of Mexico: An Essay on the Apostolate and the Evangelizing Methods of the Mendicant Orders in New Spain, 1523–1572* (Berkeley: University of California Press, 1974), 144–5; Borah, *Silk Raising in Colonial Mexico*, 9–10, 25. Viceroy Mendoza also blamed some religious sceptics for slowing enthusiasm by complaining about respect of Lent and preaching disdain for 'worldly goods'. Pacheco et al., *Documentos Inéditos de Indias*, 6: 491–2.

the Nahua, Otomi, Tarascan, Zapotec, and above all Mixtec Indians who got to grips with these worms from another world.

One of the most beautiful and revealing testaments to the diffusion of silk production across parts of New Spain is the *Códice Sierra Texupan* (see Plate 2). It is the surviving account book for the years 1551–64 of the community of Santa Catalina Texupa (now Villa Tejupam de la Unión) in the Mixteca Alta, which was initially ruled by a female *cacica* (chieftain) named doña Catalina, though her presence and power seemed to wane as Spanish-style male cabildos, priests, and governors assumed more prominence over the years.[65] A precise and continuous series, the codex was compiled using the dual stylings of traditional colourful pictographs and Nahuatl alphabetic text. Entries detail the financial debts of the community, giving a record of payments in cash and kind by way of purchases, tributes, and tithes. In the process, they reveal how great was the scale of Catholic subsidy borne by such native districts, which went far beyond daily maintenance: over half the total that Indians laid out was for church goods, food and wine for the priests, and religious feasts. The community paid, for instance, for fancy silken vestments such as a red satin chasuble and a stole for the local cleric, for twelve *varas* (yards) of red velvet to decorate the local church, and for a white damask cape for the bishop, edged with red velvet, which was sent to Oaxaca.

Although the community's earnings are not broken down explicitly in the codex until the final four years, there is no question that their yield often included raw silk. There are repeated purchases documented of both silkworm eggs and mulberry plants, alongside payments to a Spaniard who came to demonstrate how best to raise the worms. By 1561, the entry for the tributes and tithes of Texupa represented silk as of paramount importance to the community, showing a glyph with a Spaniard wearing a hat, tying the raw silk up for transport to Mexico City. As this image suggests, silk played its part in the transformation of exchange in Central America, as loaded lone mules picking their way through the rugged Mixteca became pack trains. By the 1560s, most native long-distance traders (*tay cuica*) had been outmuscled by Spanish merchants running indigenous goods along the more profitable routes

[65] Digitised by the Biblioteca Digital Mexicana at http://bdmx.mx/documento/codice-sierra-texupan. Matthew Restall, Lisa Sousa, and Kevin Terraciano, *Mesoamerican Voices: Native-Language Writings from Colonial Mexico, Oaxaca, Yucatan, and Guatemala* (Cambridge: Cambridge University Press, 2005), 82–93; Borah, *Silk Raising in Colonial Mexico*, 48–50; Kevin Terraciano, *The Mixtecs of Colonial Oaxaca: Ñudzahui History, Sixteenth through Eighteenth Centuries* (Stanford, CA: Stanford University Press, 2001), 186–90.

which branched into the trunk line connecting Guatemala and Mexico City, though at the local level a mixture of petty traders operated.[66]

The Texupa community bought their silkworm seed at a price of between 23 and 28 pesos per pound, and their largest supplier seems to have been Juan de Villafañe of Mexico City (perhaps from his father's *encomienda* at Jaltepec). They paid to maintain a Spaniard 'who cultivates the silk here, because we agreed to it this way', which suggests that Spanish silk expertise had featured continuously in the town since the arrival of the Marín brothers who had brought 3 lb of eggs in 1538, from which they generated 225 lb of raw silk.[67] Payments were also recorded in the codex for dedicated buildings and equipment for raising and reeling: 'iron for the silk spinning wheel and other things' (62 pesos, presumably including cauldrons), wood 'needed there for the silk house' (162 pesos, perhaps for shelving and fuel), and 'reeds from Tuctlan . . . all needed for the silk house' (22 pesos, perhaps for decking for the cocoons). That such investments later brought rewards is demonstrated in the 1561 outlay of over 41 pesos for 'rope, mats, packframes, and palm baskets' to pack up the harvest, and 'food for all those who carried it' north-west to Mexico. Although the value in pesos is sometimes disfigured in the codex, a sense of the quantity of raw silk is nonetheless apparent in the representations of each load delivered, and silk accounted for nearly three quarters of the community's income in the last four years documented, when the yield averaged around 400 lb, each lb worth 4.2 pesos. Ten specified 'people who take care of the silk' were given 10 pesos each in 1561, totalling 100 pesos, suggesting that while the harvest was viewed as a community effort, and drew on community labour (*tniño*), some individuals warranted particular payment, presumably for the scale and skill of their efforts in reeling.[68]

One of the important attractions of sericulture for Central American populations was that, though able to absorb significant labour input at peak seasonal moments and furnish work across gender and age divides, it was not labour-intensive throughout the year. The microbes that had accompanied Europeans from the 1520s brought such heavy mortality that it was impossible to sustain impressive pre-conquest projects such as the extensive terracing of Meso-American hills and their accompanying irrigation. The siphoning off of labourers (especially men) to fulfil Spanish-imposed quotas likewise undermined, sometimes literally, earlier land-use practices. Yet there was no dramatic rush to sell off lands to

---

[66] Terraciano, *The Mixtecs of Colonial Oaxaca*, 245–7.
[67] Las Casas, *Arte nuevo para criar seda*, xxvii.
[68] Restall, Sousa, and Terraciano, *Mesoamerican Voices*, 88, 90, 91, 93; Borah, *Silk Raising in Colonial Mexico*, 49; Terraciano, *The Mixtecs of Colonial Oaxaca*, 201–9, 234.

Spanish settlers, especially outside the agricultural hinterlands of the Valleys of Mexico and Puebla, and though much acreage was donated to religious establishments (particularly Dominicans and Jesuits), leasing only became popular in the later seventeenth century. For Indians in the mid-sixteenth century, the establishment of mulberry plantations and silk-raising operations on either household or community lands could therefore provide a flexible resource. They offered the capacity to ride out moderate fluctuations in patterns of labour availability, and production of a commodity that was in high demand, while also non-perishable, and lightweight – explaining in part the prevalence of such operations, especially in areas such as the Mixteca Alta and Valley of Oaxaca, which were distant from major Spanish markets. Whereas 'few native communities' chose to cultivate wheat, another Spanish introduction popular amongst *encomenderos*, many Indian communities flocked to silk.[69]

Besides the good environmental fit between the concentration of mulberry trees and patterns of land availability, the native populations themselves possessed specific characteristics and experiences that were readily transferable to the new pursuit – traits which went beyond the wider trade, transport, and cultural integration of the region that eased parasitic Spanish colonialism. Most importantly, it is no coincidence that silk became most firmly and profitably established amongst the Meso-American groups who held the most impressive portfolio of pre-conquest textiles. As one Dominican friar put it, 'even though silk was unknown in this country, the people were extremely skilled in weaving, embroidering, and painting cotton cloth'.[70] The Mixtecs were quintessentially experts in creating luxury cloth, their reputation apparent in their symbolic representation on codices, and in the complex weaving patterns required of them as Aztec tribute. Working mostly with cotton fibres acquired along coastal regions, they had established an efficient gendered infrastructure that held female labour paramount and made use of the household unit to specialise, with spinning and weaving technology widely dispersed, and complemented by processes of trading, finishing, and marketing of yarn, woven goods, and other related materials.[71]

---

[69] Terraciano, *The Mixtecs of Colonial Oaxaca*, 234.

[70] Diego Durán, *The History of the Indies of New Spain*, ed. Doris Heyden (Norman, OK: University of Oklahoma Press, 1994), 203.

[71] Patricia Rieff Anawalt, *Indian Clothing before Cortés: Mesoamerican Costumes from the Codices* (Norman, OK: University of Oklahoma Press, 1981), 95–146; María Romero Frizzi, *Economía y vida de los españoles en la mixteca alta: 1519–1720* (Mexico: Inst. Nacional de Antropología e Historia, 1990), 148–50; Richard J. Salvucci, *Textiles and Capitalism in Mexico: An Economic History of the Obrajes, 1539–1840* (Princeton, NJ: Princeton University Press, 1987), 48.

One related dyestuff in particular, cochineal, had been mastered by these Meso-American producers, and would go on to revolutionise European consumption from the mid-sixteenth century, not least because of its particularly robust adherence to the protein fibres of silk. In time, cochineal would go on to become Mexico's second most profitable export after silver in the seventeenth and eighteenth centuries. The long-standing seasonal harvesting of cochineal meant that Indians of the Mixteca (and neighbouring regions) were familiar with the peculiar demands of textile-related entomological agriculture. The cochineal insects, which feed parasitically on particular host *nopal* cacti, require careful oversight to generate an effective yield of their red dye. Meso-American Indians had mastered the symbiosis of these plants and insects, along with practices of selective breeding, protecting from predators, adapting to moments of seasonal intensity, and adopting methods of killing the creatures most effectively at the appropriate point in their lifecycles, by boiling, steaming, or baking. All of these experiences made the conceptualisation and the carrying through of *Bombyx* sericulture a more feasible adaptation, one that required minimal expense and did not demand wholesale Spanish involvement. The raw silk, in effect, followed the cochineal to Spanish merchants clustered in urban centres. It would invite much investment and economic pressure from *encomenderos*, but would become for a time a preoccupation of embattled indigenous communities – in Antonio Garrido Aranda's neat formulation, 'silk became the gold of the Indians'; they were a comparatively cheap, partly willing, and highly skilled and adaptable labour force with strengths in key areas.[72]

The neighbouring settlement to the south-east of Texupa was Yanhuitlán, which was another site of considerable Oaxacan silk production and had furnished its own distinctive source, this time in the European mode. Yanhuitlán was the centre of a significant *encomienda*, which in the late 1540s had a tributary population of some 16,000, and by the 1560s would extend its influence to encompass 26 dependent pueblos mostly to the south-east, when it was labelled an 'encomienda muy buena'. The energetic *encomendero* since 1546 had been Gonzalo de Las Casas, the descendant of one of Hernán Cortés's first cousins from

---

[72] Carlos Marichal, 'Mexican Cochineal and the European Demand for American Dyes, 1550–1850', in *From Silver to Cocaine: Latin American Commodity Chains and the Building of the World Economy, 1500–2006*, ed. Steven Topik, Carlos Marichal, and Zephyr Frank (Durham, NC: Duke University Press, 2006), 76–92; Luca Mola, *The Silk Industry of Renaissance Venice* (Baltimore, MD: Johns Hopkins University Press, 2000), 120–1, 130–1; Raymond L. Lee, 'Cochineal Production and Trade in New Spain to 1600', *The Americas* 4, no. 4 (April 1948): 449–73; Las Casas, *Arte nuevo para criar seda*, xxviii.

Trujillo, and Gonzalo took up numerous local official roles in the Mixteca and would go on to more prominent roles, ultimately being elected municipal magistrate (*alcalde ordinario*) of Mexico City. In 1581 Las Casas published the first-ever surviving silk manual for the Americas: an original work of agricultural improvement rooted in experience and informed by theory, entitled *Arte nuevo para criar seda* that he had compiled in New Spain in the mid-1570s, and had printed in Granada. Las Casas spent some of the opening passages retracing silk's early arrival in New Spain, and was especially keen to link Spanish women to silk culture's origins, as when he claimed that it was his mother, Lady Maria de Aguilar, who had launched sericulture in the Mixteca by propagating a pound of silkworm seed – given to her by no less than Hernán Cortés himself – in the 1530s. Las Casas also dedicated the first edition of his manuscript to doña Catalina de Galvéz, who had been in Guatemala where her husband was president of the *Audiencia* between 1570 and 1573, and who, like his mother, had shown a special interest in the pioneering of silk. Between the local quantitative drawings from the Indian community of Texupa and the qualitative textual musings from the *encomendero* of Yanhuitlán, much of the shape of New Spanish silk production can be inferred.[73]

Sericulture in New Spain exhibited many features that linked it to its Spanish and Moorish origins. These included preferred processes such as the frequent reeling of cocoons with the larvae still alive inside (known as *verde*, not *ahogado*), techniques such as the use of the hands (instead of whisk-like implements) to pick out the next bobbing cocoon to attach to the thread, and technical terms such as *embojarse*, whose provenance was unclear even to experienced New World silk raisers.[74] But there remained a number of distinctive elements. Even though the proportion of American trees declined with the growing reliance upon imported mulberries, American sericulture was at the mercy of American conditions, and allowance had to be made for different seasonal timings. In the Mixteca, silkworms were retrieved from storage in early February (two months earlier than in Granada), often being blessed during the Catholic 'Feast of the Purification of the Virgin' on 2 February, which appropriately involved their ritual cleansing with water and preparation for

---

[73] Las Casas, *Arte nuevo para criar seda*, xvii–xx, xxiv–xxv, 210.

[74] This term described the point at which silkworms had reached their fullest and began to mount and locate sites for cocooning. Las Casas suspected 'it is taken from the name of the broomstick that you put up, which in some parts of Spain is called "boja"'. Other terms such as *azarja* (reeling machine) or *azache* (floss silk) can be traced to Granada and its Morisco heritage. Las Casas, 225v, 226–226v; Juan Martínez Ruiz, *Inventarios de bienes moriscos del reino de Granada (siglo XVI): lingüística civilización* (Madrid: Consejo Superior de Investigaciones Científicas, 1972), 40, 62.

hatching. Sensible silk raisers, however, waited before fully exposing the eggs to the necessary heat (via sun or skin) until an adequate number of local mulberries were leafing, usually later in the month; one observer emphasised the need to wait also for a new moon (following Pliny).[75]

Besides the season being earlier in the calendar in Central America, practitioners needed to guard against particular local dangers, which ranged from fires to leaf-munching livestock (especially goats), caterpillar-eating lizards, and even iniquitous human predators, as when Gonzalo de Las Casas warned that 'not only will the Indians steal them to take advantage of the cocoons, but also to eat the worm, which they know how to roast like shrimps'. He advised the use of traps and poison, but not the acquisition of cats, to cope with the threats from troublesome Mexican rodents and lizards. Materials also differed, with the improvisation of adobe and pine building structures, and baskets (*paneras*) for the growing silkworms made of thatched straw, hair, or hemp. Meso-American silk raisers sometimes burned copal, a Nahuatl-derived term for aromatic tree resin, which was used as incense, to revive, or to warm silkworms. Likewise when they destroyed chrysalids, because they could not guarantee reeling before these hatched out, the silk raisers sometimes drew on steam suffocation techniques or the use of Indian sweat lodges (*temazcal*). Defective cocoons were dexterously removed from hot-water basins using *una puya de maguey*, the sizeable thorn on a local agave, most likely *Agave americana* var. *oaxacensis*. Las Casas, clearly schooled in the humoral understanding of living beings and their life cycles, spent long portions of his treatise advising how to counter the greater moisture found in Mexico and the problems it presented compared to the drier conditions in Granada. He recommended the selection of higher and drier lands for the pursuit, and frequent exposure of growing silkworms to the sun, or natural fire (of wood or charcoal).[76]

Practices in sericulture also evolved distinctive qualities, in spite of efforts to follow Granadan traditions, that reflected the different organisational features of the labour force and the different physical and resource environments. Las Casas warned Spanish entrepreneurs of the imperative of knowing or learning indigenous languages, so that employers could pass on information, guard against damaging idiosyncrasies, and monitor levels of diligence and efficiency amongst their workers. Meso-American communities operated along what might described as

[75] For accounts of this timing: Las Casas, *Arte nuevo para criar seda*, 218v–220; Motolinía, 'Historia de Los Indios', 239. Spanish domestic sericulture typically saw silkworm hatching begun on the Feast of St Mark, 24 April, and running through to the end of June.
[76] Las Casas, *Arte nuevo para criar seda*, 211, 212, 214v, 217, 225v, 226v; Borah, *Silk Raising in Colonial Mexico*, 58.

either collective or diffusional models. By the first, as at Texupa, resources were pooled from the purchase (or hatching) of silkworm eggs onwards, and activities centralised using collective nurseries and silk houses, leading one scholar to describe it as 'a sort of paternalistic socialism' guarding against the predation of either Spanish or native powers. This system, along with the large silk houses constructed by *encomenderos* and entrepreneurs, involved an unusually high proportion of sizeable enterprises when compared with older Mediterranean silk-raising patterns. It reflected the creative economic practices – especially in relation to labour and space – that accompanied Atlantic colonialism, while remaining not too demanding in terms of capital outlay. The gravitation towards economies of scale pushed these operations into the kinds of efficiencies that Las Casas described in his treatise: large multipurpose buildings, long elaborate shelving, standardised reels of oak or sapodilla wood (*ruedas*), and contracted specialists.[77]

The less common diffusional model, as practised at Jaltepec, involved the parcelling out of silkworm seed to individual households. There the worms were raised by families, most likely using baskets rather than shelving, who delivered up the cocoon harvest or sold it to traders or entrepreneurs to be disposed of and reeled. Though Borah ridiculed this method as preserving a 'farcical equality' and being 'blundering, [and] wasteful' since 'one would have to hunt far to find a worse raiser than the individual peon', there seems little evidence to affirm that the quality of the silk was inferior.[78] Indeed, assuming a base level of proficiency instead of a base opinion of the workers, there were certain advantages in spreading risk and assuring future stocks of seed, and this method of quota distribution and return by a local peasantry was closer to contemporary practices in many Old World silk-raising regions. It perhaps lent itself particularly well to districts where the mulberry trees used for leaves were somewhat spread out, or of the indigenous variety. Long after the nucleated or collective approach had disappeared, occasional Indian households and hamlets continued to raise cocoons for local use into the seventeenth and eighteenth centuries, drawing on the seasonal spread of experience and stocks that had been a function of the diffusional model.

Some features of Gonzalo de Las Casas's treatise revealed less about the nature of New Spanish sericulture than about contemporaries' theoretical appreciation of what forces were acting upon their caterpillar charges. The fact that he was operating in an extra-European and

---

[77] Las Casas, *Arte nuevo para criar seda*, xxxiii, 216v, 225v; Borah, *Silk Raising in Colonial Mexico*, 45 (quote).
[78] Borah, *Silk Raising in Colonial Mexico*, 46.

improvisational setting meant that the Spaniard – like the French and Anglo-American commentators who would follow in centuries to come – was emboldened to test older theories or propose new ones. This creativity and open-mindedness applied both in scientific terms and when it came to the tendency to anthropomorphise the silkworms. Las Casas was adamant that constant monitoring of the silkworms' appearances and behaviours, particularly through their colouration, could lead to swift diagnoses and responses on the part of their human carers. Since the silkworms were changeable, chromatic and translucent creatures, he reasoned that 'at any time it holds its colour according to its mood, complexion, or quality' and therefore any threatening humoral imbalances could be offset by deducing whether to apply heat or cold in response. On the basis of experience, he dissented from conventional views, as when he criticised Italian humanist and historian Raffaello Maffei of Volterra ('Bolaterrano') for claiming in his selective description of animals and plants in the early sixteenth century that silkworms enclosed themselves in their cosy cocoons because they felt cold. Las Casas also showed considerable conviction in the power of astrological forces, not least the sun, which he held to have restorative powers, partly because its heat and dryness could counteract excessive moisture and cold. He believed the silkworms passed through vaguely defined stages of sleep, fear, love, and sadness, and that they only developed visual awareness when they metamorphosed.[79]

Las Casas would also blaze a trail in using the fragile silkworms as a way of reflecting on the physical and metaphysical impact of transatlantic relocation: what happens when a species is transferred from one part of the globe to another? He believed that silkworm eggs had lost something of their essence in their removal from the Old World to the New. 'Having traded and transferred things in the past from some lands to others', he opined, 'while in their first locale they remain complete, where they are transplanted they do not, retaining only the principal part'. Silkworm eggs differed from place to place even in the Iberian Peninsula, with some parts of highly valued Granada deemed to be better than others, and anything secured around the Guadalquivir River, to his mind, being 'vile fruit'. Ultimately, Las Casas felt that Mexican raw silk was somewhat inferior as a product, and the insect labourers more prone to disease, a fact we now should most likely ascribe to the spatial concentration and genetic narrowness of the silkworm population. But Las Casas felt that there was no need to persist with trying to perfect the seed coming from

[79] Las Casas, *Arte nuevo para criar seda*, xxxiv, 215v, 217v–218. Cf. Raffaelo Maffei, *Commentariorum rerum urbanarum octo et triginta libri* (Rome, 1506) esp. book 24.

Spain, since 'it is better and more healthy to be in one's natural environment, as seen in livestock, which always do best where they are raised'. He advocated a mixture of risk-averting strategies, including guarding, conserving, and diversifying stock in the Americas, and refreshing it frequently from Europe.[80]

Though the output of colonial sericulture between 1540 and 1580 is difficult to gauge statistically, its rise to prominence can be easily vouched for by triangulating a mixture of sources with those above. Perhaps the first indications of increase lay in the collection of tithes (*diezmos*) and tributes by Spanish authorities. Back in 1501, Ferdinand and Isabella had creatively compiled a list of tithes for Hispaniola, in which they stipulated that, as in Granada, one silk cocoon in every ten should be reserved to the Catholic Church (whose tithes they were authorised to dispose of). Like a drifting caiman, these ambitions resurfaced when sericulture edged into view as a realistic prospect for fiscal predation. In 1539, Spanish settlers were ordered to pay this tenth on any silk their raised or obtained as tribute.[81] In 1544, though Indians were exempted from tithes on native crops grown for subsistence, a royal decree insisted that New Spain's indigenous communities pay their tithes in silk, livestock, and wheat to the archbishop and the *cabildo* of Mexico, forbidding the subcontracting of this collection to exploitative landlords.[82] A like decree was still active in Panama forty years later, stipulating that Indians should pay their tithes in cattle, wheat, and silk, and that neither the bishops nor anyone else should send proxies (tax farmers) to collect them, in case of the likely wrongs that could accompany this.[83] The awkward solution brokered in the silk-raising regions was that diocesan authorities either directly or via trustworthy Indians collected the tithes in the form of raw silk or cocoons, where necessary conceding some ground to religious orders.[84]

---

[80] Las Casas, *Arte nuevo para criar seda*, xxxvi, 228v, 229v. On likely silkworm diseases and infections, with 'grasserie' a particularly strong candidate – a gruesome nuclear polyhedrosis virus (also known as the *Borrelina* virus) which kills larvae in 12 to 15 days and involves jaundicing, wilting, and internal liquefaction, and is known to attack several species of wild Central and North American insects, being transmittable by skin or effluence, see Yoshinori Tanada, *Insect Pathology* (San Diego: Academic Press, 1993), 173–95; Borah, *Silk Raising in Colonial Mexico*, 63–5.

[81] 'En la Nueva España se pague diezmo de la seda que se cogiere en ella como en el reino de Granada', August and October 1539, Pacheco et al., *Documentos inéditos de Indias*, 20: 183.

[82] Real Cédula, 8 August 1544, AGI, Indiferente, 427, 30: 31r–31v.

[83] 'Carta de la Audiencia de Panamá', 4 June 1584, AGI, Panama, 13, 23: 161; for similar attention to hoped-for silk returns elsewhere, 'Tributos y diezmos de los indios de Perú', 5 December 1557, AGI, Lima, 567, 8: 299r–300r.

[84] Borah, *Silk Raising in Colonial Mexico*, 81–3.

As far as labour obligations went, *encomenderos* were likewise swift to capitalise on raw silk production, with one observer recounting that in the 1540s many had seven or eight dedicated silk-raising buildings of significant proportions, 'more than two hundred feet long and very wide and very high' which held thousands of feet of shelves and trays to house the silkworms.[85] Cortés's personal efforts were increasingly concentrated on his estates south of the Valley of Mexico, using a central mulberry nursery at Cuernavaca tended by another expert (Cristóbal de Mayorga) from which thousands of saplings were transplanted to new satellite groves to facilitate Indian leaf-collection. Operations began in earnest in 1546 by which time a customised silkworm rearing house had been constructed and equipped, being 204 feet long by 30 feet wide, of adobe reinforced by wood, stone, and lime.[86] The scale and grievances associated with this kind of expansion and centralisation brought a new royal decree of 1549, instructing the New Spanish government to ensure that labour obligations imposed on the Indians in relation to silk, as well as tributes expected of them, must be fair.[87] Gonzalo de Las Casas was one of the culprits in 1550, when he was reprehended for abuses in relation to his tributes, though unsurprisingly he omitted to mention this in his pioneering tract.[88]

The sorts of abuses generated by Spanish exploitation of Indian labour in raising silk are shown in an episode that occurred in Metztitlán, a district north-east of Mexico City about midway to the Gulf of Mexico (now northern Hidalgo). Thanks to its defensible mountainous terrain and limited economic appeal, this pugnacious Otomi region had narrowly avoided subjugation to the Aztec empire. By the early sixteenth century it had become something of a refuge for Meso-American dissidents, but could not hold out against the new European power. In 1552, it was under the shared control of three powerful *encomenderos* spearheaded by Alonso de Mérida, whose brutal maltreatment of their workers and notorious exactions became the subject of a controversial investigation by a royal commission headed by Diego Ramírez. The paperwork generated by this power struggle between metropolitan and local Spanish powers, in the context of an Indian community with a particularly strong tradition of resistance, swept up the kind of historical dust and dirt that usually lies hidden beneath layers of colonial oppression. One of the unsavoury

---

[85] Motolinía, 'Memoriales', in *Colección de documentos para la historia de México*, ed. Joaquín García Icazbalceta, vol. 1 (Mexico City: Librería de J. M. Andrade, 1858), 11.

[86] Borah, *Silk Raising in Colonial Mexico*, 18–19; William B. Taylor, *Landlord and Peasant in Colonial Oaxaca* (Stanford: Stanford University Press, 1972), 113–16.

[87] 'Real Cédula', 22 June 1549, AGI, Mexico, 1089, 4: 80r–80v.

[88] Las Casas, *Arte nuevo para criar seda*, xix.

episodes that Ramírez aired was the whipping to death of an Indian, Martín Ozumatl, a few years earlier. Ozumatl had doggedly refused to acquiesce to Spanish demands that he and his fellow labourers must water the trees in a nursery of imported mulberries that de Mérida had illegally seized on native lands. In response, the *encomendero* and his enslaved black had apparently tied Ozumatl to a tree, and inflicted such fierce punishment that he expired some days later, leaving two orphaned young children. After a long battle to establish jurisdiction, Ramírez ordered de Mérida to pay compensation to a guardian on behalf of these victims, and theoretically stripped him of his *encomienda* for a wide range of other exploitative behaviours, but the mulberry tyrant seems to have evaded the punishment.[89]

The decline of the *encomienda* system in many parts perhaps alleviated some of the more direct exploitation, which had prompted at least one exasperated cleric to wonder why Spaniards chose to abuse the labour of 'those poor Indians, whom they should take care of like silkworms'.[90] The first district in the Mixteca Alta to revert to the Crown, Teposcolula, used its silk to furnish thousands of pesos by way of annual royal taxation in the early 1560s.[91] But as with *encomenderos*, entrepreneurs, and occasional native authorities, the success of communities raising silk made them a primary target for the Spanish officials (*alcades mayores*) who acted as tribute collectors. Though formally barred from trading in their dominions, officials nonetheless orchestrated the flow of many raw, finished, and semi-finished textile materials to suit their private interests. Their wide range of powers allowed them especially to pressurise female textile activity and to appropriate labour and production illegally, as when the Indians from Achiutla complained in 1601 of being forced to work silk, spin cotton, and weave cloth for the profit of the *alcalde mayor*.[92]

Indian grievances therefore accompanied the rise of silk production, frequently reaching the higher echelons of government, and helping to generate growing regulation of the industry in the final quarter of the

[89] María Justina Sarabia Viejo, *Don Luis de Velasco, virrey de Nueva España, 1550–1564*, Publicaciones de La Escuela de Estudios Hispano-Americanos de La Universidad de Sevilla (Seville: Escuela de Estudios Hispano-Americanos, 1978), 368–71; Walter V. Scholes, 'The Diego Ramírez Visita in Meztitlán', *The Hispanic American Historical Review* 24, no. 1 (1944): 30–8; Francisco del Paso y Troncoso and Silvio Arturo Zavala, *Epistolario de Nueva España, 1505–1818*, 16 vols. (Mexico: Antigua librería Robredo, 1939), 7: 99–102, 121, 182–3; 9: 19.

[90] Motolinía, 'Historia de Los Indios', 115.

[91] María Romero Frizzi, *Economía y vida de los españoles en la mixteca alta: 1519–1720* (Mexico: Inst. Nacional de Antropología e Historia, 1990), 73. Gonzalo de Las Casas reported that this town produced 'the best silk, and more clean than other communities' in the early 1570s. Las Casas, *Arte nuevo para criar seda*, 226.

[92] Terraciano, *The Mixtecs of Colonial Oaxaca*, 240–1.

sixteenth century, as viceroys found themselves trapped between Indian producers' protests against interference on the one hand and urban Spanish manufacturers' calls for professionalisation of the quality of raw silk on the other. In 1579, for instance, Viceroy Martín Enríquez, who three years before had issued extensive instructions to regulate silk production, received a complaint from two Indians in the town of Tilantongo. They complained against the magistrate, Juan de Bazán, who had imprisoned, whipped, and banished them from the town for their having refused to render up a mule load of silk. The viceroy ordered Juan de Bazán to allow the expelled Indians to return and instructed that he should take no reprisals against them, under penalty of suspension of his office. Similar protections were secured for silk-producing Yanhuitlán Indians in 1591–2 under Viceroy Luis de Velasco, who granted a general licence to those living under the rule of *cacique* Gabriel de Guzmán to trade in Castilian merchandise, and expressly named ten native men and five women whose textile activities were not to be impeded. Velasco insisted in 1592 that the profits of silk production were not to be channelled to communities but rather 'that each Indian may profit for themselves'.[93] Such discussions of 'profit' from raw silk, and the underhand attempts to appropriate it, demonstrate that *Bombyx* sericulture had successfully transferred to New Spain – having eventually fulfilled the prerequisites discussed in the opening chapter relating to materials, climate, expertise, and labour. The transfer had been eased by the depth of experience in Spanish territories in the Old World, and the opportune fit to indigenous populations in these parts of the New World, which were sedentary, dense, and skilled in interconnected areas. These distinctive advantages had helped outweigh the challenges apparent in the transoceanic passage, the problems of coordinating symbiosis, and the embryonic nature of the market for the raw product.

Consolidation

The rise and consolidation of sericulture from the 1540s was borne out not just in taxation and protective measures, but in the observations of residents and travellers through New Spain. Motolinía wondered at the speed with which mulberry plantations were transforming parts of Oaxaca, being 'that which makes these lands most rich'. He estimated that more than 15,000 lb of silk were being harvested in 1541, its quality

---

[93] Hortensia Rosquillas Quilés, 'El sello de la seda en la mixteca alta', *Restuara: Revista electrónica de conservación* 1 (2000): 1–10. For other interventions to assist Indian silk raisers in the face of exploitative authorities, Borah, *Silk Raising in Colonial Mexico*, 49, 72–3; Frassani, 'The Church and Convento of Santo Domingo Yanhuitla', 82.

comparable or superior to that of Granada, and marvelled that production could take place through 'all seasons of the year', anticipating that it would soon expand into the environs of Puebla.[94] Juan Lopez de Zárate, the bishop of Antequera (Oaxaca), noted in 1544 that the community of Teposcolula was raising 2,000 lb of raw silk (worth 900 pesos). This being some years before the bishopric was receiving the woven silk goods and expensive support mentioned in the Texupan codex, he complained that Mixtecan relations were topsy-turvy, for 'contrary to what ought to be the situation, the natives are rich and well-treated, and the Spaniards the poorest and most restless'.[95] The same year, Bartolomé de Zárate, a municipal representative (*regidor*) of Mexico City, estimated that the output of the Mixteca Alta and Valley of Oaxaca totalled 9,000 lb of 'reeled silk' that came mostly from indigenous mulberries.[96] Outside the heartland of Oaxaca, sources document extensive mulberry plantations in the decade after 1545 in an array of locations, including concentrations in Guerrero, Colima, Mexico, Michoacán, Nayarit, Guadalajara, Huasteca, Hidalgo, Yucatán, and Puebla.[97] Joining these historical dots, groves, and profits shows silk raising initially spreading through central and southern Mexico, before contracting back to a core area rooted in the temperate highlands of the Mixteca Alta. Whereas the north and west were increasingly dedicated to silver mining from the late 1540s and the tropical lowlands favoured the cultures of cacao and indigo, silk production maintained a significant presence in between. Its retreat to districts that were buttressed by geographic and demographic advantages followed a similar pattern to that which prevailed in Murcia.[98]

Atlantic colonialism brought a distinctive combination, however, when it came to the relationship between raw silk production and manufacturing. Given the wealth wrung out of the New World and the desire to attain social improvement that was a motivation for migration for many Spaniards, it was not long before the major urban locales in Spanish America began to serve as sites of manufacture as well as conduits of Atlantic trade. But New Spain did not exhibit the characteristics of earlier new sites in silk's great sweep westward, whereby the industry tended to arrive in reverse, with weaving workshops paving the way for greater interest in and demand for raw materials. Rather, the leap across the

---

[94] Motolinía, 'Historia de Los Indios', 8, 236–8.
[95] Letter from Mexico City, 30 May 1544, Pacheco et al., *Documentos inéditos de Indias*, 7: 551.
[96] Las Casas, *Arte nuevo para criar seda*, xxvi.
[97] Las Casas, *Arte nuevo para criar seda*, xxviii.
[98] Borah, *Silk Raising in Colonial Mexico*, 26–7; Pérez Picazo and Lemeunier, 'El caso murciano', 103.

Atlantic prompted development from the bottom up: the initial innovation and expansionism was in relation to the production of raw materials, and processing and manufacturing centres followed in their wake, being largely emulative and limited.

The preamble to the first-ever measures to regulate a silk industry in the Americas, issued by Viceroy Mendoza in Mexico City in 1542, explicitly justified the ordinances on the grounds that 'this city and all its lands begin to raise and work up silk'.[99] As this suggests, sericulture stimulated manufacturing, and the basket-laden carriers winding their way into the city in the late spring, congregating from near and far, with raw silk from *encomiendas* and Indian communities alike, presented an obvious entrepreneurial opportunity. Silk had arrived in the Americas as a novelty that marked out class and fairly quickly also become an available raw product: the region had not first, as had happened in earlier spreads of the commodity, gradually acclimatised to the new fibre (in finished or semi-finished form), then organically integrated it with dress cultures, then adapted to its use with local textile interests to stimulate a new manufacturing industry, then finally pursued and refined raw silk production. The 1542 regulations, which largely remained in shape for the duration of New Spain's production of silk, were put together by a silk raiser (Jerónimo Ruíz de la Mota) and an administrative veteran from Granada (Gonzalo de Salazar), and the shadow of the Spanish domestic industry loomed large. Mexico's silk industry was explicitly to emulate the kind of industry restrictions that were operational in Granada, which held primacy in matters of Spanish silk manufacturing and later secured an export monopoly on silk goods to the New World.[100]

To follow the trickle of such specialists as Ruíz de la Mota who migrated from Spanish silk centres to set up operations in New Spain offers a useful measure of this distinctive relocation of the cycle of industry. The scattered pattern of licences by royal decree shows the arrival of many expert silk raisers and reelers, followed by throwers and dyers, alongside weavers who congregated in the cities of New Spain. This was a logical progression through the stages of silk manufacture, but not one that had typically characterised earlier regional or transnational relocations. In 1557, a Gabriel López of Toledo was allowed to travel to the Indies, though no strings were attached to this 'silk reeler' who was leaving a region that one contemporary described in 1561 as having 'felled its black mulberries and relocated its silk-raisers'. In February of 1563,

[99] 'Ordenanzas de Antonio de Mendoza sobre géneros de seda', 7 February 1542, AGI, Patronato, 181, 2–3.
[100] Borah, *Silk Raising in Colonial Mexico*, 32–3; Sarabia Viejo and Moreno de Del, *Los inicios de la agricultura europeana en el nuevo mundo, 1492–1542*, 298.

Juan de Madrid was permitted to take his wife, children, and sister to New Spain so long as they practised 'the art of silk'. Further permissions were granted a week later to Francisco de Escobar (along with his wife, children, and one María Ruiz), listed as 'reeler of silk', and in April to Mateo de Benavente. The preponderance of travelling wives, women, and children amongst these silk-raising or silk-reeling licensees contrasts with contemporary listings of male silk artisans known to have left wives in Spain (such as the two dozen listed by Bishop Zumárraga).[101]

Mendoza's 1542 regulations generously granted a monopoly to the capital city where early migrant artisans concentrated, making it the sole location with the right to employ silk looms. Soon silk producers and merchants in Mexico City were recruiting silk throwers and weavers under contract from Spanish silk-manufacturing centres, who brought looms and introduced a broadening range of products. They expanded from thread and narrow-ware to satins, taffetas, and velvets, in large part stimulated by what Salazar described as 'the abundance of silk that is being raised'.[102] The capacity of the Mexican looms to absorb raw material ensured that domestic silk producers could find robust market prices for their output, and that only diminutive amounts of Mexican raw silk were licensed to be exported to Peru, Guatemala, or back across the Atlantic to the manufacturers of Seville. By 1547, an official inspector from the Council of Indies, Francisco Tello de Sandoval, commented that the local reserves of silk ('granjería de la seda') played a major role in the city's activities, 'maintaining a great number of people, with Spaniards as well as Indians profiting'.[103]

It was another signal of the importance of local sericulture to this fledgling manufacturing that over the next decade, the two cities closest to silk-raising centres and Mexican raw silk trading routes, Puebla de los Ángeles (1548) and Antequera (1555), successfully overturned Mexico City's monopoly and won the privilege to dye and weave silks. Fortified with guilds, these three cities became the focal points for the purchase of Indian-raised American silk for the remainder of the sixteenth century. They also served a useful function by effectively creating a legal and racial

---

[101] Luis Hurtado cited by Montemayor, 'La seda en Toledo en la época moderna', 121. 'Real Cédulas' or 'Licencia de Pasajeros' AGI, Indiferente, 1965, 13: 458; 1966, 14: 324v, 328, 367v; 1967, 16: 11v; 1968, 20: 263v. For Zumárraga's list of wifeless weavers, see Borah, *Silk Raising in Colonial Mexico*, 32.

[102] Cited in Borah, *Silk Raising in Colonial Mexico*, 33.

[103] 'Fragmento de la visita de Tello de Sandoval', Joaquín García Icazbalceta, *Coleccion de documentos para la historia de Mexico*, 2 vols. (Mexico, 1858), 2: 136–7. Decline of exports to Seville mentioned in Bernardo de Ulloa, *Restablecimiento de las fabricas, y comercio español* (Madrid: Por A. Marin, 1740), 233. For licences for American trade, see Borah, *Silk Raising in Colonial Mexico*, 139n52, 140n53.

barrier to many of the artisan vocations. The very first Mexican ordinances of 1542 had barred enslaved people (both Indian and other) from apprenticing in or practising silk weaving, a restriction that was extended twenty years later to exclude free blacks and those of mixed race from dyeing and weaving. Mendoza had not deemed it sensible to lock out the prospect of Indian specialists, but Spanish artisans nonetheless prevented their access to technology and training. The upshot was a system whereby cheap Indian labour could be mobilised and Indian skills exploited from mulberry planting as far as the silk-reeling stage, whereupon Spanish artisans clustered in the three cities commandeered the subsequent processes from throwing to weaving.

From the 1560s expansion and specialisation in these urban centres yielded guilds or regulated subdivisions of silk ribbon makers (*listoneros*), embroiderers (*bordadores*), taffeta weavers, cap makers (*gorreros*), and others. Nonetheless, the wide availability of raw silk and the possibilities of working up waste silk gave rise to significant pockets of Indian manufacturing, especially of craft goods. These have sometimes been unfairly disdained by scholars looking, as it were, through Spanish or European eyes. Home-raised yarn, mixed-fibre weaving, and Meso-American embroidery may not have challenged the growing Spanish silk hegemony in urban artisanry, but they were not necessarily 'aside[s]' that held little meaning or 'never developed great skill'.[104] Indeed, these were the first of many occasions in pockets of the Atlantic world when the creative repurposing and adaptation of local silk production and exchange would become meaningful: commercial 'failures' could nonetheless became sources of aesthetic, personal, and communitarian pride. Regulation, consistency, and profitability may have ruled in silk industries and silk literature, but other criteria could determine value in localities less inured to them.

Silk manufacturing in New Spain benefited in the 1560s from the tribulations that were imposed on the industry back in Spain and on its infrastructure and labour force. The city and silk districts of Granada experienced a disastrous collapse in the wake of Philip II's renewed campaigns against the Moriscos, which saw his heavy taxes on silk contributing to the Alpujarras rebellion in the late 1560s, and culminated in the brutal deportation of much of the specialised labour force to the rest of Castile and Aragon – in spite of Crown attempts to authorise hundreds of 'women for raising and reeling the silk' to remain. Granada's collapse, which lasted for decades and as a result of which the sector never returned to pre-rebellion levels, even after a recovery in the early seventeenth

---

[104] Las Casas, *Arte nuevo para criar seda*, xxix; Borah, *Silk Raising in Colonial Mexico*, 34–6 (quote on last).

century, saw capacity decline precipitately, with the number of looms dropping from 4,000 to less than 400 in the space of five years, while the cost of generating a pound of raw silk had more than quadrupled by 1572. Workshops stood empty, merchants disappeared in droves, and the relocations reinforced manufacturing in other towns such as Córdoba, Toledo, and Valencia – just as the later external expulsion of Moriscos from 1609 would boost production in the cities of North Africa.[105] The upheaval clearly had ramifications for Atlantic trade and manufacture, for Granada held an export monopoly in the trade of silk textiles that it was in merchants' interest to bypass. Contraband activity had prompted a royal decree in 1569, which reminded viceroys and other officials to abide by the terms of an agreement with one Hernando Díaz de Alcocer, licensing him the sole privilege of 'the sale of silk of the kingdom of Granada ... and of the export of silk to the Indies'.[106] A letter jointly written by several royal officials in Nombre de Dios, which had become the great Atlantic transhipment port on the Isthmus of Panama, complained of fraud in the silk trade in 1581, amongst other problems arising in the conduct of commerce. They wrote that 'no silks travel here from Granada, the merchants have no need of it, preferring to sustain their trade by bypassing the regulations secretly, as last year's fleet showed they had done and some admitted ... they don't pay any notice to strictures'; they requested a clearer system of licensing.[107] Granada's ineffective supply of semi-finished or finished textiles from the 1560s represented an opportunity for Mexican silk manufacturers and, soon after, Pacific traders, and in 1591 its monopoly was finally officially removed at the behest of Sevillean merchants.[108]

---

[105] Coleman, *Creating Christian Granada* 8, 185; David E. Vassberg, *Land and Society in Golden Age Castile* (Cambridge: Cambridge University Press, 1984), 177–9, 181; A. Katie Harris, *From Muslim to Christian Granada: Inventing a City's Past in Early Modern Spain* (Baltimore, MD: Johns Hopkins University Press, 2007), 12–14, 24–6; Garrad, 'La industría sedera granadina en el siglo xvi y en conexión con el levantamiento de las Alpujarras (1568–1571)', 74–5; Garzón Pareja, *La industria sedera en España*, 249 (quote); López de Coca Castañer, 'La seda en el reino de Granada', 57; Martín Corrales, 'Comercio de la seda entre España y Mediterráneo', 161.

[106] For examples of fraudulent trading practices in silk textiles, 'Autos de Lope Ruiz de Lecea [Loja, Peru] ... y Francisco García [Potosí, Peru]', in 'Autos entre partes,' 1570 and 'Autos fiscales', 1596, AGI, Contratacion, 712, 11; 5731a, 4. Final quote from 'Real Cédula de ejecutorias a los virreyes y demás autoridades', 10 July 1569, AGI, Indiferente, 426, 25: 13–13v. On the effect of the Granada monopoly on Toledo and illicit trade with the Americas between 1569 and 1591, Montemayor, 'La seda en Toledo en la época moderna', 128.

[107] 'Cartas y expedientes de oficiales reales: Panama y Portobelo', 27 May 1581, AGI, Panama, 33, 122: 7.

[108] Eufemio Lorenzo Sanz, *Comercio de España con América en la época de Felipe II* (Valladolid: Servicio de Publicaciones de la Diputacion Provincial de Valladolid, 1980), 440–1.

A final stage in the consolidation of a comprehensive silk industry in New Spain was the standardisation of practices of regulation and inspection in the 1570s and 1580s, which focused particularly on two critical determinants of raw silk's quality: the adeptness of the cocoon reeling and the generational hardiness of the stock of silkworm eggs. Silk was a frequent subject of discussion in the letters home of the diligent Viceroy Martín Enríquez de Almanza, as he sought guidance on royal policy amidst the transformative years of the 1570s, when the Atlantic world came to terms with a nascent Pacific trade and commercial routes were recalibrated according to shifting patterns of population growth, mineral extraction, and commodity production. In 1572, he wrote 'in regard to that which touches on the profit of silk, it neither flourishes nor declines', the year later that the silk 'could be up to 20,000 pounds, in which case it is neither growing nor diminishing', and in 1574 that 'there is no great agitation'.[109] All of which suggests a fairly stable and impressive output in the early 1570s. In April 1576, Enríquez appointed 'two experts' to improve the yield of silk, confirming them as silk inspectors (known at times as *jueces de la seda* and *veedores*). The responsibilities officially designated to these new inspectors give detailed insights into the high level of specialisation and standardisation that had already evolved in the silk industry, and were repeatedly promulgated into the early seventeenth century.[110] Despite some fraud occurring during the term of the Count of Coruña, which involved the two inspectors being replaced for a time by a single judge (one *licenciado* Melchor de Vargas y Cordona), by 1587 the inspectors had been reinstated. The new viceroy, the Marquis of Villamanrique, reported then that 'in the previous year in many towns in the Mixteca' there was a fine yield of silk, 'in good quantity', and that he felt the judge unnecessary but the inspectors essential, and less expensive, in the efforts to counter the likelihood of 'great dangers and clandestine frauds in silk'.[111]

---

[109] 'Cartas del virrey Martín Enríquez', *c.*1572, 11 June 1573, and 23 October 1574, AGI, Mexico, 19, 74: 24v, 116: 3 and 142: 17.

[110] 'Testimonio de los nombramientos e instrucción que se hicieron por el Virrey Martín Enríquez para jueces de la seda', 12 April 1576, AGI, Mexico, 21, 19: 95–95v; 'Copia de un nombramiento e instrucción que dio el virrey, conde de Coruña, para veedor de la seda', 22 September 1581, AGI, Mexico, 21, 19: 91–2; 'Relación de los despachos remitidos por el marqués de Villamanrique', 13 November 1587 (confirmation in letter of 20 October), AGI, Mexico, 21, 16: 2v. Repeated in 1600 by Viceroy Gaspar de Zúñiga, adding the appointment of José de Arranzola in place of Tristán de Luna y Arellano as keeper of the seal of the Mixteca Alta, on which see Rosquillas Quilés, 'El sello de la seda en la Mixteca Alta.'

[111] 'Carta del virrey marqués de Villamanrique', 20 July 1587, AGI, Mexico, 21, 19: 13–13v. The identification of Melchor de Vargas y Cordona as the *licenciado* is on account of his inventory, which listed him as a sometime 'corregidor y juez de la seda del partido de Nochistlán en la Mixteca Alta'. 'Inventario de bienes: Vargas y Cardona, Melchor de', 16 July 1622, AGI, Mexico, 262, 258. Cf. Borah, *Silk Raising in Colonial Mexico*, 75. Another man listed as an inspector in the 1590s was Luis de Morales Beltrán ('oficial del

The package of measures first set up by Enríquez sought to improve relations between the merchants who purchased raw silk and Meso-American producers, and to iron out inconsistencies in practices of production, collection, manufacture, and sale. Indian raisers and reelers (known as *rescatadores* and *hiladores*) were commanded to be more diligent in separating and sorting cocoons such that fine ones and mediocre ones were not reeled off together. This had been a problem reported by Gonzalo de Las Casas in his treatise, when he spitefully observed that 'particular Indians, friends of deceit', had included defective cocoons, silk floss, and conjoined cocoons in their skeins, 'as they are in the habit of behaving in all such cases'.[112] Enríquez sought further quality control by mandating that floss or waste silk (*escobilla* or *desperdicio*) was not to be worked into the yarn, but rather 'removed to spin separately'. Reelers were ordered to maintain the same tally of cocoons unwound together throughout the skein, and to 'avert fraud ... so that the yarn is equal and does not come out in a sticky or heaped way', presumably because such features reflected either careless reeling or, potentially, deliberate efforts to increase weight and therefore sales value to the detriment of actual quality.

The two *veedores*, Lorenzo Marroquín and Damián de Torres Zorrilla, had lived in the provinces of Yanhuitlán and Teposcolula, and were affirmed by Enríquez and later viceroys to be the most knowledgeable in silk culture. Enríquez conferred a seal to them and warned that no one should dare sell or work up silk without receiving this seal of authorisation (stamped upon the cords binding the skeins), under pain of confiscation of the product, though the resolutions did not always deter Indians from attempting to market their silk without registration, nor Spaniards from attempting to exploit the trade, as we have seen. Later on, the viceroy gave instructions to the overseers to visit the producers to help them bring the output to perfection, threatening to punish them and remove them from office if they did not comply. Besides this quality control at the point of reeling, which was to be paid for by Spanish merchants and traders, guild inspectors were appointed to ensure that the throwers and weavers in the manufacturing cities purchased only from these recognised suppliers, and to stamp out illicit trade via Indians, enslaved people of African origin, mulattoes, or others.[113]

---

arte de la seda') in a lawsuit, 'Bienes de Difuntos: Francisco de Palma y Luis Morales', *c.*1590–1, AGI, Contratacion, 923, 18.

[112] Las Casas, *Arte nuevo para criar seda*, 226.

[113] Viceregal act of 4 March 1576, confirmed a month later. Rosquillas Quilés, 'El sello de la seda en la Mixteca Alta', 6; Juan Barrio Lorenzot Francisco del, *El trabajo en Mexico durante la epoca colonial* (Mexico: Secretaría de gobernación, 1920), 48–9.

The flourishing state of Mexican silk manufacturing actually showed that consumer demand for silks in the New World far exceeded the supply of raw silk. Trying to keep pace with high local consumption and the orders coming in from each part of the Americas as they expanded (especially Peru and Guatemala), the silk artisans of Mexico City, Puebla, and Antequera competed not only within the regulatory framework, but also often outside it to secure raw materials with which to work.

The involvement of the state in brokering the various stages in silk production was in step with the Spanish Crown's increasingly systematic approach to information, science, environment, and colonial efficiency under Philip II. In 1577, the king commissioned detailed surveys of his holdings in the Indies, and in reply to the fifty-item questionnaires, local officials across the Viceroyalty of New Spain produced over 150 responses, the *Relaciones Geográficas*. Invited explicitly in the questionnaire to describe the extent of sericulture, they indicated in 1581 that silk constituted a principal commercial product in some areas, 'the trade and engagement of those naturals in all of this Mixteca province' according to one Oaxacan magistrate.[114] The Spanish raw silk traders who purchased so much of this product had to register their stocks, bring them to Spanish towns, and put them on public sale, from 1558 dividing the costs of carriage with the artisans who bought it up and who were obliged to work it up without stockpiling. Under other circumstances, such a restrictive system may have been a disincentive to merchants, but the ability to masquerade as silk producers (which allowed better terms), comparatively light taxes (compared to Spain), and the continuing rises in the price of raw silk meant that their activity was profitable. The sketchy information on raw silk prices suggests that the commodity's value increased, probably peaking in the decade between 1575 and 1585, before falling away dramatically by the start of the seventeenth century.[115]

---

[114] Rodolfo Pastor, *Campesinos y reformas: La Mixteca, 1700–1856* (Mexico: Colegio de México, 1987), 139; Howard F. Cline, 'The Relaciones Geograficas of the Spanish Indies, 1577–1586', *The Hispanic American Historical Review* 44, no. 3 (1964): 361; René Acuña, *Relaciones Geográficas Del Siglo XVI*, 10 vols. (Mexico: Universidad Nacional de Mexico, 1982), 1: 29 (wording of questions on silk and fruit trees), 2: 145, 158, 369, 4: 64–5.

[115] Silk exported from Granada paid taxes in the region of 15 per cent. Mexican silk was subject only to the export *almojarifazgo* (of 2.5 per cent on leaving New Spain and 5 per cent on entering other colonies) and the sales *alcabala* (of 2 per cent on commodities exchanged, including Mexican and imported silks), beside the tithe. Borah, *Silk Raising in Colonial Mexico*, 76–9.

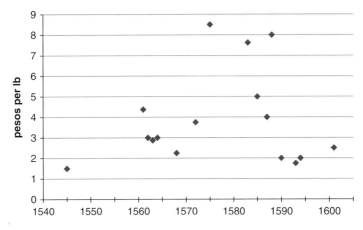

Figure 2.1 Oaxacan raw silk prices (*c*.1550–1600). Derived from figures from: Gonzalo de Las Casas, *Arte nuevo para criar seda*, 209, *Códice Sierra Texupan*, 'Libro de cargo y descargo del mayordomo', 1563–1604, MS in Archivo de la Catedral, Oaxaca (cited in Borah, *Silk Raising in Colonial Mexico*, p. 91), converted into pesos. I have assumed that the figure Las Casas gives for 'today's price' is for 1575, and that the value of 1.5 pesos that he gives for 'back then' in the district of 'Tipuzque' refers to 1544, when widespread production was mentioned in another source

Pacific Challenge and Collapse, *c*.1580–1640

By 1605, the crop of Mixtecan silk that viceroy Enríquez had estimated at 20,000 lb in 1573 had fallen to less than 1,500 lb.[116] Spanish-American silk production was dropping at a precipitate rate, alongside prices, and it would never recover. What had gone wrong? The collapse in the last two decades of the sixteenth century arose from a set of exogenous shocks, any one of which would probably have constituted a mortal blow. Firstly there was an acceleration in the succumbing of Mixtecan and other producers to disease, which hampered the availability of labour, and its flexibility and sustainability. Secondly – and perhaps related to the first – recent findings in environmental history give evidence of extreme weather in this period, with global cooling linked to some major volcanic eruptions around the Pacific Rim. Lastly, and perhaps most critically of all, the regularisation of trade between Spanish America and China would serve to undercut

---

[116] King to Marquis of Montesclaros, Valladolid, 6 June 1605, AGN, *Boletín*, VI, 843–4, cited in Borah, *Silk Raising in Colonial Mexico*, 87.

Mixtecan silk's commercial viability and would compromise political support for silk production. When raw silk failed in New Spain, then, it failed because of largely exogenous factors: pathogens, climate change, and rapid commercial reconfiguration, which all undermined competitiveness and viability. Unlike later attempts by Europeans in the Americas, this was more a question of a successful endeavour being interrupted than a gradual discovery of internal flaws in silk projection.

The colonial production of all commodities in the Americas, of course, was constantly pressurised by the phenomenon of the native population succumbing to waves of disease, a situation unprecedented in the history of the world let alone the history of sericulture. In the Mixteca Alta alone, the Indian population dropped in the century after 1520 from around a third of a million to just 35,000. Falls of this magnitude across Native American populations had colossal consequences for cultures and economies, proving unfathomable to contemporaries and, in different ways, historians. The continual decline of the silk raisers disrupted any sense of equilibrium between supply and demand, and affected quality and quantities of raw silk. But the 1570s in particular brought great plagues that scythed down Meso-American producers (measles, typhus, smallpox, and in 1576 a severe epidemic known as *cocoliztli*, which was likely a viral haemorrhagic fever).[117] Agreed tributes or schedules for silk were soon out of date and out of reach, placing an unanticipated and even unintentional squeeze on native workers, and ensuring that the terms of exchange moved from those favourable to Indians to those favourable to the Spanish by around the 1580s. In 1583, for example, Tilantongo found its official quota of silkworm eggs reduced from 6 to 4 lb, partly reflecting the fall in the town's population (to somewhere above 1,000) and the consequent strain on labour availability during the peak period of leaf gathering and feeding. Falling population contributed to many of the local and regional disputes discussed above over trade, treatment, and regulation. Knowledge of the difficult art of reeling cocoons may have spread to a large degree, but the fact that proficiency remained concentrated amongst a few individuals even within Indian communities – something preferred by Spanish authorities – left reeling particularly vulnerable to the scourge of pestilence.[118]

---

[117] Rodolfo Acuna-Soto, Leticia Calderon Romero, and James H. Maguire, 'Large Epidemics of Hemorrhagic Fevers in Mexico 1545–1815', *American Journal of Tropical Medicine and Hygiene* 62, no. 6 (2000), 733–9.

[118] Las Casas, *Arte nuevo para criar seda*, xxviii–xxix, 225v; Borah, *Silk Raising in Colonial Mexico*, 40; Joseph Patrick Byrne, *Encyclopedia of Pestilence, Pandemics, and Plagues* (Westport, CT: Greenwood Press, 2008), 1: 414; J. N. Hays, *Epidemics and Pandemics: Their Impacts on Human History* (Santa Barbara: ABC–CLIO, 2005), 85.

Strong evidence exists to suggest that the final two decades of the sixteenth century also brought environmental pressures that may well have impacted upon vulnerable pursuits such as silk raising in New Spain. Papua New Guinea's Billy Mitchell volcano erupted in 1580, followed by several others, including in Colombia and southern Peru, events which had global impacts: ash in the stratosphere reduced solar radiation substantially, leading to a series of bad years globally – visible in low crop yields, price spikes, famines, and diseases, with heightened death rates apparent even in distant (though well-documented) European regions. The 1590s were the coldest decade of the sixteenth century, and a particularly heavy toll was taken in the Americas through severe drought cycles and low temperatures – wrecking the wine industry of Peru, for instance, as well as maize growing in western North America, and compromising the bedraggled early English colonists in Virginia discussed below. As one survey summarises, on either side of 1600, 'Central Mexico was experiencing the worst multi-decadal climate anomaly of the last millennium.' Such testing conditions put pressure on food supply, and changed the logic of cash crop production and exchange, perhaps helping explain the irregular raw silk harvests and redirection of efforts, as would later occur in the second half of the eighteenth century when producers in the same region opted to turn away from cochineal.[119]

Equally important, within the space of a few decades of the arrival of *Bombyx* silk as a raw product in the Americas, silk's oceanic encirclement of the globe as a trade good had been completed. Mapping out the eastward four-month return passage (*tornaviaje*) of nearly 9,000 miles, from the Philippines to the Pacific coast of the Americas, had cost much in the way of lost Spanish ships and crews. Even after the passage's discovery in 1565, long after the first abortive attempt to cross it in 1522, it remained a perilous and unpredictable journey. In 1574, there seem to have been few indications of any sericultural catastrophe around the corner, for although viceroy Enríquez's letters betrayed the rise of Pacific competition, he stated dismissively that year that the Chinese trade was only worth 'a few silks of very poor quality (most of which are very coarsely

---

[119] Wolfgang Behringer, *A Cultural History of Climate* (Cambridge: Polity, 2010), 87, 133–5; Brian M. Fagan, *The Little Ice Age: The Prelude to Global Warming 1300–1850* (Boulder: Basic Books, 2000), 90–105; Brian R. Hamnett, 'Dye Production, Food Supply, and the Laboring Population of Oaxaca, 1750–1820', *The Hispanic American Historical Review* 51, no. 1 (February 1971): 51–78; Bradley Skopyk, 'Rivers of God, Rivers of Empire: Climate Extremes, Environmental Transformation and Agroecology in Colonial Mexico', *Environment and History* 23, no. 4 (November 2017): 491–522 (quote on 492).

woven), some imitation brocades, fans, porcelain, writing desks, and decorated boxes'.[120] Gonzalo de Las Casas made no mention of it. But growing regularisation and expansion of trade across La Mar del Sur between Manila and Acapulco demonstrated, beyond all doubt, that Chinese silks were desirable in bulk as cargo: the silks and spices which Columbus had set sail to find were finally viable, and the Manila galleons (*naos de China*) were inaugurated. All of which meant that silk, the fibre until recently unknown to the Americas, was suddenly arriving from the Pacific as well as the Atlantic. From the late 1570s, the imports of finished and raw silk products directly challenged the delicately regulated world of Mexican production and manufacture.[121]

The settlement of Spanish enclaves in the Philippines from the late 1560s – enclaves in which one commentator recorded that soon 'all, both men and women, [were] clad and gorgeously adorned in silks' – and the possibilities surrounding Pacific trade sparked extensive discussions and debates amongst Spanish imperial authorities.[122] As far as the silk trade was concerned, policymakers grappled with powerful new overseas forces that included the scale and quality of Chinese production, high consumer demand for Asian silk products (especially in the Americas), and the emerging silk-manufacturing and mercantile interests of New Spain. Domestically, vested interests clamoured equally loudly for attention: the struggling Spanish silk industry sought to protect its threatened position, while export merchants moved to keep hold of markets and clientele, and political economists fretted over the outflow of specie. They were heartened by a royal decree in 1616 which ordered the eastward shipping of as little 'quantity of silk of China' as possible, in order not to undermine that which was produced in Spain.[123] Amidst this cacophony of lobbyists, each steeped in different ways in the rhetoric of cultural nationalism, there was little chance of the beleaguered indigenous silk raisers of Central

---

[120] Letter to the king, 9 January 1574, Emma Blair, James A. Robertson, and Edward G. Bourne, eds., *The Philippine Islands, 1493–1898: Explorations by Early Navigators, Descriptions of the Islands and Their Peoples, Their History and Records of the Catholic Missions, as Related in Contemporaneous Books and Manuscripts*, 53 vols. (Cleveland: A. H. Clark Co., 1903), 3: 226n75.

[121] José Luis Gasch Tomás, 'Global Trade, Circulation and Consumption of Asian Goods in the Atlantic World: The Manila Galleons and the Social Elites of Mexico and Seville (1580–1640)' (PhD thesis, European University Institute, 2012).

[122] Antonio de Morga (1609) in Blair, Robertson, and Bourne, *The Philippine Islands*, 16: 143. For other comments on the extensive general and symbolic use of silk textiles in Spanish Manila, see the Italian description (1699) of impressed traveller Giovanni Francesco Gemelli Careri, *Giro del mondo* (Naples: Stamperia di Giuseppe Roselli, Presso Francesco Antonio Perazzo, 1709), 5: 23–4.

[123] 'Aviso y orden sobre carga de la armada de socorro', 10 October 1616, AGI, Filipinas, 340, 3: 155.

America getting a hearing. To make matters worse, when the Crown of Portugal joined those of Castile and Aragon united under a Habsburg monarch (Philip II) in 1581, the extensive Portuguese silk-trading infrastructure out of Macao added greater Asian export power to the mix in Manila. Iberian officials in the Philippines tried to make clear through interpreters exactly what kinds of quality and quantity of raw and finished silks they preferred, but whether their messages made any difference or not, they eagerly disposed of what came their way from growing numbers of Chinese traders and ships.[124]

The overland route connecting the new Pacific and old Atlantic shipping lanes ran between Acapulco and Veracruz, via Mexico City, and it would soon be known as the road of China (camino de China). It literally and metaphorically cut across New Spain's decades-old indigenous silk trading paths. Uncertainty and vaguely positive statements around the turn of the century, such as Herrera's that 'in this valley of Oaxaca ... there grows much silk, wheat, and maize' soon turned to scepticism. By 1605, one of the appointed Mexican inspectors of raw silks, Luis Calbacho, whose domestic fees had doubtless been waning dramatically, made the point explicitly that raw silk from China was strangling sericulture in New Spain, undercutting its value.[125] Plenty of commentators have promoted other explanations to a position higher up the chain of causality than they deserve, often fuelled by insistent biases such as anti-Indian, anti-Spanish, or anti-ecclesiastical sentiments, or postcolonial censure – for it is true that both Spanish authorities and some religious orders would go on to reverse their earlier support of silk raising from the

---

[124] Sanjay Subrahmanyam, 'Holding the World in Balance: The Connected Histories of the Iberian Overseas Empires, 1500–1640', *American Historical Review* 112, no. 5 (2007): 1359–85; Rui D'Avila Lourido, 'The Impact of the Macao–Manila Silk Trade from the Beginnings to 1640', in *The Silk Roads: Highways of Culture and Commerce*, ed. Vadime Elisseeff (New York: Berghahn Books, 2000), 209–46; Katharine Bjork, 'The Link That Kept the Philippines Spanish: Mexican Merchant Interests and the Manila Trade, 1571–1815', *Journal of World History* 9, no. 1 (1998): 25–50; Antoni Picazo Muntaner, 'El Comercio sedero de Filipinas y su influencia en la economía de España en el siglo xvii', in *La declinación de la monarquía hispánica. VIIa reunión científica de la fundación española de historia moderna*, ed. Francisco J. Aranda Pérez (Cuenca: UCLM, 2004); Gasch Tomás, 'Global Trade, Circulation and Consumption,' 213–26; Dana Leibsohn, 'Made in China, Made in Mexico', in *At the Crossroads: The Arts of Spanish America & Early Global Trade, 1492–1850*, ed. Donna Pierce and Ronald Y. Otsuka (Denver Art Museum, 2012), 18–19.

[125] Herrera y Tordesillas, *Descripción de las Indias ocidentales*, 19. See also 'Carta del virrey conde de Monterrey', 4 August 1597, AGI, Mexico 23, 86: 21. Calbacho cited in Borah, *Silk Raising in Colonial Mexico*, 90–1. For other claims about price differentials, see Muntaner, 'El comercio sedero de filipinas y su influencia en la economía de España en el siglo xvii', 502, though as Gasch notes these are assumed rather than evidenced.

1590s onwards.[126] But indigenous American sericulture, already undermined by Atlantic microbes and weather patterns, was one of the first
victims of the dawning of a new global economic system.[127]

Belying Enríquez's initial disparagement, Chinese silk fabrics soon
constituted a major component of trade whether determined by volume
or by value, as appreciation of the quality and range of Asian silk products
became more nuanced. The arrival of the Manila galleons (or singular
galleon from 1593) annually transformed the quiet thoroughfares of
Acapulco into thronging, swarming markets, with the ships' cargos serving as the bait in a spectacular commercial feeding frenzy starting in late
January: mule trains descended from Mexico and merchant vessels from
South American ports. Most silks would end up being consumed by
peninsular and American-born Spaniards (*criollos*) as well as elite mesti-
zos, especially in Mexico City, though large proportions were also disseminated to major provincial towns in the Viceroyalty of New Spain
(such as Puebla and Guadalajara) and down the coast to Peru (especially
silver-rich Lima) or across to other Spanish possessions, in spite of the
attempts of the Crown to restrict re-exports.[128] Amongst the semi-
finished and finished silks arrived large numbers of velvets, satins,
damasks, and taffetas, the finest fabrics being tightly packed into half-
chests (*medio cajones*), while inferior grades were bundled or baled
(*fardos*).[129] Antonio de Morga, a senior official in Manila, recorded the
Spanish orders of 'quantities of velvet, some plain, and some embroidered
in all sorts of figures, colours, and fashions – others with body of gold, and
embroidered with gold; woven stuff and brocades, of gold and silver upon

[126] For recent discussions which outline these different explanations and biases, see: Las
Casas, *Arte nuevo para criar seda*, xxix–xxx; Teresa de Campos and Teresa Castelló
Yturbide, *Historia y arte de la seda en México: Siglos xvi–xx* (Mexico, D. F.: Banamex,
1990), 34–60; Borah, *Silk Raising in Colonial Mexico*, 87–101.
[127] Debin Ma, 'The Great Silk Exchange: How the World Was Connected and Developed',
in *Pacific Centuries: Pacific and Pacific Rim History since the Sixteenth Century*, edited by
Dennis Owen Flynn, Lionel Frost, and A. J. H. Latham, 38–65 (London: Routledge,
1999), 52.
[128] William L. Schurz, *The Manila Galleon* (New York: E. P. Dutton & Co., 1939), 362;
Borah, *Silk Raising in Colonial Mexico*, 97.
[129] The goods inventory of merchandise traded by one prominent merchant back to
Acapulco gives an example of the many different classes of silks. 'Inventario de los
bienes de Sande depositados por Diego López', 17 February 1581, AGI, Filipinas, 34,
35. A detailed discussion of the silk and mixed-silk goods was provided in the 1637
memorial by Juan Grau y Malfalcon, noting headdresses and stockings in particular, in
Blair, Robertson, and Bourne, *The Philippine Islands*, 27: 184–203. On packing and the
nature of goods, Carmen Yuste López, *El Comercio De La Nueva España Con Filipinas,
1590–1785* (Mexico, D. F.: Instituto Nacional de Antropologia e Historia, 1984), 25–6;
Edward R. Slack Jr., 'Orientalizing New Spain: Perspectives on Asian Influence in
Colonial Mexico', *México y La Cuenca Del Pacífico* 15, no. 43 (2012): 97–127; Gasch
Tomás, 'Global Trade, Circulation and Consumption', 219.

silk of various colours and patterns'.[130] Little wonder that the Viceroy of Peru informed Philip III that his people lived luxuriously, recording that 'all wear silk, and of the most fine and costly quality', with women's gala costumes more numerous and more excessive than in any other kingdom of the world. These American Hispanic elites were instrumental in the early market shaping of the European consumption of Asian goods that would explode from the late seventeenth century, though its trans-Pacific component stagnated somewhat after the 1630s.[131] But the question remains: to what extent was their flamboyant consumption – detailed in probate inventories and tax records – an unthinking decision when it came to the sourcing of their raw materials?

It is fair to say that the finished silks of China ferried across the Pacific were better appreciated by some consumers than by others. For all their novelty, artistry, and technical brilliance, these Asian imports could and did raise cultural hackles. Complaints about the influx of Chinese fabrics were mounting in the early seventeenth century, when globetrotting Bishop Martín Ignacio de Loyola grumbled that all classes in South America were dressing in the silks of China, above all the poorest people, and that they were used to adorn churches.[132] Another cleric explicitly requested that decorative liturgical materials for Catholic masses be sent to the Philippines all the way from Spain, preferably along with more friars, because 'although there are many ornaments here, they are of false Chinese silk and gold'.[133] Nonetheless, the cargos of silk goods shipped across the Pacific had a dramatic impact, with finished silk garments found in around 40 per cent of Mexico City inventories, and often dominating artistic and cultural depictions of the city.[134] Across the Atlantic, the steady trickle of Asian silk orders from New Spain, spread onwards from Seville as elite gifts to the Castilian aristocracy, suggested a proto-commercial metropolitan appetite for innovative luxury products that was perceptibly growing. In a short time, on the East Asian mainland,

[130] Blair, Robertson, and Bourne, *The Philippine Islands*, 16: 178. Morga explained that the price of both raw and woven silks was settled in silver and reals, and the trading completed by the end of May such that the *nao de China* and most of the Sangley traders could depart for their onwards legs in June and July. Ibid., 182.

[131] For excellent recent analyses: Gasch Tomás, 'Global Trade, Circulation and Consumption'; Elena Phipps, 'The Iberian Globe: Textile Traditions and Trade in Latin America', in *Interwoven Globe: The Worldwide Textile Trade, 1500–1800*, ed. Amelia Peck (London: Thames and Hudson, 2013), 28–45.

[132] 'Carta de Martín Ignacio de Loyola, obispo del Rio de la Plata', n.d. [1607–9], AGI, Filipinas, 35, 47: 823v.

[133] 'Petición del agustino Pedro de Solier de mercedes para agustinos de Filipinas', *c.* October 1614, AGI, Filipinas, 79, 109: 1–2.

[134] Gasch Tomás, 'Global Trade, Circulation and Consumption', 258, 260; Leibsohn, 'Made in China, Made in Mexico.'

the Chinese were adapting their silk workshops to emulate Spanish tastes and Christian motifs, and this export product adaptability would position them well for the upsurge in the westward-bound Asian textile trade that took place over subsequent centuries.[135]

Just as important as these ready-woven silks, and arguably far more culturally transmissible, were the spiralling shipments of raw silks arriving in New Spain. Long before the arrival of the Spanish, the Philippines had served as an international transhipment point for raw silks, and though Pacific cargos were farther in distance and more concentrated, they fitted with the long-standing pattern of re-export established by the archipelago's Sangley traders to Japan. Historically, raw and semi-processed silk yarns were amongst the most prized offerings brought each year from China by the dozens of trading vessels that arrived in clusters with the monsoon in March (now growing to as many as fifty junks or *somas*).[136] One Spanish official, negotiating precarious early relations with China recorded that 'the great bulk of our purchases' consisted of raw silk.[137] Antonio de Morga, in his inventory of Spanish procurements at Manila, likewise emphasised the 'raw silk in bundles, of the fineness of two strands [*dos cabecas*], and other silk of coarser quality; fine untwisted silk, white and of all colours, wound in small skeins'.[138] Practically the full range of raw silk (*seda cruda*) was therefore catered for, from the cocoon floss that could not be wound as filament (*seda floja*) through to high-quality silk yarn that was virtually ready for dyeing or weaving and suited to either warp (*seda torcida*) or expressly for weft (*seda de tramas*). In 1599, the licenciate in Manila, Hieronimo de Salazar y Salcedo, wrote an extensive report discussing the ins and outs of the silk trade, recommending to the king that raw silk from Manila – because damaging to Atlantic trade – be restricted to five picos per ship, 'which is a very small quantity' but was still liable to make an estimated 400 per cent profit upon sale in Mexico.[139]

---

[135] Shirley Fish, *The Manila–Acapulco Galleons: The Treasure Ships of the Pacific, with an Annotated List of the Transpacific Galleons, 1565–1815* (Milton Keynes: AuthorHouse, 2011), 440–4; Ma, 'The Great Silk Exchange: How the World Was Connected and Developed', 51–2; Gasch Tomás, 'Global Trade, Circulation and Consumption', 53–6, 65–8, 70–3.

[136] Blair, Robertson, and Bourne, *The Philippine Islands*, 16: 177. 'Instrucción a los procuradores de Manila en la corte', 15 July 1611, AGI, Filipinas, 27, 85. The rich Japanese market itself was destabilised by the arrival of Europeans, as noted by the *procurador general* of the Philippines, Martin Castaño, who lamented the loss of the chance to sell silks there in 1618 because the Spanish had been trumped by the combative Dutch. 'Memoria impresa de Martín Castaño', 1618, Filipinas, 27, 107.

[137] Letter from Hernando de los Ríos Coronel, cited in Blair, Robertson, and Bourne, *The Philippine Islands*, 15: 172.

[138] Blair, Robertson, and Bourne, *The Philippine Islands*, 16: 178.

[139] 'Carta del fiscal Salazar sobre oficios, comercio, Hacienda', 21 July 1599, AGI, Filipinas, 18b, 9, 127: 19–20. A like-minded assault on the loss of silk revenue due to

The report seems to have made little impression: most of the growing quantity of Chinese raw silk continued to be bought up by the rising manufacturing industry in New Spain, which by the early seventeenth century was reportedly employing in excess of 14,000 workers in its three silk cities, where they worked up Chinese skeins, thread, and *trama* into 'velvets, veils, headdresses, passementaries, and many taffetas'.[140] In Mexico, one enthusiastic sailor reported to his father in 1590 that he had earned 2,500 ducats (then around £1,250) from the *nao de China* voyage in spite of the spoilage of one pack of silk by salt water.[141] But such private ventures were small fry compared to the commercial orders, and the officially acknowledged orders were a decreasing proportion of the overall trade, as smuggling and fraud increased substantially into the seventeenth century.[142] Merchants formed close links and sometimes partnerships with silk-manufacturing artisans, as when master silk-weaver Fernando de Padilla agreed to supervise the production of silk at one of the Mexico City stores of wholesaler Juan de Castellete: the former providing the labour and expertise, and the latter the capital.[143] By the early seventeenth century, Chinese petty traders and artisans (*chinos*) clustered into growing ghettos in Mexico City and Puebla, offering competition and expertise in the marketing and finishing functions of the silk trade.[144] In another nod to a world in which silk was breaking free of regional containment, a writer in Manila related that master silk-weavers had been leaving Toledo and Granada to set up workshops (*obrajes*) in New Spain, where they benefited from Asian raw silk.[145] Ironically, the stagnation of their Iberian home industries had also been caused in part by the profusion of Asian silks, because the pesky Dutch and other East Indies Companies were transporting them back westwards in increasing

---

the organisation of the Manila trade was made by the Dominican missionary Diego Aduarte to the Council of Indies: 'Carta del dominico Diego Aduarte sobre comercio de Filipinas', May 1619, AGI, Filipinas, 85, 34: 1–4.

[140] Memorial of Juan Grau y Malfalcon, 1637, in Blair, Robertson, and Bourne, *The Philippine Islands*, 27: 199.

[141] Sebastian Biscaino to Antonio Biscaino, 20 June 1590, Mexico, cited in Richard Hakluyt, *The Principal Navigations, Voyages, Traffiques, and Discoveries of the English Nation*, 16 vols. (Edinburgh: E. & G. Goldsmid, 1885), 15: 319.

[142] Dennis O. Flynn and Arturo Giráldez. 'Silk for Silver: Manila-Macao Trade in the 17th Century', *Philippine Studies* 44 (1996): 52–68.

[143] Louisa Schell Hoberman, *Mexico's Merchant Elite, 1590–1660: Silver, State, and Society* (Durham, NC: Duke University Press, 1991), 128–31.

[144] Edward R. Slack Jr., 'The Chinos in New Spain: A Corrective Lens for a Distorted Image', *Journal of World History* 20, no. 1 (2009): 42–4, 47.

[145] Blair, Robertson, and Bourne, *The Philippine Islands*, 27: 203.

volume, beginning to undermine long-standing European circuits of production and distribution.[146]

A significant proportion of Chinese raw silk was also ferried onwards across the Atlantic to provide materials for some of the looms of the Iberian Peninsula. There, in a sense the raw materials were culturally whitewashed by being worked up into Spanish fabrics, an apt expression since one of the enduring strengths of Chinese silk that was early recognised was its whiteness or purity and consistency of colour, which meant that it lent itself readily to dyestuffs. Chinese silk began with symbolic novelty value, by which knowledge of the silk's Asian provenance would add to the originality and social reception of fabrics worked up and then sported by Castilian elites.[147] But it soon became a commercial talking point. The Viceroy of Peru, Marques de Montesclaros, identified one important reason to allow the influx of Asian silks to continue in his lengthy contemplations on the Manila trade in 1610. He was by no means an apologist for China silk, warning that saturating the market with Asian silks might 'cease the present industry [in Spain] of the raising of silk, its weaving and trade', and replace sturdy Iberian products with 'what is so much poorer and of so little durability'. He explained that Spaniards in the Indies had discovered 'the harm caused by even a small quantity of silk of this class [i.e. thinner Chinese yarn]', which when mixed 'in almost all the velvets and taffetas brought from Spain' rendered them useless after two days. Yet de Montesclaros accepted that in light of the struggles of Spanish domestic production and the rise of European competition, should the door to Pacific trade be shut, 'the bulk of silk stuffs would have to be brought from France and Flanders', both powers who had proved extremely 'skilful in getting this product away from us' in the Mediterranean and beyond. This was a dangerous prospect indeed, and reason enough to sustain a Pacific silk trade: French and Dutch power could bite, whereas 'the Chinese do us no other harm than to keep the silver', albeit an astonishing quantity of it. Within a decade of Monteclaros's 1610 report, taxed imports of Chinese raw silk to Seville from New Spain had more than tripled, valued at over 60 million *maravedís* in 1618 (or 2,000 times the reward offered to the first Spaniard to produce raw silk 100 years earlier). It was another testament

---

[146] Occasional Portuguese merchants are recorded bringing raw silk back from India at the very end of the sixteenth century for use by Toledo manufacturers. Montemayor, 'La seda en Toledo en la época moderna', 121; Mariano Bonialian, 'La "ropa de La China" desde filipinas hasta Buenos Aires. Circulación, consumo y lucha corporativa, 1580–1620', *Revista de Indias* 26, no. 268 (2016): 641–72.

[147] See, for examples, small amounts of raw silk recorded in Gasch Tomás, 'Global Trade, Circulation and Consumption', 57–8.

to how quickly Meso-American production had collapsed in the past four decades that de Montesclaros prefaced his discussion of the future of Iberian silk with only the most half-hearted of reminders, that silk 'may be obtained in great abundance, without begging it from anyone' in any of Mexico's provinces and especially the Mixteca.[148]

Rekindling sericulture, in fact, had not been entirely abandoned, and several protagonists in the seventeenth century sought to re-energise it through the Pacific transhipment of Asian silkworm seed. Naturally, the rising appetite for raw, semi-finished, and finished silks in New Spain had led to considerable interest in the nature of Chinese production.[149] In 1609, Hernando de Los Ríos Coronel informed the king that a new and more valuable type of silk was on the market at Lanquin (Nanjing), writing that the seed was very fertile and 'they have worms whose cocoons are so large that they seem greater than hundreds of others'. He relayed that it was grown at a latitude of forty degrees and that 'it would be easy to bring this seed ... and it would be most useful for this kingdom'.[150] He was wrong. In 1610 the governor of the Philippines, Juan de Silva, had been instructed to seek out and send home some of this silkworm seed, with a request not only for the stock but also for insights into how the Chinese raised their silk, but this seemed to come to nothing.[151] Occasional later references also recorded attempts to bring away Chinese silkworm seed. The Dominican friar, Manuel Trigueros, wrote about his trip to Fujian on the south-east coast of China in 1682, during which he sought to procure seed and dispatch it to the Philippines governor Juan de Vargas, like an eastwards variant of Justinian's mythologised Nestorian monks. Trigueros tormented himself with his attempts to identify the quickest sailing combination to get the eggs to their destination, trying to find the journey that involved the fewest 'steps for it to reach Manila with dispatch: all is in vain if the Canton ship leaves so late that the worms hatch'. But he and others who attempted to convey the seed in this direction were facing an impossible task, given the travel involved. As he rightly and diplomatically predicted, 'I fear greatly that time is set against His Majesty's wishes in this matter', adding for good

---

[148] Blair, Robertson, and Bourne, *The Philippine Islands*, 17: 214–212; Flynn and Giráldez, 'Silk for Silver: Manila–Macao Trade in the 17th Century', 59–60; Gasch Tomás, 'Global Trade, Circulation and Consumption', 100–1 (figures for raw silk imports).

[149] 'Relación sobre el reino de China de Juan Bautista Román', 28 September 1584, AGI, Filipinas, 29, 49: 215–29.

[150] 'Petición de Ríos Coronel sobre variedad de seda de China', 24 January 1609, AGI, Filipinas, 27, 72: 513r–514v. Briefly mentioned in John N. Crossley, *Hernando de Los Ríos Coronel and the Spanish Philippines in the Golden Age* (Farnham: Ashgate, 2011), 88.

[151] 'Orden de enviar a España semilla de seda china', 1 November 1610, AGI, Filipinas, 329, 2: 118r–118v.

measure the disclaimer that the importation had not been his idea: his superior in Macao had charged him with the duty.[152]

Rather like these larvae, Mexican sericulture was left behind as Spanish subjects in the New World adapted Pacific materials to reconstruct the sartorial models of materialism that they had imported across the Atlantic. One writer in 1637 argued that only imports shipped from Manila would suffice in the absence of Mixtecan produce; they complained that by the time Atlantic silks reached Peru from Spain, especially black, brown, and silver-coloured goods, they apparently 'arrived in bad shape, because the sea rots them'.[153] Gradually, tastes and fashions amongst Spanish *criollos* were embracing new colours, styles, weaves, and creating a hybrid material identity, to the point that occasional European silk textiles at the start of the seventeenth century were even sent back home across the Atlantic, having failed to charm discerning American consumers. Andean peoples also co-opted available silks into their production and fashion cycles, as indigenous groups had done a few decades earlier in New Spain, for example in the use of imported silk weft in the weaving of the shimmering *tornesols* (overspun camelid warp-faced black fabrics) that became highly popular in the southern highlands.[154] Rather than contemplating revived silk-raising projects, silk consumers in South America pressed on several occasions to be allowed to open their own direct trade across the Pacific which might also negate smuggling.[155]

At the national level, the Spanish debate over the pros and cons of suppressing the Manila trade continued. An alarmist six-page pamphlet, printed in Spain in 1628, called for a blanket ban and warned of the pernicious 'dangers and inconveniences' which would accrue from

[152] 'Expediente sobre el comercio con Macao', 7 January 1682, AGI, Filipinas, 24, 4, 27: 1–2.

[153] Memorial of Juan Grau y Malfalcon, 1637, in Blair and Robertson, *The Philippine Islands, 1493–1803*, 27: 199.

[154] Fish, *The Manila–Acapulco Galleons*, 90. On cultural and material crossover, see: Héctor Rivero Borrell Miranda, *The Grandeur of Viceregal Mexico: Treasures from the Museo Franz Mayer* (Houston, TX: Museum of Fine Arts, Houston, 2002); Gasch Tomás, 'Global Trade, Circulation and Consumption', 223 (cargoes returned), 318–29 (adaptation of fashions); Armella de Aspe, 'Artes asiáticas y novohispañas', in *El Galeón del Pacífico: Acapulco–Manila 1565–1815*, ed. Fernando Benítez (Mexico City: Biblioteca del Sur, 1992), 203–39; Leibsohn, 'Made in China, Made in Mexico', 23–4. Elena Phipps, '"Tornesol": A Colonial Synthesis of European and Andean Textile Traditions', in *Textile Society of America, Seventh Biennial Symposium, Santa Fe, New Mexico 2000 Proceedings*, ed. Textile Society of America (Earlville, MD: Textile Society of America, 2000), 221–30; Elena Phipps, Johanna Hecht, Cristina Esteras Martín, et al., *The Colonial Andes: Tapestries and Silverwork, 1530–1830* (New York: Metropolitan Museum of Art, 2004), 190–1, 276; Arteaga, 'Vestido y desnudo', 202–3.

[155] 'Autos fiscales', 1629, AGI, Contratacion, 5737, 6: 3, and 1635, AGI, Contratacion, 650, 5; 'Los oficiales reales de Quito sobre diversos asuntos', 11 May 1632, AGI, Quito, 20a, 19; Fish, *The Manila–Acapulco Galleons*, 48–9, 268.

allowing even a limited exchange – up until then, the choice of moderates – that would permit the stealthy penetration of China's 'wild and rough' silk. The pamphlet conveyed a sense of class war, warning of price hikes and the self-interested officials in Spanish America – viceroys, generals, and justices – who had collaborated in the Chinese saturation of the markets there. It lamented the consequences for Spanish silk raisers (*criadores*), and warned that the domestic industry would likely collapse in a few years, crippling populations and revenue streams, especially in Granada. The author walked back through the consequences: the wasted skill, the poverty, and ultimately the death of the mulberry trees for lack of care that would render it impossible to reconstruct the industry in the future.[156]

Survival, c.1640–1700

By the 1640s, sericulture in Spain's New World possessions was therefore no longer associated with large-scale commercial ambitions. The vast majority of the mulberry trees that had been so carefully planted out in the sixteenth century had either been progressively destroyed or, more commonly, simply neglected. It was telling that there was virtually no discussion of sericulture's revival, even when the Acapulco-Manila trade was at its most insecure, or when Asian raw silk declined in step with the collapse of the Ming dynasty – an event that itself lessened the tide of Chinese silk production and contributed to a contraction in international commerce and the numbers of vessels arriving at Manila.[157] By 1679, when a royal edict formally ordered the physical uprooting of all trees in the Viceroyalty of New Spain 'whose leaves would feed silkworms' it could be safely ignored because it would have virtually no added impact.[158]

But though its extent was vastly reduced, silk raising nonetheless persisted, being embedded particularly in the economic and cultural life of a small number of Mixtecan townships. The output of raw silk was enough in 1608 to warrant an explicit mention in a guild order of the hat and silk workers of Lima which insisted that 'the silk sellers did not combine Mixteca silk with China silk in fringes or other items'.[159] Specialisation brought sensitivity to the origin and quality of raw

[156] 'Razones para no admitir el comercio con China', signed by a Juan Velázquez Madridejos, October 1628, AGI, Filipinas, 40, 5: 1–6.
[157] Hoberman, *Mexico's Merchant Elite, 1590–1660: Silver, State, and Society*, 15.
[158] Borah, *Silk Raising in Colonial Mexico*, 99.
[159] Francisco Quiroz and Gerardo Quiroz, *Las Ordenanzas de Gremios de Lima (s. XVI–XVIII)*, Historia Serie Documental (Lima: s.n., 1986), 19.

materials, and at other points Meso-American silk was clearly in demand on its own, being mentioned explicitly in purchase orders amongst the merchants of Cuenca, who sold it alongside China silk to a range of clients in the 1600s – many of them from the lower orders.[160] The last testament of a wealthy Mixtec merchant from Yanhuitlán in 1621 recorded his trade of silk fabrics from 'the Mixteca, Tlaxcala, Europe and Asia'.[161] In the early eighteenth century, foreign visitors reported that the province of Oaxaca still 'affords much Silk', besides wheat and maize – Edward Cooke described the country as 'wholesome and pleasant', adding that it 'produces much Silk, being full of Mulberry-Trees'.[162] Local raw silk was still being used to pay a small portion of parish tithes in the late eighteenth century in such places as Texupa and Teposcolula, but the quantity was minimal and declining. One view of this persistence has been to characterise it as little more than a slow, lingering death of the pursuit, what Woodrow Borah described as 'degenerate remnants' whose value seeped away.[163] Seen in the light of global market integration, and the increasingly transcontinental flows of goods and technologies, this view has its merits.

However, the fact that for a century or more, Mixtecan raw silk lapsed into a niche commodity produced and traded by Indians, also highlights a profound Atlantic adaptation and a sort of reclamation. Even if figures permitted (which they don't), we could not infer qualitative cultural value in the same way we might chart quantitative output, but there are a few signs that suggest Mixtecans' exclusive ownership of their silk raising was highly significant to them. Caciques placed high symbolic value upon silk vestments, as recorded in the will of Don Gabriel de Guzmán who wanted a Yanhuitlán silk item returned that had been loaned out to the cacique of Mistepec and passed on to the governor of Tlaxiaco.[164] One seventeenth-century historian recorded that the most important items ritually exchanged as gifts during festival celebrations were silk mantles.[165] And though hard to track definitively, the legacy of this local usurpation of and persistence in silk production is perceived to be of great importance to

[160] These included 'seda de mixteca floxa y torcida', and 'seda colorada floxa de la mixteca', which were offered to poor janitors and Spanish aristocrats alike. Arteaga, 'Vestido y desnudo', 195–7.

[161] Cited in Frassani, 'The Church and Convento of Santo Domingo Yanhuitla', 57.

[162] Edward Cooke, A Voyage to the South Sea, and Round the World Perform'd in the Years 1708, 1709, 1710, and 1711, 2 vols. (London: Printed by H. M. for B. Lintot and R. Gosling etc., 1712), 1: 393–4.

[163] Borah, Silk Raising in Colonial Mexico, 101.

[164] Last will and testament of Don Gabriel de Guzmán, 1591, translated in Restall, Sousa, and Terraciano, Mesoamerican Voices, 108.

[165] Francisco de Burgoa, Geográfica Descripción (Mexico: Talleres Gráficos de la Nación, 1934), 1: 289.

producers today, who cherish an art that they and their ancestors have nurtured through the ages. They place great emphasis on the fact that their *criollo* silkworms are descended from those brought by the Spanish in the sixteenth century, as opposed to the hybrid Japanese *mejorado* silkworms provided by government programmes.[166]

Spain had offered an effective model of how to bring silk production to the New World, thanks in large part to the substantial involvement of these indigenous collaborators, whose practices persisted. But choreographing projection, production, and exchange had been complicated by diverse forces and discoveries to the point where it was no longer desirable. As for peninsular silk producers in Spain and later Portugal, their fortunes in the long seventeenth century varied somewhat from region to region, pushed and pulled by wider trends that included the upsurge in Asian imports, economic stagnation as silver declined, loss of foreign markets, and growing domestic-market penetration of Italian silk yarn and north-western European manufactured silk and mixed-silk products. The decline in some districts, such as Toledo, was offset by the consolidation of a domestic silk industry chain from moth to cloth, especially in vibrant Valencia and Cataluña, but one which was strong in the middle range and lacked either high quality at the top end or low enough price at the bottom to fend off commercial rivals. The Spanish raw silk export trade, meanwhile, increasingly gravitated northwards to France, with Marseille becoming a favoured destination, until exports were strategically banned in 1699. By that stage, the more northerly European powers had long had their own plans in motion for introducing silk production to their Atlantic empires.[167]

---

[166] Alejandro de Ávila Blomberg, 'Threads of Diversity: Oaxacan Textiles in Context', in *The Unbroken Thread: Conserving the Textile Traditions of Oaxaca*, ed. K. Klein (Los Angeles: The Getty Conservation Institute, 1997), 87–151; Careyn Patricia Armitage, Silk Production and Its Impact on Families and Communities in Oaxaca, Mexico (Ames, IA: Iowa State University, 2008), 50–1.

[167] Martín Corrales, 'Comercio de la seda entre España y Mediterráneo', 162; Carl A. Hanson, *Economy and Society in Baroque Portugal, 1668–1703* (Minneapolis: University of Minnesota Press, 1981), 167–8.

3 England and Virginia

A defence against the Dutch not necessary 'till now, for they [Virginians] begin to make those rich commodities which may hereafter tempt the army of Princes. Have made great & unexpected progress in silk which they shall double every year till they make 100,000 lbs. weight yearly: in want of good wheels (the French call them Mills) from Marseilles or Messina. Shall shortly make as much as 40,000 people in the world can do, for they are provided with innumerable trees which in four or five years will come to their perfectest.

– Governor William Berkeley, Virginia, 1665[1]

A Fibre Fit for a King

England's distance from global sites of silk production and its overwhelmingly woollen textile heritage stood in stark contrast to Spain's centuries-long familiarity with sericulture. Nonetheless, between the late sixteenth and late seventeenth centuries, dramatic enlargement in commerce, manufacturing, and territory encouraged this peripheral north-western European power to view it as not only desirable but practicable to secure to itself a silk industry and to supply itself with home-grown silk. Elite consumption and cultural familiarisation with the product, encouraged at the very centre of the state, drove projects to domesticate sericulture, increasingly buttressed by newer arguments about trade and labour that carried consensus, even through periods of social upheaval. Significant efforts were made to secure replenishable stocks of silkworm eggs and to add mulberries to English estates, but production was jeopardised by the absence of sufficient expertise and by recurring environmental problems that undermined uptake. In Virginia, England's first permanent colony, whose warmer climate and forested interior were more promising than the British Isles, attempts to establish sericulture would become a rallying point for grand visions of Atlantic

---

[1] Governor William Berkeley to Sir Henry Bennet, Virginia, 1 August 1665. 'Virginia in 1662–1665', *Virginia Magazine of History and Biography* 18 (1910): 427.

colonialism. Drawing on English patronage more than Spanish experience, they solved problems with trees and symbiosis, initiated distinctive migrant streams, and established a new literature to challenge presuppositions – acting as a laboratory and an archive for future experimentalism. By the century's end, however, Virginian exploits had largely come and gone, many planters having boldly tried but failed to escape the all-consuming dominance of tobacco and the structural inadequacies of the available labouring population. That it was endogenous factors that largely undermined the earliest English production – unlike the external shocks visited upon sericulture in New Spain – allowed belief to persist in silk's viability as a potential product of the British Atlantic. The upshot was that silk would remain a primary target of American colonial projection, opening the door to varied new projects and permutations in the long eighteenth century.

It was not a coincidence that the first widespread interest in silkworms in England followed a pronounced rise in the domestic consumption of silk goods. In January 1617, the exasperated sixty-two-year-old privy councillor Lord Carew complained of the changing habits in textile consumerism that had percolated through English society in recent decades: 'there is suche a madnes[s] in England as thatt we cannott endure our homemade clothe, but must needes be clothed in silke'. Carew linked self-control, production, and national identity together, in a formulation that harked back to an era when society had rationally and patiently worn traditional English products. The heyday of woollen cloth, however, had just begun to wane, as British textile manufacturing adjusted in the mid-sixteenth century to diversify beyond this classic staple and its continuing dominance of exports from London, most of them through the hub of Antwerp.[2] Stimulated partly by an economic depression that stifled wool and cloth exports around the time Carew was born in 1555, and partly by an influx of craftspeople, methods, and technologies that permitted lighter-weight fabrics and mixes, textile production in the British Isles was kicking into a new gear that was fast enough to compete in international marketplaces. Imports of silks reached over 100,000 lb in weight in 1601, and a growing portion of these were raw silk or thrown silk then worked up by manufacturers in England (including many 'Strangers').[3] By this time, luxury cloths had

[2] Lawrence Stone, 'Elizabethan Overseas Trade', *Economic History Review* 2, no. 1 (1949): 37. Silk luxury textiles, mostly Italian, constituted just 6 per cent of listings of imports into London in the 1560s.

[3] Arthur Newton, ed., *Calendar of the Manuscripts of Major–General Lord Sackville: Preserved at Knole, Sevenoaks, Kent* (London: His Majesty's Stationery Office, 1966), 1: 124; Stone, 'Elizabethan Overseas Trade.'

become by far the most significant group of imports, and sumptuary decrees about who could wear them had come (1597) and gone (1604).[4] Carew was therefore long enough in the tooth to be pragmatic about England's deepening madness for silk, concluding that it ought at least to be furnished as cheaply as possible: 'itt cannot be gayne-sayed but the silks bought att the first hand is the best husbandrye'.[5] Leaping in to buy raw silk at its point of origin offered the opportunity to bypass the many charges and challenges that came with brokers, carriers, or third parties, and that left English manufacturers and consumers at the whim of foreign powers and merchants – particularly Dutch, Portuguese, Italian, and French.

Late Tudor and early Stuart monarchs were thin on capital and paranoid about the need to cement dynastic standing in the face of various credibility gaps, and so generally supported attempts to interfere with the foreign sourcing of many luxury fabrics. This helped to bring to the surface a fresh political economy at the start of the seventeenth century – spearheaded by writers such as Francis Bacon, who were acutely mindful of inhabiting an age of discovery, and of the possibilities of equating enlargement of the rational with enlargement of the national. Rather than unthinkingly maligning merchants or the exotic materials they brought home, attention had increasingly turned to how to harness profitable private activities into the service of the state, and how to understand and manage systems of exchange. In this particular case, Carew was agreeing with Sir Thomas Roe's 1616 proposal – co-initiated by the Safavid Shah Abbas – to open a new English trade in Persia and redivert the silk trade that flowed overland through the Ottoman Empire or exited by sea via Portuguese control of the Strait of Hormuz in the Persian Gulf. Roe was convinced that there was no

---

[4] Maxine Berg, *Luxury and Pleasure in Eighteenth–Century Britain* (Oxford: Oxford University Press, 2005); Negley B. Harte, 'Silk and Sumptuary Legislation in England', in *La Seta in Europa. Secc. XIII–XX*, ed. Simonetta Cavaciocchi (Florence: Le Monnier, 1993), 801–16.

[5] George Carew, Thomas Roe, and John Maclean, *Letters from George Lord Carew to Sir Thomas Roe, Ambassador to the Court of the Great Mogul. 1615–1617* (Westminster: Printed for the Camden Society, 1860), 77; Iosif K. Hamel, *England and Russia: Comprising the Voyages of John Tradescant the Elder, Sir Hugh Willoughby, Richard Chancellor, Nelson, and Others, to the White Sea* (London: R. Bentley, 1854), 124–5. On the wider changes in textile production and luxury sensibilities: Alison V. Scott, *Literature and the Idea of Luxury in Early Modern England* (Routledge, 2016), 142; Linda Levy Peck, *Consuming Splendor: Society and Culture in Seventeenth-Century England* (Cambridge: Cambridge University Press, 2005); Berg, *Luxury and Pleasure*; Jane Stevenson, 'Texts and Textiles: Self–Presentation among the Elite in Renaissance England', *Journal of the Northern Renaissance* 3, no. 1 (2011): 39–57.

better 'place for the benefitt of our Nation to settle a trade for venting cloth and buying silke'.[6]

The Persian enterprise that prompted Carew's musings on silk was by no means the first such attempt by English commercial agents to solve the dilemma – which had long plagued several northern European powers – of their distance from the global supply of silk. Already by the 1560s, English mercantile interests had begun to make considerable inroads in the European scramble for Levantine silk (concentrated in Aleppo and Smyrna), and attempts were underway to cement an 'overland' route (largely via the Volga) through Muscovy to the great silk-producing regions around the Caspian Sea, leading to the establishment of an English factory (trade post) in Shamakhi (Shirvan province, now in Azerbaijan) and six trade delegations before 1580. These had secured small privileges and small quantities such as the '11 packes of rawe silke' (around five mule loads) which Arthur Edwards sent back in 1567 and reported to be 'fine and good'.[7] In turn, the New Lands Company (chartered 1551), Muscovy Company (1555), Turkey Company (1581), Venice Company (1583), Levant Company (1592), and East India Company (1600) all expressly targeted importing silk – whether via Russia–Persia, Mediterranean–Turkey–Persia, or longer maritime routes to the Persian Gulf, Indian Ocean, and China.[8]

Their efforts and privileges helped drive forwards not only access to silks but also cultural familiarity in the British Isles with silk production. *Bombyx* silkworms and mulberry trees broke into English poetry and literature, where they were often expressly linked to themes of national or global expansion, kingship, and labour and prosperity. Thomas Lodge noted in his *Wits Miserie, and the Worlds Madnesse* (1596) how English ploughmen now expected to have 'garters of fine silke of Granado', and common farmers sold livestock 'to buy him silken geere for his credit'. Elizabethan favourite Michael Drayton, fighting an uphill battle to endear himself to James I, extolled the silkworm as a creature who '[f]rom small beginnings . . . have rear'd / To be the strength and maintenance of Kings' and anticipated a future in which England overtook the European

---

[6] Thomas Roe, *The Embassy of Sir Thomas Roe to the Court of the Great Mogul, 1615–19, as Narrated in His Journal and Correspondence* (London: Hakluyt Society, 1899), xlvi–xlviii, 96 (quote).

[7] Richard Hakluyt, *The Principal Navigations, Voyages, Traffiques, and Discoveries of the English Nation*, 16 vols. (Edinburgh: E. & G. Goldsmid, 1885), 3: 293. Mules calculated on the basis that Edwards estimated twenty-six 'batmans' in each pack and, separately, sixty 'batmans' to a laden mule. Ibid., 199.

[8] Kenneth R. Andrews, *Trade, Plunder, and Settlement: Maritime Enterprise and the Genesis of the British Empire, 1480–1630* (Cambridge: Cambridge University Press, 1984), 84–7, 99, 275–6.

gatekeepers of silk: 'Naples, Granado, Portugale, and France / All to sit idle, wondering at our trade.' Shakespeare's King Lear sought to understand his humanity by reflecting on nakedness and obligation: 'Thou owest the worm no silk'; his Othello valued the handkerchief he gifted as a token to Desdemona by claiming '[t]he worms were hallow'd that did breed the silk'. These and other writers, like the merchants before them, drew creative inspiration from the idea of working back from the point of silk's display to the point of its production.[9]

This was a path most clearly mapped for the first time in English by Thomas Moffett in his 1599 poem, *The Silkewormes and Their Flies*. Moffett's work, while being heavily derived from Vida's 1527 Latin verses, and inspired by a trip to Tuscany and Spain where he witnessed silk production first-hand, carefully anglicised the subject matter and tacked it to the constructive, competitive national rivalry apparent in the commercial ambitions of English trading companies. 'Up Britaine blouds', he has his silkworm cry, 'rise hearts of English race, / Why should your clothes be courser then the rest?' Moffett's silken nationalism drew upon the sorts of physiological and racial assumptions that elsewhere buttressed early Anglo-Protestant imperialism – celebrating the divine whiteness of the silkworms alongside the 'feature tall, and high aspiring face, / Aime[ing] at great things' of Englishmen; these were observations befitting Moffett's background as an accomplished physician. But most importantly, his work put forward a concrete argument in support of the domestication of raw silk production – going a step further than the mere capture of commerce or manufacturing. Moffett's silkworm, spinning a new kind of Renaissance trope that applied the form and message of Virgil's classical Georgics, promised to transform his readers and their economic landscapes: '[it] shall enrich your selves and children more, / Then ere it did Naples or Spaine before'.[10]

---

[9] Thomas Lodge, *Wits Miserie and the Worlds Madnesse: Discovering the Devils Incarnat of This Age* (London: A. Islip, 1596); Olivier de Serres and Nicholas Geffe, *The Perfect Use of Silk–Wormes, and Their Benefit: With the Exact Planting, and Artificiall Handling of Mulberrie Trees Whereby to Nourish Them, and the Figures to Know How to Feede the Wormes, and to Wind off the Silke* (London: Felix Kyngston, 1607); Todd A. Borlik, 'Plants: Shakespeare's Mulberry: Eco–Materialism and "Living On"', in *Shakespeare and the Human*, ed. Tiffany Jo Werth, Tom Bishop, and Alexa Huang (Aldershot: Ashgate, 2015), 123–46.

[10] Thomas Moffett and Victor Houliston, *The Silkewormes and Their Flies*, vol. 61 (Binghamton, NY: Renaissance English Text Society, 1989); K. A. Craik, '"These-Almost-Thingles-Things": Thomas Moffat's The "Silkewormes", and English Renaissance Georgic', *Cahiers Elisabethains*, no. 60 (2001): 53–65; Monique Bourque, 'Thomas Moffett and Insect Sociality', *Quidditas* 20 (1999): 137–54; Janice Neri, *The Insect and the Image: Visualizing Nature in Early Modern Europe, 1500–1700* (Minneapolis: University of Minnesota Press, 2011), 70–3.

Around the turn of the seventeenth century, English projectors began in earnest to pursue an even more radical option than banning silk or monopolising its trade: the 'husbandrye' or direct production of silk within English territories. Raw silk came belatedly to join a suite of commodities (amongst them woad, raw iron, flax, and hops) that had already been driven forwards by a growing state preoccupation with self-sufficiency, much of it orchestrated by William Cecil in the late Elizabethan era.[11] But the call for English-raised silkworms arrived with more fanfare than the logic of import substitution might have brought alone, because it became a particular preoccupation of the royal household. From the point that King James I fell in love with the prospect of homespun silk, efforts to bring mulberry trees and *Bombyx* silkworms across the English Channel deepened, and arguments in favour of sericulture broadened: the case for a healthier balance of trade and import substitution was joined by concerns about the volatility of long-distance supply chains and what this might mean for the expanding silk (and silk-mixed textile) industries in London, Canterbury, Norwich, and elsewhere. Since the 1560s, when two individuals in Aldersgate were reputed to be 'the first Silk-throwers in London, and brought the Trade into England', capacity for silk throwing had increased dramatically, culminating in the incorporation of a guild in 1629.[12] High demand for silk made it possible to link prospective sericulture to employment, promising remunerative work for labourers – particularly the idle, women, and children, who could fulfil roles leafing, feeding, cleaning, and reeling, as their counterparts did in southern Europe. This had been a point expressly made by Moffett, who composed his work during the agriculturally traumatic 1590s, when population growth collided with economic instability and swelling pauperism in the parishes, hence his insistence that sericulture would 'enrich both people, priest, and king'. Lastly, the challenge of transplanting wholesale a foreign commodity promised to yield technological, scientific, and reputational benefits for the nation, and glory for its monarch. It would be a move in step with a king pursuing modernisation and recognition, and seeking to align and integrate economic and intellectual pursuits. Besides being 'pleasing to our owne disposition', it would also be a move that made James's rowdy kingdoms more civilised, more European, because it expressly took inspiration from

---

[11] Stone, 'Elizabethan Overseas Trade.' Native woad production was successful in Hampshire, Berkshire, Wiltshire, and Sussex. Joan Thirsk, *Alternative Agriculture: A History from the Black Death to the Present Day* (Oxford: New York, 1997), 72–103.

[12] John Strype and John Stow, *A Survey of the Cities of London and Westminster*, orig. 1598 (London: A. Churchill et al., 1720), 1: 112.

top-down efforts in France to enlarge the acreage of mulberry trees and the extent of high-quality raw silk production.[13]

Nicholas Geffe bundled most of these economic, social, and welfare gains together in a 1607 publication that, more than Moffett's poem eight years earlier, was intended to foster action. Much of his *Perfect Use of Silk-Wormes* was a translation of Olivier de Serres's French tract (discussed in Chapter 4), which served as an instruction manual for those unfamiliar with the pursuit of sericulture. But as would occur frequently in anglophone publications on silk over the next two centuries, the instructional dimensions tended to be fairly generalised, and preceded, or intermixed with, more localised claims and suggestions. These were sometimes of a quasi-literary character (in which imagination, morality, and creativity were in the foreground) and sometimes of a quasi-scientific character (in which empiricism, comparison, and technology figured prominently), though by no means were these characteristics mutually exclusive, particularly in the seventeenth century. Geffe played with alliteration and analogy to ram home a nationalistic point about England's historic dependence upon sheep, lamenting the 'mass of money . . . which strangers fleece from us' and urging that 'we may as well be silke-masters as sheepe-masters', beginning by 'plentifully plant[ing]' marginal lands with mulberry trees.[14]

The royal household played a direct role in fostering sericulture and introducing the two species on which it depended to British landscapes, operating simultaneously through patronage, prescription, and example. King James I, who sponsored Geffe's translation and was its dedicatee, was quite open about emulating 'our brother the French king' Henri IV's actions in expanding the province of silk, 'whereby he hath won to himself honour, and to his subjects a marvellous increase of wealth'. That James was influenced by a French model was also borne out in his support of a series of schemes led by opportunistic Frenchmen to accelerate uptake in England, brokered by Ludovic Stewart (the French-raised Duke of Lennox). The initial intercession was made by François de Verton, a horticultural entrepreneur who operated under the rather thin alias of 'Monsieur de la Foret' (Mr Forest) and had the backing of two prominent English figures who well understood the commercial profitability of silk: Robert Cecil (who held the customs farm on imports of silk from 1602 until 1609, when he underleased it to merchant syndicates) and William Stallenge (controller of customs).[15] In 1606 Stallenge and de Verton were

---

[13] William Stallenge, *Instructions for the Increasing of Mulberie Trees, and the Breeding of Silke–Wormes for the Making of Silke in This Kingdome* (London: Printed by E. A. for Eleazar Edgar, 1609), [5–6].

[14] Serres and Geffe, *Perfect Use of Silk–Wormes*.

[15] Lionel Cranfield eventually took over this role in 1612. Newton, *Sackville Manuscripts*.

granted a patent to bring mulberries into England, on condition that they imported 'only the white mulberry' and plants of at least one year's growth, with a price cap of one penny apiece, and an expectation that 1 million would be brought in per year. The deal changed over time, dropping to 10,000 mulberry plants put out to the main towns across 13 southern counties, and settling on a more open agreement that involved a 5-year monopoly on selling trees and an undertaking to supply worms and instructions and, in due course, to buy raw silk back from English producers at a fair price.[16] Considering that some black mulberries had been introduced to England by the Romans, and that there was an ongoing dispute in parts of Spain over which species was preferential for sericulture, the contract's insistence on *M. alba* and planting in warmer southern counties suggests a mindfulness of conventional best practice in northern Italian and French zones.

The first projectors and pioneers of domestic English silk production were in circles close to court, or amongst groups quick to perceive the current preoccupation of the monarch. King James issued a prescriptive circular letter to the Deputy Lieutenants in every county in 1607, timed to coincide with Geffe's publication and the de Verton initiative. The instruction required each landowner to buy and plant 10,000 mulberry trees, which would be made available in the spring of 1608 at a subsidised rate of six shillings per hundred. Hot on the heels of James's letter was Mr Forest himself, taking orders for transplanting tree slips from (what he promised was) a beautiful, fertile nursery in Languedoc. De Verton also seems to have sourced the silkworm eggs, for in August 1609 he undertook 'to bring into this kingdom not only a great number of silk worms but great store of mulberry trees for the maintenance of the worms, whereby an exceeding great benefit will redound as well to all sorts of labouring people as to others'.[17] De Verton had some successes, much depending on which notables he was able to convert. Unsurprisingly they included Robert Cecil, the Earl of Salisbury himself, who arranged for 500 mulberries to be laid out by John Tradescant at Cecil's magnificent Hatfield House estate in Hertfordshire, where de Verton began. In all his travels, de Verton estimated he had covered 1,100 miles and distributed 100,000 trees to

---

[16] Cecil Papers (Hatfield House Archives), CP 193/28 (1606).

[17] Cecil and the Privy Council issued him a warrant to bring in 'as many mulberry trees as to him shall seem good for five years, all other persons being forbidden to bring in the same'. Cecil Papers, CP 130/173, 140/204 (August 1609).

the English gentry, roaming as far north as Lancashire, and scoring particular support from the Earls of Southampton, Essex and Huntingdon, and Lords Shrewsbury, Cavendish, and Derby.[18]

For his part, William Stallenge, a Plymouth merchant with strong European connections who was now around sixty years old, focused his energies on London, where he published an instructional pamphlet in 1609 for the 'publike weale' (common good), largely translated from a French text. Alongside the pamphlet, Stallenge was employed in laying out an impressive four-acre Mulberry Garden 'for His Majesty's use, near to his palace of Westminster … together with the charge of walling, bevelling and planting thereof with mulberry trees etc.' Stallenge would take primary responsibility for this site, for which he was handsomely rewarded to the tune of over £1,300 between 1609 and 1613, planting out thousands of mulberries from all parts of Europe, charging for silk-worms, labourers, and items to nurture them (such as sweet woods whose incense reportedly restored their health), and ultimately producing 9 lb of English silk in 1611. In 1613, management passed onto his nephew Jasper Stallenge, who was still being paid a fee of £60 in 1617 'for keeping the garden for the silk-worms', until in 1628 the office – probably now as a sinecure – was granted to Sir Walter Aston.[19]

English efforts to this point had done little to unleash the gendered claims and implications that would follow, which held that silkworm and cocoon work were peculiarly suited to women's domestic labour. Geffe wrote of 'silke-masters', and Stallenge's work seemed mostly to have been aimed at a male readership, offering little discussion of women's suitability as a labour force, and also eschewing the many claims in foreign literature about 'women possess[ing] a specific heat', to hatch silkworm eggs by placing them between their breasts or around their throats (see Fig. 3.1). Instead Stallenge recommended the more gender-neutral laying them in fabric, or 'carrie[ing] them in some warme place about you, in a little

[18] UK National Archives (hereinafter NA) SP/14/47/109–110 (Letters and Papers: Jul.–Aug. 1609); M. A. E. Green, ed., *Calendar of State Papers, Domestic, James I*, 5 vols. (London, 1872), 1603–10, pp. 344, 398, 540; 1611–18, pp. 246, 555; British Library Harley Manuscripts 4807, nos. 25, 29, 30.

[19] Stallenge, *Instructions for the Increasing of Mulberie Trees*. Transcribed in: *The Harleian Miscellany* (London: Dutton, 1809), 3: 80–7. Largely translated from Jean Baptiste Letellier, *Mémoires et instructions pour l'establissement des meuriers & art de faire la soye en France* (Paris: Jamet & Pierre Mettayer, 1603). On Jasper Stallenge and Aston: Walter Scott, *A Collection of Scarce and Valuable Tracts on the Most Entertaining Subjects*, Vol. 2, 2nd ed. (London: T. Cadell and W. Davies, 1809), 390; J. Bruce, W. D. Hamilton, and S. C. Lomas, eds., *Calendar of State Papers, Domestic, Charles I*, 23 vols (London, 1897), 1628–9: 192. The role of Keeper of the Mulberry Gardens was apparently passed on to Lord Goring in 1640. Peck, *Consuming Splendor*, 98–9.

Figure 3.1 Detail of the bosom method of silkworm hatching, from engraving of plate 3 of the series of six illustrations of the perfection of the silk industry in Europe and Italy by Flemish artists Johannes Stradanus and Karel van Mallery, *Vermis Sericus* (Antwerp: Phillips Galle, *c*.1580). Shows women preparing bags of silkworm eggs for warming and hatching through body heat, a method which excited much interest and observation that was often sexualised. Accession No. 49.95.869(2), The Elisha Whittelsey Collection. Metropolitan Museum of Art

safe boxe'.[20] The need to encourage uptake and the newness of the endeavour perhaps discouraged early writers from yet narrowing the gendered parameters of the language of production.

A handful of other sites besides Stallenge's Westminster plantation became flagship projects for advancing English sericulture in the 1610s, mixing horticultural and entomological dimensions. Payments were issued for mulberry trees planted at St. James's Palace in the summer of 1609, but a more substantial operation developed at Greenwich Palace, which the king and queen visited in 1608 during a busy 'royal progress' (a trademark regional tour) during the summer. Queen Anne seems to have been just as gripped as her husband, and may well have chosen the lavish dress embroidered with silkworms worn in a portrait the next year in order to manifest her interest in and patronage of not only expensive clothing, gardens, and buildings, but also the caterpillars and leaves themselves (see Plate 3). Just as elaborate were the plans advanced at the royal palace at Oatlands in Surrey, where Anne personalised the challenge of silkworm raising. By 1618, Oatlands boasted not only extensive mulberries but state-of-the-art shelving, heating, and ventilation in a bespoke building constructed by its keeper Sir John Trevor for 'the Queenes Silk woormes', complete with chimney and 'Ironwoorke of Severall Sortes' for cocoon reeling. The grandiose silkworm house featured the queen's coat of arms and was two stories high, containing four small rooms and a larger space upstairs where the shelving was installed for the growing silkworms. Here, they could feed while admiring the craftsmanship of a host of artisans: the oval and arched wainscoting, the frieze, the symmetrical painted doors, glasswork, and carved mantels.[21] Outside of London, James also sought to establish sericulture at his favourite country estates, particularly Theobalds Palace in Hertfordshire, where he employed the head gardener, Munton Jennings, 'for making a place for the silkworms and for providing mulberry leaves' in 1618. Though the queen was increasingly absent from the royal progresses around the provinces – where James concentrated on profile raising, politicking, and a lot of hunting – he literally took silk projection on the road, for he was accompanied during summer months

[20] Marcus Hieronymus Vida, *The Silkworm: A Poem, in Two Books*, trans. Samuel Pullein (Dublin: S. Powell, 1750); Maggino Gabrielli, *Dialoghi Di M. Magino hebreo venetiano. Sopra l'utili sue inventioni circa la seta* (Rome: Heredi di G. Gigliotti, 1588); Ulisse Aldrovandi, *De Animalibus Insectis Libri Septem: Cum Singulorum Iconibus Ad Viuum Expressis* (Bologna, 1602); Stallenge, *Instructions for the Increasing of Mulberie Trees*.
[21] On St. James: NA E351/3244 (Works and Buildings: A. Kerwyn, 1 Apr. 1609–30 Sep. 1610). On Denmark House plans: NA: E351/3243 (Works and Buildings: A. Kerwyn, 1 Oct. 1607–31 Mar. 1609). On Oatlands, NA: AO 1/2485/344 (Works and Buildings: J. Trevor, 10 Aug. 1616–30 Sep. 1618), and Jennifer Potter, *Strange Blooms: The Curious Lives and Adventures of the John Tradescants* (London: Atlantic, 2006), 211.

between 1615 and 1624 by a contingent of 'his Majestie's silke-wormes', for which he paid Richard Lecavill (Groom of the Chamber) an increasing sum for the 'paines and charges in carying'.[22]

French migrant expertise was important to sustaining these early English efforts concentrated close to the Crown, but the numbers of such experts were limited. Besides de Verton's role, from 1614 sericulture at Greenwich was under the supervision of Jean and François Bonoeil, who were granted the office of 'Keepers of the Royal Gardens, Vines, and Silkworms', and were paid £60 and issued letters of naturalisation in 1617, as was another French expert, 'keeper of his majesty's silkworms', Jean Laurien.[23] Fresh stocks of mulberry trees were also secured through special permissions granted to French nurserymen: one Languedoc-born Anthony Barbatier was issued a licence in 1618 to transplant the trees 'to his best advantage; with proviso that it be not prejudicial to grants formerly made to other men'.[24] The involvement of these experts continued to shape English attempts at sericulture into a French likeness, with illustrations in anglophone printed works, for instance, typically replicating French woodcuts (see Fig. 3.2).[25] The foreign specialists and their networks were clearly necessary to the launching of Jacobean initiatives in English sericulture, but as compared with other points of silk's transregional migration, they were insufficient in number to generate rapid economic impact. Knowledgeable people were the most effective means of transfer, for explanatory publications and even the finest technical illustrations could only carry efforts so far, as demonstrated by the seeming lack of English attention to Vittorio Zonca's intricate description of a water-powered silk throwing mill (in northern Italy in 1607), despite its being available in print at least as early as 1620.[26] That none of the named specialists in silk who migrated to England were female was also a shortcoming, and one that jarred with the woodcut representations that starkly showed the gendering of the practices of feeding and reeling silkworms in France and Italy.

---

[22] Lecavill was paid £10 16s in 1615, £20 in 1616, £18 in 1620 for 106 days' attention, and £25 in every year between 1621 and 1624. J. R. Dasent et al., eds., *Acts of the Privy Council of England, 1542–1631*, 45 vols (London: H. M. Stationery Office, 1964), 34: 129; 35: 88; 36: 214; 37: 53, 330; 38: 54, 33; 39: 118, 419.

[23] Scott, *Collection of Scarce and Valuable Tracts*, 390.

[24] Thirsk, *Alternative Agriculture, 126; W Shaw*, ed., *Letters of Denization and Acts of Naturalization for Aliens in England and Ireland, 1603–1700* (Lymington: Huguenot Society, 1911), 23, 25.

[25] For example, reprints in Stallenge, Bonoeil, and others of woodcuts from Letellier, *Mémoires et instructions*. Peck, *Consuming Splendor*, 95.

[26] Vittorio Zonca, *Nouo teatro di machine et edifici* (Padua: Pietro Bertelli, 1607); Carlo M. Cipolla, *Before the Industrial Revolution: European Society and Economy, 1000–1700*, 3rd ed. (London: Routledge, 2004), 121.

Figure 3.2 Reprinted woodcut showing cocoon reeling (1622). Illustration of 'the fashion of the Engine, how to wind off the silke from the cods', in John Bonoeil and Virginia Company of London, *His Maiestie's Gracious Letter to the Earle of South-Hampton, Treasurer, and to the Councell and Company of Virginia Heere Commanding the Present Setting Vp of Silke Works, and Planting of Vines in Virginia* (London: Felix Kyngston, 1622), page 15 in LOC F229.B71. Cf. earlier version in Letellier, *Mémoires et instructions* (1603) and later variant in Edward Williams, *Virginia: more especially the south part thereof, richly and truly valued* (1650). Library of Congress

A larger reserve of female immigrants from silk-producing regions might have minimised some early losses and prevented the genesis of questionable claims about silk cultivation amongst English and Irish populations over the course of the following century. In the absence of a fund of traditional knowledge such as that provided by Granadans and Murcians in New Spain, the English struggled to diagnose unfamiliar problems they encountered. This surfaced in the 1600s, when William Stallenge confessed that he lacked the knowledge even to describe second-hand how to reel silk properly from cocoons, and the 1620s, when horticultural writer John Parkinson cautioned about misunderstandings, urging 'that respect must be had to change your [silkworm] seede, because therein lyeth the greatest mysterie'. In the 1650s, even in the process of celebrating English experimentation at sites including Charing Cross and Ratliffe Cross (London), Oxford, and Duckenfield (Cheshire), the well-connected intellectual and silk enthusiast Samuel Hartlib acknowledged that 'they have had little skill in the managing of them'.[27] Human failings were also identified when it came to appetite for learning: Richard Bradley echoed John Evelyn in bemoaning 'our own insuperable Sloath' and wishing that 'the indigent or young Daughters in proud Families are as willing to gain three or four Shillings a Day for gathering Silk, as some are to get four Pence or six Pence a Day for hard Work, at Hemp, Flax, and Wool'.[28]

In summary, the early English efforts at silk raising scored reasonably well when it came to securing mulberry plants and ferrying silkworm seed across the Channel, and succeeded in relocating some experts, albeit in quite small numbers that permitted a perceptible but limited diffusion of knowledge (largely confined to the southern counties). English gardeners did grow in prominence alongside French silk projectors, demonstrating their skill at transplanting, nurturing, and managing the growth of mulberry orchards and sometimes silkworms across estates.[29] But while initial access to materials and manpower was fairly straightforward – especially for larger landholders and while relations with France were cordial – sericulture's medium-term prospects were seriously hampered by the lower temperatures, frequent summer rainfall, and seasonal differentiation found in the changeable environment of the British Isles. The likelihood is that even the finest oversight could not sustain large numbers of thriving white mulberries in a climate that was too cold for them to prosper for long, and in an environment (whether landscaped garden or rural estate) in which plenty of other plants pushed for space.

Additional expertise and uptake might have prolonged efforts in England, but the key differentials almost certainly lay in a few degrees of climatic warmth, a few too many late frosts, and their implications for disrupting the delicate symbiosis of silkworm and mulberry. Hampshire's noted agronomist, John Worlidge, dealt to some extent with adverse English conditions in his tract of 1668, noting that mulberries 'are difficult to propagate' and insufficient numbers of mulberry trees were concentrated to allow leaf collection on a meaningful scale, echoing

[27] John Parkinson, *Paradisi in Sole, Paradisus Terrestris; or, A Garden of All Sorts of Pleasant Flowers* (London: Humfrey Lownes and Robert Young, 1629), 575. Samuel Hartlib, *Samuel Hartlib His Legacie* (London, 1652), 64–5. Other sites with documented trees or trials included Tunbridge. Robert Boyle, *The Works of the Honourable Robert Boyle*, ed. Thomas Birch, 6 vols. (London: J. & F. Rivington et al, 1772), 6: 95.

[28] Richard Bradley, *Dictionnaire Oeconomique, or, The Family Dictionary* (London: D. Midwinter, 1725), n.p. (entry on 'Mulberry').

[29] NA E404/153 (Warrants for Issues), pt. 2, f.29. Potter, *Strange Blooms*, ch. 16.

a complaint made by Ralph Austen in his experimentation in Oxford in 1654, which involved trying plantation 'by Seed, Inoculating, Grafting, &c.'[30] Worlidge proposed that a royal or public orchard might be set aside to allow more intensive propagation, and derided some of the claims forged in the furnace of Hartlib's can-do spirit of mid-century, including the suggestion that lettuce or other garden or fruit-tree leaves might be substituted for mulberry in the silkworm's diet. It is telling that English writers like Worlidge offered suggestions for how to cope with dew and rain, and 'in case you live remote from Mulberry-trees, or the weather prove casual'.[31] Though they rarely made it into Hartlib's publications, critiques were also apparent in his own correspondence, as when a Mr Middleton objected that some of the positive results had occurred 'in the last drye extraordinary summer, wher[e]as in wett ordinary summers they would never doe'.[32]

White mulberries seem to have been especially hard to sustain for any length of time, and leaved too late for the needs of hatching silkworms. Outside areas such as London and Huntingdonshire that had enjoyed widespread plantings in the first sweep of enthusiasm, numbers must have declined, for later English experimenters could find it difficult to secure new stock.[33] Supporters such as Sir Robert Moray, the courtier and 'learned Scotchman', sought to rejuvenate 'Silk-making heretofore begun in England' by targeting new ways of planting out white mulberries, perhaps 'by cuttings put in good ground' or by investigating occasional successes, such as that of the minister in Coventry who had 'so much Silke made by his Family, that they furnished themselves with Silk-Stockings'.[34] One reverend in Wiltshire hoped to take it up but ended up writing in frustration to the author of a botanical survey of trees, having failed in his search for 'some seed of the whiter kind'.[35] But even where

[30] Letter from Ralph Austen to Samuel Hartlib, 18 February 1654, cited in Samuel Hartlib, *The Reformed Virginian Silk-Worm* (London: Printed by J. Streater, for G. Calvert, 1655), 10.
[31] Worlidge parroted Stallenge and earlier writers adapting for the English readers when he talked of tiles on the roofs of houses, but offered original tips such as inserting paper cones rather than Provençal sprigs of lavender as a material to which mature silkworms could affix their cocoons. John Worlidge, *Systema Agriculturae, the Mystery of Husbandry Discovered*, 4th ed. (London: Printed for Thomas Dring, 1687), 115, 199–201.
[32] Samuel Hartlib, *The Hartlib Papers* (originally published as CDs in 1996 that have since been digitised at: www.dhi.ac.uk/hartlib/), Ephemerides, 1652, 28/2/39B.
[33] John Beale, 'Some Agrestic Observations and Advertisements', *Philosophical Transactions of the Royal Historical Society of London* 12 (1677): 817.
[34] On Sir Robert Moray, David Stevenson, ed., *Letters of Sir Robert Moray to the Earl of Kincardine, 1657–73* (Aldershot, England: Ashgate, 2007), 44. Minutes of the Royal Society, 26 May 1663; Archives of the Royal Society, JBO/1/132.
[35] Rev. Nicholas Jameson to John Evelyn, Credwell (Wiltshire), 11 April 1670, in Evelyn, *Diary and Correspondence of John Evelyn*, 3: 226–7.

black mulberries offered a viable alternative – some contemporaries claiming 'the leaves of the blacke will doe as much good as the white' – historian Joan Thirsk has also pointed to structural issues within the English economy, and particularly the rising profitability of grain eroding the appetite for diversification in agricultural production.[36] Ultimately, the evidence suggests that the English did not fail at silk raising because they possessed the wrong trees; they failed mostly because they possessed the wrong weather.

Nonetheless, the mulberry-planting burst in England left environmental and cultural legacies. By the mid-seventeenth century, the original Mulberry Gardens near Westminster had become an elite location upon which 'ladys and gallants' seasonally descended, complete with bowling alley and maze; part of the site would later be given up to the building of Buckingham House, which became today's palace.[37] By the eighteenth century, the Jacobean mulberry carried a particular provenance and generated popular interest because of the association with William Shakespeare, fostered by actor-celebrity David Garrick: mulberry 'relics' of a tree supposedly planted by the Bard in Stratford-upon-Avon were sold to eager devotees, usually after having been crafted into serviceable objects such as pipes, card-cases, tobacco boxes, and memorial goblets.[38] Trees with purportedly Jacobean origins were ubiquitous in the nineteenth century and can still be found across a handful of country estates, where they are celebrated as living testaments to aristocratic pedigree and continuity.[39]

More immediate an impact than gnarled boughs or feted mementos was the way that raw silk as an economic goal provided a sense of

[36] Thirsk, *Alternative Agriculture*, 129; Parkinson, *Paradisi in Sole*.

[37] John Evelyn, *Diary and Correspondence of John Evelyn, F.R.S.*, ed. William Bray, 4 vols. (London: Henry Colburn, 1882), 2: 69. 'The Mulberry Garden: Plan of the Mulberry Garden whereon the Housing-thereto belonging stood as described in the Parliament Survey taken in July 1651', Royal Collection Trust, RL 18909. Historic England Legacy Record for Buckingham Palace: https://historicengland.org.uk/listing/the-list/list-entry/1000795.

[38] Peter Hewitt, 'The Material Culture of Shakespeare's England: A Study of the Early Modern Objects in the Museum Collection of the Shakespeare Birthplace Trust' (PhD thesis, University of Birmingham, 2014), 44, 57.

[39] For nineteenth-century listings, J. C. Loudon, *Arboretum et Fruticetum Britannicum; or, The Trees and Shrubs of Britain*, 8 vols. (London: Printed for the author, 1838), 3: 1345. For examples of these claims for Fulham and Blackheath, see letters from 'A. J. K.' and 'E. D. S.': Gentleman's Magazine, 24 (1845), pp. 488 (Nov.), 591–2 (Dec.). For today: Chilham Castle (Digges estate in Kent), Sayes Court Garden (John Evelyn's at Deptford), Charlton House Park (Greenwich), Hogarth's House (Hounslow), Bethnal Green, Charterhouse, Hatfield House. Many of these can be seen in photographs at: http://spitalfieldslife.com/2016/06/29/a-brief-history-of-londons-mulberries/. Stephanie Green and Zoe Meyer, *Mulberry & Silk* (Rye: Sage Press, 2003), 22–3.

connectivity between disparate forces within the expanding and evolving English state. The silk trade and luxurious clothing more broadly were certainly politicised in the maelstrom of mid-century civil wars. A hard-hitting parliamentary petition, for example, from seventy 'Silk Thro[w] sters of London' and on behalf of the 200,000 'poore people … doublers, turners, thre[a]d makers, winders, spinners, and others' whom they claimed to support in silk manufacturing, railed against the decay of trade and being 'disinabled to buy raw silk' because of Charles I's policies.[40] However, across the upheavals, sericulture tended to offer an agronomic narrative that roped together groups in spite of their differing political and religious outlooks – royalists and parliamentarians, Anglicans and Calvinists, metropolitans and provincials – for all could share in the mutually recognised but unrealised ambition to domesticate the raw product.

As an apolitical subject that embraced national self-improvement without threatening existing interests, the dream of silk was an agent of continuity and occasionally of integration. Its advocates – whether kings, merchants, scientists, or gardeners – could and did celebrate one another's input to what was becoming a perpetual British mission. Calvinists and Commonwealthmen in the mid-1650s both figuratively and physically took over where royal initiatives had left off: Samuel Hartlib pulled strings through his extensive correspondence, while some individual parliamentarians took the lead on confiscated royal estates that harboured numbers of mulberry trees; an example of this was Major General John Lambert, who was described as 'a huge undertaker about the design of silkworms' at Wimbledon.[41] Interest in the potential and properties of silk meanwhile inspired Anglican royalists such as the Ferrar family (discussed below) and Robert Hooke to conduct experiments with silkworms, the latter admiring silkworm eggs as 'an easie thing' to hatch and 'a pretty Object for a Microscope', and pondering the possibility of artificial silk.[42] Silkworms in England had proved easier to hatch than to

---

[40] The guild was incorporated by Royal Charter in 1629. Silk Thro[w]sters of London, *A Very Considerable and Lamentable Petition* (London, 1641); W. M. Stern, 'The Trade, Art, Mystery of Silk Throwers of the City of London in the Seventeenth Century', *Guildhall Miscellany* 5 (1955): 25–8; Strype and Stow, *A Survey of the Cities of London and Westminster.*

[41] Peck, *Consuming Splendor*, 91; David Farr, *John Lambert, Parliamentary Soldier and Cromwellian Major–General, 1619–1684* (Boydell Press, 2003), 198–9; Thirsk, *Alternative Agriculture*, 128.

[42] Robert Hooke, *Micrographia: Or, Some Physiological Descriptions of Minute Bodies Made by Magnifying Glasses. With Observations and Inquiries Thereupon* (London: J. Martyn and J. Allestry, 1665), 7, 181–2.

sustain, and better for the microscope than the open countryside, but their real resilience within developing arguments about political economy would allow them to become prominent imperial missionaries.

Virginia: Ambitious Beginnings

The Atlantic world offered the English a new and exciting domain in which to both imagine and undertake silk production. Indeed, the late Tudor and early Stuart crowns' preoccupations with comparative prestige and advancing overseas 'plantation' synchronised closely with ambitions for sericulture. In 1607, the first fleet of three ships were sailing up the James River in Virginia to establish an English presence in the Chesapeake Bay, even as the king launched his domestic scheme to plant out thousands of mulberries. Silk held particular appeal for the advisers who constructed rationales for colonial settlement, for merchants and adventurers who put their cash and lives on the line in hope of profitable trade or booty, and for state interests (like the king himself) who sanctioned charters and voyages. Silkworms first appeared in earnest in Richard Hakluyt's advocacy of Atlantic colonialism to Queen Elizabeth in 1584, the *Discourse of Western Planting,* in which he stressed that the Americas possessed 'silke wormes, fairer then ours of Europe', and listed the value 'in mayneteynaunce and increasinge of silke wormes for silke, and in dressing the same'.[43] Such claims were empirically reinforced by incoming reportage from the short-lived Roanoke colony (North Carolina) in the late 1580s, from which Governor Sir Ralph Lane and his scientific adviser Thomas Harriott identified 'Silkewormes faire and great, as big as our ordinary Walnuts' and anticipated 'as great profit in time to the Virginians, as thereof doth now to the Persians, Turks, Italians and Spanyards'.[44]

These and other claims about indigenous wild silk moths, sometimes conflating silk with silk grass (probably *Apocynum cannabinum*), gradually permeated the growing anglophone literature of colonisation.[45] From these uncertain beginnings, a number of influential ideological figures

---

[43] Hakluyt, *Principal Navigations*, 13: 193, 195.
[44] Lane and Harriott, 'A Briefe and True Report of the New Found Land of Virginia' (1588), in Hakluyt, *Principal Navigations*, 13: 331.
[45] See, for example, Walter Raleigh's fantastical *Discovery of Guiana* (1596) which stated that 'all places yeeld abundance of cotton, of silke, of balsamum, and of those Cotton, silke, kindes most excellent, and never knowen in Europe'. Excerpted in Hakluyt, 10: 427, 458. On silk grass, see Helen C. Rountree, *The Powhatan Indians of Virginia: Their Traditional Culture* (Norman, OK: University of Oklahoma Press, 1989), 65; William S. Powell, *John Pory, 1572–1636: The Life and Letters of a Man of Many Parts* (Chapel Hill, NC: University of North Carolina Press, 1977), 101–2.

connected the domestic efforts at sericulture to early English colonies in
the Atlantic world, making for a loose but supportive net that offered
social capital and generated intellectual credibility for silk projection
during the long seventeenth century. Francis Bacon, Robert Cecil, and
Richard Hakluyt (Cecil's personal chaplain) were linked through projec-
tor Nicholas Geffe, man of letters John Pory, and plantsman John
Tradescant. Tradescant and other silk-related royal office holders, such
as Jean Bonoeil, forged close friendships with early Virginian adventurers
and Virginia Company officials, amongst them captains John Smith and
Samuel Argall. These and other personal relationships and convictions
were instrumental to providing a foothold for sericulture in the New
World. It helped that the prime movers within the Virginia Company
conceived of their project as a distinctive public undertaking – though
borrowing methods and structures from fellow joint stock corporations
and trading companies.[46]

Given silk's enduring prominence in the political economy
espoused by the Virginia Company (which administered the colony)
and later the royal colony (once it reverted to direct rule in 1625),
there was surprisingly little explicit discussion in much of the
Virginia literature of the success of Spanish sericulture in Mexico,
though New Spanish silk manufacturing was seemingly known
about. A first-hand English report mentioning silk production in
New Spain was published in Hakluyt's 1589 compendium of
voyages, in which merchant Robert Tomson (who had arrived in
New Spain in 1556), found time amidst his dodging of the
Inquisition to mention that 'there is a place called the Misteca, fiftie
leagues to the Northwest, which doth yeeld great store of very good
silke, and Cochinilla'. That no opportunist seems to have latched
onto and recycled this claim may reflect either ignorance or
a misapprehension on the part of the English that the origin of
New Spain's silk industries lay in Spanish or Chinese raw silk.
Henry Hawks, an English merchant, commented that in Mexico
City 'they have muche silke and make all maner of sorts thereof',
and Miles Philips, who had been abandoned by John Hawkins near
Veracruz in 1568, likewise testified to production, having himself

---

[46] For discussion of English silk projection links involving Geffe: Peck, *Consuming Splendor*,
95. On the Tradescant links to Virginia, Potter, *Strange Blooms*, esp. ch. 9;
Warren M. Billings, 'Sir William Berkeley and the Diversification of the Virginia
Economy', *The Virginia Magazine of History and Biography* 104, no. 4 (1996): 436–8.
On the Virginia Company more broadly, Andrew Fitzmaurice, *Humanism and America:
An Intellectual History of English Colonisation, 1500–1625* (Cambridge: Cambridge
University Press, 2003), 61; Wesley Craven, *The Virginia Company of London,
1606–1624* (Charlottesville: University Press of Virginia, 1957).

learned to weave in the city's silk quarter.[47] In contrast to sketchy information about raw silk production, the English had long been finely attuned to the value of the silk trade operating out of both the Atlantic and Pacific sides of the Spanish Americas. Silks were amongst the most highly valued goods sought by the English pirates and buccaneers who preyed on Spanish shipping, famously illustrated when Sir Thomas Cavendish returned home in triumph in 1587 having picked off the Manila galleon, the *Santa Ana*. Though tons of silk had regrettably had to be consigned to the waters off Baja California for want of space in the hold, Cavendish's flagship, aptly named *The Desire*, sailed up the Thames some months later, magnificently festooned with sumptuous Chinese fabrics draped from all parts of its decks and rigging.[48]

Some scholars have suggested that the Iberian model in New Spain was a direct influence on English colonial reformers pushing for silk production in Virginia, but the evidence base is rather thin. It is true that scrawled observations about silkworms appear in the margins of a copy of the *Mercator* atlas, where they wend their way round a page showing New Spain. The writer, John Ferrar – a merchant who became an instrumental figure as deputy treasurer of the Virginia Company from 1619 – and others did occasionally compare the prospect of Virginian raw silk with Peruvian silver, but these were generalised observations about extractive wealth and the advantages of Atlantic colonialism rather than belying close knowledge about practice. If creative and obsessive types such as John Ferrar, who waxed lyrical about silkworms and their potential, had known of the trajectory and extent of Spanish experiences in sericulture in the New World, or known of Gonzalo de Las Casas's pamphlet published in Granada, they would have made far more direct reference and drawn on them more explicitly and meaningfully. The referential framework for attempting to produce silk in Virginia was therefore not based on successful New World projects (the Spanish in the late sixteenth century) but on French and then English projects in *c.*1600–1630, the latter of which turned out to be unsuccessful for the reasons outlined above. As a consequence,

---

[47] Hakluyt, *Principal Navigations*, 14: 154, 181, 215. On the partial state of English insights into Spanish developments: David B. Quinn, *The Hakluyt Handbook*, 2 vols. (Cambridge: Cambridge University Press, 1974).

[48] Accounts of Cavendish's circumnavigation by Master Francis Pretty and Cavendish himself, in Hakluyt, Principal Navigations, 16: 5–55, 80–1. See also Shirley Fish, *The Manila–Acapulco Galleons: The Treasure Ships of the Pacific, with an Annotated List of the Transpacific Galleons, 1565–1815* (Milton Keynes: AuthorHouse, 2011), 191–7, 495–6; William L. Schurz, *The Manila Galleon* (New York: E. P. Dutton & Co., 1939), 303–14.

the English mirrored Spanish struggles in several respects as they began to explore the possibility of Atlantic sericulture: they experimented with first native and then imported trees, relied on royal incentives and fell back on authoritarian directives, and persistently struggled to sustain eggs across the Atlantic. And much more than the Spanish, they lacked adequate specialists and a serviceable labour force.[49]

Silk was not mentioned explicitly in the instructions that accompanied the first fleet to Virginia in 1607, though the pioneers' commercial and agricultural targets were framed to accommodate it: navigators were to seek out large rivers and 'make choice of that which bendeth most toward the North-West' in anticipation of a passage to the Pacific and its silken riches, while settlement sites were to be chosen for experimental production of commodities not available in England, drawing clearly on Portuguese and Spanish exemplars (particularly sugar, ginger, and wine).[50] Silk's profile climbed up the pecking order of potential commodities when news filtered back confirming the presence of indigenous mulberries around the James River, as when John Smith and William Strachey later recorded 'some great Mulbery trees' around Algonquian villages such as Kecoughtan (Hampton Roads) and others 'found growing naturally in prettie groves'.[51] Just like Las Casas had done on Hispaniola, Sir Thomas Gates returned from the Chesapeake in September 1610 to proclaim to the Virginia Company that there were enough wild trees (red mulberries, *M. rubra*) 'to cherish and feede millions of silke wormes, and returne us in a very short time, as great a plenty of silks as is vented into the whole world from al the parts of Italy'. Gates also reported favourably on prospects for silkworms in Bermuda (then the Somers Isles), where he and a contingent of Virginia settlers aboard the *Sea Venture* had been wrecked, stating in 1610 that '[t]he Country yeeldeth ... great plentie of Mulberries, white and red: and on the same are great store of silke-wormes, which yield cods of silke, both white and yellow, being some course, and some fine'.[52]

---

[49] For a less sceptical reading of the evidence on linkages to New Spain, see Allison M. Bigelow, 'Gendered Language and the Science of Colonial Silk', *Early American Literature* 49, no. 2 (2014): esp. 290–9.

[50] On associations between a Northwest Passage and silk benefits, see for example: Hakluyt, *Principal Navigations*, 12: 61.

[51] John Smith, *The Complete Works of Captain John Smith (1580–1631)*, ed. Philip L. Barbour, 3 vols. (Chapel Hill, NC: University of North Carolina Press, 1986), 1: 151; William Strachey, *The Historie of Travell into Virginia Britania (1612)* (London: Printed for the Hakluyt Society, 1953), 61.

[52] Hakluyt, *Principal Navigations*, 15: 187. For other early references to Bermuda mulberries and caterpillars (1610 narratives of Silvanus Jourdan and William Strachey who reported 'We oftentimes found growing to these [palmetto] leaues, many Silk-wormes inuolued therein'): J. Henry Lefroy, *Memorials of the Discovery and Early Settlement of the*

Though these were not *Bombyx* cocoons, and he was misidentifying as *M. alba* unripe white berries on Bermudan *M. rubra* trees, Gates's and others' claims soon prompted action – for they echoed around a receptive court engaged in its own extensive mulberry plantings, and a paranoid Company whose project was miscarrying.

The plight of Jamestown, where colonists were dying in droves, had forced the Virginia Company to request a new charter and new powers in 1609, and embark on an idiosyncratic publicity campaign involving dozens of promotional books and pamphlets to try to generate capital and recruit settlers. The subtle shifts these brought inclined the Company's divided leadership to treat sericulture seriously and favourably as a prospect in the colony, emphasising patriotic profit, economic and social conversion, and national benefit in the medium to long term. Also important was the developing emphasis upon privatising acreage and issuing large swathes of it to settlers and investors rather than promising cash or stock. By the mid-1610s, it had become a commonplace to associate Virginia with silk projection (see Fig. 3.3), as Richard Hakluyt himself had noted in his translation of Hernando de Soto's sixteenth-century forays into North America: after gold, pearls, and oxen, '[a] fourth chiefe commoditie wee may account to be the great number of Mulberrie trees, apt to feede Silke-wormes to make silke'.[53] On Bermuda, after initial trials had been conducted, silk was ranked amongst the top five products from which royalties were expected, alongside pearls, ambergris, whale oil, and tobacco, and reports back likewise celebrated the mulberry trees as being 'altogether resemblant to thoes I haue seene in the best silck makeinge places'.[54]

The first attempt at raw silk production occurred in British North America in the spring of 1609, under the oversight of specialist 'Silkemen, with [not only] all their appurtenances but materials'. They had arrived in Jamestown in 1608, probably in the autumn, as part of the Second Supply whose seventy passengers included targeted European craftsmen comprising 'eight Dutch men and Poles' skilled in the production of potash, glass, and naval stores (tar, pitch and turpentine), along 'with some [unspecified] others'. The *Bombyx* silkworm eggs they brought were presumably sourced from the domestic projects on estates around London. Unlike those first parcels sent from Seville to Hispaniola a century before, the first English eggs survived their Atlantic passage, and

Bermudas or Somers Islands, 1515–1685, 2 vols. (London: Longmans Green and Co., 1877), 1: 18–19, 33, 102.
[53] Hakluyt, *Principal Navigations*, 13: 541.
[54] W. F. Craven, 'An Introduction to the History of Bermuda', *William and Mary Quarterly* 17 (1937): 329; Nathaniel Butler, *The Historye of the Bermudaes or Summer Islands*, ed. J. Henry Lefroy (London: Hakluyt Society, 1882), 218.

Figure 3.3 Historic photograph of Jamestown mulberry. Unknown photographer. Keystone photo print, 1926, titled 'Government Monument on Jamestown (Shows Mulberry Tree) the First Permanent Colony of the English People, the Birthplace of Virginia and the United States, May 13 1607.' Keystone-Mast Collection, UCR/California Museum of Photography, University of California at Riverside

were hatched in the early spring of 1609, Captain John Smith relating that 'there was an assay made to make silke, and surely the wormes prospered excellent well' – by which he presumably meant they fed on the local mulberries and progressed through the stages of growth in reasonable health, without yet cocooning. But when the unnamed 'master workeman' fell sick in April or May, the silkworms were left unattended, and helplessly eaten – like so much else in the colony – by the plague of rats which had arrived with the ships.[55]

Such was the ongoing plight of white labourers and the pathetic fragility of white settlement that the prospect of introducing sericulture to the increasingly unreceptive Native Americans of Tsenacommacah (the Powhatan confederation of Tidewater Virginia) was a distant one, unlike the very different intercultural and economic circumstances that had prevailed in New Spain. Although the Algonquian-speaking locals were less versatile than their Mixtecan counterparts in intricate textile and textile-related processes, observers remarked upon Indian familiarity with relevant indigenous mulberries in the Chesapeake. When the bedraggled remnants of the Jamestown and Bermuda settlements were forced to return to the fort they had abandoned on account of famine in 1610 (by the arrival of a new transatlantic fleet they met on the James River), they noted that the Indians 'had nothing to trade withal but mulberries'.[56] Amongst the limited words translated by William Strachey from Algonquian to English were *Muskimins* (a mulberry tree), *Paskamath* (mulberries), *Maangwipacus* (leaves), *Mohwhaiok* (moth), *Mowsah* ('a little worme or magot'), and *Pasqwuxxaws* (to reel). He did not record an actual translation of the term 'silk', perhaps underscoring that production was viewed by the English, at least initially, as an undertaking for the settler population.[57]

The brief thriving of a cohort of silkworms and the large indigenous red mulberries identified along the James River and on Bermuda in 1609 and 1610 transformed sericulture into a primary economic target for the Virginia Company – something that William Strachey tellingly described in 1612 as now 'seriously considered of, and order taken that yt shalbe duly followed'.[58] Companies issued repeated instructions to Virginia's and Bermuda's governors to prioritise silk production, and facilitated the procuring of experts and materials

[55] Smith, *Complete Works of John Smith*, 1: 151.
[56] Lefroy, *Memorials of the Bermudas*, 11.
[57] Strachey, *Historie of Travell into Virginia*, 191, 194, 206, 207.
[58] W. Strachey, *The Historie of Travell into Virginia Britania (1612)*, ed. R. H. Major (London: Printed for the Hakluyt Society, 1849), 117.

required for sericulture.[59] In fact, the arrival of one such expert on Bermuda in 1613 temporarily dashed hopes there, for a Frenchman (later named as Peter) hired in England for his knowledge of mulberries took a dim view of the trees' fitness for silkworms, and 'returned an answer of dislike, as that they wer altogether improper for that effect'. Nonetheless, the colonial companies and those seeking their goodwill found ways to bypass objections and persist with experimentation – their transatlantic remoteness complicating the process of learning from setbacks closer to home.[60]

The redoubled efforts to establish silk in the early 1610s in Virginia depended to this point upon wild stocks of mulberry trees. Beginning with silkworm eggs that were successfully shipped across the Atlantic in late 1613 and hatched between March and June the following spring, Ralph Hamor reported that there were 'thousands of them grown to great bigness, and a spinning, and the rest well thriving', though it is unclear who took responsibility for them before the arrival of a servant trained by Jean Bonoeil at Oatlands in around 1615.[61] At some point in this period 'there was a house built to p[re]serve the Wormes' as they grew and cocooned, making it the first dedicated textile building in English North America.[62] Perhaps it was the Frenchman's servant, under the strict governorship of Sir Thomas Dale, who ensured that by 1616 a sample of Virginia-grown silk could triumphantly be sent back to England with John Rolfe (and Pocahontas); more followed the next year when Governor Samuel Argall reported that 'silk wormes thrive exceedingly'.[63] What happened to this first Anglo-American raw silk is unclear: one of the complaints retrospectively fired at the prolific overseas trader, financier, and Virginia Company Treasurer Sir Thomas Smith (amidst the factional disputes in the Company in 1623) was that 'silke in some quantitie ... was spunne in Sir Thomas Smiths Hall'.[64] The colonists probably reeled it themselves, likely in the bespoke silkworm house, and it was shipped as raw silk to Thomas Smith, who took charge of throwing and weaving it in Kent through his extensive textile operations.[65]

[59] Charles E. Hatch, 'Mulberry Trees and Silkworms: Sericulture in Early Virginia', *The Virginia Magazine of History and Biography* 65 (1957): 7.
[60] Butler, *Historye of the Bermudaes*, 30. Simon Jones, 'Mulberry Tree Mystery Is Solved', *Royal Gazette* (Bermuda), 21 March 2015.
[61] Ralph Hamor, *A True Discourse of the Present Estate of Virginia* (London, 1615), 35. Lefroy speculated that the Bermuda Frenchman was likewise connected to Bonoeil in Lefroy, *Memorials of the Bermudas*.
[62] Virginia Company of London, *Records of the Virginia Company of London*, ed. Susan Myra Kingsbury (Washington: Govt. print. off, 1906), 4: 142.
[63] Virginia Company of London, 3: 74; Hatch, 'Mulberry Trees and Silkworms', 8.
[64] Virginia Company of London, *Records of the Virginia Company*, 4: 142.
[65] Cf. assumption that this was cocoons in Hatch, 'Mulberry Trees and Silkworms', 9.

In time, however, as in New Spain, English experimentation shifted from haphazard harvesting of indigenous leaves to extensive plantings of new mulberry trees, 'neere the habitacons of o[u]r people'.[66] This was partly to rationalise the time costs of leaf collection, and partly in recognition that Old World mulberries were better suited to high-quality raw silk, whereas planters found pragmatic drawbacks with American ones – albeit few as sensational as the claim that they 'have a prickle in their leaves w[hi]ch destroyed the Silkworms when itt grew to biggnes'.[67] By January 1623 the Virginia council reported that 'great store' of mulberries had been planted, 'and shalbe yearly inclosed', though the vines had largely failed.[68] On Bermuda, mulberry seed was shipped with new governor Captain Daniel Tucker in 1616, along with clear stipulations for planting them '10 foote asunder', anticipating that their leaves could be gathered 'neere your houses, that you may have meat at hand for the Wormes'.[69] The Somers Isles Company in 1625 noted that it had been very difficult to procure white mulberry saplings from England to send to Bermuda, as they were very expensive and unfit to remove – underscoring the lack of availability of *M. alba* about which English projectors later complained. Instead, the Company sent a box of new seeds of 'the greate black and best sorty of mulberrye' and arranged to distribute to planters.[70] By the 1620s then, the English had emulated the earlier Spanish experience: their views of native mulberries had partially sobered, and there was a growing willingness to substitute American trees with imported saplings or seeds. Their method promised to bring order to the colonial landscape not through clearing land so much as through selective reforestation.[71]

Planting experimental mulberries, like planting almost anything else in Virginia, would be significantly stifled by the all-consuming rise of tobacco production, which took place after 1612 when John Rolfe and his fellow planters proved the quality of the *Nicotiana tabacum* leaf that could be raised in the rich Tidewater soil. Tobacco both saved and condemned the Virginia Company, and in a larger sense, the English Chesapeake. But its success was not a spontaneous phenomenon, being

[66] Virginia Company of London, *Records of the Virginia Company*, 4: 142.
[67] Virginia Company of London, 2: 396.   [68] Virginia Company of London, 4: 15, 24.
[69] Lefroy, *Memorials of the Bermudas*, 117. W. F. Craven, 'Lewis Hughes' "A Plaine and Trve Relation of the Goodnes of God Towards the Sommer Ilands"', *William and Mary Quarterly* 17 (1937): 84.
[70] Lefroy, *Memorials of the Bermudas*, 1: 358, 373.
[71] Some additional confusion about mulberries may have derived from Bonoeil's claim that 'notwithstanding the difference of the colour of the fruit, [the three kinds of trees] beare but one name of the white Mulbery tree'. John Bonoeil, *Observations to Be Followed for the Making of Fit Roomes, to Keepe Silkwormes in* ... (London: Kingston, 1620), 6.

a product of precisely the same experimental approach that drove wider Atlantic commodity projection, as English preconceptions evaporated: trial and error shaped by socio-economic capacity, environmental limitations, and cultural sensibilities. In contrast to other crops, it was well suited to unskilled (if intensive) labour, newly cleared land and garden patches, and local weather conditions and soil (though draining the latter of fertility), and offered a reliable turnaround from sowing to harvest (typically a year and a half), with very easy steps for managing reseeding and quality control, and relatively easy processing steps before the product could be shipped in hogsheads of dried, cured, and packed leaves. In short time, tobacco literally as well as figuratively became the currency of the colony, used to pay taxes and salaries, which put pressure on regulating its quality. Within five years, the settlement was indulging in 'tobacco mania' and within a decade, some 60,000 lbs of tobacco were being shipped annually from Virginia, sold as a cash crop that allowed purchases of land, labour, and manufactured goods, all of which in turn were ploughed back into tobacco – a frenzied extractive cycle which left discarded and broken fields, tools, and bodies in its wake.[72]

Tobacco's dominance was not lauded in all quarters, and new leadership within the Company challenged the colony's direction with a suite of measures under Sir Edwin Sandys in 1619, designed to foster social and economic stability in the medium and long term. As a result, Jamestown would famously receive its first legislative General Assembly, receive boatloads of new migrants including women for marriage to provide a demographic base, and receive more targeted support and materials to encourage the diversification of the economy. For their part, the Company concentrated on those commodities which had shown potential, but in which investment had lately dried as fast as tobacco leaves: silk, hemp, pitch and tar, wine, and glass. Importantly, this encouragement was not just in the form of instructions or pamphlets, but driven forwards by a set of key figures who linked Company policy to actions and plantations on the ground in Virginia – including dutiful governors, and officials with strong personal or factional connections to Sandys, such as his youngest brother George Sandys, John Pory (colonial Secretary and Speaker of the Assembly), and John and Nicholas Ferrar (influential Company officials). Large amounts of the Company's thinning resources

[72] Lorena S. Walsh, *Motives of Honor, Pleasure, and Profit: Plantation Management in the Colonial Chesapeake, 1607–1763* (Chapel Hill, NC: University of North Carolina Press, 2010), esp. 36–44 (quote on 38); David S. Hardin, "'The Same Sort of Seed in Different Earths": Tobacco Types and Their Regional Variation in Colonial Virginia', *Historical Geography* 34 (2006): 137–58; Karen Ordahl Kupperman, *The Jamestown Project* (Cambridge, MA: Belknap Press of Harvard University Press, 2007), 1622 figure on 297.

and goodwill were spent between 1619 and its ultimate collapse in 1624 chasing a programme of economic development – extending at times to sugar, indigo, olive oil, and rice – on the Company's own public lands and a handful of private estates, all in the face of the upsurge in tobacco.

The reforms particularly encouraged the pooling of associations of planters, who undertook to settle larger areas, and were given considerable acreage and administrative freedom to use their own joint-stock funds and manage new districts. The Berkeley Hundred, a collective land grant of some 8,000 acres on the north bank of the James River, was one corporate plantation enterprise which sought to explore silk production amongst its other activities around the inevitable core of tobacco cultivation. The directives originally issued by one of the major shareholders in September 1619, Sir William Throckmorton, insisted that the first lands be settled with a view to healthy air, access to waterways, and advancing not just tobacco but new commodities including 'mulberry trees for no[u]rishing of silke wormes'; six months later he paid six shillings and sixpence for 'one pound of worm seed' shipped aboard the *London Merchant*.[73] Administrative support for such initiatives arrived with John Pory, who proved an able official during governor Sir George Yeardley's tenure (1619–21), having spent much of his earlier career in European and Levantine silk regions acting as secretary to English ambassadors and becoming intimately immersed in the Levant Company's raw silk trade.[74] Pory's influence and experience encouraged the Company to consider Virginia in light of Italian and Persian sericulture – not just French and Spanish, and he characterised it in June 1620 as 'a marvellous hopefull commodity'.[75]

The new faction pushing for Virginian diversification and stability found silk production a particularly welcome topic to revisit because of the king's long-standing support for it, which pointedly contrasted with James's verdict on consuming tobacco as 'sinning against God, harming your selves'.[76] They were therefore quick not only to occupy the moral high ground when it came to arguments about socio-economic consolidation, but also to involve the monarch and his patronage – a pattern which repeated the Spanish Crown's involvement in incentivising production in the 1530s. They proudly recorded in May 1620, for instance, that 'his Maiestie hath beene gratiouslie pleased now the second time (the former haveinge miscarried) to bestowe upon the Company plenty of Silkewormes seed'. These silkworms were set against tobacco in both

---

[73] Virginia Company of London, *Records of the Virginia Company*, 3: 208, 261.
[74] Virginia Company of London, 3: 254; Powell, *John Pory*, 34–6, 42.
[75] Virginia Company of London, *Records of the Virginia Company*, 3: 303, 308.
[76] Final paragraph of King James I, *A Counterblaste to Tobacco* (London: A. B., 1604).

a macroeconomic and a physical sense: recipients of the king's 'owne store' of silkworm seed shipped aboard the *Duty* were advised 'especially to keep the Wormes from the aire of Tobacco, which is mortal to them'.[77] Royal favour also manifested itself in James's support of a publication authored by his Master of Silkworms at Oatlands, Jean Bonoeil, for which the king wrote an accompanying foreword in strong terms – described as a 'royall comandment' to the Virginia council that would guarantee 'a speedie course be taken for the setting vpp of Silkworms ... throughout the whole Colony', and urged planters to 'rather bestow their travail in compassing this rich and solid commodity than in that of tobacco'.[78] The king took pains to recommend Bonoeil's tract to the Somers Islands Company as well as Virginians. The Company, in turn, offered a parallel bounty to try to stimulate competition and thereby jumpstart production – promising fifty pounds sterling 'to him that shall first obteyne and send over ten pounds of silke or ten gallons of *coccoons*'.[79]

The difficult task of arranging shipment of silkworm seed and 'men skillfull in the orderinge of the Wormes' fell to two of the Virginia Company's London merchants in July 1620, Abraham Chamberlain and Richard Wiseman, who attempted to synchronise the two so that worms and experts travelled in a fast pinnace in October, at no small price.[80] Procuring specialists in France stretched Chamberlain's networks, though happily, an apprentice of Jaspar Stallenge who had since 1615 become 'very skillfull in breedinge of the wormes and in wyndinge of their Silke' had been given his master's approval to complete his three years of contract in Virginia. The Company paid Stallenge £20 for his servant's time, inserting the proviso that he must undertake to instruct others.[81] By the end of 1620, eight Frenchmen from Languedoc had indeed agreed to migrate, described as '*Vignerons* ... who are very skilfull also in breeding of the *Silke*-wormes, and making *Silk*', along with 'some Englishmen sent that haue been trayned vp therein' (presumably including Stallenge's apprentice).[82] Planters who had shown the most forwardness in building 'fitt houses for Silkwormes and in plantinge Mulberie Trees' were given the first pick of new apprentices, so as to provoke others 'to contend for the like favour & reward hereafter'.[83] French and other

[77] Virginia Company of London, *Records of the Virginia Company*, 1: 353; 3: 279.

[78] Virginia Company of London, 2: 101.

[79] Lefroy, *Memorials of the Bermudas*, 1: 500.

[80] Virginia Company of London, *Records of the Virginia Company*, 1: 392–3. £1,000 was set aside to procure specialists for silk, wine, salt, flax, and hemp, and a further £250 for a suitably rapid pinnace.

[81] Virginia Company of London, 1: 431–2.   [82] Virginia Company of London, 3: 240.

[83] Virginia Company of London, 1: 432. For example of placing, see Peter Arondelle to Thomas Nuce in June 1621. Virginia Company of London, 3: 463.

specialists were also recruited by individual planters, such as John Pory (whose tenant Estinien Moll helped him to inspect fitting mulberry lands on his 'Secretary's Plantation'), and John Berkeley, who brought several Frenchmen in 1620.[84] Not wishing to delay the experts from Languedoc, it was long after their departure that the Company actually approved their contract for wages and other allowances.[85] Viewed in the round, the aim of transplanting silk culture across the Atlantic therefore conducted to Virginia and later other parts of British America a set of European people and skills who would otherwise have had little reason or capacity to migrate. Even when production ultimately failed, the determination to make earnest trials had served to diversify British outposts' cultural, linguistic, and skills bases.

The profile of the limited silk experts in the English Chesapeake contrasted noticeably with Spanish efforts that had not only tapped a far larger skilled population, but had also allowed them greater positional authority relative to labour in sixteenth-century New Spain. The Virginia Company's proactive emphasis on providing printed anglophone instructional material also reflected the difficulties they had in safeguarding against the dearth and death of specialists. Amidst the redoubled engagement with silk, Edwin Sandys requested that a new publication be translated from French books and 'dispersed among the Planters soe as everie houshold might have one', along with a list of stipulated commodity rates and other agricultural advices. According to the rates, Virginian silk cocoons were to be valued at two shillings and sixpence per pound, and raw silk at thirteen shillings four pence per pound.[86] For his part in helping translate and support silk production, and particularly in procuring 'Frenchmen from Languedock', the Virginia Company admitted Jean Bonoeil into the Virginia Company and granted him two shares of land in the spring of 1621.[87]

The foreign specialists established at sites such as Elizabeth City were as quickly disabused of their Virginian expectations as most English indentured labourers. Their spokesperson, Peter Arondelle, wrote directly to Edwin Sandys in December 1621 pointing out that the ready-built structures, provisions, and cattle he had been promised had never materialised, and that the Frenchmen were surviving on 'a pinte and a halfe of musty meale' per day and foraging for oysters. Remarkably, he had nonetheless persisted in 'erecting a silke house at his owne charge and

[84] Powell, *John Pory*, 97.
[85] Virginia Company of London, *Records of the Virginia Company*, 1: 466.
[86] Virginia Company of London, 1: 422, 432, 543; 3: 237 (rates); Hatch, 'Mulberry Trees and Silkworms', 12; Bonoeil, *Observations to Be Followed*.
[87] Virginia Company of London, *Records of the Virginia Company*, 1: 459, 470; 3: 63.

in cherishing of silkewormes' according to a report in the spring of 1623.[88] The Languedoc specialists seem to have been young, and although they were sent additional provisions and equipment in June 1622, the Company paid their wages in London to Jean Bonoeil, leaving little scope to further incentivise them in 'the instructing and training vp of many in their skills and arts'.[89] Unlike the oversight of tobacco, which could be fairly easily imparted and in which many accrued experience, overdependence on a handful of defensive, struggling experts meant that silkworks and glassworks were much more vulnerable. This was emphasised by George Sandys, who explained to John Ferrar in March 1623 that silk had been his main priority, and he had 'set for to do nothing else', preparing his rooms for that purpose, but that he had been held back by the peculiar monopoly of knowledge these workers held. He complained that in spite of having been called rascal to his face for scolding them, he dared 'not punish theise desperate fellowes, least ye whole dessigne through theire stubbornesse should p[er]ish'.[90] It was already in George Sandys's mind that the Frenchmen's contracts were elapsing the subsequent year (1624), and he urged John Ferrar to extend them and 'send more of their quality' in order to generate a regular output of silk.[91]

Arondelle's letters must have been a source of enormous vexation to John Ferrar, for they informed him that new silk houses were complete, that 'Our Wormes are well hatched & very hopefull' and that the Frenchman's 'hope for silke is greater than euer', even as they recounted how the key specialists lacked basic provisions and were living in the shadow of 'Great men' and corrupt government. Not only were many planters inactive, but some were actively obstructive, as when news emerged of 'some quarrells betweene Capt Whitakers chiefe man and Mr Anthony Bannall [perhaps a Bonoeil] who went to gather Mulberrye leafes vpon the said Capt[ain's] ground'. Arondelle outlined his plans to return to England to bring some raw silk and put his case to the Company, including demonstrating a method 'for the easier hatching of the wormes then yet hath be[e]n found here or in England', but he announced his ill health and forewarned that in the event of death his eldest son John would 'follow the silke worke for I find him very fitt for it'.[92] In response, the Company pressed the governor and council to lend their full support to the French specialists on whom meaningful progress in silk depended, and to persuade them to continue beyond

[88] Virginia Company of London, 3: 534; 4: 92.
[89] Virginia Company of London, 3: 651.   [90] Virginia Company of London, 4: 24.
[91] Virginia Company of London, 4: 108.   [92] Virginia Company of London, 4: 230–1.

their 'covenanted times ... if not for ever[,] yett at least so long, vntill theire skill and knowledg in those things may be deriued into such numbers of o[u]r people, as may be sufficient for a large imployment'. They worried particularly that should the French return discontented, given the parlous state of the Company's finances in August 1623, it would be impossible to locate and send across new experts, though they stopped short of recommending their detention by 'violence, or any vniust meanes'.[93]

Authoritarian directives did, however, accompany this package of supportive measures. The creation of a landmark General Assembly in Virginia, which broke new ground in July 1619 as English settlers elected their first representatives to an American legislature (comprised of twenty-two burgesses and four additional members including John Rolfe and John Pory), quickly prompted the first Anglo-American laws to advance silk production: every household head was instructed to 'plant and maintain in growth six mulberry trees at the least' for a period of seven years, subject to censure by the government.[94] According to the printed 'Orders and Constitutions' of 1620, which synthesised much of the existing sociolegal framework, all grantees receiving lands were obliged to 'covenant to employ their people in great part in Staple Commodities ... and not wholly or chiefly about *Tobacco*'.[95] Instructions to the governor and council in July 1621 insisted that they ensured great numbers of new mulberries be planted in every plantation and those already growing be preserved, which they acceded to through directives in January 1622 when the burgesses and 'the whole Countrey was very well affected to the plantinge of both, and to the receavinge of Silke worme seede', in contrast to other economic targets such as pitch, tar, and potash.[96] Sumptuary laws complemented these strictures: no Virginian was technically allowed to 'wear silk till they make it themselves', excepting the council and heads of districts ('hundreds').[97] This was a way of demarcating power that was both archaic, because dispensed with in England, and forward-looking, because it creatively sought to link American production to new forms of status display in the New World.

---

[93] Virginia Company of London, 266–7.
[94] Powell, *John Pory*, 87; William Waller Hening, *The Statutes at Large: Being a Collection of All the Laws of Virginia, from the First Session of the Legislature in the Year 1619* (Charlottesville: University Press of Virginia, 1969), 1: 119; H. R. McIlwaine, ed., *Journals of the House of Burgesses of Virginia*, 13 vols. (Richmond, VA: The Colonial Press, E. Waddey Co., 1915), 1: 10.
[95] Virginia Company of London, *Records of the Virginia Company*, 3: 360; repeated in May 1622, 3: 628.
[96] Virginia Company of London, 3: 581–6.
[97] Virginia Company of London, 3: 474; Hening, *The Statutes at Large*, 1: 114.

Raw silk's role as a potential economic diversifier and a cure for mono-culture in Virginia was mirrored in Bermuda in the 1620s, where those arguing against sugar production and concerned about tobacco quality returned to the subject. Governor Nathaniel Butler urged the abandon-ment of sugar and vines (vulnerable to the high winds), pointing to the rate of growth of mulberry trees, and going so far as to expressly contradict the stated opinion of the expert Frenchman on the mulberries in 1613, report-ing that credible informants had told Butler they had heard 'Peter' confess in London that 'ther are not better trees nor a better place in the world than thes Ilands for that end', and that he had lied to the Company because he wanted to go home, throwing in the allegation that Peter had starved the silkworms 'on purpose to that entent'. Having denounced the earlier expert verdict, Butler made new 'experiment', and a later open letter addressed to the governor and council in May 1623 referred to a 'good beginninge' and affirmed that 'the *mulberrye leaves* doth soe well agree with the silke wormes'.[98] The new Bermuda Assembly followed its Virginian counter-part in insisting in the years that followed that every owner or occupier of lands in the islands must plant fifty mulberry trees, but by March 1630 the measures needed tightening because it was apparent that the planters had not treated their mulberries very assiduously – sometimes technically ful-filling the act's terms, but doing so by 'thrusting mulberry slipps into the ground under fences and other waste places'.[99] Bermudan authorities no doubt fed off the literature advocating diversification in Virginia, also drawing on their islands' inability to compete with Chesapeake and St Kitts tobacco production in quality or quantity.[100] In 1630, environmental adversity in the form of storms were also invoked in silk's favour: an act claimed that 'God doth as it were leade us by the hand to the setting on foote that noble design of the Silkworke'. In case God's indication were not sufficient, the law imposed a fine of thirty pounds of tobacco and impri-sonment for those neglecting their mulberry planting, to be monitored by two officials in March each year.[101]

There is only sketchy evidence of any product generated by all of this extensive attention to silk production in early English Atlantic outposts. Russell Fenne, a labourer in Hambleton Tribe, Bermuda, was sentenced to death for stealing a diminutively priced 'skeane of silke' from Robert Haies, amongst other more costly items, in the assizes of July 1626, though this may have been imported sewing silk rather than the product of Bermudan mulberries.[102] Firmer evidence was apparent in Virginia,

---

[98] Butler, *Historye of the Bermudaes*; Lefroy, *Memorials of the Bermudas*, 1: 297.
[99] Acts for 'the preservation of timber' and 'for the Advancement of the Silke worke', in Lefroy, 1: 411, 499–500.
[100] Lefroy, 1: 398.   [101] Lefroy, 1: 500–1.   [102] Lefroy, 1: 391.

where – besides the samples already mentioned – a 1621 report affirmed that 'silke, began to be planted ... [and] prospered with soe good successe', though there is no record of a ship's captain refusing tobacco and insisting that they be paid for the transit of indentured servants in 'corn, silk codds, silk grass, hemp, [or] flax' as Edwin Sandys desired in November 1620.[103] Some silks were apparently shown to the king on Easter Monday of 1623, but commissioners were tasked in June 1623 to check whether 'the silkes ... were not made in Engl[and]'. By this time, James had announced his plans to challenge the wider mismanagement by the Virginia Company, and two other commissions followed – appointed by the Privy Council – which sought to identify 'what Hopes may be truly and really conceived of that Plantation'.[104] By a writ of *quo warranto*, the Virginia Company's charter was nullified in May 1624 and its operations devolved to the Crown. Having been closely associated with the discredited administration of the colony and the king (who died early the next year at Theobalds), support for raising silk in Virginia suffered an incapacitating blow that would have the effect of mothballing the initiative until mid-century.

Obstacles

Early English Virginia, put bluntly, fulfilled virtually none of the preconditions that were necessary for the successful transfer of sericulture from one region to another, and the infant state of English colonialism and English silk manufacturing was in poor condition to compensate for its various shortcomings (as had been possible in New Spain). The biggest handicap facing attempts to produce silk in Virginia, of course, lay in the colony's appalling mortality rate and its impact on the shape of settlement: there *was* no reserve of labour, let alone a suitable one. Some 351 settlers remained in 1616 of more than 1,500 who had been transported, not only 'a small number to advance so great a work' as John Rolfe lamented, but a woefully imbalanced, ill-equipped, vulnerable, and makeshift social group that understandably oriented itself to desperate self-preservation and short-term enterprises. The shift in management in 1618 had brought many more bodies – perhaps as many as 4,000 arriving by 1624 – but most of these unfortunates had suffered similar fates,

---

[103] Virginia Company of London, *Records of the Virginia Company*, 1: 504; Virginia Company of London, Conway Robinson, and Robert Alonzo Brock, *Abstract of the Proceedings of the Virginia Company of London* (Richmond, VA: The Society, 1888), 1: 92.

[104] Virginia Company of London, *Records of the Virginia Company*, 4: 211; Dasent et al., *Acts of the Privy Council*, 39: 108.

succumbing to a mixture of disease, malnutrition, and labour exhaustion, to leave the overall population at a paltry 1,000 souls that year.[105] As a consequence, labour was expensive, hard to come by, and channelled intensively into the work of clearing, and planting corn and especially tobacco. The uncertainty of title and precarious nature of settlement added to a reluctance to draw off labour into projective undertakings which required more patience. As the Bermudan Assembly recorded in 1630, 'The main let and obstacle of this noble worke may seeme to bee the doubt which the inhabitants here haue of the enioying of the Labors and benifit thereof to them or theire children.'[106]

Indian hostility helped not only to slow population growth but also had a pronounced impact on silk production. On 27 March 1622, the Virginia Company in London had trumpeted reports that its efforts were yielding results, 'their hopes . . . nowe greater than euer [of] a flourishinge Country in a short time with that rich Comodity of Silke'. But unbeknownst to them, five days earlier, one of the most emphatic coordinated Native American attacks of the colonial era had taken place in Virginia, killing nearly 350 colonists, and taking its heaviest toll on newer settlements spread out along the James River, which included several of the sites committed to economic diversification within the districts of Henrico and Elizabeth City.[107] The Powhatan raids caused profound damage, though they fell short of their ultimate aim of obliterating or confining European settlers to a minimal regional presence.

In the short term, the deaths and the destruction wrought upon the more innovative plantations cut short many developing silk initiatives: the attacks killed prominent figures involved in silkworm importation (such as George Thorpe), and wreaked havoc on people, livestock, and buildings on the Berkeley, Bennett, Ferrar, Peirce, Nuce, and Yeardley lands. As John Pory put it, 'having made these preparations, and the silke-Wormes ready to be covered [i.e. making their cocoons], all was lost, but my poore life and children, by the Massacre'.[108] In the medium term, the urgent need for a coordinated response from the Virginia Company absorbed executive energy, manpower, and resources and channelled these away from experimental investments. Whole areas were abandoned, as English groups consolidated and militarised, retreating to a narrower and more

---

[105] James P. Horn, *A Land as God Made It: Jamestown and the Birth of America* (Basic Books, 2005), 234–6; Kupperman, *The Jamestown Project*, 310–11.
[106] Lefroy, *Memorials of the Bermudas*, 1: 500.
[107] Virginia Company of London, *Records of the Virginia Company*, 1: 623.
[108] Smith, *Complete Works of John Smith*, 2: 312. See also claims about the massacre's economic impact in response to Nathaniel Butler's critique of colonial diversification: Virginia Company of London, *Records of the Virginia Company*, 2: 381–5.

ethnocentric model of occupation. One veteran settler, John Martin, put forward outlandish proposals in December 1622 for 'Howe to Bringe the Indians into Subiection', that did not involve extirpation, suggesting that they could be persuaded to produce raw silk, being 'apter for worke then yet o[u]r English are, knowinge howe to attayne greate quantitie of silke, hempe, and flax'.[109] But the prospect of benign Anglo-Indian relations proved to be another of the massacre's hapless casualties, as the English retaliated ferociously in the months and years that followed. From the point of the Indian attack, there was a retreat in silk projection to concentrate energy on those who 'haue the most desire & the best meanes to cherish' silkworms, and surviving shipments of seed were more narrowly disbursed, while the governor and council ordered certain planters 'to build a large house of 2 storyes, well seiled, for silkewormes'.[110]

Besides inadequate human labour reserves, a second major practical hindrance throughout the first decades of Chesapeake colonisation was the difficulty of conveying silkworm larvae to planters. The only reliable feature of shipments of silkworm seed was that they were unlikely to survive the transatlantic voyage in adequate quantity, creating challenges for both packaging and commissioning stocks from France, Italy, and Spain.[111] It took 'extraordinary care and provision' to safeguard the eggs' welfare, as recorded in September 1618 when eighty ounces were received safely and distributed 'through the whole plantation'.[112] As pressure on the Company's economic policies mounted, paranoia about their transit increased, and Edwin Sandys urged John Ferrar in September 1620 to '[a]boue all have in remembrance the matter of Silk woorm seed'; the said cargo was to be conveyed carefully under the personal care of Ferrar's associate the physician Lawrence Bohun. On this occasion, the voyage of the *Margaret and John* fell victim to Spanish attack in the West Indies in March 1621, with Bohun and the silkworm larvae amongst the casualties.[113] As a consequence, George Thorpe and John Pory determined to save all of the 'verie small quantitie'

---

[109] Virginia Company of London, 3: 704–6. For a contextual discussion of the visions articulated in the wake of the massacre, see: Alexander B. Haskell, *For God, King, & People: Forging Commonwealth Bonds in Renaissance Virginia* (Durham, NC: UNC Press, 2015), 214–24.

[110] Among these persisters was George Sandys in James City. Virginia Company of London, *Records of the Virginia Company*, 4: 15, 24, 68.

[111] Virginia Company of London, 1: 431–2. Likely sources for the continental seed were Marseille and Livorno, where olive plants were also procured, as in 3: 315.

[112] Virginia Company of London, Robinson, and Brock, *Abstract of Proceedings of Virginia Company*, 2: 149.

[113] Virginia Company of London, *Records of the Virginia Company*, 3: 407.

they were able to preserve in Virginia (from the separate Bristol supply) and give preference to replenishing the stock rather than reeling raw silk.[114] Such oceanic and endemic risks of the Atlantic world played havoc with fragile cargo, and it is little wonder that this tactic of preserving stock (rather than reeling off raw silk, thereby killing the moths) quickly became advice within Anglo-American instructional literature.[115]

Company officers conscious of previous miscarriages in slower ships recommended the specific hiring of a fast pinnace to carry the silkworm seed across the Atlantic later that year.[116] Chamberlain's trading connections were again called on to source six pounds of silkworm seed, narrowing the target region to Valencia, whose silkworms had a hardier reputation than others for travel.[117] But this superior stock arrived too late in the season and the Company were forced to hatch the silkworms in London, promising to ship a hundred ounces to Virginia before Christmas 1622.[118] Concerns over the silkworms on occasion actually delayed the dispatch of vessels to Virginia, as when 'the hope of Silkworme seed ... hath kept the Shipp longer than we meant'. English pigeons, rabbits, beehives, and mastiffs were easy enough, but 'of thinges so farr remote [as silkworms] we are not absolutely maisters'.[119] The geographic challenge of transhipment, especially via England, thus undermined efforts, though – as with experts – the fight to secure stocks was prompting English merchants to enter new markets and develop innovative methods within Atlantic circuits.

Failure to master the procurement of silkworm seed, in time, became one of the charges levelled by critics of the Virginia Company administration, who alleged serious mishandling in 1623.[120] This may have been a minor allegation relative to other grievances about the Company, but it stood to offer disproportionate harm because of the king's interest in the endeavour. The king's patience had noticeably thinned by 1622, when the Company warned the council that his majesty 'aboue all things requires from vs a proofe of Silk; sharply reprovinge the neglect thereof'. By May 1623 the failure to increase raw silk production was causing 'much shame and dishonor to the Plantation ... especially in regard of

---

[114] Virginia Company of London, 3: 447.
[115] Lefroy, *Memorials of the Bermudas*, 1: 359.
[116] Virginia Company of London, *Records of the Virginia Company*, 1: 483, 490; 3: 502.
[117] Virginia Company of London, 1: 510.   [118] Virginia Company of London, 3: 647.
[119] Edward D. Neill, *History of the Virginia Company of London with Letters to and from the First Colony Never Before Printed* (New York: B. Franklin, 1968), 264, 270. For similar issues in the Somers Isles Company in 1625, Lefroy, *Memorials of the Bermudas*, 1: 358–9.
[120] Virginia Company of London, *Records of the Virginia Company*, 4: 147.

his Ma[jes]t[y']s iust resentment therein' and the Company in London 'deservedly feare[d] a diminution of his Royall grace and loue to the Plantation'.[121]

The view from Virginia showed several planters feeling harangued by the stream of silk-related requests and instructions, and offering their own explanations for failure. Recognising it was impolitic, one frustrated progressive planter in Elizabeth City, Captain Thomas Nuce, could not help but vent his anger in May 1621 at the mismatch between the verbal encouragement of silk and the fixed values ascribed to it by the Company. These were certainly not 'indifferent good rates and prices', which Sir Edwin Sandys had promised they would be in 1620 when he arranged a committee of merchants to set them, and likely reflected instead the 'prices as they are now sold at here in England' – if anything adjusted downwards to induce English merchants to buy up any Virginia silk.[122] The meagre pricing model reflected that the Virginia Company was simply not well enough capitalised to artificially create a market that might stimulate uptake. Far from overpricing the product to generate interest, Nuce warned that the low rates were discouraging people, and pointed out that the high price of labour in the colony made a mockery of the two shillings sixpence one notionally earned for a pound of Virginia cocoons. He cited the three shillings per day cost 'for the labor of a man' and wondered sardonically whether the merchants who set the rates 'thought themselues in Italie, Spayne, or ffraunce: Countries plentifull and populous: wher[e] are thousands of women and children and such ydle people to be hyred for 1d or 2d a day'. Lastly, even had the values been more promising, Nuce warned that the hatching of silkworm eggs and availability of mulberry leaves in Virginia 'falls out to be iust at such a season as wee are busiest about our Corne: so as no man but he that means to starue will once looke after them'. Coming from a willing, organised and respected official, having newly relocated from Ireland and in command of a respectably sized labour force, this was a major blow to Sandys and his Company's ambitions, and it coincided with the intensifying clamour against their management of people and projects.[123]

Nuce's letter summarised several of the structural forces hindering silk production (labour cost, fragility of supply, low initial return), but it also

---

[121] Virginia Company of London, 3: 647; 4: 163.
[122] Virginia Company of London, Robinson, and Brock, *Abstract of Proceedings of Virginia Company*, 1: 94.
[123] Virginia Company of London, *Records of the Virginia Company*, 3: 457; 4: 147 (criticism echoed by Alderman Johnson); Martha W. McCartney, *Virginia Immigrants and Adventurers, 1607–1635: A Biographical Dictionary* (Baltimore, MD: Genealogical Pub. Co., 2007), 519.

demonstrated how, even in the most straitened circumstances, trial and failure shaped the evolution of Atlantic colonialism, making it a distinctive laboratory for self-advancement. Nuce himself died in 1622, widely admired for his estate management in spite of dramatic losses during the massacre. But his wider proposals for reorganising the terms of labour in the colony had a lasting legacy, giving the owners of labour a more complete jurisdiction over their charges in Virginia by forcing sharecroppers and tenants into more straightforward and exploitative bonded servitude. His attempts at silk, in other words, contributed arguments and evidence to the wider campaign that resulted in much harsher livelihoods for indentured servants, a shift supported by the opportunistic burgesses, and sanctioned by the desperate Virginia Company.

The sorts of practical shortcomings identified by Nuce and others that were compromising silk production tended to be lost amidst the larger swirl of grievances and accusations of mismanagement aimed at the Virginia Company. This proved important because the (manifestly untrue) allegation that 'little hath beene done' to encourage production allowed others to revisit sericulture in decades to come without accepting or addressing its deeper defects.[124] It was not so much a question of learning from failure as failure at learning, for many of the partial, lobotomised claims made about Virginian silk would – ironically – become a justificatory platform for later experimentation. Edward Waterhouse reported in his pamphlet published in 1622 that Virginia had 'whole Woods of many miles together of Mulberry trees' and gave out stock phrases that would echo in encouragement literature for over a century, including John Pory's comparison with 'Silkes of *Persia* and *Italy*' and Peter Arondelle's observations about 'excelling . . . their owne Country of *Languedocke*'.[125] The signs of progress or minor victories were remembered – such as the transplanting of mulberry trees, the occasional silk samples, and the glowing expert testaments – but the more fundamental obstacles above were often conveniently overlooked or forgotten.

Virginia: A Second Wave

For a time the mulberry trees – whether indigenous *M. rubra* in the forested interior or the smaller numbers of imported *M. alba* and *M. nigra* on estates – stood on the perimeter of the relentless march of armies of tobacco plants. Even the remaining French silk experts, once free from their

---

[124] Virginia Company of London, *Records of the Virginia Company*, 4: 147.
[125] Edward Waterhouse, *A Declaration of the State of the Colony in Virginia* (Amsterdam: Theatrum Orbis Terrarum, 1970), 4, 10.

original contracts, seem to have quietly transitioned to tobacco, deliberately concealing their silk skills, according to one letter in 1628, for which they were threatened with forfeiture of their estates and eviction from the colony in 1632.[126] Contemporaries displayed some interest in and attention to the trees, often reflected in the naming of estates and use of mulberries as common boundary markers, and botanists such as John Parkinson and John Tradescant went so far as to identify and name a *Morus virginiana* ('Virginia mulberry') between 1629 and 1634, which has seemingly confused some claims.[127] The trees' silent testimony as to the landscape's suitability for sericulture helped a second wave of interest in silk production to break over Virginia at mid-century.

A precipitate drop in tobacco prices in the late 1630s offered the other required motivational energy for planters to recontemplate silk production, and it is telling that Governor Francis Wyatt described the colony as 'againe beginning with silk worms' in 1639, referring triumphantly to a sample of Virginian raw silk that had been dispatched to the Secretary of State, Sir Francis Windebank, to be presented to King Charles I.[128] The new-found attention was part of a wider flush of experimentation, more successful than during the Company years because its commodity targets had narrowed, and it now depended upon planters' own economic calculus and a less tempestuous demographic and environmental landscape. English wheat and livestock production (principally cattle, hogs, and goats) increased considerably in the 1640s, often taking up lands fatigued by tobacco, and these products joined maize as a Virginian export to markets in other growing parts of the colonial Atlantic, while other crops (oats, barley, and several vegetables) secured a domestic presence, helping feed a human population that was pushing 20,000 by mid-century. Put together, the provincial concern about overproduction of Chesapeake tobacco (and its falling price), the new conviction that economic diversification was practicable, and the interest in impressing metropolitan powers at a time of radical domestic and imperial upheaval

---

[126] America and West Indies, Colonial Papers (General Series) NA CO 1/4/45; Hening, *The Statutes at Large*, 1: 161; Hatch, 'Mulberry Trees and Silkworms', 23.

[127] John Parkinson, *Theatrum Botanicum: The Theater of Plants* (London: Thomas Cotes, 1640), 1491–2; Maggie Campbell-Culver, *A Passion for Trees: The Legacy of John Evelyn* (London: Random House, 2006), 104. For illustrative confused claims: Philip Alexander Bruce, *Economic History of Virginia in the Seventeenth Century* (New York: Macmillan and co., 1896), 91. David Childs, *Invading America: The English Assault on the New World 1497–1630* (Seaforth Publishing, 2012). For regulations on fencing: Hening, *The Statutes at Large*, 1: 126. For examples of boundary-marking mulberries: Hatch, 'Mulberry Trees and Silkworms', 43.

[128] NA CO 1/10/5. The governor's instructions of 1639 and 1642 specified the planting of 'white Mulbery Trees'. Hatch, 'Mulberry Trees and Silkworms', 45.

(prompted by the British Civil Wars in 1638–60) all meant that silk spectacularly re-emerged as a frontrunner for uptake and investment in Virginia in the 1650s and 1660s.[129]

One of the distinctive features about this second wave of Virginian interest was that it was preceded by a spate of creative English publications (see Fig. 3.4). These produced an artful chorus of arguments in print that demanded Virginian attention to sericulture (amongst other products), combining economic, environmental, scientific, social, and cultural rationales, and collectively generating a political vision of what the colony could become under a new productive regime. As far as silk went, some of these works replicated the instructional content of earlier pamphlets (by Geffe, Stallenge, and Bonoeil), and it is fair to view them as part of an emerging anglophone canon, whose very existence in print was a reflection of the absence of practical or folk know-how about cultivating silkworms in the English-speaking world. It is telling that the English works were overwhelmingly projective whereas similar literatures in French and Spanish tended to be summative or reflective, emerging after sericulture had been established in some regions, and usually proposing models of best practice to transmit to new zones. The re-proposing of English silk production for mid-century Virginia encouraged fresh thinking about colonialism, environment, and the imperial economy, throwing up an intense and creative series of propositions specific to the historical moment that bridged factional interests.[130]

The second generation of efforts to foster Virginian sericulture retained an umbilical link to the Virginia Company, for much of it was authored by John Ferrar, who continued to monitor if not choreograph projective activity.[131] John and Nicholas Ferrar's administrative involvement with Virginia had ended painfully with the termination of the Company, and over the next quarter of a century they had withdrawn from mercantile preoccupations to set up an idiosyncratic High Anglican community at Little Gidding in Huntingdonshire, committed inwardly to routinised

---

[129] For a recent overview of the political economy of the colony, L. H. Roper, *The English Empire in America, 1602–1658: Beyond Jamestown* (London: Routledge, 2009). For a classic explanation of the impact of English upheavals on the colony's government and direction, Wesley Frank Craven, *The Southern Colonies in the Seventeenth Century, 1607–1689* (Louisiana State University Press, 1970), 224–69.

[130] For the best recent consideration of the novel literary, gender, and cultural dimensions of this literature, see Bigelow, 'Gendered Language'; Allison Margaret Bigelow, 'Colonial Industry and the Language of Empire', in *European Empires in the American South: Colonial and Environmental Encounters*, ed. Joseph P. Ward (Oxford, MI: University Press of Mississippi, 2017), 8–36; Sarah Irving, *Natural Science and the Origins of the British Empire* (London: Routledge, 2015), 53–6.

[131] Peter Thompson, 'William Bullock's "Strange Adventure": A Plan to Transform Seventeenth-Century Virginia,' *William and Mary Quarterly* 61, no. 1 (2004): 118.

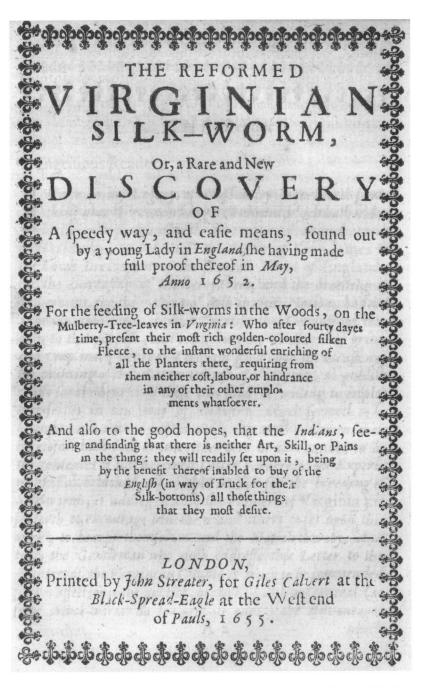

THE REFORMED

VIRGINIAN
SILK–WORM,

Or, a Rare and New
DISCOVERY
OF

A speedy way, and easie means, found out
by a young Lady in *England* she having made
full proof thereof in *May*,
Anno 1 6 5 2.

For the feeding of Silk-worms in the Woods, on the
Mulberry-Tree-leaves in *Virginia*: Who after fourty dayes
time, present their most rich golden-coloured silken
Fleece, to the instant wonderful enriching of
all the Planters there, requiring from
them neither cost, labour, or hindrance
in any of their other employ-
ments whatsoever.

And also to the good hopes, that the *Indians*, seeing and finding that there is neither Art, Skill, or Pains
in the thing: they will readily set upon it, being
by the benefit thereof inabled to buy of the
English (in way of Truck for their
Silk-bottoms) all those things
that they most desire.

LONDON,
Printed by *John Streater*, for *Giles Calvert* at the
Black-Spread-Eagle at the West end
of *Pauls*, 1 6 5 5.

Figure 3.4 Title page to Samuel Hartlib, *The Reformed Virginian Silk-Worm*
(1655). One of the many works of economic reform and sericultural projection
issued with Virginia in mind at mid-century. Printed as appendix to Samuel
Hartlib, *The Reformed Common-wealth of Bees* (London: Giles Calvert, 1655).
University of Wisconsin–Madison Libraries.
Image from Hathi Trust: https://catalog.hathitrust.org/Record/005783174

prayer and local charity and education. After his brother's death in 1637, the short, swarthy, 'priest-like' John Ferrar remained for twenty years the patriarch of the family – with a short interruption when he fled into exile during the English Civil War. He had become a sort of intense archivist and soothsayer, leaping at any chance to reflect on sericulture and its meanings and possibilities, as if the prospect of Atlantic silk had itself become an article of faith.[132] Ferrar took issue with the published claims of William Bullock in 1649, who had critiqued the Virginia Company's earlier policies, and who had urged smaller planters to pursue known cereals instead of persisting in tobacco or attempting new exotic products, Bullock warning 'we are not all . . . Masters of the Silk-worme mystery'.[133] Ferrar angrily scribbled defensive marginalia in his copy, protesting that they had 'do[n]e all that Couldbe / donn' in the 1620s to push new products, including silk, and that the commodity was suitable to the whole population, not just the planter elite. Ferrar had remained in close contact with a number of Virginia planters, including Captain Samuel Mathews Sr., who established plantations pursuing textiles, which Ferrar complimented in his own (anonymously published) work, *Perfect Description of Virginia* (1650).[134] The specific experiences, peculiar household, and copious papers of John Ferrar provided a core of evidence and activity on which much of the Virginia reform literature of the 1650s drew – sometimes through Ferrar himself, and otherwise through his daughter, ostentatiously named Virginia, who similarly consulted about silk production with a number of Chesapeake, English, and Irish contacts in the late 1640s and 1650s, when she conducted and publicised her own experiments on silkworm raising.[135]

---

[132] For the description of John's appearance, see Peter Peckard, *Memoirs of the Life of Mr. Nicholas Ferrar* (Cambridge: J. Archdeacon, 1790), 287.

[133] William Bullock, *Virginia Impartially Examined* (London: John Hammond, 1649), 8, 32–3.

[134] John Ferrar, *A Perfect Description of Virginia: Being, a Full and True Relation of the Present State of the Plantation* (London: Printed for Richard Wodenoth, 1649). John Ferrar, 'Questionnaire & Excerpt', 30 August 1646, The Ferrar Papers, 1590–1790, [hereafter FP] David R. Ransome editor, microfilm edition by Microform Academic Publishers, Wakefield, Yorkshire, 1992. Mathews discussed Virginian silk in 1650 in Hartlib Papers, Ephemerides, 1652, 28/2/39A.

[135] Edward Williams, *Virginia: More Especially the South Part Thereof, Richly and Truly Valued . . .* (London: Printed by T. H. for John Stephenson, 1650); Edward Williams, *Virgo Triumphans, or, Virginia Richly and Truly Valued . . .* (London: Printed by Thomas Harper, for John Stephenson, 1650); Edward Williams, *Virginia's Discovery of Silke-Wormes, with Their Benefit . . .* (London: Stephenson, 1650); Samuel Hartlib, *A Rare and New Discovery of a Speedy Way and Easie Means . . . for the Feeding of Silk-Worms in the Woods* (London: Richard Wodenothe, 1652); Hartlib, *Reformed Virginian Silk-Worm.* John Hammond, *Leah and Rachel, Or, the Two Fruitfull Sisters of Virginia and Maryland* (London, 1656), 5. For a full overview of the various editions and distinctions, Danielle C. Skeehan, 'Creole Domesticity: Women, Commerce, and Kinship in Early Atlantic

The literature of Chesapeake reform showed some divisions over where and how silk might best be established in the mainland colonies. But in sharing the core idea that the Chesapeake was a natural extension of England, and that the region's false course ought to be corrected to suit, the works were able to embrace economic, moral, and demographic enlargement all at once. Silk became a coming-of-age story, cut to fit a nation and an empire rising to maturity: 'as the Mulberry Trees grows up, which are by every one planted, Tobacco will be laid by, and we shall wholy fall to making of Silk', predicted John Hammond, linking this to the fact that 'Children increase and thrive so well there, that they themselves will sufficiently supply the defect of Servants.'[136] These writers usually began with grand economic arguments, in which they ascribed to the colonial Chesapeake not just an opportunity, but the principal responsibility for raising England's civilisational profile and productive capacity, through establishing raw silk production – 'to show to the World that wee may equall the best of the Westerne Kingdomes', as Edward Williams put it.[137] Their novelty was in merging the earlier political economy put forward by Jacobean writers with new-found claims based on the natural environment of English North America.

Attention to the historical spread and organisation of sericulture in European regions where it had proven profitable was much fuller in these works, and there were the beginnings of recognition of environmental hazards associated with northerly climes, with silkworms viewed as 'weaker' in France than in Italy.[138] This north–south axis found expression in another vital biogeographic claim that remained a fixture of projection in the centuries to come: that British American territories occupied a latitude commensurate with the great silk-producing empires of China and Persia.[139] Williams argued that Virginia, like its Asian forebears, was 'particularly assigned' by Nature 'for the production, food, and perfection of this Creature'.[140] Advocating the proper exploitation of the Chesapeake's untapped silk potential often involved the use of muscly, masculine language that squared with wider English designs in the Atlantic in a period of violent competition with rival European

---

Writing' (PhD thesis, Northeastern University, 2013) esp. chapter 1; Bigelow, 'Gendered Language.' See also Peck, *Consuming Splendor*, 104–5.

[136] Hammond, *Leah and Rachel*, 15, and again 18.

[137] Williams, *Virginia Richly and Truely Valued*, 29.

[138] Williams, *Virginia Richly and Truly Valued*, 30.

[139] Anya Zilberstein, *A Temperate Empire: Making Climate Change in Early America* (Oxford: Oxford University Press, 2016), 19–38.

[140] Williams, *Virginia Richly and Truely Valued*, 31. This prompted conjectures about the prospect of a double (or bivoltine) harvest in silk cocoons later in the work, 39–40. On bivoltine aspirations, see also Hartlib, *Reformed Virginian Silk-Worm*, 16.

powers: 'Singly in her selfe' the Chesapeake stood to 'outvy France, Spaine, and Italy'.[141] The overall framing of the pro-silk case thus showed many continuities, but aspects of the political economy had been noticeably sharpened, including propositions relating to England's place in the world and to the specificity of Virginian strengths.

That indigenous temperatures, trees, and insects became important justificatory agents placed great weight on their presence, health, and distribution in the Chesapeake. Correspondingly, authors showed great initiative and effort in order to secure information about American estates, forests, and insects, being very attentive to any findings, news, or rumour on which they could pin suppositions. These would be the thin platforms from which they could legitimately leap to their conclusions, and there is a sense at times of an internal appreciation of this dilemma, as when Ferrar commented that 'Wee must not ... conforme the nature of the [Virginian] Climate to our Rules, but our Rules to it.'[142] Amongst the claims which resurfaced in the 1640s and 1650s were the inferences made about species of indigenous silk moths in Virginia, whose existence – as with the *M. rubra* trees before them – was taken to show the natural fitness (and often presumed superiority) of the American environment for sericulture. Reflecting on William Bullock's note that Virginia's silkworms were larger than walnuts, John Ferrar jotted down that 'alsoe are the[re] Silke / Wormes Found that live Feede / and Spinn Naturally In / the woods of them selves' – creatures he and his daughter claimed were ten (sometimes twenty) times larger than European *Bombyx mori*, but were almost certainly from another family of lepidopterans, the cecropia moth (*Hyalophora cecropia*).[143] Finding new species opened fanciful new theories, like the idea that Virginia mulberry trees somehow internally produced these silkworms, or that Virginia indigenous silkworms had appetites that went beyond mulberry leaves to those of other fruit trees.[144]

The Ferrar family, particularly Virginia, made strenuous efforts to locate meaningful evidence from which they could extrapolate claims about the Chesapeake environment and its fit to silk production. Virginia Ferrar's collaborative and experimental approach (shared through John Ferrar and then Samuel Hartlib) formed the basis of

[141] Williams, *Virginia Richly and Truely Valued*, 31.

[142] Williams, *Virginia Richly and Truely Valued*, 34.

[143] For examples of the Ferrars elucidating these claims, see: Thompson, 'William Bullock's "Strange Adventure"' web supplement with Ferrar marginalia: https://oieahc .wm.edu/wmq/Jan04/ThompsonWeb.pdf. Hartlib, *Reformed Virginian Silk-Worm*, 14, 31–2, 36. For a list of claims and descriptions, and identification of the cecropia moth: D. R. Ransome and D. C. Lees, 'The Virginian Silkworm: From Myth to Moth. Or: How a Businessman Turned into a Naturalist', *Antenna* 41, no. 3 (2017): 120–7.

[144] Hartlib, *Reformed Virginian Silk-Worm*, 22, 25.

much relentless subsequent promotion, reflecting a pattern that would become common in the history of silk attempts: female labour appropriated and thrown by male publicists. Ferrar actually did better at securing recognition than many later women involved in Anglo-American silk experimentation, seizing with both hands her distinctive opportunity to link the empirical with the imperial agenda.[145] Her efforts to demonstrate that silkworms could be reared freely on the trees were overzealously celebrated in print as 'a rare and new discovery', an 'Experiment' with 'full proof', and an 'invention' of someone who had once 'kept them [silkworms] by the Book-rules' but had now transcended the rules (with divine assistance, of course).[146]

It is her unpublished papers that perhaps offer the highest accolade to Virginia's methodical exertions, as she fired off over twenty questions to multiple planters, trying to find out 'Informations' about the timings, extent, habits, predators, and preferences of Chesapeake caterpillars. Persistent in her correspondence, careful to log her data, and constantly searching for patterns of behaviour and response, Virginia spent a considerable time trying to make sense of the problems and possibilities that her insect charges and transatlantic information yielded. One John Stirrup informed her in January 1650 that the mulberry trees tended to 'grow uppon old plantations and in old ffeilds', an Edward Johnson (of Mulberry Island) was pushing others to respond to Ferrar's queries and agenda in March, and a Michael Upchurch responded that in his district 'Silkwormes here be some but they make noe use of them'. A physician, John Pykering, sent her his 'own contentions and observations' about the health and functionality of Virginian worms, and the timings of their developmental cycle, while Michael Sharman charmingly confessed to not having been able to get his to hatch in spite of three weeks' efforts.[147] Ever mindful of the gendered dimensions of silk and empire, Virginia even wrote to the governor's wife, Lady Berkeley, trying to recruit her to lend her patronage to noble designs, by mentioning great women associated with projects of Atlantic colonialism, such as 'Lady Queene Isabella' who had endorsed Columbus's discovery 'in her most deepe and profound judgment . . . to the Eternall honor of her Sexe (and Shame of men)'.[148]

In the spirit of Europeans conforming rules to the Virginian environment, not expecting Virginia to fit to European rules, several mid-century

---

[145] On Virginia Ferrar's triangulation of gender, nature, and scientific enquiry, see Skeehan, 'Creole Domesticity: Women, Commerce, and Kinship in Early Atlantic Writing', esp. ch. 1; Bigelow, 'Gendered Language', 280.
[146] Hartlib, *Reformed Virginian Silk-Worm*, 1, 3, 11, 12.
[147] FP: 1152, 1160, 1182, 1190.   [148] FP: 1176, 1205.

authors returned to the proposals put forward by John Martin in 1622 which had provocatively recommended subcontracting silk labour to neighbouring Native American populations. Beginning with the presumption that Indians could 'gather the Mulbery leaves and bringe them to the Englishe to Sell da[i]ly', John Ferrar stretched this to the idea that Indians could rear the silkworms directly themselves, using houses of boards 'sett up in the woods' that would act as a cocoonery 'and in them the Indian taught how to feed the worme'. This model would have the advantage of not leaving the silkworms vulnerable to greedy birds, as had occurred when the Company had apparently conducted experiments leaving silkworms unattended in the wild.[149] Edward Williams elaborated a seven-point plan whereby selected Indian men could be used as supplementary labourers, 'cunningly divided' amongst white settlements pursuing sericulture. Although the men were work-shy (in his archetypal view), by spreading the practice and involving Indian women and children, it was possible to imagine 'our Trade with them for silke' as outstripping the value of the fur trade, and a future in which working to grow silk had brought widespread new plantations of mulberry trees, and, in tandem, brought civility to the 'savage'.[150] Virginia Ferrar's 'new invented' proposal to rear silkworms on the trees, with its minimal labour input, was quickly linked to indigenous peoples, whom it was assumed would imitate the practice 'with all alacrity' and develop strategies to guard against birds.[151] Such notions prompted Laurence Ward in January 1653 to invite three visiting Indian 'great men' back to his estate to show them European silk cocoons; he was disappointed when they did not 'know any such in the woods at any time'.[152]

Authors also recognised by now the limitations of instruction manuals, and so urged experimenters not to be dogmatic about 'observing the Booke Rules, and written Precepts'.[153] They encouraged Virginians and others to improvise 'your owne inventions' and make use of the materials around them, proposing for instance that the well-constructed Algonquian mats could be used as fitting roofing for cocooneries, or that families could construct mutualised lodges in the woods during the feeding season, such that silkworms could be fed and protected with the swiftest and easiest access to leaves – the wooden buildings perhaps

---

[149] For examples of Ferrar elucidating these claims, see: Thompson, 'William Bullock's "Strange Adventure"'. Also FP: 1187, p. 3. See also Hartlib, *Reformed Virginian Silk-Worm*, 1–2, 17–18.

[150] Williams, *Virginia Richly and Truely Valued*, 38–9.

[151] Hartlib, *Reformed Virginian Silk-Worm*, 13.

[152] Laurence Ward to Virginia Ferrar, 7 February 1653, FP: 1216.

[153] Williams, *Virginia Richly and Truely Valued*, 33.

palisaded and patrolled by half a dozen hounds, according to one pamphlet.[154] Such precautions suggest that, in spite of long-term hopes for interracial collaboration, the shadow of the 1622 massacre and its impact on silk operations remained, with some works recommending 'a sufficient defence against all the Natives of the Countrey' or cautioning against Indians being involved in 'Remoter Works'.[155] But regardless of their incongruity and naivety, these suggestions for how to manage the spatial configuration of silkworm rearing at least demonstrated a willingness to address known hindrances in Virginia, and to embrace opportunities associated with the Virginian environment and its indigenous peoples.

Another key area in which the mid-century works hinted at new thinking was in relation to the nature of labour in silk production. Greater research attention was focused than before on the coordination of labour in existing sericultural zones: the English observed that poor people in some Italian provinces were forced to buy their mulberry leaves from noble landowners, but in other regions were allowed access to trees in return for a share of the profit of the raw silk generated. Which model might work best, they asked, in British America? This second generation of anglophone works on silk also made a more explicit and comparative effort to contrast silk's labour requirements (light, easy, and inexpert) against those of other commodities that had become or were becoming plantation fixtures in the Atlantic world, including tobacco, sugar, indigo, and rum.[156]

Perhaps most fundamentally, as has already been intimated, in the process of articulating these claims, the question of gender rose to occupy a central position in the literature on silk encouragement. Silkworms, though historically masculinised in many publications, themselves began to be gendered feminine throughout their life cycle.[157] This brought them in line, of course, with the flamboyant gendering of the Chesapeake colonies as a whole under reform programmes – Williams, for instance, had likened Virginia to 'the Eldest Daughter of Nature', whose 'unwounded wombe' awaited the attention of ardent 'Gentlemen'.[158] But it also brought silkworms in line with the slowly changing demographics of Chesapeake society, where female bodies and female labour were beginning to have a major impact on production,

---

[154] Williams, *Virginia Richly and Truely Valued*, 37.
[155] Williams, *Virginia Richly and Truely Valued*, 37.
[156] Williams, *Virginia Richly and Truely Valued*, 49; Hartlib, *Reformed Virginian Silk-Worm*, 16–17.
[157] Bigelow, 'Gendered Language', 274.
[158] Williams, *Virginia Richly and Truely Valued*, 50. For overview, Kathleen Brown, *Good Wives, Nasty Wenches, and Anxious Patriarchs: Gender, Race, and Power in Colonial Virginia* (Chapel Hill: University of North Carolina Press, 1993).

reproduction, and notions of sustainability. It had made perfect sense for John Ferrar, veteran of the testosterone-swamped demographics of early Virginia, to model 'a man and a boy' in his case studies or hypothetical projections about silk; the female reeler depicted in Bonoeil's published illustrations of the 1620s (at work in teasing out warmed cocoon filaments) was borrowed from French plates.[159] But the models were changing, and Ferrar's man-and-boy scenario was largely formulaic, for the purpose of proving silk's higher labour return, compared with tobacco. Bullock recommended that English fathers ought to 'keepe his Sonnes in England, and send his Daughters to Virginia'.[160] Hammond noted that 'Women are not (as is reported) put into the ground to worke, but occupie such domestique imployments and houswifery as in England … yet som wenches that are nasty, beastly and not fit to be so imployed are put into the ground.'[161] Silk encouragers placed a growing emphasis on the suitability of the pursuit for women of all classes: 'a most fit recreation for Ladies, especially being begun and ended in the two pleasantest Months of the year, *March* and *April*'.[162] John Ferrar wrote directly 'To the *Virginian* Ladies', urging them: 'O let not envious men deprive you / Of what to you so properly is due. / Of silk the Winder, Twister, and the first Weaver.'[163]

Through the prism of gender, then, silkworms metamorphosed from a redemptive economic force into a redemptive social force. Like industrious women, and in contrast to beastly 'wenches', they promised to transform Virginia's morals and upgrade civil society. As one poetic rendering put it, feminised silkworms were both self-contained and selfless. The creatures had learned 'how to unself thy self, & be / Reneu'd into fresh vivid puritie; / How to put off that old & rotten Man / Which overgrows thou with corruption.'[164] Notions of whiteness also lurked tellingly amidst many of the claims about these creatures, considering the creeping institutionalisation of racial slavery in the Cheseapeake: one author claimed silkworms 'loveth any thing that is white and luminous', while another associated their whitening skins with health and vigour, unlike those darkened and retarded in development by tobacco smoke.[165] In laboured

---

[159] Williams, *Virginia Richly and Truely Valued*, 32. Cf. Ferrar's marginalia in 1649 that silk was a pursuit 'donn by women and / Children w[i]th noe labour / in a house in six weeks / time' (Thompson, 'William Bullock's "Strange Adventure"') and observation that the work was 'admitting of all Ages (for a childe can doe all yt belongs to it), Sexes, Qualitys & Callings'. FP: 1186.

[160] Bullock, *Virginia Impartially Examined*, 54.   [161] Hammond, *Leah and Rachel*, 9.

[162] Hartlib, *Reformed Virginian Silk-Worm*, 25.   [163] FP: 1192.

[164] John Beaumont, verses 'Upon the Silkworm', FP: 1191.

[165] Williams, *Virginia's Discovery of Silke-Wormes*, 11. Letter from John Pykering to Virginia Ferrar, *c.*1650, FP: 1190.

poetry and repetitive prose, the worms themselves were held up as models of hard work, resilience, natural beauty, and self-sacrifice – the implication being that if only the male workers of Virginia could match some of these qualities rather than indulge their idleness, vanity, selfishness, and slavish addition to tobacco, the colony would become a healthier, nobler place.

Virginia Ferrar's high profile in the literature on silk – in which she is often referred to as 'the Lady' – helped to secure this shift, but she was perhaps less exceptional a figure than her father and supporters would have us believe.[166] For one thing, Virginia Ferrar demonstrated through her epistolary activity and secondary references that there existed a potent network of female practitioners and experimenters across Britain and Ireland. An Irish kinswoman of one of the Ferrars' Dublin correspondents kept 'great store' of silkworms and affirmed that they could thrive on lettuce (and possibly dandelions) as an alternative food source, claiming that they would 'spin as much Silk'. Virginia's cousin Jane Collett was the source of further insights through her Chesapeake planting relatives. Oftentimes, though letters were exchanged through male hands, women were clearly the targets and lead experimenters, as when Edward Johnson lamented that 'the gloves came after to my wives hands but not the silk-worm eggs'.[167]

The correspondence of Laurence Ward in 1653 exposed the full breadth of colonial involvement: in the process of elaborating on the origins of Virginian silk moths that his wife Mary had sent to the Ferrars, he explained that the cocoons had been first found by 'one of o[u]r negros beinge triminge of some ap[p]le trees in the orchard', where-upon Mary had 'tooke her s[c]isers & cutt it open', before hanging it up in a paper bag on the wall.[168] The eagle eye of a bondsperson of African origin, and their inquisitive mistress, were therefore the real originators of the 'rare and true discovery' attributed glowingly in print to Virginia at Little Gidding. On a separate occasion while scouring for promising indigenous caterpillars, Mary informed Virginia that an Indian had retrieved and supplied her with cocoons.[169] Far from being 'palpably incompetent' of adapting to sericulture, as Gertrude Working claimed in 1932, Native Americans and Africans had actually played important roles in the earliest forays in both Spanish and English America, and the

---

[166] On the literary and gendered idealisation of Virginia Ferrar, Bigelow, 'Gendered Language', 283, 306.

[167] Hartlib, *Reformed Virginian Silk-Worm*, 25, 29–30. For examples of this network of female correspondents, FP: 1121, 1134 (Jane Collett), 1144 (Ann Ffraisle), 1187 (Anne Mapletoft), 1194 (Abigaill Clement), 1202 (wife of Johnson), 1209 (Mary Hill).

[168] Letter from Laurence Ward to Virginia Ferrar, 7 February 1653, FP: 1216.

[169] Letter from Mary Ward to Virginia Ferrar, 4 April 1656, FP: 1261.

profile of the latter would grow as racial slavery and southern plantations expanded.[170]

As with new emphases on labour and gender, England's deepening global experiences – through the Levant and East India Companies in particular – helped to inform new claims and hopes about Atlantic seri-culture, the objective becoming 'To reape Persian harvests in America'.[171] Hartlib and the Ferrars, for instance, drew on the reports of gentlemen travellers and merchants who had accrued experience of the silk trade and witnessed silk production in the Near East.[172] They also relayed discov-eries by other European powers, as when Portuguese traders had demanded of peoples from the Kingdom of Congo 'what numbers of Silk Wormes they had in their country, and how and of what they feed their Worms' – being surprised and disappointed to learn that their African trading partners 'never heard of Silk Wormes, nor such things' and had woven their textiles out of plant fibres.[173] Atlantic schemers expressly consulted the board of the East India Company (EIC) in 1652, asking – as the Portuguese had asked the Central West African traders – under what conditions silkworms were raised, and what was the size, colour, fre-quency, and consistency of their Asiatic raw silk yield? The twenty ques-tions put to the EIC pointedly exposed awareness of English failings, with Ferrar asking whether silkworms were kept 'by all sortes of Peopell' in Persia, what coloured fruit the Asiatic mulberries bore, whether much raw silk came from 'Tartaria w[hi]ch is but a Cold country', and 'by what kind of Instrument or Invention' the cocoons were reeled.[174] Alongside the new lines of questioning, Virginian silk encouragement prompted creative thinking in political economy; Hartlib recommended that Virginian raw silk be granted a ten-year exemption from customs export duties, and that successful producers be allowed to import goods custom free to the Chesapeake (to the value of their silk), in an effort to reduce expenditure on 'doubtfull friends, or Heathen Nations'.[175]

For all of their exposition of greater information and detail about the practices and possibilities of sericulture, however, the works encouraging silk in the Chesapeake showed little progress in their assumptions about expertise and practical knowledge exchange. 'One skilfull in this noble mystery', wrongly anticipated Williams and Ferrar, 'is sufficient for the employing, overseeing, and directing hundreds under him', and they

---

[170] Gertrude Brown Working, 'The History of Silk Culture in the North American Colonies' (PhD thesis, Radcliffe College, 1932), 38.

[171] Verse by John Pickering, c.1650, FP: 1190.

[172] Hartlib, *Reformed Virginian Silk-Worm*, 21.   [173] FP: 1188.

[174] John Ferrar to 'Gentlemen . . . of the East Indian Company', 23 August 1652, FP: 1213.

[175] Hartlib, *Reformed Virginian Silk-Worm*, 15.

expected that six weeks of experience under such a silkworm rearer would perfect 'full understanding of the mystery'. The ratio of teacher to learner, time period to proficiency, and the blithe hope that 'arguments of honour' buried in pamphlets would incentivise either party were all far wide of the mark.[176] Also problematic was the support and advice offered for the critical moment of reeling off the cocoons. Hartlib reissued instructions from the first wave of literature, which at times dodged the issue entirely: 'the making of the Wheel, as likewise the way to winde the said silk from the bottoms, can hardly be set down so plainly as to be rightly understood'.[177] John Mapletoft conversely proposed that reeling was 'so easy & plaine that the meanest head is capable of learning it & practising it at the first'.[178] In the aggregate, the literary and imperial push was therefore forceful but imbalanced – bringing hypothetical assistance more than material aid to silk trials, and neglecting some of the vital areas that required attention and understanding.

The Wood for the Trees

As a consequence of renewed efforts by prominent planters, governors, and self-modelled improvers, the 1650s and 1660s saw extensive plantings of mulberry trees in the Chesapeake numbering in the tens of thousands, and the production of hundreds of pounds of Virginian raw silk. Early on, Sir Henry Chicheley (Lancaster County), Lt. Col. Thomas Ludlow (York County), Col. William Bernard (Gloucester County), Major John Westrope (Charles City County), and a George Lobb (Isle of White County) all lent their authority to supporting initiatives, for which they were given poetic recognition in an awful rhyming verse by Virginia Ferrar's brother.[179] At its height in the mid-1660s, the progress was described by Governor William Berkeley as 'great & unexpected' and he believed the commodity's prospects were another reason to invest in 'a defence against the Dutch' – who raided Virginian exports during the Anglo-Dutch Wars, notably in 1667 and 1673. Indeed, Berkeley felt that Chesapeake production in future would only be held back by the 'want of good wheels (the French call them Mills) from Marseilles or Messina'.[180] At the request of the Virginia assembly in June 1666, Berkeley oversaw

---

[176] Williams, *Virginia Richly and Truely Valued*, 32. For Virginian correspondents reporting a lack of engagement with the literature, see letters from Laurence Ward (Nansamond) and Ed Johnson (Mulberry Island) in 1651, FP: 1200, 1202.
[177] Hartlib, *Reformed Virginian Silk-Worm*, 9.   [178] FP: 1187.
[179] Hartlib, *Reformed Virginian Silk-Worm*, 34.
[180] Letter from William Berkeley to Sir Henry Bennet, 1 August 1665, in 'Virginia in 1662–1665', 427.

the gifting of 300 pounds of raw silk to the king in October 1668, which
Charles II apparently ordered 'to be wrought up for the use of our owne
person' – a fitting outcome for his grandfather's dreams, if not quite the
coronation robes claimed in Virginian cavalier legend.[181]

The legislative footprint of silk encouragement was unmistakable
from 1656, when the House of Burgesses stipulated that planters must
tend to a quota of ten mulberry trees for every hundred acres in their
possession; they must set their trees out twelve feet apart and guard
them from foraging livestock and weeds. The penalty for non-
compliance for the two-year period of the act was 10 lb of tobacco for
each neglected tree.[182] The act, in all likelihood, reflected the particular
enthusiasm of one of Virginia's interim governors, Edward Digges, who
led the colony for a short time between 1655 and 1656 during the
Commonwealth years either side of the lengthy governorships of the
staunch royalist Sir William Berkeley. Digges, who hailed from
a prominent gentry family in Kent which had invested in the original
Virginia Company, had migrated to Virginia and bought up extensive
lands in York and Gloucester counties in 1650. A respected newcomer
who had not given offence to either side, Digges was a good candidate
for the governorship. At the assembly's request he returned to England
in December 1656 to help negotiate a resolution to political contentions
in the Chesapeake, but not before the assembly had passed the mulberry
legislation, and approved the payment of 4,000 pounds of tobacco to
one 'George the Armenian' to persuade him 'to stay in the country' to
support silk production.[183]

The serious experimenters such as Edward Digges, unlike several of the
overconfident pamphleteers, did not take lightly the matter of expertise,
and invested heavily in securing key people to advance their silk ambitions. The presence of Armenian silk specialists in Virginia was in some
ways a function of the reach of the East India and Levant Company
connections that wealthy Atlantic colonists could draw on. From a less

[181] McIlwaine, *Journals of Burgesses*, 2: 31 (request on 5 June 1666); 2: 39 (committee to
progress on 6 Nov. 1666); King Charles II to Governor and Council of Virginia,
25 November 1668, NA CO 1/23/87. For examples of claims that repeat the myth
first propounded by Robert Beverley, that Charles II wore coronation robes made of
Virginia silk, see: Robert Beverley, *The History and Present State of Virginia, in Four Parts*
(London: R. Parker, 1705), 57; John Leander Bishop, Edwin Troxell Freedley, and
Edward Young, *A History of American Manufactures, from 1608 to 1860*, 3 vols.
(Philadelphia: E. Young & Co., 1866), 1: 33; Mary Thomas McKinstry, 'Silk Culture
in the Colony of Georgia', *Georgia Historical Quarterly* 14 (1930): 225; John
Esten Cooke, *A Life of General Robert E. Lee* (New York: Applewood Books, US,
1883), 8. For a variant featuring 'bed furniture': 'Manuscripts of S. H. Le Fleming,
Esq., of Rydal Hall', *Virginia Magazine of History and Biography* 20 (1912): 199.
[182] Hening, *The Statutes at Large*, 1: 420.   [183] Hening, *The Statutes at Large*, 1: 425.

Eurocentric perspective, it also reflected the deepening commercial ambition of Armenian merchants and their silk-growing suppliers, as both groups took advantage of more relaxed Safavid controls and squabbling European maritime powers in mid-century to grow global opportunities.[184] By the summer of 1654, Digges seems to have recruited at least 'two *Armenians* out of *Turky*' who helped to develop his output and ensure a proof of quality, even if limited quantity, as some 400 pounds of cocoons were reeled into 8 pounds of Virginian raw silk. In a report to John Ferrar that June, Digges was polite and indulgent on the subject of the miraculous New World silkworm species the Ferrars sought (which he could not find), but he also hinted at the persistence of two of Virginia's structural problems with silk cultivation: the diffuseness of mulberry trees, and the struggle to secure reliable silkworm seed. The leaves were 'far scattered from my present Plantation' meaning he had to send workers far afield, while the 'want of Eggs' had prompted Digges to concentrate much of his crop of cocoons on breeding. He informed Ferrar that he was giving out as much as ten pounds of seed 'to diverse Planters, that are very earnest (seeing so great a benefit before their eyes) to become also Silk-masters', and ended on an upbeat note about uptake and prospects. The coup, as he explained, lay not in persuading Chesapeake planters to give up tobacco for silk – so often the metropolitan line – but in persuading them to 'proceed with both together'.[185]

The House of Burgesses took further measures over the next two years to add incentives and clarify the strictures about mulberry trees. In March 1658, in an act entitled 'Encouragement for Staple Comodities', silk was the first product enumerated in a list of those targeted to compete for labour and acreage with tobacco. The assembly – blithely sidestepping the irony – offered a prize of 10,000 pounds weight of Virginia tobacco for diversifying output, to be awarded to anyone who exported 200 pounds sterling's worth of silk, flax, or hops (or two tons of wine). A separate act promised half this sum, not for exporting, but merely for making 'one hundred pounds of wound silke in one yeare' in recognition that 'the making of silk will much conduce to the good of this colony'. A third measure gave a little more time to orphans who had only just come into their lands, allowing them five years before they were expected to have planted their mulberries. But local objections clearly persisted about the mulberry quota and the fines that accompanied it, for in March 1659 the Virginia assembly repealed the act, deeming it 'rather troublesome and

---

[184] R. W. Ferrier, 'The Armenians and the East India Company in Persia in the Seventeenth and Early Eighteenth Centuries', *The Economic History Review* 26, no. 1 (1973): 38–62.
[185] Letter from Edward Digges to John Ferrar, Virginia (21 June 1654), repr. in Hartlib, *Reformed Virginian Silk-Worm*, 26–7.

burthensome'. At the same time, they boosted the reward on the statute books for sericulture, now offering 10,000 pounds of tobacco to whomsoever reeled just 50 pounds of raw silk, '*Provided* he prove it to be all of his owne 'making'.[186] These different permutations suggest a legislature grappling with some uncertainty with the issue of whether sericulture was best pursued as a collective or an individual endeavour.

The Restoration of Charles II and soon thereafter of Berkeley as Virginia's royal governor brought with it some greater clarity, and the 'act for mulberry trees' was swiftly revived in 1661 and consolidated and strengthened the next year, the terms expressly noting that 'his majestie hath taken perticular notice of the greate folly and negligence of the country'. Berkeley's assembly not only committed to a grand jury 'strictly' policing any breaches of the tree quota, but also democratised further the raw silk incentives, creating what amounted to a bounty, by approving a payment of fifty pounds of tobacco raised from 'the publique levy' for each pound of reeled raw silk.[187] In effect, the ingenious system would compensate successful silk experimenters by fining failed mulberry – or incorrigible tobacco – planters. The circuit in the political economy of Virginia silk was one loop that reflected a deepening willingness in the 1660s and beyond to shape imperial production and specialisation through the manipulation of economic policy. While in London, both Edward Digges and William Berkeley were appointed to the first Council of Foreign Plantations (forerunner to the Board of Trade), and both would consistently press for measures to restrain tobacco overproduction and support diversification. Though Digges did not return to Virginia until late 1669, Berkeley's championing of new exports injected energy and, for a time, political will into the affair, and he hoped to lead by example as well as by proscription, cultivating an array of products at his pioneering Green Spring Plantation – including raw silk from as early as 1649.[188]

By September 1663 it had become apparent that supplying the requisite number of white mulberry trees for Virginian estates was not going to be possible from existing stock, and the assembly approved a welcome extension of time until the end of 1666 – with the sting in the tail that the fine for non-compliance would be doubled. The measures were evidently bearing some fruit, as witnessed in the payments made out to those who had reeled raw silk, including George the Armenian, but they were also

[186] Hening, *The Statutes at Large*, 1: 470, 481, 487, 520, 521.
[187] Hening, *The Statutes at Large*, 2: 32, 121.
[188] Billings, 'Sir William Berkeley and the Diversification of the Virginia Economy'; Joan Leonard de Lourdes, 'Operation Checkmate: The Birth and Death of a Virginia Blueprint for Progress 1660–1676', *The William and Mary Quarterly* 24, no. 1 (1967): 44–74.

generating opposition in some quarters.[189] Col. Edmund Scarborough, a long-standing member of the House of Burgesses from Accomack County on the Eastern Shore, objected to a suite of Berkeley's measures that damaged the profitability of tobacco estates, and viewed the 1663 mulberry act as 'very prejudicial to such as want clear grounds and are not in a capacity at present to fulfil' its terms. He and others saw little place for the managed economy that Berkeley and others sought to engineer, arguing that if silk were profitable, 'men as they find themselves in a capacity will fall upon it without constraint'.[190]

One such man was the Reverend Alexander Moray, a Scottish royalist who developed extensive mulberry plantations on Ware Neck, jutting out into Mobjack Bay (Gloucester County). Writing to his kinsman, Sir Robert Moray, in February 1665, Moray was in optimistic mood, and full of ideas as to how to plant out more of these young trees so as to maximise their potential in the seasons to come. Using cuttings, Moray felt he had the edge on those who were planting mulberries from seed, and another innovation was 'to plant them all, as if they were curran[t]s or goosberries, so thick as in hedges' to allow one labourer to collect leaves most efficiently, using 'a pair of sissers' (shears). Importantly, these were not the armchair musings of an absentee philosopher: Moray reported he had conversed with many others in Virginia about the virtues of hedge-style moriculture over dispersed orchards of single trees, and that 'having discoursed of this new way to all here, they may be inclinable this way'. Also revealing of wider uptake and experimentation was Moray's derision for the Virginian methods of killing the insects before they ruptured the cocoons. He noted that 'here is a great difficulty, they lying sometimes 3 or 4 daies in the sun, before they dye, and bring many inconveniencies' for planters who 'have endevored the work'.[191] In this way, silk as an experimental product opened up cultural and discursive space for planters to contemplate land use, labour disposal, and rearing practices – offering creative testing grounds, often with low risks indexed against low expectations.

As the act's 1666 deadline approached, with heavy fines in prospect for those, unlike Moray, who had not fulfilled or exceeded their mulberry obligations, the matter once again required legislative intervention. On the positive side, there was no doubt that significant progress had been

---

[189] McIlwaine, *Journals of Burgesses*, 2: 21; Hening, *The Statutes at Large*, 2: 191, 199.
[190] Hening, *The Statutes at Large*, 2: 202.
[191] Mr Muray, dated at Mockjack Bay in Virginia, to Robert Moray, 1665 (read 28 March 1666), Archives of the Royal Society, EL/M1/36a. An extract of this letter was published as 'An Extract of a Letter, Sent Lately to Sir Robert Moray out of Virginia', *Philosophical Transactions of the Royal Society* 1, no. 12 (1666): 201–2.

made: in November 1666 the House of Burgesses certified that Major Thomas Walker had planted 70,397 white mulberry trees between 1664 and 1665 in Gloucester County alone.[192] But the burgesses preferred to cancel the penalties for mulberry neglect, when faced with the reality of levying unpopular and potentially substantial charges at a point when tobacco prices were tanking, taxes were rising, internal and external defences required urgent investment, and Berkeley's faction and other planters were struggling to secure social stability. Reasoning that there had been 'successe' in 'evident demonstrations' (without specifying whom or when), they conveniently determined that proof of concept had now done away with the need for further sanctions, repealing the fine for failing to plant mulberry trees two months before it came into effect, on the basis that 'every one [who] intended to make silke will now propagate [trees] voluntarily'.[193] The lifting of mulberry proscriptions coincided with the assembly's determination to send the public gift of Virginia silk to Charles II, and they were left in no doubt as to the monarch's approval: in light of his glowing letter of November 1668 commending their 'laudable industry [which] … We esteeme much', the House of Burgesses reissued the bounty of fifty tobacco pounds for each pound of raw silk produced, describing it in October 1669 as a commodity which brought present 'honour and reputation' and future 'benefitt and profit'.[194]

Evidence of production bears out some of the claims in the improvement literature about the leadership and labour offered by women, such as Elizabeth Burbage Streater on her extensive plantations at Elizabeth City.[195] The demands placed on their domestic management could be significant. One husband worried that his wife, in trying 'to be an Instrument to sett forward the designe of silke', had taken on too much additional workload, besides the 'Care of house Keepinge', managing a large household and 'a greate da[i]ry the Charge where of lyeth all upon her'.[196] Some three years later Mary Ward was still persisting, but had not wound off the cocoons she had raised because she deemed them too few to be worth making a reel. She was trying to assess the relative value of either selling the cocoons or reeled raw silk, but in an apologetic

[192] McIlwaine, *Journals of Burgesses*, 2: 39. Malcolm Hart Harris, *Old New Kent County: Some Account of the Planters, Plantations, and Places* (Baltimore, MD: Genealogical Publishing Co., 2006), 456.

[193] Hening, *The Statutes at Large*, 2: 241.

[194] King Charles II to Governor and Council of Virginia, 25 November 1668, CO 1/23/87; Hening, *The Statutes at Large*, 2: 272.

[195] Hartlib, *Reformed Virginian Silk-Worm*, 34. Hening, *The Statutes at Large*, 1: 405.

[196] Laurence Ward to Susannah Chidley, 12 July 1653, FP: 1231.

note about prices, a female correspondent noted that nobody sent cocoons 'to ye merchant'.[197] Other women passed on their knowledge or resources in ways that revealed their involvement – as when Sarah Thompson Willoughby (of Lower Norfolk County), on her death in 1674, bequeathed a book with 'directions for planting mulberry trees' to her children.[198] Though more circumstantial, the wife of Alexander Moray was dispatched from Virginia five weeks after his letter to Sir Robert Moray about sericulture on his estate, which described her as a capable agent to 'acquaint you of my endevors'.[199] That a thirteen-year absence in England did not interrupt Edward Digges's Virginian silk exploits is also a strong indicator that his mulberry estates and silk production were being co-directed by others, probably his wife Elizabeth; one Virginian remembered in the early eighteenth century that when they reached 'where a great gate stood near a mulberry tree, they were then in Madam Diggs' land'.[200]

In the course of their limited production, Virginia silk experimenters took steps that addressed claims and possibilities raised in the reformist literature. Fears that silkworms were damaged by Virginian thunderstorms were felt to be overstated – though the apocalyptic hurricane recorded by Thomas Ludwell in August 1667 must have ravaged the many thousands of young white mulberry saplings, having ruined plantations, fields, fences, houses, and orchards.[201] Older claims about the human nurturers – like Bonoeil's that 'even the very breath of one that hath taken' tobacco could cause seizures and mortality amongst the silkworms – were likewise challenged, Digges noting that 'I never observed that the smell of tobacco, or smells which are rank, did any ways annoy the Silk-Worms, which is contrary to the general received opinion.'[202]

---

[197] Letter from Mary Ward to Virginia Ferrar, 4 April 1656, FP: 1261.

[198] Edward W. James, 'Libraries in Colonial Virginia', *The William and Mary Quarterly* 3, no. 1 (July 1894): 44; Warren M. Billings, ed., *The Old Dominion in the Seventeenth Century: A Documentary History of Virginia, 1606–1689* (Chapel Hill: University of North Carolina Press, 1975), 141.

[199] Mr Muray, dated at Mockjack Bay in Virginia, to Robert Moray, 1665 (read 28 March 1666), Archives of the Royal Society, EL/M1/36a.

[200] Digges letters cited in Barham, *An Essay upon the Silkworm*, 99, 101. Deposition of Richard Smith, 1 March 1738, Charles County Court Records, Maryland State Archives, Book T2 (1735–1739): 426.

[201] Thomas Ludwell to Lord Berkeley of Stratton, 4 November 1667, 'Virginia in 1667–1669',*The Virginia Magazine of History and Biography* 19, no. 3 (1911): 251. See also damage to trees mentioned in Thomas Glover, 'An Account of Virginia, Its Scituation, Temperature, Productions, Inhabitants, and Their Manner of Planting and Ordering Tobacco &c.', *Philosophical Transactions of the Royal Historical Society of London* 11 (1676): 635.

[202] John Bonoeil and Virginia Company of London, *His Maiesties Gracious Letter to the Earle of South-Hampton, Treasurer, and to the Councell and Company of Virginia Heere*

Adjustments were also proposed to offset the lower quality of raw silk reeled off by novices, as when instructions suggested combining fifteen, eighteen, or twenty cocoons together (rather than the lower numbers of filaments preferred for thin raw silk of higher value).[203]

These positive steps to dismiss erroneous theories or advance useful knowledge were not only necessary to any hope of colonial development, but also of interest to a growing body of intellectuals in Europe (see Plate 4). Virginian planters were assaulted with demands from 1660 by the group of virtuosi from England, Ireland, and Scotland who met at Gresham College (receiving institutional recognition in 1662 as the 'Royal Society of London for the Improvement of Natural Knowledge'), first in response to a gift of silk sent by the Virginia councillor Col. Thomas Pettus.[204] It was silk that offered the entry point for Virginians into this illustrious group, when Edward Digges's letters on his experiments were read out by Dudley Palmer in September 1663.[205] In response, members of the Royal Society proposed ways to understand and improve production: John Pell suggested sending Virginian silkworm seed to Languedoc 'to see how that would thrive there'; others compared Digges's findings with those lately shared by a French gentleman, Balthasar de Monconys; Robert Hooke appropriated some of the sample to look at through his microscope. Lastly, Abraham Hill undertook to get the 'parcel of coarse silk' from Virginia wrought up 'into a Stuffe for a Cover to the Mace', the proud instrument of regal approval cherished by the Royal Society.[206] Until it was presumably discarded or replaced, unsheathing this piece of American silk marked the opening of each Royal Society meeting, as the mace was ceremonially placed on the table before the President.

If these connections constituted a cultural and intellectual breakthrough of sorts, what of the enduring failure to generate produce in quantity from Virginia? Deficiencies in mulberry availability and location

---

Commanding the Present Setting Vp of Silke Works, and Planting of Vines in Virginia (London: Printed by Felix Kyngston, 1622), 10. Digges cited in Barham, *An Essay upon the Silkworm*, 98–9.

[203] FP: 1187.

[204] T. Povey, 'Letter from Mr. Povey Concerning the Naturall Product of Virginia in Behalf of the Royall Society', *The William and Mary Quarterly* 1, no. 1 (January 1921): 66.

[205] Edward Digges to Dudley Palmer, 29 September 1663 (read 30 September 1663), Archives of the Royal Society, EL/D1/1. Raymond Phineas Stearns, *Science in the British Colonies of America* (Chicago: University of Illinois Press, 1970), 177.

[206] Minutes of the Royal Society, 30 September 1663, Archives of the Royal Society, JBO/1/150. Samples of the Virginian silkworms and their 'bags' were also kept and documented as part of the Royal Society's collection, as recorded in Nehemiah Grew, *Musaeum Regalis Societatis, or, A Catalogue & Description of the Natural and Artificial Rarities Belonging to the Royal Society* (London: W. Rawlins, 1681), 175–6.

had been significantly redressed in mid-century Virginia, and there were far fewer complaints about problems with stock. However, exchanges in the 1660s suggest that the lack of expertise in silkworm rearing and raw silk reeling was much harder to overcome (enigmatic Armenians excepted). Securing experts was paramount on the agenda in 1663, when one tract pressed the Crown to 'procure us on good Salaries able men for Silk'.[207] And even when the king's Virginian silk arrived in the summer of 1668, it was accompanied with an appeal for the monarch to command 'men better skilled in that and other Staple Comodities . . . to come and reside amongst us'.[208] William Berkeley used the enquiries sent out to governors by the streamlined Council of Foreign Plantations in 1670 to reiterate the point, observing that 'of late, we have begun to make silk', and that given the high uptake in mulberry plantations, Virginia lacked only 'skilfull men from Naples or Sicily to teach us the art of making it perfectly'. He despaired that the mercantilist system of Navigation Acts had the effect that 'we cannot procure any skilfull men for one now hopefull commodity, silk'.[209]

Lacking experts who could foster sustainable production in a period when political winds were fair, the pursuit of silk would be further compromised when the edifice of cultural and economic power that Berkeley had constructed in Virginia began to show cracks in the early 1670s. It would come crashing down (with much of Jamestown) in the 1676 rebellion against him led by Nathaniel Bacon and a cadre of planters and labourers who had been locked out of the route to self-advancement accessible to earlier generations like Edward Digges. Digges had died the year before, leaving his widow Elizabeth to erect a gravestone commending his ingenuity as an 'introducer and promoter of the silk manufacture in this colony'. But few were unaffected by Bacon's Rebellion, and the Royal Commission's post-facto report mentioned Elizabeth as having 'suffered considerably in her estate for her sonnes Loyalty', as had another Berkeley councillor, and silk producer, Sir Henry Chicheley.[210] Ultimately, the fact that William Berkeley and his circle had associated themselves so vigorously with diversification and sericulture meant that their political and personal discreditation from 1676 undermined further

---

[207] William Berkeley, *A Discourse and View of Virginia* (London, 1663), 8.
[208] Governor, Council, and Burgesses to King Charles II, 22 July 1668, NA CO 1/23/24–5.
[209] Hening, *The Statutes at Large*, 2: 514–15.
[210] J. L. Hall, 'Ancient Epitaphs and Inscriptions, in York and James City Counties, Virginia', *Proceedings of the Virginia Historical Society*, 1892, 107; 'Persons Who Suffered by Bacon's Rebellion: The Commissioners' Report', *Virginia Magazine of History and Biography* 5, no. 1 (1897): 64, 68.

will to experiment – either with laws, trees, or worms.[211] One survey that year highlighted that there was 'good store' of mulberry trees around many planters' houses, but that the silk 'design failing, they are now of little use amongst them'.[212] Berkeley was recalled to England in disgrace and died in 1677, buried in a crypt in Twickenham encased in his own lead cocoon. Like the sericulture he supported, he had once represented the grandeur of Virginia, but had aged beyond his usefulness, having failed to adapt to a changeable, competitive, and impatient environment.

Beginnings and Endings

By the 1680s, though tens of thousands of mulberry trees remained, raw silk had largely dropped out of agricultural and aspirational landscapes in England, the Chesapeake, and Bermuda. Absent the large reservoirs of expertise and indigenous labour that had made production in New Spain feasible in previous decades, and in the face of adverse environments – notably the climatic environment in the British Isles and the demographic environments in the Chesapeake and Bermuda – experimenters had made many hopeful beginnings but few satisfying endings. What function had the pursuit of silk served? As a target commodity it had energised and concentrated new ways of thinking about production, environment, labour, political economy, and colonialism. English silk had become an important rallying point for those seeking metropolitan credibility and for those embracing an alternative vision for regional productive relations and the imperial economy. In the process of engaging with – and sometimes surmounting – challenging shortfalls in resources (such as mulberry trees or silkworm supplies), proponents had forged new contacts and created and implemented new strategies: fast pinnaces, sumptuary regulations, intricate systems of fines and bounties. In the process of trying to understand why and how they failed at their endeavours, they plugged more extensively into emerging imperial bodies, scientific associations, and commercial circuits than they otherwise would have. Through the labour of the English writers and propagandists who sought to situate Virginia within a grander context, or the French and Armenians who joined Africans and Indians in the idiosyncratic quest for viable cocoons, the ambition of silk production brought visibility, monarchical kudos, and international reach to the English Atlantic.

Of course, how we measure the full impact of these efforts is problematic, for they were messily and indiscernibly incorporated into historical behaviours and outcomes. Even if the pursuit of silk production had possessed

---

[211] Billings, 'Sir William Berkeley and the Diversification of the Virginia Economy', 452–3.
[212] Glover, 'Account of Virginia', 628.

a determinative endpoint – such as the geological end point involved in the search for gold mines (which the Virginia Company also sanctioned, and which also ended disappointingly, with an embarrassing transatlantic consignment of a cargo of pyrite) – the journey up to that point was absorbing resources and energies, creating distractions and expectations, channelling knowledge and human capital.[213] Successful Atlantic plantation was not only delayed by failures, it was built on failures, and then defined and understood in reference to failures. In sericulture's case, the attempts in Virginia showcased many of the same qualities that would support the colony's rapid expansion: the creativity with which governing authorities adapted (or had to adapt) to economic opportunities; the willingness to treat the New World environment as a laboratory; and the exploitative flexibility with which elites disposed of available land and limited labour.

In the space of a few decades, and from a baseline of virtually no knowledge or practice, being far removed from stocks of white mulberries or *Bombyx mori*, the British had firmly embedded sericulture within their view of emergent Atlantic empire. An entire print literature had grown up around sericulture, broadening to incorporate gender and race into its parameters. The subject contributed to innovations in political economy and scientific discourse, forming an evidence base for future projection in British America, and new forms of botanical, biological, and commercial enquiry within the empire. Nor was its legacy entirely textual or theoretical: there were material products and by-products, in the form of exports, textiles, raw silk skeins, orchards, and buildings. William Berkeley boasted to John Evelyn about having 'presented the king with as much of silk made there, as made his Majesty a compleat suit of apparel'.[214] Occasional planters and servants, a growing proportion of whom were probably female, inhabited bizarre worlds within worlds during their Chesapeake seasons of experimentation: they repurposed their interior spaces, moistened mulberry leaves to make them more palatable to needy insects, built arbours and harried birds, selected moths for mating, and struggled to solve an array of problems in the colonial wilderness, often with little sense of how their improvised solutions might affect their final product. Bread ovens became abattoirs (for terminating pupae), cooking cauldrons became manufactories (for loosening cocoon filaments), caterpillar cadavers and cocoon husks became chickenfeed. And long after the deaths of Virginia's agricultural visionaries and sericulturists such as Edward Digges and William Berkeley, the

[213] David T. Rickard, *Pyrite: A Natural History of Fool's Gold* (New York: Oxford University Press, 2015), 14–20.
[214] John Evelyn, *Sylva: Or a Discourse of Forest Trees*, 4th ed. (London: Arthur Doubleday & Co., 1706), 213 (Evelyn got Berkeley's name wrong).

mulberry trees of all varieties continued to thrive – Robert Beverley characterising them in 1705 as growing 'there like a Weed'.[215]

Only after the deeper-lying challenges to silk production were again exposed during the second wave – relating to the deficiencies of the labour force, resource stock, and environment – did Virginia largely retreat from sericultural aspirations, completing its move in the 1670s, in step with other constitutional and socio-economic reforms in the region. Rejecting silk at the time had been a thinking, not an unthinking decision, and a decision reached after fairly extensive deployments of land and labour in the enterprise by some, watched closely by others. But because there was this legacy of meaningful investment in Virginia, and because there was no definitive or agreed article to blame for silk's failure to take hold, each new region breached by the British and several other European powers tended to have silk ambitions associated with it – like a kind of genetic abnormality carried in the DNA of Atlantic colonialism. When Swedish governor Johan Printz discovered his commission for settling the Delaware River region (as New Sweden) in 1643 contained an instruction to 'raise silk worms', he responded huffily that he had 'not been able to find an opportunity' and that the climate was cold, but found colonial authorities to be very insistent, citing first-hand evidence of the existence of mulberry trees in the region and reports from English Virginia.[216] The nagging hope, to which American projectors would return in regions beyond the Chesapeake, was that 'there may be rules found out' specific to the American environment that were yet unknown, that permitted successful silk production.[217] To Rev. Hugh Jones in 1724 – who ought to have been well qualified to pontificate, as a professor at the College of William and Mary who had studied geography, geometry, and astronomy at Oxford – Virginia's historical lack of silk was bewildering. He reflected that 'the only Reason that I know' related to the historic value of tobacco, which had now fallen so much that 'I can't imagine why the Silk Trade is

---

[215] Beverley, *History of Virginia*, 15, 58 (quote); see also William Byrd, *William Byrd's Natural History of Virginia: Or, The Newly Discovered Eden* (Richmond, VA: Dietz Press, 1940), 35; James Blair, Henry Hartwell, and Edward Chilton, *An Account of the Present State and Government of Virginia* (London: John Wyat, 1727), 4.

[216] Hampton L. Carson, 'Dutch and Swedish Settlements on the Delaware', *Pennsylvania Magazine of History and Biography* 33, no. 1 (1909): 10; Randall M. Miller and William Pencak, *Pennsylvania: A History of the Commonwealth* (University Park: Pennsylvania State University Press, 2002), 50. Amandus Johnson, ed., *The Instruction for Johan Printz, Governor of New Sweden* (Philadelphia: The Swedish Colonial Society, 1930), 90, 112, 129. Printz's successor Johan Rising was interrupted by the seizure of New Sweden by the Dutch before he could 'observe whether or not the climate will allow that silk worms can be reared'. Amandus Johnson, *The Swedish Settlements on the Delaware, 1638–1664*, 2 vols. (Baltimore, MD: Genealogical Pub. Co, 1969), 2: 744.

[217] Williams, *Virginia Richly and Truely Valued*, 35.

not there revived; which I am very positive would turn to a very great Account, if carried on by good Managers'.[218] Such logic, based exclusively on the success of tobacco (and the assumption of male labour), constituted a typically partial view of the problems and realities that had accompanied silk experimentation in the Chesapeake. And even as Jones wrote, French projectors some thousand miles to the south-west were endeavouring to build a new colony based around tobacco and silk, drawing on a very different national experience of sericulture.

[218] Hugh Jones, *The Present State of Virginia, 1724* (New York: Joseph Sabin, 1865), 60, 130 (quote).

4   France and New France

We implore your mercy God Almighty, in deigning to bless these silk-worms' eggs, whose work is necessary for the needs of Man and the glory of thy Church. May thy blessed power protect them, that they may hatch, and be shielded from destructive predators, from deadly diseases, and from all evils that might torment them. That by thy blessing, and the invocation of thy most Holy name, and by the grace of the Blessed Virgin Mary, they may be fertile. And that they may, in time, fulfil well their mission, for thy glory, and for the good of thy Church and thy faithful believers. In the name of Christ our Lord, Amen.

– 'Benedictio seminis bombicis' (benediction of the silkworm seed), translated from anonymous French Latin manuscript, 1695[1]

Early Modern Foundations, c.1500–1700

The murmuring of such prayers, at the end of the seventeenth century, echoed around many of the parish churches of rural southern France in the early summer. The practice of sericulture had taken a long time to find a niche within the crowded seasonal activities of the French peasantry, and to nestle in areas that had the requisite environmental and cultural attributes. But these idiosyncratic benedictions – tributes to both the value and the fragility of the creatures – reflected a sort of institutional appreciation that the silkworm had by now become a recognisable part of the landscape, the economy, and the society. From one viewpoint, south-eastern France lay at the end of the long hemispheric process of transmission described in the prologue. Its embracing of mulberries and silkworms originated in the pincer-like arrival of resources and expertise across both its Spanish and Italian borders, and would last through to the end of the

---

[1] Mistitled in Hervé Ozil, *Magnaneries et vers à soie: La sériciculture en pays vivarois et cévenol* (Lavilledieu: Ardèche, 1986) as 'femelle' (female), an error in the transcription of the first letter in the Latin 'semina' (seeds). Translation by the author. For other examples of such Catholic silkworm benedictions, see Noël Chomel, *Dictionnaire oeconomique* (Lyons, 1709), 69; J. J. Boucher, *Arts & techniques de la soie* (Paris: Editions Fernand Lanore,1996), 137–40.

nineteenth century. From another viewpoint, France's conversion to sericulture during the *Ancien Régime* owed more to top-down initiatives pioneered by ambitious monarchs, ministers, and agronomists. It was a story, usually told as a success story, of targeted patronage that culminated in the rise of Lyons and the creation of fashion, technical and technological mastery, and reputational hegemony in the world of luxury textiles. This second perspective on the spread of sericulture within provincial France, with its stress on effective intervention, partly explains why it served as a model for subsequent efforts in northern European states and their Atlantic colonies. Yet even as French silk policies and publications were being plagiarised elsewhere, French merchants and their powerful elite clients over the course of the seventeenth century remained deeply conscious that they had not secured an adequate quantity or quality of raw product. In a world of uncertain supply, precarious borders, and regional rebellion, the French state would also turn to the Atlantic as a means of satisfying its craving for raw silk.[2]

The arrival of sericulture in southern regions of France, as so often the case in Eurasia, had followed on the heels of the development of domestic silk manufacturing. But these were not heels that had walked smoothly or rapidly, but rather, from the late thirteenth century, stumbled and tottered forwards – occasionally lurching, sometimes halting, before gaining in poise and pace in the second half of the fifteenth century. Initially, early silk-processing operations and silk-weaving workshops were hard to sustain in French territories, drawing hostility from the merchants who monopolised the importing of foreign silk fabrics. They only really gained traction with the arrival of significant numbers of Italian workers and weavers in response to the dramatic upheavals of the fourteenth century. Amongst these upheavals was the establishment of the Papacy at Avignon in 1309, which was surrounded by the lands of the papal fief of Comtat Venaissin, and brought with it a rich clientele with great demand for high-quality silk fabrics, as well as a number of experts from Lucca. Silk manufacturing in France, and its corresponding demand for raw or semi-finished silk, thus largely arrived in a triangle defined by the peculiar enclave of Avignon and the Mediterranean trading centres of Marseille and Montpellier. As it happened, the triangle pointed to the commercial future of the fibre in France, straight up the River Rhône to the market city of Lyons, which was host to a number of key Florentine interests. The

---

[2] This section and the passages below owe much to the following sources: Beauquis, *Histoire économique de la soie*, 9–13, 51–5; Boucher, *Arts & techniques de la soie*, pp. 34–53; Salvatore Ciriacono, 'Silk Manufacturing in France and Italy in the XVIIth Century: Two Models Compared', *The Journal of European Economic History* 10, no. 1 (1981): 167–200; Molà, *The Silk Industry of Renaissance Venice*.

domestic silk industry grew to noticeable proportions over the course of the fifteenth century, when French royal authority began to establish a more effective presence in the country's southern provinces, and greater numbers of Italian artisans and entrepreneurs sought out new opportunities in French cities. When François I favoured Lyons with letters patent in 1536, welcoming with generous terms the relocation of experts from Piedmont, Genoa, and Avignon, Lyons soon become the primary site of both trade and manufacture.

The expansion of silk manufacturing in a number of cities, notably Avignon, Lyons, Saint Chamond, Tours, and Aubenas, far outstripped any development of sericulture in French territories. The spread of silk raising remained slow, and seemingly confined to a few regions in which mulberry leaves were being used as early as the thirteenth century, as in Anduze in Languedoc, where a 'trahendius' (silk reeler) was listed in a notarial act in 1296 and a silk throwsters' guild subsequently appeared.[3] French sericulture began by furnishing supplementary raw materials, an occasional trudging of mules down the dusty hill roads to Avignon workshops or the early mills of Nîmes. The increasing quantities of 'mountain silk' from Anduze and other sites in the Cévennes were raised from black mulberries and of a rougher and coarser nature, valued less for its use in the cutting-edge loom-woven fabrics than its use for sewing silk, embroidery, and as a component of mixed stuffs or heavy silks.[4] White mulberries, however, were also soon trickling into France, with plants brought from Naples and small nurseries established in parts of Provence and in the Comtat, near Montélimar, often initially by French noblemen seeking to emulate the cultures of contemporary Italy.[5] Emmanuel Le Roy Ladurie described a 'mulberry mania' breaking out in 1540–50, linking this to a 'craze for silks … with the influx of American silver and the spread of luxury'.[6] New plantations, almost certainly of white mulberries, were established at Montpellier, Narbonne, and in the Comtat and parts of Provence and the Vivarais, though these were young trees and not in the kinds of quantity that would yet have a major bearing on the wider market. They catered for small local industries, as in locations such as Nîmes, Toulouse, Orange, and Aix-en-Provence.

[3] Boucher, *Arts & techniques*, 40; Emmanuel Le Roy Ladurie, *The Peasants of Languedoc* (Urbana: University of Illinois Press, 1974), 71.
[4] Line Teisseyre-Sallmann, *L'industrie de la soie en Bas-Languedoc: XVIIe–XVIIIe siècles* (Paris: École nationale des chartes, 1995), 21–4.
[5] Pierre Clerget, 'Les industries de la soie dans la vallée du Rhône', *Les études rhodaniennes* 5, no. 1 (1929): 1–2.
[6] Le Roy Ladurie, *The Peasants of Languedoc*, 71.

This meant that weavers in France had to source raw and semi-finished silk for their looms from farther afield, a costly outlay. Around a third of the silk used by the industries of Lyons, Tours, and papal Avignon was of Persian or Spanish origin in the second half of the sixteenth century, while the majority came from Italian centres, including a significant quantity from the Venetian Terraferma, Lombardy and Piedmont.[7] Wars along the major trading routes particularly showed up French susceptibility to long raw silk supply chains, as when maritime Venetians and Turks contested the eastern Mediterranean (in 1537–40 and 1570–73) or when the Ottoman Sultan blocked the overland access of Safavid Persia to major markets in Syria (in 1514–18, and often in the later sixteenth century). One solution to this supply problem was for French interests to enter directly into the silk trade, and sure enough French ships – alongside the English and the Dutch – were soon challenging in the Levant, and French merchants competing in Aleppo to secure the greatest possible slice of the Persian yield. Italian sources of raw silk, though closer at hand, could also be temperamental, with total prohibitions issued on foreign exports of cocoons, raw silk, waste silk, silk thread, or all of the above by each of the states of Genoa, Tuscany, Savoy, Bologna, Mantua, and Milan in one or more years between 1560 and 1578.[8]

The French appetite for raw silk was one of the factors that drove them to turn westwards to the Atlantic Ocean and its possibilities in 1534. The year before, King François I had harassed Pope Clement VII into amending an earlier papal bull (*inter caetera*) of 1493 which had notionally limited European sovereignty over the 'unclaimed' New World to just Spain and Portugal. Now the French monarch dispatched Breton seafarer Jacques Cartier to the uncharted waterways of the north Atlantic, and though his commission has not survived, it is clear from other sources that Cartier was tasked with two priorities, both heavily influenced by the thriving Iberian example. The first was to search for precious gems and metals in the northern lands scouted out by the likes of Verrazano and Cabot, where there was little Spanish presence beyond large numbers of Basque fishermen. The second was to locate a shipping route to the Far East that would allow French traders to import fine products, notably silks and spices, into Europe, bypassing older Eurasian Silk Roads and rival oceanic routes around the Capes. Returning from a first foray in the autumn of 1534, Cartier was convinced that the St Lawrence River held the key to a transcontinental passage, and when frustrated by the rapids near Montreal in 1535, named them *Lachine* for China. Jean Alfonse,

---

[7] Molà, *The Silk Industry of Renaissance Venice*, 59, 241.
[8] Molà, *The Silk Industry of Renaissance Venice*, 255.

a navigator who piloted the expedition that followed Cartier's in 1542, was likewise convinced that the Saguenay River 'runneth into the sea of Cathay [China]' on account of the rapid tides at its entrance, and felt that the lands 'stretch[ed] toward Asia, according to the roundness of the world'.[9] It was an idea that died hard, and led Jean Nicollet more than ninety years later to pack a grand robe of finest damask silk, 'all strewn with flowers and birds of many colours' (either brocaded or embroidered) in anticipation of encountering Chinese diplomats or silk traders, as he set off to seek out a western exit to the Great Lakes in 1634.[10]

The first clear-cut expression of French hopes for silk production in the New World occurred while the English were still devoting most of their Atlantic plantation energies into subduing parts of Ireland. In 1562, Jean Ribault established the short-lived French Huguenot colony of Charlesfort in present-day Port Royal Sound (South Carolina), his report hinting at rich prospects of silk cultivation. Ribault justified this outpost to his patron, the Admiral Gaspard de Coligny, by emphasising the prospect of economic production and 'the commodities that may be brought thence'. He purportedly left a small garrison of around thirty men there with a rousing speech, urging them to 'make triall in this our first discoverie of the benfites and commodities of this newe lande'. Ribault felt that Terra Florida was a land 'of such fruitfulness, as cannot with tongue be expressed: and where in short time great and precious comodities might bee found', and had already identified 'Silke wormes in merueilous number, a great deale fairer and better then be our silk wormes.'[11] The Spanish stepped in to terminate this experimental threat, though their capacity to plug other whistling European punctures in their New World dominions would gradually decline in the decades to come. In a 1565 letter informing King Philip II of the brutal eradication of the French, and his establishment of a mission-fort Santa Elena in their stead, Pedro Menéndez de Avilés likewise listed silkworms amongst the potential high-yield products of the region that would make it 'of more value to Spain than New Spain or even Peru'. But the hardships of sustaining a fledgling settlement amongst often hostile Indians apparently precluded

---

[9] Jacques Cartier, Henry Percival Biggar, and Ramsay Cook, *The Voyages of Jacques Cartier* (Toronto: University of Toronto Press, 1993), 118; Hiram B. Stephens, *Jacques Cartier and His Four Voyages to Canada: An Essay, with Historical, Explanatory and Philological Notes* (Montreal: W. Drysdale & Co., 1890), 121, 125.

[10] Reuben Gold Thwaites, ed., *The Jesuit Relations and Allied Documents*, 73 vols. (Cleveland: Burrows Bros. Co, 1896); Norman K. Risjord, 'Jean Nicolet's Search for the South Sea', *Wisconsin Magazine of History* 84, no. 3 (2001): 34–43.

[11] Richard Hakluyt, *Divers Voyages Touching the Discovery of America and the Islands Adjacent*, ed. John Winter Jones (London: Printed for the Hakluyt Society, 1850), 113, xcvii, 109, 101.

any actual Spanish attempts at silk cultivation in future South Carolina before Santa Elena was abandoned in 1587.[12]

From 1564, even as Ribault and Avilés were spilling blood over the potential of Florida, one man seems to have played an important part in advancing the potential contribution of Languedoc and Provence to French silk yields. A professional gardener from Nîmes, François le Traucat, who received sanction from the city council keen to encourage local silk production, then began planting out a number of very large nurseries of white mulberry trees (perhaps as many as 4 million feet). Traucat's and his fellow nurserymen and landowners' less popularised efforts provided a maturing resource base for sericulture and a stock to facilitate future expansion in a crescent that eventually ran from the Swiss border to the Pyrenees. The diffusion of white mulberries first occurred in areas nearest the Mediterranean, and by the 1590s, was mainly spreading through lower Languedoc, often based on partnerships of merchants, landlords, and peasants operating a kind of sharecropping (*métayage*). In their reliance upon neighbouring materials, the transmission of expertise, and the availability of labour, these steps fulfilled the typical prerequisites of sericulture's transregional spread.[13]

The appetite and market for French-raised silk encouraged these introductions at the end of the sixteenth century. A concerted effort to address import dependency was made during the reign of the pragmatic Henri IV (1589–1610), a Protestant who had abjured his Calvinism to pacify the realm but retained a clique of Huguenot advisors and adopted a number of progressive agricultural policies. Barthélemy de Laffemas, as the king's one-time honorary tailor and valet, was all too well aware of the spectacular cost of arraying princely courts, and in his capacity from 1601 as Henri IV's controller-general of commerce, went to great lengths to try to popularise and systematise protectionist precepts across the kingdom, especially in relation to silk. The first measures were aimed outwards, as foreign-wrought silk imports were notionally prohibited, and silk merchants and weavers in Tours and Lyons encouraged with new privileges. But Laffemas aimed at nothing less than self-sufficiency in silk, and

---

[12] Avilés to Philip II, 15 October 1565, in Eugenio Ruidaz y Cara, *La Florida, Su Conquista y Colonización Por Pedro Menéndez De Avilés* (Madrid: Los Hijos de J. A. Garcia, 1893), 2: 98–9. For a wider discussion of Avilés's plans, see Woodbury Lowery, *The Spanish Settlements within the Present Limits of the United States: Florida, 1562–1574* (New York: Russell & Russell, 1959), 211–13. The *adelantados* (governor-explorers) and some Spanish royal officials had good contractual reasons to pursue remunerative agricultural projects, because their salaries were to be paid out of the produce of the country. 'Asiento', 30 March 1565, Ruídaz y Cara, *La Florida*, 2: 420.
[13] Le Roy Ladurie, *The Peasants of Languedoc*, 72–3, 130–1; Teisseyre-Sallmann, *Industrie de la soie en Bas-Languedoc*, 23.

brooked no dissent from his conviction that France's climate was perfect for raising silkworms, considering any claims to the contrary to be 'evil designs of certain French merchants, retailers of foreign silks'. Laffemas was largely ambivalent about whether the mulberry revolution should be of the white or black variety: he acknowledged that the whites could grow taller and be more troublesome to leaf-pick, but also that they were more universally to the taste of the silkworms, especially when young. He advocated a law compelling all property owners (including ecclesiastical) to plant mulberries, not just as fodder for silkworms, but also for their aesthetic beauty and medicinal properties – which apparently included curing toothache, indigestion, burns, and repelling poisons and vermin. Some of these ideas likely derived from the ageing (but horticulturally astute) Traucat himself, who was extended some royal patronage.[14]

A more intellectual influence behind many of these measures to more effectively nationalise silk cultivation was a Huguenot gentleman from the Vivarais (now Ardèche), Olivier de Serres, who would become a founding father of French agricultural science by virtue of his groundbreaking weighty publication, *Le théâtre d'agriculture et mésnage des champs* (1600), based on his experiments as a minor landowner at Pradel.[15] Serres's writings had come to the attention of Henri IV, and after some background checks, the king ordered him to print a pamphlet excerpting his encouraging sentiments and guidance on the planting of mulberry trees for the benefit of his subjects.[16] Moreover, in 1600 the king liaised with Serres

---

[14] Barthélemy de Laffemas, *Reiglement général pour dresser les manufactures en ce royaume et couper le cours des draps de soye et autres marchandises qui perdent et ruynent l'état* (Paris: C. de Monstroeil, 1597); Barthélemy de Laffemas, *Le tesmoignage certain du pofiict & reuenu des soyes de France: Par preuues certifiees du païs de Languedoc* (Paris: Pautonnier, 1602); Barthélemy de Laffemas, *Lettres et exemples de feu la reine mère, comme elle faisoit travailler aux manufactures et fournissoit aux ouvriers de ses propres deniers* (Paris, 1602); Barthélemy de Laffemas, *Preuve du plant et profit des meuriers, pour les parroisses des généralités de Paris, Orléans, Tours, et Lyon, pour l'année 1603* (Paris: Pautonnier, 1603), 5, 10, 12, 13; Barthélemy de Laffemas, *Le naturel et profit admirable du meurier* (Fauxbourg S. Germain-lez-Paris: F. Bourriquant, 1604); Barthélemy de Laffemas, *Instrvction dv plantage des mevriers povr messievrs dv clergé* (Paris: David Le Clerc, 1605). On the myths and realities of Traucat, see Teisseyre-Sallmann, *Industrie de la soie en Bas-Languedoc*, 25–6. For the similarities of claims about the wonders of mulberries: François le Traucat, *Discours abrégé tant sur les vertus et propriétés des mûriers, tant blancs que noirs ...* (Paris, 1606).
[15] Olivier de Serres, *Le Theatre d'agricvltvre et mesnage des champs d'Olivier de Serres, seignevr dv Pradel* (Paris: A. Savgrain, 1617). For a recent consideration, Jonathan Patterson, 'Avarice in the Moral Landscape of Olivier de Serre's Theatre d'Agriculture et Mesnage Des Champs (1600)', *Forum for Modern Language Studies* 49, no. 3 (2013): 244–56. More comprehensive treatments are: Jean Boulaine and Richard Moreau, *Olivier de Serres et l'évolution de l'agriculture*, Les Acteurs de La Science (Paris, France: L'Harmattan, 2002); Henri Gourdin, *Olivier De Serres: Science, expérience, diligence en agriculture au temps de Henri IV* (Arles: Actes Sud, 2001).
[16] Olivier de Serres, *La cueillette de la soye par la nourriture des vers qui la font* (Paris, 1599).

over the transformation of a number of royal gardens, whose parks would shortly be littered with white mulberry saplings. Thousands soon sprung up on the grounds of the Château de Madrid adjoining the Bois de Boulogne, the royal Arsenal in Paris, and at the spectacular Palace of Fontainebleau. Tens of thousands were installed at the royal behest (and cost) in several central and northerly regions with little prior engagement with moriculture, including Touraine, Orléanais, Lyonnais, and Beaujolais, with Laffemas estimating 60,000 alone transported from Languedoc to the environs of Paris. Under Laffemas's guidance, the king also ordered each French diocese to create a nursery of 50,000 trees, spending over 140,000 *livres* (approximately £10,000) on the project, and in theory at least, creating a reservoir in excess of 6.5 million mulberries. Large stocks of silkworms were secured and distributed through commissioned entrepreneurs, and premiums were offered for the purchase of the raw silk that, it was hoped, would soon be denting the import trade.

Measured against its national objectives, the project ended in failure. Many of the trees failed to prosper or died, like those in England, where environmental forces hindered usability. As in Virginia, the notion that silk raising could be learned by manual was also exposed as unsound, though in Laffemas's defence, he had cautioned his readers that in spite of silk's facility, 'it is necessary to undertake a little apprenticing ... from people expert in the said Art'. Nonetheless, in France's southerly regions, colloquially known as Le Midi, longer and warmer summers were more conducive to the successful symbiosis of leaves and their dependent silkworms, and significant numbers in nurseries lived on, as did the dream of an interventionist policy. Amidst the flurry of activity, de Serres also established that the white mulberry was the preferred variety on which political economists supportive of sericulture should concentrate – though he was careful not to disrespect the silk spun from black mulberry leaves, which remained 'necessary, in spite of its coarseness, to many works'.[17]

Not all policymakers welcomed these initiatives, and Henri IV's leading minister, the Duc de Sully, recorded in his 1638 memoirs that he had 'exclaimed loudly against this scheme', being particularly sceptical about the French climate which 'it is certain ... refuses silk', on account of its late spring and excessive moisture. He recalled a hot debate with the king

---

[17] Serres, *Le Theatre d'Agriculture*, 419–20. Isnard echoed that white mulberries were preferable for feeding silkworms on account of their leaves' tenderness, density, speed of growth, and superior product. Isnard, *Mémoires et instructions*, 52–3. By the mid-eighteenth century, French white mulberries themselves were divided into three types by Pomier: 'le Murier-sauvageon, le Murier-franc ou gressé, & le Murier d'Espagne', all of them described as superior to the black mulberry, but the best being the Murier-franc. L.Pomier, *L'art de cultiver les mûriers-blancs: D'élever les vers à soye, et de tirer la soye des cocons* (Paris: Lottin & J. H. Butard, 1754), 3–4.

in 1603 over the costs of importing silk weavers, increasing silkworm breeding, planting white mulberries, and erecting expensive buildings for reeling, though it is difficult to judge how much of this was being wise after the event. Sully took issue with what were becoming staple arguments in favour of silk: far from praising the easiness of labour, he was worried about introducing an occupation that might effeminise the stock of peasants from which French soldiers were drawn. While weakening the countryside, Sully expected the initiative would also damage the moral fibre of French cities, sketching again in heavily gendered terms the prospect of slothful townspeople flouncing about, whose glittering silk habits would conceal 'the manners of weak women'. Sully, who remained a staunch Calvinist, preferred to suppress the use of silks entirely and to turn the clock back to the austerity of earlier reigns than to somehow democratise them in the interests of the state, but the king informed him that he would 'rather choose to fight the King of Spain in three pitched battles' than create more sumptuary, 'whimsical' regulations that he struggled to defend. The royal will triumphed; nor would the king be diverted from his expensive plans to alter the Hôtel des Tournelles and its enclosure to fit it out as a model silk-raising site and manufactory. It accompanied the raised terrace known as the 'allée des Mûriers' added by Henri IV and his gardener Claude Mollet to the Jardin des Tuileries, which ran along what is now the Rue de Rivoli, and was imposingly planted with a double row of white mulberry trees, numbering in the thousands (and home now to two replanted replicas).[18]

Later Protestant political economists including Antoine de Montchrestien would continue to echo Laffemas's cries for self-sufficiency in silk, claiming in his 1615 *Treatise of Political Economy* that the subsidisation of sericulture in the reign of Henry IV had only collapsed in many regions because of the indifference of certain advisors. He viewed the initiative nonetheless as constituting a great success that ought to be revisited, having generated extensive output across Provence, Languedoc, Dauphiné, Touraine, Lyonnais, Beaujolais, and elsewhere. The poet in Montchrestien wished royal power might again 'give birth to forests of Séres' (the ancient name for the Chinese) and that this time the delivery might be seen through to its glorious conclusion, rather than 'losing all our courage in our designs, in coming across some difficulty'.[19] But royal power was moving definitively against the interests of France's Protestant population, with renewed Catholic

---

[18] *Memoirs of Maximilian de Bethune, Duke of Sully, Prime Minister of Henry the Great*, 5 vols. (Edinburgh: A. Donaldson, 1770).

[19] Antoine de Montchrétien, *Traicté de l'oeconomie politique: Dédié en 1615 au roy et à la reyne mère du roy* (Paris: E. Plon, 1889).

repressions climaxing in Cardinal Richelieu's remorseless siege of Protestant stronghold La Rochelle, and the disenfranchising Peace of Alès of 1629. Retreating beyond the reach of the state, at least one refugee, Antoine de Ridouet, the Baron de Sancé, wanted to settle families on the Carolina coast chartered by English King Charles I, 'upon a river where they can traffic in silk and other merchandise', listing the advantages to be gained from exploiting the 'great quantities of mulberry trees for silkworms' found south of Virginia. Largely because of inadequate recruitment, de Sancé's visionary plan and English partnership quickly collapsed.[20]

The preoccupation with nationalisation that characterised both the Protestant-conceived reforms of the silk industry and the French Catholic 'reforms' of the Protestants took on a new impetus of centralisation in the mid-seventeenth century. Willingness to revisit the idea of harnessing French domestic silk production was spurred on by the growing volume of imported raw silk coming in through the Mediterranean to Marseille, which doubled between 1613 and 1642, and the busy overland trade from Italy via Susa (Piedmont) and the Pont-de-Beauvoisin (Savoy), both catering to the increasing demands of the flourishing manufacturers in Tours and Lyons.[21] At Lyons, the silk industry was becoming ever more refined, with a *corporation* (guild) established by royal ordinance in 1600 that went on to codify and regulate working practices in the region. Reeling women (*dévideuses*), for instance, could take work to supply up to three master throwsters, and the Council of Masters kept a close eye on any waste or theft of raw silk along the way – mindful that compared to almost all other industries, the value of the raw material was proportionally hefty relative to the other costs of production.[22] The city's snaking rivers were themselves co-opted into service in the classification of international raw silk, with Italian products and those of the Comtat Venaissin channelled through the eastern Porte du Pont du Rhône while those from Spain had to enter by the southwestern ports of Saint-Just and

---

[20] America and West Indies, Colonial Papers (General Series) NA CO 1/5/68. Like its ill-fated precursor at Charlesfort, this plan was predominantly orientated towards economic ambitions (silk, salt, wine and olives), with the religious element operating only as an organising and recruiting structure. Bertrand Van Ruymbeke, *From New Babylon to Eden: The Huguenots and Their Migration to Colonial South Carolina* (Columbia, SC: University of South Carolina Press, 2006), 2–5.

[21] M. Morineau, 'Flottes de commerce et trafics français en Méditerranée au xviie siècle (Jusqu'en 1669)', *XVIIe Siècle* 86 (1970): 135–71; Junko T. Takeda, *Between Crown and Commerce: Marseille and the Early Modern Mediterranean* (Baltimore, MD: Johns Hopkins University Press, 2011).

[22] Paul Chartron, *Le Moulinage de la soie et la corporation sous l'Ancien Régime, xviie et xviiie siècles* (Lyons: A. Rey, 1943), 5–8, 17.

Saint-Georges.[23] The increase in the scale of activity and technical improvements, including Claude Dangon's draw loom for weaving luxury figured silks, augured well for what Salvatore Ciriacone has neatly described as Lyons's 'commercial emancipation' from Italian influence. But Lyons would continue to depend on supplies of Italian raw silk, much of it from Messina and Milan, and, for its most illustrious fabrics, upon the distinctive regularity of the silk yarn thrown in Bolognese mills, a trade which remained under the control of Italian merchant houses for much of the seventeenth century.[24] The pattern was strikingly reminiscent of Japan's reliance on neighbouring Chinese raw silk for a bedrock of consistent silk yarn for its looms, supplemented by cruder and rougher domestic local product that was about to have improvement imposed from above.[25]

The principal architect of silk centralisation was Louis XIV's councillor from 1649, the great financial and fiscal reformer Jean-Baptiste Colbert, who energetically addressed the silk industry along with almost every other site of commerce and manufacture in the kingdom. Colbert sought to more effectively control and connect together French economic activity at all levels, to cut back on corruption and local variation, and to systematise a new order that placed heavy emphasis on revitalising French colonialism and manufacturing (especially textiles). He and his administrative successors linked national power, wealth, and commerce in a kind of realpolitik that set little stock by morality when it came to the market, viewing luxury, including silks, as just another field of international competition.[26] The bundle of ordinances and regulations, especially between 1667 and 1687, that sought to protect and reshape the silk industry has been documented elsewhere.[27] Lyons was raised further ahead of the pack to become the only *bureau des douanes* (tax office) for overseas silk goods, with interior customs between the provinces suppressed in favour of Lyons officials acting as the supreme guardians of quality and revenue, cementing the city's pre-eminence and paving the way for its golden era in design and manufacturing.[28]

[23] Clerget, 'Les industries de la soie dans la vallée du Rhône', 20.
[24] Ciriacono, 'Silk Manufacturing in France and Italy in the XVIIth Century: Two Models Compared', 171–5.
[25] Souza, *The Survival of Empire: Portuguese Trade and Society in China and the South China Sea, 1630–1754*, 59; Debin Ma, *Textiles in the Pacific, 1500–1900*, The Pacific World (Aldershot, Hampshire, England: Ashgate/Variorum, 2005), 37–8.
[26] John Shovlin, *The Political Economy of Virtue: Luxury, Patriotism, and the Origins of the French Revolution* (Ithaca, NY: Cornell University Press, 2006), 20–1.
[27] Ciriacono, 'Silk Manufacturing in France and Italy in the XVIIth Century: Two Models Compared', 176–7.
[28] Boucher, *Arts & techniques*, 50; Teisseyre-Sallmann, *Industrie de la soie en Bas-Languedoc*, 46–53.

Colbert approached sericulture with no less purpose than he did the silk trade and silk manufacture. He pursued a campaign of plantation, hoping to foster new nurseries, including in areas north of Le Midi (Berry, Angoumois, Orléanais, Maine), by offering an incentive of twenty-four *sols* (roughly two shillings) per foot of land planted in white mulberry trees of three years' growth. He also encouraged the plantation of mulberries such that they lined the great highways of the realm and the riversides and canals. At Colbert's insistence, Marseille invited Levantine silk merchants and experts to resettle within French borders from 1669 bringing their skills, Ottoman connections, and materials to aid in the contest for silk sovereignty, though the door of naturalisation did not remain open for long, partly reflecting Marseillais qualms.[29] Structural factors were equally important, however, for French silk-throwing operations expanded into new regions of the Rhône valley in the late seventeenth century to benefit from market opportunities and water power, in the process stimulating and underwriting silk raising. In due course, the output of domestic silk rose noticeably, with major raw silk fairs taking place in the summer at Alès and Beaucaire in Languedoc, and the commodity offering an important source of cash income for peasants being squeezed by margins and taxes elsewhere. Gradually, through trial, error, and investment, pockets of the French countryside – such as the villages of the Drôme valley – developed familiarity and competence in sericulture, providing they could access mulberry trees, sustain silkworms at an adequate temperature, and draw on a cheap, diffuse, and flexible labour force able to devote intensive time seasonally to a cash crop.[30]

Colbert's measures were accompanied by a second tranche of publications, the most significant of which was Christophle Isnard's lengthy 1665 work, dedicated to Colbert, entitled *Reports and Instructions for the Planting of White Mulberries, and the Nourishing of Silkworms*. On its title page it paid tribute to the example of Henri IV, and included an image showing the progression of mankind and silk, from a naked woman clasping leaves (under a banner reading 'nature begins') to a distinguished tailor holding forth a bolt of silk fabric ('art achieves') on either side of a flourishing mulberry tree (see Fig. 4.1).[31] For all its grandeur, Isnard's work, in truth,

---

[29] An edict that year insisted that silks from the Mediterranean and Near Asia (including Italian, Levantine (Turkish and Persian), and North African silks) could only arrive into France through Marseille or Rouen. Takeda, *Between Crown and Commerce: Marseille and the Early Modern Mediterranean*, 80, 96–102.

[30] Production of raw silk would muscle in on alternatives such as wine, oil, and grain. E. Le Roy Ladurie *Les Paysans de Languedoc* (Paris: SEVPEN, 1966), 1: 441. For the museum, see: www.atelier -museedelasoie-taulignan.com/musee/accueil/index.html.

[31] Isnard, *Mémoires et instructions*, 204.

Figure 4.1 Imaginative frontispiece to French sericulture tract (1665).
Frontispiece from Christophe Isnard, *Mémoires et instructions pour le plant des meuriers blancs* (Paris, 1665). Exergues read 'Nature Begins, Art Achieves' and 'True Metamorphoses', suggesting the spontaneous generation method of silkworms through feeding cows mulberry leaves.
Collection Bibliothèque municipale de Lyon

was derivative and pedestrian. Isnard apologised for his 'provincial' background, explaining that he had admired Paris's mulberries over the last fourteen or fifteen years, and justifying his propagation of the silken gospel because of the direct encouragement of the king after witnessing his own silk samples in the early 1660s. He stressed that the same arguments that had motivated Henri IV and his advisors were now amplified by the 'sums incomparably greater' spent on silk in the kingdom by the late seventeenth century.[32] Isnard depicted silk as a means of sustaining the Parisian poor, and alleviating the burden on lowly families, giving them an incentive not just in terms of income but also in ennobling themselves by virtue of matching the sericultural activities of 'personnes de condition' in the provinces.[33] His vision of an energised silk-raising industry in the north made space for home manufacturing, proposing that the lower orders might bypass merchants to generate their own clothing and upholstery (part silk, part wool) – though this chimed less well with Colbert's economic tenets.[34] Isnard also prefigured later, more desperate pamphlets (and echoed Laffemas), by listing a host of other uses to which mulberry trees might be diverted besides sericulture – the trunks fit for masts, the bark for cordage, the fruit for animal forage, and the leaves for sustaining other beasts, particularly hogs. Isnard hoped that new projects might rejuvenate the avenues planted out by gardeners at the start of the seventeenth century, implying that the Phoenix-like metamorphoses of the silkworms might be paralleled in the ascension to greatness of a new silk region.[35]

Where his writing was original, it tended to relate to recommendations for Paris, such as his suggestion that because of the city's poor air, silkworms would prosper best in higher rooms, and be sheltered from the loud noises of artisanal workshops such as blacksmiths.[36] Isnard recommended that the best silkworm seed be secured from Spain, also commending sources in Piedmont and Bologna, which benefited from new stocks secured from Sicily and the Levant. But he made the point, salient for future Atlantic experimenters, that it was very hard to discern from the eggs what the quality would ultimately be.[37] His comments on the care of silkworms, like his cover illustration, were suggestive of the kinds of heavily gendered assumptions that increasingly guided conventional wisdom on sericulture, including in the work of English writers. For instance, his recommended method of hatching the eggs was by warming them in female cleavages or armpits for two days, and he advised that women were not only not to touch the worms during their periods of menstruation, but

---

[32] Isnard, *Mémoires et instructions*, 17.   [33] Isnard, *Mémoires et instructions*, 23.
[34] Isnard, *Mémoires et instructions*, 24.
[35] Isnard, *Mémoires et instructions*, 39–40, 283, 287.
[36] Isnard, *Mémoires et instructions*, 90, 100.   [37] Isnard, *Mémoires et instructions*, 104–7.

not even to enter the rooms, 'because they would make them die' in a kind of associative purgation.[38] Isnard also warned that it was important to be able to replenish the variation of stocks of silkworm seed, for though they were at their best in the second year in France, by their fourth or fifth cohort, the quality of worms (and their silk) tended to deteriorate.[39] Figures from 1688 seem to attest to this practice, for Jacques Savary des Brûlons (Louis XIV's inspector-general of customs) estimated that silk producers in Provence and Languedoc consumed 250 lb of silkworm seed annually – partly from their own sources, but also from Spain and Portugal by land and sea, valued at 30–35 *sols* (just over two shillings) per ounce.[40]

The extension of French domestic sericulture in the seventeenth century – that either coincided with Colbert's reforms or derived from them – was ultimately not enough to keep pace with the nation's growing silk manufacturing. Even after Colbert's mulberries had time to mature, in 1697, of 6,000 bales of silk entered at Lyons, only 1,200 were of French origin.[41] The progress was a matter of import complementation rather than import substitution, and Savary des Brûlons noted that most of the raw silk produced in Languedoc tended to be worked up in provincial manufacturing centres, and particularly those of Toulouse, Montpellier, Nîmes, Alès, and smaller towns along the Rhône. There, French-grown silk figured prominently in the manufacture of sewing thread, trimmings, embroidery and passementerie, ribbons, small fabrics and various stuffs and flowered taffetas akin to those of Florence and Avignon.[42] Meanwhile, imports of raw silk and thrown silk continued to pour in overland from Italy (of high grade) and through Marseille (of variable quality, see Fig. 4.2). For while some Italian centres were manifestly in decline by the seventeenth century, many continued to thrive, exporting silk yarns that depended on generations of knowhow alongside great technological sophistication and commercial infrastructure. Such

---

[38] Isnard, *Mémoires et instructions*, 125–6, 165. Caution about menstruation repeated by Chomel, *Dictionnaire oeconomique*, 67.

[39] Isnard, *Mémoires et Instructions*, 278–9.

[40] Jacques Savary des Brûlons and Philémon Louis Savary, *Dictionnaire universel de commerce: Contenant tout ce qui concerne le commerce qui se fait dans les quatre parties du monde . . . le detail du commerce de la France en general et de la ville de Paris en particulier*, 3 vols. (Paris: Estienne et fils, 1748), 1: 158, 168, 172.

[41] Estimate of *intendant* Herbigny, cited in Clerget, 'Les industries de la soie dans la vallée du Rhône', 3. Jean Peyrot notes that recorded weights of silk bales never reached their administrative weight, usually being around 110 lb, and also arriving in smaller 'ballotins' of 40–50 lb. Jean Peyrot, 'Les techniques du commerce des soies au xviiie siècle, à travers les documents commerciaux et comptables des fabricants de soieries', *Bulletin du Centre d'histoire Économique et Sociale de la Région Lyonnaise* 1 (1973): 35.

[42] Savary des Brûlons and Savary, *Dictionnaire*, 1: 213–14.

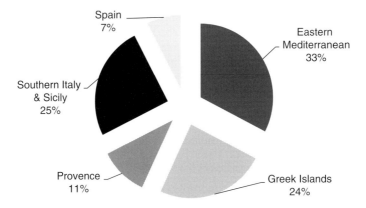

Figure 4.2 French raw silk sources registered proportionally through Marseille (1688). This chart is based on estimates of the origin of 1,320.5 bales (*c.*250 lb each) of silk (overwhelmingly raw but including 175 bales of silk worked into 'organsin' from Messina). A further 517.5 bales arrived as 'ardasse' silk, but these had mixed origins so were excluded from the proportional estimate. This gives a total of 1,838 bales or 459,500 lb of raw silk. The major sources were Smyrna (now Izmir), Aleppo, Cyprus, the Cyclades, Messina, Palermo, and Calabria, and for the Spanish silk, Catalunia, Valencia, and Majorca. Savary des Brûlons, *Dictionnaire universel de commerce*, 1: 158, 168, 172, 190, 194–8.

conditions were unrealisable in the socio-economic environment of rural meridional France in the short term, especially with the additional handicap of the formal hegemony of Lyons as an epicentre through which all silk materials must theoretically pass.[43]

In spite of their failure to secure an adequate domestic source of raw silk for their manufacturers in the second half of the seventeenth century, and the haemorrhaging of Huguenot expertise to rival producers, the continued success of the French industry was assured thanks to its pioneering of what has been termed a 'fashion cycle'. Powered by the splendour of the court of the Sun King, this involved close collaboration between the patterned-silk manufacturers centred in Lyons and their principal customers, Paris's influential *marchands-merciers*, and it focused on the rolling out of inspirational new designs in such a way as to impose a fashion. Design innovation became a driving force, dragging silk consumers in its wake, and jealously guarded in the hands of the professionally trained designers and artisans associated with major firms. Each step of the

[43] Teisseyre-Sallmann, *Industrie de la soie en Bas-Languedoc*, 35–43, 48–9.

process played its part in the creation of these exquisite fabrics: novelty in the fine arts lubricated technical ingenuity in weaving, which powered innovative practices in business organisation and marketing, which relayed cutting-edge preferences back to designers. Like greyhounds inured to an artificial hare, from the 1670s, wealthy clients in Paris and beyond now found themselves chasing in patterns largely controlled by the industry, which supported around 10,000 looms in the 'Grande Fabrique' of Lyons alone by the 1680s.[44] Lingering French frustration at needing to import lots of Italian raw silk and organzine yarn was offset by the knowledge that the Italian peninsula was becoming a dependent market for French-exported silk fabrics of various types.

Neither the quickening integration of the French silk industry, nor the fashion cycle, however, ever resulted in watertight systems impervious to external influence. For one thing, geography and a shortfall of primary materials determined that raw and semi-finished silks arrived not just in Marseille and Lyons but entered the kingdom through Nantes, Toulouse, Lille (via Antwerp), and elsewhere, leading to bitter municipal squabbling over the nature of exemptions and duties.[45] There was an unresolved tension between the desire to create a national luxury industry (which required concentration) and the desire to generate national production (which required diffusion). The dream of impermeable silk integration receded dramatically with the 1685 Revocation of the Edict of Nantes, whereby France inadvertently sponsored the establishment of a suite of silk industries in ambitious Protestant countries by ejecting thousands of Huguenots. The damaging effects of the Revocation on the French silk industry has been well mapped out – it heralded a long and intense crisis,

---

[44] Carlo Poni, 'Fashion as Flexible Production. The Strategies of the Lyons Silk Merchants in the Eighteenth Century', in *World of Possibilities. Flexibility and Mass Production in Western Industrialization*, ed. C. F. Sabel and J. Zeitlin (Cambridge: Cambridge University Press, 1997), 37–74; Lesley Ellis Miller, 'Paris–Lyons–Paris: Dialogue in the Design and Distribution of Patterned Silks in the Eighteenth Century', in *Luxury Trades and Consumerism in Ancien Regime Paris*, ed. R. Fox and A. Turner (Aldershot: Ashgate, 1998), 163–5; Ciriacono, 'Silk Manufacturing in France and Italy in the XVIIth Century: Two Models Compared', 180–5. For a classic statement on the design cycle in silks and its rolling out to other centres, see Peter Thornton, *Baroque and Rococo Silks* (London: Faber and Faber, 1965).

[45] At Lorient, the base of the Company of the East Indies, silks tended to be purchased by Parisian firms while Nantes merchants bought up the Indian cottons and cowries that were central to the French African trade. Paul Butel, 'France, the Antilles, and Europe, 1700–1900', in *The Rise of Merchant Empires: Long-Distance Trade in the Early Modern World, 1350–1750*, ed. James D. Tracy (Cambridge: Cambridge University Press, 1990), 170. On municipal complaints and adjustments to some of the rules and regulations describing the tariff system for raw silks between 1664 and 1713, see Savary des Brûlons and Savary, *Dictionnaire*, 3: 206–7; Teisseyre-Sallmann, *Industrie de la soie en Bas-Languedoc*, 49–53.

worsened by Louis XIV's incessant wars, while leaking vital manufacturing expertise and capital to neighbouring states, whose competition in a short time would prove surprisingly strong. Though some silk raisers fled, a higher proportion of emigrants comprised those farther up the industrial chain: spinners, throwsters, dyers, ribbon-makers, weavers, and their correlate workforces who poured into Switzerland, the Low Countries, German states, the British Isles, and farther afield. Nonetheless, by undermining the foundations of the urban industry and its demand, the Revocation deepened the existing economic malaise in the Midi, and dealt body blows to silk production, especially in the Protestant cantons.[46]

The yearning to diversify the sources of French raw silk supply reached out across and around the Atlantic between 1670 and 1730. At the close of the seventeenth century, with all of this new competition in motion and some disastrous European weather patterns in the 1690s wiping out several domestic raw silk harvests, it was more apparent than ever that the French industry needed to secure reliable sources of raw silk from abroad. Increasing market share in the Levant, in Persia, and in the East Indies was one way forward, though the latter (cheap Indian and Chinese raw silks) were somewhat contaminated by concerns about yarn quality and wider contemporary fears of market saturation by Far Eastern finished goods. Another way forward was to sustain a dominant position in the buying up of Italian raw silks and silk yarns, though this meant having to rely excessively upon wily Genoese merchants.[47] In his analysis, Jacques Savary des Brûlons therefore categorically recommended not only that his compatriots pursue 'all sorts of goods and works of silk' for consumers in the Atlantic world (especially silk stockings), but aim to transform French possessions overseas into a zone of silk production.[48] Hoping that an effort by the French East Indies Company interests to settle Madagascar might foster sericulture exchanges, Isnard acclaimed in 1669 that 'We travel the Seas from one side to the other', and attention would soon turn westward.[49]

As in New Spain and Virginia, between 1670 and 1730, eager French planters and settlers would latch on to this imperial ambition with vigour, seizing opportunities that offered preferential treatment and patronage. The French attempts bore some of the hallmarks of the Spanish,

---

[46] Beauquis, *Histoire économique de la soie*, 11; Le Roy Ladurie, *The Peasants of Languedoc*, 299; Ciriacono, 'Silk Manufacturing in France and Italy in the XVIIth Century: Two Models Compared', 191–3; Owen Stanwood, *The Global Refuge: Huguenots in an Age of Empire* (Oxford: Oxford University Press, 2020).

[47] Ciriacono, 'Silk Manufacturing', 196.

[48] Savary des Brûlons and Savary, *Dictionnaire*, 1: 388–98 (quote), 483, 487, 491, 506, 515.

[49] Christophle Isnard, *Les vers à soie presentez au roy* (Paris: By the author, 1669), 2.

including their familiarity with (and access to) silkworms and an experienced Old World reservoir of labour (see Plate 5). They also shared some features with the English efforts, in their grappling with environmental difficulties, struggle to overcome difficulties of oceanic transit, and exposure of demographic deficiencies within vulnerable settler societies. The efforts to raise silk in France's Atlantic outposts also revealed that female initiative was central to experimentation and to the limited production that was achieved.

Prospecting the New World, 1665–1740

Silk's occasional appearance in early New France – and the vast indigenous interior it encroached upon – initially acted as a means of impressing upon inhabitants and indigenous peoples the power of the church and state, as when Jesuit fathers carried 'the most beautiful silk fabric' with them to add to the majesty of services performed or improvised amongst Indian peoples.[50] By the mid-seventeenth century New France – occupied sporadically by the English and ravaged by Haudenosaunee (Iroquois) Indians – was a disorderly scarecrow of a colony whose mismatched clothes and limbs bespoke the eclectic interests that had been drawn to the northeastern corner of the continent in earlier decades. Centred on Quebec (Canada), which was no more than a large village by European standards, it incorporated fishing communities around Newfoundland, a handful of farming settlements in Acadia, fur traders and merchants delving into the interior along the waterways of the St Lawrence, and Jesuit priests prospecting the harvest of Native American souls that had enticed them into the heart of the continent, via the Great Lakes and the Mississippi River.

The arrival of a new *intendant* hand-picked by Colbert in 1665, Jean Talon, marked a turning point in how the French state treated its Atlantic possessions, and from 1669 they were placed under the direction of the newly created Ministry of the Marine. No longer left to half-hearted early companies or impetuous governor-adventurers, they would fall more squarely within the purview of the French Crown. Talon would go on to set in motion a number of projects that breathed commercial life into New France, and under other circumstances we might very well have expected silk production to have numbered amongst them. But, hardened by their own domestic attempts at moriculture, the French seem to have been more mindful than the English of the climatic disadvantages

---

[50] See numerous silk ornaments and furnishings recorded in Thwaites, *Jesuit Relations*, 42: 269–87; 66: 84–6, 215–17.

of the northerly latitudes of the eastern seaboard, and though occasional sources mention the presence of indigenous mulberries, they were not instantly linked to sericulture.[51] That silk does not seem to have figured as a target product was also perhaps a reflection of the fact that Talon still fervently believed in the imminent discovery of a route to the raw silk supplies of China, something he pushed particularly in his second term as *intendant* (1669–72). Deepening awareness of the impact of regional climates and global trade routes, in other words, were beginning to influence expectations about what was achievable when it came to transplanting sericulture to the New World.

It was in the Caribbean where raising silk became a preoccupation of French authorities, as Colbert hoped to diversify French economic activity, promoting a range of island products besides sugar (whose price had slumped and in the 1670s was in low demand in France). The French – like other European powers – had initially subcontracted much of the dirty work of founding settlements on the Atlantic archipelago of the Antilles to trading interests and freebooters, and it would be some time before royal authority was meaningful, and some time again before the plantation complex emerged as the dominant model. Uncertainty about what was profitable, sustainable, and controllable on the islands in the seventeenth century gave rise to many permutations of economy and society. It was an experimental world of micro-societies contested by native Caribs, European opportunists and vagabonds, and people of African descent (most in bondage), all finding their fates closely tied to what plants and what microbes might flourish. In 1670, white and black population numbers were approximately matched amongst the French possessions, somewhere over 15,000 apiece.[52]

The newly created French 'governor-general' of all Caribbean possessions from 1667, Jean-Charles de Baas, did not perform his duty with quite as much acquiescence as Talon in Canada, but midway through his decade in post, he was nevertheless repeatedly prodded to make progress in sericulture in the islands. Colbert informed de Baas in 1674 that an earlier correspondent, named Pélissier (a director of the Compagnie des Indes Occidentales whom Colbert seemed to treat like an *intendant*), had pursued some company trials with silkworms, which had been compromised by the aggressive ants on Martinique (probably

[51] For example, Thwaites, 13: 12 (1637, Indians picking fruit); 51: 123 (1668, mulberries abundant in Iroquoia and fruit dried).
[52] Philip P. Boucher, *France and the American Tropics to 1700: Tropics of Discontent?* (Baltimore, MD: Johns Hopkins University Press, 2008), 190–1, 234 (population); James S. Pritchard, *In Search of Empire: The French in the Americas, 1670–1730* (Cambridge, UK: Cambridge University Press, 2004), esp. 123–87 on production.

Azteca delpini) which covered the ground throughout. Colbert told de Baas that he might expect the imminent arrival of two specialists, a man and a woman who were to be hand-picked by the Duchess of Modena (Laura Martinozzi) on behalf of King Louis XIV, and who would be tasked in future with trying to sustain the silkworm eggs in the face of this predatory threat. Colbert felt that the introduction of foreign specialists was well worth the cost of their travel, not least because of the reluctance of French women in the islands to occupy themselves in spinning or working up textiles. This was something which exasperated Colbert, both as a workaholic and a political economist with hopes for Caribbean spun fibres (including silk, linen, and hemp); he lamented that 'even the poorest prefer to go and die in the hospital than wanting to work'.[53]

In the 1680s, Michel Bégon, another of Colbert's colonial placemen (married to the minister's first cousin), who had been appointed *intendant* of the French West Indies, was pleased to announce that a new parcel of silkworms which he had himself brought to Saint-Pierre on Martinique, had exceeded his hopes, producing 'silk as beautiful and also as fine as that of Persia'. Bégon reported that 'we will work at multiplying the seed', anticipating that if it worked, 'I don't doubt it will be a great boon for the islands.'[54] In spite of Colbert's passing, with the king's direct support, the next few years witnessed a brief but active extension of silk culture into this corner of the French Caribbean.[55] Bégon and the new governor-general, the Comte de Blénac, wrote in June 1684 that settlers were applying themselves diligently to planting out mulberries on Martinique, themselves having led the way by example with 'a great clearance'.[56]

One of the foremost planters to commit to silk was François Picquet de La Calle, who had arrived as the company's *commissaire* in 1664 and subsequently become a member of the sovereign council; he invested substantial labour and capital in his efforts at Sainte-Marie (on the

---

[53] Only one woman, a Madame de Lavale, had shown adequate perseverance for his liking, and he recommended that she be sent any equipment from France that might assist in perfecting her designs. Letter to Baas-Castelmore, 8 February 1674, 'Correspondance à l'arrivée en provenance de la Martinique', C/8/A, f.263v–264v, Archives Nationales d'Outre Mer, Aix-en-Provence (hereafter ANOM).

[54] Letter from Bégon (Michel), intendant des îles d'Amérique, 29 May 1683, C/8/A, f.243v–244, ANOM.

[55] According to one source, it was Seignelay who actually initiated silk experiments. Louis Philippe May, *Histoire économique de la Martinique 1635–1763* (Paris: Librairie des Sciences, n.d.).

[56] Letter from Blénac (Charles de La Roche-Corbon, comte de), gouverneur général des îles d'Amérique, et Bégon (Michel), intendant des îles d'Amérique, 18 June 1684, C/8/A/ 4, f.18, ANOM.

northeast coast of the island).[57] La Calle eventually sent a number of raw silk skeins to the ministry, brought home in triumph by Bégon in 1684, and when they reached the king's attention, Louis XIV awarded him a premium of 500 *livres* (roughly £38). The monarch also rewarded La Calle for his efforts by raising his estates to a fiefdom, officially for having planted more than '4,000 mulberry trees, the leaves of which nourish a very great number of silkworms'.[58] Louis XIV's generous encouragement for La Calle, however, was not simply a royal gesture so much as a kind of compensation, as revealed in a report jointly compiled in 1685 by Governor Blénac and the new French Antilles *intendant* Gabriel Dumaitz de Goimpy. After long passages explaining the religious disputes amongst missionary orders (Jesuits, Dominicans, and Capucins), the buccaneering exploits of Saint-Domingue *filibustiers*, and the marital problems associated with racial intermixture in the French Caribbean, the officials stressed that La Calle had sacrificed much to make Martinique silk, and that other silkworms had not prospered so well. His enslaved labour force, in working with mulberries or silkworms, were of necessity neglecting sugar production or subsistence farming, and therefore occasioning him losses to the point where 'we cannot hope that he will be able to continue this manufacture unless we give him exemptions'.[59] Strikingly reminiscent of Edward Digges's exploits and accolades in Virginia some twenty years earlier, La Calle's willingness to take on the challenge of sericulture may have constituted pioneering agronomy but was also a calculated piece of imperial entrepreneurship.

La Calle let it be known that he wished to escape head taxes on his 200 enslaved people and customs taxes on his sugar output, which would help repay him for the high-quality mulberry trees he had secured from the Comtat region in France and the customised buildings he had apparently erected in pursuit of raw silk. He would go on to write a grovelling letter of thanks to Louis XIV, in which he promised to sustain his silk-raising activity. Administrators, however, were much more particular in acknowledging the role of his wife in their endeavours.[60] Dumaitz

---

[57] Pierre François-Régis Dessalles and Bernard Vonglis, *Les annales du conseil souverain de la Martinique* (Bergerac. J. B. Puyncsgc, 1786), 1: 65, 105 6, 147, 153, 191.

[58] 'Erection en fief de la terre du sieur de la Calle', C/B/13, f.40, ANOM; Sydney Daney, *Histoire de la Martinique depuis la colonisation jusqu'en 1815*, 6 vols. (Fort-Royal: E. Ruelle, 1846); C. A. Banbuck, *Histoire politique, économique et sociale de la Martinique sous l'ancien régime 1635–1789* (Paris: M. Riviere, 1935).

[59] 'Mémoire pour le Roy', Blénac et Dumaitz de Goimpy (Gabriel), 30 September and 1 October 1685, C/8/A, f.50, 58–58v, ANOM.

[60] Letter from La Calle (François Piquet de), 18 February 1687, C/8/A/4, f.396–7; Letter to Dumaitz de Goimpy, 'Au sujet de la culture des mûriers et de l'élevage du ver à soie, à propos des essais faits par madame de La Calle', 30 March 1687, B/13, f.14v, ANOM.

exported some of La Calle's output in 1688, suggesting that there was continued progress as workers developed experience in some of the processes, notably reeling. Dumaitz mentioned that there were many qualities of raw silk, but that the reelers had now rectified some of their shortcomings, and further that La Calle had successfully bred silk moths on the island whose offspring had worked very well.[61] Reading between their enthusiastic lines in 1685, Blénac and Dumaitz did express some pertinent qualifiers in their comments on silk production on Martinique. While they were encouraged by the reception and professional verdict on the quality of West Indian silk, they warned that settlers held debts in sugar (by then a currency of sorts), which inhibited planters from expanding their range of products. Moreover, planters could be disillusioned due to the long time it took for mulberries to mature: it would do them no harm to witness the king's particular intervention to reward La Calle.

The battle to provide mulberry trees for settlers wanting to diversify and grow silk seemed to be going well initially. Thousands of white mulberry seedlings were available for transplantation in 1684, some of them no doubt via the large nurseries created by Bégon and La Calle. Other planters such as François Hurault de Manoncourt, envious of the change in the status of La Calle's lands, likewise sought to mobilise their many enslaved labourers, in his case growing 'a great quantity of mulberries' on his *habitation* named Fonds Plumet at Case Navire (now Schœlcher). Having already dispatched 'very fine' samples of raw silk back to France in 1687, he confidently outlined his plans to plant between 4,000 and 5,000 new mulberries, to construct buildings 'of the length and size necessary' for the silkworms, to import more silkworm varieties, and to bring 'people instructed in the manufacture of silk'.[62] As a consequence, Hurault de Manoncourt was likewise rewarded by royal decree in 1687, his efforts at silk bringing enfeoffment of his lands, which in turn brought a tax break on his enslaved population.[63] Thereafter, rather than targeting existing landholders, the king insisted that the terms of all future grants must oblige landholders to plant a certain quantity of mulberries in proportion to the amount of land they were given, and moreover to nurse these trees to maturity and the point where their leaves could nourish silkworms. The flipside of this obligation was

[61] Letter from Dumaitz de Goimpy, 5 May 1688, C/8/A/5, f.87, ANOM.
[62] 'Mémoire du sieur François Huraut de Manoncourt sur l'établissement de manufactures de soies à la Martinique', 6 March 1687, C/8A/4, f.405–405v, ANOM.
[63] 'Extraits des lettres écrites des îles entre le 15 août 1686 et le 6 mai 1687', C/8/A, f.253, ANOM; on landholding and the rarity of enfeoffment, see Liliane Chauleau, *Dans les Îles du vent: La Martinique (XVIIe–XIXe siècle)* (Paris: L'Harmattan, 1993), 138–40.

that the king declared all silks manufactured in the Antilles exempt from duties.[64] In the second half of the 1680s, French imperial authorities shipped mulberry trees and silkworm seed in large numbers to all parts of the French Caribbean.[65]

The response, however, was distinctly underwhelming, as colonial correspondents on different islands described the various difficulties they encountered on their patches. On Guadeloupe, where there was some willingness to diversify beyond sugar production and a number of labourers who hailed from silk regions, Governor Pierre Hinselin found that aridity had destroyed nearly all the mulberry seeds and cuttings he had distributed.[66] On the still fledgling colony of Saint-Domingue, whose larger land mass seemed to augur better for mulberry nurseries than the Lesser Antilles, the governor reported in 1689 that in spite of having promised advantages to those who raised silkworms, he had been unable to convince them to try it. Most of the feisty and disreputable planters there had never encountered the culture, and much preferred to pursue indigo production (which was selling well).[67] Far more positive sounds were heard from the islet of Marie-Galante, whose planters assembled in 1687 and identified some 12,000 feet of lands fit for mulberries, planning to house silkworms in buildings abandoned as a result of recent wars. But as it turned out, the inter-colonial carnage in the Antilles was only just warming up, and any such plans, along with nearly everything else on Marie-Galante, was wiped out by a subsequent English attack in February 1690 that saw the entire island depopulated.[68] Indeed, the wrenching upheaval of the Nine Years' War (1689–97), which pitted France against the allied marine powers of the Dutch and English (amongst others) and was the backdrop to much displacement and destruction in the Caribbean, proved to be a brake even on the places where silk production had begun. *Intendant* Dumaitz de Goimpy guesstimated in 1691 that had it not been for the war, more than a million feet of mulberries would have been planted, but explained in a report for the

---

[64] Arrêt du Conseil d'Etat, 22 August 1687 and 9 February 1688, as recorded in Dessalles and Vonglis, *Annales du conseil de Martinique*, 1: 296–7.

[65] 'Le ministre à l'intendant Bégon au sujet de l'envoi aux îles d'Amérique de graines de mûrier', 23 February 1687, B/13, f.7; 'A monsieur Du Maitz de Goimpy sur les différentes cultures à pratiquer aux îles d'Amérique', 19 March 1687, B/13, f.11v, ANOM.

[66] Letters from Pierre Hinselin, governor of Guadeloupe, 12 August 1687 and 9 May 1688, C/7/A/3, f.146, 162.

[67] Letter 'A monsieur de [Tarin de] Cussy au sujet des affaires de Saint-Domingue', 30 September 1686, B/12, f.102v; 'Extrait d'une lettre de Cussy' [1689], C/8/A/5, f.335v, ANOM.

[68] Blenac, 'Procès-verbal de visite des terres de Marie-Galante propres aux plantations de mûriers blancs', 10 December 1687, C/8A/5, f.57

king that people did not dare invest in the requisite buildings until 'the war has moved on'. Other correspondents likewise mentioned handicaps to production during wartime, which included continual patrols, corvées imposed on enslaved labourers, and the prioritisation of subsistence commodities.[69]

Gradually, in spite of occasional successes, including the shipment of a few more skeins that were received with acclaim at the French court, a consensus emerged that environmental conditions were defective for silk. The sovereign council of the French islands made the point that mulberries refused to grow everywhere, which seriously complicated the idea of attaching conditions to land grants.[70] Although the heat was always strong enough and the seasons reasonably uniform, the high winds that prevailed for a good part of the year, and the frequent storms and tropical cyclones of the summer, made it impossible to imitate silk production on the scale of the Levant; they were obliged instead to emulate the economically supplementary type of silkworm raising in Languedoc. But many of the trees which had been planted out had begun dying off, as on Guadeloupe, causing problems for the supply of adequate mulberry leaves. Lastly, French planters were sceptical that silkworm raising would be compatible with Caribbean slavery: they worried on the one hand that the enslaved Africans would not pay adequate attention to the needs of their charges. On the other hand, planters had it on good authority that such was the great 'délicatesse' (fragility) of the silkworms that they would not support the 'strong and disgusting smell of the blacks of our colonies'.[71]

Colonial Caribbean authorities conceded defeat definitively in the mid-1690s, becoming more strident in their defiance of metropolitan encouragement. In the spring of 1694 Governor Blénac and Dumaitz de Goimpy – admittedly themselves both increasingly ill and grumpy – summarised the situation in a few rather blistering lines, explaining that however Herculean their cheerleading, it could not offset the fact that 'silkworms only promise imaginary profits', 'the earth refuses the trees, and 'the insects killed the enterprise'. They requested that a fund of 2,000 francs a year (about £150) that had been amassing unbeknownst to them, intended for those who planted out mulberries, be rediverted to assist

---

[69] Dumaitz de Goimpy, 'Mémoire pour le Roi', 16 February 1691, C/8A/6, f.337; Charles de Pechpeyrou-Comminges de Guitaud and Dumaitz de Goimpy, 'Mémoire pour le Roi', 4 October 1691, C/8/B/2, f.29–29v; letter to 'monsieur Bégon au sujet de l'élevage des vers à soie aux îles d'Amérique . . . ', 13 May 1693, B/14, f.486v, ANOM.

[70] 'Extraits des lettres . . . ', C/8/A, f.253, ANOM.

[71] 'Ils auroient bien de la peine à supporter l'odeur forte & dégoûtante des Negres de nos Colonies.' Dessalles and Vonglis, *Annales du conseil souverain de la Martinique*, 2: 297.

victims and the poor of the islands. In a separate report, Dumaitz de Goimpy elaborated on how the protection of the silkworms from the ants required 'a number of blacks occupied solely at this work', without which it was impossible to replace those that died. The predatory insects on Martinique put paid to the idea of silk raising as a supplementary activity, for the real cost of sustaining just 2,000 silkworms a year precluded *habitants* from fulfilling ordinary duties.[72] Even where the mulberry trees did not entirely die off, and seemed to come on well, as on Martinique, Dumaitz de Goimpy's successor as *intendant*, Sieur François-Roger Robert, was warned that their leaves were soon too rough and bitter for the silkworms' palate, and that the silkworms suffered from the stifling conditions and produced little seed, even if they managed to survive the onslaught.

In some ways the experiences of the silkworms were made to echo the narratives of French-blooded men and women whose lives disintegrated upon exposure to the vices and vicissitudes of the tropics. The difficulties of silk raising in the French Caribbean were described as 'very different to those which have been overcome in some provinces of France, when the people there were keen to learn silk manufacturing'. Rather, the venomous insects, unforgiving climate, and brutal labour regime with few 'large families as in France' made the project unworkable, and it was unceremoniously dropped, its thousands of trees soon felled in the rush for timber to facilitate the developing surge of sugar. The environmental legacy of silk efforts in the French West Indies was written off the landscape, unlike in other locales where sericulture was attempted. More mixed was the conclusion about combining sericulture with slavery – for African labour had both been mobilised and vilified in the processes of experimentation.[73]

Louisiana's Mulberries

On the North American mainland, despite metropolitan preferences for a more integrated and compact model of French colonial development that remained mostly coastal, neither seasoned administrators like Talon

[72] Letters from Dumaitz de Goimpy, 1 March 1694, and Blénac and Dumaitz de Goimpy, 19 April 1694, C/8A/8, f.17, 152v, ANOM. Pritchard concluded that the 'evidence of a mass dying off of young mulberry trees suggests they failed to adapt to their new environment'. Pritchard, *In Search of Empire*, 127.
[73] 'Mémoire pour server de response aux ordres du roy constenus dans l'instruction de Sa Majesté du 12 octobre 1695 remise au sieur Robert', 12 May 1696, C/8A/9, f.328–330, ANOM. On the evolution of tree species, see Françoise Hatzenberger, *Paysages et végétations des Antilles* (Paris: Editions Karthala, 2001), 175, 361. Mulberries are now an endangered species on Martinique, surviving only on protected islets on the east coast.

nor restless Jesuits, *coureurs des bois*, and explorers could resist the temptation to stride or canoe onwards into the continent.[74] This persistence, which developed its own geopolitical logic as the French connected up their system of small forts, missions, and trading posts into an imperial thin blue line, eventually gave rise to the only documented efforts at silk raising that the French pursued on the North American mainland. Talon, followed by the single-minded Governor Louis de Buade de Frontenac, sanctioned voyages of exploration, hoping that the Mississippi River might lead to the Pacific. The reports that came back from the likes of *voyageur* Louis Jolliet and Father Jacques Marquette in 1673 brought disappointing news about the Mississippi emptying into the Gulf of Mexico, but tempered this with a high commendation of the fertility of the newly charted lands. Marquette mentioned extensive mulberries along the banks of the Mississippi, 'as large as those of France', a domestic reference point that the English were never able to invoke. Later priests described how the Tunica Indians (then situated around the Yazoo River) used strands from these mulberries to make clothing, spinning it 'like hemp and flax' into 'a strong and thick cloth'.[75] Early advocates of a new French colony at the Mississippi Delta – a territory named 'Louisiana' with much pomp by the flamboyant explorer René-Robert Cavalier de La Salle in 1682 – wrote to Colbert's son and ministerial successor, the Marquis de Seignelay, of the region's prospects: 'cotton, sugar, cochineal, indigo, entire forests of mulberry trees'.[76] One of La Salle's party, his able subordinate Henri de Tonti, even suggested in his journal that the vibrant Indian trade might be twisted to generate silk, proposing that 'as these savages are stationary, and have some habits of subordination, they might be obliged to make silk in order to procure necessaries for themselves'.[77] With no accompanying reports of evil ants, poor soils, pilfering competitors, dry conditions, or destructive

---

[74] P. Margry, ed., *Découvertes et établissement des français dans l'ouest et dans le sud de l'Amérique septentrionale, 1614–1754*, 6 vols. (Paris: D. Jouaud, 1886), 1: 257. C. Jaenen, 'Colonisation compacte et colonisation extensive aux xviie et xviiie siècles en Nouvelle-France', in *Colonies, territoires, sociétés: L'enjeu Français*, ed. A. Saussol and J. Zitomersky (Paris: L'Harmattan, 1996), 15–22.

[75] Thwaites, *Jesuit Relations*, 58: 91–107; 59: 137; 65: 129; 66: 225. Other references to the use of the inner bark of mulberry trees being used by Apalachees and Houmas to make female clothing: B. F. French, *Historical Collections of Louisiana and Florida: Including Translations of Original Manuscripts Relating to Their Discovery and Settlement, with Numerous Historical and Biographical Notes* (New York: A. Mason, 1875), 80n, 257n; H. W. Beckwith, *Documents, Papers, Materials and Publications Relating to the Northwest and the State of Illinois* (Springfield, IL: H. W. Rokker, 1903), 140. Letter from Hubert, C/13A/5, f.287, 25 April 1719, ANOM.

[76] French, *Historical Collections of Louisiana*, 9.   [77] Beckwith, *Illinois Documents*, 144.

hurricanes, the French imperial dream of Atlantic silk that lay listless in the Caribbean began to pick up a second wind.

By the start of the eighteenth century, a limited French presence on the Gulf Coast was established by the intrepid Jean-Baptiste le Moyne, Sieur de Bienville, but Louisiana was largely neglected by the state and suffered because of the weakness of the French navy during the War of the Spanish Succession (1701–14). Positioned between expanding British colonies to the north-east and lucrative Spanish possessions to the south-west, and commanding the entrance of the Mississippi (with its access to many near and far Indian populations), Louisiana was too well placed to allow to fail and too marginal to warrant serious investment in the context of a war that stretched from Quebec to Vienna. Its few hundred French settlers eked out a living via trade with Indians, but optimism about its commercial potential was initially just another immigrant who died or moved on. It was telling that one of the foremost brains in Atlantic oceanic business enterprise, the financier and royal counsellor Antoine Crozat, who had made a fortune out of the slave, tobacco, and sugar trades, took a hard look at Louisiana for five years between 1712 and 1717, hoping to establish mines in Upper Louisiana and a commercial entrepôt for trade with New Spain, but quickly reined in his involvement.[78]

Between 1717 and 1731, Louisiana and its vaunted mulberry trees at last fell under the purview of commercial companies who made more of a concerted effort to generate productive capacity.[79] The first company, the Compagnie d'Occident (also known as the Mississippi Company), was chartered in 1717 and placed under the control of a remarkable character, the extravagant Scots economist and gambler John Law, who, in an era of great fiscal innovations, had managed to convince the French Regent that he had a watertight plan to wipe out the extensive French national debt by deploying a system of credit based on paper money. Like several other contemporary high-profile joint-stock schemes, such as the Scottish Darien Company (1698) or the British South Sea Company (1711), Law's company used the medium-term expectation of lucrative Atlantic commerce to entice investors and rapidly accumulate a capital base. Law's state-sponsored financial system began with promise, and its oceanic commercial prospects were expanded with

[78] Gilles Havard and Cécile Vidal, *Histoire De L'Amérique française* (Paris: Editions Flammarions, 2008), 105–29.
[79] Marcel Giraud, *Histoire de la Louisiane Française*, 4 vols. (Paris: Presses universitaires de France, 1953), 1: 157. See, for example, François Le Maire, *Mémoire sur la Louisiane, pour estre présenté, avec la Carte de ce Pais, au Conseil Souverain de Marine* (1717), Français 12105, Western Manuscripts Division, Bibliothèque Nationale de France, Paris [hereafter BnF].

the creation of the Compagnie Perpétuelle des Indes in 1719, a fusion of existing French chartered commercial companies that was granted extensive rights and domains and used the port of Lorient as its operative base. The share price, which had begun at 500 *livres*, climbed to a height of 10,100 (approximately £750) in 1720, and then, like several of its soon-to-be suicidal victims, plummeted. The so-called 'Mississippi' bubble burst as confidence evaporated upon the realisation that the Banque Royale was massively undercapitalised in specie and the company was significantly overvalued. John Law himself, having only just converted to Catholicism and become the Controller-General of Finances (akin to the Prime Minister of France), escaped the mobs baying for his execution and scuttled off to gamble elsewhere, and on a much smaller scale.[80]

The feasibility of these giant initiatives depended in large part upon their directors' ability to convince potential punters of the imminent prospect of American gains. Louisiana therefore became the subject of an enormous propaganda campaign and correspondingly enormous public interest, and writers returned to the commodities that the likes of La Salle and Tonti had identified as potential winners. If subscribers were bemused at first in 1717, they were soon to be informed in a torrent of publicity. The propaganda made occasional mention of possible gold and silver mines in the Illinois country, as well as lead and copper, but dwelt particularly on the prospects of tobacco and silk, the pairing that had so preoccupied Virginians in the mid-seventeenth century, followed by indigo and rice. A typical report of 1719 listed tobacco, silk, indigo, and silver as the four first fruits expected of the delightful climate and rich soils.[81] Newspapers such as the *Nouveau Mercure* repeatedly trumpeted the luscious latitude of Louisiana, using the forests of mulberry trees as evidence of its fertility.[82] 'Within 50 Leagues of the Sea', promised one defensive tract authored in 1720, 'you meet with some Mulberry-Trees, which increase to that Degree as you go farther up the Country, that in some Provinces, the Mulberry-Trees are alone equal in Number to all the other Trees of different Kinds'. Mention was made of 'some Cods of Silk-Worms, which perpetuate there naturally', and the fact that some had

[80] Gavin John Adams, *Letters to John Law* (Washington, DC: Newton Page, Inc., 2012), xix–lxviii.

[81] Anon., *Mémoire instructif des profits et avantages des interessez dans la Compagnie des Indes & de Mississippy* (1719), 4. Folder 32, Kuntz Collection, Howard–Tilton Memorial Library, Tulane University, New Orleans.

[82] Giraud, *Histoire de la Louisiane*, 3: 135–52; Pierre Berthiaume, 'Louisiana, or the Shadow Cast by French Colonial Myth', *Dalhousie French Studies* 58 (2002): 10–25; Paul Mapp, 'French Geographic Conceptions of the Unexplored American West and the Louisiana Cession of 1762', in *French Colonial Louisiana and the Atlantic World*, ed. Bradley G. Bond (Baton Rouge: Louisiana State University Press, 2005), 134–74.

been successfully 'cultivated' in 1717, 'and the Silk that was sent to *Paris* from *Louisiana* prov'd very good'. The leaves of the mulberries were deemed 'excellent' for silkworms, and the pamphlet reported the testimony of local specialists that, unlike in European regions, the silkworms would not be 'subject to Sickness'.[83]

Besides the hot air and the paper currency, the dramatic economic events in France did generate some real investment and activity under the auspices of the Compagnie des Indes and its precursors, as the mention of silk samples and specialists suggests. In spite of the credit collapse in 1720, enough capital had been committed by the company to allow it to persist with attempts to fulfil its colonial ambitions, albeit operating on a skeleton budget and with a much more constrained profile. In all, the company transported an eclectic mix of some 7,000 Europeans to Louisiana between 1717 and 1731 (when the French Crown took over direct administration of the colony). These included a small number of officers, recruited specialists and volunteers, some 1,300 industrious German Catholics, and the bulk made up of *engagés* – French conscripts, vagrants, and convicts consigned to servitude, whose crimes varied from petty theft and prostitution to political dissent and tax evasion. Deposited upon the humid, swampy lands of the lower Mississippi valley and tasked with the hard labour of clearing dense vegetation, these unfortunates certainly were 'subject to Sickness', less than a third of them remaining after the hazards of the voyage, malnutrition, dysentery, and malaria had taken their toll. Between 1719 and 1743, and especially from the late 1720s, this unwieldy and distrustful mix of whites also absorbed some 6,000 enslaved Africans, the majority embarked from Senegambian ports (including Wolof and Bambara peoples in significant numbers), with a smaller proportion from the Bight of Benin and West-Central Africa, and a few hundred transferred from the French Antilles.[84]

Agricultural production was minimal in the early years, for as had occurred in English Jamestown, surviving Louisiana settlers were incapable of feeding themselves let alone producing much for commercial export. They relied desperately on trade with the Indians, on sporadic

[83] *A Full and Impartial Account of the Company of Mississippi; or of the French India Company, Projected and Settled by Mr. Law* (London: Printed for R. Francklin, 1720), 77. See also Mapp, 'French Geographic Conceptions', 168n14.
[84] Paul Lachance, 'The Growth of the Free and Slave Populations of French Colonial Louisiana', in *French Colonial Louisiana and the Atlantic World*, ed. Bradley G. Bond (Baton Rouge: Louisiana State University Press, 2005), 204–43; Havard and Vidal, *Histoire de l'Amérique française*, 242; Cécile Vidal, 'French Louisiana in the Age of the Companies', in *Constructing Early Modern Empires: Proprietary Ventures in the Atlantic World, 1500–1750*, ed. L. H. Roper and Bertrand Van Ruymbeke (Leiden: Brill, 2007), 133–61.

French provisioning vessels, and on the small amounts of maize, peas, and beans that survived floods and droughts, or what trifling livestock they could sustain.[85] From 1717, the company granted large portions of land to *concessionaires*, individuals, or partnerships (often from the nobility) who then undertook to develop estates as private business enterprises. Many concessions were administered by resident directors (*régisseurs*), themselves usually shareholders, who managed operations across the Atlantic and reported back to their patrons or the associations (including *sociétés des colonisation*) who employed them and held capital in France. The concessions – including John Law's own hefty holding near Arkansas Post on the lands that Henri de Tonti had so enthused about – were buffeted and reshaped by the financial storms in France (which played havoc with investors) and by problems on the ground in Louisiana – not least of which was the colony's notoriously corrupt and inefficient administration. The fluctuating concession system, and the eclectic cluster of *habitations* that snaked around the most fertile sections of the lower Mississippi, thus offered a pretty brittle framework for the trial of unproven Atlantic products.

Mississippi Silk's Trials

Evidence of meaningful engagement with silk cultivation in French Louisiana dated back to the late 1710s, and the final years of Crozat's control of the colony. In a 1716 report on the region's economic potential, Crozat emphasised that after the certain prospects of mines and peltry, Louisiana possessed many white mulberries fit for raising silkworms, and that Indian women were very skilful 'at spinning it', seeming to base this observation on 'the example of the English' who had by then established silk cultivation in Carolina (discussed below).[86] Crozat's governor, Antoine Laumet de La Mothe (Sieur de Cadillac), a man with long-standing interests in botany and zoology, reported that he had discovered two kinds of mulberry tree around the bay of St Louis, differentiated by their bearing of fruit. He believed that the leaves of the fruitless tree (which he named 'Meurier Masle') were very suitable for silkworms, being similar to those of Piedmont and Provence, and noted that there was a great quantity amongst the Natchez Indians and further north as far as the Illinois. De La Mothe recommended that more mulberries be

---

[85] Giraud, *Histoire de la Louisiane*, 3: 349–50.

[86] 'Mémoire sur la Colonie de la Louisiane porté au Conseil de Regence le 11 Fevrier 1716', C/13A/4, f.33, ANOM. See also 'Le Mémoire du Sr. Crozat sur la Louisiane', 11 February 1716, C/13A/4, f.914, which explained how hopes of silk were well founded, 'because the English have been making it in Carolina for several years'.

transplanted to the uplands around the Natchez, where their leaves and consequently the silk would be finer and of higher quality.[87]

Mindful of such testimony, the subsequent company enshrined silk encouragement in its mandates for Louisiana. It wanted its settlers to concentrate their efforts on a handful of viable products, and to avoid threatening the domestic economy or associated royal privileges, so proscribed the pursuit of a number of other commodities in Louisiana. Settlers caught cultivating vines, hemp, or flax – products which in British America were often targeted alongside silk – were subject to a fine of 500 *livres* for each contravention.[88] The instructions issued to concession holders, somewhat standardised in 1719, stipulated that they should plant at least ten mulberry trees per *arpent* of land they had cleared (a French measurement of area, equating to roughly 6/7 of an acre), later insisting that these be transplanted 'around their households', since it had emerged that many were left inaccessible in forests or heavy cane thickets. These did not specify whether the mulberries were to be of the imported white or the indigenous red variety (mostly found in moist soils of hardwood forests), though both would be used to feed silkworms. Given that *concessionaires* also had to improve a minimum of 50 arpents, this meant in theory that each grant would deliver at least 500 mulberry trees.[89] Another novel measure taken by the company was to award concession holders the right to establish silk-manufacturing operations – a permission which ran contrary to the usual proscription of such activities in the colonies, making silk exceptional.[90] Towards the end of its existence, the company would introduce another policy that illustrated how aspirational commodities prompted colonial authorities across European nations to think creatively, insisting that any residents to whom they delivered enslaved Africans would be obliged to plant a certain number of contiguous mulberry trees in proportion to their bondspeople.[91]

Many societies in the late 1710s expected quick returns from extracting mineral resources and establishing basic silk-manufacturing operations. The well-capitalised concession headed by financier Joseph Pâris-Duverney in 1718 was placed under the direction of the Dubuisson family, whose background was in silk production, and who oversaw the

---

[87] De La Mothe-Cadillac, 'Meuriers, tabac et feüille nommée Apalachine', 11 July 1716, C/13A/4, f.615, ANOM.

[88] 'Ordonnance des directeurs', 9 January 1721, C/A/23, f.31, ANOM.

[89] 'Mémoire pour servir d'instruction au Sr Duvergier', 15 September 1720, C/13A/6, f.21v, ANOM.

[90] See model contract, 'Lettres de concession aux Srs J.-B. et Michel Delaire', 12 September 1719, C/13C/4, f.219v–221, ANOM.

[91] Proceedings of the Directors' meeting, 3 June 1729, C/13A/11, f.350–350v, ANOM.

establishment of a large plantation on the site of an old Bayagoulas settlement some twenty-eight leagues upriver from New Orleans, discussed in detail below. A number of other *concessionaires* (such as Claude Le Blanc and the Comte de Belle-Isle) and associations (such as the Société de Mézières) likewise targeted personnel with expertise to 'work in silks' or undertake the 'raising of silks' in Louisiana. The partnership of the brothers d'Artaguiette d'Iron sent over at least forty colonists before 1720, including a number of artisans and dedicated silk-reeling experts, who were spread across their different plantations, which included sites around Baton-Rouge and New Orleans. They included for example the twenty-three-year-old Pierre Desjeans from Saillant (near St-Étienne), a 'worker for the raising of silk' who signed a three-year contract in 1719 and later became the director of d'Artaguiette's plantation. The Marquis d'Ancenis hired nine 'men for silk' from the silk town of Uzés, while John Law sought out experts from other plausible sericultural zones, finding ten 'workers in silk' from Alès, Tours, Turin, and Lausanne. Perhaps the most comprehensive plans for establishing silk production in Louisiana were formulated by the partnership of Étienne Demeuves, who contracted with a silk merchant's son, Pierre Coutaud, from Annonay in the Dauphiné, to create on their concession 'a silk-making establishment', procuring whatever people and materials he required from his homeland.[92]

It is clear from these instances that *concessionaires* appreciated that to target certain crops (notably silk and tobacco) they needed to expand their recruitment base, to make the most of French experience in sericulture in Le Midi. The bulk of the French labour force sent to Louisiana was taken from western provinces (especially concentrated in the region around La Rochelle and Lorient), with a good proportion also from Paris and its hinterland, but smaller representation from the south and southeast. One undated report urged the company to send more ships directly from Provence precisely 'because of women for the making of silk' and 'the proximity of Lyons' with its depth of silk workers, as well as the abundance of French convicts available in Marseille.[93] Special efforts needed to be made to counter the natural skew towards French Atlantic and company entrepôts – as when the Kolly-Vernesobre enterprise brought over a portion of workers who were Italian, Swiss, and from the lands around Lyons. Incentives for silk specialists included better

[92] Giraud, *Histoire de la Louisiane*, 3: 159, 179, 232; Marie-Claude Guibert, Gabriel Debien, and Claude Martin, 'Notes d'histoire Coloniale No. 178', in *Actes Du 97e Congrès national des sociétés savantes, Nantes 1972* (Paris: Bibliotheque Nationale, 1979).

[93] 'Mémoire Instructif que le Sr. Bertrand donne touchant les operations ... n.d.' C/13C/1, f.216v, ANOM.

contracts than their hard-up peers from Brittany parishes, and they could expect annual salaries, with even female 'workers in silk' occasionally receiving 100 *livres*, while men with target vocational experience could expect salaries that were inflated, and especially so where their wives or children offered a 'supplementary craft' as we might expect with the silk raisers from Languedoc and Dauphiné.[94] Amongst the passengers listed on *La Seine* were four 'inspectors in silk and in tobacco' who would share the transatlantic voyage with the Marquis d'Ancenis's nine specialists, several of whom brought wives. Aboard *Le Chameau*, another *fluyt* which also departed Port-Louis for Louisiana in August 1720, were three workers whose metiers were also listed as 'for the silk'.[95] Finding the extra investment that was needed to target specialist labour would become virtually impossible with the depreciation of the French paper currency and the paralysis of exchange, as one after the other the *sociétés de colonisation* collapsed and the company was placed under tight administration in 1721.[96]

Silk ambitions, however, survived the company's reorganisation and stricter controls, reflecting both a sense of the progress that had already been set in motion and a growing appreciation of the botanical merits of the forests of the interior. Samples of the silk produced under the Dubuissons' management in 1720, described as 'very fine and of a good quality', as good as the finest manufactured in the kingdom, were sent back to France, where they so delighted investors that the Compagnie des Indes arranged a special exhibition in Paris.[97] Though probably of higher quality than those that had preceded them, these were not the first silken products to travel eastwards across the Atlantic, however, for some skeins of raw silk were carried to France by the wife of Jacques Lochon, raised from silkworms in the Illinois country.[98] A report in the summer of 1721 stressed the importance of not cutting down a single mulberry (later strengthened by fines and corporal punishments), and of planting them out wherever possible to sustain the most silkworms, encouraging Indian women and children to pursue the matter.[99] This was part of a growing

[94] Giraud, *Histoire de la Louisiane*, 3: 225–7, 237–9.
[95] 'Liste de tous les passagers pour la Louisiane depuis le 4 janvier 1720 jusqu'en compris le 24 janvier 1721', Fonds du Dépôt des papiers publics des colonies, G/1/464, nos. 21, 22, 44, 46, ANOM.
[96] Giraud, *Histoire*, 4: 10–11, 19.
[97] 'Recensement et commentaire annexe de New Orleans', 24 November 1721, DPPC, G/1/464, f.4v, 6, ANOM.
[98] Giraud, *Histoire*, 4: 306.
[99] 'Mémoire sur la colonie de la Louisiane … n.d.', C/13C/1, f.341–341v; 'Arrêt du conseil supérieur de la Louisiane qui interdit aux habitants de couper des arbres fruitiers sans permission (n. 112)', 29 July 1727, C/A/23, f.86, ANOM.

recognition that introducing silk required its proponents to play the long game: in a comprehensive report and census at the end of 1721, the discussion of silk took up more space than either indigo, tobacco, rice, or 'vegetables' – the company insisting that Louisianans must view silk as 'a considerable object'.[100] It advocated that a few years later, once mulberries had matured, there should be also be a renewed importation of female silk reelers (*tireuses de soye*).[101]

From 1723, under the new *régie*, the company tasked a particular councillor, Paul Perry (likely with a textile background) with overseeing economic order in Louisiana, with a particular emphasis on nurturing production of tobacco but also tar, silk, indigo, and minerals, though precious little funding was set aside to help. Perry's instructions reminded him how easy silk raising was in Louisiana, being merely a question of transplanting mulberries 'around the habitations' in order to collect leaves, and having families instructed in reeling the cocoons. They ordered him to consult with the Dubuissons and follow their example, finding out what wages were paid to 'each white girl, or each Negresse' working in silk raising, and to 'learn their mystery'.[102] Councillor Perry subsequently sent home to the company 'some magnificent cocoons' in 1724, along with a pack of silk reeled by 'negresses'.[103] No mention was made in Louisiana of earlier French planters' occasional indictment of black labour as unsuitable for silkworms, underscoring that this claim had been a convenient excuse to forestall further pressure to diversify production in the Caribbean. Where silk was pursued in earnest in 1720s Louisiana, as elsewhere in the Atlantic world, enslaved labour was readily and creatively mobilised.

Two locations in particular seem to have been flagship projects whose silk production allowed political economists to continue to press for measures in support of the commodity, in the face of the colony's wider challenges. Within a few months of leading some thirty settlers to the Pâris-Duverney concession at Bayagoulas in the spring of 1718, Étienne Dubuisson had planted out a number of mulberry orchards which explorer Jean-Baptiste Bénard de la Harpe admired, believing they would soon bring fame to the region.[104] Silk was the first of a number of products that the Dubuissons (Étienne, his younger brother François

---

[100] 'Règlement de la Compagnie . . . ', 2 September 1721, C/A/23, f.32, ANOM.
[101] 'Recensement et commentaire annexe de New Orleans', 24 November 1721, DPPC, G/1/464, f.7, ANOM.
[102] 'Instructions for P. Perry', C/B/43, f.203–4, ANOM.
[103] 'Projet anonyme de régie pour la Compagnie de la Louisiane', 14 August 1724, C/13A/8, f.184, ANOM.
[104] William D. Reeves, *From Tally-Ho to Forest Home: The History of Two Louisiana Plantations* (Bayou Goula, LA: D. Denis Murrell and David R. Denis, 2005), 17; Bernard de La Harpe, *Journal historique de l'établissement des Francais á la Louisiane*, ed. A. L. Boimare

from 1721, and two sisters) pursued with determination, but like many others, their efforts were undermined by the demographic disintegration of the labour force: only four white workers remained alongside some fifteen to twenty enslaved people in 1721. To counter this, the next year Étienne brought in a number of Dauphinois silk raisers, planning to capitalise on the growing trees. When the noted explorer and historian of New France, Father de Charlevoix, stopped at Bayagoulas in January 1722, he stressed 'the estate ... is magnificent', and noted the orderly rows of white mulberries, adding that 'very beautiful silk had already been made there'. He anticipated that silk, along with tobacco and indigo – the latter lately begun with success – would soon turn around the concession's fortunes.[105]

François Dubuisson duly arrived with 'two workers and three women specialising in the raising of silk', amongst eight servants whose freight costs were personally covered by Étienne, and one memorialist cited a silk manufactory established at Bayagoulas in 1722.[106] It is likely that this building was an adaptation of the thirty by twenty foot kitchen unearthed by archaeologists at the site, a structure that once had a first floor and in which large copper basins were found.[107] In the course of a few months, however, the number of *engagés* dwindled to six. Besides the impact of disease and the Dubuissons' failure to honour contractual obligations to supply them with flour, the remaining Bayagoulas silk workers were also thwarted by the difficulty of transporting silkworms across the Atlantic, managing to produce just three *écheveaux* (skeins) weighing half a pound in 1723.[108] Although the original white mulberries continued to thrive, by 1725 when a new director took over the plantation, silk had fallen away from its major interests, and the remaining Dubuisson brother, François, had his hands full quarrelling with rival figures – notably the new Basque manager Louis Cavelier de Verteuil and his replacement Claude Trénonay de Chanfret. Pâris-Duverney finally gave up on the enterprise in 1729. Still, François Dubuisson remained convinced of the viability of silk cultivation in the Bayagoulas region, and he secured substantial

(Paris: Hector Bossange, 1831), 142. *Mémoire concernant la Louisiane* (1721), M 1026, Centre d'Accueil et de Recherche des Archives Nationales (hereafter CARAN).

[105] Pierre-François-Xavier de Charlevoix, *Histoire et description generale de la nouvelle France: Avec Le journal historique d'un voyage fait par ordre du roi dans l'Amérique septentrionnale*, 3 vols. (Paris: Nyon fils, 1744), 3: 436–7.
[106] Jean-Baptiste Lemascrier, *Mémoires historiques sur la Louisiane* (Paris: Cl. J. B. Bauche, 1753), 58; Giraud, *Histoire de la Louisiane*, 4: 247.
[107] Reeves, *From Tally-Ho to Forest Home: The History of Two Louisiana Plantations*, 17.
[108] Letter from Jacques de la Chaise, 8 March 1724, C/13A/7, f.26v, ANOM. A few of the silk workers seem to have returned to France later in 1723: Giraud, *Histoire de la Louisiane*, 5: 128.

support from the Compagnie des Indes for a new enterprise on his own account in 1728. None of the original female silkworm specialists remained with Dubuisson, so that year he offered to bring more over 'for silk making', though at the extravagant cost of 300 *livres* (roughly £23) per year for each girl, wages which would cover both the cost of raising silkworms and educating bondspeople in the pursuit. Dubuisson further demanded of commissioners Périer and Delachaise that the company should pay him a limited-term bounty for each ounce or pound of silk that he raised.[109]

It was a measure of the increasingly desperate conviction about Louisiana silk that even in an era of spiralling company debts, Dubuisson's project was supported. The directors considered his propositions in June 1729, and then issued instructions to furnish Dubuisson with twelve enslaved Africans from the next four ships to arrive at Louisiana, with the express objective of offering a demonstration to other settlers of the methods of 'raising worms, preserving seed, and reeling silk'. Two female reelers (*tireuses de soye*) were to be paid 600 *livres*, and in addition François Dubuisson's sister was invited to return to Louisiana. Equipment was also commissioned by the company, including a reeling engine or filature, copper basins, and a substantial amount of precious silkworm seed. The company refused only Dubuisson's final and rather vague request, they insisting that any silk produced in the first two years be furnished for free to the company, after which the company would set a reasonable price for Dubuisson's output.[110]

Ultimately, the project was undermined by the difficulty of transporting silkworm eggs across the Atlantic, leaving an expert silk reeler with nothing to wind off. The English had eventually managed to get enough eggs to Virginia but struggled to secure experts; for the French it was the other way around. To her great dismay, Dubuisson's sister-in-law, Marie Anne Dubuisson Bonnaud, could not prevent the eggs from hatching and spoiling when her ship put in at Saint-Domingue in 1729. She reported the disaster on 10 December, explaining that the precautionary measure of placing the silkworm seed within a sealed bottle of water to keep them cool had failed. The bottle had cracked, and once fully exposed to the heat of the hull, the eggs had hatched and died. She proposed in future using a little marble box instead, and recommended sending them in smaller quantities, noting that a handful would be enough 'to furnish the whole colony with seed'. Despite failing in her commission to bring the seed, she

---

[109] Letter of Périer and Delachaise, 1 November 1728, C/13A/11, f.118–118v, ANOM.
[110] Proceedings of the Directors' meeting, 3 June 1729, C/13A/11, f.350–350v, ANOM.

hoped to soon bring news of progress in Louisiana, and passed on an address in Dauphiné that could be used to acquire further supplies.[111]

The second principal site of some French Atlantic raw silk yields was on the fertile elevated lands around the Natchez, where settlers arrived to evade the sandy Gulf Coast and the problematic floodplains around New Orleans. Arriving on his concession in early 1720, the *commissaire-ordonnateur* (Commissary General) Sieur Marc-Antoine Hubert experimented with grain, tobacco and mulberries and silkworms, with the help of his wife and a substantial workforce that included dozens of indentured servants and bondspeople. Hubert had first considered silk raising in 1717, approving of the quality of local mulberry leaves, and his wife had successfully harvested twenty-eight ounces of silkworm eggs in 1719. However, then based on the small Dauphin Island, he appreciated that little could be done until both people and mulberries were transplanted to the mainland, and anticipated that there would be a need for enslaved labourers to pursue the work with any momentum.[112] Assisting the Huberts with their relocation to St Catherine Creek in the Natchez country was Antoine-Simon Le Page du Pratz, who likewise obtained a concession and lived there for most of the 1720s, later publishing a history of Louisiana which recorded in some detail his neighbours' silk-raising efforts.

Le Page du Pratz explained that Madame Hubert was from a part of Provence 'where much silk is made', though other records attest that Hubert's wife was Elizabeth de Lesterier, originally from Montpellier in the neighbouring region of Languedoc, with whose silk-raising practices she was familiar.[113] Once in Louisiana, she undertook a series of careful experiments in silk raising. The first was to test a cohort of silkworms by offering them both the leaves of the prevalent local red mulberries and the rarer trees with white fruit. She attentively examined the silkworms' behaviours, noticing little preference for either leaf, until she further added a third type of mulberry leaf which derived from 'indigenous' white mulberries with a sweeter fruit: all of the silkworms seemed to prefer this one instinctively.[114] A second experiment was to raise silkworms in two batches, one of which was given the plain and the other the

---

[111] Letter from Mme du Buisson and report (no. 24 and no. 25), 16 December 1729, C/9B–9, f.15, ANOM.

[112] Letter from Hubert, 26 October 1717, C/13A/5, f.53v; Letter from Bienville, 15 April 1719, C/13A/5, f.209v, ANOM.

[113] Samuel Wilson, Mary Louise Christovich, and Roulhac Toledano, *New Orleans Architecture*, 8 vols. (Gretna, LA: Pelican Pub. Co., 1971), 6:3.

[114] Various possibilities explain Hubert's descriptions here: misattribution, naturalisation from Spanish introduction, or hybridisation. For over-confident pronouncements on their being Mexican escapees from cultivation, see Edna F. Campbell, 'New Orleans in Early Days', *Geographical Review* 10, no. 1 (1920): 35n3.

sweeter white mulberry leaves, to see if she could perceive a difference in the quality of their raw silk. Finally, Elizabeth Hubert located varieties of wild silkworms found on these indigenous mulberry trees and experimented with feeding them. Her findings, that the native worms 'did nothing but rush here and there, & their nature led them no doubt to live amongst the trees', comported well with French conceptions of America's native peoples; the indigenous silkworms' greater mobility caused her consternation that they might mix with 'those of France'. All of Elizabeth Hubert's scientific trials were directed at the end product, the reeling off of raw silk, and the 'industrious Lady' received high plaudits from Le Page du Pratz, who felt privileged to witness some of her successes.[115]

She directed reeling operations herself, and quickly concluded that the wild silkworms rendered less silk than those from France: in spite of constructing larger cocoons, they produced a silk that was thick and rough, which she attributed to their having failed to eat diligently because they were too busy running here and there. Hubert believed, contrary to many contemporary experimenters in other colonies, that the cocoons produced from red mulberry leaves were made of stronger and finer silk than those in the Old World, and she felt there was little difference between the Louisiana silkworms fed on red or plain white mulberry leaves. However, the silkworms fed up on the sweeter white mulberries produced a silk that was so fragile and thin that it was troublesome to reel off, and hardly worth persisting in. Le Page du Pratz, in relaying these details in his *Histoire*, emphasised how valuable such information should be in the future, making the point that societies owed much to such people as Elizabeth Hubert, who 'gave all their efforts to study Nature', in the process improving the lives of their fellow citizens and instructing 'le Public'.[116] It was a rare moment in which female scientific experimentation as well as female labour was acknowledged as seminal to the production of raw silk.

Capt. Jean Béranger also witnessed the Huberts' efforts and success in the Natchez country, concluding that no place was better suited to 'soieries' (silk-manufacturing enterprises) than Louisiana, and lamenting Hubert's death in 1723 all the more because 'I witnessed much application from them to make this Commerce pay.'[117] A *régisseur* to whom the Huberts sold lands and 'utensils' was adamant that silk thrived in the region and sent home 'a sample of silk' in July 1721.[118] For her part, the

---

[115] Antoine Le Page du Pratz, *Histoire de La Louisiane*, 3 vols. (Paris: Lambert, 1758), 3: 349–351.

[116] Le Page du Pratz, 3: 352–3.

[117] 'Mémoire des connaissances que le Sr [Jean] Béranger a tirées … ', C/13C/4, f.95v, ANOM.

[118] Excerpt from letter from Faucond du Manoir in Various, 'Concession of Ste Catherine at the Natchez', *Louisiana Historical Quarterly* 2, no. 1 (1919): 169.

widowed Elizabeth wrote pressingly in 1723 about their successes, stating that her five years' of production of fine silk was 'incontestable' evidence of the value of the product, along with the 'infinite' number of mulberries in greater Louisiana's vast forests. She argued that the colony could furnish France with all of its raw silk, 'and even all of Europe'. She felt that only the absence of population hindered silkworm raising, and that once enslaved workers were provided in sufficient number, and foodstuffs locally secured, 'they would occupy themselves with it'.[119] She would bring more Louisianan silk samples to France upon leaving the colony, but only outlived her husband by a year.[120]

After Hubert's death, his promising lands were purchased and developed by the large Sainte-Catherine association. Though safe from river water, the growing settlement was far from secure from the flowing resentment of the populous nearby villages of Natchez Indians, especially the Anglo-orientated villages to the northeast. In 1729, the Natchez were able to shelve their factional tensions in response to the abusive and shortsighted activity of a local French commandant, and with brutal efficiency wiped out the French settlements. Turning enslaved Africans free and taking white women and children captive, in its opening stages the Natchez 'rebellion' killed over 200 whites (mostly men), along with what residual pursuit of silk there was in the vicinity. The collapse of Dubuisson's scheme along with the Natchez revolt left French hopes for sericulture in Louisiana alive again largely in theory, with only one small last foundation in practice.

Given the company's willingness to support Dubuisson and others, Governor Étienne Périer expressed a certain defensiveness in his letter of August 1730, responding to the allegation that he had neglected to stimulate progress in silk and indigo. He pointed out that the *habitants* much preferred to take up tobacco and cotton, and that there could only be indigo and silk once there were adequate seed of one or other, after which it would still take a few years of acclimatisation.[121] In the report that accompanied the retrocession of the colony to the Crown, Périer wrote highly of silk prospects, insisting it was imperative to 'transmit to them silkworm seed' but only in ships leaving in the final quarter of the year when the silkworms would suffer less from heat in the tropics or Saint-Domingue. Périer explained that the community of Ursuline nuns based at New Orleans were employing the orphans under their charge in the 'raising of silk', and since these girls were destined to

[119] Letter from widow Hubert, 11 April 1723, C/13A/7, f.243v, ANOM.
[120] Giraud, *Histoire de la Louisiane*, 4: 307.
[121] Letter from Périer, 1 August 1730, C/13A/12, f.335v, ANOM.

marry settlers once in their early teens, he anticipated that they would eventually be able to direct enslaved women (household economics being one of the reasons, besides moral improvement, the company had placed them with the nuns).[122] After the retrocession of the colony to the Crown, in 1735, two women in New Orleans were reported to be raising silk-worms, but despite calls to send more silkworm eggs to the Ursulines, no take-up was apparent.[123]

Still, silk managed to creep ineluctably back into projections for French Louisiana from the 1730s until its cession to Spain at the close of the Seven Years' War in 1763. Later commentators and administrators, while operating from a more candid appreciation that the province's chief *raison d'être* was geopolitical, sought to consign past nightmares to history and to rehabilitate greater Louisiana's prospects as a site for agricultural experimentation and diversification. An anonymous 1733 memoir on Dutch and French commerce in the Atlantic proposed that Louisiana would be suitable for tobacco and silk, a verdict shared in the influential 1751 report on France's North American colonies by the realist Comte de La Galissonière (governor of Canada in the late 1740s). No doubt encouraged by the successes that British Americans were reporting in the mid-eighteenth century (discussed below), other contemporary writers came to the same conclusion, with one memorialist emphasising that cause for optimism over Louisiana lay not in the unknown quantities of the western regions but in the known quantities of silk, livestock, timber, and beavers in the east.[124]

Dictionaries, encyclopaedias, and travel literature increasingly returned to positive representations of Louisiana, lauding the prevalence of white mulberries, and the potential of upriver lands.[125] The mulberries

---

[122] 'Mémoire sur l'état présent de la Louisiane', 1731, 4/DFC/12, f.37–8 (Fonds du Dépôt des fortifications des colonies), ANOM. The customary marriage age of girls in 'the devil's empire' was estimated in Marie Madeleine Hachard, *Voices from an Early American Convent: Marie Madeleine Hachard and the New Orleans Ursulines, 1727–1760*, ed. Emily Clark (Baton Rouge: Louisiana State University Press, 2007), 83.

[123] Khalil Saadani, *La Louisiane française dans l'impasse: 1731–1743* (Paris: L'Harmattan, 2008), 124; Giraud, *Histoire de la Louisiane*, 5: 307; 'Sidelights on Louisiana History', *Louisiana Historical Quarterly* 1 (2013): 92. One source claims that in 1734, 'the Indians and the Negresses, who came every afternoon from 1:00 to 2:30 were instructed in reading, writing, catechism, the care of silkworms and the making of silk fabric', *Louisiana Writers' Project, Louisiana: A Guide to the State* (New York: Hastings House, 1941), 117.

[124] Reports cited in Mapp, 'French Geographic Conceptions', 139, 147. 'Description de l'Amerique meridional tant des côtes de la Mer du Nord que d'une partie de celle du Sud ...', 70v, 106r–107v, 111, 113v–126r, in 'Mémoires et documents', Amérique, 2, *Archives des Affaires étrangères*, Paris.

[125] See for example Antoine-Augustin Bruzen de la Martinière, *Le grand dictionnaire géographique, historique et critique*, 6 vols. (Paris: G. Le Mercier, 1741), 3: 201; Lemascrier, *Mémoires historiques sur la Louisiane*, 58, 63.

in Louisiana found other uses besides awaiting generations of silkworms that never arrived. Alongside cedar, the mulberry wood was used by French settlers for the construction of simple *poteaux-en-terre* (earthen post) houses and for fences and palisades, because both woods were particularly resistant to moisture and rot when placed directly in the ground.[126] But it was a measure of the particular silk-facilitating value associated with white mulberries in France that visitors such as Charlevoix were shocked to find the trees being used in America 'to build their houses', especially when other timber was readily available.[127] Amongst other *philosophes*, Voltaire was particularly taken with Louisiana's possible agricultural staples – on several occasions clustering silk, indigo, cacao, and tobacco as natural assets that made the colony infinitely preferable to the cold of Canada. These target commodities were valued by Voltaire and his peers, not just as agricultural or commercial objects, but as emblems of sophistication that signalled Enlightenment civilisation.[128] As the Abbé Raynal concluded looking back from 1770, the 'successful trials' had 'constantly invited' the French to undertake silk cultivation in Louisiana; but the mulberry-clad province, ceded to Spain in 1762, was a lost opportunity to recover all her former losses.[129]

Domestic Frontiers: Consolidation in the Early Eighteenth Century

Such worries about 'lost opportunities' in the French Atlantic colonies underlined that, for all its dominance, throughout the eighteenth century the domestic French silk industry remained heavily reliant upon foreign sources of raw and thrown silk. But what allowed the French to call time on further significant transatlantic efforts at raw silk production – in contrast to the Anglo-American attempts, which deepened and diversified significantly in the eighteenth century – boiled down to European geography and settler-colonial demography. Put simply, France was better positioned than those in northern Europe to adapt domestic and nearby supply sources of raw materials, while worse positioned than others in the Americas, on account of the demographic precarity of its colonial

---

[126] Charles E. Peterson, *Colonial St. Louis: Building a Creole Capital* (Tucson, AZ: Patrice Press, 1993), 39.
[127] Charlevoix, *Histoire de la nouvelle France*, 3: 395.
[128] Berthiaume, 'Louisiana, or the Shadow Cast by French Colonial Myth', 22.
[129] Abbé Guillaume Raynal, *A Philosophical and Political History of the Settlements and Trade of the Europeans in the East and West Indies*, ed. J. Justamond, 6 vols. (London: T. Cadell, 1776) 5: 49–51.

population. French experimentation in Atlantic silk production had never achieved the scale of output and throughput to New World silk manufacturing that had encouraged Spanish American persistence. Having failed to find a niche amidst Caribbean plantations, and in the absence of a sustainable settler population of any size on the mainland, attention reverted to retrenchment and consolidation in pre-existent supply chains. French sericulture in Le Midi may never have furnished a majority of the domestic demand, probably plateauing at 40 per cent of the total quantity of raw silk worked up, but by the late eighteenth century it had deepened and improved in scale and (to a lesser degree) in quality.[130]

The most obvious quickening of French domestic sericulture occurred in the Cévennes, where white mulberry cultivation had made comparatively little arboreal headway before the winter of 1709. But the year's disastrously cold frosts devastated the region's chestnut trees (*châtaigniers*), which to that point had dominated the richest and best-exposed soils, closest to homesteads, paving the way for their dramatic displacement by over 400,000 mulberries by mid-century.[131] It was not a simple substitution, for the mulberries required more intensive management, and were increasingly treated to more elaborate plantations, planted out in terraces that allowed for better springtime irrigation and fertilisation.[132] In this way, the kinds of sericultural projecting pursued by southerners in the New World – the likes of Picquet de La Calle, the Dubuissons, and Madame Hubert – became an increasingly realistic prospect on home soil, in sites such as Peyreleau, Millau, Aguessac, Compeyre, and Rivière-sur-Tarn. Perhaps the growing conviction that white mulberry trees were 'superior because they are more tender' in itself owed to frustrated experiences with other varieties overseas.[133] From the 1730s, the royal administration concentrated its considerable power and state support on advancing this revitalisation in southern sericulture, proving able to reach what the Languedoc silk inspector Buffet termed 'the common cultivator' through institutions such as the Bureau de Commerce in Versailles and the Intendance of Languedoc in Montpellier.[134]

---

[130] Savary des Brûlons and Savary, *Dictionnaire*, 3: 578; Chomel, *Dictionnaire oeconomique*, 70; Pomier, *L'art de cultiver les mûriers-blancs*, xiii, 81; Matthieu Thomé, *Mémoires sur la manière d'élever les vers à soie et sur la culture du mûrier* (Paris: Vallat-la-Chapelle, 1767), 35, 260, 276, 361–2.
[131] Le Roy Ladurie, *The Peasants of Languedoc*, 67.
[132] Clerget, 'Les industries de la soie dans la vallée du Rhône', 2; Pomier, *L'art de cultiver les mûriers-blancs*, 37.
[133] See for instance Savary des Brûlons and Savary, *Dictionnaire*, 386; Chomel, *Dictionnaire oeconomique*, 65.
[134] Cited in E. Stockland, 'Patriotic Natural History and Sericulture in the French Enlightenment', *Archives of Natural History* 44, no. 1 (2017): 3.

The uptake in silk raising began through the adaptation of existing buildings: owners seasonally reorganised their homes and barns to make space for the insect invasion, though they were rarely very fit for their purposes and often inefficient and inconvenient for families. Over time, however, as the pursuit flourished, larger proprietors invested in the iconic *magnaneries* that still punctuate the landscape (see Plate 6), two-storey buildings devoted to silkworm rearing – whose name derives from the Occitan word 'magnan' (*Bombyx mori*). Leaves were deposited and stored on the lower floor, while the caterpillars themselves usually occupied the second level, known as the *espélidor* (hatchery), where they were safer from predators and could be more effectively ventilated. In the public markets of some Languedoc towns, mulberry leaves themselves were reportedly exchanged like grains or vegetables.[135] The harvesting of cocoons after a successful season took the form of a customary party, the *décoconnage*, at which friends, family, and neighbours gathered to pool and pack up their yields, accompanied with drinking, socialising, and thanksgiving.[136] As with the benedictions that opened this chapter, wherever French silk experts played instrumental roles in supporting fledgling American sericulture – as they continued to do over the next century – we might expect variants of such buildings and rituals to have been modelled.

Environmental adequacy, an appropriate labour pool, and the changing market conditions in these southern regions of France – in conjunction with their pre-existing easy access to materials and expertise – now fulfilled enough of the prerequisites to allow silkworm raising to prosper, accompanied by local reeling operations, as small filatures sprang up to process the harvests, and market towns and larger communities located on transport nodes developed silk-processing and silk-manufacturing operations – the Cevenols region, for instance, becoming noted for its silk stockings. The numbers of cocoon filaments reeled together and the consequent thickness of the yarn depended upon the intended product, with eight used for ribbons, twelve to fourteen for heavier fabrics, and so on.[137] Much of the silk worked its way steadily outwards: from rural smallholders dotted across the countryside through reeling, spinning,

---

[135] Thomé, *Mémoires sur la manière d'élever les vers à soie*, 366–7.

[136] Michel Wienin, *Magnaneries cévenoles* (Vézenobres: Parc National des Cévennes, 1995); Écomusée de la Cévenne, *Magnanerie de la roque: Le fil de la mémoire* (Florac: Parc National des Cévennes, 2011).

[137] Savary des Brûlons and Savary, *Dictionnaire*, 3: 184–5. Savary estimated that two experienced and cooperative workers could wind and reel up to 3 lb of raw silk in one day. For detailed descriptions of traditional French reeling practices and the machinery, along with the innovative reel introduced by Vaucanson which improved French raw silk consistency and brought it closer to Piedmontese quality, Pomier, *L'art de Cultiver Les Mûriers-Blancs*, 172–216.

and throwing operations (performed by *dévideurs*, *filateurs* and *mouliniers*) to more centralised and regulated urban weaving operations.[138]

French authors in the eighteenth century built on the framework provided by the likes of De Serres and Isnard, taking every opportunity to link progress in sericulture with technological and botanical advances, and to share models of best practice and circulate ideas about artisanal techniques and entomological behaviours, often thanks to the patronage of institutions such as the Académie des Sciences.[139] Under their scrutiny, earlier proscriptions that supposed the female menstrual cycle to be damaging to silkworms were deemed unfounded, though careful choice of the women nominated to bear responsibility for hatching silkworm seed still betrayed gendered assumptions.[140] They also began to integrate information about Asian silk practices, which had been steadily if eclectically trickling back to Western Europe since Jesuit reports in the seventeenth century, later supplemented via merchants in the French East India Company. As one influential botanist put it in justifying his Asian references, 'the Chinese must be regarded as our Masters in the art of managing the silkworms and reeling their silk'.[141] He felt it astonishing that after so many voyages to the Far East by missionaries, by merchants, and explorers from all across Europe, no one had yet brought home any of the three identified Chinese species of silkworms.[142] Another, in response to questions posed by the royal agricultural society of Lyons, stressed that the peoples of China, Tongking, and Bengal 'must be our guide' rather than traditionalist claims derived from the French peasantry.[143] Where once the Atlantic had been an appealing site for policy and projection, the research that developed now looked to the East not the West, including the groundbreaking questionnaire disseminated at mid-century from

[138] For a microhistorical snapshot of silk production circuits in Bagnols, see Michel Cointat, *Rivarol (1753–1801): Un écrivain controversé* (Editions L'Harmattan, 2001).

[139] Besides Pomier, see: Chomel, *Dictionnaire Oeconomique*, 62–71; Pierre Augustin Boissier de Sauvages, *Mémoires sur l'éducation des vers à soie* (Nimes: Gaude, 1763); Thomé, *Mémoires sur la manière d'élever les vers à soie*; Denis Diderot and Jean le Rond d'Alembert, *Encyclopédie; Ou dictionnaire raisonné des sciences, des arts et des métiers*, 28 vols. (Paris: Briasson, 1751), 15: 268–306; Jean Paulet, *l'art du fabriquant d'étoffes de soie* (Paris: Academie Royales des Sciences, 1773).

[140] Thomé, *Mémoires sur la manière d'élever les vers à soie*, 66–8. In other settings, silkworm rearers were less inclined to break with sacred traditions that barred menstruating women from direct contact. John Walsh, *A History of Murshidabad District (Bengal) with Biographies of Some of Its Noted Families* (London: Jarrold, 1902), 106.

[141] Pomier, *L'art de cultiver les mûriers-blancs*, xxiii; Donald F. Lach and Edwin J. Van Kley, *Asia in the Making of Europe*, 3 vols. (Chicago: University of Chicago Press, 1998), 3: 1191, 1259.

[142] Pomier, *L'art de cultiver les mûriers-blancs*, 68.

[143] Thomé, *Mémoires sur la manière d'élever les vers à soie*, 66.

Languedoc to Continental Europe, throughout the Ottoman Empire, parts of Central and East Asia, and the Mascarene Islands.[144]

Evidence of Chinese influence was beginning to show by the mid-eighteenth century in French sericulture, notably in the use of netting, the design and temperature management of *magnaneries* (to reduce the period of silkworm feeding, *l'élevage hâté*), and some aspects of moriculture, especially in Provence. But it would take time for intercultural scientific claims and technological insights to reach practitioners and to challenge traditional practices, and it was not until the end of the eighteenth century that substantial progress would be made, paving the way for the golden era in French domestic sericulture in the early nineteenth century.[145] Agronomists themselves were resigned to an ongoing battle, and anticipated 'meet[ing] with abundance of opposition, especially amongst people bigotted to old customs'.[146]

In the meantime, if it was not worked up locally, much of the expanding domestic French raw silk of the early eighteenth century snaked its way by water or by mule to the increasingly dominant Grande Fabrique of Lyons.[147] French-raised silk, processed with increasing finesse into semi-finished yarn that was of respectable quality, found itself deployed alongside the lesser Italian yarns (of Milan, Modena, and Venice) typically in the weft of silk fabrics.[148] The triumph of Lyons had created the greatest single market for raw and semi-finished silk across Europe, shaping global perceptions not just of France but of fashion, finery, and industry. But it was a precarious pole position, threatened by the establishment of rival European industries, vulnerable to scarcities in raw materials, and challenged by the rising star of Oriental textile imports and designs. If by the midpoint of the eighteenth century, French raw silk production had increased marginally, it was only diluting the supply risk at the lower end of the quality spectrum, and still frequently required stocks of foreign

---

[144] Pierre-Etienne Stockland, 'Statecraft and Insect Oeconomies in the Global French Enlightenment (1670–1815)' (PhD thesis, Columbia University, 2018), 130–46.

[145] Mau Chuan-Hui, 'Les techniques séricicoles chinoises dans le développement de la sériciculture française de la fin du xviiie siècle au début du xixe siècle', in *Artisans, Industrie. Nouvelles Révolutions Du Moyen Âge à Nos Jours*, ed. Natasha Coquery et al. (Lyons: ENS Editions, 2004), 409–20; Mau Chuan-Hui, 'Enquêtes françaises sur la sériciculture chinoise et leur influence, fin xviiie–fin xixe siècles', *Documents pour l'histoire des techniques* 14 (2007): 24–36.

[146] Goyon de la Plombanie, 'Memoir upon the Manner of Breeding Silk-Worms in France, and All Other Climates Where Mulberry-Trees Can Be Cultivated', in *Select Essays on Commerce, Agriculture, Mines, Fisheries, and Other Useful Subjects*, ed. Tobias Smollett (London: D. Wilson & T. Durham, 1754), 485.

[147] Beauquis, *Histoire économique de la soie*, 12; Savary des Brûlons and Savary, *Dictionnaire*, 3: 190.

[148] Peyrot, 'Les techniques du commerce des soies', 34.

silkworm seed – often illegally secured across the Spanish border.[149] The caravans arriving in Smyrna each January with the finest raw silks from Persia remained vital, as did the distinctive Italian processed yarns (from Bologna, Piedmont, and Messina destined for Lyons and Tours) and raw silks (from Parma, Modena, Lucca, and Reggio), and even the Spanish raw silks (known as 'Soye de Grenade') that were spun, twisted, and thrown in France.[150] Like the Spanish before them, the French had reluctantly abandoned ideas of American sericulture to consolidate a mixture of domestic production and distinctive high-volume imports (to which they had particularly strong access). For other nations, the dream of Atlantic sericulture persisted and grew stronger in the eighteenth century, a dream inspired in part by the French model of expanding production, and in part by envy of the long shadow of Lyons.

---

[149] Stockland, 'Patriotic Natural History and Sericulture in the French Enlightenment', 6.
[150] Savary des Brûlons and Savary, *Dictionnaire*, 3: 197.

Part II

Persistence

5 Persistence

> In our Manufacture of Silk, it is true, the grand and fundamental
> Materials are foreign. But then, the Silk Manufactures are but of late
> called our own; it is an Improvement, and it is within the Reach of our
> Memory, that we bought all our wrought Silks, a few Ribbands
> excepted, from Abroad, to the Value of near two Millions a Year; and
> it may not be long before an improving Nation, as we are, may raise the
> Silk at Home too, or at least in our Colonies, as well as other Countries
> have done, which had none before, *viz. France, Italy* and *Spain.*
>
> Daniel Defoe, *A Plan of the English Commerce* (1728)[1]

Trading Demand and Supply

Spanish, English, and French agents had set themselves the challenge of
transplanting sericulture to new regions in the growing Atlantic world, in
each case pursuing experiments and plantations between 1500 and 1730
that reflected their own national histories of production. In spite of much
greater access to expertise, the Spanish and French eventually abandoned
the pursuit, frustrated by global trade and environmental or labour-
related hindrances, and by the second third of the eighteenth century,
both would be retrenching largely in domestic consolidation and quality
improvement, as the Italians had done before them (without the longer-
range forays). The English, much more heavily compromised by the
difficulties of sourcing materials and expertise for sericulture, had probably produced the smallest output and yet had at least succeeded – largely
through projection in Virginia – in creating an enduring literature of
colonial ambition, and a myth propounding the suitability of sericulture
for northern climes.

Between the mid-seventeenth and late eighteenth centuries, this ambition and myth was carried to all corners of northern Europe and the
Atlantic world in a range of different polities: Sweden, New England,

---

[1] Daniel Defoe, *A Plan of the English Commerce: Being a Compleat Prospect of the Trade of This
Nation, as Well the Home Trade as the Foreign* (London: Charles Rivington, 1728), 76.

Russia, Ireland, Prussia, the Carolinas, and Poland. The attempts to bring forth a new domestic sericulture in these regions were driven by the same core cultural and economic impulses that had long helped silk to spread, often stimulated by investment from state authorities interested in import substitution. The heightened sense of investment opportunity that characterised these efforts, however, was new. It was magnified in the century after 1650 by the dramatic acceleration in the global consumption of silk goods, and by the opening of new agricultural lands across the Atlantic and new textile markets in Africa and the East Indies. It was amplified by the diaspora of silk manufacturing skills and technology throughout Europe, and by the growing conviction that a functional and sustainable European economy ought to possess its own domestic supplies as a matter of status and power. The selectively remembered snapshots of production in England and Virginia in the earlier seventeenth century also encouraged other non-Mediterranean European powers to give credence to their domestic silk dreams and to act on their ambitions.

Ultimately, few European states persisted across time and space as extensively as did the British. The case for introducing sericulture to this 'improving Nation' (in Defoe's description of 1728) would be relentlessly reinforced over the long eighteenth century because of Britain's distinctive territorial reach into the Atlantic and Indian Ocean worlds, and its simultaneous development of an expansive hybrid silk industry at home that serviced global markets. Britain's persistence in trying to introduce mulberries and silkworms to many of its diverse Atlantic territories would overcome some of the initial hurdles encountered in the early seventeenth century, and have significant impacts on colonial lives and landscapes from the Carolinas to New England, albeit without quite bringing the metamorphosis that was hoped for by imperial authorities and entrepreneurial colonists. The attempts to introduce sericulture encouraged diverse colonial populations to confront the relationship between their worlds of material consumption and production, and exposed regional inflections relating to culture, labour, and environment. Persistence in trying to raise silkworms in America continued to bring new peoples to fledgling British colonies, to create new networks of knowledge, and to provide distinctive permutations of household labour – including significant roles for women.

The Gospel of Silk Production in Northern Europe

The increase in silk manufacturing activity in northern Europe after 1650 – such as the growing industries in the British Isles, the

Netherlands, and Switzerland – enhanced the vigour with which existing silk-raising regions attempted to control their supply of the raw material.[2] The silk-raising provinces of Mediterranean Europe – located predominantly in south-eastern Spain, southern France, and throughout Italian territories as far north as the Tyrol – obviously stood to benefit by manipulating their market position. Spain banned the export of its raw silk in 1699 and when it did so again in 1739, denying access to Valencia's dominant output (which likely harmed the prospects of its own silk raisers), it prompted other European powers to scuttle to find new sources of equivalent raw materials, probing in the Mediterranean markets of Salonica, Alexandria, and Cyprus as well as enlarging imports from farther afield.[3] The French monitored their raw silk production and the commodity's flow through privileges granted to Lyons in 1687 that were reinforced in 1721 and 1758.[4] They sought to make the most of domestic production, as we have seen, and to reduce their dependency on raw silk raised on the other side of the Alps, for fear of thriving cities being 'destroyed and impoverished by the disappearance of silk' as one royal official put it.[5] From the other direction, in northern Italy, numerous stoppages and bans were imposed – including in the Kingdom of Savoy (and Sardinia) in 1722, and Tuscany in 1693, 1697 (renewed in 1699), and 1749 – which affected what was available in any given year to take off from ports such as Leghorn (Livorno).[6] A British parliamentary commission determined in 1750 that damaging raw silk export prohibitions 'throughout all the *Italian* Principalities and States, as well as in

---

[2] See the various relevant regional chapters in Dagmar Schäfer, Giorgio Riello, and Luca Molà, eds., *Threads of Global Desire: Silk in the Pre-Modern World* (Woodbridge: Boydell and Brewer, 2018).

[3] Ricardo Franch Benavent, 'La sedería valenciana en el siglo xviii', in *España y Portugal en las rutas de la seda* (Barcelona: Universitat de Barcelona, 1996), 202–6; Martín Corrales, 'Comercio de la seda entre España y Mediterráneo', 162, 173; Natalie Rothstein, 'Silk in the Early Modern Period, c.1500–1780', in *The Cambridge History of Western Textiles*, ed. David Jenkins (Cambridge: Cambridge University Press, 2003), 556.

[4] Teisseyre-Sallmann, *Industrie de la soie en Bas-Languedoc*, 51–3; Jeff Horn, *Economic Development in Early Modern France: The Privilege of Liberty, 1650–1820* (Cambridge: Cambridge University Press, 2015), 53–4.

[5] 'Mémoire sur le commerce des soies', ANF F/12/1432A, Archives Nationales de France, Paris (hereinafter ANF). Paola Bertucci, 'Enlightened Secrets: Silk, Intelligent Travel, and Industrial Espionage in Eighteenth-Century France', *Technology and Culture* 54, no. 4 (2013): 820–52.

[6] Giuseppe Chicco, *La seta in Piemonte 1650–1800. Un sistema industriale d'ancien regime* (Milano: Angeli, 1995), 79; Vittorio Marchis, Mario Cordero, and Lucia Dessi, *Storie di fili di seta. Ovvero non tutti i bruchi diventano farfalle* (Milan: Silvana Editoriale, 2008), 20–6; Francesco Battistini, *Gelsi, Bozzoli e Caldaie: L'industria della seta in Toscana tra citt . . ., Borghi e Campagne (sec. xvi–xviii)*, L'officina Dello Storico (Firenze: L. S. Olschki, 1998), 60–71, 210–11; Corey Tazzara, *The Free Port of Livorno and the Transformation of the Mediterranean World, 1574–1790* (Oxford: Oxford University Press, 2017), 182.

Spain ... including the Papal Dominions' were drying up the raw silk market or driving up the thrown silk price to such an extent that looms and weavers were being laid off.[7]

Any advantage for states controlling raw silk production, however, was somewhat diluted by the particular conflicts that raged in many of these zones in the early part of the eighteenth century. The War of the Spanish Succession (1701–14) brought war and disruption to northern Italy (especially Milan and Savoy) and to Portugal (damaging a small region of production at Trás-os-Montes), and eventually parcelled off the Kingdom of Naples and the Duchy of Milan to the Habsburg Emperor Charles VI of Austria, and the Kingdom of Sicily to Victor Amadeus II of Savoy (until 1720 when he was forced to exchange it for Sardinia). The Ottoman–Venetian War (1714–18) involved armies rampaging through the silk-producing Greek lands of Morea (lost to the Turks), and much war-induced stagnation.[8] Farther east, access to Persian silk was repeatedly compromised between 1722 and 1747 on account of a host of obstacles – rebellions, wars between Ottomans, Russians, and Safavids, and famines and plagues amongst key producer populations – which encouraged merchants to look to alternative sources (not just of silks but also cottons and coffees).[9] Cumulatively, these disruptions served to reinforce the sense amongst nations without stable supplies of raw silk that they ought to prioritise sericulture within their territories if practicable, and if not, do what they could to spread the risk.[10]

The changing equations of supply and demand even encouraged the revisiting of attempts to grow silk in the British Isles in the early eighteenth century. The most coordinated effort began in 1718 and was exhaustively described by Henry Barham, a Fellow of the Royal Society whose interests in national commodity innovation had already emerged during his time as a physician in Jamaica, when he wrote on logwood.[11] Between 1718 and 1724, Barham and one John Appletree established a joint-stock

---

[7] House of Commons, *Journals of the House of Commons*, 56 vols. (London: H. M. Stationery Office, 1803), 25: 996 (February 1750).

[8] Charles W. Ingrao, Nikola Samardžić, and Jovan Pesalj, *The Peace of Passarowitz, 1718* (Ashland, OH: Purdue University Press, 2011), 65; Fernando de Sousa, 'The Silk Industry in Trás-Os-Montes during the Ancient Regime', *Journal of Portuguese History* 3, no. 2 (2005): 1–14.

[9] Syrian silks were one such alternative for several powers. David Hancock, *Citizens of the World: London Merchants and the Integration of the British Atlantic Community, 1735–1785* (Cambridge: Cambridge University Press, 1997), 122; Matthee, *The Politics of Trade in Safavid Iran*, 203–30.

[10] For a discussion of these issues of raw silk supply and political economy influencing French policy and practice, see Stockland, 'Patriotic Natural History and Sericulture in the French Enlightenment.'

[11] Jennifer L. Anderson, *Mahogany: The Costs of Luxury in Early America* (Cambridge, MA: Harvard University Press, 2012), 218–20.

company with a view to a major new sericulture initiative based at Chelsea Park (see Plate 7), upon which a 122-year lease was taken out, with the support of a patent from King George I that granted a monopoly 'to manage and produce raw Silk of the growth of England'.[12] Their proposals attracted over 500 subscriptions that made small speculative contributions. This was enough to launch the project with the plantation of over 2,000 white and black mulberry trees by 1718 and the construction of a number of state-of-the-art buildings the next year that together occupied a third of the park. The company seems to have devoted particular attention to sustaining the right temperatures for silkworms, through installation of an evaporating stove and the patenting of 'a certain engine called the Egg Cheste', likely for the storage of silkworm seed.[13]

Barham did not lack in confidence. He prefaced his 1719 essay on the project by claiming that 'all objections and difficulties against this glorious undertaking, are shewn to be mere phantoms and trifles', and affirming that the 'glaring facts, and unerring experience' that he recounted would dispel them. His long and passionate essay – part history, part marketing brochure – began by ridiculing the sceptics who doubted the line of 'worthies' from whom Barham saw himself descending, including James I, Samuel Hartlib, and Edward Digges. Barham did much more than replicate English-language works on the subject of sericulture. He integrated them with the publications of Isnard and Malpighi, and therefore offered what amounted to a creative work of synthesis whose tone would be emulated in many works on silk that followed, for Anglo-American readerships. Barham had explanations for everything, beginning with how silkworms must have crept into Noah's Ark, which he used to support claims that the ark's descendants had initially settled and prospered in China; in the process, he subordinated Chinese origin myths about silk into European world views.[14] He was especially preoccupied with notions of national guilt, in failing to exploit sericultural potential. He explained how the Spanish had thrown away their advantages in silk, having once 'had the best Silk-Worms eggs in *Europe*', but claimed that people had become distracted by the easier gold and silver of America.[15] He put English failure in the mid-seventeenth century down to 'unnatural

---

[12] Henry Barham, *An Essay upon the Silkworm* (London: J. Betterham and T. Bickerton, 1719), 175.

[13] Barham, *An Essay upon the Silkworm*; Henry Barham, 'A Letter of the Curious Mr. Henry Barham, R.S. Soc. to Sir Hans Sloan', *Philosophical Transactions of the Royal Historical Society of London* 30 (1719): 1036–8. 'On the Attempts that have been made to Introduce the Culture of Silk in This Country', *European Magazine & London Review* (August 1798), 934.

[14] Barham, *An Essay upon the Silkworm*, 8–18.

[15] Barham, *An Essay upon the Silkworm*, 43–4.

wars and broils, which were the cause why it did not succeed', though as we have seen, there was little evidence for this.[16]

The Chelsea Park scheme may have been dressed up as an English venture, but Barham made mention of foreign expertise in an accompanying scientific paper that offered insights into his raw silk yields. It recorded that in late April 1719 the silkworm seed had arrived from Languedoc, and 'Hatcht of themselves' on 6 May – which Barham attributed to a warm southerly wind. After a dutiful spell of feeding and rearing, the silkworms spun their cocoons in the final week of June and first week of July. Barham then reported that '*Mons. Lachivre* began to wind off their Silk-Balls with a Machine that made great dispatch, winding much fine Silk in a Day.' No mention had been made of Lachivre in the much longer essay, perhaps because it would have compromised the nationalistic tone. But the novelty of the machine and fineness of the product suggest an accomplished hand – as well as a reeler with a good amount of patience, considering Barham insisted four times on counting exactly how many cocoons weighed 3 lb (it averaged 830), and then how much reeled raw silk they produced in aggregate (17 oz of fine silk, with 7 oz of waste). Barham's conclusion was that English silk matched the proportional quality of that reeled in Calabria (at 12 lb of raw silk per ounce of silkworm eggs), and was superior to Languedoc, Provence, and Brescia in Italy. That his sample was ludicrously small did not seem to bother him.[17]

The only thing Barham seemed not to have an explanation for was how his silkworm operation at Chelsea failed, and it is not known when the directors met for the last time, as they had been doing on a monthly basis at the house of a Mr Foulks near Chancery Lane.[18] The Chelsea Park scheme clearly did generate some output of raw silk – described by one writer as 'a han[d]some quantity' in 1722–4, in their bid to bring it to the attention of politician Sir Robert Walpole.[19] A silkworm experimenter later in the eighteenth century, Henrietta Rhodes, noted that many of the trees remained in the 1780s, and advocated another trial in the area, while admitting that 'how it miscarried, I have not learnt'.[20] Another later commentator pointed to the more general collapse in investment in speculative schemes in the aftermath of the South Sea Bubble, which

[16] Barham, *An Essay upon the Silkworm*, 70.
[17] Barham, 'A Letter of the Curious Mr. Henry Barham, R.S. Soc. to Sir Hans Sloan.'
[18] Barham, *An Essay upon the Silkworm*, 180.
[19] T. Thomsby to Lord Hercourt, 12 March 1724, NA SP 35/42/1/f 67. Thomsby claimed, wrongly, that the raw silk 'is ye first yt has bin knowne to have bin raised in England'.
[20] Letter from Henrietta Rhodes, Bridgnorth, 28 December 1786, *Journals and Transactions of the RSA* 5 (1787): 69.

coincided with Barham and Appletree's project, suggesting this 'contributed to derange the original design'.[21] But over the course of a four- or five-year period, we might presume that the same environmental hazards that had compromised seventeenth-century efforts in England took their toll, in spite of the attempts to anticipate low temperatures and inclement weather.

The English had again proved better at holding the silkworm up as a mirror to reflect on national virtue than treating it as a filter with which to understand environmental determinism. As one tongue-in-cheek newspaper letter put it, assuming the perspective of silkworms, 'we like the climate … yet whether it be your indolence and sloth, your backwardness to improvement, or your aversion to have foreigners come among you … we have met with very barbarous usage here'.[22] Barham and others' over-exaggerations about the hardiness of *Morus alba* and *Bombyx mori*, however, would help lead others in northern Europe down similar cul-de-sacs. The hopes of the Chelsea investors to end up exporting 'great quantities' of British raw silk 'to *Holland, Germany, Muscovy,* and other places' was more than matched by those regions' ambition to generate their own supplies (see Map 2).[23]

Russia had been some fifty years behind England in seeking to domesticate sericulture, beginning experiments in the 1660s, and gaining significant momentum under the auspices of the reformist Peter the Great. The emperor extended patronage to a small Russian silk-manufacturing industry, luring Iranian and Armenian weavers to set up new manufactories in the 1710s, as Moscow and St Petersburg developed niche silk industries that catered for elite demand. Under Peter, Russia also advanced plans for improving trade to neighbouring sericultural zones, winning the right to purchase silk in Gilan and Shirvan in a Russo-Iranian commercial deal in 1720, before opting for outright war two years later when his forces invaded the Caspian littoral.[24] Attempts to establish silk raising in Russian territories in the eighteenth century concentrated on the Volga-Akhtuba floodplain, between Tsaritsyn (now Volgagrad) and Astrakhan, as well as the nearby Terek river valley (especially at Kizlar) which also drains into the Caspian Sea. Russian authorities approved proposals by two French entrepreneurs and a German for developing sericulture and stocking manufacture near Saratov, where 50,000 mulberries were planted by 1769. Any hopes to create a 'Russian Ghilan',

---

[21] Thomas Croker, *A Walk from London to Fulham* (London: William Tegg, 1860), 90–1.
[22] Letter from 'Silkworm', *Mr. Mist's Weekly Journal or Saturdays Post* (London), issue 101, 15 November 1718.
[23] Barham, *An Essay upon the Silkworm*, 179.
[24] Matthee, *The Politics of Trade in Safavid Iran*, 219–22, 228.

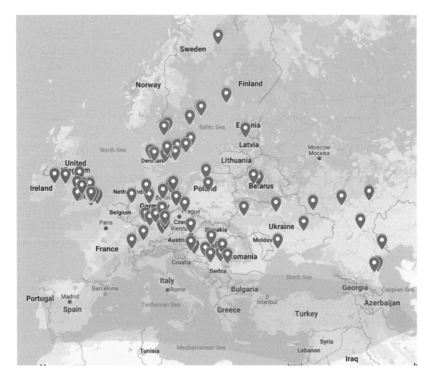

Map 2 Indicative map of European sites pursuing silk production. Known new sites of plantation of mulberries and attempted raising of silkworms, *c.*1650–1800. Excludes those in existing areas of sericulture (such as Spain, France, and Italian regions), whose main concentrations are shown in the shaded Mediterranean band

however, met with environmental obstacles in a climate less forgiving (drier and colder) than that of the humid and warm silk heartlands of Transcaucasia. Mismatched against their productive neighbours, from whom they could at least procure silkworm stocks easily, inhabitants of the Russian North Caucasus preferred to pursue securer income through livestock and fishing, and experiments were therefore fleeting and produced only small amounts in 1720, 1756, and 1782. Smaller mulberry and silkworm operations were later attempted around the Donets river at Belgorod and the Dnieper river in the vicinity of Kiev (Ukraine), including on imperial gardens where plantations of mulberries were established, though probably compromised by spring frosts. At the end of the century, Catherine the Great's minister Grigory Potemkin pursued hopes for silk production in the Taurida region (Crimean lands annexed from the Ottomans in 1783). But the Crimea, like the Volga-Akhtuba before it, did not quite match up to the environmental exoticism which Russian rulers wishfully imagined for their southern conquests.[25]

The realm of Brandenburg-Prussia also sought to engineer a domestic silk industry, beginning with the chance to capitalise on the arrival of upwards of 20,000 Huguenots who were invited to settle in Hohenzollern lands through the generous Edict of Potsdam in 1685. Although French silk weavers and others struggled to thrive in Berlin, royal backing allowed a flagship state manufactory to continue to operate, because King Frederick William I deemed the reputational value worthy of the loss of investment. He raised tariffs on foreign imports and granted special privileges to selected silk manufacturing interests, including a small number of Jewish specialists in Potsdam who sourced goods through the Leipzig fair and were running 100 silk looms, including velvet production, in the 1730s. A second, more organic, centre of silk production arose in Crefeld (a Rhineland city that passed to Prussia in 1702), where Mennonites who had migrated from Holland in the late seventeenth century – particularly the von der Leyen family – made a less directed transition from silk merchants to manufacturers.

Under Frederick the Great in the mid-eighteenth century, Prussian state interventionism and patronage of silk deepened spectacularly. New centres at Magdeburg and Bernau supplemented Potsdam, Berlin, and Crefeld in the second half of the century, while bans were placed on silk imports, including of goods onward-bound to Poland and Russia (which encouraged widespread smuggling). Attempts to produce Prussian raw silk correspondingly intensified and reached a substantial scale, with the plantation of perhaps a million mulberry trees, as dutiful royal agents within Prussian dominions fought hard to counter the environmental deficit they faced on account of low temperatures. Decrees coerced public officials, institutions, and spaces, especially around Berlin, into supporting the initiative: teachers, ministers, orphanages, monasteries, and cemeteries were reconfigured to supply leaves and experiment with silkworm raising. The levels of state investment in sericulture became

---

[25] William Tooke, *View of the Russian Empire during the Reign of Catharine the Second, and to the Close of the Present Century*, 3 vols. (London: T. N. Longman and O. Rees, 1799), 3: 276–85; Simon S. Montefiore, *Catherine the Great & Potemkin: The Imperial Love Affair* (Hachette UK, 2010), ch. 17; I. Zonn, A.Kostianoy, A.Kosarev, and M.Glantz, *The Caspian Sea Encyclopedia* (London: Springer, 2010), 79; Andreas Schönle, 'Garden of the Empire: Catherine's Appropriation of the Crimea', *Slavic Review* 60, no. 01 (27 January 2001): 1–23; Roger P. Bartlett, *Human Capital: The Settlement of Foreigners in Russia, 1762–1804* (Cambridge: Cambridge University Press, 1979), 132, 155–8; Philippa Scott, *The Book of Silk* (London: Thames and Hudson, 1993), 209–10.

unsustainable in the 1780s, in spite of the best efforts of the elder states-
man Count Hertzberg to bolster activity, which had reached 11,000 lb of
output in one year. But long before then a small national silk industry had
at least been founded, which generated persistent demand for raw and
thrown silk in the expanding Prussian lands of the eighteenth century –
furnishing many of Frederick's castle interiors, and turning Crefeld into
a major export centre that capitalised on cheap regional labour, albeit
never threatening to turn Berlin into a new Lyons.[26]

Further west, the restless and competitive rulers of German principalities had been no less eager to create luxury industries to demonstrate
their credibility, drawing on translations of works such as Isnard's.[27]
Samuel Hartlib recorded attempts in Cologne in 1655, where women
'have a Priviledge to sell their Silk which they make with their silk-
wormes', though an exile from the Duchy of Cleves, Joachim Hübner,
reported experiments in such 'cold countries being difficult to initiate'.[28]
Karl Ludvig, the Elector Palatinate who had spent much time and perhaps been influenced in Stuart England, issued regulations for planting
mulberries in the Rhineland in 1664 but on poorly chosen lands. Only in
Heidelberg did the trees prosper, leading to further attempts in the
Palatinate in 1728 and 1748, employing Italian experts and offering
monopolies to manufacturers, the latter firmly supported by Prince-
Elector Karl Theodor whose support helped to generate a few thousand
pounds' weight of cocoons. Projectors elsewhere in German lands tried to
introduce sericulture, including in Schaumburg-Lippe, Anhalt-Köthen,

[26] Liah Greenfeld, *The Spirit of Capitalism: Nationalism and Economic Growth* (Cambridge, MA: Harvard University Press, 2001), 176–8; Cinzia Lorandini, 'Family, Partnerships, and Network: Reflections on the Strategies of the Salvadori Firm of Trento (17th–18th Centuries)', Department of Economics Working Papers 0707Department of Economics: University of Trento, Italy, 2007), 4–6, www.academia.edu/7438515/Family_Partners hips_and_Network_Reflections_on_the_Strategies_of_the_Salvadori_Firm_of_Trent o_17th-18th_Centuries; Herbert Kisch, 'Prussian Mercantilism and the Rise of the Krefeld Silk Industry: Variations upon an Eighteenth-Century Theme', *Transactions of the American Philosophical Society* 58, no. 7 (1968): 3–50; Jeffry M. Diefendorf, *Businessmen and Politics in the Rhineland* (Princeton: Princeton University Press, 1980), 30–2; Florian Schui, *Early Debates about Industry: Voltaire and His Contemporaries* (London: Palgrave Macmillan, 2005), 71–6; Karola Paepke, 'Die Brandenburgisch-Preuáische Seidenindustrie im 17. und 18. Jahrhundert', in *18th-Century Silks: The Industries of England and Northern Europe*, ed. Regula Schorta (Riggisberg: Abegg-Stiftung, 2000), 197–210.
[27] Christoph Isnard and Georg Kapfer, *Kurtze und Gründtliche Underweisung / Wie die Weisse Maulbeer-Bäum / in disen Landen auff Underschidliche Weiß / Zu Erzüglung der Seyden-Würmen, dem Allgemainen Wesen zum Besten / Sollen Gepflantzt Werden* (Vienna: Kürrner, 1669); Christophle Isnard, *Neue Seiden-Manufactur, Das Ist, Ausführliche Erzehlung Wie Maulbeer-Bäume und Seiden-Würme Gepfleget, Gewartet, Fortgepflantzet, und die Darzu Bereitete Seide Recht Zugerichtet und Genutzet* (Leipzig: Winckler, 1693).
[28] Hartlib Papers, Ephemerides, 1652, 29/5/34A; Extracts of Letters, 61/7/9A.

Cologne, and the larger Duchy of Saxony (where some 35,000 trees were planted between 1744 and 1755), and the Landgraviate of Hesse-Kassel (where the landgrave Frederick II planted over 6,000 mulberries, including outside the state orphanage) amongst others. In many of these locations, the strictness with which ruling authorities enforced mulberry plantation and the 'spirit of monopoly and of tyranny' that artificially lowered cocoon prices or introduced taxes in labour turned local populations against the endeavour – to the point where mulberries were sometimes targeted and felled.[29]

Huge Swedish demand for thrown and finished silks from the East Indies and Italy in the early eighteenth century prompted governing authorities and naturalists to turn their attention to home manufacture, and domesticating sericulture. Nurturing a luxury weaving industry was a priority for the mercantilists who sought to regenerate the state from the 1720s, beginning with the recruitment of foreign specialists from Holland and northern German states. The Riksdag (Swedish parliament) introduced high duties in the 1740s, culminating in a total ban on Chinese silk imports in 1754, as an emphasis grew on supporting and wearing Swedish products, such as those produced by almost 900 looms in Stockholm. Much of the silk produced in Sweden was channelled through Queen Lovisa Ulrika – who, like her daughter, Sophia Albertina, was celebrated for supporting the industry and extending royal promotion and patronage. Lovisa Ulrika is often described in unfairly passive terms, as having been induced into patronising sericulture by her brother Frederick of Prussia, or captivated by Voltaire. But the active agency and impetus that she brought to the pursuit of Swedish sericulture was independent and important.[30] As a consequence of this political support and wider market demand, between the 1730s and 1760s, Mårten Triewald, Carl Linnaeus, and his botanical apostle Eric Gustaf Lidbeck intensively pursued efforts to sustain white mulberry trees

---

[29] H. M. Scott, ed., *Enlightened Absolutism: Reform and Reformers in Later Eighteenth-Century Europe* (Basingstoke: Palgrave Macmillan, 1990), 232–3; Charles W. Ingrao, *The Hessian Mercenary State: Ideas, Institutions, and Reform under Frederick II, 1760–1785* (Cambridge: Cambridge University Press, 2002), 67–8, 116, 3. Ogilvie, 'The Beginnings of Industrialization', in *Germany: A New Social and Economic History, Vol. II: 1630–1800*, ed. S. Ogilvie (London: Edward Arnold, 1996), 263–308; Anders Johansson Åbonde, 'Drömmen Om Svenskt Silke: Silkesodlingens Historia i Sverige 1735–1920' (Alnarp, 2010), 149–51. Final quote from memoir of Bailiff Hout to Agricultural Society of the Grand Duchy of Baden, Manheim, 6 April 1825, reprinted in Joseph Hazzi, *Letter from James Mease* (Washington: Printed by D. Green, 1828), 43.

[30] Some of the fabrics they reportedly wore, designed by Jean Eric Rehn and woven by the workshop of Bartholomé Peyron, were part-manufactured from Kanton and Lund raw silk in 1766, and survive at the Nordic Museum Collections.

and silkworms at a number of chosen sites.[31] That Sweden's brief window of Atlantic colonialism in the mid-seventeenth century had closed without opening new territories for Swedish silk production became part of a wishful situational narrative linked to the eighteenth-century trials.[32]

Triewald, one of the founders of the Royal Swedish Academy of Sciences, began inauspiciously when a dozen black mulberry trees froze dead in the winter of 1735. Although he managed to secure silkworms from Malaga and an all-important reel from Marseille, a cold spring in 1741 dashed his modest progress, again obliterating the mulberries that he had planted – this time a mix of black and white. Triewald's experiments initiated a Swedish intervention in the debate about the relative properties of mulberries, and he drew on Virginian insights in proposing how best to plant the trees, recommending planting them in hedges and as fences so that they did not intrude upon soil for mainstay crops. Carl Linnaeus was convinced that moriculture was practicable 'Even in the North', as the text of a 1755 prize gold medallion handed out by the queen put it. Linnaeus encouraged Triewald to undertake further experiments, sent acolytes abroad to conduct research on mulberries (Per Kalm to North America in 1747, John Gustaf Hallman to Italy in 1749, and Lidbeck to Brandenburg and Saxony in 1752), exchanged a number of letters on the subject, and authored a twelve-page synthetic work on silk moths in 1756. His thesis concluded: 'since our climate is good enough to sow white mulberry, it follows by logical inference that silkworms could and ought to be raised in the country'. But both the precept and the associated claim were problematic.[33]

[31] Johansson Åbonde, 'Drömmen Om Svenskt Silke', esp. 23–58; Sten Lindroth, *Kungl. Svenska Vetenskapsakadamiens Historia 1739–1818*, 3 vols. (Stockholm: Almqvist & Wiksell, 1967); Elisabet Stavenow-Hidemark, 'The Silk Industry in Sweden in the 18th Century', in *18th-Century Silks: The Industries of England and Northern Europe*, ed. Regula Schorta (Riggisberg: Abegg-Stiftung, 2000), 163–72; 'Affairs in the North, in Germany, &c.', *The Scots Magazine* 16 (1754): 540–2; Hanna Hodacs, *Silk and Tea in the North: Scandinavian Trade and the Market for Asian Goods in Eighteenth-Century Europe* (Palgrave Macmillan, 2016); H. Arnold Barton, 'Canton at Drottningholm: A Model Manufacturing Community from the Mid-Eighteenth Century', *Scandinavian Studies* 49 (1977), 81–98.
[32] Daniel A. Backman, 'The Benefits which our Dear Fatherland might have derived from the Colonies in America formerly called New Sweden', thesis of 1754, translated in P. Collinson and Esther Louise Larsen, 'Peter Kalm, Preceptor', *The Pennsylvania Magazine of History and Biography* 74, no. 4 (1950): 507–11.
[33] Carl Linnaeus and John Lyman, *Dissertatio Academica, de Phalaena Bombyce* (Uppsala: L. M. Hojer, 1756), 12. For examples of correspondence: Johan Gustaf Wahlbom to Carl Linnaeus, Berlin, 12 June 1753, L1604; Mårten Kähler to Carl Linnaeus, Naples, 8 October 1754, L1826; Peter Hernquist to Carl Linnaeus, Lyons, 13 August 1764, L3438, Linnaean Correspondence Online.

Royal sources and the government's new manufacturing department soon funded schemes that went well beyond Triewald's. These included a model complex near Stockholm, named Kanton, which (amongst other pursuits) employed a French specialist, Jean Meaurin, to try to nurture mulberries and furnish raw silk to the small on-site workshops that manufactured sewing silk, stockings, ribbons, and lace. Support paid for a plantation of white mulberries at the Academy of Sciences at Ladugårdslandet, which had 25,000 trees in 1758, but this had fallen to 6,000 a decade later, and dwindled to just 300 trees in 1797. The department also offered bounties to the general population for sustained mulberry plantation and raw silk production, requiring certification from Lidbeck, now installed as the director of the botanical garden at Lund. Lidbeck tried to use his university nursery as a launch pad for mulberry plantation throughout Sweden, laying out over 8,000 white mulberry plants at a nearby site named 'Paradislyckan' (Paradise Happiness), and firing off seeds and slips as far north as the subarctic Skellefteå. A local wrote back triumphantly that 'they stand in their snowstorms as well as they fare in Italy!' In Turku (Finland), professors Pehr Adrian Gadd and Pehr Kalm planted over a thousand mulberries, acting, like Lidbeck, as suppliers for smaller operations typically pursued by nobles, priests, and local officials in nearby estates.

The educational and literary background of the key Swedish projectors ensured that they left extensive insights about their trials, revealing problems and obsessions particular to northern experiments on either side of the Atlantic. Prominent amongst these again was the problem of securing expertise, for in spite of the touring botanists, Lidbeck could not secure funds to send someone to study sericulture in Piedmont and Languedoc as he wished in 1758. Certain of their observations reveal a reliance upon dated manuals, and gaps between theory and practices. Swedish chickens apparently turned their beaks up at the idea of eating spent silk moths, though Swedish spiders, mice, and even frogs were happy to prey on the caterpillars when left unattended. When they were attended, the reports suggested extensive involvement of female labour. Two Swedish authors also independently noticed that the presence of menstruating female workers did not seem to damage silkworms, an observation which led Triewald not to dismiss the theory that menstruation in the workers was detrimental, but to differentiate between cleanly Scandinavians and slovenly French. At Paradislyckan, Lidbeck expressly hired women to pick the mulberry leaves for a daily wage.

But if this was paradise, it was cold, and sooner or later, the temperatures took their toll. Swedish silkworm eggs needed warming around tiled ovens to persuade them to hatch, and, once the insects were feeding,

Lidbeck stressed the need for special heated silk houses – on one occasion bringing boxes to his bedroom to prevent their freezing. The white mulberries, mostly from Piedmont, might not leaf fully until the end of June, leading to the need for substitute food that inevitably led to sub-standard silk. Tips in the literature – such as advice on how to cover young plants in winter – might tide growers over for a season, but every few years a bad winter (like that of 1759–60) wrecked prospects. Because of these inescapable but oft-unstated environmental constraints, Swedish silk attempts produced little by way of raw product – Lidbeck reaching a maximum of some 25 lb of raw silk in 1780, by which time the political environment had also cooled. By the end of the decade, the commoners of Lund were invading Paradislyckan and, as in some German territories, felling white mulberries to use as fuel.

Other parts of central Europe also took up experimentation in silk production, drawing naturally on models and resources spread outwards from northern Italy: silkworms were brought to Jičín (north-east of Prague) by Bohemians in the 1620s, Brody (near Lviv) by Polish Lithuanians a few years later, and Denmark–Norway in the 1670s and 1720s, in experiments whose course, output, and duration was similar to those pursued in the British Isles.[34] Only in one locale, the Banat region (centred in what is now western Romania), which became a province of the Austrian Habsburgs in 1718, was it clear that sericulture had spread successfully to colonise a virgin territory in the early eighteenth century as it had in parts of southern France. Its establishment owed to the coming together of the prerequisites identified in the prologue: firstly, a workable environment, thanks to the peculiar geographic protection offered to the Pannonian Basin by the Alps and the Carpathian Mountains, with good soils, adequate moisture, and warm summers. Migrant labour and exper-tise, in adequate numbers, were also important to the progress, and was accounted for by significant numbers of Italians led by an abbot from

---

[34] John Mitchell, *The Life of Wallenstein, Duke of Friedland* (London: James Fraser, 1837), 93. Malgorzata Lochynska, 'History of Sericulture in Poland', *Journal of Natural Fibers* 7, no. 4 (2010): 334–7; Elena Karpenko, 'The Golden Century of Silk Weaving: Kontush Belts and Portraits of the Nobility from the Collection of M. K. Chiurlionis National Art Museum (Kaunas)', online catalogue archive (2015): www.artmuseum.by/eng/vyst/the-last-exhibitions/archive-2015/. Kjell Lundquist, 'Reconstruction of the Planting in Uraniborg, Tycho Brahe's (1546–1601) Renaissance Garden on the Island of Ven', *Garden History* 32, no. 2 (2004): 163–4; Paul Douglas Lockhart, *Denmark, 1513–1660: The Rise and Decline of a Renaissance Monarchy* (Oxford: Oxford University Press, 2007), 136; Leonora Christina Ulfeldt, *Jammers-Minde*, ed. Soph. Birket Smith and Johan Waldstein Wartemberg (Copenhagen: Gyldendalske Boghandel, 1869), 220–1, 243; Anne Kjellberg, 'English 18th-Century Silks in Norway', in *18th-Century Silks: The Industries of England and Northern Europe*, ed. Regula Schorta (Riggisberg: Abegg-Stiftung, 2000), 135–45; Johansson Åbonde, 'Drömmen Om Svenskt Silke', 154–5.

Mantua, who were concentrated around the village they renamed Carani in 1735. Extensive supplies of white mulberry trees were ensured by decree of the first governor, Count Claudius de Mercy, and subsequently reinforced by Empress Maria Teresa in the 1760s, who insisted mulberries be planted along roadsides (and protected them with a death penalty). And labour density was addressed through the deliberate sponsored settlement of colonial populations, including Swabian, French, and dozens of further Italian families from Trentino, some 600 miles due west, who raised silkworms at Dudeștii Noi and Charlottenburg (a model village whose mulberries are still prominent) – delivering either raw silk or cocoons to the throwing works at Vršac (now Serbia).[35] In comparison, while Maria Theresa spent more than 33,000 florins in the six years from 1749 on distributing over 300,000 mulberry saplings in the vicinity of Vienna, the injection did not last, or accomplish its aim of 'the winning of silk for the Imperial-Royal hereditary lands' as her advisor Johann H. G. Justi put it in the title of one of his policy proposals.[36] It was easier to swallow up pre-existing Italian silk regions into the Habsburg domains by diplomatic exchange or intermarriage.

Situational Innovation: British Opportunities

In its quest for new sites of production and sources of raw silk, the British silk industry clearly had plenty in common with many rival powers in northern Europe frustrated by problems of supply. But three features placed Britain in a distinctive situation in the early eighteenth century: the pace of its domestic manufacturing upswing, the reach of its oceanic trade in the East Indies, and the dynamic growth of its colonial populations in the Atlantic world. Against a backdrop of falling access to Levantine and Mediterranean raw silk, then, and under the political spotlight of the growing demand of British silk throwers and silk weavers, two very different imperial scenes would be acted out simultaneously. In the theatre of the East Indies, British merchants sought to capture a substantial market share of Persian, Bengali, and Chinese raw silk, and to influence its composition to fit it for English processing. In the theatre of the Atlantic, in a much less well-known performance that is the

---

[35] Urdea, 'Sericiculture in Romania between Tradition and an Uncertain Future'; John Paget, *Hungary and Transylvania: With Remarks on Their Condition, Social, Political, and Economical*, 2 vols. (London: John Murray, 1839), 2:141; *The Literary Panorama, Vol. 2* (London: Cox, Son, and Baylis, 1807), 1023–4.

[36] M. Bucek, *Geschichte der Seidenbarikanten Wiens im 18. Jahrhundert* (Vienna, 1974), 97–100; Johanna M. Menzel, 'The Sinophilism of J. H. G. Justi', *Journal of the History of Ideas* 17, no. 3 (June 1956): 300.

focus of the chapters that follow, British colonists broadened and deepened their quest to introduce raw silk in the European style, experimenting with species and environments as they tried to make sericulture work alongside other forms of colonial production.

The period between roughly 1660 and 1740 witnessed huge increases in the quantity of silk passing through English ships and ports, and correspondingly large increases in the amount of raw or semi-finished silk worked up by throwers and weavers in the British Isles, which would be consumed domestically or exported to foreign markets. Silk imports stood at more than a third of a million pounds in weight already in the early 1660s, when silk throwsters were amongst the foreigners who secured naturalisation rights after the Restoration, adding to a domestic pool of perhaps 40,000 labourers.[37] In the final third of the seventeenth century, English traders and particularly the East India Company were effectively muscling in on the seaborne commerce in silk exported from India, Bengal, and later China, bringing both wrought goods and raw silk and silk yarns back to London in increasing volume and value, which the company sold off at four great auctions each year.[38] At the same time, the gulf between the luxuriance and range of fabrics created in Italian cities and those woven or knitted in northern Europe was narrowing rapidly, thanks in no small part to the outmigration of Huguenot manufacturers from French centres such as Tours and Lyons with their capital, connections, designs, and experience. Their influx into Spitalfields added huge additional impetus and capacity to the fledgling silk industry in London that was already export-oriented.[39] The concentration in the metropolis eventually absorbed or smothered some older silk operations such as Canterbury's broadlooms. But the expansion was complemented by specialised silk or part-silk manufacturing centres in provincial locations, such as ribbons in Coventry, thread and buttons in Macclesfield, Leek, and Congleton, stockings in Nottingham, Derby, and Tewkesbury, part-silk products in Dublin, Norwich (such as its famous *bombazine*), and Canterbury, and plenty of other sites involved in manufacturing narrow

[37] Ralph Davis, *Aleppo and Devonshire Square: English Traders in the Levant in the 18th Century* (London: Macmillan, 1967), 125. Shaw, *Letters of Denization*, 78, 123; John Raithby, ed., *Statutes of the Realm: Volume 5, 1628–80* (London: Great Britain Record Commission, 1819), 407–9.

[38] K. N. Chaudhuri, *The Trading World of Asia and the English East India Company, 1660–1760* (Cambridge: Cambridge University Press, 1978), esp. ch. 20.

[39] Nuala Zahedieh, *The Capital and the Colonies: London and the Atlantic Economy, 1660–1700* (Cambridge: Cambridge University Press, 2010), 267; Robin D. Gwynn, *Huguenot Heritage the History and Contribution of the Huguenots in Britain* (London: Routledge & Kegan Paul, 1985), 67–9; Zara Anishanslin, *Portrait of a Woman in Silk: Hidden Histories of the British Atlantic World* (New Haven: Yale University Press, 2016).

ware (including lace, fringe, braid, trimmings, and embroidery). By selecting winnable battles – for instance leaving the top-end furnishing silks as the province of Italian and Turkish manufacturers – the young hybrid British silk industry made commercial and manufacturing inroads into mid-range dress goods, and secured a presence in domestic, colonial, and foreign marketplaces, claiming to employ 200,000 persons in London alone in 1689.[40] As historian Ralph Davis put it having scoured the records of the Levant Company, 'in the early part of the eighteenth century the best prospects for growth among the English textile industries appeared to lie in silk rather than cotton manufacture'.[41]

The records of silk imports (see Fig. 5.1) highlight how the English industry at the start of the eighteenth century had become divided into three substantial dimensions (represented in the chart's columns, each of which was worth more than £70,000 in value): firstly throwsters worked up large quantities of Levantine raw silk into yarn, mostly for weft or coarser goods such as stockings; secondly broadloom weavers worked with high-quality Italian thrown silk; and thirdly English merchants and consumers disposed of high volumes of Asian finished silks. The shape of raw silk imports also reflected the very different valuations ascribed to regional produce. Officials set the value in 1697 of Italian *organzine* silk at between 20 and 25 shillings per pound, Italian standard product at 16 shillings, Turkish raw silk at 15 shillings, and East Indies raw silk at a paltry 5–6 shillings, underscoring the low esteem in which extra-European yarn was held for the purposes of much manufacturing, though this galled merchant companies.[42] A fourth pillar – invisible in these statistics but unquestionably of substantial magnitude – involved the high volume of clandestinely imported silks, such as the smuggling in of French products (which had been banned comprehensively in 1693–6), and Asian wrought silks (initially burdened with heavy duties and

---

[40] Natalie Rothstein, 'The 18th-Century English Silk Industry', in *18th-Century Silks: The Industries of England and Northern Europe*, ed. Regula Schorta (Riggisberg: Abegg-Stiftung, 2000), 10; Frank Warner, *The Silk Industry of the United Kingdom: Its Origin and Development* (London: Drane's, 1921), esp. 107–376; David Mitchell, '"What d'ye Lack Ladies? Hoods, Ribbands, Very Fine Silk Stockings": The Silk Trades in Restoration London', in *Threads of Global Desire: Silk in the Pre-Modern World*, ed. Dagmar Schäfer, Giorgio Riello, and Luca Molà (Woodbridge: Boydell and Brewer, 2018), 187–222. Claim of 200,000 found in 'Petition of the Silkthrowsters, Weavers, and Dyers, in and about London', in *Journals of the House of Commons*, 10: 280 (6 November 1689) and repeated in 10: 385. Peter Earle downgraded this estimate to some 50,000: Peter Earle, *The Making of the English Middle Class: Business, Society, and Family Life in London, 1660–1730* (Berkeley: University of California Press, 1989), 20.

[41] Davis, *Aleppo and Devonshire Square: English Traders in the Levant in the 18th Century*, 134.

[42] London prices for 'Antioch' (Levant) silk in London, for example, varied from 13 shillings 6 pence in 1729 to 26 shillings 6 pence in October 1752. Much depended on both English demand and Turkish supply. Davis, 164–5.

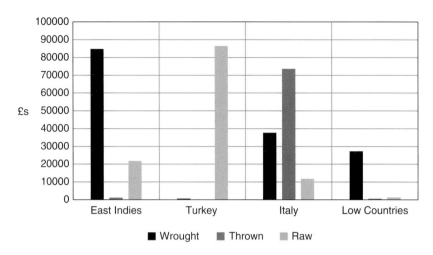

Figure 5.1 English customs records, silk imports by value (1697–8). Based on the aggregation of silk goods, with the crude addition of half the value of silk and cotton mixed piece goods from the East Indies (such as romals and elatches), running from 29 September 1697 to 24 December 1698. Cust 3/1-2 (1697–1698, 1698), Ledgers of Imports and Exports, UK National Archives

eventually proscribed from wear in England, though allowed for re-export under the Calico Acts).[43]

The parallel pillars, as revealed in the import figures, could not comfortably be relied upon to sustain the English silk industry for two main reasons, even setting aside the problem of illicit trade. Firstly, the growing weight of East Indies silks and cottons threatened to swamp the domestic textile industry. Secondly, the dependency on Italian thrown and Levantine raw silks left the English processing chain very vulnerable to breaks in supply – especially given the high carrying competition with the Dutch and the high manufacturing competition with the French, who dominated several European markets. Both of these problems ultimately led political economists and silk throwsters and weavers between 1690

[43] 2 Will. & Mary, c. 4 and c. 9 (1690); 5 Will. & Mary, c. 3 (1693); 8 & 9 Will. & Mary, c. 36 (1697); 11 & 12 Will. III, c. 3 (1700); 1 Anne, c. 27 and c. 28 (1702); 5 Anne, c. 27 (1706); 6 Anne, c. 19 (1707); 7 Anne, c. 8 (1708); 8 Anne, c. 13 (1709); 9 Anne, c. 21 (1710). Ralph Davis, 'The Rise of Protection in England, 1689–1786', *The Economic History Review* 19, no. 2 (August 1966): 309; William Farrell, 'Smuggling Silks into Eighteenth-Century Britain: Geography, Perpetrators, and Consumers', *Journal of British Studies* 55, no. 02 (11 April 2016): 268–94; W. H. Manchée, 'Some Huguenot Smugglers: The Impeachment of London Silk Merchants, 1698', *Proceedings of the Huguenot Society of London* 15, no. 3 (1937): 406–27; Warner, *The Silk Industry*, 521–6.

and 1740 to fight hard for political and imperial reforms or innovations that would negate the threats. The protective and proactive legislative response helped foster recognition of the domestic silk industry as a source of national wealth and national pride – as one law encouraging silk exports put it in 1721, 'one of the most considerable branches of the manufactures of the kingdom'.[44]

Silk throwers had won a preliminary battle in 1690, when in response to their objections, Parliament forbade the importation of thrown silk from Turkey, Persia, and the East Indies. After much debate and counter-petitioning, Parliament did allow the continued import of Italian thrown silks whose exceptional quality (because of their evenness and strength) made them the only fit choice for the warp threads used in the manufacture of the most accomplished fabrics, such as the brocades and damasks of Spitalfields.[45] The Italian exception – vigorously argued for by the Weavers' Company and Italian merchants – marked out, in effect, the chasm that separated 'fine Italian, Sicilian, & Naples thrown silk' from that thrown by the rest of the world.[46] It eventually gave English weavers access to the *organzine* 'from any port or place whatsoever without any restriction (excepting the Ports of France)' in 1693, while ensuring that English throwsters would not be undercut in their operations by lower-grade thrown silk processed in the East.[47]

But British silk throwing, the technique of doubling and twisting skeins of raw silk thread into thicker yarns, itself took a substantial leap forward in the early eighteenth century. For the first time, the industry moved beyond the rudimentary methods that allowed the throwing of 'tram' silk, a form of yarn that was suitable only for the weft in many broadloom fabrics, and therefore had to be intermixed with imported ready-thrown silk (usually Italian *organzine*) for the warp. The throwing of silk tram in England had long relied on hand or pedal mills operated by large numbers of throwsters in London, but had begun to take place in more distant locations where labour was available, and to incorporate technical improvements, some of them borrowed from the Dutch, as watchful merchants and

---

[44] 8 Geo. I, c. 15 (1721). Raymond L. Sickinger, 'Regulation or Ruination: Parliament's Consistent Pattern of Mercantilist Regulation of the English Textile Trade, 1660–1800', *Parliamentary History* 19, no. 2 (17 March 2008): 227; Jonathan P. Eacott, 'Making an Imperial Compromise: The Calico Acts, the Atlantic Colonies, and the Structure of the British Empire', *The William and Mary Quarterly* 69, no. 4 (2012): 731–62.

[45] *Journals of the House of Commons*, 10: 280 (6 November 1689), 285.

[46] *Journals of the House of Commons*, 10: 735 (7 December 1692).

[47] *Journals of the House of Lords*, 15: 340 (11 January 1693); *Journals of the House of Commons*, 10: 359 (29 March 1690).

manufacturers shared insights.[48] The advances meant that more varieties of raw silk could be absorbed and processed in a way that suited demand farther on in the textile production chains. As one report put it in relation to overseas raw silk in 1711, 'the manufacturers could not find the way of working it ... but now they are fallen into a better method and it begins to rise in value'.[49]

In 1704 in one such location at Derby, a manufacturer named Thomas Cotchett sought to establish a more modern mill that deployed water power to save labour. For centuries, Italian producers had jealously guarded the designs and operational specifications for complicated circular water-powered throwing mills (*filatoi*), often known as 'Bolognese' machines. Alongside the hydraulic wheels and multi-storey facilities, these required the raw silk to be wound on bobbins, and an attentive and dextrous labour force to feed the machine – monitoring spindles, reels, tension and yarn breakages, and quality control. Manufacturers were well aware that this technology to create *organzine* yarn, together with the exceptional quality control applied to the reeled raw silk it relied upon, constituted a critical market advantage because of its combination of labour-saving motion and regularity of output.[50] But in the latter decades of the seventeenth century, with dozens of mills spreading through the Piedmont region, the secret had begun to leak more widely. When, upon Cotchett's bankruptcy in 1714, an associate named John Lombe took up the Derby mill's lease and equipment, the Lombe family opted to pursue a much bolder construction to replicate in full the Piedmont mills and machines. Following some brazen industrial espionage in 1714–16, which actually helped prompt the Kingdom of Savoy to ban its exports of raw silk in 1722, and an unprecedented capital investment of some £30,000, Thomas Lombe's silk-throwing mill opened for business on the river Derwent. It was employing around 300 workers by 1730. It had stolen the designs (which Lombe shrewdly patented in 1718), the headlines, and the historiographical limelight – even as less

[48] Eric Kerridge, *Textile Manufactures in Early Modern England* (Manchester, UK: Manchester University Press, 1985), 141–2; Carlo Poni, 'L'occhio esterno: l'indagine di un mercante inglese sui mulini da seta, i filati di seta e le pratiche mercantili nell'italia settentrionale (1677–78)', *Quaderni di storia della tecnologia* 4 (1995): 9–51; Mitchell, 'The Silk Trades in Restoration London', 192–3.
[49] EIC official cited in Chaudhuri, *Trading World of Asia and the EIC*, 349.
[50] For the fullest English attempt to describe its properties: William Aglionby, 'Of the Nature of Silk, as It Is Made in Piedmont. Communicated by William Aglionby, Esq; F. R. S.', *Philosophical Transactions of the Royal Society of London* 21 (1699): 183–6.

sensational and smaller silk-throwing mills were established throughout many parts of the country.[51]

The Lombes' Derby mill has often been heralded as the first recognisable British factory because of its incorporation of water power, large-
scale technology, and centralised labour – as silk's iconic contribution to
the Industrial Revolution, before other fibres appropriated mechanisation
more fully towards the end of the century.[52] But what impressed about
the Lombe mill, when considered in the context of the technology of silk
throwing, was less its copycat machinery and operation (for similar plants
existed by now in the Netherlands, France, and elsewhere); it was its
bizarre geography. Nestled away in the landlocked English Midlands, this
was probably the farthest away from a production region of raw silk that
any throwster had dared to operate on such a scale, showing unprecedented industrial temerity borne out of unprecedented commercial confidence. Parliament eventually denied Lombe his monopoly on British
use of the raw silk throwing machines, but awarded him £14,000 'as
a Reward and Recompence to him for the eminent Service he has done
this Nation'.[53] In a short time, new partnerships, new buildings, and new
employment opportunities were opening up that could work up raw silk at
even farther distances from London, such as the mills built at Stockport
with the help of Nathaniel Gartrevalli in the 1730s (one of the Italian
experts the Lombes had recruited) or the four-storey construction established in Macclesfield by Charles Roe in the 1740s, which copied the
Derby machinery, forged new links with silk merchants, and was valued at
over £19,000 in 1764.[54] Empire had made the Lombes' vision

---

[51] For sites of new silk British throwing: Kerridge, *Textile Manufactures in Early Modern
England*, 171; Gail Malmgreen, *Silk Town: Industry and Culture in Macclesfield, 1750–1835*
(Hull, England: Hull University Press, 1985), 10–16. On the Italian knowledge capital,
technical proficiency, and its leakage: C. Zanier, 'The Sericulture of Mediterranean Europe
from World Supremacy to Its Decline – Commercial Competition between East-Asia and
Europe', *Quaderni storici* 25, no. 1 (1990): 7–53; Chicco, *La seta in Piemonte*, 79; Carlo Poni,
'The Circular Silk Mill: A Factory Before the Industrial Revolution in Early Modern
Europe', *History of Technology* 21 (1999): 65–85; Riello, 'Textile Spheres: Silk in a Global
and Comparative Context.' On the Lombe mill in particular: Anthony Calladine, 'Lombe's
Mill: An Exercise in Reconstruction', *Industrial Archaeology Review* 16, no. 1 (18 October
1993): 82–99; W. H. Chaloner, 'Sir Thomas Lombe and the British Silk Industry', *History
Today* 3 (1953): 778 85; Warner, *The Silk Industry*, 198–207.
[52] S. R. H. Jones, 'Technology, Transaction Costs, and the Transition to Factory
Production in the British Silk Industry, 1700–1870', *Journal of Economic History* 47
(1987): 75.
[53] *Journals of the House of Commons*, 21: 795 (11 February 1731).
[54] William Hutton, *The History of Derby: From the Remote Ages of Antiquity to the Year 1791*,
2nd ed. (London: Nichols, Son, and Bentley, 1817), 167; Malmgreen, *Silk Town:
Industry and Culture in Macclesfield, 1750–1835*, 13–14; Jones, 'Technology,
Transaction Costs, and the Transition to Factory Production in the British Silk
Industry, 1700–1870', 77.

conceivable, and now, it was hoped, would be instrumental in making it profitable. But what options were available to secure the raw materials for this new silk-throwing capacity?

The East India Company (newly consolidated in 1708) was highly responsive to the growing English demand for raw silk. It had long chased options to source a reliable product for the market and to work around existing interests. Early in the eighteenth century it sent out agents with experience in the Levant trade to try to 'divert the current of silk' including the knowledgeable Francis Coppin (after many years of experience of the Syrian market), who promised but failed in 1712 to locate 'raw silk from Gilan as good and as cheap as that purchased at Aleppo'.[55] The company was alert to the difficulties that English traders experienced in securing Persian and Turkish raw silk as the century progressed, indicated in the erratic nature of imports through the Ottoman Empire that were documented by travelling merchant Jonas Hanway. His figures showed wild oscillation from around 230,000 lb in 1736 plummeting to 88,000 in 1737, recovering to 170,000 in 1738 and 1739, and then dropping to virtually nothing in 1740 and 1742, with a bumper year of some 320,000 in between.[56] Such fluctuation influenced the East India Company's instructions to supercargoes of its Bengal-bound ships.[57] Whereas the company continued to find it tricky to influence the Persian trade directly then, they were proactive (see Fig. 5.2) in seeking to increase the volume of raw silk of different types coming direct from major producers in Bengal (mainly through Cossimbazar) and China (through Canton).[58]

From the 1720s, the company's directors tended to instruct their agents to secure large quantities of Bengal raw silk from Kumarkhali and Cossimbazar; the standard request was over 40 per cent apiece, with a further 15 per cent from the district of Rangpur and from Gujarat merchants.[59] The company encouraged its officials in Kolkata

---

[55] Company orders to Mr Coppin, 4 April 1712, India Office Records, British Library, E/3/97. Ferrier, 'The Armenians and the East India Company in Persia in the Seventeenth and Early Eighteenth Centuries', 61–2; Davis, *Aleppo and Devonshire Square: English Traders in the Levant in the 18th Century*.

[56] Jonas Hanway, *An Historical Account of the British Trade over the Caspian Sea* (London: T. Osborne et al., 1754), 321. William Farrell, 'Silk and Globalisation in Eighteenth-Century London: Commodities, People and Connections c.1720–1800' (Birkbeck, University of London, 2014), 47–9.

[57] India Office Records, E/3/107/f 186v.

[58] Chaudhuri, *Trading World of Asia and the EIC*, 348–9; Edmund M. Herzig, 'The Iranian Raw Silk Trade and European Manufacture', in *Textiles: Production, Trade and Demand*, ed. Maureen Fennell Mazzaoui (Aldershot: Ashgate, 1998), 27–43.

[59] See for example: India Office Records, E/3/109/f 130.

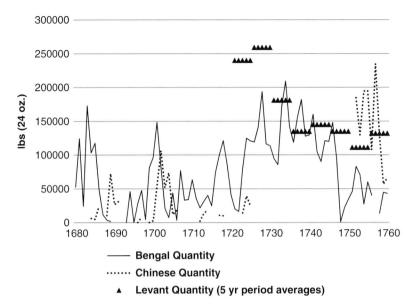

Figure 5.2 East Indies and Levant raw silk imports (1680–1760). Chart compiled by author from figures in Chaudhuri, *Trading World of Asia and the EIC*, 533–7; Davis, *Aleppo and Devonshire Square: English Traders in the Levant in the 18th Century*, 139

and Cossimbazar to intercede actively in productive processes to main-tain quality, including reeling, sorting, and appraising.[60] For the first time in February 1743, the directors instructed the President and Council at Fort William to 'send us for a Tryal a few bales of Raw Silk wound off from the Worm, and made up in Skains'.[61] But there continued to be worrisome feedback about the Bengal raw silk's lack of suitability for onwards processing. 'This Important Staple may be brought into Disrepute among the Manufacturers', warned the directors in 1744; this would have disastrous commercial consequences, if on-site servants at Cossimbazar were unable to redress problems of evenness, dryness, and crossed threads. Inferior reeled raw silk was likely to break or entangle

[60] 'Instructions to the Richmond, and Lynn', 13 December 1738, India Office Records E/3/107/f 266; E/3/109/f 45v.
[61] India Office Records, E/3/108/f 313 (quote), 322v (sample sent). The Dutch VOC had pursued such an experiment as early as the 1650s at Cossimbazar: Om Prakash, *Bullion for Goods: European and Indian Merchants in the Indian Ocean Trade, 1500–1800* (New Delhi: Manohar Publishers & Distributors, 2004), 303.

when rewound during throwing operations in Britain.[62] However, any ability to influence production in the decade after 1741 was compromised by the disruption of war, as Maratha armies rampaged six times through the Nawab of Bengal's territories, prompting company officials in Kolkata to recommend shifting sericulture east of the Padwa River so that 'the Marathas or any other country power' could not 'destroy the mulberry plantations or disperse the winders of raw silk'.[63]

Until mid-century, the East India Company's imports from China were at a disadvantage because of higher duties, but it still showed the same intention to try to secure reeled raw silk in as close a condition to Italian imports as possible. In 1723, the East India directors drew on experienced authorities to compile a comprehensive set of directions for supercargoes to refer to in making decisions about their raw silk purchases at Canton. The instructions preferred Chinese 'Three Mass' silk, which was parcelled into fewer bundles and carried the best reputation in England. The expert author warned buyers not to be distracted from the all-important fineness and evenness of the thread by issues to do with pureness of white colour, which was a secondary consideration, and recommended opening a sample up 'because very often the outside is good where the inside is bad'. They also armed the supercargoes with three samples of Italian raw silk – some of it reeled into thread from just four or five cocoon filaments – in hopes that these materials would impress upon Chinese silk traders the importance of thinness and consistency, and perhaps make it easier 'for them to imitate'.[64] The company tweaked its instructions about raw silk in 1730, offering further tips to monitor fraudulent practices by Chinese exporters (for instance trying to inflate their bundles' weight) courtesy of 'memorandums and further instructions [that] were received from Mr Thomas Lombe' himself. They added a notice that a much larger quantity of raw silk was being ordered that year, wrongly hoping that Parliament was going to offer some relief on their import duties.[65] Lombe, however, was apparently unimpressed by what arrived back from Canton, leading the directors to instruct the next year that 'what you purchase must exceed them as much as possible in goodness, or else

[62] 'Instructions to the President and Council at Fort William', 20 March 1745, E/3/109/ f 170.
[63] Cited in Sujit Chandra Guha, *Silk Industry of Malda and Murshidabad from 1660 to 1833: A Study of Its Production Organisation, Production Relations, Market and the Effect of Decline on the Economy of the People* (Shivmandir: N. L. Publishers, 2003), 84.
[64] 'Estimate of a Cargo for the Macclesfield to be purchased in China for Europe', 27 December 1723, India Office Records, E/3/102/f 54v–56v. Repeated, for instance, for ships Caesar and Houghton, 21 December 1724, ibid., 199v–200.
[65] 'Orders and Directions', 4 December 1730, India Office Records, E/3/105/f 27-27v. On duties, Chaudhuri, *Trading World of Asia and the EIC*, 351.

send no great quantity', and to insist that the raw silk directives were 'strictly' complied with.[66]

The specific demands of Lombe and other European silk throwsters meant that such instructions for raw silk were fastidiously derivative, in stark contrast to instructions for wrought silks, which encouraged the East India supercargoes to ship any 'new thing that has not been seen in Europe before'.[67] By the mid-1730s, only an estimated one eighth of China raw silk was suitably fine 'to serve the purposes of the thrown silk of Italy', while the remainder equated to the slightly coarser raw silk of Turkey or Persia. The company continued to propose innovative experiments – for instance, lettering five samples of Chinese raw silk thread from A to E according to whether they were reeled from 4, 5, 6, 7, or 8 cocoons, to explore which was viable, or trying to locate the source of the raw silk that did prove most like Italian, and could be adapted for 'winding per engine'.[68] As the import figures show, all this market research and product specificity would reap dividends when Chinese raw silk became an important replacement in the 1740s and 1750s, in the face of the Spanish and Italian raw silk bans, and the disruption caused by the brutal Maratha invasions in Bengal. The surge in Chinese raw silk in the early 1750s owed to its rate of duty being reduced to match other imports, following a concerted campaign that emphasised its partial capacity to match Italian material in the throwing machines.[69]

The experimental, partially successful, and variegated approaches taken by the East India Company to importing raw silk in the first half of the eighteenth century remind us that at this juncture it remained a risky enterprise that English officials could never really control. For large parts of the eighteenth century they were at the mercy of the Indian market, Dutch competitors making headway out of the intra-Asian trade, changeable Chinese policies, and Bengali producers (who themselves were dependent upon weather conditions).[70] The East India Company would go on to conquer territories in India from the late 1750s, allowing it to secure wider powers of coercion, political authority, and economic control. These would dramatically change the extent to which it could impose demands and influence production within the textile trade – as well as locking out other European trading companies, including the

[66] 'Instructions to the Council for China', 10 December 1731, India Office Records, E/3/105/f 189, 190v.
[67] Letter from Frederick Pigou, c. December 1731, India Office Records, E/3/105/f 194.
[68] 'List of Investment for the Ship Grafton', 5 December 1733, India Office Records, E/3/106/f 53–54v. See also E/3/106/f 171, 179v, 272, 279, 282; E/3/107/f 50, 59, 168, 172, 173, 180, 296, 307v; E/3/108/f 29, 37, 38, 124v, 328v, 330 (quote); E/3/109 f 56v, 59, 116v (Pigou sent out as a supercargo).
[69] 23 Geo. II. C. 9.   [70] Chaudhuri, *Trading World of Asia and the EIC*, 355–8.

French and the Dutch.[71] As has been well documented elsewhere, the result was that by century's end, the East India Company would grow into the pre-eminent commercial force in the global transhipment of raw silk.[72] But before then, trading circumstances required a short-term and opportunistic mentality that operated from ship to ship and from season to season. As Samuel Lloyd – an experienced silk mercer-manufacturer who had once acted as Thomas Lombe's agent in Italy, and had bought the Derby throwing mill upon Lombe's death in 1739 – put it before a parliamentary committee in 1750, 'Supply from thence is precarious, the *East-India* Company not knowing what Species of Goods they shall import.'[73]

The discussions and outcomes in Parliament in February 1750 emphasised how the two imperial theatres – the Atlantic and the East Indies – were viewed as interconnected at mid-century. Lloyd's was one of several prominent testimonies from experts in the silk trade. Many of them began by stressing the centrality of Atlantic markets to the growth of the silk industry: consumption in Ireland, Africa, and the Americas unquestionably offered a profitable end point for Asian goods transhipped by merchant companies and processed or finished by British manufacturers. But as Lloyd warned, even if Britain could 'receive a certain Supply [of raw silk] from *China* it would not answer all Purposes'. The consensus of the most influential figures within the British silk industry in 1750 thereby recognised that the harder, longer path to ensuring sustainable sources of the right kinds of raw silk involved developing sericulture within Britain's Atlantic dominions. The act which lowered duties on Chinese raw silk was intended as a short-term fix, and it had an American corollary, in legislation passed in the same session, 'for the encouraging of the Growth and Culture of Raw-Silk in his Majesty's Colonies or Plantations in America'.[74]

Ambitions to produce American raw silk had not declined in the way that other Asian target commodities – notably raw cotton – perhaps had for Britain's colonies in the years after the Calico Acts.[75] English silk throwers and weavers had their hands full enough without choking off a potentially lucrative imperial supply – preoccupied as they were with combatting their loss of market share in the face of impossibly cheap, comfortable, and hard-wearing new products in cotton and linen, with trying to expose and assault (often literally) the illegal wrought silks sauntering around British streets, and with fending off foreign

[71] Om Prakash, 'From Negotiation to Coercion: Textile Manufacturing in India in the Eighteenth Century', *Modern Asian Studies* 41, no. 6 (2007): 1331–68.
[72] Chandra Guha, *Silk Industry of Malda and Murshidabad*; Karolina Hutková, *The English East India Company's Silk Enterprise in Bengal, 1750–1850* (Woodbridge: Boydell Press, 2019).
[73] *Journals of the House of Commons*, 25: 996 (February 1750).
[74] *Journals of the House of Commons*, 25: 986 (Chinese act), 996 (Lloyd) (February 1750).
[75] Eacott, 'Making an Imperial Compromise', 747–8.

competition.[76] Besides, such was the variegated demand of the textile industry for all types and styles of silk – to the point that waste silk (from discards or broken cocoons) had now begun to be worked up by British manufacturers – that it is hard to imagine an addition that would not have been welcome and workable.[77] British American sericulture therefore possessed a distinctively strong rationale for experimental persistence, buttressed by the wider ethos of patriotic agrarianism that dominated British imperial networks and institutions as the eighteenth century progressed.[78]

At the parliamentary hearing, one by one, they had come forward to present their evidence. John Delamare brought invoices that showed the increase in the cost of bales of Piedmont and Bologna thrown silk. Job Rothmahler and Philip Lee testified to the existence of suitable mulberries, and 'many Silk-worms' in South Carolina, Virginia, and North Carolina, having personally borne witness to households that 'made a great Quantity of Silk'. Attention then moved to the product itself. Harman Verelst recounted the boxes of raw silk that had been shipped to him from Georgia. James Crockatt and John Nicholson affirmed that they had acquired hundreds of pounds' weight from South Carolina which, according to Nicholson's broker, 'answered all the Purposes of *Piedmont* Silk'. Lastly, the master weavers stepped up with the hardest evidence of all: fabrics wrought from colonial American raw silk. Thomas Mason laid out a piece of light-brown velluret, Peter Freemont two pieces of paduasoy, Lewis Chauvet a piece of black taffeta 'worked after the *Indian* manner' and silk handkerchiefs in various colours, and Daniel Gobbé a piece of scarlet damask, noting that it was entirely American silk, 'Warp and Shute: [and] That the same worked as well as any *Italian* Silk, and with rather less Waste'. Samuel Lloyd closed this bizarre February fashion show at the House of Commons with 'several Samples of organzine' produced by the groundbreaking Derby throwing mills from Carolina and Georgia raw silk.[79] Where had all this come from? Far from a reduction in sericultural projection in the opening decades of the eighteenth century, as the subsequent chapters explain, remarkable persistence and creative ambition had continued to characterise colonial aspirations, as authorities and households in different regions took up the challenge.

---

[76] On complaints about wrought silks, see for instance 'The humble Petition of the Bailiffs, Wardens, Assistants, & Comonalty of the Trade, Art, & Mistery of Weavers, London', to the Board of Trade, 17 Oct. 1719, CO 389/27, pp. 229–31, NA.

[77] On waste silk's use: Warner, *The Silk Industry*, 399–401; Barham, *An Essay upon the Silkworm*, 166–7.

[78] Richard H. Drayton, *Nature's Government: Science, Imperial Britain, and the 'Improvement' of the World* (New Haven: Yale University Press, 2000), 63–6.

[79] *Journals of the House of Commons*, 25: 996–8 (February 1750).

Whoever shall make any Silk Worms this Year to dispose of, may apply
to John Lewis Poyas near the Watch House in Charles Town, who has
Occasion for 4000 Bushels, and will pay (a reasonable Price) ready
Money. Provided, That the Worms shall be brought two or three Days
after they have done working, and before they have Time to break thro'.
He will also buy some Silk Balls, if good.

– *South Carolina Gazette*, 10 April 1742

Origins in South Carolina, 1660–1730

Captain Mathias Halstead was clearly not the right man for the job.
Commissioned to scout out viable agricultural products for settlers to
pursue in 1671, it turned out that whenever he was not being argumenta-
tive or self-interested – which was rare – he was an 'idle fellow'. The new
proprietors of Carolina, a settlement that was part of a flurry of
Restoration colonies in the 1660s, had sent Halstead off with specific
instructions about what he was to search out and bring back to eager
settlers on the Ashley River. Through Halstead's research and insights,
they hoped that they might implement new colonial practices in husbandry and manufacturing. The authorities 'particularly' instructed Halstead
to bring back information from the neighbouring northward colony of
Virginia about the different sorts of mulberry trees they possessed, and
how to propagate them, about the silkworms they used there, and basi-
cally anything that related to 'ye right way of making ye best Silk'. They
wanted him to bring back samples of both trees and worms with which
Carolina colonists might launch sericulture, but they would be
disappointed.[1] The episode illustrated how silk projection, right from
the inception of the Carolina colony, sought to unlock a potential that
contemporaries unquestionably felt lay within their reach.

---

[1] Langdon Cheves, ed., *The Shaftesbury Papers and Other Records Relating to Carolina and the
First Settlement on Ashley River Prior to the Year 1676* (Charleston, SC: Tempus Publishing
Inc., 2000), 318–21.

Over the next century, like Tantalus – the figure from Greek myth, punished for offending the gods – Carolinians contorted in different ways to stretch towards this fruit. Although they never definitively grasped it, the motions towards sericulture left cultural, material, and environmental legacies within many households, markets, and estates in the region, as mulberries proliferated. They played a significant part in influencing schemes for and arguments about economic development in the Lower South, which would blossom in neighbouring Georgia and beyond (being referenced, as we have already seen, in French Louisiana). They generated innovation in the justification and practice of state investment: taxes paid for public enslaved labourers and their training, bounties, filatures, and the global sourcing of technical knowledge, experts, and technology. As with the French and Armenian immigrants to Virginia, stretching towards silk helped to bring Huguenots, Swiss, and Italians to early Carolina, to shape schemes for westward expansion, and to broaden the employment of enslaved people. By recognising silk, then, in both the aspirational and productive worlds of Carolina, we see rehearsals of the same muscular triggers and motions that would allow the colony to successfully reach to grasp rice and indigo (which became major commercial exports). From its earliest days, Carolina offered up to the English quest for Atlantic sericulture some promising new permutations that involved the intermeshing of political will, environmental resources, and labour assets. And in the process of reaching for silk, they gave the larger imperial textile ambition a new lease of life, as Samuel Lloyd had advocated in Parliament.[2]

The Lords Proprietors and their propagandists in the late seventeenth century identified silk from the outset as one of the natural bounties of Carolina, justifying their claims, much as their Virginia antecedents had done, with empirical evidence of wild mulberry trees and native silkworms, and the testimony of expert commentators. In 1666, the year that Capt. Robert Sanford took formal possession of Carolina for England (and the Lords Proprietor), Robert Horne informed readers in his *Brief Description of the Province of Carolina* that 'Mulbury-Trees and the *Silk-worm* breeding naturally upon them' were amongst the many sorts of fertile fruit trees that settlers would find.[3] Virginia's prior experience in

---

[2] For an insightful exploration of South Carolina's formative relationship with globalization, see Peter A. Coclanis, 'Global Perspectives on the Early Economic History of South Carolina', *South Carolina Historical Magazine* 106, no. 2 (2005): 141. On the globalisation of silk between the seventeenth and nineteenth centuries, see Zanier, *Where the Roads Met. East and West in the Silk Production Processes (17th to 19th Centuries)*.

[3] B. R. Carroll, *Historical Collections of South Carolina*, American Culture Series (New York: Harper, 1836), 2: 12; Cheves, *Shaftesbury Papers*, 176.

sericulture strengthened the argument that Carolina's even more southerly latitude would suit it admirably to the pursuit, and unlike their Chesapeake counterparts, projectors in Carolina would not have to surmount the noxious effect of a tobacco economy. Indeed, the Proprietors emphasised that silk was one of 'those commodyties that will not injure nor overthrow the other plantations' – seeking to allay the fears of Caribbean sugar producers as well as tobacco planters, and to attract willing migrants.[4]

Leading proprietor Anthony Ashley Cooper (Earl of Shaftesbury from 1672) strongly encouraged a spirit of agricultural experimentation. A member of the Royal Society, Shaftesbury was quite willing, as he put it, to 'throw away some money in making some experiments' on his plantations, albeit in the expectation that high-minded advances in the natural sciences would eventually return an economic profit.[5] He and others directed Carolina storekeepers and botanists to obtain a plethora of cuttings, roots, and seeds from a range of regions, and to plant them at different intervals and in different seasons and soils to establish what products most thrived.[6] Silk recurred as a product of great potential in these early experiments, alongside tobacco, grape vines, olives, indigo, rice, hemp, flax, and ginger.[7] Fittingly, the council journals recorded at a meeting in March 1673 that the 12,000 acres marked out for Shaftesbury on a western branch of what became the Cooper River was 'com[mon]ly called ye Mulberry tree' – later made more grandiose by subsequent owners as the Mulberry Plantation (now a National Historic Landmark). Shaftesbury was soon receiving positive indications about the climate and soil: whereas Joseph Dalton reported to Shaftesbury after his first few seasons that winters were too cold for sugar canes and cotton, he affirmed that 'Wine Oyle and Silke' could be 'propagated to great perfection and profit'.[8]

The Proprietors introduced a range of crude incentives to encourage production of target commodities. They passed on exemptions in their royal charters that freed certain crops from export taxes – with silk top of

---

[4] Duke of Albemarle to Thomas Modyford and Peter Colleton, 30 August 1663, Cheves, *Shaftesbury Papers*, 13–14.

[5] Quoted from a letter to Thomas Lynch, Governor of the Bahamas, in relation to his plantations in the Bahamas, in Charles H Lesser, *South Carolina Begins: The Records of a Proprietary Colony, 1663–1721* (Columbia, SC: South Carolina Department of Archives and History, 1995), 29.

[6] Cheves, *Shaftesbury Papers*, 125; William Noel Sainsbury and A. S. Salley, eds., *Records in the British Public Record Office Relating to South Carolina, 1663–1782*, 36 facsimile (Columbia: South Carolina Department of Archives & History, 1928), 1: 53–9.

[7] Converse D. Clowse, *Economic Beginnings in Colonial South Carolina, 1670–1730* (Columbia: University of South Carolina Press, 1971), 58–9.

[8] Lesser, *South Carolina Begins*, 29; Cheves, *Shaftesbury Papers*, 125, 386–7, 420, 445.

the list.[9] Perhaps believing their own propaganda, however, they left damaging restrictions on who could qualify for this customs exemption, insisting that producers of 'Wine, Silk, Raisins, Currance, Oyl, Olives, and Almonds' could only claim it after four tons of any of these were imported in one ship.[10] This benchmark, ludicrously high in the case of raw silk, illustrated how deeply the spectacular recent Atlantic production booms had bitten colonial projectors; tobacco was carefully denied a similar customs exemption for fear it would provoke a mass exodus from the mother country.[11] Rulings about currency were another indication of a Carolina expectancy that raw silk would feature prominently in economic exchanges from an early point. In 1669 the proprietors authorised Governor Joseph West to treat selected commodities as currency, with a list of rates that valued silk at ten shillings per pound. They reiterated this when they were hoping for quit-rent payments in 1690 and 1695, indicating they would accept silk, cotton, Spanish money, or indigo in lieu of specie.[12]

The Atlantic successes in production of new agricultural commodities (especially in the Caribbean), as well as the list of partial failures – which included Virginian silk – left Carolina's administrators in no doubt that importing the right experts was amongst the most vital contributions that they could make to introduce new products. In 1679, thanks in part to the scheming of his associate John Locke, Shaftesbury quietly supervised the pinball of a petition from two Normandy gentlemen that was bouncing around the halls of colonial power, requesting English support to transplant a number of Huguenot families to Carolina.[13] The petition met with the warm approval of the Lords of Trade, the Carolina Proprietors, and the Commissioners of Customs; the process culminated in King Charles II agreeing to stump up £2,000 and lending two frigates to transport the Huguenots. This was not entirely a blank check, as certain stipulations were attached: the migrants had to possess genuine skills, were barred from interference in Virginia tobacco, and were expected to refund the loan through the customs return on their specialist

---

[9] For relevant line in royal charters, see Thomas Cooper and David J. McCord, eds., *The Statutes at Large of South Carolina*, 3 vols. (Columbia, SC: A. S. Johnston, n.d.), 1: 26 (1663); 1: 36 (1665). This was also made manifest in item four of the 'Barbadoes Concessions' of January 7, 1664, Cheves, *Shaftesbury Papers*, 41.

[10] Carroll, *Historical Collections of South Carolina*, 2: 15.

[11] George Chalmers, *Political Annals of the Present United Colonies from Their Settlement to the Peace of 1763* (London: J. Bowen, 1780), 541.

[12] This weight was presumably to be of raw silk. Cheves, *Shaftesbury Papers*, 128; Sainsbury and Salley, *Records in the BPRO*, 2: 289–90; Clowse, *Economic Beginnings*, 97–8.

[13] Van Ruymbeke, *From New Babylon to Eden*, 34–7.

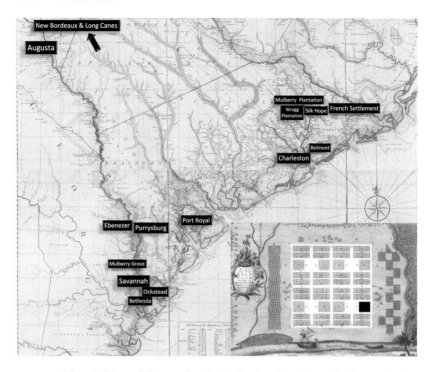

Map 3 Map of Lower South, indicating locations of silk production
mentioned in text. Adapted from John Gerard William De Brahm,
A Map of South Carolina and a Part of Georgia (London, 1780). G3910
1780 .F3. Library of Congress Geography and Map Division.
Combined with elements of Matthaeus Seutter, *Plan von Neu Ebenezer*
(Augsburg, 1747). Image No. 12040110. David Rumsey Map
Collection. The orphanage at Ebenezer, in which silkworms were
raised, is the blacked-out square in the township plan

manufacture of silk, oil, and wine in due course.[14] The Huguenots
boarding the *Richmond* were under no illusions about their anticipated role in the young colony, for each household head had signed
an 'undertaking' that agreed 'for to settle there ye manufactures of
Silke, oyle, Wines &c which many of us are skilled a[nd] practised
in'.[15] The Proprietors instructed their officers to give these newco-
mers preferential treatment (including especially choice lands),

[14] Sainsbury and Salley, *Records in the BPRO*, 1: 69, 71, 74, 75, 79.
[15] St Julien R. Childs, 'The Petit-Guérard Colony', *South Carolina Historical and
Genealogical Magazine* 43, no. 1 (1942): 1–17 (quotation on 1).

anticipating 'that the English will by them learne to become Skilled in those comodityes'. Shaftesbury's precipitate fall from metropolitan grace amidst charges of treason in 1681, and his death in the Netherlands in 1683, may have slowed but by no means quashed the support, for the next year another influential proprietor, Peter Colleton, instructed the Charleston governor to give 'all manner of Incouragem[en]t' to the newly arrived 'skillful' Frenchman named Baille, 'for hee Perfectly well understands Silke'.[16]

There is good evidence that the supply base of mulberry trees in the colony began to diversify in the 1680s as a consequence of this injection of expertise and resource, as planters systematically pursued moriculture and introduced new species. As John Ferrar had noted decades earlier, there were extensive red mulberries (*M. rubra*) indigenous to Carolina, and Thomas Ashe (a clerk aboard the *Richmond* in December 1679) recorded them growing wild 'every where amidst the woods'. In terms of Eurasian species, prior to the arrival of the *Richmond*, Maurice Mathews reported that he knew 'bot of two white Mulberrie trees in the Countrey'. The frigate, however, brought plentiful white mulberry (*M. alba*) seeds, and another source, Samuel Wilson, reported that white mulberries were thereafter 'propagated with a great deal of ease' either by cuttings or seed. By 1682, a number of planters had relocated either these new *M. alba* or stocks of *M. rubra* 'near their Plantations, in Rows and Walks ... for Use, Ornament and Pleasure', and Wilson was claiming 'by experience' that both species fed 'the Silkworm very well'.[17] Surveying the mulberries in 1709, John Lawson extended his description to three sorts: the 'common red' (*M. rubra*) which grew wild in great quantities, and two others with smoother leaves better for sericulture, one of which was probably *M. alba* which by now was 'common' and the other, now also introduced in Carolina but in smaller numbers, the black mulberry (*M. nigra*).[18] That Carolina contained more white than black mulberries set it apart from English trials, and perhaps explains

---

[16] Sainsbury and Salley, *Records in the BPRO*, 1: 95, 306.
[17] Maurice Mathews, 'A Contemporary View of Carolina in 1680', *South Carolina Historical Magazine* 55, no. 3 (1954): 156; Samuel Wilson, George Larkin, andFrancis Smith, *An Account of the Province of Carolina in America Together with an Abstract of the Patent, and Several Other Necessary and Useful Particulars, to Such as Have Thoughts of Transporting Themselves Thither: Published for Their Information* (London: Printed by G. Larkin for Francis Smith, 1682), 18. Thomas Ashe, *Carolina; or a Description of the Present State of that Country, and the Natural Excellencies Thereof ...* (1682), repr. in Carroll, *Historical Collections of South Carolina*, 1: 25, 65.
[18] John Lawson, *A New Voyage to Carolina; Containing the Exact Description and Natural History of That Country ...* (London: s.n., 1709), 103.

why one Englishwoman went so far as to complain in 1702 that the Carolinian 'sort of Mulberys' were all well and good for silkworms but 'very inferior' for their fruit.[19]

As these comments suggest, proprietary support and Huguenot involvement was sufficient to generate Carolina raw silk production before the end of the seventeenth century, despite the assertions of some historians that the French settlers entirely failed.[20] A telling feature within these glimpses of attempts at raw silk, which helps explain the higher level of early progress in Carolina compared to England and Virginia, was the involvement of colonists from silk-raising regions. Louis Thibou wrote from Charles Town (later Charleston) in glowing terms of the Carolina environment in his French circular to 'Gentlemen and Dear Friends' in September of 1683, informing a Madame Poupé that her brother had produced some 30 lb of raw silk.[21] A 1688 letter from an unknown Huguenot to Dutch noblewoman Agnes van Wassenaer Obdam, describing the fledgling French settlement along the Santee River, placed silk alongside rice as the likeliest candidates for economic success, and relayed the positive reports of those with knowledge of silk. These included a Monsieur Gaillard who expected 'to make a very good trade here', and another Frenchman – likely Jean-François Gignilliat from the Pays de Vaud – who had planted between 10,000 and 12,000 mulberries and was waiting for them to grow in 1690. The letter identified as the main stumbling block the fact that 'great investment is required because of the need for large houses' where the silkworms would be housed, and where cocoons could be reeled off.[22] French Protestant Durand de Dauphiné, for instance, who sailed for the New World in 1686, recalled that on his flight from France he was joined by a widow from Languedoc who was proficient in managing

---

[19] Elizabeth Hyrne to Burrell Massingberd, 2 April 1700, LAO 2MM/B/7/5 (Lincolnshire Archive Office, Lincoln, UK).

[20] Edward McCrady, *The History of South Carolina under the Proprietary Government, 1670–1719* (New York: The Macmillan Company, 1897), 181, 350. Cf. Van Ruymbeke, *From New Babylon to Eden*, 39.

[21] Louis Thibou to 'Gentlemen and Dear Friends', 20 September 1683, South Caroliniana Library.

[22] Molly McClain and Alessa Ellefson, 'A Letter from Carolina, 1688: French Huguenots in the New World', *The William and Mary Quarterly*, 3rd Ser. 64, no. 2 (2007): 392–3; Robert Cohen and Myriam Yardeni, 'Un suisse en caroline du sud ... la fin du xviie siècle', *Bulletin de la société de l'histoire du protestantisme français* 134 (1988): 70. Joachim Gaillard was from Montpellier, Languedoc, and brought with him to Carolina his Lyonnais wife Esther Paperel; both of them likely brought considerable sericultural experience. The 'Monsieur Gaillard' here, however, is probably their son Barthelemy, who later became a surveyor. Thomas Gaillard, 'Immigrants from 1690 to 1700', *Transactions of the Huguenot Society of South Carolina* 5 (1897): 14–18.

silkworm raising.[23] He remarked upon his arrival in the Chesapeake that 'they could walk upon gold, for in every province there are enough mulberry-trees to produce silk for their own use, & in those of the south there could be four times as much as they need'. But although Carolina played host to a larger number of immigrants from European silk regions than did Virginia, there apparently still remained insufficient depth of knowledge throughout the labour pool and through the silk-raising processes. Dauphiné bemoaned that 'not one woman in the whole country knows how to reel'.[24]

One of the explanations for less pronounced uptake in American sericulture than many hoped for, was that the Carolina Huguenots were not quite what they claimed to be. We have already explored the potent impact that the late-seventeenth-century Huguenot *Refuge* had on the silk industries of neighbouring European states, and the assets they transferred with them in the fields of commerce and manufacturing (particularly weaving, dyeing, design, and so on). Many of the regions of France through which silk raising or silk throwing had spread between the late sixteenth and early eighteenth centuries had contained notable, resilient Protestant populations – with Protestant entrepreneurs controlling, for instance, the silk industry of Nîmes and Tours, and with Protestants maintaining a strong presence in the provinces of Vivarais and Languedoc.[25] So there were good grounds for colonial schemers to connect French Protestantism with sericulture. But many of those with skills in raising and reeling raw silk, a pursuit dominated by women, were from the struggling pool of agricultural labouring families that were unlikely to have the capital and connections to emigrate, and faced heavy pressure to abjure. In most of the urban locations to which Huguenots fled in northern Europe, and most famously in the Spitalfields community in London, they did not raise silk themselves but rather processed or manufactured silk stuffs using imported raw silk from abroad.

The geographic spread of those able to escape also compromised the chances of Huguenot silk raisers reaching the British Atlantic. Protestants from the Vivarais and Dauphiné – who were viciously treated by the *dragonnades* of Louis XIV in the 1680s – tended to flee to Switzerland, and onwards into German states, while those in the Cévennes took advantage of their rugged mountainous environment to fight a remarkable

---

[23] Durand de Dauphiné, *A Huguenot Exile in Virginia, or, Voyages of a Frenchman Exiled for His Religion with a Description of Virginia & Maryland, from the Hague Edition of 1687*, ed. Gilbert Chinard (New York: Press of the Pioneers, 1934), 86.

[24] Durand de Dauphiné, *Huguenot Exile*, 112.

[25] Warren Candler Scoville, 'The Huguenots in the French Economy, 1650–1750', *The Quarterly Journal of Economics* 67, no. 3 (1953): 431.

rearguard action. Indeed, the Huguenots who actually sought refuge in North American colonies tended to be even more urban, more orientated towards the Atlantic (rather than Mediterranean) economy, and more heavily from the artisan and merchant classes than most emigrating Huguenots, making it unlikely that they would be as experienced in silk raising as colonial proponents hoped. While colonial administrators and political economists therefore had some foundation for imputing key sericultural skills to Huguenots, there was a heavy degree of inflation of their expertise (often indulged by the migrants themselves), and a serious discrepancy between authorities' high expectations and the actual experiences of those crossing the Atlantic, which became further complicated by the Carolina Commons House of Assembly's hard-line stance on naturalisation.[26]

Early Carolina sericulture was by no means confined to Huguenots, however, and evidently spread beyond them: by the start of the eighteenth century a peculiar mix of people was busy each springtime. The most significant planter to pursue the challenge was Englishman Sir Nathaniel Johnson, a tough, experienced administrator, who arrived in Carolina under a political cloud as the ousted governor of the Leeward Islands (tainted by his loyalty to the deposed James II). As William Berkeley had done when politically marginalised in Virginia, Johnson initially devoted his impressive energies to private projects, which he was well set to pursue in light of his international trading contacts and substantial capital (including enslaved people).[27] According to one of the earliest historians of South Carolina, Johnson was 'particularly allured by the hope of making silk' and made 'considerable quantities of that commodity', encouraging others in the process.[28] A fellow governor credited him

---

[26] Around two thirds of French immigrants arrived from urban regions, especially the northern or western port towns of Dieppe, Le Havre, La Rochelle, and Bordeaux. Van Ruymbeke, *From New Babylon to Eden*, 207; Bertrand Van Ruymbeke, 'The Huguenots of Proprietary South Carolina: Patterns of Migration and Integration', in *Money, Trade, and Power: The Evolution of Colonial South Carolina's Plantation Society*, ed. Jack P. Greene, Rosemary Brana-Shute, and Randy J. Sparks (Columbia, SC: University of South Carolina Press, 2001), 32, 37; McClain and Ellefson, 'A Letter from Carolina, 1688: French Huguenots in the New World', 383–4. Sainsbury and Salley, *Records in the BPRO*, 4: 114.

[27] Richard S. Dunn, 'The Glorious Revolution and America', in *The Origins of Empire*, ed. Nicholas Canny, The Oxford History of the British Empire (Oxford: Oxford University Press, 1998), 457; Mabel L. Webber, 'Sir Nathaniel Johnson and His Son Robert Governors of South Carolina', *South Carolina Historical and Genealogical Magazine* 38, no. 4 (1937): 109–10; Ian Steele, 'Governors or Generals?: A Note on Martial Law and the Revolution of 1689 in English America', *The William and Mary Quarterly*, 3rd Ser. 46, no. 2 (1989): 309–10.

[28] David Ramsay, *The History of South-Carolina, from Its First Settlement in 1670, to the Year 1808*, 2 vols. (Charleston: David Longworth, 1809), 2: 476.

with being 'the principal Promoter' of sericulture in the colony at the turn of the century, and with good reason: within a year of his arrival from Antigua, the determined Johnson had planted 24,000 mulberry trees on his new estate, pointedly named 'Silk Hope'.[29] According to one source, by the early 1700s Johnson was apparently generating 'yearly 3 or 400 l. in silk only'.[30] Johnson's commitment reaped dividends, as his status improved in the eyes of the Proprietors: they thanked him in October 1699 for a 'present of Silke which was very acceptable and which wee make use of to your honour & that of Carolina', closing their letter by stating his ingenuity and industry 'have made us, Sr, yo[u]r assured Friends'. The political warmth that Johnson's silk exploits generated was evident in their willingness to suspend proceedings in law against him that month, though others who owed dues were followed up.[31]

John Stewart, a Scottish Indian trader, proprietary propagandist and experimenter, had initially aided Johnson, apparently improving the consistency of his raw silk by developing metal plates to support his wooden reels.[32] He experimented with varying degrees of success with cotton, silk, and rice in the early 1690s, making extensive notes from his trials on the eastern shore of the Cooper River, and the Proprietors likewise rewarded him with land grants, some of them substantial.[33] Stewart's agricultural know-how was matched by a deep-seated frustration at the cold reception his findings received from planters, especially uneducated ones. His close involvement in the factional disputes that gripped the colony during the decade, which had him at one stage sleeping for weeks with a 'naked sword befor me and charg'd gun', also limited his ability to spread the seed of agricultural enlightenment.[34]

Even admitting that Stewart was a more-than-capable self-publicist, it appears he made substantial inroads into silk cultivation both on his own estates and by encouraging others, especially through the distribution of silkworm seed. Initially, he described his verbal attempts to spread the pursuit as futile because the settlers understood little 'of nature art or ingenuity'. In Stewart's rather egotistical world, only his persistence and

---

[29] Carroll, *Historical Collections of South Carolina*, 2: 118.
[30] John Oldmixon, in Carroll, *Historical Collections*, 2: 460.
[31] Sainsbury and Salley, *Records in the BPRO*, 4: 117–18.
[32] John Stewart, 'Letters from John Stewart to William Dunlop', *South Carolina Historical and Genealogical Magazine* 32, no. 1 (1931): 17. For a full discussion of Stewart's career in Carolina, see Alan Gallay, *The Indian Slave Trade: The Rise of the English Empire in the American South, 1670–1717* (New Haven: Yale University Press, 2002), 156–68.
[33] Sainsbury and Salley, *Records in the BPRO*, 2: 284. For a rice-centred discussion of Stewart's experimentation, see S. Max Edelson, *Plantation Enterprise in Colonial South Carolina* (Cambridge, MA: Harvard University Press, 2006), 72–3.
[34] Stewart, 'Letters', 27.

his demonstration of 'personall practice on that wonderfull Insect did show them', leading to more than sixty planters pursuing silk by April 1690, and buying silkworm seed from him in significant quantities. Stewart reported that many Carolinians chose not to plant white mulberries, but 'wo[u]ld try only upon wild leaves in the woods' – perhaps an unsurprising phenomenon given the barrage of positive environmental propaganda about the trees that had been directed at them. He estimated that as many as 1 million trees would be planted by the following spring, justifying this weighty figure by pointing out that Nathaniel Johnson and his unidentified 'silkman' had been forced to send boats and canoes to all neighbouring plantations to secure more wild and planted leaves to feed the 'Immense number of worms they have'. As in Johnson's case, Stewart's advice and progress in silk led to a dramatic (though transient) increase in prestige, and for a while Stewart found himself 'cares't everywhere for my success and discovery in silk', including 'eve[n] esteem from my Goosquill enemys'. His social barometer would plummet again when he turned from agriculture to politics.[35]

Besides the kudos, Stewart was also keen to hatch his own schemes to profit more directly from Carolina silk. His most simple commercial aim was to monopolise the sale of silkworm eggs, for which purpose Stewart decided to breed almost all of his first cohorts of silkworms (thereby generating eggs for the next season, rather than killing the worms and reeling off their cocoons). This ambition was apparently thwarted by the machinations of Stewart's political enemies. Maurice Mathews, leader of the powerful Goose Creek planter faction, contrived (by a seemingly irreconcilable combination) to undersell Stewart, give away silkworm seed for free, and hamper interest in sericulture by spreading false gossip about the necessity of using older mulberry trees – not newly planted orchards. Stewart complained that Mathews caused the loss of '9 parts of 10 of my seed', as no retailers or 'chapmen' (pedlars) would take on his stock.[36] The only feature the episode revealed in a good light was that Carolinians were not struggling to secure transatlantic access to supplies of silkworm seed in the way that their earlier counterparts had done.

John Stewart's correspondence also offered evidence of South Carolinians trying to deploy Native American labour in raising silk, something which had been an increasingly common aspiration in Atlantic silk writings, but one that nobody seems to have taken forwards practically

---

[35] Stewart, 'Letters', 6–7.
[36] Michael J. Heitzler and Nancy Paul Kirchner, *Goose Creek, South Carolina a Definitive History 1670–2003* (Charleston, SC: History Press, 2005), 67; John Stewart, 'Letters from John Stewart to William Dunlop', *South Carolina Historical and Genealogical Magazine* 32, no. 2 (1931): 102.

since the successful Mixtecan adaptation of Spanish sericulture. Whether seeking to implement the hypothetical scenarios that the likes of Edward Williams and John Ferrar had proposed for English Virginia, or to take advantage of the local Yamasee Indians' traditional economic activities being disrupted by their increasing dependence upon slave-taking and trading, Stewart's 'darling projection and pregnant hope' was to enter into a contract with the Yamasee chief Altamaha to provide 300 Amerindian labourers who would be directed to 'work to mee in silk and cotton'. This group of Yamasee, a multi-ethnic conglomerate tribe of significant strength, had relocated to the Savannah river region in the 1680s, where they formed close relationships with a number of Scots settlers and traders involved in the colonisation of Stuarts Town (1684); until the early eighteenth century the Yamasee enjoyed good relations with South Carolina on account of their shared hostility to the Spanish and Spanish-allied Indians. Stewart proposed to pay a certain amount in Indian trade goods 'for every hand in silk' and every acre for cotton tended under his supervision, making this a highly innovative and open-minded scheme, especially in light of the low opinion that most contemporaries had of Indians as agricultural labourers. Though he apparently sat on the idea for some months, Stewart could not initiate such a scheme without the patronage of the governor, and only begrudgingly revealed his design.[37]

Apprised of the scheme, the governor, James Colleton, apparently at first agreed to a partnership with Stewart, but then, to Stewart's dismay, took the project on as his own, bringing 'Alatamoha to mak the bargan with himselfe, excluding me, for 300 hands for 7 years!' At the point of Stewart's bitter letter, Colleton had not yet completed the contract, and Stewart retained hope that he might yet negotiate a role and a profit for himself, urging his correspondent: 'keep all to yorselfe for nev[e]r a soull here dreamt of it'. Ultimately though, Stewart's secret scheme evaporated with the precipitate removal of Colleton after his political authority collapsed in the colony in 1690, which also brought Stewart's Goose Creek enemies to power.[38] To some extent then, these more radical proposals for silk cultivation became a victim of the stormy factionalism of early Carolina politics.[39]

---

[37] Stewart, 'Letters', 94 (and later quotes from Stewart). For the best account of the Scots' relations with the Yamasee, see Gallay, *The Indian Slave Trade: The Rise of the English Empire in the American South, 1670–1717*, 77–91.

[38] L. H. Roper, *Conceiving Carolina: Proprietors, Planters, and Plots, 1662–1729* (New York: Palgrave Macmillan, 2004), 106.

[39] William J. Rivers, *A Sketch of the History of South Carolina* (Spartanburg, SC: Reprint Co, 1972), 428.

By the 1690s, besides the pioneer planters and agronomists, all the looms in Carolina were reported to be 'at work with silk cotton and wooll either simple or complex', and a dozen families in the growing port of Charleston were listed as raising silkworms. One woman in particular, Mary Fisher Bayly Crosse, had apparently mastered the art, having indulged in a remarkable career of transatlantic metamorphosis herself. Crosse was a long-suffering Quaker who had converted to the faith in 1652 as a young servant-woman in Selby, Yorkshire, and subsequently travelled around the Atlantic and Mediterranean worlds facing down persecution. She died a widow in 1698, having married a third husband (a cordwainer) twenty years earlier and migrated to Charleston. There, the Crosse household initially included Mary's son and two daughters by her first marriage, and went on to own as many as ten enslaved people, both African and Indian. It was headed by Mary from 1695, who besides feeding silkworms continued to play a significant role in the small but growing Quaker community.[40] Silk cultivation in Carolina in this formative period was clearly attracting an odd transnational mélange of experimenters – of different faiths, ethnicities, and origins – who together worked up significant amounts, as reflected in the descriptions of commentators in the early eighteenth century.

It was a measure of Carolina's eclectic but persistent production of raw silk, at low levels and in middling households, that much of the output seems to have been crudely reeled and then worked up locally – leaving more evidence of this than was left by progress in Virginia or Louisiana. John Archdale noted in 1707 that 'Silk is come into great improvement, some families making 40 lb. or 50 lb. a Year and their plantations not neglected; little Negro children being serviceable in Feeding the silk worms.' The extent of cultivation was also disguised because much silk was not exported but rather used locally. Archdale related that silk was worked up with wool into druggets (or *droguets* for Huguenots), which he described as 'an excellent Wear for that Country', presumably because the mixed fabric combined the coarse durability of wool with the comfort and softness of silk.[41] A report sent by the governor and council to the Board of

---

[40] For references to her life, see 'Mary Fisher', in John A. Garraty and Mark C. Carnes, *American National Biography* (New York: Oxford University Press, 1999), 8: 15–16. On her various travels and travails: Carla Gardina Pestana, 'The City upon a Hill under Siege: The Puritan Perception of the Quaker Threat to Massachusetts Bay, 1656–1661', *The New England Quarterly* 56, no. 3 (1983): 323–53; Timothy Marr, *The Cultural Roots of American Islamicism* (Cambridge: Cambridge University Press, 2006), 84; Randy J. Sparks, 'Mary Fisher, Sophia Hume, and the Quakers of Colonial Charleston', in *South Carolina Women: Their Lives and Times*, ed. Marjorie Julian Spruill, Valinda W. Littlefield, and Joan Marie Johnson (Athens: University of Georgia Press, 2009), 44–5 (quote).

[41] Carroll, *Historical Collections of South Carolina*, 2: 118 (both quotes). See also William Laurence Saunders, *The Colonial Records of North Carolina* (Raleigh: P. M. Hale etc. State Printer, 1886), 1: 664. This fabric mix also mentioned in Raynal, *A Philosophical and*

Trade in 1706 explained that only 'a little silk' was exported, but that some planters 'for their own use only make a few stuffs of silk & cotton & a sort of cloth . . . to clothe their slaves'. Writers later in the eighteenth century (see Fig. 6.1) also emphasised this domestic application, such as William Bull, who recollected that 'French Protestants . . . made and manufactured silk here for their own use.'[42]

Besides these anecdotal reports, the account book of Nicholas de Longuemare offers some evidence of an active low-level production and exchange system in silk amongst early Carolinians. The Longuemare family, goldsmiths by trade from Dieppe (Normandy), took up land on the Santee River and along the Cooper River some thirty miles upstream of Charleston. Nicholas's involvement in silk dealing seemed to originate in his remarriage to Marie (née Söyer), who likely brought experience in sericulture, and had been earlier married to Jean Aunant, a Languedocian silk thrower who owned a larger neighbouring plantation. In 1708 the Longuemares' account book recorded – in wonderful Franglais – exchanges of silk-related products at all levels, from ounces of silkworm eggs ('de la graine a vers') to boxes of cocoons, and on to raw silk, and different colours and grades of processed silk (such as 'soÿe blance fine') and silk thread. Many of the transactions involved neighbours such as weaver Pierre Du Tartre and a Madame Poulain, from whom they received three boxes of cocoons valued at fifteen 'schelins' (shillings) in May 1710.[43] The Longuemares were also likely amongst those reported as deploying enslaved labour in silk, for Marie manumitted an enslaved Indian and her children in her will of 1712.[44]

Such production elicited metropolitan comment and excitement given that Britain, as we have seen, was in the midst of a great leap forward in silk manufacture and trade. Edmund Randolph concluded his report to the Board of Trade with a firm commendation of Carolina's progress: '[t]hey are very much improved in making Silk & everybody has planted Mulberry Trees to feed their Wormes'.[45] News filtered through to prospective English settlers: Elizabeth Massingberd Hyrne, preparing to depart for Carolina, expected that 'we shall be in a way to rais[e] money

Political History of the British Settlements and Trade in North America, from the French of Abbé Raynal, in Two Volumes, 1: 149.

[42] Sainsbury and Salley, *Records in the BPRO*, 5. 204, 207, II. Roy Merrens, *The Colonial South Carolina Scene: Contemporary Views, 1697–1774* (Columbia: University of South Carolina Press, 1977), 266.

[43] Samuel Gaillard Stoney, 'Nicholas de Longuemare: Huguenot Goldsmith and Silk Dealer in Colonial South Carolina', *Transactions of the Huguenot Society of South Carolina* 55 (1950): 38–69 (transactions on 63–69 and Poulain quote on 66). For a brief discussion of Du Tartre and Huguenot weaving, Van Ruymbeke, *From New Babylon to Eden*, 79–80.

[44] Will of Marie de Longuemare, 18 October 1712 (Charleston Museum Archives).

[45] Letter from Edmund Randolph to Board of Trade, Charleston, 27 May 1700, in Sainsbury and Salley, *Records in the BPRO*, 4: 190.

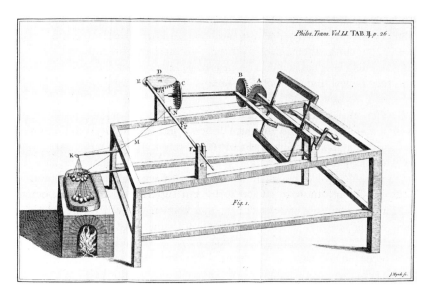

Figure 6.1 Samuel Pullein's drawing of the Piedmont reel (1759).
Drawing of the standard Piedmont silk reel, which Rev. Samuel
Pullein claimed he had innovated an improvement to, in a paper that
was published in the *Philosophical Transactions of the Royal Society*, 51
(1759–60), image a foldout on page 26. He began the paper by
expressing the hope that his new design 'will help to promote the
culture of silk in our American colonies, and to bring it to that
perfection, which at present is scarce found in any country but
Piedmont'. The innovation was to create additional motion through
use of an additional *croissure* (wooden cross) that would help prevent
reeled silk filaments from sticking to one another and generating
imperfections in the thread. It was a perennial problem for colonial silk
reelers to adapt or improvise such technology in households.

by raw silk whereof many gitt great estate by there'.[46] The output
prompted the remaining Carolina proprietors in 1709 to urge their colonists, some forty years after the first cohorts set sail, to target production,
'particularly that of Rice and Silk'.[47] What small amounts of Carolina silk

---

[46] Elizabeth Hyrne to Burrell Massingberd, 2 April 1700, LAO 2MM/B/7/5 (Lincolnshire
Archive Office, Lincoln, UK). For wider context, Pauline M. Loven, 'Hyrne Family
Letters, 1699–1757', *South Carolina Historical Magazine* 102, no. 1 (2001): 27–46.

[47] Letter from proprietors to 'Deputies and Council', 9 April 1709 in Sainsbury and Salley,
Records in the BPRO, 5: 274. The proprietors also continued their targeted sponsorship of
migrants with potential skills in the right commercial areas, offering favourable terms to
'poor Palatines ... being willing to encourage the making of Silk, Planting of Rice,
Vineards [sic], Fruit & Naval Stores'. Sainsbury and Salley, *Records*, 5: 293.

were exported, even in these early years, were clearly highly valued in qualitative terms by metropolitan markets: in 1716, Benjamin Godin sold several bales of silk at 33 shillings a pound, while a memorial from Richard Beresford in 1716 declared that Carolina silk 'has been manufactured in London and proves to be of extraordinary Substance and Lustre'.[48] Six years later, Francis Yonge predicted that Carolinian commerce was in danger of stultifying, forecasting that with rice and tar exports threatened by trading restrictions, and the provisions trade ruined by Indian attacks, 'there remains now nothing but silk'.[49]

Silk production had established and maintained a precarious foothold in early Carolina because, compared to efforts in seventeenth-century Virginia, the colony had proved to have a superior environment, better access to resources and expertise, and a more variegated population. Yonge's pamphlet though, while emphasising silk's presence in the Carolina economy, was actually an expression of the growing power of rice.[50] During this first period of limited silk production between the 1680s and 1719 (when Carolinians threw off proprietary rule), the colony's rulers and settlers navigated a range of precarious internal and external battles for survival, as the relationship between local planters and state power stabilised. The final years of this maelstrom and those that followed witnessed the meteoric rise to dominance in the Lowcountry (the geographic and cultural region along the coastline) of rice cultivation: silk had proved possible, but rice had proved profitable. The emergence of rice as a region-defining staple owed much to rice being a versatile food for which there was a growing appetite in Atlantic markets, to white planters being innovative with capital and technology, and brutally exploitative with labour, and to enslaved Africans bringing a degree of experience and knowledge. The expansion also depended in good measure on planters' enlistment of state power to support their interests and their persuading of imperial bodies to treat the needs of the plantation economy as paramount.[51]

---

[48] Sainsbury and Salley, *Records*, 6: 286; Saunders, *The Colonial Records of North Carolina*, 2: 232.

[49] Francis Yonge, *View of the Trade of South-Carolina* (1722) in Merrens, *Colonial South Carolina Scene*, 68–75 (quote on 72).

[50] Yonge was part of a prolonged lobbying effort which secured a parliamentary decree in 1730 that eased the passage of Carolina rice to markets south of Cape Finisterre. Kenneth Morgan, 'The Organization of the Colonial American Rice Trade', *The William and Mary Quarterly*, 3rd Ser. 52, no. 3 (1995): 433–52; Peter A. Coclanis, 'Rice Prices in the 1720s and the Evolution of the South Carolina Economy', *The Journal of Southern History* 48, no. 4 (1982): 531–44.

[51] Proprietors to Deputies and Council, 9 April 1709, Sainsbury and Salley, *Records in the BPRO*, 5: 271–4. On the rise of rice, see Edelson, *Plantation Enterprise*, 53–91; R. C. Nash, 'South Carolina and the Atlantic Economy in the Late Seventeenth and Eighteenth Centuries', *Economic History Review* 45, no. 4 (1992): 677–702; Peter A. Coclanis,

What contributed to the advent of Carolina rice as an export staple, and especially how significant a role was played by West Africans' pre-existing proficiency in risiculture, has stimulated extensive and sometimes passionate debate amongst scholars trying to unpick blurry patterns of Atlantic innovation, migration, and adaptation. African farmers already cultivated rice extensively in the fifteenth century before the Portuguese arrived on the Upper Guinea coast, which they had not done with tobacco, sugar, or cotton, and had adapted the crop to a range of environments (including uplands and wetlands). This made 'black rice' in some ways distinctive from several other staples with which, from around 1700, it collectively spurred on the slave plantation complex in the Atlantic world. Some African techniques and practices, especially in sowing, threshing, and basket winnowing, diffused extensively and were hybridised by planters alongside other technologies in New World rice cultivation. If African labourers' experience had been a critical determinant, however, slave purchasers did not seem to target African rice-growing regions as systematically as one would expect.[52]

For all that is contested about what people, regions, and decisions were instrumental in the uptake of rice, we can say definitively that the regions of Africa from which Carolina's earliest enslaved workers had been savagely wrenched had no familiarity with *Bombyx* sericulture.[53] The fact that West Africans did not bring experience in raising silkworms can only have aided the triumph of rice in early Carolina – for supposing they had, there would unquestionably have been opportunity to apply expertise, and appetite amongst planters to appropriate it, potentially prolonging the search for a primary export staple. The reverse was not true: the fact that Africans lacked direct experience in sericulture, like many English

'Distant Thunder: The Creation of a World Market in Rice and the Transformations It Wrought', *The American Historical Review* 98, no. 4 (1993): 1050–78; Gary L. Hewitt, 'The State in the Planters' Service: Politics and the Emergence of a Plantation Economy in South Carolina', in *Money, Trade, and Power: The Evolution of Colonial South Carolina's Plantation Society*, ed. Jack P. Greene, Rosemary Brana-Shute, and Randy J. Sparks (Columbia: University of South Carolina Press, 2001), 49–73.

[52] For major contributions: Judith Ann Carney, *Black Rice: The African Origins of Rice Cultivation in the Americas* (Cambridge, MA: Harvard University Press, 2001); David Eltis, Philip D Morgan, and David Richardson, 'Agency and Diaspora in Atlantic History: Reassessing the African Contribution to Rice Cultivation in the Americas', *American Historical Review* 112, no. 5 (2007): 1329–58; 'AHR Exchange: The Question of "Black Rice"', *American Historical Review* 115, no. 1 (2010): 123–71.

[53] Yoruba and Hausa peoples did harvest indigenous silk from nests spun by wild *Anaphe* caterpillars, but the processes required to generate yarn (degumming, drying, carding, and spinning) bore little resemblance to *Bombyx mori* raw silk production and reeling. McKinney and Eicher, 'Unexpected Luxury: Wild Silk Textile Production among the Yoruba of Nigeria'; Colleen E. Kriger, *Cloth in West African History* (AltaMira Press, 2006), 25–6; J. Chunwike Ene, 'Indigenous Silk-Weaving in Nigeria', *Nigeria Magazine* 81 (1964): 127–36.

migrants, was no barrier (as we shall continue to see) to the mobilisation of enslaved people and their skill sets in attempts to progress silk production through the eighteenth century. But in order for Carolina sericulture to secure continued support from the 1720s, the commodity would need to find a way to compete in an agricultural world dominated increasingly by rice and slaves.

Townships and Creative Models, 1730–1750

From the 1730s until the mid-century, attempts to grow silk in the Lower South not only persisted but became more systematic, rigorous, and meaningfully state-sponsored than they ever had before. Much of the renewed vigour was borne out of British mercantilist concerns, for, as we have seen, in the mother country raw silk imports were becoming increasingly precarious even as demand and manufacturing capacity continued to rise. So Parliament, the Board of Trade, colonial governors, and independent organisations all offered considerable support to schemes to increase the amount of silk produced in the Lower South. The growing pool of continental European settlers acted as an added stimulus to new projects, for instance at new townships in Purrysburg, Ebenezer (Georgia), and New Bordeaux. Also important was the decline of rice prices after 1738, which inclined planters in Lowcountry areas more pointedly to explore alternative and complementary products to their major staple, mirroring the effect of tobacco saturation on silk projection in the seventeenth-century Chesapeake.

In South Carolina (which formally became a Crown colony separate from North Carolina in 1729), public funds and energies continued to be channelled into securing labour that was knowledgeable in new commodities and amenable to raising silk and wine, carrying forwards the legacy of the earlier proprietary support of Huguenot arrivals. In their efforts from the 1720s to strengthen and fortify the precarious Lowcountry, Carolinians and imperial officials alike consistently expressed a preference for migration streams that promised to transplant silk growers. Governor Robert Johnson, who had inherited his father Nathaniel's 'Silk Hope' in more ways than once, provided the model for populating these western areas of South Carolina.[54] His orderly 'township scheme' was an exercise in urban planning that shared much in common with other contemporary

---

[54] Richard Philip Sherman, *Robert Johnson, Proprietary & Royal Governor of South Carolina* (Columbia: University of South Carolina Press, 1966), 107–30; Robert Lee Meriwether, *The Expansion of South Carolina, 1729–1765* (Philadelphia: Porcupine Press, 1974), 31.

propositions, such as Robert Montgomery's imagined colony of Azilia (1717) and the Board of Trustees' distinctive ambitions for Georgia (discussed later in this chapter).[55] It proposed the laying out and populating of ten 20,000-acre townships on Carolina's frontiers, along strategic rivers. Restrictions were placed to discourage speculators and planters from exploiting these lands, while generous provisions particularly courted non-British subjects, for instance by offering them grants according to family size at low cost, and equal voting privileges. Although the implementation of the township scheme was somewhat haphazard, it received the sanction of the Board of Trade, and put in place a framework that succeeded over the coming decades in bringing about a degree of social and economic diversification. The promise of silk, alongside other diversifier commodities (such as wine and flax), strengthened the whole concept of new buffer zones in the southern interior.

The first township to be populated from 1732, Purrysburg (on the north bank of the Savannah River), was the culmination of decades of frustrated pamphleteering and scheming by its founder, Jean-Pierre Purry. Purry hailed from the French-speaking Protestant canton of Neuchâtel (Switzerland), which had placed itself under Prussian sovereignty since 1707 in an effort to help fend off the threats from Catholic neighbours. Like many parts of the Swiss Confederation, Neuchâtel had provided a sanctuary for large numbers of French Protestant refugees, and Purry had pestered innumerable officials across three empires with his climatological theories and plans for administering an overseas colony for these countrymen.[56] Now, though a wine man by trade who had promised vineyards for other potential settlements, Purry fine-tuned his proposals aimed at British and Carolinian readers to accentuate silk prospects.[57] He also penned an influential promotional tract for Swiss families that exalted Carolina's fertile environment. He made it plain that he required resourceful migrants to take advantage of the location's fertility, and particularly to attend to planting white mulberries since he believed there was 'perhaps no Country in the World where those Trees

---

[55] Robert Montgomery, *A Discourse Concerning the Design'd Establishment of a New Colony to the South of Carolina* (London, 1717); Trevor R. Reese, ed., *The Most Delightful Country of the Universe: Promotional Literature of the Colony of Georgia, 1717–1734* (Savannah, GA: Beehive Press, 1972).

[56] Purry to Duc de Bourbon, 1723, C/13A/7, f.292v–293, ANOM.

[57] Purry's earlier writings, such as his two memorials 'On the Country of Kaffraria and the Terre de Nuyts' make little specific mention of silk, and are more firmly aimed at wine. Jean Pierre Purry and Arlin C. Migliazzo, *Lands of True and Certain Bounty: The Geographical Theories and Colonization Strategies of Jean Pierre Purry* (Selinsgrove, PA: Susquehanna University Press, 2002), esp. 15–17 on wine, 118, 128.

grow better nor where the Silk is finer'. Purry was a zealous exponent of the latitudinal logic which held that 'all the best Countries in the Universe' – including Barbary (north-west Africa), Crete, Syria, Persia, Moghulistan, and China – were situated on a certain climatic axis. In his promotional claims about Carolina and its 'lots of silkworms', he not only theorised this but also grounded it with hard, local examples: the trunk of a seven- or eight-year-old white mulberry tree round the back of one house at Port Royal was already grown to a circumference of five feet; other four- or five-year-old trees there had foot-wide diameter trunks, as did those on plantations in Goose Creek and Wassamsaw. Purry thus constructed an enticing mix of old arguments and new evidence, to cast Carolina silk as a missed opportunity that was now again come around – 'the major commodity from which one can certainly enrich himself'. With proprietary disputes, pirates, Spanish invasions, and Indian wars behind it, Purry emphasised that the newly stable, peaceful, and expanding province evinced an appetite for manufactures.[58]

In spite of much exaggeration and mischaracterisation, enough knowledge and perseverance arrived with non-English settlers in these lands to ensure that they developed into real sites of silk production. Indeed, over the course of the next decades, clustered in and around these townships on either side of the Savannah River, the French settlers, French- and German-Swiss, German speakers from various principalities, and Piedmontese Italians, probably made the most substantial contribution to silk production of any group in the Lower South. One visitor to Purrysburg reported he had seen more than 1,200 lb of cocoons raised in 1749, predicted to yield 120 lb of raw silk, whose quality was equal 'if not preferable, to any foreign growth'.[59] Participation in Purrysburg silk-raising was extensive, thanks in part to the township's position near a major centre of Georgia production (Ebenezer, discussed below), and the possibility of marketing produce to either Savannah or Charleston. It persisted even when the region began its transition to a plantation and

---

[58] Purry, 'A Brief Description of the Current State of South Carolina', in Purry and Migliazzo, *Lands*, 143–4, 153–4, 162. His pamphlet was published in numerous editions in multiple languages, including circulation in the *Gentleman's Magazine*, 2 (August 1732), 886, 894–6.

[59] R. T., 'Extracts of Some Letters from South Carolina', *Gentleman's Magazine* 19 (1749): 410. For later examples of positive publicity linking Swiss emigrants to silk culture, John Tobler and Walter L. Robbins, 'John Tobler's Description of South Carolina (1754), Translated and Edited by Walter L. Robbins', *South Carolina Historical Magazine* 71, no. 4 (1970): 257–65; John Tobler and Charles G. Cordle, 'The John Tobler Manuscripts: An Account of German-Swiss Emigrants in South Carolina, 1737', *The Journal of Southern History* 5, no. 1 (1939): 83–97.

slaveholding economy.[60] Persuading settlers to take up sericulture, how-ever, required more than just latitude and aptitude.

The South Carolina assembly was proactive and imaginative in setting up direct bounties to reward silk production in the 1730s and 1740s, aiming for a product 'fit for any foreign market' and raw silk that was 'bright, well cured and cleansed from the swingle, fit for use'.[61] The assembly's incentives to promote the likes of olives, silk, and wine have proved an easy target for economic histories to disparage, but they did not just sit on the statute books.[62] The first evidence of payments can be found in a short line in the provincial budget of 1736–7, which noted a payment 'To Peter Bonneau for Bounty of 23 lbs. Raw Silk ... £29 10s' and subsequent payments followed, including to merchant and slave dealer Job Rothmahler, who would go on to testify about American production before the parliamentary committee on raw silk in London in 1750.[63] Though quite unfashionable by the start of the nineteenth century, bounties had played a significant role in channelling colonial Carolinian economic energy: production of pitch and tar had dramati-cally increased in response to a British bounty offered from 1705, and uptake of indigo was encouraged by a bounty during King George's War (1744–8) which was afterwards lowered without affecting the crop's new-found profitability. The silk bounties were also forerunners of textile-supporting measures that followed for hemp, flax, linen, and cotton, several of which were perceived as successful interventions when lifted in the 1770s.[64] Seen in this light, sericulture was not a whimsy but a dynamic testing ground for legislative intervention.

[60] Arlin C. Migliazzo, *To Make This Land Our Own: Community, Identity, and Cultural Adaptation in Purrysburg Township, South Carolina, 1732–1865* (Columbia: University of South Carolina Press, 2007), 209–15, 232–8 (quote on 232).
[61] Cooper and McCord, *Statutes at Large*, 3: 436–7.
[62] Hewitt, 'The State in the Planters' Service: Politics and the Emergence of a Plantation Economy in South Carolina', 49. Cooper (the compiler) himself criticised the measure: Cooper and McCord, *Statutes at Large*, 3: 786.
[63] Rothmahler had produced 16 lb of mixed-quality output in 1739 in Georgetown, on which he claimed the bounty. J. H. Easterby, R. Nicholas Olsberg, and Terry W. Lipscomb, eds., *Journal of the Commons House of Assembly, 1736–1757*, 14 vols. (Columbia: Historical Commission of South Carolina, 1951), 1: 322, 379, 447, 732; 2: 317. Hereinafter cited as *Commons Journal, 1736–1761*.
[64] 'An Act to repeal several Acts of the General Assembly and Resolutions of the Provincial Congress of South Carolina, granting bounties on the culture and manufacture of Hemp, Flax, Linen, Thread and Cotton', 28 March 1778, Cooper and McCord, *Statutes at Large*, 4: 428. On pitch and tar, see Russell R. Menard, 'Economic and Social Development of the South', in *The Cambridge Economic History of the United States*, ed. Stanley L. Engerman and Robert E. Gallman (Cambridge and NY: Cambridge University Press, 1996), 276. For the successful incentivisation of indigo, see wording of 'An Act to revive and continue the several Acts therein mentioned, and to repeal that part of an Act which gives a bounty upon Indigo', Cooper and McCord, *Statutes at Large*,

The structure of bounties for mulberry trees, cocoons, and raw silk was closely debated in the South Carolina assembly, and revealed a high degree of confidence in the sericulture initiatives, based on an expanding pool of experience and capital. This was indicated by Hercules Coyte's sale of up to 200,000 mulberry trees 'of the best White sort' in an advert of 1736, designed to coincide with the announcement of the first bounty – Coyte having built up his white mulberry reserves over ten years of silk production.[65] Only one bill fell through completely upon debate in the assembly; this would have made it compulsory for all planters to plant a specified number of mulberry trees in proportion to their enslaved males, and thereby starkly linked capital in human beings to progressive economic credentials. This proved too radical for the larger slaveholders in the Upper House, who dressed their reluctance up in the kind of noble rhetoric that only the myopia of slave ownership could render unironic: 'we think everything that relates to settling the Province, and encouraging Trade should have all the Air of Liberty and Freedom imaginable'.[66] The most comprehensive system of state-sponsored incentives in South Carolina was erected in the 1744 'Act for the Further Improvement and Encouraging the Produce of Silk', which appointed a set of ten named commissioners (mostly rice planters), any three of whom were authorised to purchase 'on behalf of the public' all cocoons and evenly reeled raw silk produced in the province, at set rates in local currency. The law instructed the commissioners to accept the produce 'tendered unto them by any person or persons whatsoever', a deliberately open-ended constituency that included women, free blacks, and possibly enslaved people also – whether such persons were producing the most inferior 'knubbs'

---

3 670–1; also Ramsay, *History of South Carolina*, 1809, 2: 210–12. The best surveys of its introduction are David L. Coon, 'Eliza Lucas Pinckney and the Reintroduction of Indigo Culture in South Carolina', *The Journal of Southern History* 42, no. 1 (1976): 61–76; Joyce E. Chaplin, *An Anxious Pursuit: Agricultural Innovation and Modernity in the Lower South, 1730–1815* (Chapel Hill: University of North Carolina Press, 1993), 190–208; Virginia Gail Jelatis, 'Tangled up in Blue: Indigo Culture and Economy in South Carolina, 1747–1800' (University of Minnesota, 1999). R. C. Nash has challenged the linking of protectionism to production in some of the historiography: R. C. Nash, 'South Carolina Indigo, European Textiles, and the British Atlantic Economy in the Eighteenth Century,' *Economic History Review* 63, no. 2 (2010): 362–92.

[65] *South Carolina Gazette* (hereinafter *SCG*), 18 December 1736, 15 January 1737, 2 November 1738.

[66] Easterby, Olsberg, and Lipscomb, *Commons Journal*, 2: 522 (Pinckney introduction), 523, 524, 535, 546–7, 548, 552, 554 (clauses not struck out), 555, 560 (Upper House message), 562, 563; 3: 35, 38, 39, 40 (bill rejected definitively). The average number of enslaved people owned by the nine royal councilors for whom we have slave-owning records 1720–1763 was 234. M. Eugene Sirmans, 'The South Carolina Royal Council, 1720–1763', *The William and Mary Quarterly, 3rd Ser.* 18, no. 3 (1961): 373–92.

(unreelable cocoons) or international-quality raw silk suitable for 'organ-zining' in throwing mills.[67]

As has already been made clear, South Carolina's efforts to introduce sericulture repeatedly and pointedly treated silk and slavery as mutually compatible, proposing innovative models that would later extend to Georgia. There is absolutely no substance in the arguments offered by later commentators, such as George Richardson Porter, that the 'princi-pal difficulty with which the Americans had to contend in producing silk in these southern colonies arose out of . . . negro slaves, who could not be made sufficiently attentive and skilful in the management of the business', though this falsehood crept into twentieth-century scholarship, even about the English silk industry.[68] Black people in eighteenth-century Carolina were not viewed as 'palpably incompetent to pursue such an occupation', as Gertrude Working claimed in 1932. Marguerite Hamer's assertion three years later that 'Negro labor was not used in the cultivation of silk, for the "smell from the negroes" was found to "be offensive to the Worms"' involved an outrageous omission of the previous qualifier, since the source reads in full: 'For, upon Trial, it appears there is not the least Ground for the Apprehension, some People have had, that the Smell from them Negroes would be offensive to the Worms.'[69] Rather, planters and enslaved people – disproving occasional racialised claims such as those raised in the French Caribbean – deployed enslaved labour in silk in a number of ways and locations that sought to make the most of pre-occupations about estate development, profit, civility, and reputation – whether at the colonial or the personal level.

Between 1737 and 1741, the assembly underwrote a remarkable experiment, paying for two Piedmontese silk experts (John Louis Poyas and his wife Susanne) to train a handful of publicly purchased

[67] Hercules Coyte was appointed as a special inspector, who would countersign a certificate verifying the produce (whether cocoons or reeled raw silk) and its quality. Easterby, Olsberg, and Lipscomb, *Commons Journal*, 4: 258, 305, 342, 351, 507, 509, 510, 530, 533, 540, 549, 551, 552–4; 5: 43, 51, 96, 171, 178, 181–2, 188, 190–1, 194, 195, 196–7, 202; Cooper and McCord, *Statutes at Large*, 3: 613–16. Records of payments made: Easterby, Olsberg, and Lipscomb, *Commons Journal*, 5: 428, 6: 61, 157; 7: 363; 8: 380; 9: 162. After expiry of the act, ad hoc bounties continued to be granted, as in the case of Anthony Camuse, an expert who had relocated from Georgia and in 1749 'wrought up eighty-five Pounds Weight of best organzined Silk' for which he sought reward and was granted around £600 (SC): Easterby, Olsberg, and Lipscomb, 9: 381–2, 404.

[68] Porter, *A Treatise on the Silk Manufacture*, 40; Gerald B. Hertz, 'The English Silk Industry in the Eighteenth Century', *The English Historical Review* 24, no. 96 (1909): 718.

[69] Working, 'History of Silk Culture', 36; Marguerite B. Hamer, 'The Foundation and Failure of the Silk Industry in Provincial Georgia', *North Carolina Historical Review* 12, no. 2 (1935): 140; Allen D. Candler et al., eds., *The Colonial Records of the State of Georgia*, 31 vols. (Atlanta and Athens: Various printers, 1904), 33: 574.

enslaved people along with white apprentices. The Poyases had originally taken up a commission to work with the Swiss in Purrysburg, but instead sought to set up operations in Charleston, contracting themselves to the assembly for seven years, for which Poyas would be paid £100 in cash for the first three years, and receive all the profits as payment for the remainder. According to the act's terms, a number of enslaved people would be bought by the public purse and constitute the Poyases' initial labour force and their first trainees. Poyas would be given provisions for his family and the public slaves for a year, in the expectation that after this the bondspeople would provision themselves (a common phenomenon). Poyas undertook to instruct apprentices 'in the whole Art and Manufacture of Silk from the Egg to the Organzining thereof inclusive', who would be put to him by the silk commissioners. Moreover, to maximise the take-up that it was hoped would follow Poyas's success, the workings were to be permanently laid open to 'all Persons ... in order to inform themselves in the said Manufacture'.[70] Conscious that this project would be looked on favourably by the Board of Trade and enlightened political economists in Britain, the assembly directed the colony's agent, Peregrine Fury, to 'sollicit the taking off the Duty on Raw Silk exported from America' as a means of further encouraging potential profitability.[71]

The Poyases began operations some five miles outside Charleston on the eighty-acre plantation of Joseph Wragg, an experienced slave dealer who also procured 'six Negroes' for the project at a cost of £900 (South Carolina currency).[72] Much of the early work no doubt involved planting out and tending substantial numbers of mulberry trees to add to the stocks on Wragg's lands, building a filature, and sourcing silkworm eggs and machinery from Europe. Poyas owed Sarah Trott over £29 for various building materials 'for the Use of the Silk Work', including 625 feet of boards that were carted from town and made into special feeding benches for the worms.[73] In

---

[70] Easterby, Olsberg, and Lipscomb, *Commons Journal*, 1: 336–7, 344, 395, 423 (first two quotes), 424 (third quote), 447, 464, 465, 479, 514, 528, 534, 536, 541, 542, 543; Cooper and McCord, *Statutes at Large*, 3: 487 ('An Act for encouraging the Manufacture of Silk in this Province, under the direction of Mr. John Lewis Poyas, for seven years' listed as passed on 11 March 1738 but original not to be found).

[71] Easterby, Olsberg, and Lipscomb, *Commons Journal*, 1: 562.

[72] Easterby, Olsberg, and Lipscomb, 1: 634 (quote), 660; for Wragg's actions as a slave-trading agent, James A. Rawley and Stephen D. Behrendt, *The Transatlantic Slave Trade: A History, Revised Edition* (Lincoln: University of Nebraska Press, 2005), 160.

[73] Easterby, Olsberg, and Lipscomb, *Commons Journal*, 3: 317 (quote), 375. *Commons Journal, 1736–1761*, III, 317 (quotation), 375.

1739 the newspaper reported that the training school had indeed opened, and would that year be admitting up to ten apprentices, some maintained at public expense from any of the townships, and others 'at the Charges of their Parents'.[74]

By 1741 though, it was clear that the Poyas project was falling short of expectations, and both parties accepted that there were some mitigating factors: Poyas referred in a petition to his 'Loss of Time &c' while the commissioners acknowledged the plantation they provided had been 'not very suitable to the Work' and that there had been 'several cross Accidents concurring'.[75] Charleston had undoubtedly been hit hard by substantial disruptions in this period: smallpox tore through the population in 1738 and still dogged the colony at the start of the next year, followed by an epidemic of yellow fever in the summer which caused such chaos that the assembly was prorogued, schools were closed, newspapers were cancelled, and the townsfolk fled. Perhaps these events contributed to the more than £14 spent on medicines for the treatment of the 'Negroes belonging to the Public ... Silk Work'.[76] Stimulated at least in part by this carnage, the Stono slave rebellion on 9 September 1739 itself provoked widespread upheaval. Also interconnected with the rebellion was the outbreak of the War of Jenkins' Ear between Britain and Spain. This largely naval conflict, which lasted in effect until 1742, had potentially serious ramifications for Poyas, for it massively disrupted transatlantic trade and communications, cutting off potential sources of silkworm eggs in the Iberian peninsula, and making procurement from anywhere in the Mediterranean problematic as a result of large-scale and ruinous Spanish privateering.[77] Finally, in November 1740 a great fire burned out a good portion of Charleston in the waterfront district.[78] The commissioners also evidently felt that the Poyas family was underperforming, not fulfilling their mission 'to teach and instruct certain Apprentices': they eventually withheld

---

[74] *SCG*, 15 February 1739. The commissioners 'ready to treat with the Parents of any Children who are willing' were Ralph Izard, Isaac Mazyck, and Benjamin Whitaker.
[75] Easterby, Olsberg, and Lipscomb, *Commons Journal*, 2: 481, 484.
[76] Peter H. Wood, *Black Majority: Negroes in Colonial South Carolina from 1670 through the Stono Rebellion* (New York: Norton, 1975), 312–13. The account for medicines for the treatment of the enslaved people was presented by physician Dr Peter Delmestre in January 1741, in Easterby, Olsberg, and Lipscomb, *Commons Journal*, 2: 480.
[77] Carl E. Swanson, *Predators and Prizes: American Privateering and Imperial Warfare, 1739–1748*, Studies in Maritime History (Columbia, SC: University of South Carolina Press, 1991), 142.
[78] Matthew Mulcahy, 'The "Great Fire" of 1740 and the Politics of Disaster Relief in Colonial Charleston', *South Carolina Historical Magazine* 99, no. 2 (1998): 135–57.

Poyas's salary and requested he return the 'Slaves, Machines and other Things purchased'.[79]

The Poyas project had been launched at a deeply unpropitious time, but it had showed an explicit willingness to try to synchronise slavery with sericulture. Poyas himself remained convinced of future success, and evidently persisted for a few years without public support, as suggested in his offer post-dismissal to pay £4 a bushel to 'any Persons' who had made 'any Silk-Worms this Year ... provided they have been baked in an Oven, and not in the Sun'.[80] The assembly publicly auctioned off the six trained bondspeople, and aggregation of payments made out of the proceeds of these sales, from 1741 to 1744, suggests that they brought in over £1,135 (SC).[81] It is tempting to speculate that this increase in the value of the enslaved people (around 26 per cent) reflected their having acquired new skills, a notion supported by probate inventory analysis which suggests slave prices in South Carolina collapsed in the years after 1739, dropping to their lowest level of the century. So these six bondspeople were worth noticeably more in a period when the average price of enslaved people was dropping and the paper currency was stable.[82] Subsequently, the assembly and its long-standing 'Committee of Silk Manufacture' tried again to find trustworthy experts capable of centralising and managing reeling in the colony, and again these initiatives involved important contributions made by planters and their enslaved labourers.

In areas with fewer enslaved people, Carolina silk was commonly associated with white female labour. This reflected that silkworm rearing had to be accommodated within households, and involved tasks of nurturing and reeling that were typically described in maternalistic or feminine terms. Having seen 'exceeding good' Carolina silk samples in Britain in 1737, worth '18 shillings the pound', transatlantic botanist Peter Collinson urged Carolinians that silk 'is not to be feared' and strongly framed his arguments around the mobilisation and empowerment of

[79] Easterby, Olsberg, and Lipscomb, *Commons Journal*, 2: 481 (second quote), 483–4 (first quote), 500, 501. Joseph Blake was later paid £75 'for the Hire of a Plantation for the Use of the Silk Work'. Easterby, Olsberg, and Lipscomb, *Commons Journal*, 2: 531, 542.

[80] *SCG*, 7 May 1741 (all quotes), 10 April 1742.

[81] Easterby, Olsberg, and Lipscomb, *Commons Journal*, 2: 500, 551; 5: 146.

[82] Peter C. Mancall, Joshua L. Rosenbloom, and Thomas Weiss, 'Slave Prices and the South Carolina Economy, 1722–1809', *The Journal of Economic History* 61, no. 3 (2001): 616–39 (quote on 627); on the paper currency: Richard M. Jellison, 'Paper Currency in Colonial South Carolina: A Reappraisal', *South Carolina Historical Magazine* 62, no. 3 (1961): 134–47; John J. McCusker, *Money and Exchange in Europe and America, 1600–1775: A Handbook* (Chapel Hill, NC: Published for the Institute of Early American History and Culture, Williamsburg, Va., by the University of North Carolina Press, 1978), 220–3.

female labour. Collinson bemoaned silk's status as a peripheral product, and in a letter to merchant Samuel Eveleigh, he argued that 'I see no way so effectual to introduce it by degrees into a staple manufacturer; but by making it the good woman's property.' There is no suggestion that Carolinians took up Collinson's radical proposition to give women exclusive 'disposal' of their profits from home-raised silk, but many glimpses of Carolina production point to women's dominant role.[83] John Oldmixon reported in 1708 that amongst their other domestic tasks, '[t]he ordinary women ... wind silk from the worms'.[84] Moravian Johann Ettwein commented in his 1765 travelogue that amongst the European townships, '[a] good housewife with three or four children can get about three ounces of seed, and from that, if they are successful, they can get from £20 to 30 Sterling worth of cocoons'.[85] Given that activities within illiterate and poorer homesteads were poorly documented, especially when under the auspices of women, we might expect that domestic production of raw silk was also somewhat underreported.

Even where any commercial profit seemed distant, sericulture's high currency in the overlapping worlds of natural science and political economy offered important incentives for many planters to persist in their own efforts, and in their proxy patronage of townships, schemes, and filatures. It particularly drew the interest of both amateur and renowned botanists, physicians, horticulturists, and scientists such as James Petiver, John Brickell, Peter Collinson, Robert Pringle, and Alexander Garden.[86] Garden closely inspected the mechanics of silk production, and the relative contributions of its plant, insect, and human functionaries from 1752, paying close attention to the worms spinning (to 'Ocularly Learn their Oeconomy'), and also to Carolina women reeling the cocoons off, whose 'Method of winding the Silk off from the bottoms ... was new to me.' After numerous experiments and dissections of silkworms in various states of development, Garden posited that feeding them on native red

---

[83] Letter from Peter Collinson to Samuel Eveleigh, London, 22 April 1737. Linnean Society, Peter Collinson's Larger Commonplace Book, Item 119, copied in File 30–02-3, titled 'Silk Cultivation' (South Carolina Historical Society, Charleston).

[84] John Oldmixon, *The History of Carolina: being an Account of that Colony* (London, 1708), in Carroll, *Historical Collections of South Carolina*, 2: 460.

[85] George Fenwick Jones and Johann Ettwein, 'Report of Mr. Ettwein's Journey to Georgia and South Carolina, 1765', *South Carolina Historical Magazine* 91, no. 4 (1990): 247–60 (quote on 259).

[86] W. H. G. Armytage, 'Letters on Natural History of Carolina 1700–1705', *South Carolina Historical Magazine* 55, no. 2 (1954): 59–70 (esp. 60, 62); John Brickell, *The Natural History of North-Carolina* (Dublin: Printed by J. Carson for the author, 1737), 29; Robert Pringle, *The Letterbook of Robert Pringle*, ed. Walter B. Edgar, 2 vols. (Columbia: University of South Carolina Press, 1972); Walter B. Edgar, 'Robert Pringle and His World', *South Carolina Historical Magazine* 76, no. 1 (1975): 1–11.

mulberries from time to time 'purges them gently', allowing for a healthier and more efficient crop.[87] Such naturalists linked Carolinians to wider circles of association that facilitated the transfer of technical literature and resources, as well as experimental ideas: physiologist Stephen Hales, for instance, sent Gov. William Lyttleton 'a Proposal to keep Silkworms eggs from hatching too soon, by keeping them, in well glazed large Jarrs, in Wells, and blowing down some times fresh air to them'.[88] Irish cleric and improver Rev. Samuel Pullein part-translated and part-authored a substantial synthetic guide to silk cultivation in 1758, which became highly prized amongst Carolina women, as did newly rediscovered observations by John Locke on sericulture.[89]

In terms of its overall dispersal, and in spite of its commercial failure, silk cultivation in South Carolina in the mid-eighteenth century therefore involved a small number of planters, a disproportionately high number of women, a substantial number of white European migrants, and plenty of enslaved people (especially those unfit for more conventional springtime labour). As a consequence, we find diffusion of the subject into the everyday fabric of life in the colony of a type that was distinctive from many other regions, in which sericulture was more fleetingly attempted. By 1746, newspaper printers themselves offered to sell 'Very good SILK WORM SEED' for ready money.[90] A physician reported that Carolina silkworms were useful as medicine, claiming that when 'dried, powder'd and laid to the Crown of the Head [they] are good in *Megrims, Virtigoes* and *Convulsions,* and the Ashes of the Silk cleanseth Wounds, *&c*'.[91]

The pursuit of silk influenced how planters marketed their estates, and what international news was deemed of interest to Carolinians. Mulberry trees were held to be important bonus selling points for estates, as indicated by the emphasis on the 'great quantity of mulberry' situated on a plantation listed in 1761. As early as 1736, a 200-acre plantation on

[87] Alexander Garden and Joseph I. Waring, 'Correspondence between Alexander Garden, M.D., and the Royal Society of Arts', *South Carolina Historical Magazine* 64, no. 1 (1963): 18.

[88] 'Letter from Dr Stephen Hales to Royal Society of Arts on Book on Silk Worms', 8 April 1755, in Guard Book (PR.GE/110/1/16), Royal Society of Arts Archive, London.

[89] Samuel Pullein, *The Culture of Silk: Or, An Essay on Its Rational Practice and Improvement* (London: A. Millar, 1758). Pullein was referred to, for instance, in letters between Harriott Pinckney, Becky Izard, 'Miss R.', Eliza Huger, and Eliza Pinckney: Eliza Lucas Pinckney, *The Letterbook of Eliza Lucas Pinckney*, ed. Marvin R. Zahniser (Columbia, SC: University of South Carolina Press, 1997), 239, 254. On Pullein and silk promotion in Ireland: Samuel Pullein, *Some Hints Intended to Promote the Culture of Silkworms in Ireland* (Dublin: S. Powell, 1750); Mairead Dunlevy, *Pomp and Poverty: A History of Silk in Ireland* (New Haven: Yale University Press, 2011). For Locke, *SCG*, 21 July 1766, extracted from the London *Universal Museum and Complete Magazine*.

[90] *SCG*, 10 March 1746. Offer repeated on 17 and 24 March.

[91] Brickell, *The Natural History of North-Carolina*, 155.

Goose Creek was recorded as including 'a nursery of 5 or 600 mulberry trees about two years old, fit to plant out'. John Francis Triboudet declared his plot 'sufficient to raise 4 or 500 pounds of cocoons' though this was trumped by Patrick Mackay's 1762 notice that '[o]n this plantation are several hundreds of large white mulberry trees, sufficient for making many thousands of cocoons'.[92] Besides influencing the shape of estates, the pursuit of silk influenced what international news was deemed of interest to Carolinians, who were informed in 1741, through letters from Turin, that a freak cold snap had done widespread damage to Italian mulberries.[93] In later years, Carolinians were updated on progress in sericulture in Minorca, Ireland, Naples, Sweden, Persia, India, and Sicily, and of course when silk was taken up more fervently by other American colonies, news of their exploits was closely monitored.[94] The creation and marketing of mulberry orchards, and the communication of their international linkages, would not only facilitate sericulture but also demonstrate the kind of dominion over marginal landscapes that helped elites stake their claim to social authority.[95]

The Georgia Colony

The most sustained and creative model to emerge out of silk aspirations in the Lower South was not a migrant stream, project, or estate, but an entire colony, claimed in 1732 out of lands lying between the Savannah River and Spanish settlements in Florida. Georgia's founders and administrators literally stamped silk on Georgia's formative identity. The Trustees (who were granted the charter by George II) selected a design

[92] *SCG*, 19 June 1736, 28 November 1761, 11, September 1762 [Mackay], 9 April 1763 [Triboudet]. Mackay's 2,300-acre plantation in the township of Purrysburg was still listed for sale on 27 August 1763. See also similar examples on 17 November 1758, 12 November 1764, 14 February 1769.

[93] *SCG*, 10 October 1741.

[94] *SCG*, 21 May 1750 [update on duties on Chinese raw silk], 16 March 1752 [Georgia exported 496 lb], 7 May 1753 [Georgia], 9 June 1759 [Georgia filature received over 10,000 lb of cocoons], 7 May 1763 [Georgia exports from 5 January to 5 April 1761 listed '10 chests and 5 bales of raw silk'], 14 January 1764 [Mobile], 12 November 1764 [Floridas & Georgia], 25 May 1765 [New York & Philadelphia reportedly to establish 'manufactures for silk'], 1 June 1765 [Minorca], 21 January 1766 [Stockholm], 1 September 1766 [Etna], 16 September 1766 [China], 4 November 1766 [Persia], 3 December 1771 [Georgia produced 438 lb raw silk for export], 10 September 1772 [New Jersey: an excerpt from Gov. William Franklin's speech on silk encouragement], 27 October 1772 [India], 31 December 1772 [Minorca]. Charleston *South Carolina and American General Gazette*, 5 September 1766 [Ireland & Naples], 12 June 1769 [Connecticut: a discussion of the progress made by several gentlemen in Connecticut in planting mulberry orchards, building filatures, and making gowns], 31 July 1769 [discussion of Shakespeare's mulberry].

[95] For a discussion of elite gardens and orchards, see Edelson, *Plantation Enterprise*, 146–51.

for the new colony's first seal whose reverse showed a symbolic mulberry leaf, pointing upwards like the ace of spades, with a silk cocoon and a silkworm climbing upon it – so positioned to indicate the ascendant hopes of establishing silk as a mainstay of the province's economy. From its inception, the Georgia colony was a unique experiment, designed to make a distinctive contribution to the British Atlantic empire. Promising no proprietary profit, the venture was geared to offering a new line of defence to vulnerable British American possessions, to offering a haven for suitable British and European colonists struggling in the Old World (for reasons of debt, religious persecution, or economic strife), and to offering a new economic model that would fit with imperial needs for target commodities and avoid the social imbalances that plagued neighbouring plantation slave societies. Many of the Trusteeship's distinctive features eroded, including its ban on slavery, when subjected to the powerful neighbouring influences of Caribbean and Carolinian migrants and models, but silk investment and iconography persisted. When the remaining Trustees surrendered their charter and seal back to the Crown in 1752, signalling a complete overhaul in the province's government, a new royal Deputed Great Seal was created; again, silk was selected to feature prominently. On the seal's image, which was re-engraved more modestly in 1767 for George III, a semi-nude female Native American figure hangs a symbolic skein of raw silk onto the belt of the king, representing the theoretical abundance, prosperity, and dutiful submission of the province's lands and peoples. It neatly captured themes of gender, patronage, and production that remained important to Georgia sericulture for the duration of the colony's existence (see Plate 8).[96]

The Trustees' selection of silk as an economic lynchpin for Georgia was based in large part on the episodic production of high-quality silk in South Carolina in past decades. Also important was their recognition that silk and wine would be looked upon very favourably by metropolitan authorities and constitute a useful weapon in their continuing campaign for financial support for the Georgia project. If some of their projections were exaggerated and fanciful, such as the profit figure of £500,000 that was bandied about in some of their promotional pamphlets, they were nonetheless careful, before they committed resources to the goal of silk, to secure the approval of relevant experts. In January 1732, some months before their charter came into existence, the Trustees wrote to the now-famed English silk thrower Sir Thomas Lombe, asking his opinion of the idea of raising silk in Georgia, of 'the Probability of succeeding therein',

---

[96] Ben Marsh, 'The Meanings of Georgia's Eighteenth-Century Great Seals', *Georgia Historical Quarterly* 96, no. 2 (2012): 195–232.

and his verdict on 'the Nature, Quality, and Use of the Raw Silk produced in Carolina'. Lombe was adamant on all counts that silk in Georgia could succeed. After conducting several experiments on Carolina output, he vouched that it could bear the demands of organzining and therefore supply the most valuable warp thread required in silk weaving. He did, however, caution that the 'very great Probability' of success was dependent upon pursuing proper measures to assist, instruct, and encourage colonists. People with suitable experience should be sent out to teach reeling in the Italian style, aiming for 'short Skains, a fine, clean and even Thread'.[97]

The Trustees took these suggestions seriously, and went to extraordinary lengths to give Georgia sericulture the kind of running start that had proved impossible in Virginia or South Carolina. These involved wide stipulations in relation to landholding, the contracting of experts from silk regions, the continuous provision of materials (trees, eggs, books, reeling machinery), measures intended to encourage production, and measures taken to foster the training and diversification of silk producers. The Georgia Trustees saturated their correspondence with references to silk, dealing with the minutiae of operations as much as the grander visions captured on the seals. Indeed, one consequence of their heavy prioritisation of silk culture was that Georgia production, from the outset, was heavily state supported and heavily centralised; these features swelled further with the transition to Crown colony. Packaged as a staple product, and often dependent on a handful of individuals tasked with responsibility for reeling operations, Georgia silk was channelled outwards towards the Atlantic. As a result, even though this investment mobilised the labour of many hundreds of settlers and many millions of worms between the 1730s and 1770s, and almost certainly produced more raw silk than any other contemporary colony (in spite of its youth), no material fabric seems to have survived, only hanks and skeins mentioned in probate inventories.[98]

---

[97] Thomas Lombe to Georgia Trustees, Old Jewry, 31 January 1732, included as appendix four in Benjamin Martyn, *An Impartial Enquiry into the State and Utility of the Province of Georgia* (London: W. Meadows, 1741).

[98] This high profile of silk means that there exists for Georgia, more than other regions, something of a literature on sericulture: Madelyn Shaw, 'Silk in Georgia, 1732–1840: From Sericulture to Status Symbol', in *Decorative Arts in Georgia: Historic Sites, Historic Contents*, ed. Ashley Callahan (Athens: Georgia Museum of Art, 2008), 59–78; Ben Marsh, *Georgia's Frontier Women: Female Fortunes in a Southern Colony* (Athens: University of Georgia Press, 2007), 53–61; Chaplin, *An Anxious Pursuit*, 158–65. For earlier works of mixed quality and accuracy, see: William B. Stevens, 'A Brief History of the Silk Culture in Georgia', in *Biographical Memorials of James Oglethorpe: Founder of the Colony of Georgia in North America*, ed. Thaddeus Mason Harris (Boston: Printed for the author, 1841), 177–89; McKinstry, 'Silk Culture in the Colony of Georgia'; Hamer, 'Foundation and Failure'; Pauline Tyson Stephens, 'The Silk Industry in Georgia,' *The*

Nobody reading the many promotional pamphlets circulated by the Trustees in the 1730s could realistically have evaded the subject of silk. Authors such as James Oglethorpe and Benjamin Martyn explained at length the desirability and feasibility of silk production, linking it carefully to long-standing domestic, industrial, commercial, and imperial agendas. Many of their arguments, though, were fresher and related to more recent developments: the tightening constraints on access to superior raw silk markets overseas, the new-found capacity for British silk throwing, and the growing clamour to address pauperism and its social and economic costs through parish relief. They pulled statistics out of the air, such as the 20,000 Georgia colonists to be gainfully employed for four months a year in sericulture, and the additional 20,000 jobs that would be created for silk manufacturers in the home country. They also spun the existence of Carolinian silk production, holding it up as evidence of achievability even as they caricatured the production taking place across the border as being compromised by 'the Negroe Slaves being both dull and careless and not capable of winding it with that nicety which it requires' (an argument with no grounds in reality and which obviously and intentionally mutually reinforced the Trustees' prohibition on slaves).[99] The promoters were neither unaware nor disregardful of prior attempts in other southern colonies, as once assumed.[100]

Besides idiosyncratic prohibitions on slavery, rum, lawyers, and Catholics, the Trustees sought to control the socio-economic profile of their colony by using the principal capital at their disposal: Georgia land.

Georgia Review 7 (1953): 39–49; Joseph Ewan, 'Silk Culture in the Colonies: With Particular Reference to the Ebenezer Colony and the First Local Flora of Georgia', *Agricultural History* 43 (1969): 129–42; James C. Bonner, 'Silk-Growing in the Georgia Colony', *Agricultural History* 43, no. 1 (1969): 143–7; Joan W. Krispyn, 'The Silkworm Bombyx Mori (Linn.) in Colonial Georgia', *Journal of the Georgia Entomological Society* 13, no. 2 (1978): 124–8; W. Calvin Smith, 'Utopia's Last Chance? The Georgia Silk Boomlet of 1751', *Georgia Historical Quarterly* 59 (1975): 25–37.

[99] Figures and quotes in Benjamin Martyn, *Reasons for Establishing the Colony of Georgia: With Regard to the Trade of Great Britain, the Increase of our People, and the Employment and Support it Will Afford to Great Numbers of our Own Poor, as Well as Foreign Persecuted Protestants* (London: W. Meadows, 1733), 5, 8–11; James Edward Oglethorpe, *A New and Accurate Account of the Provinces of South-Carolina and Georgia* (London: Printed for J. Worrall, 1732), 51 (quote on poor relief), 55–63; James Edward Oglethorpe, Rodney M. Baine and Phinizy Spalding, *Some Account of the Design of the Trustees for Establishing Colonys in America* (Athens: University of Georgia Press, 1990), 15 (quote on slaves), 44–5. For a discussion of the figures and literature, see Milton L Ready, 'Philanthropy and the Origins of Georgia', in *Forty Years of Diversity: Essays on Colonial Georgia*, ed. Harvey H. Jackson and Phinizy Spalding (Athens: University of Georgia Press, 1984), 56–7; Rodney M. Baine, 'James Oglethorpe and the Early Promotional Literature for Georgia', *The William and Mary Quarterly* 45, no. 1 (1988): 100–6.

[100] Lewis Cecil Gray, *History of Agriculture in the Southern United States to 1860*, vol. 2 (Gloucester, MA: Peter Smith, 1958), 1: 186.

Those male colonists sent across the Atlantic 'on the Trust' were entitled to their passage, provisions for one year, tools, and a tract of fifty acres of land in return for their labour – the support for servants and apprentices including cheap clothing which consisted of one frock and trousers made of linsey-woolsey, another made of coarse heavy linen ('oznabrigs') with a matching shirt, and three pairs of shoes (one 'English' and two 'Country').[101] So-called 'adventurers', the minority of settlers of independent means who paid for their own crossing, were awarded land by petition, though their grants were capped at 500 acres. This liberal distribution of land, however, came with unpopular provisos that the Trustees designed with their wider goals in mind: they connived against absenteeism, female landownership, and anything that might reduce Georgia's capacity to defend the southern frontier of British America or damage its social stability. As had occurred over a century before in Virginia, the Trustees also used land regulations to foster silk cultivation. To avoid their lands reverting to the Trust, the dutiful yeomanry had to clear and cultivate 10 acres in their first 10 years, planting at least 100 white mulberry trees in the process. Nor did adventurers escape constraints, for they had to reside on their estates, and within 10 years plant 2,000 'White Mulberry-trees or Plants' on 200 cleared acres. All in all, this policy promised to establish a ratio of ten white mulberry trees to every cultivated acre in the colony, with 'the Trustees obliging themselves to furnish the Plants'.[102]

This kind of commitment to moriculture required careful supply planning, which the Trustees engineered via the financial support of staffed nurseries in different locations across the province. From its creation on 9 June 1733, the 'Trustee Garden' in Savannah swiftly became one of the important vehicles for facilitating sericulture in Georgia, being a 'publick Garden . . . designed as a Nursery, in order to supply the People for their several Plantations with White Mulberry-trees, Vines, Oranges, Olives, and other necessary Plants'.[103] Boasting by 1734 an official botanist and a permanent staff of gardeners and servants, the ten-acre agricultural experiment station was modelled after the botanical gardens at Oxford and London. It had several mandates, one of which was to conduct research on what cultivars might prosper out of the various crops, drugs and dyestuffs whose seeds were carefully collected and planted out. Besides receiving a range of seeds from the renowned Scottish horticulturist Philip Miller of the Chelsea Physic Garden, ambitious expeditions

[101] Candler et al., *Col. Rec. Georgia*, 20: 37.
[102] Candler et al., *Col. Rec. Georgia* 3: 375–6, 412.
[103] Candler et al., *Col. Rec. Georgia* 3: 382.

were organised to the northern coast of Brazil, the Caribbean islands, and Spanish possessions in Central America in a bid to compete in the production of the popular dye cochineal and fever-dousing 'Jesuit bark' from the cinchona tree (later known as quinine).[104]

The Garden soon housed important collections of targeted semitropical plants, becoming a miniature vineyard, orchard, and most importantly a nursery of white mulberry trees for the colony. Between September 1733 and April 1734, Miller sent two parcels of white mulberry seeds from Italy, as well as 'a Tub of White Mulberry Plants'.[105] Trustee Gardeners were designated as the point men in the supply of mulberry seedlings for distribution to the settlers, without whom landholders would struggle to fulfil the terms of their grants. By 1735, they had planted out nearly 3,000 'Virginia white Mulberry Trees' and a further 100,000 seedlings in Savannah alone. Many hundreds of trees and thousands more seedlings were sourced that year in Charleston, where they were loaded up on flat-bottomed 'periagua' boats, and relocated to nurseries and plantations via the Savannah River.[106] Other regional nurseries soon emulated the Savannah original, including the one developed in the township of Ebenezer. There, Francis Moore described 'vast quantities of mulberry trees' planted in orderly squares in 1735 such that 'every planter that desires it has young trees given him gratis from this nursery'.[107] Paulo Amatis recorded that these white mulberries from Italy, Virginia, and Carolina were indeed finding their way onto private plantations, informing the Trustees that 15,000 plants had been given out 'to the Inhabitants' in the summer of 1736, and that most of a further 25,000 were to be 'distributed this Autumn'.[108]

---

[104] Renate Wilson and David L. Cowan, 'Trustee Garden', *New Georgia Encyclopaedia*, 2003, www.georgiaencyclopedia.org/nge/Article.jsp?id=h-813; Julie Anne Sweet, 'A Misguided Mistake: The Trustees' Public Garden in Savannah, Georgia', *Georgia Historical Quarterly* 93, no. 1 (2009): 1–29; Thomas Pinney, *A History of Wine in America: From the Beginnings to Prohibition* (Berkeley: University of California Press, 1989), 44.

[105] Candler et al., *Col. Rec. Georgia*, 1: 130, 3: 59–60.

[106] Estimates of tree numbers and relocation: Candler et al., *Col. Rec. Georgia*, 20: 22, 71, 88, 152, 251; Sarah B. Gober Temple and Kenneth Coleman, *Georgia Journeys: Being an Account of the Lives of Georgia's Original Settlers and Many Other Early Settlers from the Founding of the Colony in 1732 until the Institution of Royal Government in 1754* (Athens: University of Georgia Press, 1961), 127; David S. Shields, *Oracles of Empire: Poetry, Politics, and Commerce in British America, 1690–1750* (Chicago: University of Chicago Press, 1990), 52.

[107] Francis Moore, *A Voyage to Georgia, Begun in the Year 1735: Containing an Account of the Settling the Town of Frederica, in the Southern Part of the Province; and a Description of the Soil, Air, Birds, Beasts, Trees, Rivers, Islands, &c* (London: Jacob Robinson, 1744), 30.

[108] John Perceval Egmont, *The Journal of the Earl of Egmont: Abstract of the Trustees Proceedings for Establishing the Colony of Georgia, 1732–1738*, ed. Robert G McPherson (Athens: University of Georgia Press, 1962), 179.

Amatis himself was an important early lynchpin in the pursuit of silk production in Georgia, being the first of a stream of well-remunerated experts, most of them from Piedmont (the silk-rich principality within the lands of the House of Savoy), who were tasked with directing operations from Savannah. Mindful of Thomas Lombe's warnings, the Trustees used their excellent social networks to track down these 'experienced persons', and one of their most important connective figures seems to have been Samuel Lloyd, the agent and later proprietor of Thomas Lombe's Derby throwing mill, who in 1747 was himself appointed a Georgia Trustee.[109] The Amatis dynasty was amongst the most prominent families of silk merchants in Turin, and two brothers, Paolo and Nicola, reached agreements and agreed terms with the Trustees between 1732 and 1733, the former departing on the first ship to settle the new colony with founder James Oglethorpe in November 1732.[110] Paolo first busied himself in South Carolina – another testament to continued local production there – where he sourced not only mulberry trees but also silkworms and cocoons to help launch Georgia production. In a notice in the *South Carolina Gazette* on 27 April 1734, he offered, on behalf of the Georgia Trustees, 'to give 3 Pounds currency [in SC cash] to every Bushel of good Silk Balls' brought to him in Broad Street in Charleston. Paolo had agreed with Oglethorpe that his brother would 'bring with him 2 Men and 4 Women who understand the whole of the Silk Business', and that the Trustees would reimburse Nicola for the cost of travelling from Turin to London with these experts and bringing several pounds of silkworm eggs, a 'copper for boiling' and a reeling machine.[111] As the Earl of Egmont, one of the most prominent early Trustees, declared in his diary in January 1733: 'we build great expectations on these two brothers'.[112]

Nicola Amatis arrived in London via Lyons in February with a complement of 'seven persons ... who were well skilled in the silk', amongst them expert Savoyard reelers (the Camosso family) and Giacomo Ottone, 'a Man of Experience in making the Silk Machines'. These Italians were interviewed by none other than Sir Thomas Lombe, and departed in April, excepting Ottone. The Trustees agreed to defray the cost of the Atlantic passage and initial subsistence of any Piedmontese silk experts who followed (at least five were expected), but not to cover their

---

[109] On Lloyd, see *Gentleman's Magazine*, 57, part 2 (1787), 835; R. B. Prosser, 'Lombe, Sir Thomas (1685–1739)', Oxford Dictionary of National Biography, 2004, www.oxforddnb.com/view/article/16956.

[110] Chicco, *La Seta in Piemonte*, 82–3.   [111] Candler et al., *Col. Rec. Georgia*, 20: 3.

[112] John Perceval Egmont, *Manuscripts of the Earl of Egmont* (3 vols., London: H. M. Stationery Office, 1920), 1: 309.

relocation from Italy. Instead of crossing the Atlantic, Ottone's construction skills were retained in the Old World: he brought a reeling machine 'such as is used in Italy for spinning silk' before the London Trustees in May, and they paid him three pounds, six shillings and sixpence for each Piedmontese reel they commissioned thereafter.[113] Besides these Italians, the Earl of Egmont recorded in his diary that several English colonists with silk skills were amongst the first Georgia settlers, agreeing to 'follow the manufacturing of silk, and one of them assured us that he had worked Carolina silk for many years in London'. These included 'the two Elringtons and two Lacys' who were awarded grants of 400 acres 'to go over with four servants each, if not more, and make silk yarn', stocking-maker Joseph Stanley who could also 'Draw and reel silk', and a thirty-year-old silk throwster Samuel Grey, with two apprentices (whose stay was short-lived). The highest home-grown hopes seem to have been pinned on James Lacy, whom the Trustees approved to take over 'twenty charity children as [ap]prentices for the silk affair' in May 1733, but he and his son succumbed to the malarial climate of Thunderbolt, where they settled.[114] In late 1733, as the Carolina proprietors had before them, the Trustees also tried to absorb some forty emigrants from the Vaudois region, the alpine valleys south-west of Turin. This niche population had been alternately persecuted and invaded by French and Savoy authorities since 1685, and many would flee to British lands in a second diasporic wave in the early eighteenth century. They were 'useful and experienced hands in the silk trade', but the migrants refused to bow to Georgia's strict rules barring female land inheritance, so this opportunity was lost and some of the migrants likely instead headed to neighbouring colonies, as some Trustees feared they might.[115]

With the supply of stocks of mulberry trees, experts, and silkworm eggs taken care of, to move forwards with production the Trustees next needed to drum up interest in pursuing silk cultivation amongst their hard-pressed colonists, and particularly amongst the women, whom they had expressly targeted. They found a useful supporting crutch in a pamphlet published in 1733 by Thomas Boreman (see Plate 9), a natural history writer and

---

[113] Egmont, *Manuscripts*, 3: 327, 336, 339, 378; Candler et al., *Col. Rec. Georgia*, 1: 100; 2: 26–28, 38, 41, 44; 3: 381. The Giovannoli family embarked for Georgia in August 1735. E. Merton Coulter and Albert Berry Saye, *A List of the Early Settlers of Georgia* (Athens: University of Georgia Press, 1949), 18, 75.

[114] Egmont, *Manuscripts*, 1: 297–8, 303, 305, 379 ('Elrington' should probably be 'Hetherington' on 305); Coulter and Saye, *List of Early Settlers*, 20, 78, 81; Shaw, 'Silk in Georgia, 1732–1840', 61.

[115] Egmont, *Manuscripts*, 1: 463; 2: 103, 106. William Stephen Gilly, *Waldensian Researches during a Second Visit to the Vaudois of Piemont* (London: C. J. G. & F. Rivington, 1831), 253–60.

publicist of children's books, who had initially determined to write a 'small treatise, on the Management of the *Silk-Worm*' predominantly aimed at a domestic audience but not geared to commercial production, on account of the failures of attempts 'by several worthy Gentlemen' at Chelsea and elsewhere in England. Boreman expressed delight that his work 'may be of more general Use than it was at first intended', and praised the Trustees for seeking to enrich the nation 'with this golden Fleece' in Georgia. Lamenting the neglect in Virginia and elsewhere of the silkworm, Boreman reminded readers how important patronage was. Sericulture's introduction to Italy, he stressed, had depended upon the involvement of 'Persons of the first Rank' alongside magistrates. In his extended historical introduction, he noted the improvement of silk in Carolina, where some families were producing forty or fifty lb per year, and was careful to link his practical guidelines to the wider goals of the Georgia Trustees.[116]

Any Georgia colonists who used Boreman as a manual would have followed the conventional wisdom, bagging up silkworm eggs into linen pouches when the mulberry trees began to bud, and carrying them in sweaty cleavages or pockets during the day, or next to warm pillows during the night. Woken by this 'natural' heat, they would nourish the silkworms with fresh mulberry leaves, and once of an adequate size, move the caterpillars to shelves without touching them by hand. Boreman relayed advice about constructing the wooden scaffolding to best guard against predators, and issued warnings about the importance of the tenders having good hygiene and 'smell[ing] not of Garlick, Onions, or any other strong offensive Smell'. Colonists were to use a pan of 'Small-coal Dust' mixed with some sweet-smelling incense to fortify the feeding caterpillars against colder weather or rain, and gradually disperse them as they increased in size. At the point of cocooning, some forty-five days after their first hatching, the tenders were to scatter and affix arches of dried twigs and branches on the shelves upon which the now corpulent and part-translucent caterpillars could fix their cocoon. If they followed Boreman to the letter, the huts and sheds of Georgia silk raisers would for a short time thereafter smell of vinegar and sweet herbs, used to encourage the slothful silkworms to finish their constructions. Boreman gave a range of options for terminating the pupae, including stifling by laying out in the midday sun, baking in an oven, or, as practised in Sicily, steaming using specially adapted cauldrons.[117]

---

[116] Thomas Boreman, *A Compendious Account of the Whole Art of Breeding, Nursing, and the Right Ordering of the Silk-Worm* (London: J. Worrall, 1733), i–iv.

[117] Boreman, *Compendious Account*, 14, 18–23. French writers at this point were breaking with some of these long-standing guidelines, for instance in suggesting that hatching eggs through closeness to body parts could damage the pupae. 'Mémoire du S. Baron

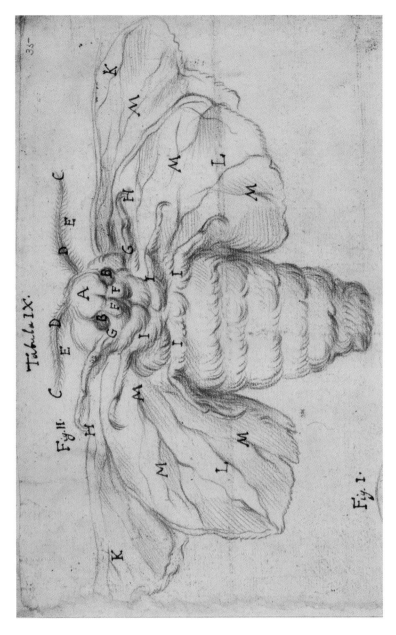

Plate 1 Taxonomic drawing of a silk moth (1669). Original drawing from the manuscript of Marcello Malpighi, *Dissertatio epistolica de bombyce* (London, 1669). MS/104. Image RS.9505. © The Royal Society

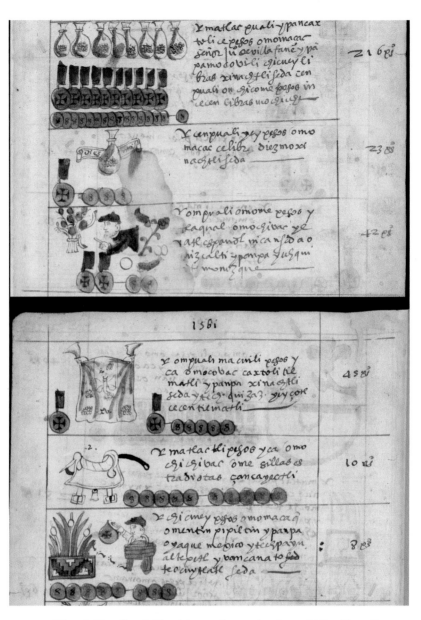

Plate 2 Details of silk raising and expertise from *Códice Sierra Texupan* (1561). Compiled payment records in Nahuatl text and pictographs, 1551–64, of the community of Santa Catalina Texupan in the Mixteca Alta, Oaxaca. Details showing bags of silkworm seed, Spanish instruction, Spanish conveyance, and seed hatching, from pages 37, 38. Biblioteca Histórica José María Lafragua

Plate 3 Portrait of *A Lady of Rank* at Parham House (1609). Now attributed to artist Robert Peake the Elder, but attributed to Paul Van Somer in T. B. Pugh, 'A Portrait of Queen Anne of Denmark at Parham Park, Sussex', *The Seventeenth Century* 8, no. 2 (1993): 167–80. Jemma A. J. Field, 'Anna of Denmark and the Arts in Jacobean England' (University of Auckland, 2015), 328. © Parham House & Gardens, West Sussex

Plate 4 Painting of a silkworm for the Royal Society (1669). Unknown artist, attr. Jan Swammerdam. Watercolour, included in manuscript copy of Malpighi, *de Bombyce*, 1669. MS/104. Image RS.16274. © The Royal Society

Plate 5 Silkworms feeding in French style at the *Musée de la Soie*, in Saint Hippolyte du Fort, Gard (France). These sorts of arrangements, with large raised trays (to protect from predators including ants) and small boughs arranged to allow the larger silkworms to climb and cocoon, were likely introduced amongst larger operations or those with dedicated spaces in Atlantic colonies. Photo by author

Plate 6 Ruined *magnanerie* near Quissac, Gard (France). Structures used to store and centralise the raising of silkworms in French areas of sericultural concentration, such as the Cévennes. Quissac lay between the Cévennes and regional centres of processing and manufacture such as Nîmes. Photo by author

Plate 7 Photo of mulberry tree in Elm Park Gardens, Chelsea. Vestige of the sericultural scheme in Chelsea in the 1720s. Photo by permission of Peter Coles

Plate 8 Deputed Great Seals for Georgia colony, reverses, 1754 (left) and 1767 (right). Engravings by John Pine (1754) and Christopher Seaton (1767) in which 'A figure, representing the Genius of the Colony, is described, offering a skein of silk to his Majesty'. These were used for formal and legal matters relating to the colony once it reverted to Crown rule following the Trusteeship, which had created its own iconic seal featuring silkworms and a mulberry leaf. Photos by author. Courtesy The Royal Mint Museum, Llantrisant (UK)

Plate 9 Explanation of silkworm cycle from Georgia manual. Engraving by George Child, plate 2 of the work distributed to settlers by the Georgia Trustees by Thomas Boreman, *A Compendious Account of the Whole Art of Breeding, Nursing, and the Right Ordering of the Silk-Worm* (London: J. Worrall, 1733), page 12. Beinecke Rare Book and Manuscript Library, Yale University

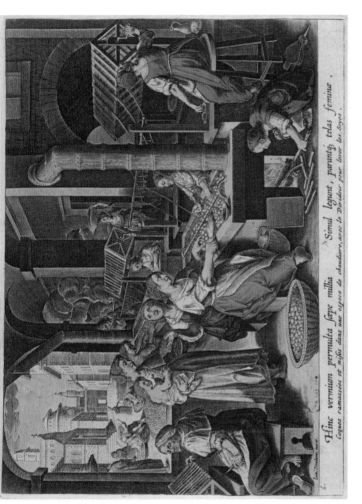

Hinc vermium permulta ſæpe millia   Simul legunt, parantíq; telas feminæ.

Coques ramassices et mises dans une eſpèce de chaudière, avec le Dèvidoir pour tever les Soyes

Plate 10   Scene from an early modern silk filature. Hand-coloured engraving of plate 6 of the series of six illustrations of the perfection of the silk industry in Europe and Italy by Flemish artists Johannes Stradanus and Karel van Mallery, *Vermus Sericus* (Antwerp: Phillips Galle, c.1580). Shows an Italianate filature, the scene of busy activity and multiple furnaces and reeling machines as cocoons are sorted, steamed, reeled, dried, etc. Note the overwhelming predominance of women, the presence of occasional children, and the need for furnaces, basins, piping, large reels, high ceiling, and firewood. A variant of this scene would have been played out in those American locations and buildings where centralisation was attempted. Object No. 2044374. Beinecke Rare Book and Manuscript Library, Yale University

Plate 11 Eliza Lucas Pinckney dress (*c*.1760). Sacque or sack dress comprised of three individual pieces (opened-front dress, matching petticoat and stomacher). The raw silk for this gown was reportedly made from silkworms raised on the Pinckney plantation near Charleston, involving the labour of enslaved bondspeople - though it was thrown and woven in England. Catalogue no. 2008.0002.001. Division of Cultural and Community Life, National Museum of American History, Smithsonian Institution

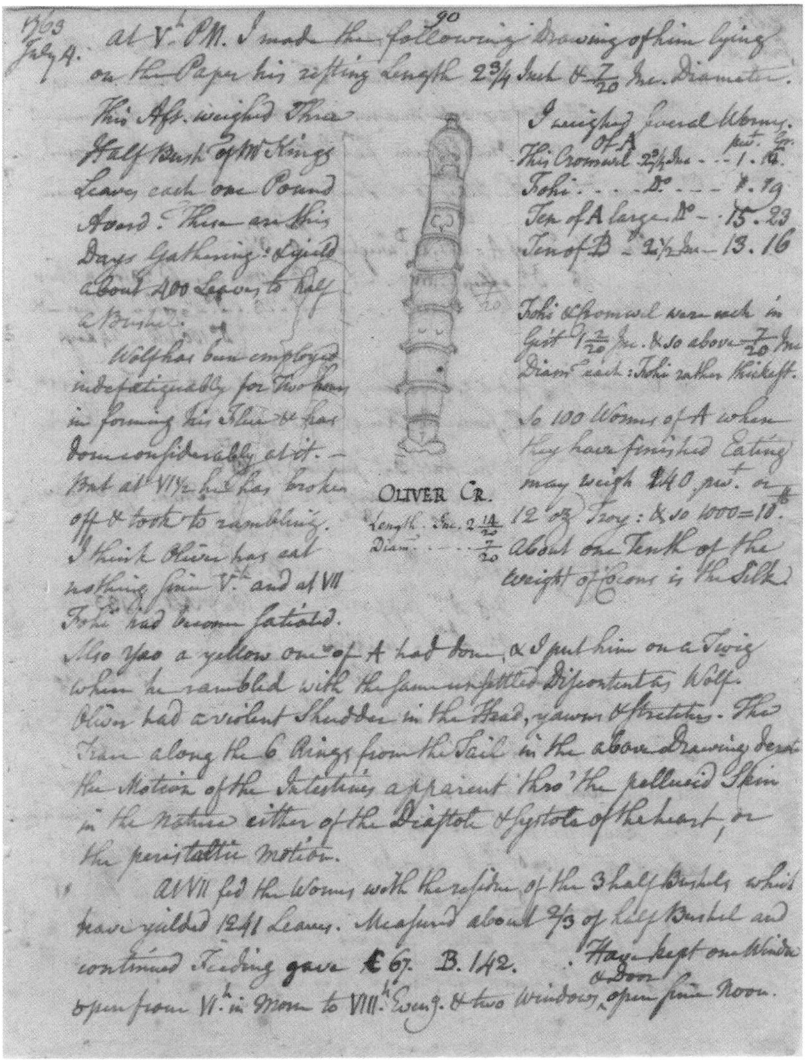

90

1763 July 4. at V. P.M. I made the following Drawing of him lying on the Paper his resting Length 2 3/4 Inch & 7/20 Inc. Diameter.

This Aft. weighed Three Half Bush of Mr Kings Leaves each one Pound Avoird.: These are this Days Gathering: & yield about 400 Leaves to half a Bushel.

Wolf has been employed indefatigably for Two hours in forming his Silk & has done considerably at it. — But at VI 1/2 he has broken off & took to rambling.

I think Oliver has eat nothing since V. and at VII Tohi had become satiated.

I weighed Several Worms of A. pwt. gr.
This Cromwell 2 3/4 Inc . . . 1.16.
Tohi . . . Do . . . 1.19
Ten of A large Do - 15.23
Ten of B - 2 1/2 Inc - 13.16

Tohi & Cromwell were each in Girt 1 2/20 Inc. & so above 7/20 Inc Diamr each: Tohi rather thickest.

So 100 Worms of A when they have finished Eating may weigh 240 pwt. or 12 oz Troy: & so 1000=10 lb. About one Tenth of the weight of Cocons is the Silk.

Also Yao a yellow one of A had done, & I put him on a Twig when he rambled with the same unsettled Discontent as Wolf. Oliver had a violent Shudder in the Head, yawns & stretches. The Train along the 6 Rings from the Tail in the above Drawing denot the Motion of the Intestines apparent thro' the pellucid Skin in the nature either of the Diastole & Systole of the heart, or the peristaltic motion.

At VII fed the Worms with the residue of the 3 half Bushels which have yielded 1241 Leaves. Measured about 2/3 of half Bushel and continued Feeding gave C 67. B. 142. Have kept one Window & Door open from VI h. in Morn to VIII h. Even. & two Windows open since Noon.

Plate 12 Oliver Cromwell, the silkworm (1763). Pencil sketch of a silkworm named Oliver Cromwell (2 and 7/10 inches long) amidst other observations by Rev. Ezra Stiles, 'Journal of Silkworms', Miscellaneous Volumes & Papers #318, Ezra Stiles Papers, Beinecke Library, page 90. Beinecke Rare Book and Manuscript Library, Yale University

Plate 13 Swatches of fabrics made from New England raw silk (1772–87). Samples of silk fabric and silk mixes woven from raw silk raised in New England households. The green swatch (original *c.*3 x 5 inches) is almost certainly from the dress pattern manufactured for Elizabeth Stiles in 1772. Other swatches (*c.*1 x 2 inches) marked 'Dr. Foot of Northford, 2 Gowns 14 yds, 1787' and 'Mr. Fowler, 1787' and recorded by Rev. Ezra Stiles, 'Journal of Silkworms', Miscellaneous Volumes & Papers #318, Ezra Stiles Papers, Beinecke Library, pages 158–9. Beinecke Rare Book and Manuscript Library, Yale University

Plate 14 Photograph of Hanks Silk Mill, relocated to Greenfield Village at the Henry Ford Museum, Dearborn, Michigan (titled Hanks Silk Mill IMG_9292). The mill was first built by Rodney and Horace Hanks in 1810 in Mansfield, Connecticut – one of the first American silk mills, to generate twist with machines powered by a water wheel, and a reflection of the existing familiarity with sericulture and production of raw silk in the community. The mill is 12 x 28 feet in size, and was relocated to the Museum in 1930 where it was reassembled. Created by OZinOH under CC BY-NC 2.0 licence, Flickr

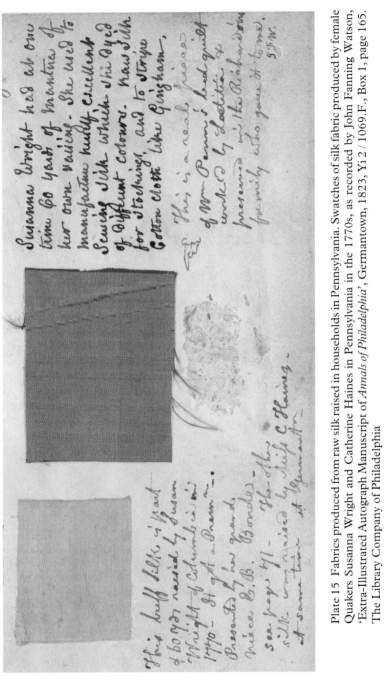

Plate 15 Fabrics produced from raw silk raised in households in Pennsylvania. Swatches of silk fabric produced by female Quakers Susanna Wright and Catherine Haines in Pennsylvania in the 1770s, as recorded by John Fanning Watson, 'Extra-Illustrated Autograph Manuscript of *Annals of Philadelphia*', Germantown, 1823, Yi 2 / 1069.F., Box 1, page 165. The Library Company of Philadelphia

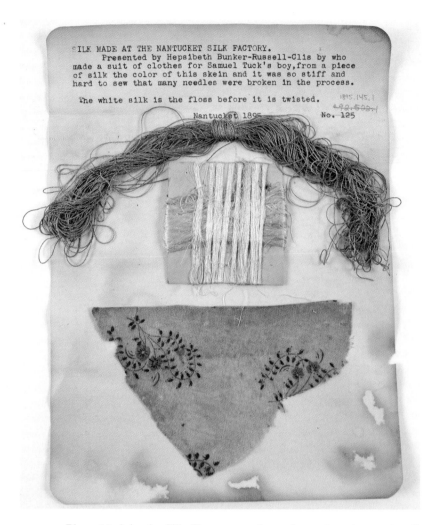

SILK MADE AT THE NANTUCKET SILK FACTORY.
Presented by Hepsibeth Bunker-Russell-Clis by who made a suit of clothes for Samuel Tuck's boy,from a piece of silk the color of this skein and it was so stiff and hard to sew that many needles were broken in the process.

The white silk is the floss before it is twisted.
1895.145.1

Nantucket 1895   No. 125

Plate 16 Atlantic Silk Factory products from American raw silk (c.1837). Samples of products made at the Atlantic Silk Factory, including untwisted white floss, tan-coloured skein silk, and cream-coloured silk ground with floral spray pattern. Mulberries were planted from 1832 in Quaise and other locations on Nantucket (including Academy Hill and Polpis), and a silk factory was founded by William H. Gardner and Aaron Mitchell which survived until 1844, mostly employing female labour. Samples presented by Hepsibeth Bunker-Russell-Clis in 1895, who had made a suit of clothes for a local boy and found the silk 'so stiff and hard to sew that many needles were broken in the process'. Accession No. 1895.0145.001. Courtesy of the Nantucket Historical Association

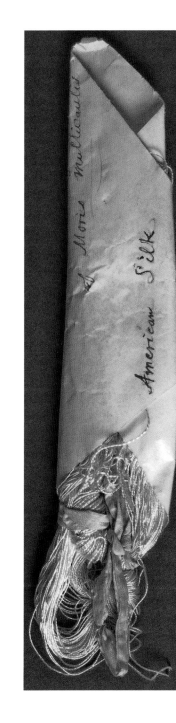

Plate 17 Skein of American raw silk reeled from silkworms raised on *M. multicaulis*, dating from the mid-Atlantic region in the late 1820s (dimensions 5.5 x 1.25 inches), as affirmed by mention of the *Morus multicaulis*. Collected by John Fanning Watson, 1800–30, Museum purchase, 1958.0102.014, and included in his 'Relic Box' with other silk textile fragments (1958.0102.012-015). Courtesy of Winterthur Library

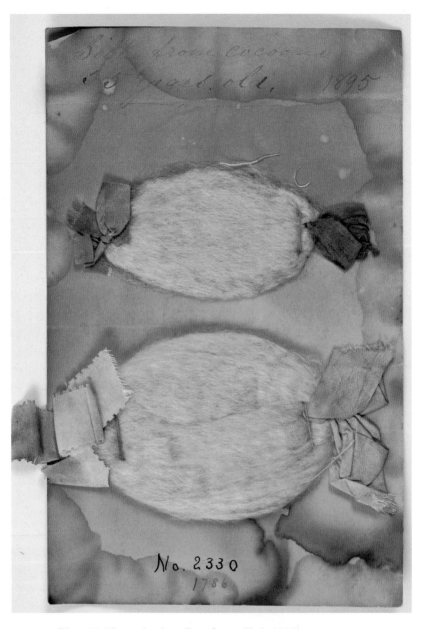

Plate 18 Nantucket bundles of raw silk (*c.*1838).
Two bundles of cream-coloured raw silk from Nantucket, linked to the raising of silk on the island and the associated Atlantic Silk Company, which was operational from mid-1836. Accession No. 1913.0022.003b. Courtesy of the Nantucket Historical Association

Boreman may have had little new or specialist advice to offer, beyond his compendium of images and insights from earlier European publications, and the verdict of Harry B. Weiss in 1939 on his entomology elsewhere was certainly rather damning: 'Boreman was interested in sales.'[118] But though opportunistic, the publicity and concision of his work also offered something to the Trustees and their settlers. James Oglethorpe and Benjamin Martyn were quick to draw attention to Boreman's work, citing it already in 1732 as a forthcoming 'Treatise' that would deal more fully with 'this method of Agriculture', and it is likely that Oglethorpe himself subsidised the appearance of Boreman's tract. The Trustees stored and sent copies in bulk to the new colony, on one occasion in 1745 ordering twenty-five of them to be distributed to those 'most intelligent and desirous of being instructed'. Non-English communities particularly expressed their appreciation of the work, as when two German women 'succeeded very well . . . in winding according to the Direction given by some Author of the Treatise concerning Silk Manufacture'.[119]

All of these measures supporting trials at silk production cost money, of course, and the Trustees reached deep into their pockets, their charitable funds, and the considerable parliamentary appropriations that proved necessary to support the administration of the colony (once public contributions were dwindling). Though it is hard to untangle different components of the Trustee accounts, it is clear for instance that at least £3,312 sterling were spent between July 1732 and June 1751 on charges for the production of silk, which included the salaries and expenses of Italian experts, some technology and materials, and payments for silk cocoons, bounties, and apprenticeships. Other silk-related charges for stocking and sustaining white mulberry nurseries also came to over £3,000 in just the five years between July 1734 and June 1739. When the rewards of all this investment (regular packages or trunks of silk) began to trickle back in the 1740s, the Trustees also picked up the various bills for 'Charges on Raw Silk received from Georgia, and of working it in England for Sale into

sur l'élevage des vers à soye' (12 January 1743), cited in Stockland, 'Patriotic Natural History and Sericulture in the French Enlightenment', 7.

[118] Harry B. Weiss, 'The Entomology of Thomas Boreman's Popular Natural Histories', *Journal of the New York Entomological Society* 47, no. 3 (1939): 216. Boreman's sources included works by Letellier (1603), Stallenge (1609) discussed earlier, and the prints of Eleazar Albin, an English illustrator who became something of a naturalist after instruction by silk weaver Joseph Dandridge, publishing *A Natural History of English Insects* (London: William and John Innys, 1720).

[119] James Edward Oglethorpe, Rodney M. Baine, and Phinizy Spalding, *Some Account of the Design of the Trustees for Establishing Colonys in America* (Athens: University of Georgia Press, 1990), 22. Known recipients included settlers in Acton, Vernonburgh, and Ebenezer. Candler et al., *Col. Rec. Georgia*, 2: 449, 482–3; 25: 61; Baine, 'James Oglethorpe', 105–6; Hamer, 'Foundation and Failure', 127.

Organzine &c', and for its 'freight and Insurance' across the Atlantic.[120] All of this constituted unprecedented state investment in the Atlantic production of a target imperial commodity, in a colony which itself enjoyed unmatched governmental support.[121]

At the beginning of 1735, the silk part of the Georgia plan seemed to be progressing well. On 12 January, Paulo Amatis dispatched to the Trustees a 'little piece of silk, consisting of three qualities, ordinary, fine and superfine', weighing 9 lb 10 oz, which arrived three months later. He sent instructions for James Oglethorpe, who had departed for London the previous year, in a letter in which he likened sericulture to 'gold and silver mines in this country ... for every one of both sexes', and directing Oglethorpe to have it worked up at Lombe's Derby 'manufactory' to see whether it was surpassed by Italian 'fineness, quality and neatness'. The Georgia silk passed the test, the Trustees informing Amatis in May 1735 that the silk 'proves entirely to his [Lombe's] satisfaction' by being robust enough 'through all the operations' of the machinery, and that summer they presented an organzined specimen to Queen Caroline, who expressed 'a great satisfaction for the beauty and fineness of the silk'.[122]

Much to the gratification of the Trustees, the queen wore Georgia silk to King George II's birthday levee, now wrought up into a 'beautiful pattern' of her choice by Daniel Booth, an affluent silk weaver in Little Moorfields, London, who had been one of the earliest customers of famed designer Anna Maria Garthwaite even before he married into wealth.[123] The Rev. Samuel Wesley, Jr, was quick to capitalise on the moment, issuing a poem titled *Georgia* that celebrated how 'was never so Majestick seen, / As in her home-wrought Silks, the *British* QUEEN'.[124]

---

[120] Figures collated from Candler et al., *Col. Rec. Georgia*, 3: 16, 54, 86, 116, 117, 145, 169, 170, 191, 192, 211, 227, 255, 269, 281, 305, 316 (quote), 317, 329, 341, 354, 367 (quote).

[121] Trevor Richard Reese, *Colonial Georgia: A Study in British Imperial Policy in the Eighteenth Century* (Athens: University of Georgia Press, 1963), 30; Paul Pressly, *On the Rim of the Caribbean Colonial Georgia and the British Atlantic World* (Athens: University of Georgia Press, 2013), 26.

[122] Candler et al., *Col. Rec. Georgia*, 3: 130; 20: 69, 152, 211–12. There is some confusion about how many parcels of silk were carried over in 1734–5, with Shaw stating Oglethorpe carried a separate parcel with him in 'early 1735' (though he left Georgia in May 1734 and embarked again in December 1735) and Stevens claiming Oglethorpe brought 8 lb in June 1734. Shaw, 'Silk in Georgia, 1732–1840', 61; Stevens, 'A Brief History', 178.

[123] Marriage announcement in London *British Observator*, 17 August 1734; Randolph Vigne and Charles Littleton, *From Strangers to Citizens: The Integration of Immigrant Communities in Britain, Ireland, and Colonial America, 1550–1750* (London: Huguenot Society of Great Britain and Ireland, 2001), 163, 164. On Caroline's choice, London *Weekly Miscellany*, 6 August 1735.

[124] John C. Stephens, ed., *Georgia, and Two Other Occasional Poems on the Founding of the Colony, 1736* (Atlanta: Emory University Publications, 1950), 327, 336. For a useful discussion of the poem, Shields, *Oracles of Empire*, 52–3.

There is sadly little description of the court dress's appearance or style, but the silk's provenance was challenged on more than one occasion. The queen herself quizzed the Earl of Egmont at court in April 1737, when she affirmed that the Georgia gown was 'indeed the finest she ever saw, but that she's told the silk in truth came from Italy'. Egmont explained the confusion, pointing out that 'we debauched two Italians, Piedmontese, away, and sent them to Georgia to cultivate the silk', which appeased Queen Caroline. Yet in later years, after the queen's death, Egmont acknowledged that the silk was not the sole product of Georgia but had relied upon a large number of South Carolina cocoons that were reeled in Savannah.[125] Later parcels of raw silk intended to showcase Georgia's output would be accompanied by extravagant affidavits and measures to prevent any intermixture in the throwing processes.[126]

This unravelling of the fibres of the queen's dress was paralleled in the temporary collapse of silk efforts in Georgia. Even as metropolitan excitement was growing in the summer of 1735, in Savannah, Paulo Amatis wrote two letters to the Trustees that did not bode well: in the first, he requested 'about thirty thousand bricks ... to build a fabrique in the manner as is done in Italy', a laudable ambition, but one that showed questionable appreciation of the realities of the infant settlement.[127] In the second, dated 15 August, he announced that he had dismissed his brother Nicola, who had allegedly acted contrary to his orders, begging the Trustees to 'have no regard to him nor to what he may say against me'.[128] One contemporary source reported that Nicola, now released from his £25 per annum contract to reveal 'the secret of making Raw Silk' to others, resentfully 'stole away the machines for winding, broke the coppers and spoiled all the eggs which he could not steal, and fled to South Carolina'. But this seems to have been exaggerated.[129] Nicola's absconding need not have been a major blow, and partly reflected a wider loss of faith amongst Georgia settlers once Oglethorpe's domineering presence had faded from view (as he had returned temporarily to England). Many others in this peculiar corner of the British Atlantic world, looking enviously across the Savannah River and reinterpreting

[125] Egmont, *Manuscripts*, 2: 387; Shaw, 'Silk in Georgia, 1732–1840', 61.
[126] Letterbook of Lloyd, Wilson & Co., BA677, Derby Local Studies and Family History Library. 7 August 1749. Transcripts by Griff Everett generously shared with the author by Derby Museums.
[127] This did reflect Amatis's appreciation, however, of the risk of fire, which proved prophetic. Chicco, *La Seta in Piemonte*, 84.
[128] Candler et al., *Col. Rec. Georgia*, 20: 411, 459.
[129] Contract in 2: 27; Moore, *A Voyage to Georgia*, 31. For historians mentioning this sabotage: Chicco, *La Seta in Piemonte*, 85; Shaw, 'Silk in Georgia, 1732–1840', 74.

their own awkward circumstances and their frustrations with Trustee officialdom, likewise moved on.[130]

Paolo Amatis remained confident, reminding his employers (who were fond of classical comparisons) that 'Rome was not built in a day' and looking two years ahead to when he hoped there would be 'a Sufficient quantity of balls or Coquons, a building erected for the purpose, and Spinners enough'.[131] Unfortunately he did not survive to see it, succumbing to disease in December 1736. Rumours again reached the Trustees of an Amatis (this time Paolo) having burned 'all the worms and machines before he died', ostensibly because 'the magistrate would not allow him a priest in his sickness', a story that hints strongly at elements of both Catholicism and anti-Catholicism featuring in English settlers' dealings with the Piedmontese. However, the Trustees were relieved to learn in person from Elizabeth Stanley in March 1737 that these accounts were 'entirely false'. Stanley, the public midwife (and wife of a gardener) was with him at his death, and reported not only that he 'demanded no priest' but also that his Protestant wife (formerly his maid servant) 'gave up to the magistrate all the machines and eggs'.[132] All in all, it is hard to describe Paolo Amatis's efforts as anything less than foundational to the Georgia production that would begin at more or less the time he had predicted it would.

Martha Causton, the wife of the Trustees' storekeeper in Savannah, provided a rare insight into the development of silk production in the year after Amatis's death. She had some 1,000 four-year-old mulberry plants in her own 'garden' on the grounds of Ockstead plantation, but these and other trees had seemingly proved inadequate to provision the colony's impressive stock of silkworms, which were kept in a bespoke cocoonery. Causton described the two-storey wooden house in Savannah, some twenty-four foot in length, along which were placed five tables 'of the full Length and Width of the House' that were completely 'covered with the Worms, as are likewise the upper Floor'. Visitors were apparently amazed by this insect farming, and Causton reported that the silkworms' 'Number, regular Disposition, and Manner of working' attracted much admiration. In years to come, Causton would be fiercely protective of her mulberry trees, and was outraged in April 1739 when trustee official Thomas Jones ordered them stripped of their leaves (at the rate of three

---

[130] For a comprehensive and damning survey of the state of the Georgia economy, whose only redemption lay in deerskins, lumber, and artificial support thanks to the presence of the military, see Pressly, *On the Rim*.

[131] Egmont, *Journal of the Earl of Egmont*, 179.

[132] Egmont, *Manuscripts*, 2: 370. It is possible, though unlikely, that the Amatises were amongst the tiny minority (144 out of 63,819) of Protestants in Turin in 1726, many of whom were merchants. Paola Bianchi and Karin Elizabeth Wolfe, eds., *Turin and the British in the Age of the Grand Tour* (Cambridge: Cambridge University Press, 2017).

pence per tree), which task was clumsily performed by three German female indentured servants. Causton complained that the servants had 'with their Fingers stript every Branch naked, by drawing it through them', rather than picking off individual leaves, a more laborious technique but much less damaging to the trees. Causton pointed out how the injurious stripping method had previously spoiled many mulberries in the public garden, and did not refrain from 'foul Language' in her objections.[133]

Causton's letter reported that a delegation of Chickasaw Indians were amongst the visitors to the cocoonery, and that the Indians were 'in an exceeding Manner delighted with them, never failing their Attendance at the House twice a Day'. An interpreter explained how the silk was harvested for clothing, and one of the Chickasaws observed that 'they had not those Worms in their Nation, but if they had, and knew the Method of keeping them, they could return us yearly Canoes laden with Balls [i.e. cocoons], having a great Abundance of Mulberry-Trees up in the Country, to supply them with Food'. Whereas in sixteenth-century New Spain the subcontracting of sericultural labour had been forced on Amerindians, and in seventeenth-century Carolina a reciprocal contract proposed by European authorities, in eighteenth-century Georgia the idea was mooted by Indians. For Southeastern Indians, the mulberry tree had always had profound significance, a fact which helps explain the Chickasaws' particular fascination with the caterpillars. The Muscogee calendar included a 'mulberry month' (Kē-Hvse) in the spring, and the sweet berries of female red mulberry trees were described by William Bartram as 'in great estimation with the present generation of Indians', who not only ate them fresh but dried and stored them in large patties (as did the Haudenosaunee and other Iroquoian tribes), later to be baked with bread or mixed with oil. According to John Brickell, mulberry wood was also used to make bows when locust wood was not available. Little wonder that the idea of further exploiting the leaves of the extensive Kē trees of the interior was a particularly appealing prospect to the Chickasaws when other resources were diminishing.[134]

---

[133] Egmont, *Manuscripts*, 2: 477; Candler et al., *Col. Rec. Georgia*, 1: 314; 4: 310–11; 39: 480.

[134] William Bartram, *Travels through North & South Carolina, Georgia, East & West Florida, the Cherokee Country, the Extensive Territories of the Muscogulges or Creek Confederacy, and the Country of the Chactaws* (Philadelphia: James and Johnson, 1791), 38; Bill Grantham, *Creation Myths and Legends of the Creek Indians* (Gainesville: University Press of Florida, 2002), 64, 69; James Treat, 'Kē-Hvse, "Mulberry Month"', Muscogee Nation News, 2011, http://mvskokecountry.wordpress.com/tag/ke-vpe/; Esther Louise Larsen, 'Pehr Kalm's Description of the North American Mulberry Tree', *Agricultural History* 24 (1950): 224–5; Brickell, *The Natural History of North-Carolina*, 67. Silk was also later

In 1739, just six years after Georgia's first settlers had set foot in the colony, the first silk grown exclusively in its borders, which came from the northerly settlements, arrived back in London.[135] Its conveyor, Samuel Augspurger, a gentleman from Bern who had migrated to Purrysburg but found employment as a surveyor in Georgia, swore an affidavit about the silk's origins, reflecting continuing sensitivity about the provenance of the commodity.[136] He confirmed that the 'Bag of Raw Silk ... containing about 20 pounds weight' he brought had been received in person from a Savannah official, and that while in the town he had witnessed first-hand its reeling by an Italian family. Like earlier specimens, the silk was swiftly submitted for evaluation, once again to weaver Daniel Booth and also to John Zachary, a leading raw silk importer. To the Trustees' delight, they declared it as fine as any Italian silk, and worth a similar price of at least 20 shillings per pound.[137] At the Trustees' annual sermon that year, William Berriman acclaimed the Georgians' shipping of their first silk to the Trustees by comparing it approvingly to the Hebrews offering up their first fruits to the Almighty as thanks for their deliverance.[138]

The Italian family mentioned by Augspurger were the Camossos (often anglicised as Camuse or Camuche), who by virtue of the Amatises' untimely exits had entered centre stage. They unquestionably made full use of the limelight. On the positive side, in the five years between 1739 and 1744 the Camossos processed and transhipped over 100 lb of raw silk of prime quality back to the Trustees.[139] On the negative side, their mastery of the technical aspects of silk reeling was more than matched by their appreciation of their monopolistic position. Husband Giacomo Luigi and wife Maria Giovanna Camosso had brought three sons to Georgia with them, added a daughter and two sons thereafter, and they liked to keep things in the family.[140] This meant that opportunities to broaden and improve silk production in early Georgia never reached the levels they might have, given the extensive investment. Unusually, Maria Camosso was by far the more prominent actor in the historical record. Perhaps because reeling was overwhelmingly treated as a feminine 'art'

---

recommended in Carolina as suitable for 'the Cherokee women who set no great value on their time'. Merrens, *Colonial South Carolina Scene*, 266.

[135] For evidence of lag in southern settlements, Egmont, *Manuscripts*, 3: 60, 155.

[136] George Fenwick Jones, *The Georgia Dutch: From the Rhine and Danube to the Savannah, 1733–1783* (Athens: University of Georgia Press, 1992), 64–5.

[137] Candler et al., *Col. Rec. Georgia*, 1: 362; 3: 220, 398; Egmont, *Manuscripts*, 3: 110, 117.

[138] Phinizy Spalding, 'Some Sermons Preached before the Trustees of Colonial Georgia', *Georgia Historical Quarterly* 57 (1973): 337.

[139] Aggregated from 20 lb in 1739, 45 lb 2 oz in 1740, 19 lb 14 oz in 1742, and 23 lb in 1744. Candler et al., *Col. Rec. Georgia*, 3: 249, 275, 287.

[140] The three children born to the Camossos in Georgia were anglicised in the Earl of Egmont's list as Margaret, Isaac, and Jacob. Coulter and Saye, *List of Early Settlers*, 67.

ascribed to women and children, and perhaps because of the particular relational and linguistic dynamics of the family, it was Maria whose dealings with fellow colonists most clearly frustrated Georgia authorities. Bereft of recourse to alternative specialists, they frequently found themselves at an impasse.[141]

Male officials, who felt themselves doubly superior to Maria Camosso on account of their sex and their social position, particularly struggled to cope with her positional influence, and often commented on the unwelcome inversion of gender. A 'Wicked Woman [who] domineer[ed] over all', according to the Trustees' main Savannah administrator, William Stephens, she also drew comment from key leaders in the southern districts, such as Major William Horton, who warned the Earl of Egmont in July 1740 that if 'that woman' should die, 'the art would be lost'. At the other end of the colony, in the distinctive north-western Indian trading town of Augusta, where white mulberry seedlings were planted in 1740, Thomas Christie felt that silk had a real future, 'for which purpose the Italian family should be obliged to instruct them by taking more apprentices, there being enough of bastard orphans belonging to the Indian traders to apply that way'. Particularly vexed were the leaders who had first-hand experience of Camosso's absolute refusal to adhere to the terms of her generous contracts. These stipulated that she must undertake the training of other women who were put to her as apprentices to learn key techniques, as many as ten instructees in 1743. But rather than serving as a transnational conduit of commodity-specific skills to the New World, Camosso manifested instead the flipside of silk's global history: the experience of protectionism, suspicion, and a powerful awareness of the value of her specialist knowledge and labour in new regions. Indeed, William Stephens eventually ascribed her obstinacy to her subscription to long-standing Italian rulings: 'If I am rightly informed 'tis Death for any Piedmontors ... who shall divulge the Art (of winding silk) in another country.'[142] Her salary rose from £20 to £60 with an assurance of a pension, reaching £100 in 1743 when authorities in Savannah capitulated to 'her perverse Temper Rather than hazard the loss of a Manufacture always designed by their Honours as a Staple of the Country' though she pressed for £200 in 1746; she was also supported by

---

[141] Chicco, *La Seta in Piemonte*; Marsh, *Georgia's Frontier Women*; Shaw, 'Silk in Georgia, 1732–1840.'

[142] William Stephens and E. Merton Coulter, *The Journal of William Stephens* (3 vols., Athens: University of Georgia Press, 1958), 2: 83, 88. On Italian prohibitions with death penalties, Molà, *The Silk Industry of Renaissance Venice*; Bertucci, 'Enlightened Secrets: Silk, Intelligent Travel, and Industrial Espionage in Eighteenth-Century France.'

numerous special measures such as the cash and provisions advanced her in 1741 because she 'must not be disobliged'.[143]

What did the Trustees get for their money, including the servants and the gratuities offered to Camosso for every person certified to have been trained in silk reeling? Even allowing for descriptive exaggeration and the very real practical and linguistic difficulties inherent in training novices up to high standards of consistency, Camosso had thwarted uptake. She refused to permit her reeling machine to be copied, prevented others from studying her finger movements, took on fewer apprentices than she was supposed to, and those she did employ ended up doing housework or basic tasks. The usually sanguine Lutheran pastor, Rev. Johann Martin Bolzius, repeatedly complained of Camosso being 'unwilling to tell us the least Article concerning this Art', fed back the grievances of German-speaking female apprentices, and eventually sought to bypass the Camossos' monopolistic Savannah operations completely by instituting an independent filature farther up the Savannah River, where his wife Gertrude would ensure that no woman could likewise 'pretend a Monopolium'.[144]

Raw silk production in the first half of the 1740s averaged 14 lb per annum rising to 41 lb in the second half of the decade, and though it was confined to the northern segments of the small colony, it did spread beyond Savannah.[145] William Stephens commented on a 'promising great Increase of our Silk Affair' in 1741, with an 'Abundance of Worms, more than hitherto, fed at Camuse's' and noted several other families in Savannah 'where there were careful Housewives … busy in feeding no inconsiderable Quantity of the Worms' – by May their houses 'fully taken up with feeding worms'. He had little doubt that 'it will every Year appear more and more an Employment worth taking in Hand'.[146] Small and large parcels of cocoons alike, totalling over 220 lb, were brought in during late May, carried in boxes, loaded on pack animals, or waterborne via the Savannah River.[147]

[143] Stephens and Coulter, *Journal of William Stephens*, 2: 84; Egmont, *Manuscripts*, 3: 155, 196; Candler et al., *Col. Rec. Georgia*, 1: 406; 2: 416–21, 428; 4a: 134; 6: 6–7, 85–6; 25: 125–6; 30: 281. Only at the end of August 1747 was Camosso's salary eventually suspended. Ibid., 6: 190. For other references to Camosso: Marsh, *Georgia's Frontier Women*, 204n64.
[144] Samuel Urlsperger, George Fenwick Jones, and Renate Wilson, *Detailed Reports on the Salzburger Emigrants Who Settled in America* (Athens: University of Georgia Press, 1968), 18: 201; Candler et al., *Col. Rec. Georgia*, 25: 62, 181.
[145] Working, 'History of Silk Culture', 112–13.
[146] Candler et al., *Col. Rec. Georgia*, 4a: 134, 136, 141, 164.
[147] Candler et al., *Col. Rec. Georgia*, 1: 392.

The incentives for ordinary families lay in the inflated prices that the Trustees offered for their cocoons, which were graded upon delivery to Savannah according to their quality, beginning at four shillings per pound for the highest quality. Given that experts had valued the best Georgia raw silk at 20 shillings per pound, and recommended a ratio of 12.5 lb of cocoons to 1 lb raw silk, we might estimate that each pound of cocoons (even if of the highest quality, and with no cost added for the considerable expense of Camosso reeling, transatlantic transport, insurance, etc.) was at most worth only one shilling and seven pence. Whenever the Trustees sought to lessen the gulf between subsidised and 'real' value, they faced falling yields and vocal opposition from key supporters. They did partly succeed in 1742, however, in reducing the bounty to two shillings (or eight pence for each pound of the worst-quality cocoons) and in formally closing off the artificial Savannah market to cocoon producers in Purrysburg, South Carolina, judging it a 'Misapplication' of Georgia's public money.[148] Some South Carolina cocoons probably continued to be furtively transported across the river in the springtime, criss-crossing some illicit furs that came the other way, destined for Charleston. Overall, the operations were heavily centralised, and there is no mention of silk producers in Georgia working up their own yarn or manufacturing home-spun garments as in other regions.

The fitful progress in silk should be weighed against the wider stagnation of the Georgia economy and population in the 1740s, as people, capital, and confidence drained away from the project. Like other early European settlements (and as we have seen in English Virginia and French Louisiana), a combination of disease, demographics, and geopolitical vulnerability quickly eroded ambitions – with Georgia threatened and invaded in 1742 by Spanish forces from neighbouring Florida. It is telling, for instance, that amidst the vituperative debates that swirled around the Georgia Trustees' management of their colony, even the most critical of the 'Malcontents' chose not to attack the possibility of silk production – preferring to concentrate on issues of its direction and support. They complained that in spite of 'so great Time and Charge' invested in sericulture, 'there are not so many Mulberry-Trees in all the Province of *Georgia*, as many one of the *Carolina* Planters have upon their Plantations; nor so much Silk made there in one Year, as many of those Planters do make'.[149] Hugh Anderson (the one-time botanist at the Trustees'

[148] Candler et al., *Col. Rec. Georgia*, 1: 527–8, 539; 4a: 134; 24: 295–300, 415–17.
[149] Patrick Tailfer, Hugh Anderson, and David Douglas, *A True and Historical Narrative of the Colony of Georgia, in America, from the First Settlement Thereof until This Present Period* (Charles Town, South Carolina: Printed by P. Timothy, for the authors, 1741), 27.

Garden) and Patrick Tailfer chose to interpret Samuel Wesley's poetry about Georgia silk as satirical rather than a piece of Georgic utopianism – as they put it, 'a satyr upon the mismanagement of those manufactures [silk and wine]; since no measures were taken that seemed really intended for their advancement'. But they were careful to insist that 'we no wise question the possibility of advancing such improvements in Georgia, with far less sums of money'.[150] Unlike Virginia, where silk and most other products were eclipsed by tobacco planting as the colony stuttered forwards, silk remained central to Georgia's future.

In light of the Camossos' communal failings, much of the credit for upholding the prospects of silk culture in this corner of the Atlantic world lay not with English matrons and maids nor Italian experts but with desperate German-speaking women and exploited orphans. The Ebenezer settlement several miles up the Savannah River from Savannah, and just across from Purrysburg (SC), was initially established by Protestant refugees mostly from the Archbishopric of Salzburg between 1734 and 1737. It remained a steadfast community despite the plantation town (*Pflanzstadt*) becoming home to a number of other migrants, both German-speaking and others, over the ensuing years, and numbered approximately 300 people for much of the 1740s. The community around Ebenezer has left excellent records of its day-to-day affairs, which were more closely scrutinised and monitored than many others because of its particular circumstances. The Salzburg migration was supported by the British Society for Promoting Christian Knowledge and provided with dutiful ministers from Halle by the Pietist Francke Foundations in Brandenburg-Prussia, ensuring that their colonial experiences could be publicised by Samuel Urlsperger (in the German Imperial City of Augsburg) and avidly followed by his Lutheran networks amongst the Protestant congregations in Europe. One Pietist leader back in Halle described the township in 1743 as 'a City on the Hill' and prayed for 'the grace to excel ... before all other European inhabitants of America'. The diaries of the Ebenezer pastors offer a unique window into the history of community development, and because Ebenezer's religious leaders also acted as the township's governors, therapists, poorhouse overseers, teachers, and magistrates, their insights reveal much about the economic workings of the Georgia colony and the township's persistent engagement with silk production. Its transnational residents were subject to the same general rulings on land grants and mulberry plantations as others, but had more incentive and more

---

[150] Cited and discussed in Shields, *Oracles of Empire*, 53–4.

support to act out the imperial dream of model colonists than many of Georgia's other embittered arrivals.[151]

Virtually none of the German-speaking population of Georgia came from regions with experience in sericulture, but thanks to a mixture of a lack of alternatives and targeted encouragement by the community's leaders, by the early 1740s, Ebenezer was developing into a noteworthy site of cocoon production – by 1744 second only to the Camossos' operations.[152] Besides the number of widows and orphans engaged in the pursuit at the orphanage (discussed below) in 1742, Rev. Bolzius listed 'the widow Helfenstein, the Rheinlander woman, the clockmaker's wife [Christina Muller], the Swiss woman's girl [Magdalena Meyer], and [Thomas] Bacher's two daughters' who apparently sometimes used 'wild' (*M. rubra*) and sometimes 'cultivated' (*M. alba*) leaves.[153] Two other younger Salzburger women, chosen for their good English and dexterity, were sent by boat down to Savannah for the Camosso instruction experience.[154] When impeded at Savannah, the Salzburgers resolved to take more direct ownership of their efforts in silk raising. This involved firstly seeking out another Piedmontese expert, a widow named Baricco who was apparently one of the Italians enticed by the Trustees into an Atlantic crossing in 1734 (then with a husband and children), and who had relocated to South Carolina. But Bolzius discovered Baricco made heavy demands, and was 'with Mrs. Camuse of one & the same principle viz. to get much money for no, or little work'.[155] Bypassing the Italians seemed the only option, so led by the pastors' own wives (who were sisters), between 1744 and 1750 Salzburger families launched on a drive that saw them secure copper basins, get reeling machines from Samuel Lloyd, and apply a range of special bonuses and subsidies for winding proficiency, mulberry trees, and private cocooneries. In 1749, they produced 464 lb of cocoons, and in 1750 in excess of 72 lb of raw silk, albeit of variable quality and

---

[151] Renate Wilson, 'Public Works and Piety in Ebenezer: The Missing Salzburger Diaries of 1744–1745', *Georgia Historical Quarterly* 77, no. 2 (1993): 342, 351 (Francke quote); Jones, *The Georgia Dutch: From the Rhine and Danube to the Savannah, 1733–1783*; George Fenwick Jones, *The Salzburger Saga: Religious Exiles and Other Germans along the Savannah* (Athens: University of Georgia Press, 1984).

[152] Egmont, *Manuscripts*, 3: 186; Candler et al., *Col. Rec. Georgia*, 2: 357; 24: 297–8.

[153] Urlsperger et al., *Detailed Reports*, 9: 85.

[154] These two were Anna Magdalena Ott and Thomas Bacher's youngest daughter. In 1745 the trainees were 'Leitner's oldest daughter' and 'Rieser's youngest daughter'. 18: 24, 30, 216.

[155] Candler et al., *Col. Rec. Georgia*, 24: 319, 343.

consistency, winning a grant of £100 from the Trustees to erect their own public filature in 1751.[156]

The buildings and gardens of the Ebenezer orphanage (located in the north-east corner of the township, the building indicated as blacked out in Map 3) were initially used as an effective focal point, socialising resources and skills for the enterprise in spite of its complexity. The orphanage, a two-storey building at the centre of the community, measuring 45 by 30 feet and 22 feet high, had been completed and opened in January 1738. By 1744 some 10,000 silkworms were housed at the orphanage, where they occupied the children and several widows along with three new wives who had taken up sericulture (Kalcher, Lackner, and Kogler) who put in as much time as they could 'when they can get away from their other housework and chores with their children'. At first the space used for rearing silkworms was the cramped attic, where Bolzius reported in 1741 that 'some times the Heat, some times cool and wet Weather, as also several sorts of bad Vermins have distroy'd a great many Silk Worms'. The prioritisation of the insects' welfare was bad news for the boys, whose dormitory was subsequently commandeered and remained a cocoonery even after the orphans had been moved elsewhere.[157]

The German-speaking children who helped to raise silkworms at Ebenezer were not the only Georgia orphans so deployed. Georgia's grander Bethesda orphanage was set up by the celebrity itinerant Rev. George Whitefield in 1740, for which he collected huge sums at the close of his exhilarating and well-attended sermons all over the British Atlantic world. Given the appalling rates of mortality amongst European migrants in their first years in the Lowcountry, Georgia had a pressing need to support the welfare of its many dozens of orphaned children, though Bethesda's expensive and remote construction ten miles south of Savannah brought dogged criticism in the years after it opened (housing forty children) in 1740. The Bethesda orphans had a fairly gruelling schedule, but time was found in the spring to try to synthesise the social dream of rehabilitating Anglican orphans with the economic dream of generating raw silk, and one Mrs Gautire was later rewarded for her 'great Care' in directing the raising of high-quality Portuguese silkworm eggs at

---

[156] The Salzburgers got approval for building a separate 'large house for the use of widows and orphans to be employed in making silk at Ebenezer' in 1746. 25: 62; 31: 43. For references to the progress and activity of these silk raisers up to 1750: 1: 527–8, 539–40; 6: 325; 25: 169–71, 179–81, 270–2, 287–90, 369–73, 378, 500; Det. Rep. 11: 27, 46; 14: 74; 15: 55; 16: 28; 18: 217, 220; Wilson, 'Public Works and Piety', 360–1; Shaw, 'Silk in Georgia, 1732–1840', 63–4.
[157] Candler et al., *Col. Rec. Georgia*; Wilson, 'Public Works and Piety'; C. E. Buckingham, 'Early American Orphanages: Ebenezer and Bethesda', *Social Forces* 26, no. 3 (1 March 1948): 311–21.

the orphanage.[158] Conviction about Bethesda's contribution to silk raising in the province was also reflected in the Trustees' insistence to Whitefield that the remote and largely self-sufficient operation ought to gear its raw silk output outwards, towards 'our Manufactures in England', though this did not preclude the carding and spinning of wool and cotton, and sewing or knitting of yarn.[159]

In the final years of the collapsing Georgia Trusteeship, though council attendance plummeted, parliamentary subsidies were withdrawn, and slavery was reluctantly permitted in 1750, silk remained a flickering beacon of optimism. In Savannah, the dismissal of Maria Camosso (who seems to have left for South Carolina and to have died sometime before June 1749) and the maturing of various white mulberry plantations left space for a democratisation of sericulture, as operations were channelled through the more amenable widow Elizabeth Anderson.[160] Samuel Lloyd presided over the sale of over 133 lb of 'Organzine, Tram, Single, Knittings, and waste Silks' worked up from Georgia produce, which brought in over £159 in 1748 – some of which was likely manufactured into the two pieces of paduasoy shown before the parliamentary committee in 1750.[161] The testimony in the private letterbook of his Derby silk-manufacturing company (Lloyd, Wilson & Co.) perhaps above all affirmed the impressive quality of several of the American raw silk skeins – recording that they wound 'exceeding well' in the machines, and one observer remarked, 'I don't remember to have seen a Better of that kind of Silk ... as clean[,] even[,] fine and good as any real Pie[d]mont I ever saw.' The lead partner in Derby, William Wilson, lamented that 'I sincerely wish, we had large quantities of it, it wou'd make an Exceeding good Commodity either in Tram or Org[anzin]e.'[162] The valiant efforts of early Georgia's multinational women and children, especially the

---

[158] Candler et al., *Col. Rec. Georgia*, 26: 238–30. Jane Dupree Gautire (sometimes Gautier) arrived very ill from Purrysburg and eventually married the Bethesda gardener Anthony. Edward J. Cashin, *Beloved Bethesda: A History of George Whitefield's Home for Boys, 1740–2000* (Macon: Mercer University Press, 2001).

[159] Candler et al., *Col. Rec. Georgia*; Buckingham, 'Early American Orphanages: Ebenezer and Bethesda.' On the orphanage and its foundation and workings more broadly: Cashin, *Beloved Bethesda*.

[160] Camosso's death mentioned in Candler et al., *Col. Rec. Georgia*, 6: 251. On Anderson, see Marsh, *Georgia's Frontier Women*, 50, 59, 112; Candler et al., *Col. Rec. Georgia*, 1: 547; 6: 166, 190–1, 206, 218, 251, 323; 25: 140–1; 26: 145, 426–31.

[161] 3: 327; Natalie Rothstein, *Silk Designs of the Eighteenth Century in the Collection of the Victoria and Albert Museum, London, with a Complete Catalogue* (Boston: Little, Brown, 1990), 292, 342.

[162] Letterbook of Lloyd, Wilson & Co., BA677, Derby Local Studies and Family History Library: 16 March 1747, 15 and 22 Feb 1748. American silk's quality and output also discussed in letters on 6, 13, 27 April, 4 May 1747; 29 February, 5, 26 March 1748; 5, 12, 24 June, 15, 24, 31 July, 7, 12, 21, 26 August, 11 September 1749.

springtime labour of many orphans, 'Careful Housewives' around Savannah, and the wives, widows, and daughters who were 'the principal Persons' around Ebenezer, had therefore sustained an economic activity that would otherwise have had little prospect of surviving during the Trusteeship. But it would suffer new pressures when the province opened – like rice-field sluice gates – to the wretchedly effectual model of plantation slavery in South Carolina.[163]

Persistent Production and Filatures, c.1750–1770

Over the next two decades, authorities in Georgia and South Carolina both took significant steps to support silk raising alongside the core economic activities pursued in the Lower South. They generated innovative working models and new constructions that used silk to situate themselves more firmly within empire – as evidence of their productive potential and their cultural civility. This happened even while Georgia was swiftly changing shape, growing rapidly into a patriarchal slave society that fell into step with its formative Caribbean and Carolinian neighbours; a visitor to Savannah in the late 1760s would barely have recognised the province from its earlier incarnation. But if they were observant, they might have spotted the high number of white mulberry trees in the vicinity, and even if they were not, they would have noticed the quirky structure of the Savannah filature on the town's skyline (see Plate 10). This centrepiece of Georgia's silk production was a two-storey building some 36 by 20 feet long that was designed, built, and kitted out at great cost, under the oversight of James Habersham (a merchant and former manager of the Bethesda orphanage), and other similar structures would emerge in South Carolina in the 1760s. Both provinces, rightly confident of having successfully navigated the problems of supply and expertise that had held back earlier efforts, ploughed resources into the undertaking – especially through the support of these centralised filatures that were flexible enough to process the produce of either enslaved labourers in the Lowcountry or interior townships.

The amount of state funding lavished on enabling silk production in Georgia was substantial, and showed a continuity of scale with the Trusteeship. At the beginning of the royal period in 1752, the funds set aside for 'Purchasing from growers cocoons of raw silk as an encouragement to silk culture' constituted £1,000 – roughly equal to the bill for the support of the governor and officeholders – comprising over a third of the entire parliamentary appropriation for Georgia. The support of silk

---

[163] Candler et al., *Col. Rec. Georgia*, 4a: 134; 30: 276.

remained extraordinarily high, fixed at £1,000, which was still around
a quarter of the annual parliamentary appropriation in 1758–67. Such was
the generosity of the bounties on cocoon production that even these
sums did not cover the outlay, as shown by the accounts provided by
Georgia's agent John Campbell, which listed over £1,625 paid out in cash
in 1765, £1,936 in 1766, and £1,101 (anticipated) in 1767. In return, in
these peak years, the raw silk sales generated £639 in 1765 and £999 in
1767, therefore covering only about half of the cost.[164] These funding
streams ensured that Georgia was able to continue to secure plentiful access
to white mulberry trees and new stocks of silkworm eggs: Savannah officials
secured American eggs from South Carolina, Ebenezer, and from Mary
Jones (daughter of a Georgia councilman); they purchased Italian and
Portuguese stocks in Charleston, and other Portuguese stocks were sourced
via London 'in extraordinary good Order' through Samuel Lloyd.[165]

South Carolina's assembly likewise backed new silk initiatives with
public finances, approving £1,000 (SC) to support production in the
piedmont, where the New Bordeaux settlement brought hundreds of
Huguenots to Hillsborough Township from 1764.[166] Its settlers reported
progress, in spite of being pressed by sickness and Indian fears, and one of
the settlement's leaders, Rev. Jean Louis Gibert, carried back to England
some of the raw silk to show its quality.[167] Fresh from his successful
London exposition of Carolina township production, Gibert proposed
in a 1766 petition to erect two new filatures, one at Charleston and one at
Long Canes, which would prevent the spoilage of cocoons needing to
travel long distances to the seaboard.[168] Gibert presented samples of
wrought silk, along with 'Certificates of the goodness', and informed
the assembly he had sent for three people from southern France, experts

---

[164] These figures derived from Percy Scott Flippin, 'The Royal Government in Georgia,
1752–1776: IV. The Financial System and Administration', *Georgia Historical Quarterly*
9, no. 3 (1925): 187–91. For information on the bounties offered for cocoons: Candler
et al., *Col. Rec. Georgia*, 7: 115.

[165] Candler et al., *Col. Rec. Georgia*, 26: 331; Stevens, 'A Brief History', 181; Shaw, 'Silk in
Georgia, 1732–1840', 65.

[166] The town was located at the confluence of Long Cane Creek and Little River, tributaries of
the Savannah River in present day McCormick County. Edward M. Riley, *Survey of the
Historic Sites of the Clark Hill Reservoir and of South Carolina and Georgia* (Athens: University
of Georgia, Laboratory of Archaeology Manuscript 40, 1949), 10–11; Walter B. Edgar,
South Carolina: A History (Columbia, SC: University of South Carolina Press, 1998), 54;
Nora Marshall Davis, 'The French Settlement at New Bordeaux', *Transactions of the
Huguenot Society of South Carolina* 56 (1951): 28–57; Bobby F. Edmonds, *The Huguenots
of New Bordeaux* (McCormick, SC: Cedar Hill Unltd, 2005).

[167] *SCG*, 8 October 1764. Petition of Jean Louis Gibert, 24 June 1766, in 'Journal of the
Commons House of Assembly, MS 1761–1776' (Manuscript volumes: South Carolina
Department of Archives & History, 1761), 37(pt. 1): 145, 177.

[168] *SCG*, 7 July 1766.

in reeling, who were expected later in the year, and would manage the filature operations with him.[169] Over the next year, the assembly transformed buildings and furnished Gibert with 'materials and necessarys' – large copper basins and reeling machines were probably amongst the 'great Number of Implements Proper for the Cultivation of raw Silk' shipped from London in August 1766.[170]

Anticipating the filature's first year of production in 1767, the silk commissioners arranged a further public loan of £3,000 (SC) to purchase planters' private cocoons, which sum would be refunded from the sale of the reeled silk back to Britain, with any shortfall covered by the Carolina treasury.[171] Some felt this was too little investment, including Rev. Charles Woodmason, who believed that a premium should have been granted 'on all Cocoons, brought there which would set all our Young, Idle, lazy People to work'.[172] In 1769, the sale of 330 lb of Carolina silk in London brought in over £2,173 (SC), and at Henry Laurens's suggestion, this sum was immediately returned to the commissioners for purchases in the subsequent year.[173] Hopeful that public support could coax the industry to the point of take-off, the assembly voted £1,000 (SC) towards establishing another filature at Purrysburg in February 1770, and a further £3,000 (SC) in October 1771 to enable them to purchase 'raw Silk of the produce of this Province, to be transported to Great Britain for Sale'.[174] The establishment of these state-sponsored filatures from the early 1750s in Georgia and 1760s in South Carolina promised to unlock the potential of the bounty system and to link into a production cycle the various enclaves that had proved willing to undertake sericulture – including township settlers, occasional planters, and 'a considerable number' of their bondspeople.[175]

Once slavery was permitted, Georgia authorities followed Carolinian precedents in seeking creative ways to use enslaved labourers to generate

[169] 'Commons Journal', 37(pt. 1): 177. Gibert had actually hoped to bring considerably more settlers with him from silk-growing regions, but many had diverted to East Florida, and his ambitious proposals dating back to 1761 were heavily reined in by first British and then Carolinian authorities. J. L. Gibert, 'Memorial of Pastor Jean Louis Gibert to the Lords of the Treasury, Read in Council, 6 July 1763', *Transactions of the Huguenot Society of South Carolina* 19 (1912): 18–23.

[170] 'Commons Journal', 37(pt. 1): 203. 'News from London' section in *SCG*, 7 October 1766.

[171] 'Commons Journal', 37(pt. 1): 374; 37(pt. 2): 633, 659, 675.

[172] Charles Woodmason, *The Carolina Backcountry on the Eve of the Revolution: The Journal and Other Writings of Charles Woodmason, Anglican Itinerant*, ed. Richard James Hooker (Chapel Hill: University of North Carolina Press, 1953), 254.

[173] 'Commons Journal', 38(pt. 2): 247.   [174] 'Commons Journal', 38(pt. 3): 543.

[175] See for instance 'Letter from Edmund Caiger of Charlestown on the Culture of Silk in Georgia', to Royal Society of Arts, 15 September 1766, in Guard Book (PR.GE/110/22/78), Royal Society of Arts Archive, London.

silk. Political economists and authorities in the post-Trusteeship period clearly indicated that they believed slavery and sericulture to be compatible and even mutually supportive, in the process reversing some of the promotional claims issued by the Trustees – which had often framed silk (and other commodity targets) as counterposed to the economics of plantation slavery. Georgia's early royal governors showed enthusiasm (particularly Henry Ellis), and such influential imperial figures as the Earl of Halifax (George Montagu Dunk), Charles Townshend, and James Oswald lent their weight. Along with Viscount Dupplin (Thomas Hay), the latter three identified a number of advantages they felt Georgia possessed in 1752 compared to the Piedmont region, not least of which was non-enslaved Georgians' ownership of their land and labour rather than having to 'work chiefly for others'.[176] Writers argued that enslaved males could furnish the ovens or copper basins (used to heat the cocoons) with firewood, while a bondswoman, 'if She is carefull', could perform the more intricate tasks of feeding and winding.[177]

An example of how this thinking translated into practice was the law in 1750 insisting that slaveholders maintain a ratio of one trained enslaved woman for every four 'Male Negroes or Blacks' they possessed, and they were to be fined if they failed to have their enslaved females 'well instructed in the Art of winding or reeling of Silk' – with any cash generated by these penalties to be added to the budget supporting sericulture. Landholders also had to sustain a planting programme of mulberry trees, and to adequately fence them 'to defend and protect them against Cattle' – for roaming livestock could threaten the leaf supply. But in contrast to South Carolina, whose council had blocked some measures supporting silk uptake, the very membership of the Georgia legislature was initially designed to advance it. No person could be elected as a deputy to the new representative assembly unless they had fenced 100 mulberries on each 50 acres they owned, had at least 'one Female in his Family' instructed in reeling, and produced a small amount of raw silk annually.[178] Many of the incoming waves of planters probably disregarded such conditions in their hurry to establish new lumber mills and Lowcountry rice operations on the best lands opening up to settlement. They recognised that these rulings, though approved by Parliament, had been partly framed by the outgoing Trustees, and perhaps anticipated that the situation would change before the qualifications for office were due to come into force in 1753.

[176] Candler et al., *Col. Rec. Georgia*, 39: 187.
[177] Candler et al., *Col. Rec. Georgia*, 30: 545–81. Betty Wood, *Slavery in Colonial Georgia, 1730–1775* (Athens: University of Georgia Press, 1984), 87.
[178] Candler et al., *Col. Rec. Georgia*, 1: 60; 2: 500. Shaw, 'Silk in Georgia, 1732–1840', 65.

But for a short time, there is good evidence that silk and slavery went hand in hand in Georgia, echoing and amplifying developments in Carolina, and even more explicitly along gendered lines. For one thing, silk profits could be an entry point into slave ownership: one Ebenezer shoemaker, Matthias Zettler, 'earned so much money by making and spinning silk, for which his wife is especially qualified, that he bought a [pregnant] female Negro slave in Carolina' in 1750.[179] More collaboratively, at the public filature in Savannah it was recorded that 'there young People, both white and black, are employed in a Work', and James Habersham, Pickering Robinson, and James Harris all made reference to planters sending 'their Daughters and Negroe Women' to acquire the art of reeling. Only lack of capacity hindered the managers from accepting more planters' 'Daughters as well as Young Negroe Slaves . . . as we have two Prentices, besides a Mistress to Each Bason, we have no Room for more'.[180] If some disregarded them, many planters evidently took seriously the regulations and opportunities associated with training their female bondspeople alongside white women. Although we might imagine patterns of socialisation, treatment, and task distribution to have been racially demarcated in the extra-domestic manufactory, there was no reference to this in existing sources.

The new filature was one of the earliest manufacturing establishments of any scale in Georgia, and the region's first textile factory, in the sense that paid employees arrived to work there during its operation.[181] Described as a 'plain, coarse Building', with few of the ornamental touches that often accompanied European constructions, it initially contained six large copper basins built into a furnace system with piping. Its specifications were extremely detailed: twenty-four new copper basins for regular cocoons were ordered to be nine inches deep, eleven wide, and twenty-seven inches long, while one dedicated to reeling double balls was to be twice as deep and exactly round (of twenty-four inches diameter), with like exactitude for their rims and flats. The upper level of the filature comprised a large room to spread the cocoons in prior to reeling, 'as it is Found, that they sweat, and take much Damage, if they are kept in Heaps or confined in Bags'. Much is likewise known about the personnel of the filature in the early 1750s. Its chief reeler was to be the 'steady and dependable' Anderson, though its best reelers were still the remaining Camossos (consisting of Giacomo, two sons, and the daughter), who had returned from Carolina and now 'appeared to be very submissive'. They

---

[179] Urlsperger et al., *Detailed Reports*, 15: 4.
[180] Candler et al., *Col. Rec. Georgia*, 26: 92–3, 231, 289, 331–2; 31: 246.
[181] In 1765 the payments were increased, moving from eighteen to twenty pence and one shilling to one shilling and twopence. Candler et al., *Col. Rec. Georgia*, 28(pt. 2): 108.

were joined by three wives from the Ebenezer township (Zettler, Bruckner, and Reiser) along with a number of planters' daughters and enslaved women, and in all likelihood one or more of the French specialists who emigrated in the last year of the Trusteeship.[182] Beside the filature proper, other funds were laid out to pay for a nearby building in which to store and sort cocoons, and a large oven and a well to streamline the operations. These subsidiary buildings were occupying several workmen in the winter of 1751–2, and the combined bills for construction and salaries came to over £1,500.[183] Upon completion, Savannah therefore possessed a state-of-the-art site for generating raw silk in which female workers of different ages, colours, and languages hunched in pairs over steaming basins, turned wooden handles, replenished cocoons and repaired threads, and ferried or filled empty baskets and skeins under watchful eyes.

The other new hand-picked manager, Pickering Robinson, was part of a new commission sounded out by Samuel Lloyd in Italy and tasked from April 1750 with professionalising Georgia silk, though Robinson ended up travelling without the more senior appointee, Andrew Faesch, who had declined the American posting and repaid his advance.[184] Robinson struck up a cordial relationship with James Habersham, who spoke highly of his qualities, and anticipated that under his supervision the filature would act 'as a Nursery . . . of well instructed Reelers'. Robinson's stamina, however, was questionable, and he came close to leaving for South Carolina on account of ill health in 1752, before finally returning to England in the spring of 1753.[185] Some years later, Robinson's experience of managing the production of first-rate raw silk in the Georgia filature would qualify him for appointment by the East India Company (EIC). His involvement in bringing the Savannah filature into a semblance of order, alongside others, played an important part in his securing a commission to take up a new post in Bengal under the auspices of the EIC in 1769.[186] There, he was again under instructions to work with Italian experts and local skills and materials to improve the organisation and quality of reeling, by centralising operations more systematically in filatures. Atlantic silk thus made a small but important contribution to the improvement of Bengalese output, on which British

---

[182] Candler et al., *Col. Rec. Georgia*, 26: 143–6, 330; Urlsperger et al., *Detailed Reports*, 15: 53.
[183] Candler et al., *Col. Rec. Georgia*, 1: 568–9; 3: 354, 367; 26: 143–6, 331.
[184] Candler et al., *Col. Rec. Georgia*, 2: 505, 509; 3: 363. Faesch's seniority is assumed from the higher wages he was to be paid originally.
[185] Candler et al., *Col. Rec. Georgia*, 6: 389–90; 26: 330.
[186] Candler et al., *Col. Rec. Georgia*, 26: 431.

overseas efforts would be more fully concentrated with the loss of North America.[187]

Replacing Robinson in the spring of 1753 was Joseph Ottolenghe, a man of unusual origins and outlook. Born Giuseppe Salomone Ottolenghi in the silk-producing town of Casale Monferatto in Piedmont, he had moved to Exeter where he converted from Judaism to Christianity, and on the recommendation of one of the Trustees, clergyman and botanist Rev. Dr Stephen Hales, appeared before them in August 1750 and contracted to travel to Georgia with his wife and an acquaintance (in lieu of a servant), with all three awarded three years' subsistence in return for 'using their utmost Endeavors to promote the Culture of Silk in Georgia'.[188] It seems that Ottolenghe soon held a dual capacity, for he was also appointed as a catechiser of enslaved people, and continued to teach them to read, write, and follow the Christian religion several years *after* education was outlawed in Georgia's harsh 1755 slave code – though in the face of planter obstinacy he devoted himself more fervently to the superintendence of silk. On more than one occasion, Ottolenghe would stick up for the underdogs, as when he lambasted a proposed reward system because he felt it was 'partial' in giving preference to silk raisers with the greatest means, and he would rather the patronage exercised its 'benign Influence on the narrow Cottage as well as the spacious Palace'. Considering these credentials, it is perhaps surprising that he managed, as he claimed in September 1753, to persuade 'Planters of different Parts of ye Colony', including particularly enthusiastic settlers in Augusta 'while their Trees are perfecting, to send Yearly Hands to Savannah, to be instructed in ye Art of Reeling'.[189]

Ottolenghe left a valuable description of the workings of the filature itself, which was a loud, humid, and unpleasant working environment. One turner was allowed to each reel, a reduction after the experiences in

---

[187] H. V. Bowen, *Revenue and Reform: The Indian Problem in British Politics, 1757–1773* (Cambridge: Cambridge University Press, 1991), 106–7; Roberto Davini, 'A Global Supremacy: The Worldwide Hegemony of the Piedmontese Reeling Technologies, 1720s–1830s', in *History of Technology*, ed. Ian Inkster (New York: Bloomsbury, 2014), 87–104; Karolina Hutková, 'The British Silk Connection: The English East India Company's Silk Enterprise in Bengal, 1757–1812' (PhD thesis, University of Warwick, 2015), 109–12.

[188] Candler et al., *Col. Rec. Georgia*, 1: 552; 2: 510; Harold E. Davis, *The Fledgling Province: Social and Cultural Life in Colonial Georgia, 1733–1776* (Chapel Hill, NC: University of North Carolina Press, 1976), 49, 142–43; Holly Snyder, 'A Tree with Two Different Fruits: The Jewish Encounter with German Pietists in the Eighteenth-Century Atlantic World', *The William and Mary Quarterly* 58, no. 4 (2001): 855–82; Chicco, *La seta in Piemonte*, 88–90.

[189] Joseph Ottolenghe to Benjamin Martyn, Savannah, 3 May 1756 (PR.GE/110/5/68), RSA.

1752 when Ottolenghe had apparently met with 'Abuses Threatnings & Insolent Behaviour' from his largely female workforce, while urging them to their duty. Ottolenghe proposed to rotate his workers through different tasks, cutting the number but allowing closer oversight, such that they sorted cocoons for one part of the day, '& Turn ye other, & at ye same Time learn to Reel'. The days were long, sometimes beginning as early as '3 & 4 O'Clock in ye morning until 8 at Night'. They were also extraordinarily hot, for on account of the constant need to keep the furnaces burning and the copper basins near boiling, 'ye Heat within ye Filature, & without is, excessive'. Little wonder that Ottolenghe found that the 'girls ... love Play better than Work, and no soon my Back is turn'd, but a Cessation of Hands immediately ensues'.[190] Compared to European filatures, the Savannah ceiling was low, meaning there was little fresh air circulating, to the point where the reeled wet silk itself was compromised by the dust and smoke affixing to it and discolouring it. The building's twenty windows and two doors offered little respite to workers in the height of summer, nor did they lessen damage to the raw silk since they were low and invited thick mist in during the mornings, which itself stiffened the drying threads and adhered them together. Ottolenghe also complained of the furnace system, which he felt was poorly designed – the original six chimneys were 'ready to tumble down' after just two years' use, and because of their excessive height allowed too much oxygen inside, which made them wasteful of wood and sent the flames too high to consistently warm the basins.[191] All these shortcomings reflected to some degree the difficulties of calibrating an Old World model to the heat, humidity, and manufacturing meagreness of the Lowcountry.

By 1757, judging by detailed existing receipts for that year's operations, the filature had received a good deal of investment and modernisation, and in the process thrown a good amount of work in the direction of Savannah's emerging artisans and servicers. Ottolenghe's new furnaces (six of twenty-four feet high and two of thirty feet) were installed, along with better measuring apparatus such as large scales for weighing parcels of cocoons that silk raisers delivered, and small brass scales used to 'weigh ye daily Portion of Cocoons for each Reelers'.[192] Masons Peter Mackay and Thomas Cross both built chimneys; carpenter Richard Milledge did over £22 worth of work in the filature (probably including repairs and new reeling units) and was paid a further £42 for building the additional house; Hugh Ross, Andrew Maxton, and James Dixey all supplied boards

---

[190] Candler et al., *Col. Rec. Georgia*, 27: 37.
[191] Candler et al., *Col. Rec. Georgia*, 26: 430–7.
[192] Candler et al., *Col. Rec. Georgia*, 26: 434–5.

or coopers' work while Thomas Baillie was paid 'for Smiths work' (likely including fitting the brass cocks and hooks); George Eyley & Co. dug out the well, and Richard Dandy was paid for a pump. Unspecified services or 'sundrys' were provided by merchants John Graham, Thomas Rasberry, and Mary Ralcher, while John Grovonole charged five shillings for baking cocoons, with transport costs including boat hire locally (two days' and four men's worth) and cargo space on the transatlantic journey. Labour charges included Ottolenghe's salary, some £42.18s paid to 'Reelers, Turners and Sorters', over £10 for 'the maintenance of the people', and, intriguingly, 'Joseph Ottolenghe for Negroe hire &c.', which came to nearly £12.[193]

Notwithstanding structural problems, the quality of the silk produced by this array of transplanted Europeans and Africans (see Fig. 6.2) was high, achieving initially an even consistency of first 6–9 filaments and later 12–14 filaments per thread. In 1751 they reeled off 6,301 lb of cocoons (the work of perhaps 2 million silkworms), of which around 60 per cent came from the Bethesda orphanage and 30 per cent from Ebenezer, with the remainder from independent households. Though some 380 lb of cocoons were lost to what William Stevens described as 'vermin, fire and mould', two trunks of raw silk (269 lb 10 oz), two bales of 'Filozel' (161 lb of processed floss silk), and two other bales of inferior silk and cocoon debris (65 lb 8 oz) were shipped to London and thrown and sold by Samuel Lloyd for over £415.[194] It is worth noting that the manufacture and export of such waste silk (or filoselle) was hardly ever listed in official records, yet on the three occasions references have been found, it constituted 60 per cent (1751), 14 per cent (1754), and 78 per cent (1766) of the poundage of raw silk, which suggests it was a significant additional output of merchantable product.[195]

Perhaps the grandest testament to the accomplishments of this motley bunch, sweating away in their custom-built corner of a frontier town which itself lay on the fringes of the wider Atlantic plantation zone, arrived in 1755. That March, 38 weavers or firms gave their verdict on the output of the Georgia filature, based on 300 lb that had lately been imported. Most of the weavers were of Huguenot descent and based in Spitalfields, many operating out of the famed Steward Street, and they included such important silk-manufacturing dynasties as the Delamares,

[193] 'Expence of the Filature in Georgia in the Year 1757' and 'List of Impliments necessary in a Filature', 1757 (PR.GE/110/7/36 and /37), RSA.
[194] Shaw, 'Silk in Georgia, 1732–1840', 65; Stevens, 'A Brief History', 182; Candler et al., *Col. Rec. Georgia*, 3: 363.
[195] The next year Ottolenghe listed 197 lb in total which included 'first Sort' silk, with 12 to 14 cocoons in the thread, 'Second-Sort' with 18 to 22, and waste silk mixed from 'Woolly ... ye Falloppia, ye Doppioni, ye Waste, & two miserable Skains drawn from ye Bags'. 26: 435–6.

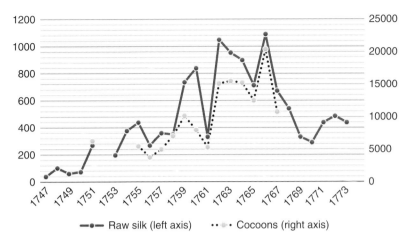

Figure 6.2 Georgia silk production for export in lb (1747–74).
Source: Allen D. Candler et al., eds., *The Colonial Records of the State of Georgia*, 31 vols. (Atlanta and Athens: various printers, 1904), I: 392, 532, 529, IVa: 134, XXV: 140–1, XXVIII Pt. 1: 125–7, 213, 341, 377, 445, XXVIII Pt. 2:49; Harvey H. Jackson and Phinizy Spalding, *Forty Years of Diversity Essays on Colonial Georgia* (Athens: University of Georgia Press, 1984), 221–2; Mary Thomas McKinstry, 'Silk Culture in the Colony of Georgia', *Georgia Historical Quarterly* 14 (1930): 225–35; Pauline Tyson Stephens, 'The Silk Industry in Georgia', *The Georgia Review* 7 (1953): 39–49; Edward J. Cashin, *Governor Henry Ellis and the Transformation of British North America* (Athens: University of Georgia Press, 1994), 118–21; James C. Bonner, *A History of Georgia Agriculture, 1732–1860* (Athens: University of Georgia Press, 1964), 16–17; W. Calvin Smith, 'Georgia Gentlemen: The Habershams of Eighteenth-Century Savannah' (PhD thesis, University of North Carolina, 1971), 111, 118, 121–2

the Guillemards, Beuzevilles, and Aubers, and such influential individuals as Peter Nouaille and John Sabatier (who alone ran around 100 looms in the 1750s, specialising in the most elaborate fabrics).[196] These collective experts had little reason to give anything other than an objective verdict – perhaps unlike Lombe and Lloyd, who had been personally connected to Oglethorpe. They declared of the Georgia silk that 'the nature and texture is truly good, the colour beautifull, the thread is even and as clean as the best Piedmont (called Novè silks) of the size, and much cleaner and evener than the usual Italian silks that are generally imported

---

[196] Anita McConnell, 'John Sabatier', Oxford Dictionary of National Biography, 2004, www.oxforddnb.com/index/57/101057817/. For the best recent overview of this world and its connections, see part two of Anishanslin, *Portrait of a Woman in Silk*.

in the greatest Quantity'. They were impressed with the whiteness of the colour, noting it was being worked 'with much less Waste than China Silk', and they averred that as much as 20,000 lb of the 'greatly wanted' product could be disposed of annually. Ottolenghe's salary went up, and occasional worried murmurs even began to appear in Italy about the birth of a new American supply threat, after Asia.[197]

Such high-profile accolades brought additional funding to Georgia silk producers, for on top of baseline imperial legislation supporting American efforts, and the extensive annual appropriations specific to Georgia, the newly established Society for the Encouragement of Arts, Manufactures, and Commerce (now the RSA, founded at a coffee house in Covent Garden in 1754 and often referred to by contemporaries as the 'Premium Society') viewed Georgia silk as the perfect kind of project on which to lavish their enlightened imperial and scientific patronage. The Society initially awarded prizes to Henry Yonge, Sir Patrick Houstoun, Benedict Bourquin (a French Swiss from Purrysburg), and Theobald Keifer for having planted and fenced the most white mulberry trees on their plantations in 1756. Thereafter, rewards became closely tied to the quality of cocoon or raw silk yield since, as Ottolenghe pointed out, 'there are several People who have Mulberry Trees upon their Land and only keep an Overseer upon it to look after their Negroes'. The monies expended by the Premium Society on Georgia silk producers between 1759 and 1767, totalling £1,374, was the largest outlay it lavished on any of its pet agricultural, industrial, or applied science projects across the British Atlantic world.[198]

The high-water mark of Georgia silk production was in the decade after 1758. At the start of this period, Governor Henry Ellis stressed that silk 'employs many poor people, and is approaching towards a Staple', and became genuinely excited about its possibilities for colony and empire.[199] Remarkably, the production quickly returned to high levels in spite of a disastrous fire that burned down the new filature in 1758 – precisely the kind of accident that Paolo Amatis had been worried about in his request

[197] Certificate of 29 March 1755, London, PR.GE/110/7/38, RSA. Candler et al., *Col. Rec. Georgia*, 7: 208 (salary to £70); Chicco, *La seta in Piemonte*, 90.

[198] James Habersham and Joseph Ottolenghe to William Shipley, Savannah, 20 May 1756 (PR.GE/110/2/123); Joseph Ottolenghe to Benjamin Martyn, Savannah, 3 May 1756 (PR.GE/110/5/68), RSA. Chaplin, *An Anxious Pursuit*, 138. A similar organisation in Ireland, the Dublin Society, likewise paid out more limited premiums for mulberry plantations after 1751. Dunlevy, *Pomp and Poverty: A History of Silk in Ireland*.

[199] Candler et al., *Col. Rec. Georgia*, 28(pt. 1): 12. Gov. Henry Ellis to Benjamin Martyn, Savannah, 27 June 1758 (PR.GE/110/7/34), RSA. Edward J. Cashin, *Governor Henry Ellis and the Transformation of British North America* (Athens: University of Georgia Press, 1994), 119.

for a brick building thirty years earlier. Some of the reeled silk was rescued, and although all the equipment, half that year's 7,000 lb of cocoons, and £40 of cash were lost in the fire, far more serious consequences for Savannah were avoided thanks to the sweat and heroism of a party of sailors who controlled it before it reached the neighbouring munitions store.[200] The disaster must have impeded the growth of the industry to some extent, but a new filature was constructed on the site of the old in time to reel a record 10,136 lb of cocoons out of 12,000 lb delivered in 1759.[201] In excess of 15,000 lb of cocoons were delivered to the filature three years in a row between 1762 and 1764, when Governor Wright estimated around 300 people were taking it up. By 1766 the number had dwindled to 264 bringing cocoons in, most of them with 'Families and little Plantations or Farms and Stocks of Cattle &c. to mind and take care of' meaning they were not available for filature work (increasingly the province of perhaps three dozen women and girls in Savannah itself).[202]

The vision of hundreds of colonists of European origin – and hundreds more of their bondspeople of African origin – busily feeding silkworms in huts, sheds, and specially constructed buildings each springtime, is not typically part of our historical picture of the society and economy of the late colonial Lower South, dominated as it was by the production of rice, deerskins, and indigo.[203] But it was a recognisable feature across many communities – from the first French family who generated 30 lb of raw silk in South Carolina in 1683, to the households Archdale reported as raising 40–50 lb in the 1690s, to the bounty claimants for dozens of pounds in the 1730s, to the patchy export records of hundreds of pounds out of both South Carolina and Trusteeship Georgia in the 1740s, and culminating in the thousands of pounds, much of it raised in townships, reeled in filatures, and graded as 'exceeding fine', exported in the late 1760s and early 1770s.[204]

[200] Candler et al., *Col. Rec. Georgia*, 28(pt. 1): 162; Cashin, *Governor Henry Ellis*, 120–1.
[201] Candler et al., *Col. Rec. Georgia*, 28(pt. 1): 213.
[202] Candler et al., *Col. Rec. Georgia*, 28(pt. 1): 377, 445; 28(pt. 2): 49, 72–6, 165–9. Shaw, from Stevens, estimates forty people involved in the filature, though this was on the basis of two apprentices to each basin whereas, as we have seen, he reduced them to one, so I have downgraded slightly while allowing for more labour in sorting the larger volumes coming in, commensurate with the filature costing list. Shaw, 'Silk in Georgia, 1732–1840', 68; Stevens, 'A Brief History', 184.
[203] Silk was ranked twelfth in the export list aggregated for the late 1740s by James Glen, *A Description of South Carolina; Containing, Many Curious and Interesting Particulars Relating to the Civil, Natural and Commercial History of That Colony* (London: R. and J. Dodsley in Pall-Mall, 1761), 50–5. See also Peter A. Coclanis, *The Shadow of a Dream: Economic Life and Death in the South Carolina Low Country, 1670–1920* (New York: Oxford University Press, 1989), 80–1.
[204] Sources of this data can be found referenced above with the exception of the following export records: Carroll, *Historical Collections of South Carolina*, 2: 237, 272. Raw silk was

Persistent Problems

Such quantification of silk production offered clear evidence of significant progress in output. But for all the imperial persistence, when set against the magnitude of what the Lower South was exporting in other commodities, or set against the magnitude of the demand of the British domestic silk industry, it remained a drop in the ocean. Neither as a staple nor as a secondary product did the collective enterprise of raw silk reach genuine commercial sustainability, as expressed in the objectives framed by imperial and colonial bodies. What accounted for the collective failure? South Carolina and Georgia did not fail to produce silk in commercial quantities because they lacked sufficient access to the core materials of sericulture (mulberry trees or silkworm eggs), because their labour force was either idle or lacking in skills or dexterity, or because of widespread natural predators. And although locating expertise in reeling was a perennial challenge, and specialists were thin on the ground, thanks to its impressive filatures and contacts, the Lower South was less compromised by a dearth of sericultural experience than earlier trials had been in Virginia, or a number of other projects in northern Europe. Rather, the Lower South failed at a colonial level because its environment was viable but not reliable, and because even with the inflated value offered by the many state bounties and enticements, other crops – notably rice and indigo – offered better prospects for estate development, especially to slaveholders, meaning that labour was available but not cheap in relative terms. While enslaved people themselves were not a hindrance, the institution of American slavery's relentless emphasis on productive efficiency, and perhaps the Lower South's high deployment of overseers, may also have helped indirectly to stall efforts. Lastly, the reconfiguration of bounty payments in the 1760s, though well intentioned, itself appears to have undermined uptake amongst non-slaveholding producers.

The climate and soils in the Lower South presented few problems when it came to moisture and humidity for the expansion of moriculture, and there was plenty of warmth in the late spring and summer when silkworms were busiest, though several observers agreed that meteorological

---

listed on one page (272) as having been exported in only six years, these being 1742 (18½ lb), 1748 (52 lb), 1749 (46 lb), 1750 (118 lb), 1753 (11 lb), 1755 (5⅓ lb). However, Glen also stated separately (237) that eight boxes of raw silk were shipped in 1747, and on the basis that in the 1770s a box of Carolina raw silk equated to 80 lb, I have assumed that these boxes represented the total of production in the years 1743–1747 inclusive, i.e. 640 lb (or 128 lb p/a). According to the recorded exports of 1769–1774, Carolinians sent to London some 2,165 lb of raw silk (361 lbp/a). *SCG*, 18 January 1770, 28 February 1771, 14 March 1771, 19 March 1771, 14 January 1772, 8 March 1773, 8 February 1774 and 'Commons Journal', 38(pt. 2): 2 47.

variability in the early spring presented a serious challenge. 'Our Climate is various and uncertain', concluded James Glen, who challenged the relevance of latitude to local conditions and warned of 'Extreams of Heat and Cold'. Glen compared his own readings with the more rigorous scientific measurements of a fellow Scot, John Lining, whose remarkable experiments in Charleston involved eleven years' monitoring of rainfall and wind direction (1737–48) and four years' tracking changes in temperature and barometric pressure. These showed 'frequent, sudden and great' temperature drops, recurrent thunderstorms, and heavy rainfall recorded in March during several years. Such weather events potentially retarded the budding white mulberry trees and infant silkworms, the consistency of cocoon winding, and especially the availability of high-quality, dry leaves for springtime feeding.[205] Sometimes silkworms hatched before mulberry trees had leafed, as in 1753 when a 'multitude of them died', or suffered from 'excessive hard and unseasonable frosts' at the start of the month as in 1761.[206] Cold and rainy weather at the end of May could also be responsible for reduced yields, retarding the later-pupating silkworms and damaging the quality of their cocoons. Such cold spells could be particularly dispiriting for silk raisers, because they could not very effectively plan for or respond to them, and because they were not paid for their labour but their produce. Governor James Wright described how 'a most extraordinary prospect' had been ruined in mid-April 1769, when 137 Georgia silk-raising families anticipated a fine harvest yet were hit with a double whammy of very cold rains for two days 'succeeded by hard black frost' that destroyed the majority of the silkworms.[207] Less commonly, fine weather allowed for good harvest years, as in 1766, and of course other agricultural output was equally dependent upon (if not quite as vulnerable to) the elements, such as marshland rice farming whose harvests could be wrecked by drought or floods. But the poor to middling non-slaveholding households in townships that concentrated on raising silk were ill placed to absorb losses of the sort that larger planters could ride out.[208]

---

[205] Glen, *A Description of South Carolina*, 11 (quote), 23 5; Edelson, *Plantation Enterprise*, 98–103; Everett Mendelsohn, 'John Lining and His Contribution to Early American Science', *Isis* 51, no. 3 (1960): 278–98 (esp. 284–92); Carroll, *Historical Collections of South Carolina*, 2: 210. Other points liable to compromise moriculture may have been the terrible hurricane of September 1700, which reportedly tore thousands of trees up at the roots. Hedward Hyrne to Elizabeth Hyrne, 19 October 1700, Hyrne Family Papers (South Carolina Historical Society).
[206] Candler et al., *Col. Rec. Georgia*, 26: 423.
[207] Wright cited in Stevens, 'A Brief History', 186.
[208] Candler et al., *Col. Rec. Georgia*, 37(pt. 1): 271.

That Carolina planters sought out silk with more energy at certain junctures reflected their own shifting economic ambitions: a handful of perennial planter 'innovators' tended to be joined during commercial crises by 'responsive' reinforcements from those usually 'bigoted to Rice & their own Notions', as shown in the Charleston filature legislation of 1738 and 1766.[209] What space existed for eighteenth-century planter investment in sericulture, however, was eroded in the Lowcountry by two important clashes. Firstly, silk and rice's respective periods of seasonal labour demand clashed: the short burst of intensive work in silk collided with the labour-hungry planting out of rice between March and May which involved drilling, planting, and extensive weeding.[210] The 'very time required to look after the silkworms', noted Gov. George Burrington of North Carolina in 1732, 'is the season of Planting and Cultivating Rice'.[211] Secondly, as Hector Berenger de Beaufain observed in 1755, after mid-century the 'unexpected success of indico seems to have left no place' for other promising exports, and writers even began to model silk hopes on indigo's success.[212] Unlike silk, James Glen remarked 'how conveniently and profitably, as to the charge of labour, both indigo and rice may be managed by the same persons', with indigo grown on higher and drier lands and needing but little weeding attention in the four months between sowing in early April and first cutting (which occurred before the intensive reaping and processing of rice from late August).[213] It was no coincidence, then, that indigo – even though plagued by deficiencies in quality – ended up as the most viable 'colleague Commodity' for rice planters desperate to diversify without

---

[209] For a discussion of these categories, see Chaplin, *An Anxious Pursuit*, ch. 6. Quote from 'Letter from Charles Woodmason about Cultivation of Various Crops in Carolina including Gum, Aromatic Bark, Sugar Maple, Hemp and Wine, Corn and Mulberry Trees', to Royal Society of Arts, Charleston, May 25, 1763, in Guard Book (PR.GE/110/4/62), Royal Society of Arts Archive, London.

[210] Dates taken from An American, *American Husbandry: Containing an Account of the Soil, Climate, Production and Agriculture of the British Colonies in North-America and the West-Indies* (London: J. Bew, 1775), 1: 392; Glen, *A Description of South Carolina*, 7; on the labour-intensity of planting and weeding, Edelson, *Plantation Enterprise*, 106–13.

[211] Burrington added tobacco, maize, and pulse as other springtime competitors for labour. Saunders, *The Colonial Records of North Carolina*, 3: 338.

[212] 'Letter from H. Beringer and William Bull on the cultivation of silk in South America', to William Shipley, Charleston, 27 September 1755, in Guard Book (PR.GE/110/2/69), Royal Society of Arts Archive, London. On writers modelling silk, see for instance William Burke, *An Account of the European Settlements in America. In Six Parts* (London: R. and J. Dodsley in Pall-Mall, 1758), 261–3.

[213] Glen, *A Description of South Carolina*, 10; Peter C. Mancall, Joshua L. Rosenbloom, and Thomas Weiss, 'Agricultural Labor Productivity in the Lower South, 1720–1800', *Explorations in Economic History* 39, no. 4 (2002): 390–424; Philip D. Morgan, *Slave Counterpoint: Black Culture in the Eighteenth-Century Chesapeake and Lowcountry* (Chapel Hill: University of North Carolina Press, 1998), 160–3.

compromising plantation organisation.[214] To add insult to injury, indigo's initial converts from the late 1740s tended to be those larger-scale rice planters best able to experiment with new crops and absorb losses.[215] In contrast, where sericulture had taken off amongst Mixtecan Indians in the sixteenth century, its uptake between February and April followed the harvest of Spanish-introduced winter cereals (wheat and barley) and preceded the peak demand for agricultural labour in planting out indigenous staple crops (maize, squash, and beans) that occurred with the rains of April to June.[216]

The proven pursuit of rice and latterly indigo production in the Carolina Lowcountry meant that the owners of the roughly 18,000 enslaved people brought to Georgia between 1751 and 1775 prioritised these over investing in silk production. Any shared multiracial conditions in the Savannah filature had lasted only a few years, for the strictures in the early 1750s about the training of enslaved women, mulberry planting, and qualification for office had been superseded by legal and political systems closely modelled on those in South Carolina. As in other sectors, racial language soon permeated the Georgia silk industry: the allowance of forty shillings to those who learned the art of reeling would become specifically offered 'To each White Woman'.[217] Within a few years, Governor James Wright was echoing his counterpart William Bull in Carolina in observing that slaveholders tended to neglect sericulture because 'People of Property can make more by Employing their Negroes about other things' – which reflected also that the pitiless Lowcountry regimen allowed little differentiation between the labour demands placed on enslaved men and women.[218] In 1772 even James Habersham, who had once written from his plantation (named 'Silk Hope') that 'Silk may with proper Care and Encouragement become as considerable, and perhaps a more beneficial Staple' than rice, admitted defeat. Until the province had a number of 'white people of middling circumstances', he concluded it would never become 'a considerable Branch of Commerce' set against a slave society.[219] If there was a path

---

[214] Easterby, Olsberg, and Lipscomb, *Commons Journal*, 9: 99.

[215] Nash, 'South Carolina Indigo, European Textiles, and the British Atlantic Economy in the Eighteenth Century', 379. For a comparative consideration of the impact of an Atlantic secondary crop, see: Michel-Rolph Trouillot, 'Coffee Planters and Coffee Slaves in the Antilles: The Impact of a Secondary Crop', in *Cultivation and Culture: Labor and the Shaping of Slave Life in the Americas*, ed. Ira Berlin and Philip D. Morgan (Charlottesville: University Press of Virginia, 1993), 124–37.

[216] Borah, *Silk Raising in Colonial Mexico*, 69–70.

[217] *Col. Rec. Georgia*, 1: 544; 2: 498–500.

[218] Candler et al., *Col. Rec. Georgia*, 28(pt. 2): 154.

[219] Candler et al., *Col. Rec. Georgia*, 26: 330; 28(pt. 2): 92, 108. Habersham to Hillsborough, 24 April 1772, *The Letters of Hon. James Habersham, 1756–1775*

forward for silk as a commercial export, Habersham, Wright, and Ottolenghe all felt that it would lie somewhere in the medium term, somewhere in the backcountry – for by the mid-1760s, raising and reeling silk had overwhelmingly reverted to the preserve of poor white women.[220]

Given that silkworms could not comfortably synchronise with the labour demands of the main Lowcountry commercial staples, nor become one, they remained a peripheral preoccupation associated with peripheral labour. Indeed, an enduring fascination for willing planters, increasingly accentuated over the course of the century, was that sericulture would not draw off prime labourers, but offer a remunerative role for women, children, and the aged and infirm, whether black or white.[221] William Bull and Alexander Garden both recorded that some slaveholders 'employ their young Negroes, unfit for field labour, in gathering leaves of mulberry to feed the worms' even though enslaved children had in fact other 'necessary business' such as 'inspection' that, if withdrawn, would cause some loss – by which Bull presumably meant, amongst many other routine chores, the springtime protection of seeds from scavengers.[222] Some settlers had even less willingness and capacity than others to invest their own labour and capital in the undertaking. In particular, plantation overseers rarely shared the positivity of some of their elite employers, and were less seduced by the imperial kudos associated with sericulture: 'managers ... like pack horses must trot in the beaten tract, which no distant, tho' beautiful prospect will invite them to quit' warned Bull.[223] His reasoning was not explicit, but there is an intuitive logic to this remark: most overseers lacked the training, knowledge, and interest of the planter-botanists and mistress-gardeners who lovingly nurtured early mulberry groves and stocks of silkworm. Even the most diligent overseers, employed on rolling contracts, were largely concerned with short- to medium-term profit and maximising labour efficiency, which left little

---

(Savannah: Savannah Morning News Print, 1904), 173–4. Ellis anticipated this a few years earlier: Candler et al., *Col. Rec. Georgia*, 28(pt. 1): 205–7.

[220] Ottolenghe claimed that at Augusta 'their Situation is extremely Propitious for ye Silk Culture', and Wright that there was merit in creating a filature there as they requested. Candler et al., *Col. Rec. Georgia*, 23(pt. 2): 212; 26: 427. Habersham elaborated, and later mentioned good prospects in Wrightsborough, where Samuel Maddock was planting white mulberry seeds in 1772. As cited in Stevens, 'A Brief History', 188; *Letters of James Habersham*, 188.

[221] See, for examples, letter of Charles Pinckney (incorrectly attributed), 'Letter from Thomas Pinckney on Plantation of Mulberry Trees in Carolina and Georgia', to Royal Society of Arts, 1 April 1755, in Guard Book (PR.GE/110/1/19), Royal Society of Arts Archive, London. For more generic works urging this: Boreman, *Compendious Account*; Pullein, *The Culture of Silk*.

[222] Merrens, *Colonial South Carolina Scene*, 266. Garden and Waring, 'Correspondence between Alexander Garden, M.D., and the Royal Society of Arts', 18.

[223] Merrens, *Colonial South Carolina Scene*, 266.

elasticity for experimental investments in complicated products with a history of failure.

These deficiencies in silk's fit to the British Atlantic plantation regime in the Lowcountry were exacerbated by Parliament's changes to the structure of American silk bounties in the late 1760s, which compromised backcountry viability. Ironically, these were motivated by a conviction that raw silk exports were increasing across the colonies, so the intention was to concentrate encouragement on the reeling of high-quality raw silk that could be machine-thrown, such as that produced in the Savannah filature.[224] But the upshot of leaning less towards payments for cocoons (which dropped by over a shilling per pound) and more towards export incentives for skeins of raw silk was to demotivate Georgia's smaller producers. 'Whilst the Poor People had their full Price it made 'em busy & happy in their little Plantations', wrote one correspondent in 1766, but once the artificial price paid for their cocoon yield fell too far, enthusiasm quickly waned.[225] The cut in bounties ate dramatically into their margins, and even the persistent Salzburgers informed Bartram that they got little now for their labour in bad seasons, in spite of the governor claiming it was 'very well worth their attention'.[226] Though the Salzburgers persisted and were still described as 'chiefly imploy[ing] themselves in the culture of silk' in 1773 under the leadership of Johann Caspar Wertsch, who helped them to install copper basins in their own filature in Ebenezer, production had fallen away sharply in many parts of the colony.[227] In Savannah, Georgians would strip the buildings of the filature complex in the 1770s to remodel them for 'public use' – a spacious and bright new public ballroom for social events.[228] Because of environmental inadequacies, the noxious logic of slavery, and counterproductive changes to the bounty system, planters now danced and gossiped on the boards once occupied by dozens of sweating silk reelers and thousands of silkworms.

---

[224] On the new system, see Bonner, 'Silk-Growing in the Georgia Colony', 147; Candler et al., *Col. Rec. Georgia*, 15: 26–9; Adam Smith, *The Wealth of Nations*, 2 vols. (London: J. M. Dent & Sons, 1920), 2: 145; Josiah Tucker, *A Letter from a Merchant in London to His Nephew in North America* (London: Printed for J. Walter, 1766), 24.

[225] Edmund Caiger to RSA, Charleston, 15 September 1766 (PR.GE/110/22/78), RSA.

[226] [Peter Collinson], 'An Extract of Mr. Wm. [*sic*] Bartram's Observations in a Journey up the River Savannah in Georgia, with his Son, on Discoveries', *Gentleman's Magazine* 37 (1767), 166–9. [Title should read *John* Bartram's]; Candler et al., *Col. Rec. Georgia*, 28(pt. 2): 154.

[227] 12: 51, 143–4. Habersham letter of 30 March 1772, cited in Stevens, 'A Brief History', 187.

[228] Wright, address to Commons House of Assembly, 19 January 1774, cited in Stevens, 187.

Legacies

Looking back, perhaps the most striking monument to silk's unlikely rise and fall across the colonial era in the Lower South was the Georgia plantation named Mulberry Grove. It was the site of an extensive mulberry nursery at the small settlement of Joseph's Town near Savannah in the 1740s, but thereafter the plantation was soon retooled for rice production by John Graham, who became one of the largest slave owners in the colony. Only a few miles away on the site of the Trustees' Garden – once the cutting edge of aspirational Atlantic botany and moriculture – Andrew Wells was using enslaved people, in a grotesque inversion of the Trustees' original vision and prohibitions, to operate a brand-new distillery that was capable of producing 200 hogsheads of rum a year. The new Georgia state legislature purchased Mulberry Grove during the American Revolution, as it had been deserted by its Loyalist owners during the war, and granted it to American General Nathanael Greene. Ironically, it was at Mulberry Grove a few years later in 1792 that Eli Whitney 'struck out a plan of a Machine' that would revolutionise the productivity of short-staple cotton as a southern plantation crop, making possible the rise of King Cotton in the American South. Cotton possessed all the assets whose absence had delayed or hindered raw silk's uptake in the region: its fit to the landscapes, seasons, and labour systems, its short-term turnaround and minimal processing at source, its potential for production at scale. All of this would allow cotton to play its well-known part in shaping global developments in capitalism, industrial manufacturing, and textile consumerism in the coming decades. At Mulberry Grove, nobody yet knew it definitively, but one fibre had triumphed on the grounds of another's failure.[229]

It is tempting to imagine how a commercially successful or sustainable model of silk production might have slowed or challenged the later regional dominance of cotton. But even without counterfactual pathways, when we adopt a snapshot rather than a retrospective viewpoint, there remains plenty worthy of harvest in the historical record of efforts at raising silk in the Lower South. The snapshots explored already have helped illustrate why, how, and when the planter elite pursued experimental economic and

[229] Mary Granger, ed., *Savannah River Plantations* (Savannah: Oglethorpe Press, 1997), esp. 57. Savannah *Georgia Gazette*, 19 October 1774. Giorgio Riello, *Cotton: The Fabric That Made the Modern World* (Cambridge: Cambridge University Press, 2013); Sven Beckert, *Empire of Cotton: A Global History* (Alfred A. Knopf, 2014); Angela Lakwete, *Inventing the Cotton Gin: Machine and Myth in Antebellum America* (Baltimore, MD: Johns Hopkins University Press, 2003), 46–57 (quote on 56); Joyce E. Chaplin, 'Creating a Cotton South in Georgia and South Carolina, 1760–1815', *The Journal of Southern History* 57, no. 2 (1991): 171–200.

agricultural practices in their quest for self-advancement and security. They have revealed a host of labourers participating in the reconfiguration of estates and domestic spaces to chase an idiosyncratic form of collective textile fibre production that left significant scope for adaptation and improvisation, throwing up opportunities and touching the lives of a multitude of interested parties, from governors to bondspeople, and from established planters to new migrant populations on the western frontiers. Silk proved much more than a persistent feature of the aspirational political economy of the southern reaches of British America: it exerted deep influence on people's social and intellectual pretensions, their domestic configurations, and their work patterns. Three closing snapshots – of a dress, a wagon, and a poem – offer a final illustration of how the challenges posed by silk culture revealed particularities and sensibilities amongst very different communities in the Lower South.

The first snapshot, a gold damask *robe à la française*, was the much-treasured material end point of raw silk produced between 1744 and 1752 by the family of Eliza Lucas Pinckney (see Plate 11). It was a fabric that would be handed down through the family as a 'silken relic', and publicly exhibited on numerous occasions through the centuries to showcase South Carolina's heritage, pedigree, and potential.[230] Pinckney's interest in sericulture was not path-breaking, nor did not come simplistically from an interest in fashion (as is sometimes assumed).[231] There are good grounds to suppose it derived at least partly from her husband, for Charles Pinckney had written an account of the silkworm in 1732 amongst other agricultural essays, and was the author of the compulsory silk bill (linked to slave ownership) that failed to get past the Upper House in 1741; two days after his marriage to Eliza in 1744 he was appointed as one of Carolina's new silk commissioners.[232] Yet although better known for her attention to indigo cultivation in her youth, Eliza unquestionably approached silk with characteristic self-confidence and entrepreneurialism, showing a tenacity

---

[230] 'Silk Culture in the United States', article in New York *Tribune*, 31 March 1902. After a long loan, this dress was finally gifted to the Smithsonian Institution Costume Collection in April 2008. Note under illustration of gold brocade 'Dress of Carolina Silk', Zahniser, ed., *Letterbook of Eliza Lucas Pinckney*, xxxv; press release entitled 'Dress from the Pre-Revolutionary War-Era Added to Smithsonian Costume Collection', dated 24 April 2008, National Museum of American History website. https://americanhistory.si.edu/press/releases/dress-pre-revolutionary-war-era-added-smithsonian-costume-collection .

[231] Frances Leigh Williams, *Plantation Patriot: A Biography of Eliza Lucas Pinckney* (New York: Harcourt, Brace & World, 1967), 155, 159; Harriott Horry Ravenel, *Eliza Pinckney* (New York: C. Scribner's Sons, 1896), 130.

[232] *SCG*, 12 February 1732. On Charles Pinckney's agricultural writings, Susan Scott Parrish, 'Women's Nature: Curiosity, Pastoral, and the New Science in British America', *Early American Literature* 37, no. 2 (2002): 230.

in her oversight of sericulture (long into her widowhood) that was perhaps protected by the sorts of feminine associations bound up in the dress.[233]

Having established an effective operation using mulberries at her Belmont plantation near Charleston, where Eliza had read up on manuals, sent for eggs, paid great attention to the best ways of destroying the pupae without damaging the cocoons, and reeled them off, the Pinckneys sought a way to use the output to raise their profile. They seized their opportunity in the summer of 1753, when during a long trip to England the family secured an introduction to present a gift to Princess Augusta (mother of George III) and her younger children at the royal gardens in Kew. In the remarkable two-hour audience that followed, Eliza recorded the 'many little domestick questions' that she had discussed with the enlightened princess, amongst which was their raising of silk, about 'w[hi]ch we answered her Royal Highness in the clearest manner we could'. Two years later, Charles Pinckney presented Augusta with 'a Piece of Silk Damask of the Growth and Product of his own Plantation ... and dyed a fine Blue with Carolina INDIGO', which the Carolina newspaper reported had been 'very favourably' approved of, with the princess undertaking to 'honour it with her own Wearing'.[234] Eliza Pinckney's gold fabric – probably worked up in the same period – returned with her to Carolina, its cultural value enhanced by this royal association and esteem.[235] The Pinckney family and their bondspeople continued to produce silk through the 1760s, and Eliza's daughter inherited the technical expertise, carrying the management, reeling, and promotion of Carolina silk into her adulthood.[236] Some white mulberries still survive, far less glorified 'relics' of the Pinckney production, that are now

[233] On Pinckney's agricultural experimentations, see: Constance B. Schulz, 'Eliza Lucas Pinckney and Harriott Pinckney Horry: A South Carolina Revolutionary-Era Mother and Daughter', in *South Carolina Women: Their Lives and Times*, ed. Marjorie Julian Spruill, Valinda W. Littlefield, and Joan Marie Johnson (Athens: University of Georgia Press, 2009), 79–108 (esp. 84–8); Sam S. Baskett, 'Eliza Lucas Pinckney: Portrait of an Eighteenth Century American', *South Carolina Historical Magazine* 72 (1971): 207–19; Coon, 'Eliza Lucas Pinckney and the Reintroduction of Indigo Culture in South Carolina.'
[234] *SCG*, 10 April 1755.
[235] A third recorded dress was not kept in the family but given as a gift to another high-profile metropolitan figure, Lord Chesterfield. Ravenel, *Eliza Pinckney*, 131. Harriott Horry mentioned only 'one of these ancient dresses of hers I still have'. Harriott Pinckney Horry to Mrs. [Margaret Anne] Waties, c.1829 MS (South Caroliniana Library, University of South Carolina, Columbia).
[236] *SCG*, 30 June 1766. On Harriott Pinckney's involvement: letter to Dolly Golightly, 20 July 1763; letter to 'Miss R' in Santee, April 1766, 14 January 1767, and n.d. (probably spring 1767), 11/332/8; letter to Becky Izard, 20 December 1766, and n.d. (probably late 1767), 11/332/8. Harriott Pinckney Horry letterbook, 1763–67, Harriott H. Ravenel Papers, 11/332/8, Pinckney-Lowndes Papers (South Carolina Historical Society).

naturalised in untended thickets dotted around the urbanised acres that used to be Belmont.[237] But the celebrated dress allows us to see how, in a colonial world always in the shadow of metropolitan manufactures, silk production could be reconstituted by the elite to bring to the foreground questions of pride, localism, and civility – a way to bridge imperial divisions and to celebrate mutual connections through material contact.[238]

A second snapshot brings into focus the way that attempts at silk stimulated technological innovation amongst backcountry communities, and illustrates how they were open to shifting their labour patterns and household practices where there was a market opportunity. Critics of the filature system in Savannah and Charleston frequently complained of the travel burden for cocoon producers or trainee reelers in western townships, pointing out that the poor white women who were at the vanguard of raw silk production were compromised by the 'great hardship' of long round trips, and could not abandon small children and economic responsibilities (such as looking after cattle and households). Such families could rarely afford the boat hire to transport cocoons down Lowcountry rivers except collectively; but in waiting for a full boatload their smaller individual harvests were liable to damage and, if the pupae were still alive (which filature managers preferred), the moths were liable to emerge and wreck the yield. They tried filling river boats to the gunwales with cocoons, making them fast and as watertight as possible with sheets, and sending them at night-time to try to offset excess warmth, but their precarious cargo was still often damaged by humidity and bruising.[239]

Alert to the need to resolve the environmental challenge of dispersed geography without compromising the distinctive cash income offered by silk bounties, German silk raisers at Ebenezer and Bethany created a custom-made long wagon, filled with many small drawers that ran the breadth of the wagon and were no more than six inches deep, 'all sides full of Holes, with lathed Bottoms'. The Salzburger cocoon-mobile, an instance of innovative adaptation to local circumstances that was typical of Atlantic silk culturists even while it typified their liabilities, 'was thus carted through the Forrests free from so strong Evaporation, as those of

---

[237] Note under illustration of gold brocade 'Dress of Carolina Silk', Pinckney, *The Letterbook of Eliza Lucas Pinckney*, xxxv.

[238] For a fuller reading of the encounter: Ben Marsh, 'Visitor from South Carolina: Mrs Eliza Pinckney', in *Enlightened Princesses: Caroline, Augusta, Charlotte, and the Shaping of the Modern World*, ed. Joanna Marschner (Yale: Yale University Press, 2017), 515–527.

[239] Pressly, *On the Rim*, 46–7; Candler et al., *Col. Rec. Georgia*, 26: 218, 330; 27: 115–16; 28 (pt. 1): 125–7.

the Stream and its Swamps and Marshes, and delivered to the Filatur[e] without damaging a single Cocoon'.[240] Given that the Lower South's backcountry could not match the transport integration or the flexibility and density of population that were so vital to systems of silk labour in regions such as Piedmont or Languedoc, the efforts to design and deploy the wagon attested to how silk production (while the bounties were available) was an important seasonal crutch for many women, including widows, and their families, around which other activities were repositioned.[241]

The final snapshot is a blurrier one, coming as it does from a suggestive poem by Sherman Shelton that drew on folk traditions and memories amongst African Americans in South Carolina. The poem, titled 'Silk Hope' and published in 1978, imaginatively reorients the reader to reflect on the effect that sericulture had on the mentalities and livelihoods of those who took up the challenge. Enslaved producers of raw silk were not motivated by the raising of profile or the prospect of profit. One wonders: what did enslaved children make of the thousands of silkworms placed under their charge, whose labour they were instructed to exploit until the silkworms' death – having to feed them, nurture them, police them, and perhaps kill them and appropriate their life's work for the indulgence and material gain of their owners? The *Bombyx* silkworm itself, in some ways, must have seemed a consummate slave. It is logical to expect that the resistance of enslaved people occasionally played a part in undermining trials, not because people of African origin were not suited to the task but because silkworms were such fragile creatures, easy to silently sabotage. No less likely is that the novelty and the comparative lightness of much of the labour in raising silk in springtime months offered tasks that were relatively welcome, sociable, or fulfilling compared to some of the mosquito-ridden, back-breaking, closely scrutinised alternative tasks in the Lowcountry.

Shelton's poetic folk tale – though a contemporary piece and somewhat awry in its description of process – offers an important way of weaving together themes of subversion and stoppage. It proposes a voice for some of the many enslaved people who were charged with sericulture, such as Eliza Pinckney's carpenters (Sogo and Pompey) who likely rigged up the

---

[240] William Gerard De Brahm and Louis De Vorsey, *Report of the General Survey in the Southern District of North America* (Columbia: University of South Carolina Press, 1971), 161–2.

[241] For instances of wealth or relief accrued from silk raising: Urlsperger et al., *Detailed Reports*, 16: 28; 17: 137, 164, 168, 173; John Bartram and Francis Harper, 'Diary of a Journey through the Carolinas, Georgia, and Florida from July 1, 1765, to April 10, 1766', *Transactions of the American Philosophical Society* 33, no. 1 (1942): 27.

shelving for her silkworms at Belmont, or the 'considerable number of Negroes' deployed in 1768 by Gabriel Manigault, who had purchased the Silk Hope estate and its mulberry trees in 1739 and was 'very active' in directing attempts at silk production.[242] Shelton's poem's narrator recounts that 'Once de old marster used to have us chilluns / picking cocoons from his Mulbery trees / and then we had to take 'em back / to the big house and unwind the little thangs / in de weave room. Some of the chilluns / got powerful tired of doing this work / so they and myself decided to do something / 'bout it.' They successfully cursed the silk in Missus Clem's lavish dress using a 'hoodooed' silkworm, and shortly after 'marster's old hag' departed for a social jaunt to Charleston wearing it, she mysteriously disappeared. The poem ends with her ghostly voice sounding in the mulberry trees, and the author reflecting: 'We aint picked / not narry one silk worm since.'[243]

The production of raw silk in South Carolina and Georgia had transformed plantation estates and townscapes, had influenced budgets and institutions, and prompted many planters and backcountry households to scrabble for ways to integrate the undertaking into their lives and seasonal cycles. It had helped justify or support the settlement of new populations and quirky specialists, and had sponsored new buildings, policies, and technologies. How colonists understood these opportunities, and how earnestly they engaged with them, varied enormously. Nonetheless, moriculture and sericulture constituted familiar pursuits across the Lower South during the period, notwithstanding the difficulties of aligning environment and labour, and the overpowering chorus of more competitive raw products that proved cultivable under plantation slavery. By persevering, settlers hardened imperial connections and networks, developed new forms of agricultural symbolism and patronage, generated new textile innovations, and – though only in small quantities – continued to produce a high quality of raw silk export which impressed metropolitan specialists. 'At some of our mills' concluded one writer in 1775, '[the silk] is preferred to any we receive either from the East Indies or Italy.'[244]

---

[242] Ben Marsh, 'Silk Hopes in Colonial South Carolina', *Journal of Southern History* 78, no. 4 (2012): 847–8; Ramsay, *History of South Carolina*, 1809, 2: 502. *SCG*, 10 August 1768.

[243] Sherman Shelton, 'Silk Hope', *Callaloo* 4 (1978): 36. Shelton was a graduate student in folklore at the University of North Carolina in the mid-1970s, and also published in *The First New England Anthology of Black Poetry and Photography* and *Hyperion*.

[244] An American, *American Husbandry*, 466; for Sheffield manufacturers using American silk, see Warner, *The Silk Industry*, 257–8. For other attestations of its worth, see: 'Correspondence of Henry Laurens', *South Carolina Historical and Genealogical Magazine* 31, no. 3 (1930): 213. Andrew Turnbull to Sir William Duncan, Charleston, 15 November 1766, Dundee City Archives.

7   New England

In this every poor man may engage, and if he fails of success, he has lost
nothing but a little attention to a curious subject, which will at least
enlarge his mind.

– Boston Evening-Post, 8 August 1768

Origins and Early Attitudes to Silk

There was a certain environmental logic to launching new attempts to
raise North American silk in British territories as they progressively
expanded southwards through degrees of latitude into warmer zones:
first Virginia, then South Carolina, Georgia, and later East Florida. But
as we have seen, the multiple, complex, and often hidden variables that
affected whether mulberries and silkworms could be successfully transplanted (or regularly produce raw silk) also acted as an incentive to
undertake trials in alternative locations. Because of silk's high profile
and value, because projectors did not have a clear sense of what caused
silkworms to work in one place rather than another, and because they
inhabited a world of commodity production in which boundaries were
constantly being broken and new crops or species domesticated, unlikely
people remained willing to try to raise raw silk in unlikely places. This
chapter demonstrates how an Atlantic region that differed greatly from
the Lower South in its origins, climatic characteristics, and demographic
make-up nonetheless embraced sericulture. Unlike the Lower South, silk
figured little in corporate or imperial plans for the political economy of
New England. Sericulture arrived late, was never really oriented towards
export, and grew out of the particular preoccupations of a small number
of local promoters. But by drawing on the region's distinctive organisation and networks, considerable progress was made in the plantation of
mulberries, and a foundation was laid that allowed New Englanders in the
late eighteenth century to engage with the larger mission (pushed by
Parliament, the Board of Trade, and the Premium Society) to convert
America into a silk-producing zone for British throwsters. Through

a compulsively well-documented case study of one particular household's pursuit of raw silk, we gain access into what Atlantic silk experimentation meant for the many thousands of families who undertook it at one stage or another across the Atlantic world, and the ways in which it affected their domestic spaces and routines. Lastly, although New England silk trials differed in so many respects from others, it was apparent that they nonetheless shared in common an overriding emphasis on the contribution of female labour – something that their more balanced demographics were better able to support than many outposts in the early South.

The Puritans who dominated the colonisation of much of New England for much of the seventeenth century did not, on the face of it, fit naturally with silken ambitions. Inspired by persecution in the Old World and the hope of creating a new model for godly society in the New, English Protestant communities had arrived since the 1620s and proceeded to spread, argue, and force their way across the region. Puritans' attitudes to silk captured some of the paradoxes of their situation as wilful exiles seeking to display their sociological credentials. John Winthrop, a Suffolk gentleman who led a large group of migrants to settle Boston, Massachusetts, and served several terms as governor, laid out a grand vision for the colony on the point of departure in 1630. Winthrop urged the colonists to 'be willing to abridge ourselves of our superfluities', reminding them of the priorities of mutual love and assistance in the challenges ahead, and of Matthew's gospel which warned that 'treasures upon earth ... are subject to the moth'. Even so, Winthrop, and many other Puritan ideologues, did not view wealthy dress as inherently evil or problematic – rather, as an expression of divine providence, and a legitimate accompaniment to status. If he wore anything like the clothes he was painted in for a portrait dated around the same time, Winthrop's audience would have well understood his first line, 'in all times some must be rich, some poor'. The portrait depicts him wearing a lavish black silk doublet and holding white silk gloves – designed to signal his wealth as much as his puritanism.[1]

Winthrop's 'City upon a Hill' sermon has become famous, a choice seasoning added to the speeches of American statesmen of all political leanings to add historical kudos to their claims. But the idea that 'the eyes of all people are upon us' carried more than metaphorical meaning to Puritan colonists when it came to their dress. As a trapping of wealth, and also a seductive superfluity – so visible, of course, in frowned-upon Catholic liturgy – silk's status and permissibility was under constant negotiation. As early as 1634, the General Court in Boston expressed its

[1] Francis J. Bremer, *John Winthrop: America's Forgotten Founding Father* (New York: Oxford University Press, 2003), 174.

disappointment at 'some newe & immodest fashions', including the wearing of overindulgent silk, and passed a sumptuary law prohibiting certain items and hairstyles.[2] The Court conferred with church elders from the townships in 1638 and asked them to warn congregations against 'costliness of apparel', but with little effect, perhaps because as Winthrop himself suspected, some of the elders' wives were culpable.[3] By 1651, the Massachusetts Bay General Court took more drastic action, reinforcing the sumptuary laws that used silk to mark out 'people of meane condition', and especially women of low rank who had the temerity to use silk to adorn sleeves, scarves, or hoods.[4] As the need for these laws suggests, the New England colonies from the outset constituted a market, albeit a slim one, for silk products from the Old World. Although woollens, worsteds, and linens dominated early New England cargoes, there was a regular if more modest influx of silk fabrics and especially decorative 'silke wares' arriving in the region, including hoods, ribbons, and bands.[5] Later sumptuary legislation gave rise to issues of enforcement and interpretation in the courts, as women of lower rank challenged rulings with their force of habit.[6] By the 1690s, when a brick-lined privy in Boston was filled in, archaeological excavation identified over a hundred fragments of discarded textiles preserved in marine clay, roughly a third of which were silk fabrics, a quarter silk ribbons or other decorative silk constructions, and another quarter silk yarns or mixed silk fabrics (the remainder being wool and cotton).[7]

---

[2] Nathaniel B. Shurtleff, ed., *Records of the Governor and Company of the Massachusetts Bay*, 5 vols. (Boston: W. White, 1853), 1: 126.

[3] John Winthrop's journal entry for 25 September 1638, in Perry Miller, *The American Puritans, Their Prose and Poetry* (New York: Columbia University Press, 1982), 40–1.

[4] Shurtleff, *Records of the Governor and Company*, 3: 243, 261.

[5] See for instance import records and poetic laments: Registry Dept Boston, *Records Relating to the Early History of Boston*, ed. W. H. Whitmore, W. S. Appleton, and E. W. McGlenen, 39 vols. (Boston: Rockwell & Churchill, 1909), 32: 395, 425–6. Governor William Bradford, 'Of Boston in New England', in Historical Society Massachusetts, *Collections of the Massachusetts Historical Society*, 90 vols. (Boston: Various, 1792), ser. 3, 7: 27–8. On Bradford's judgement on silk, Cotton Mather, *Magnalia Christi Americana* (London: Printed for T. Parkhurst, 1702), 72.

[6] Alice Morse Earle, *Two Centuries of Costume in America, 1620–1820*, 2 vols. (Rutland, VT: C. E. Tuttle Co., 1971); Laurel Thatcher Ulrich, 'Hannah Barnard's Cupboard: Female Property and Identity in Eighteenth-Century New England', in *Cultivating a Past: Essays on the History of Hadley, Massachusetts*, ed. Maria R. Miller (Amherst: University of Massachusetts Press, 2009), 154–90; Patricia Trautman, 'Dress in Seventeenth-Century Cambridge, Massachusetts: An Inventory-Based Reconstruction', in *Early American Probate Inventories*, ed. Peter Benes (Boston: Boston University Scholarly Publications, 1987), 51–71.

[7] Lauren J. Cook, 'Katherine Nanny, Alias Naylor: A Life in Puritan Boston', *Historical Archaeology* 32, no. 1 (1998): 15–19; Margaret T. Ordoñez and Linda Welters, 'Textiles from the Seventeenth-Century Privy at the Cross Street Back Lot Site', *Historical Archaeology* 32, no. 3 (1998): 81–90; Charles D. Cheek, 'Perspectives on the

Public resistance to the most flamboyant silk products remained robust throughout the seventeenth century, partly because religious associations stood firm behind the class-based prescriptions. Puritan ministers became renowned for their hard-hitting jeremiads in the final third of the seventeenth century – sermons and texts that lamented the corruption of New England society and exhorted audiences to reform their ways. One of the most influential, Samuel Danforth's 'Brief Recognition of New Englands Errand into the Wilderness' in 1671, was framed around the idea (again from Matthew) that 'Surely ye went not into the Wilderness to see a man clothed in silken and costly Apparel' and that New England 'was no fit place for silken and soft raiment', yet had become infested with 'Pride, Contention, Worldliness, Covetousness, Luxury'.[8] Others were quick to take up the theme, and the language of the jeremiad resurfaced in sumptuary legislation passed by Connecticut's General Court in 1676. Thenceforth, as in Massachusetts, wearers of silk ribbons, scarves, or trimmings stood in danger of a ten-shilling fine, unless they could prove their worth by estate value or by connection to a public officer in the colony.[9] And naturally, when the devil appeared to young New England women, he was expected to offer them money, ease from labour, worldly sights, and 'silkes'; his witch accomplices were identified at the Salem trials as wearing 'fine Cloaths in a Sad coloured Silk Mantel', and silk hoods.[10]

Samuel Sewall, a judge and businessman now remembered as a sort of moral barometer for puritanism thanks to his remorse about the Salem witch trials and published critique of slavery, captured the shifting ethical understandings of silk dress in his correspondence. Like other elites, he would commonly order silk goods, as he did for his wife Hannah in 1691 when he requested twenty ells of striped flowered silk. Two years later, he cancelled an order of silk he had placed with this factor (John Ive), stressing that 'one reason made me forbid sending [for] the Silk, out of a particular dislike I had to the wearing so much in this poor country'.

Archaeology of Colonial Boston: The Archaeology of the Central Artery/Tunnel Project, Boston, Massachusetts', *Historical Archaeology* 32, no. 3 (1998): 1–10.

[8] Samuel Danforth, *A Brief Recognition of New-Englands Errand into the Wilderness* (Cambridge, MA: Printed by S. G. and M. J., 1671), 3.

[9] J. H. Trumball and C. J. Hoadly, eds., *The Public Records of the Colony of Connecticut from 1636–1776*, 15 vols. (Hartford: Lockwood & Brainard, 1890), 2: 283.

[10] First quote from Samuel Willard's 'Account of the Strange case of Elizabeth Knapp of Groton', 2 November 1671, in Massachusetts, *Collections of MHS*, ser. 4, 8: 556. Witch-clothing silk references in Paul S. Boyer and Stephen Nissenbaum, *The Salem Witchcraft Papers: Verbatim Transcripts of the Legal Documents of the Salem Witchcraft Outbreak of 1692*, 3 vols. (New York: Da Capo Press, 1977), 2: 410, 3: 753; John M. Taylor, *The Witchcraft Delusion In Colonial Connecticut (1647–1697)* (New York: The Grafton Press, 1908), 111.

Sewall told Ive he wanted to purposely avoid pretending 'a Grandure far beyond my estate'. Yet the previous day, Sewall had written to his cousin Edward Hull, with an extensive textile order for his wife which included 15 lb weight of 'Cloth colour Silk' and sewing silk in multiple colours, along with 'a pattern of good strong colour Silk for a Jacket', 'a p[iec]e of Alamode' (glossy silk), and chequered galloon (expensive trimming)! In these two letters on successive days in 1693, Sewall marked out the point where public display of silk was winning the battle against any lingering private disquiet in New England. By the 1700s, Sewall was ordering at the most elaborate end of the market: flowered lustrings and damasks, with specified criteria – 'Let the flowers be of Herbs or Leaves; not of Animals, or artificial things.' Perhaps Sewall's misgivings lived on in his frequent preference for 'grave' colours, or the way his silk purchases were often the last call on his credit. But puritanism had never fully dominated Massachusetts and Connecticut society in the way its proponents hoped (or it is popularly imagined), let alone other colonies, and as a consequence first the consumption and then production of silk would become earnest economic pursuits in the eighteenth century.[11]

New England consumers began the eighteenth century as a marginal market, a north-west corner of the Atlantic into which silks were increasingly deposited – a bit like the Boston privy – in one way or another. But their appetites for these and other textiles would swiftly deepen and globalise, as the waning of Puritan strictures and development of maritime capacity coincided with the changing European fashions and upsurge in British silk manufacturing and Asian trade.[12] Some of the impetus came from the colonies, as when one Salem townsman encouraged his brother to migrate to Boston in 1699 and set up 'a wholesale trade of East India goods', promising a good market for 'silks for clothing and linings', albeit one whose prices were variable on account of eclectic supply.[13] From 1722, British merchants sought to incentivise colonial buyers by passing on the bounty on silk fabrics exported to the colonies, which amounted to six pence per pound, and applied to British-made silk stuffs in which at least two-thirds of the threads of the warp were silk (or enough to be apparent to the customs officer).[14] Governors complained

---

[11] Massachusetts, *Collections of MHS*, ser. 6, 1: 120, 137, 138. See also orders placed on pp. 152, 192, 299, 338 (quote on flowers and silk grass), 384 (quote on surplus); ser. 6, 2: 37.

[12] Jonathan Eacott, *Selling Empire: India in the Making of Britain and America, 1600–1830* (Chapel Hill: UNC Press, 2017).

[13] Letters from John Higginson to Nathaniel Higginson and to Matthew Collet [a linen-draper, Cornhill, London], 3 October 1699, Salem, in Massachusetts, *Collections of MHS*, ser. 3, 7: 209, 211.

[14] See for example, Rowland and Samuel Frye to Abraham Redwood, London, 3 March 1732, Massachusetts, ser. 7, 9: 26–7.

that 'we can't ascertain' what quantity of these silks arrived legitimately, though plenty of sources indicate that extensively smuggling occurred, allowing French products especially to filter through to New England communities.[15] By mid-century then, the quantity and quality of silk worn in the region remained an indispensable way of marking out elites, but increasingly silk goods tended to be distributed across the economic spectrum, and the once 'sad' colours such as russets, fawns, and olive greens had given way to livelier mixtures.[16]

Early Silk Cultivation, to 1760

Though never projected as a core economic ambition, silk production was certainly considered in New England and probably first attempted in the seventeenth century. John Winthrop Jr used silk to mark out his household's high status, like his father, and expressed a keen interest in turning natural science to a profit, largely but not exclusively through a lifetime pursuit of alchemy.[17] There is evidence to suggest this scion was amongst the first New Englanders to consider sericulture as a practicable way forward, perhaps alerted to the prospect of silk by the black mulberry tree his great-grandfather (Adam Winthrop) is supposed to have imported from Persia and planted in the late sixteenth century in their home village of Groton, or after his Mediterranean tour in 1628, which took in visits to Constantinople, Livorno, Pisa, Florence, and Venice. Just a year after he arrived in New England in 1631, Winthrop was offered 'bookes of the orderinge of silkwormes', by his friend Edward Howes, who had learned 'you have store of mulberie trees', and he evidently took up the offer.[18] In 1641 Robert Child (a Presbyterian pursuing several entrepreneurial projects in the New World) also corresponded with Winthrop Jr on the subject of silk production, announcing that he was planning a trip to the south of France to procure a 'vigneron, who can likewise manage silkewormes', and

---

[15] Gov. Talcott to Board of Trade, 9 September 1730, in Trumball and Hoadly, *The Public Records of the Colony of Connecticut from 1636–1776*, 7: 583. For episodes of silk smuggling, see testimonies in Boston, *Records Relating to Boston*, 8: 157; 17:40.

[16] Trautman, 'Dress in Seventeenth-Century Cambridge, Massachusetts: An Inventory-Based Reconstruction', 63; Margaret E. Newell, *From Dependency to Independence: Economic Revolution in Colonial New England* (Ithaca, NY: Cornell University Press, 1998), 94, 96. On the wider state of Atlantic textile consumption, Robert S. DuPlessis, *The Material Atlantic: Clothing, Commerce, and Colonization in the Atlantic World, 1650–1800* (Cambridge: Cambridge University Press, 2015).

[17] Inventory items at death of Martha in 1634 listed in Bremer, *John Winthrop*, 248.

[18] Edward Howes to John Winthrop Jr., 20 April and 1 November 1632, in Massachusetts, *Collections of MHS*, ser. 3, 9: 245; ser. 4, 6: 479. For the earliest reference to 'silk that grows in small cods', Sir Ferdinando Gorges to Earl of Salisbury, 1 December 1607, in Cecil Papers, CP 123/77.

intending when he returned to New England 'to try somewhat concerning silkewormes'.[19] Like Robert Child, Winthrop Jr was also frequently in communication with the influential intelligencer Samuel Hartlib, who sent him a 'great number of books and manuscripts' in 1660.[20] If these included any of his obsessive works on silk, then Hartlib, from his base in England, was linking Virginia silk experiments with enthusiasts in New England.[21]

Evidence of more persistent silkworm trials is apparent from around the 1730s, growing proportionately with the proliferation of silk goods. The most successful early attempts (see Map 4 for sites mentioned) were undertaken by Jonathan Law, of Milford, a prominent Connecticut judge and deputy governor of the colony when his family began experimenting in around 1731. By 1734, they had produced not only cocoons and raw silk, but had generated enough to twist silk yarn, weave fabric, and make what must have been a rudimentary waistcoat. Law sent a sample to neighbouring Massachusetts Governor Jonathan Belcher, who by virtue of his status and trading experience was a connoisseur of fine silks – often sending to London with very specific requests, which expanded with his wealth and waistline.[22] Belcher approved wholeheartedly of Law's silk sample, which, he wrote, 'I believe is the first produc'd in English America.' He requested a small cutting from a discreet part of the waistcoat 'that might not hurt it', and a report on the production of the silk which he promised to forward to imperial authorities. Law duly obliged, and Belcher received a piece of the silk and 'a very pleasing acc[oun]t of the progress of the matter from the egg to the completion by the weaver', which he sent on with a separate letter from Law and several specimens.[23] The Board of Trade, intently focused on the developing silk prospects in the Lower South, were

[19] Robert Child to John Winthrop, Jr, c.1641, in Massachusetts, ser. 5, 1:150. On Child's economic aims see Margaret E. Newell, 'Robert Child and the Entrepreneurial Vision: Economy and Ideology in Early New England', *The New England Quarterly* 68, no. 2 (1995): 223–56.

[20] Walter W. Woodward, *Prospero's America: John Winthrop, Jr., Alchemy, and the Creation of New England Culture, 1606–1676* (Chapel Hill: University of North Carolina Press, 2010), 32–3, 74.

[21] One publication claims that a fellow early Connecticut pioneer and governor (1676–83), William Leete, 'had a suit made for himself' from silk he had raised there, in Herbert Manchester, *The Story of Silk & Cheney Silks* (South Manchester, CT: Cheney Brothers, 1916), 33.

[22] Jonathan Belcher to Mr Tullit, Boston, 10 January 1733, in Massachusetts, *Collections of MHS*, ser. 6, 6: 254.

[23] Jonathan Belcher to Jonathan Law, Boston, 23 December 1734 and 12 March 1735, in Massachusetts, ser. 6, 7: 178, 192–3.

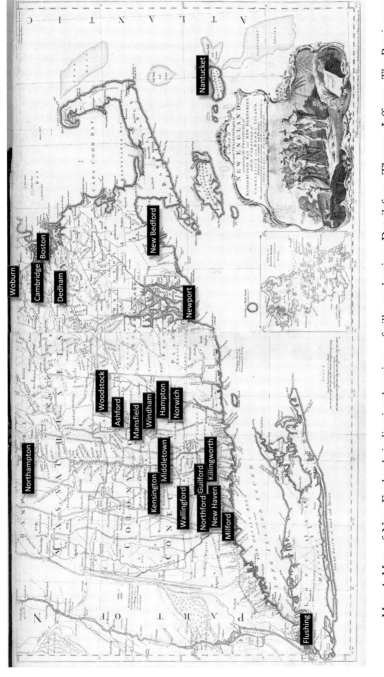

Map 4 Map of New England, indicating locations of silk production. Detail from Thomas Jefferys, *The Provinces of Massachusetts Bay and New Hampshire* (London: Sayer and Bennett, 1776). Image No. 0346018

intrigued by this package and its potential, coming as it did from an unexpected source and an unexpected region.[24]

Presumably in response to Law's pioneering efforts, by 1734, the Connecticut Assembly were sufficiently assured of silk's feasibility that they passed an act for the 'Encouragement of the raising of Silk in this Colony.' Under its terms, which lasted for ten years, the colony's public treasury offered bounties to compensate experimenters for the 'difficulty and charge' associated with establishing new products. Unlike other colonies which had tended to subsidise only early stages (such as the planting of mulberry trees or the yield of cocoons), the act attached a distinctive range of incentives to later production points. Connecticut silk raisers would be rewarded specified bounties for each ounce of 'good sewing silk', for each 'pair of silk stockings', and for each yard of woven mixed silk or 'well wrought' silks (the latter bringing nine shillings). County courts had to verify that the silks were '(bona fide) the growth and product of the silkworm bred and nourished in this Colony'.[25] Like Law's waistcoat, the novel shape of these conditions was an indication of the household manufacturing capacity already inherent in the New England colonies, which, while still overwhelmingly reliant upon Atlantic imports for their textiles, nonetheless contained a good number of wheels, looms, and labourers orientated towards domestic production. Some of the act's measures seemed to contravene the spirit, if not the letter, of the system of mercantilist rules set up by Britain, which usually sought to restrict colonial cloth production where it might compete with domestic exports.[26]

But as the parliamentary sponsorship of the contemporaneous settlement of Georgia shows, where commodity objectives promised long-term benefit (especially to the metropole), British imperialism at this point allowed for flexibility and innovation. Indeed, Law's active pursuit of British support for silk production while he was governor (1741–50) helped contribute directly to the parliamentary debates at the end of that decade, through the colony's agent Eliakim Palmer.[27] Law urged Palmer to impress upon the Board of Trade that he firmly backed an

[24] Board of Trade, *Journal of the Commissioners for Trade and Plantations*, ed. K. H. Ledward, 14 vols. (London: Public Record Office, 1920), 7: 61.
[25] Upon its expiration there were two efforts to revive the act, but there was apparently too much opposition in the Lower House. Trumball and Hoadly, *The Public Records of the Colony of Connecticut from 1636–1776*, 7: 494–5.
[26] For overviews: Claire Priest, 'Law and Commerce, 1580–1815', in *The Cambridge History of Law in America: Volume 1, Early America (1580–1815)*, ed. Michael Grossberg and Christopher Tomlins (Cambridge: Cambridge University Press, 2008), 400–46; DuPlessis, *The Material Atlantic: Clothing, Commerce, and Colonization in the Atlantic World, 1650–1800*.
[27] Albert C Bates, ed., *The Law Papers: Correspondence and Documents during Jonathan Law's Governorship of the Colony of Connecticut, 1741–1750*, 3 vols. (Hartford: Connecticut

Atlantic solution to the British demand for raw silk, and his voice and material proved important in diversifying the parliamentary view of the prospects of American silk – at a key point, as we have seen, in metropolitan debates about the global sourcing of the raw product. With adequate encouragement for American colonists, Law argued that 'there would be no necessity of ye Merchants sending up the Baltick and crossing thro Russia into the Caspian Sea for raw silk' (even as merchant Jonas Hanway was arriving back up the Volga from Astrakhan to St Petersburg, and would go on to publish a detailed account of the possibilities and pitfalls of the silk trade to the Caspian Sea in 1753). So when Parliament eventually passed its 1750 act encouraging American sericulture, Law interpreted it as a vindication of his efforts to prove productive capacity in all corners of the British Atlantic. He was sent a copy privately as soon as the act passed, though at the ripe old age of seventy-six, he would not last out the year.[28]

Law's pleasure at achieving 'that which I have labour'd Much', was combined with circumspection about whether Britain would uphold American interests, and he 'fear[ed] the Insufficiency of ye Encouragement to putt our peaple on an industrious Improvement'.[29] Investment in northerly colonies did not match the support extended to sericulture in the Lower South, meaning that in New England and later Pennsylvania, the support of silk would depend more upon internal networks than imperial backing. In contrast to the patronage of governors like William Berkeley (Virginia) and Nathaniel Johnson (South Carolina) in the late seventeenth century, or the elaborate state initiatives central to the pursuit of silk in the 1730s in Georgia and backcountry South Carolina, New England's silk advocates in the second half of the eighteenth century largely persisted through distinctive private networks that straddled religion, agriculture, education, and science. Energised by the growing integration of print culture, colonial correspondence, international academic associations, and commercial horticulture, New England silk experimenters were interested in contributing to the fund of transatlantic knowledge as well as generating profit for colony and empire. The availability of household labour and viable soils in parts of New England, where as Law put it, 'here is room for Mulbery Trees and the Climate agrees with black or white', meant that such intellectual patronage did

Historical Society, 1914), 1: xxx. Jonathan Law to Balston & Palmer, 11 July 1749, Milford, CT. 3: 322, 325 (received).

[28] Richard Partridge to Jonathan Law, 11 May 1750, London. Bates, *The Law Papers*, 3: 387, also 397 (formal confirmation from Whitehall).

[29] Jonathan Law to Richard Partridge, 25 June 1750 and 17 September 1750, Milford. Bates, *The Law Papers*, 3: 410, 414, 427.

indeed find supportive outlets in local production. 'Many of my neighbours have fallen in w[i]th it', explained Law in the 1740s.[30] In time, the
lighter dependency of these networks on the imperial state, and continuities in key personnel between 1770 and 1790, allowed New England silk
production to negotiate the American Revolution better than other areas.

Jonathan Law's fears about a scarcity of commitment to 'industrious
improvement' would have been substantially allayed had he lived to read
the published works of Jared Eliot, a Congregationalist minister of
Killingworth, Connecticut, as well as part-time physician, and agronomist
and farmer, who chose to devote one of his ground-breaking 'Essays on
Field Husbandry' to planting mulberries and growing silk in 1759. Eliot's
essays, begun in 1748, were amongst the first American publications on
agriculture, and his early pieces addressed issues such as land reclamation,
fertilisation, crop variation, technical improvement, and tillage. He was
preoccupied with marrying new scientific ideas and farming technologies
(including Jethro Tull's drill plough) to the particularities of the American
environment. This was an impulse that really only exploded in the early
nineteenth century in New England with the rise of agricultural journals
and associations, but by his sixth essay, Eliot was conscious that his 'small
tracts ... [for] a small circle of neighbours' had found their way to Britain
and were meeting with 'encouragement from abroad, and at home'. Eliot's
writing was delayed by the onset of the Seven Years' War, which dragged
thousands of New England militiamen away from their fields on campaigns
against New France. But the war also partly framed the content, for Eliot
described the planting of mulberry trees as a gendered imperial project that
would not diminish men's time and labour: 'the land we improve this way
will become more useful and profitable to ourselves, & posterity, and
render us more serviceable to our mother-country'.[31]

By the time of his sixth essay, Eliot's credentials had been enhanced by
his involvement with the Premium Society, and he was quick to cite their
encouragement of Connecticut silk in his opening pages. Both Jared Eliot
and Yale's intimidating president, Thomas Clap, had been nominated
as corresponding members of this London association, and were pre-
authorised to grant premiums of between one and three pence
per pound of cocoons (according to quality), as soon as a public filature
were established in Connecticut. The pair wrote together to the Premium
Society in 1760, informing them that 'a great Number' of households,
'some out of Curiosity, and some from a View of Advantage to themselves

[30] Jonathan Law to Eliakin Palmer, 27 January 1748, Bates, *The Law Papers*, 3: 192.
[31] Jared Eliot, *The Sixth Essay on Field-Husbandry, as It Is, or May Be Ordered in England* (New Haven: Printed by J. Parker, and Company, 1759), 3, 4.

and the Public', were procuring mulberry trees and preparing to pursue sericulture. Their letter emphasised again the growing links between consumption and production of silk in the northern colonies, for they stressed that 'much of the [New England-produced] silk is wanted here' rather than designed for Atlantic shipment. Their reports also demonstrated again that crude silk garments were being woven locally, and, judging by a 'rag o silk' which was enclosed with the letter, woven tightly:

it has been dyed or coloured twice, and worn in a gown twenty years as an holy day garment, is yet so strong that not one of many stout men who have tried with their utmost force have been able to tear it cross ways.

Eliot and Clap's letter to the Premium Society adopted a positive, careful tone in its broadly accurate predictions for New England sericulture, which highlighted some of the region's distinctive features. They noted that the climate was only adequate to raise one cohort of silkworms in a summer, but that this was viable, and that experience had overcome difficulties 'respecting hard Winter, late Frosts, Storms &c.' They anticipated that interest in silk might increase amongst farming populations once the profitable wartime boom in the provisions trade had dwindled, and explained that these farming households producing one or two pounds of silk would be happiest taking short-term payments on the spot rather than awaiting any 'further Premium for Exportation to England'. The model they proposed was for a Milford merchant, John Herpin, to buy up the household output of raw silk, and then have it shipped across the Atlantic (in some respects prefiguring the distributive role of pedlars in the antebellum period). Their letter also revealed some of the difficulties of pursuing improvement across colonial jurisdictions: both mentioned how little direct contact Connecticut had with Georgia, making it difficult to source supplies of silkworm eggs or filature technology – including reels 'more perfect than that which we have here'. Eliot was also frustrated because he was unable to compare local produce with 'old and new silk of other countrys', and therefore unable to definitively establish New England silk's relative strengths, but his publication bore out his promise to 'promote that manufacture to the utmost of my power'.[32] Clap and Eliot's exposition of the different climatic and productive environment in British America's northern colonies therefore called for novel adaptations to make silkworms work.

Eliot's sixth essay on field husbandry went well beyond repeating arguments previously rehearsed about the merits of silk for southward

[32] Letter from Thomas Clap and Jared Elliot to Mr. George Box, New Haven, 2 June 1760. PR.GE/110/9/13, Royal Society of Arts Archive.

colonies, though it retained a critical feature in common: an emphasis on female labour. Eliot offered specific insights based on local information and observation – people whom Eliot knew, or had observed – insisting that silk was not 'an empty, airy, and untry'd project', but rather a 'manufactory carried on for sundry years, and by a number of our people, in divers of our towns'. Above all, Eliot's discussion revealed that many of the pioneers were female rather than male: it was 'the family' of Captain Return Meigs in Middletown, Connecticut who had 'made silk many years' from the leaves of just two trees, or 'a woman of experience in this business' who had derived notable income. This chimed with several references to female labour that had been cloaked beneath Jonathan Law's macho swagger about his first coat and stockings made of New England silk in 1747 – such as the unnamed family member who had travelled with a silk reel to Cambridge (Massachusetts) where they 'taught Dr Wigglesworth['s] Lady to do that'. Little wonder that Eliot stressed that raising silk would not call off able-bodied men from war or husbandry, but rather mobilise 'women, children, cripples, and aged persons'.[33]

Eliot's essay put forward a number of recommendations for accelerating New England uptake of sericulture. Most urgently, Eliot pressed for the mass planting out of mulberry trees, recognising that only once this resource was established could silk production take off commercially in Connecticut. He proposed that this be accomplished either 'at the publick expence, or by agreement, each man planting a range as far as his lot extends', and that fathers should aim to give their daughters 'half an acre of land, covered with Mulberry trees', a distinctive proposition intended to link inheritance to the gendered labour pattern at the centre of his model. He explained both how to propagate mulberries and where to find good sources in the wild, such as Falkner Island in Long Island Sound, though he rather sat on the fence as to the relative merits of different species, noting 'it is a disputable point . . . [which] are the best for silk'. All the New England samples he had seen were apparently from silkworms nourished on wild mulberry leaves, about which Eliot put forward new theories – such as the idea they could 'get used to' having their leaves harvested. Influenced not by the quest to synchronise sericulture with plantation slavery but with the different cultural heritage of the northeast, Eliot closed the essay by commending the esoteric value of the

[33] Jonathan Law to Eliakin Palmer, 27 January 1748, Bates, *The Law Papers*, 3: 192. The reeling technique was presumably imparted to Rebecca, wife of Dr Edward Wigglesworth, a Harvard professor; they had apparently failed beforehand despite 'ten years Tryal'. See also information on the Law family's production in Eliot, *Sixth Essay on Field-Husbandry*.

mulberry: the evocative 'loneliness of a grove, the solemn shade, the soft murmer of the air' which conjured up the Garden of Eden, and divine approbation. He sought to enlighten and inspire New Englanders – so deeply sensible of their peripheral geographic place – about their global significance as consumers and potential silk producers.[34]

Silk Cultivation from 1760

Eliot's cry for mulberry trees did not fall on deaf ears. His work's authority and conviction provided intellectual gravitas, and others would pursue the matters of local logistical support and finding means to the ends he had outlined. In the decades from mid-century, one nurseryman in particular, Nathaniel Aspinwall, seems to have played a seminal role in distributing the white mulberries which silk raisers increasingly valued. Aspinwall's family were of long-standing Puritan stock and his ancestors had arrived with John Winthrop in the so-called 'Great Migration' of the 1630s. His branch had relocated westwards from Massachusetts to Connecticut, where his father Peter settled at Mansfield, a town incorporated in 1702, and where he married Rebecca Storrs.[35] Although he was born in 1740, we know little about Nathaniel's youth, but he acquired interests in a nursery on Long Island, and sometime after 1760 he set about transplanting white mulberries to areas where he found sufficient enthusiasm or investment.[36] Long Island was fast developing into a major centre for American horticulture: in the 1730s, Robert Prince and his son William set up a flourishing nursery business at Flushing Landing. There, they benefited from a fertile portside location, nearby Huguenot expertise, and connections to growers in Europe to create a considerable stock of fruit trees in grounds that would grow to 113 acres.[37] In 1771, when William Prince began publishing the country's first nursery catalogues,

---

[34] Eliot, *Sixth Essay.* Quotes on pp. 8, 12, 13, 19, 29, 30. For a broader context, see Christopher Grasso, 'The Experimental Philosophy of Farming: Jared Eliot and the Cultivation of Connecticut', *The William and Mary Quarterly*, 3rd Ser. 50, no. 3 (1993): 502–28.

[35] Algernon A. Aspinwall, *The Aspinwall Genealogy* (Rutland, VT: Tuttle Co., 1901), 27, 42–3.

[36] Aspinwall eventually owned his own extensive nursery on Long Island, which stood at Sands Point, near the Brooklyn Ferry. *New-York Journal, & Patriotic Register*, 9 April 1791, p. 109. On Aspinwall holdings, Jason D. Antos, *Flushing* (Charleston, SC: Arcadia Pub, 2010), 20.

[37] Claudia Gryvatz Copquin, *The Neighborhoods of Queens* (New York: Citizens Committee for New York City, 2007), 58; James R. Cothran, *Gardens and Historic Plants of the Antebellum South* (Columbia, SC: University of South Carolina Press, 2003), 290. For the population of the Trustees' Garden with white mulberry and other fruit trees, see Frances Moore, *A Voyage to Georgia* (1735).

amongst his initial listings were 'Large black English' and 'Black American' mulberries (probably *M. nigra* and *M. rubra*), and the pursuit of new varieties has left its mark on the land, for different species can still be found at Kissena Park and Flushing Meadows.[38] The more immediate upshot for New England sericulture was that Aspinwall cultivated significant stocks of mulberries at his hometown Mansfield and at his subsequent place of residence in New Haven, and later major plantations in New Jersey and Pennsylvania (discussed below).[39]

In 1783, Aspinwall advertised a 'nursery of many thousands' of mulberry trees in New Haven 'in good order', by which time he claimed that 'experience abundantly shows' that silk was a profitable pursuit in Connecticut. He timed his advert in the spring, as he would in subsequent years in the *Connecticut Journal*, with 'the season for transplanting' and was evidently receiving advance orders in 1784 and beyond.[40] More details of Aspinwall's activities were imparted in an article on silk in the *New-Haven Gazette* in 1785, which described 'a very large nursery of fifty thousand trees in New-Haven', priced at threepence apiece, and another in Kensington, some thirty miles up the Quinnipiac River. In years to come, Aspinwall sought to use his success in Connecticut as a launch pad for sales elsewhere.

Aspinwall's efforts represented perhaps a commercial vanguard for moriculture, but was by no means the only source of transplantation and propagation in New England – Jared Eliot was right about how easily the trees would grow. In July 1765, a rural Massachusetts farmer under the pseudonym 'Americus' instructed the 'good People of Boston' how to strip their mulberries of seeds in July 1765, confident after his own 'Trial at raising of Silkworms' that the trees would flourish.[41] The next year another writer, naming themselves 'Morus', conversely called on 'all our country gentlemen' to plant out their farms, promising a few years' efforts would allow Massachusetts 'to produce such quantities of Raw Silk, as

---

[38] *The New-York Journal; or, The General Advertiser*, 10 March 1774, p. 3. The trees were also offered in the *New-York Gazette, and Weekly Mercury*, 18 April 1774, supplement. Prince listed 'Large black English', 'Black American mulberry', and 'White mulberry' in subsequent listings, including, e.g. *New-York Gazette, and Weekly Mercury*, 10 October 1774, p. 2, and his broadside advertisement of 1790 which valued them at one-and-a-half shillings each. 'To be sold, by William Prince, at Flushing-Landing ...' broadsides for the nursery (New York: H. Gaine, 1771 and 1790), Hunt Institute Library (EL5 P9553L 771 and 771(2)).

[39] Aspinwall, *The Aspinwall Genealogy*, 57. Aspinwall's younger brother, Abel (1746–1807) seems also to have been involved in moriculture. Aspinwall, *Aspinwall Genealogy*, 60. See also outline of chronology of moriculture in *New-London Gazette, And General Advertiser*, 9 May 1832, p. 2.

[40] New Haven *Connecticut Journal*, 3 April 1783. Aspinwall did not specify what variety. Ibid., 5 May 1784; 27 April 1785. The 1785 advertisement mentioned trees 'of Four Year's growth', suggesting the nursery did not date back much before 1780.

[41] Boston *Massachusetts Gazette*, 8 August 1765, p. 2.

would more than pay for all the manufactured Silk used among us'.[42] In other New England papers, growing interest in silk raising was also apparent, as when the editor of the *New London Gazette* (Connecticut) acceded to a subscriber's request to reprint several paragraphs from John Locke's newly resurfaced notes on silk culture in France, even though these dated back to the late seventeenth century.[43] Reports affirmed that 'a very considerable quantity of Silk [was] made' in Massachusetts in 1768, and explained how silk raisers who lacked adequate space in their households had improved their barns to house the worms, for New England barns had space and disposable labour in the spring, whereas planters in the Lower South often faced clashes with the labour demands of other staple crops.[44] By the late 1760s, thousands of cocoons were being sold in Boston, where there was 'a ready market . . . for the pods or balls as the worm left them' and a handful of people 'that understand the true method of winding the balls'.[45]

New England silk encouragement took advantage of the competitive, crowded, market-oriented dynamics of the region, linking its mercantile and congregational heritage. A Boston merchant named William Whitwell put forward a particularly quirky scheme in August 1768. Whitwell notified the town Selectmen (administrative officers) of his intention to pass on anonymously 'One hundred Dollars or Thirty Pounds lawful Money' to whomever raised the greatest number of mulberry trees from seed over the course of the next three years. In due course, the money was handed over to John Hancock (one of the Selectmen) and an advert subsequently placed in Benjamin Edes and John Gill's *Boston Gazette and Country Journal*. The results were confirmed in April 1772, when the Selectmen duly paid Loammi Baldwin (of Woburn – a cabinetmaker and later engineer) forty dollars for the greatest number of mulberries, and proportionally smaller sums to Rev. Jason Haven (Dedham), John Hay (Woburn), and George Spriggs (Boston) – the latter a fledgling nurseryman who, like Aspinwall, would later seek financial advantage out of the communal thirst for moriculture.[46] The

---

[42] *Boston Gazette*, 21 July 1766, supplement p. 2.

[43] The contributor was confident that 'it's probable there's no one Thing we can enter into with so little Expence, or a greater Prospect of immediate Gain', *New-London Gazette*, 1 April 1768, p. 1.

[44] *Boston Evening-Post*, 8 August 1768, p. 2.

[45] *Boston Evening-Post*, 17 July 1769, p. 2. 'On the Manufacture of Silk', in Nathaniel Ames, *An Astronomical Diary, or, Almanack for the Year of Our Lord Christ 1769* (Boston: Richard Draper, Edes & Gill, and T. & J. Fleet, 1768). Reprinted in Boston *Independent Chronicle*, 9 February 1792, p. 2.

[46] *Boston Gazette and Country Journal*, 16 September 1771, p. 2. On Spriggs and Hancock's mulberries, Marshall Pinckney Wilder, *The Horticulture of Boston and Vicinity* (Tolman & White, 1881), 10.

Boston competition obligated the winners to sell to their fellow New Englanders at least ten of their mulberry trees, at a price fixed of threepence. But the scheme was as much a symptom as a cause of wider uptake: its adjudicators (who recorded over 19,000 trees even before the final tally) warned that many thousands of other trees had been planted lately that were not old enough to be eligible. Jared Eliot, long since resting, presumably six feet under some idyllic grove, was the source recommended to readers in the final newspaper notice.[47] Perhaps as a result of the competition, good fresh 'Mulberry seeds to be given away' were offered in all the Boston newspapers in the spring of 1771.[48] The competition served as an illustration of the distinctive ways in which raw silk was taken up in the north-east – less choreographed by the state and more attentive to print culture, township networks, commercial horticulture, and the high hopes and expectations of industrious farmers and neighbours who sought to maximise on the acreage, buildings, and labour, especially family labour, within their purview.

The Silkworms of Ezra Stiles

If Jared Eliot was a sort of patron saint of New England mulberry trees, one might say that his counterpart and acquaintance Ezra Stiles was the same to New England silkworms. Though over forty years Eliot's junior, Stiles was also a polymath, an open-minded reverend, and a man of extraordinary learning and breadth of interests. He went on to become a reformist President of Yale between 1778 and 1795, having spent a long time at the same institution (then under Thomas Clap) in the 1740s and 1750s as a student and then tutor. In his own life trajectory and his later presidency, he epitomised the spirit of the eighteenth-century Enlightenment. He was profoundly motivated by rationalism and a desire for self-improvement, in the process becoming a node for Atlantic networks of theologians, astronomers, natural philosophers, linguists, scientists, physicians, and many others. He was constantly hunting for opportunities to accrue information, test theories experimentally, share knowledge, and to refine his immediate, institutional, regional, or national communities.[49] But few of Stiles's many

---

[47] Boston, *Records Relating to Boston*, 20: 306 (initial offer); 23: 102 (ad placed), 112 (money transferred), 118 (payments), 121 (copy of notice), 127 (list of applicants). Advertisement, instructions for applying, and prizewinner listings can be found in: *The Boston Gazette and Country Journal*, 16 December 1771, p. 2; *The Massachusetts Gazette Extraordinary*, 9 April 1772, p. 2.

[48] Boston *Massachusetts Spy*, 2 May 1771, p. 35; *Boston Evening-Post*, 6 May 1771, p. 3; *Boston Post Boy*, 6 May 1771, p. 2.

[49] Edmund S. Morgan, *The Gentle Puritan: A Life of Ezra Stiles, 1727–1795* (New Haven: Yale University Press, 1962).

preoccupations demonstrated this quite so well as his pursuit of New England sericulture, which lasted for over thirty years. He was convinced that 'one man might bring it to perfection', and met in different ways with failures and successes, both of which he deemed equally progressive (according to the scientific method). It was typical of him that when he inadvertently trod on two of his silkworms, his response was to record in his notebook, '[t]hus some Allowance must be made for unavoidable Accidents'.[50] The notebook itself, begun in 1763, and running to over 387 pages under the title 'Observations on Silk Worms and the Culture of Silk', is a curious entity, really a mishmash of several distinct components: at times a diary, an encyclopaedia, a work of science, a business proposal, a maths exercise, and a cultural commentary. Stiles could not help himself when it came to measuring things, and little escaped his purview: caterpillars, temperatures, cocoons, leaves, times, silkworm litter, tree trunks, attendants, and pieces of fabric were all subjected to intensive observational scrutiny in the notebook's pages. If all this was not enough to feel a degree of pity for his wife and family, to make matters worse, they ended up doing much of the work themselves.

But for all its obsessive minutiae, and its particularities as the testimony of an exceptional figure, Stiles's journal is important for two principal reasons: it sheds considerable light on sericultural activities and networks during this period of widening uptake in New England (c.1760–90), and it offers us a grasp of the sorts of commonplace uncertainties, improvisations, theorisings, and adaptations that affected silkworm experimenters in their everyday lives. In looking through this window into the Stiles family and their efforts to try to secure, feed, support, kill, and process the domesticated insects with whom they cohabited each summer for many years, we can begin to imagine the emotional and pragmatic scale of the experience of experimenting with silkworms – experiences which were replicated across thousands of Atlantic households in thousands of permutations, each bringing different measures of expectation, hope, satisfaction, pride, fear, frustration, and disappointment.

Stiles was convinced, when he began with a few thousand silkworm eggs in 1763 in Newport, Rhode Island, that he could demonstrate the viability of New England raw silk production as a profitable household activity. He tabulated his experiments over ten years, in the most extraordinary detail, as he put to the test theories from China and Italy, collected local samples and insights, and corresponded with experts from all corners of the British Atlantic. Each finding led Stiles to render

---

[50] Ezra Stiles, 'Journal of Silkworms', Miscellaneous Volumes & Papers #318, Ezra Stiles Papers, Beinecke Library, Yale University, 1792, 85.

new estimates about the potential worth of the pursuit and its materials, to compare information about raw silk in Persia, Spain, Naples, and further afield. Even after his move to New Haven in 1778 and the end of his own experimentation, Stiles continued to push sericulture and meticulously add to the notebook – scrawling on its rear cover that in 1792 'I sent 4,000 Silk Worms Eggs to the Revd. W. Etwein at Bethlehem in Pennsylvania.'[51] Stiles was evidently proud of his achievements, which culminated in a symbolic piece of fabric, and intended from the start for his patronage of silk to rank amongst his most notable legacies. In 1762, the year his fourth child was born, he wrote a patriarchal 'Family Constitution' intended to bond the Stiles generations together in perpetuity. Amongst the nine commandments proposed for his progeny were 'Be religious and virtuous', 'Remember the Obelisque [an elaborate memorial erected to himself as the founding father]', and 'Plant each 100 Mulberry Trees'.[52] Although he began his notebook with a series of biblical references (in Hebrew – another of his interests), intended to establish a kind of sacred provenance to silk culture, faith itself played little role in Stiles's experiments, which quickly got down to earth.

Stiles's first harvest was the collation of information about mulberries – measuring tree trunks, height, foliage, and estimated ages – and drawing from printed sources, the local landscape, and word of mouth. Stiles planted out some 320 miniature mulberries in his garden near the Meeting House at Newport in the spring of 1763, all taken from slips and cuttings from three mulberries he had originally set out in April 1758, and he was soon busily monitoring their girth. He laboriously sketched these plantings in a quirky plan of his garden, and the next year interspersed the slips with plum-tree cuttings intended 'to keep off the sun's force'; he also tried 'inoculat[ing]' mulberry buds into other fruit trees with no effect. In the first of hundreds of references to a host of patient and obliging neighbours, Stiles recorded that he had also planted twenty of his slips on the land of William Ellery (later a signer of the Declaration of Independence) to see how they fared. Stiles drew from first-hand experience, as when Jonathan Todd of East Guilford, Connecticut, explained that his 20,000 worms had been given 'dropsy' (an excessive build-up of fluid) in 1762 by being switched to 'Forest Mulberry Leaves' which were 'more rank & not so sweet as those in the sun'. Newport merchant John Banister informed him that trees imported to the northern colonies from Virginia seemed to experience 'Seasoning' whereby

[51] Stiles, 'Journal of Silkworms', 389.
[52] Harold E. Selesky, ed., *A Guide to the Microfilm Edition of the Ezra Stiles Papers at Yale University* (New Haven, CT: Yale University Library, 1978), xv.

a certain proportion perished. Stiles also read trade literature such as Jean-Baptiste Du Halde's 1736 compilation of seventeen Jesuit missionaries' reports about the history and culture of China, which informed Stiles that the Chinese 'sow mulberry seed' and prefer soil to be 'newly broken up'. He also made inferences from the works of American explorers, concluding correctly that 'Mulberries are natural & original to the Country, & not bro[ugh]t from Europe' on the basis of his reading of French travel literature.[53]

In 1764, Ezra Stiles pre-empted the better-known Johnny Appleseed of yore – actually Jonathan Chapman – who began planting apple trees in the Old Northwest from the 1790s. Beginning with a 'journey into Connecticut', Stiles yomped across New England, distributing 10,850 mulberry seeds. Like Chapman, he was also partly in it for himself, for each recipient of Stiles's seeds undertook to return to him a quota of the trees that came up – sometimes as many as half of those they were given, which ranged from 130 seeds deposited with Amos Potter to the 2,000 taken by Helena Talcott Dorr. Perhaps counter-intuitively, Reverend Stiles's seed-spreading project was in some ways more secular than Johnny Chapman's, who would take every opportunity to impart his Swedenborgian beliefs to those he encountered. Like a growing number of intellectuals in the late eighteenth century, Stiles's was a deistic Christianity, attributing something of a distant influence to the Almighty in matters outside faith, having given humankind the gift and tool of reason. It was fitting that his Latin Vulgate was home to 3,218 silkworm eggs in 1767. Stiles's Congregationalism was of a much more tolerant disposition than that of his seventeenth-century Puritan forebears, and he tried to evade the bitter divisions which arrived with evangelical revivalism from the 1730s. But the persistent strength and vitality of religious networks across New England proved to be a real engine that Stiles used to drive sericulture forward. His first distribution of mulberry seed, as with his later and grander plans, depended on the affinity of fellow clergymen and the social capital of New England Protestantism with its distinctive organisational and geographic reach: a high proportion of the recipients were church ministers.[54]

---

[53] Stiles, 'Journal of Silkworms', 1–12; quotes on 1, 6, 8, 17.

[54] On debunking Chapman, see Howard Means, *Johnny Appleseed: The Man, the Myth, the American Story* (New York: Simon & Schuster, 2011). Stiles deposited mulberry seeds at Niantic, Killingworth, North Haven, New Haven, Cornwall, Hartford, Mortlake, Pomfret, Woodstock, Bristol, and Narragansett, as well as 1,700 seeds in 1765 in Rhode Island (Portsmouth and South Kingstown) and Charleston, MA. Stiles, 'Journal of Silkworms', 15–17 (seed spreading), 266 (Bible in which eggs were stored).

Stiles's willingness to travel was a frequent feature of his attempts to raise silkworms. He travelled three days (some eighty miles) to bring his first Connecticut eggs home to Newport on 12 May 1763. Initially enclosed in papers in his saddlebags, he tried to keep the 4,700 eggs cool by wrapping them in linen and storing them 'tho' not in a cellar yet out of way of heat' until he was ready to expose them at the start of June. He separated them into two large groups according to their day of hatching, and began to supply them with mulberry leaves, putting extra coals in his chimney because he planned to emulate the Italian method, which required intervention to ensure an even heat. The two windows in the worms' chamber were hung with blue calico curtains, to allow only restrained light, and Stiles maintains he 'chose to disturb them as little as possible' though his incessant measuring and weighing and his attempts to sex them and discover their physiognomy somewhat belied this claim. With the silkworms hatched, then began the work of locating adequate supplies of leaves as the worms fed and grew. Over the course of June Stiles scoured the countryside, gathering leaves from mulberries owned by the Nichols, the Sissons, the Rodmans, the Kings, and Francis Malbone – some of which involved six- or seven-mile rides. The leaves were brought home and 'sprinkled' – after having been counted and measured, and the time and temperature of the feeds recorded.[55]

Two weeks into his project, Stiles was struggling. His charges' escalating demand for mulberry leaves coincided with a wet spell and a Sunday, during which he had professional responsibilities ministering at the Meeting House. 'They eat so voraciously as to devour all before them', he complained, and having left them all the leaves which he hoped would 'hold them eating till we have done meeting this Afternoon', Stiles was out that evening picking fresh leaves from the Rodmans' trees. Worried about the leaves being rank or wilted because wet, Stiles tried to dry them 'between linnen cloth' and the next day experimented with other methods of drying using linen and a bottle. A tone of concern, occasionally bordering panic, characterises this section of the notebook, as Stiles fought to feed, clean ('withdrawing the moss and dung'), and protect the silkworms – having to move them as they grew. He also seemed frustrated by his inability to find order and logic, to find *reason*, in the caterpillars' evolution and behaviours. Like the silkworms, he fretted about, opening and closing chamber doors, worrying about the smell of cedar and impact of thunder, never sure whether his eclectic diet of varied tree leaves would cause instant reactions or lingering 'diminishment'. The sheer number of variables left Stiles uncharacteristically murmuring that 'I

---

[55] Stiles, 'Journal of Silkworms', 25–41, quotes on 25, 26, 41, 28.

don't apprehend', 'I can't tell', 'I don't perceive.' Gone were the halcyon times of early June when the tiny creatures seemed consistent, and he could declare '[t]his has been a good day for the worms'. By 18 June, Stiles was feeding into the night ('keeping the Candle at a distance'), his notebook's pagination had gone awry, and, heaven forfend, he was 'too busily employed to admit leisure for counting them'.[56]

Whether linked or not, the crisis of late June coincided with the first clear indication that Ezra Stiles was not tending the silkworms alone. During a 'terrible day to the Worms' who seemed to sicken and stultify, Stiles recorded that 'My Wife & self spent three hours ... in cleaning[,] removing[,] & nursing.' The notebook hereafter showed him to be heavily reliant upon his spouse Elizabeth and those within his household in sustaining efforts at silk production. Elizabeth's growing input is reflected in Ezra's increasing use over the years of the plural personal pronoun, as well as more explicit descriptors: 'My wife says she was four hours yesterday forenoon cleaning & feeding the worms: & an hour & half towards evening. She had breakfasted them the morning of 25th before I got up, & joined the numerations of the leaves to the preceding accounts.'[57] Her significance was also suggestion by omission: Ezra's record of domestic trials ended around the same time as Elizabeth's early death in Newport in 1775. Elizabeth gave birth to six children during the years of their silkworm experiments, and the notebook shows that their labour too was frequently mobilised. 'Miss Emilia' spent an hour 'Cleaning, Feeding & Tending' one July, and on another occasion we are told 'Kezia being sick did not attend much to the Worms'. Ezra mobilised the children especially when preoccupied with other concerns, such the transit of Venus in 1769.[58] He evidently sent his older daughters traipsing around New England in search of both mulberry leaves and silkworm seed, and another source narrates how two of them had collapsed trying to reach the house of his fellow Congregational clergyman and silk cultivator, Rev. Dr John Foote of Northford, Connecticut, and had to be rescued by two men on horseback.[59]

---

[56] Stiles, 'Journal of Silkworms', 42–7, quotes on 42, 39, 43, 34, 45, 31. Finding time on Sundays was a perennial problem for Stiles, who even when he laid aside a large volume of leaves in a subsequent year was horrified to discover they had begun to compost and were not usable. Stiles, 'Journal of Silkworms', 270.

[57] Stiles, 'Journal of Silkworms', 62. For other examples of her playing a major role, see 68, 80, 83, 86, 88.

[58] Stiles, 'Journal of Silkworms', 95, 244, 280.

[59] Historical Society New Haven Colony, *Papers of the New Haven Colony Historical Society* (New Haven: Printed for the Society, 1877), 2: 56. These examples disprove Edmund Morgan's claim that 'there is no evidence that any of the Stiles children were enlisted in their father's attempt'. Morgan, *The Gentle Puritan*, 151.

Besides his wife and children, the notebook reveals that Ezra Stiles also deployed an enslaved youth named Newport in silkworm-related activities from the outset. Newport had been ten years old when he was gifted to Ezra Stiles as a private venture in 1756; such enslaved arrivals were then a common sideline to the extensive Atlantic activities of Rhode Island merchants heavily involved in the African slave trade. Newport was dispatched to gather mulberry leaves from nearby estates in 1763, as when 'Newport says all he has bro[ugh]t from Col. Malbone's he pick[e]d from but one tree.' By early July he was collecting as much as five bushels a day, including leaves from the lands of the erstwhile governor of Rhode Island, Samuel Ward. He was also employed in drying wet leaves in linen to make them more palatable to the worms, though it is unclear whether Newport was directly involved in feeding and cleaning.[60] The drop in Stiles's references to his own leaf-collecting likely reflects that this key role was tasked to Newport from 1764.

Stiles's notebook provides some clues as to how awkward it could be to fit tending silkworms into typical colonial routines and lifestyles. The caterpillars were vulnerable to neglect, on account of local events – as when Ezra was 'called off on Account of the melancholy event' of the drowning of young Benjamin Searing in 1764. As the literature made clear, the caterpillars were indeed highly sensitive: one batch expired because the brown paper they were crawling upon had been in contact with ferrous sulphate (from its previous use covering woollen hats dyed using the mordant). Stiles had to be watchful of predatory insects such as spiders, whom he 'demolished', and flies, which began 'to be troublesome' from early July. One evening in 1765 'a Cat devoured the Papilios, & uncocooned Worms, & made a terrible Ravage & confusion, & put an End to this Harvest'. Even when Stiles wanted to kill the pupae himself (to prevent them breaking the cocoons), there were awkward matters of timing and technique. On 15 July 1763, he waited a quarter of an hour after his wife took her bread out of their oven at around 6.30 p.m., before shoving in 640 of his precious cocoons, laid out on three sieves. There followed an anxious wait until 8.10 p.m., when Stiles removed them, and, uncertain if the deed had been done, covered them with a double woollen baize gown 'to complete the Death of the Chrysalis by Suffocation if any should survive the heat'. Stiles opened a single cocoon and, to his relief, found the chrysalis dead. Even so, the larger and double cocoons ('doubions') he left 'because [I] intend the Precaution of exposing them to the heat of the sun'. Perhaps disenchanted with the bread oven, a second load were effectively boiled,

---

[60] Stiles, 'Journal of Silkworms', 58, 84, 85, 92.

while a final batch of 300 were soaked in soaped water for 48 hours and turned out to be the best.[61]

Stiles's notebook details the kind of improvisation and adaptation that was common amongst colonial silk raisers, who rarely had adequate technology, time, or guidance to help them through complicated problems, the most intricate of which was reeling off the silk from the cocoons. 'Not having a Filature of Italian Construction', wrote Stiles, '[we] reeled off on a common reel, the thread being brought from the vessel of hot water over a brass hook to the Reel.' With his wife, then around eight months pregnant, managing the unfurling and attaching together of cocoon filaments, Stiles guided the combined thread from the hook onto the reel, where the motion wrapped it into a rudimentary hank. Stiles ensured that the thread zigzagged or spiralled 'by hand, vibrating the thread in reeling', presumably so that the sericin had a chance to aerate slightly and prevent it sticking together in layers. This was his way of creating the lateral motion that contemporary filature technology incorporated using cogs or a lever attached to the reel. Once they had developed some degree of proficiency, he reported that on 20 July they produced a skein of 43 knots' length (over 3,400 yards) in five hours – comprised of 125 cocoons reeled in the morning and another 118 in the afternoon, and with the thread consisting of between 15 and 25 cocoons. He estimated that this was around a quarter of the speed of Italian experts, and with 25 per cent more waste.[62]

One of the most endearing features of Stiles's remarkable notebook, probably common to many novices, is that he could not resist the temptation to anthropomorphise the silkworms. This began with referring to the caterpillars' birthdays, and then found particular expression in his describing of their behavioural tendencies – the silkworms 'lounge[d] about' or 'gradually clothed' themselves. Sometimes the comparisons were more overt, as when he compared them to newborn infants, or described them as like a large company of sleeping children, 'emotions here & there, some half awake, some starting with dream, some quite awake & stretching & yawning, & some p[er]haps crawling up, & all alternately dropping into Repose'.[63] To political economists the silkworms may have been capital, but in the context of bedrooms, stables, hallways and attics where they were invested with time and attention, it was easy for them to metamorphose into objects of familiarity, into domestic pets, and quasi-children.

[61] Stiles, 'Journal of Silkworms', 192, 100, 250, 113–14, 122.
[62] Stiles, 'Journal of Silkworms', 116, 121, 122, 123. Stiles's measurements of length were explained the previous page: 1 'Run' = 1,600 yards = 4,800 feet = 20 'knots'.
[63] Stiles, 'Journal of Silkworms', 33, 34, 49, 76.

Eventually, Stiles reached the point of naming individual silkworms, and the names he chose in themselves are revealing. The first was named 'General Wolfe', after James Wolfe, who had won a famous victory at Quebec in 1759 and was celebrated in New England as the conqueror of Canada. Stiles named another caterpillar (a 'Companion' of Wolfe's) after Oliver Cromwell, also a military man, whose reputation was undergoing an American rehabilitation in the 1760s as a scourge of ineffective parliaments and monarchical despotism. The caterpillar Cromwell (see Plate 12) seems to have been less energetic than his namesake, with Stiles recording how he was 'very sluggish' and that 'Oliver spent all day in mounting about and fluing in different places, so that I despaired of his doing any Thing, expecting him a naked Chrysalis.' Later silkworms were appropriately named after prominent figures in Chinese history, including Fohi (Fu Xi, a founding patriarch whom Puritans equated with the biblical Noah), Yao (a legendarily wise emperor), and Confucius ('One clever fat fellow').[64]

Stiles found the silk moths, which he had allowed to hatch to seed future generations, at least as suitable as the caterpillars for anthropomorphising. After 'they rushed into Embraces with Fury', he ended up with an estimated 15,000 eggs, which he stored in spare folio paper or discarded snuff bottles (presumably well washed out). He closely scrutinised their copulation, noting that his American moths seemed to have two or three more days of stamina than mentioned in his eclectic guidebooks. In 1767, when there was an imbalance of male and female moths preserved for breeding, he observed that '15 or 16 furious fellows had no wives this morning & raged about, till I found <u>one couple of males in actual sodomy</u>', and went on to separate them 'by themselves into another Chamber' where they remained, apparently inseparable, for a further ten days before he 'observed the Sodomites dead'.[65] In such responses, colonists showed how the short life cycle and the mystique of the silkworms were used to revisit and refine their own assumptions about nature, sexuality, and behaviour.

Stiles took guidance from a number of writers on silk, and eagerly put a range of their theories and claims to the test. Amongst the most important authorities he used was the detailed account of a Mr Zachary, very

---

[64] Stiles, 'Journal of Silkworms', 82, 85, 88, 89, 91, 92, 93, 95, 127. On Cromwell's reputation in the colonies, see Francis J. Bremer, 'Cromwell's Ghost: The Legacy of England's Puritan Revolution in New England', in *Cromwell's Legacy*, ed. Jane A. Mills (Manchester: Manchester University Press, 2012); Brendan McConville, *The King's Three Faces: The Rise and Fall of Royal America, 1688–1776* (Chapel Hill: University of North Carolina Press, 2006), 270.

[65] Stiles, 'Journal of Silkworms', 141, 142, 145, 266–8.

likely the eminent raw silk merchant John Zachary of Cheapside, London, mentioned by the Georgia authorities in 1739.[66] Stiles followed Zachary's typologies of cocoons – which described nine kinds of varying quality and characteristics – and tried as best he could to emulate Zachary's recommendations in relation to baking and reeling the cocoons. On 9 July 1767, at Zachary's recommendation, Stiles or his wife made a bizarre omelette, consisting of eggs with onions fried in rank hogs' lard. He wafted the sizzling pan around the chamber in a bid to revive those silkworms who seemed unable to form cocoons, which perked them up but not to the point of 'recover[ing] them in spinning . . . [we] find no great effect'. Stiles hypothesised that long periods of rain soured the taste of mulberry leaves, offering support for a notion propounded by Zachary. Stiles was also closely attuned to what might be distinctive about the American environment. He was delighted to find his silkworms tended to exceed the dimensions of Italian and Persian counterparts mentioned by other writers, boasting 'as the old saying has it, an Inch in a man's nose is something', and also that his first crop constructed their cocoons 'at least two or three days sooner than in Italy'.[67]

Besides Zachary on Italian methods, Stiles also used Noël-Antoine Pluche's popular work of natural history, *Spectacle de la Nature* (first published 1732) as a source on French practices, specifically the third 'Dialogue' in the section on insects, which involved an exchange between a countess, a prior, and a knight in relation to silkworms, during which the countess explains their life cycle at length.[68] In consulting Du Halde on China and Jonas Hanway on Persia, Stiles found information about the major silk-producing regions of Asia, and by triangulating all these sources he was able to compare them and, from time to time, locate and dismiss exaggerations. For instance, while Stiles accepted that Chinese reeling must be dramatically superior, he rightly doubted the claim in Du Halde that they could produce ten pounds of raw silk from thirty pounds of cocoons. Noting that Du Halde's material was taken from a Ming dynasty author, Stiles carefully drew a map of China with prominent silk-producing regions marked up, such as HuQuang (now Hunan, noted as

---

[66] Zachary's could well have been the manuscript translation of Italian sources sent by merchants Hare and Skinner to John Morgan of Philadelphia in 1774–5. Stiles mentions that Zachary 'resided' at Turin in Piedmont. Candler et al., *Col. Rec. Georgia*, 3: 398–9.

[67] Stiles, 'Journal of Silkworms', 58 (juice), 67, 73, 77 (saying), 101 (omelette), 103 (degeneration), 111–12, 113, 123, 249.

[68] Stiles, 'Journal of Silkworms', 83, 107. The seventh edition of the *Spectacle* was translated and published by Samuel Humphreys in London in 1750: Noël-Antoine Pluche, *Spectacle de La Nature: Or, Nature Display'd*, ed. Samuel Humphreys, 7th ed. (London: R. Francklin et al., 1750), silkworm dialogue from 40.

having the 'best mulberries'), Chekyang (Zhejiang), and Shan-Tong (Shandong). Stiles admitted that British America's southernmost colonies 'seem to correspond best' with Chinese latitudes for the best culture of silk but concluded that New England and Pennsylvania 'may be enterprized with certain success' as they shared a latitude from 39th to the 42nd degree north with such sericultural specialists as Italy, Greece, and the great Persian provinces around the southern Caspian Sea. He applied the logic of Asian silk to an imaginary American setting, positing that the successful export of silk from the Safavid centre of Reshd (Rasht, in modern-day Iran) to Europe via either the Levant or St Petersburg could be a model of how 'Silk raised in the middle of an inland country finds its way to Market, & might [be transported] from the Banks of the Ohio, the Lakes Ontario, Erie, & Huron with equal success.'[69] The far-fetched silkworm literature thus became a way of experimenting not just with insects, but with Stiles's sense of the situational geography of the British Atlantic.

Stiles took every opportunity to supplement this quasi-global literature with local first-hand insights, such as those of the Rev. Jonathan Todd (Guilford, CT) and Freelove Sophia Crawford Tweedy (Newport, RI).[70] He also made efforts to locate information from well-placed individuals in other parts of the colonies. These included most notably Benjamin Franklin of Pennsylvania, who for example informed Stiles that Italians 'often shift & change their [silkworm] seed', and, most desperately, Joseph Ottolenghe of Georgia, of whom Stiles begged answers to a range of questions. Stiles wanted to know about the size of the silkworms and cocoons managed by Ottolenghe, the proportion that came to maturity, the preference for white or black mulberry trees, the degree of degeneration that occurred, and the operational capacity of the Savannah filature, though there is no record of a reply.[71] Other information arrived thanks to the particular position of Newport as a thriving hub of Atlantic

---

[69] Stiles also supposed that 'the Chinese were the first that originally invented the Raising & manufacture of Silk, which they bro't to perfection Ages phaps 2000 years before the Art reached even India & Persia'. Stiles, 'Journal of Silkworms', 124, 126, 130 (double-page annotated map), 132, 133 (last quote), 165. A much later source he consulted (p. 293), with a particular interest in the relationship between population size and raw silk production, which included coverage of Spain, Sardinia, and Turkey, was E. A. W. Zimmermann, *A Political Survey of the Present State of Europe* (London: C. Dilly, 1787).

[70] Tweedy, for example, informed him about her ratio of males to females (seven to twenty-three). Stiles, 'Journal of Silkworms', 6, 25, 44 (Tweedy ratios), 108; Ezra Stiles, 'Itineraries (6 vols.), Ezra Stiles Papers, Beinecke Library, Yale University', 1794, 2: 5 (Todd), 117 (asks Mrs. Allen 'how she whitens her silk' and how many cocoons in her thread 'for Sally Law's Gown & her petticoat').

[71] For information from Franklin, see Stiles, 'Journal of Silkworms', 98. Letter from Ezra Stiles to [Joseph] Ottolenghe, 28 March 1765, Newport (RI).

trade, sucking cosmopolitan people and their news and contacts into Stiles's purview. A Captain Dorden was at least able to outline the earlier seasonal timing and scale of silk-rearing activity on the Savannah River, while a Captain Underwood reported on silkworm rearing at the Île Bourbon (now Réunion) where he had been imprisoned during the Seven Years' War.[72]

Ezra Stiles was interested enough in New England household production to jot down comments or news about fellow silk cultivators, dating back to what he described as 'the first Silkworms raised in New England' in 1727 by the Rev. Dr Wigglesworth of Harvard. Stiles's notebook and 'itineraries' (notes he made during various journeys) underline how much contemporary local activity there was, contrary to many subsequent popular and scholarly assumptions. He rode out to Portsmouth (RI) to see thousands of cocoons raised and baked by three families there, and bought over 2 lb of cocoons from the daughter of 'Ab[raham] Antonys'. He noted 6,140 cocoons being sold by one man in Boston in 1769, and passed on silkworm eggs or worms himself to other colonists for breeding.[73] Stiles provides evidence of the developing reeling and manufacturing across New England: the wife of Rev. Rupel of Rocky Hill 'wound 28 knots of silk in 28 or 30 minutes', while a Mrs McClean sent nearly 2 lb of raw silk to Scotland (though it took her and Mrs Dor three days to wind off half a pound).[74] Stiles also documented the growing concentration of silk culture in Nathaniel Aspinwall's Mansfield, Connecticut, inserting items from newspapers which celebrated that William Hanks there had raised enough silk in 1768 'to make three women's gowns', and that there were moves afoot 'to bring on a silk manufactory. Tis said one Silk house is already erected at Lebanon'.[75] The New England world of small-scale local activity was far removed from silk culture in the Lower South, with its hub of state patronage and its state-of-the-art filatures.

Only a handful of producers seem to have escaped Stiles's attention, such as Boston's Nathaniel Appleton. Writing to the Premium Society in

---

[72] Stiles, 'Journal of Silkworms', 178, 192. Stiles also learned of two men who 'feed & take care of at least 7000 worms probably more' at Bethlehem or Nazareth, Delaware. Stiles, 'Journal of Silkworms', 132. French silk production on the Mascarene Islands was first mentioned in 1689 in royal instructions to Gov. Habert de Vaubolon, proposing silkworm eggs via Madagascar. ANOM COL C27, f.110–13. For experimentation in the mid-eighteenth century: Stockland, 'Statecraft and Insect Oeconomies', 133–7.

[73] Stiles, 'Journal of Silkworms', 210, 241, 242, 246, 279, 284.

[74] Stiles, Itineraries (6 vols.), Ezra Stiles Papers, Beinecke Library, Yale University, 2:146, 164, 181.

[75] Stiles, 'Journal of Silkworms', 279. Original notice in *New London Gazette*, 31 March 1769. This included Hanks's advertisement of 3,000 mulberry trees, mostly 3 years old, to be 'sold cheap for the speedy promoting the culture of silk'.

1766, Appleton nonetheless shared many of Stiles's opinions, avowing that American silkworms offered as fine a product as the raw silk from France or Italy. He was optimistic about the continuing spread of mulberries in Massachusetts, and anticipated that silk raising might especially 'be the department of the Female sex, who in this part of the World have not such constant employ as in many other places'. Like Stiles, Appleton also made some progress in coming to terms with the reeling process. Overcoming the 'grand dificulty with us [which] is our imperfect knowlige of winding off', by adapting a reeling machine modelled on Samuel Pullein's diagram, Appleton sent across the Atlantic 'a small sample of raw silk which is the produce of my own worms', which he hoped would meet with the Society's approbation.[76]

For his part, Stiles pursued a number of creative experiments during his years of silkworm rearing. Some of these were pragmatic and exploratory, such as placing 'about a dozen' caterpillars on his mulberry trees to see whether they might survive in the wild, using whortleberry bushes or twigs (*Vaccinium myrtillus*) for the caterpillars to climb and cocoon upon, or storing silkworm eggs in bottles over the winter rather than 'among linnen in chests' as advised by Jared Eliot.[77] Others were more theoretically grounded, as in his testing of a hypothesis about species colouration. Stiles attempted to genetically isolate silkworms who produced different colours of cocoon (respectively white and yellow), by selecting them for breeding. He concluded that it would be possible to alter the proportion of colours to create 'a predominency in a few successions'. He speculated deductively that the principles he established 'perhaps might be applied to the various coloration of the different nations of Mankind', a leap he shared with others, and that was likely influenced by the multiple colourations in his own household.[78] Elizabeth Stiles was equally willing to innovate, and Ezra proudly wrote of 'my Wifes Invention' in July 1764 of a method of stringing forty conical papers on a line of thread 'half a foot high over the worms', which the caterpillars could then climb up into to construct their cocoons. Elizabeth also found a use for the waste silk, spinning it some months later to make 'Ten Knots or half a Run' (around 800 yards) which would also have involved some labour in sorting and

[76] Letters from Nathaniel Appleton to Peter Templeman, 31 March and 28 July 1766, Boston. PR.GE/110/21/67, Royal Society of Arts Archive.

[77] Stiles, 177. Letter from Thomas Clap and Jared Elliot to Mr. George Box, 2 June 1760, New Haven. PR.GE/110/9/13, Royal Society of Arts Archive.

[78] He later referred to these as 'the laws of Degeneracy and melioration by separation & by mixture of color'. Stiles, 'Journal of Silkworms', 196–200, 221 (quotes on 196, 198). Other theories Stiles propounded but did not test included a new way of terminating the pupae by stifling in an air pump, thereby emulating a traditional Chinese suffocation method using earthen vessels and layers of salt. Stiles, 'Journal of Silkworms', 126.

hand-combing.[79] In such small trials, adaptive practices emerged that gave households a sense of productive agency and control.

Amongst his achievements, Ezra identified and sought to address a number of peculiarities of silkworm raising in colonial New England. He was able to demonstrate that it was not viable to ship cocoons back to Europe for reeling there, as the cost of freight (which he estimated at around £4 per hogshead) would eat dramatically into profit margins, so proving the need to establish filatures in North America. He corrected an 'Error' of New England planters who sowed their mulberry seed in July, which left the young plants vulnerable to winter, and advised them to sow later in the autumn or in the succeeding spring. He demonstrated that bivoltine production was impracticable in New England, as a consequence of inadequate foodstuff and overly cold temperatures for the second crop ('recolto') of silkworms, which ended up disease-prone and diminutive. In terms of solving immediate problems, Stiles found the best time to use an oven to terminate pupae was exactly twenty-three minutes after the bread was removed, and that if large volumes of leaves were laid aside for feeds, they needed to be spread out to avoid generating heat and composting themselves. Stiles also showed a growing realisation of the importance of the labour input, which so many earlier theorists and experimenters had ignored.[80]

The two achievements which Stiles probably valued the most himself, and which will be treated in turn, were the creation of a Spitalfields patterned silk dress woven out of cocoons raised in his own household, and the realisation of his regional plan to secure to New England an adequate supply of the resources necessary for widespread uptake (see Plate 13). Set alongside the production and dress commissioned by South Carolina plantation mistress Eliza Pinckney, the Stiles' material achievements reflected both core similarities (as highly valued symbols of colonial pride and performance), and distinctive regional differences. British Atlantic persistence in sericulture was like a funnel that narrowed at the metropolitan end yet spanned to accommodate wide variation across the colonies, where ascriptions of value, labour, and style diverged.

By the early 1770s, Stiles and his family had slowly amassed a respectable amount of home-grown silk. The early years, as we have seen, involved them reeling the silk off themselves, improvising around crude domestic machinery. In 1768, rather than attempting it again at home, Stiles opted to send their 11,125 cocoons down to the more professional Charleston (SC) filature to have the silk reeled. He was a bit bemused by the return of 4,065 of them at the end of October,

---

[79] Stiles, 'Journal of Silkworms', 191, 167.
[80] Stiles, 'Journal of Silkworms', 120, 140, 145, 148, 163, 164, 270, 275.

deemed too bad to reel off, but very happy at the quality of the nearly eleven ounces of raw silk wound from the remainder. He pursued this approach again in 1771, this time sending cocoons to the new filature at Philadelphia (discussed in the following chapter), for which he paid three shillings and one pence (Philadelphia currency) to Ann Powell 'For Reeling 6½ oz of Raw Silk from bad Cocoons' – again receiving some inadequate cocoons back. This varied assortment of silk yarn, grown in Rhode Island but reeled in three different colonies according to different quality criteria, was conveyed to Henry Marchant, a member of Stiles's congregation and a lawyer by profession. Marchant had travelled to London in July 1771 as a co-agent of the Rhode Island colony, with the difficult mission of securing a parliamentary grant that had been withheld because of Rhode Islanders' misbehaviour during the Stamp Act crisis of 1765, and while there he acted upon the Stiles's instructions.[81]

The Stiles had originally requested a fabric of 'the best Damask' and had sent Marchant directions in December 1771 with 'an inclosed Pattern of Green English Damask, double'.[82] A damask was a perfectly sensible choice for a colonial minister's wife, offering a longer fashion half-life than other fabrics because its patterns remained pretty consistent, the weave was durable, and it could be both reversed and adapted to other uses. That they pursued the order through Marchant was also typical of how colonial elites ordering patterned silks in this era, often placing such orders through trusted friends or familiar merchants. Marchant wrote to Ezra Stiles on 14 May 1772 to forewarn him, and more particularly his wife Elizabeth, that the finished product would not entirely match their specifications, but that 'it is I think of a good Green, and is thought by every Body to be very pretty, much more fashionable than Damasks which are not worn at all indeed in London'. The Spitalfields drawloom weaver, Samuel Laurance of Widegate Street, charged two pounds and twelve shillings for the cloth, though Marchant had expedited the work by offering an extra two shillings and sixpence 'to the manufacturer to encourage him to do his best'. This benevolence should be borne in mind when weighing up the compliments that Laurance paid to Stiles about his silk (which Stiles had underlined in his notebook): 'your Silk was of the best Kind he ever had, much better than the Philadelphia Silk ... the whole Warp is of your own, which is always of the best Silk'.[83]

[81] Stiles, 'Journal of Silkworms', 277–8, 286, 287.
[82] Stiles, 'Journal of Silkworms', 287.
[83] Stiles, 'Journal of Silkworms', 156–7, 288, 299–300 (quotes att. to weaver). On Marchant and his mission, see David S. Lovejoy, 'Henry Marchant and the Mistress of the World', *The William and Mary Quarterly, 3rd Ser.* 12, no. 3 (1955): 375–98. For an intricate analysis of the process of commissioning, designing, and delivering such fabrics from London to the colonies: Anishanslin, *Portrait of a Woman in Silk*. On the appeal of damasks to middling consumers, see David E. Lazaro, 'Fashion and Frugality: English

Upon his return, on 17 October 1772, Henry Marchant called at Stiles's house, bringing the patterned all-silk fabric, some ten-and-a--quarter yards in length and half an ell (around twenty-three inches) wide, described by the weaver as a 'Green Ducape or Mantua striped & sprigged'.[84] A measure of the Stiles's excitement at the arrival of this long-awaited fabric is that within just three days it had been '[m]ade up into a Gown for my Wife', by a local mantua-maker, leaving just under a yard surplus.[85] Judging by a small sample appended to Stiles's notebook, it was a single-coloured cloth, in dark green, in a simple weave structure of a sturdy, corded appearance. Though mostly plain woven, it contained subtle patterning and achieved extra lustre by the intermixture of a satin weave structure, akin to a damask. But unlike the dense, flamboyant damasks characteristic of recent decades, requiring fourteen to sixteen yards of length for a dress, the fabric woven by Laurance was more modest and restrained – using less than ten yards and fewer warp and weft threads.[86] Its thistle-like botanical motifs, gentle zigzags and stripes, and reflective variation offered enough to catch the eye without ostentation. Its subtlety in patterning was partly owing to wider shifts in international fashion in the final decades of the eighteenth century, as European consumers generally embraced simpler and lighter styles. But the subdued colour and plainness of design were also distinctively New England features that, as we have seen, harked back to long-standing cultural imperatives. The dress looked both forwards and backwards in another sense, too, for it was at once home raised and foreign manufactured at

---

Patterned Silks in Connecticut River Valley Women's Dress, 1660–1800', *DRESS* 33 (2006): 60, 63; Miles Lambert, 'The Consumption of Spitalfields Silks in 18th-Century England: Examples in Collections Outside London', in *18th-Century Silks: The Industries of England and Northern Europe*, ed. Regula Schorta (Riggisberg: Abegg-Stiftung, 2000), 68.

[84] Stiles, 'Journal of Silkworms', 287. Florence Montgomery lists 'Ducape' from Beck as 'a plain-wove stout silken fabric of softer texture than Gros de Naples' and cites examples in New York and Philadelphia adverts in the 1760s, noting that extant swatches from the period are frequently watered; 'Mantua' is described as 'a silk of plain weave, heavier than taffeta', and Defoe described 'plain English Mantua-silk' gowns as fitting for the tradesman's wife – 'not dressed over fine'. Florence M. Montgomery, *Textiles in America, 1650-1870: A Dictionary Based on Original Documents, Prints and Paintings, Commercial Records, American Merchants' Papers, Shopkeepers' Advertisements, and Pattern Books with Original Swatches of Cloth*, 2 vols (New York: Norton, 1984), 1: 227, 289.

[85] In his diary on 19 October 1772, Stiles also recorded that the fabric weighed 18.67 oz and had a selvedge of a tenth of an inch. Ezra Stiles, *The Literary Diary of Ezra Stiles*, ed. Franklin Bowditch Dexter, 3 vols. (New York: C. Scribner's sons, 1901), 1: 292–3. The cost of a dress in the seventeenth and eighteenth centuries lay overwhelmingly in the material and its production, rather than the dressmaking. Thornton, *Baroque and Rococo Silks*, 80.

[86] These estimate yardages lengths for strong and slight silks are taken from Rothstein, 'The 18th-Century English Silk Industry', 29.

a time when American self-sufficiency and European luxuries were being dramatically re-evaluated. On the day it was made, Elizabeth Stiles planned to give her gown '(after she is done with it) to Betsy or the oldest daughter surviving her, to be preserved as a Memorial of once having a Silk Gown made of Silk of her own Raising', though what ultimately became of it is unknown.[87]

The second major achievement of Ezra Stiles – his scheme systematising the plantation of New England mulberries using religious networks – helps us to stake out a moment of historical transition that will be explored in more depth in the following chapters. Between the point of the scheme's conception in the early 1760s and the point of its realisation in the 1790s, the persistent pursuit of sericulture in North America stopped being a set of parallel exercises in imperial projection, with differing complexions. Silk production in these regions may have shared some core features to begin with, such as the common use of female and enslaved labour, and the struggle to overcome adverse environmental conditions. But experimenters seldom intersected with one another; they tended to connect more habitually with metropolitan bodies who offered patronage, such as the Board of Trade and the Premium Society. As an instance of this regionalism, when Stiles first formulated a grand plan to drive New England sericulture forward in a letter he drafted in September 1764 (probably intended for Richard Jackson, a London agent of the Connecticut government), he began with a tirade about the wastefulness of parliamentary support for new colonies such as Georgia, Nova Scotia, and the Floridas, on which tens of thousands of pounds had been lavished, and argued that just £2,000 laid out by Parliament 'judiciously employed in the Silk culture in the Northern Provinces' would generate a much more substantial return.[88]

As suggested by this opening, which showed little appreciation of wider geostrategic British imperial goals (and little sympathy for fellow settlers), Stiles's 'Plan' was very New-England-centric. He proposed a corporate confederation across the region, with the twenty-eight New England counties each appointing a member who would meet each May to arrange the procurement and sowing of mulberry seed in orderly, fenced nurseries. Over a twelve-year period these mulberry nurseries were to be developed such that each of the 550 New England parishes had around 5,000 trees that the 'Society' would make available to families. The members were next to distribute 10,000 silkworm eggs to trusted people in each parish who would furnish them to the families with trees, while the Society procured professional 'windsters' and set them up in public

[87] Stiles, *The Literary Diary of Ezra Stiles*, 1: 293.   [88] Morgan, *The Gentle Puritan*, 150.

filatures. Stiles's bottom-line ambition, which he expected to fulfil some twenty years after the plan was initiated, was raising enough New England silk to help balance the region's colonial consumption of British goods, but the scheme initially went nowhere.[89]

The diverse schemes to introduce raw silk to new locales in northern Europe and British America between the 1690s and 1760s had grappled creatively with the different challenges that local environments, labour configurations, and agricultural production regimes threw up. They had shared in common a conviction that site-specific experimentation and targeted patronage could overcome the known obstacles to sericulture in temperate climes, and as a consequence they had built more complex models than had previously existed of everything from political economics to bounties, orchards, buildings, and machinery. The British appetite for persistence was particularly profound, on account of the substantial development in Britain's domestic silk industry and the particularities and range of its Atlantic territories and global commercial empire. Indeed, beyond the enterprises and experiments described in South Carolina, Georgia, and New England, sericulture briefly helped to shape new settler schemes in North Carolina and East Florida, where production similarly fell victim to fragile demographics, imperfect environments, and intolerant economic worlds.

In North Carolina, the Dumfriesshire-born governor, Gabriel Johnston notified the Board of Trade that in 1737 he had sent 'part of a Crop of Silk' from his estate in Bertie County to a London Scots merchant, Henry McCulloh, and when he wrote his will in 1751 he linked his estate's output to the female members of his household, hoping his widow Frances Button Johnston would continue to live with his daughter Penelope in North Carolina, in leaving her 'the Use of all my said Daughters Plantations, and for her Encouragement to Cultivate & Improve these Plantations, Especially in Raising Silk'.[90] Evidence that other North Carolinians were producing silk on their estates in the 1750s was also apparent in the correspondence of fellow Scot James Murray, while Johnston's successors as governor – who often obsessed with trying to modernise and improve the colony's faltering economy – were active in pushing silk and supporting specialists without reaching the levels of innovation, infrastructure, and take-up apparent in the Lower South.[91]

[89] Stiles, 'Journal of Silkworms', 221–9, 231–3.
[90] Saunders, *The Colonial Records of North Carolina*, 4: 919; 22: 287–8.
[91] James Murray to Richard Oswald & Co., 19 July 1756, in James Murray, *Letters of James Murray, Loyalist*, ed. Nina Tiffany and Susan I Lesley (Boston: Gregg Press, 1972), 81. Saunders, *The Colonial Records of North Carolina*, 5: 273, 293, 316, 332, 573-4, 686, 715, 855; 6: 1029; 8: 66, 87, 91, 114. Arthur Dobbs, 'An Essay on the Trade and

The brains behind the East Florida operation from 1766 was Scottish physician Dr Andrew Turnbull, whose project south of St Augustine was named New Smyrna (after the Turkish silk-trading entrepôt). He recruited significant numbers of Mediterranean indentured servants (particularly from Minorca but also Greek and Italian provinces), aiming especially at those who were experienced in producing silk, wine, and cotton. And in spite of European powers and the Levant Company limiting access to expertise in silk raising for fear of competition, he and fellow supporters made some early progress, including the orderly plantation of both Lowcountry and Mediterranean mulberry trees at New Smyrna and 'Grant's Villa' by 1772.[92] But the death of half the unseasoned European settlers in their first summer (at the forebodingly named Mosquito Inlet) encouraged a retreat to more sure-fire commodities and a concentration on indigo and later rice.[93] The prominent role of ambitious and dutiful governors, colonial agents, and Scots imperial opportunists in these smaller schemes were a reminder of how most Atlantic sericulture in the eighteenth century remained projected – through individual colonies – onto British imperial horizons of one sort or another. This would inevitably change with the sequential outbreak of protest, war, and revolution.

Back in New England, once British imperial authority was no longer in the picture, Ezra Stiles would successfully resurrect his twenty-year-old failed plan to push sericulture through the parishes. In April 1789, he distributed parcels of 4,000 white mulberry seeds to 81 ministers and 9 laypeople. He used a template or circular letter which explained the terms: three quarters of the mulberries were to be reserved to the willing nurseryman after three years, while the other quarter were to be 'distributed gratis, or given away by the minister of the Parish to about 20 or 30 families'. The overwhelming majority of seeds initially went to

Improvement of Ireland', in *A Collection of Tracts and Treatises Illustrative of . . . Ireland*, 2 vols. (Dublin: Alex Thom & Sons, 1861).

[92] On Minorcan silk potential: 'Minutes of the Society for the Encouragement of Arts, Commerce, and Manufactures', 1754, 10: 128, 143. On difficulties recruiting: Andrew Turnbull to Sir William Duncan, Leghorn, 26 June 1767; Smirna, [Turkey], 3 September 1767; Leghorn, 22 January 1768; Minorca, 21 February 1768 (incl. trees); Turnbull to the Earl of Shelburne, 27 February 1768. On progress: Alexander Skinner to James Grant, Grant's Villa, 7 April 1772 in Papers of James Grant of Ballindalloch, 1740-1819, National Archives of Scotland. Andrew Turnbull to Sir William Duncan, St Augustine, 17 July and 22 October 1768 and 9 November 1769; Archibald Neilson to Sir William Duncan, New Bern (North Carolina), 8 December 1773, Dundee City Archives.

[93] Jane Landers, *Colonial Plantations and Economy in Florida* (Gainesville: University Press of Florida, 2000); Daniel L. Schafer, *Governor James Grant's Villa: A British East Florida Indigo Plantation* (St Augustine: S. Augustine Historical Society, 2000); Carita Doggett Corse, *Dr. Andrew Turnbull and the New Smyrna Colony of Florida: With Original Correspondence from 1768-1793* ([Florida]: The Drew Press, 1919).

Connecticut parishes, but Stiles repeated the process in subsequent years, expanding to include more recipients further afield, including many in Massachusetts and in the new entity of Vermont. Stiles summarised it proudly himself, noting that between 1789 and 1793 he and his ministerial special delivery service had patronised '350 Nurseries abroad in all parts from Boston to Genesea & chiefly in Connecticutt'. One quart of mulberry seed reached Judge James Winthrop of Cambridge for him to disseminate around Boston; this Winthrop was the great-great-grandson of one of the first New England colonists to consider cultivating silk back in the seventeenth century.[94]

What had changed to make Stiles's plan workable? It cannot have been the natural environment, demographics, or technology associated with sericulture, which changed little. Rather, it was a new conviction based on the changed political and economic environment. Insofar as the colonial protest movements which culminated in American independence rejected foreign luxuries and celebrated homespun, repudiated dependency and galvanised local manufacturing, they offered a particular kind of inspiration to silk raisers, and a way for proponents in New England and elsewhere to redefine, reconnect, and re-energise their production. New balances would be struck between silk's desirability, accessibility, and innate morality, just as they had by the earliest generations of New England colonists. No less than Elizabeth Stiles's material product then, Ezra Stiles's organisational legacy for northern sericulture would be patched back together in the fabrication of a new, hybrid, American project. From the moment in the late 1760s that British-manufactured or British-imported silks began to be banned rather than bought, the pursuit of raw silk – awkwardly, gradually – would be rearticulated as an American endeavour.

---

[94] Stiles, 'Journal of Silkworms', 353, 357, 363, 364 (quote), 387 (template letter); Stiles, *The Literary Diary of Ezra Stiles*, 3: 350–1, 398–9. Letters were also sent to the newspapers in relation to this design, e.g. *Boston Gazette*, 14 June 1790, p. 4; Boston *Massachusetts Centinel*, 25 July 1789, p. 150.

Part III

Convergence

8   Convergence

If we ever mean to be truly independent, as individuals and as a nation,
like the silkworm we must spin the web from our own bowels; and,
leaving the manufactures, the fashions and vices of Europe to themselves, pursue our true interest.
                                  – Philadelphia *Freeman's Journal*, 28 May 1788

Threads in the Convergence of American Sericulture

In December 1767, Jedediah Elderkin, a fifty-year-old lawyer who had
become a prominent figure in the small town of Windham, in north-
eastern Connecticut, chaired a new self-constituted committee to help
direct British Americans towards pursuing their own manufacturing.
Like hundreds of others, Elderkin's meeting voted to restrict their
consumption of European 'Silk of all kinds for Garments' and to channel their energies into new productive ventures that were homespun.
The Massachusetts Governor Francis Bernard felt that support for such
movements was weak and would 'come to Nothing'.[1] But their
measures marked a clear point at which American political protest had
begun to converge with the worlds of textile production and textile
consumption. The fallout of this convergence was wide-ranging
over the course of the next thirty years, as fibres and fabrics accrued
new moral and commercial values in the course of what Thomas
Paine termed the 'age of Revolutions'.[2] First the American and then
the French Revolution threw open new prospects when it came to
transnational systems of silk production and distribution.

The chapters that follow address how American sericulture was twisted
into new forms in the final third of the eighteenth century, in the wake of
the many challenges posed by these Atlantic revolutions. Disrupted patterns of imperial consumption encouraged both the pursuit of new sites of

---

[1] Boston, *Records Relating to Boston*, 16: 220–1. Letter from Gov. Francis Bernard to the
Earl of Shelburne, Boston, 30 October 1767, CO 5/756, ff. 144–5.
[2] Thomas Paine, *Rights of Man* (London: J. Johnson, 1791), 162.

raw silk production and the pursuit of new trade and manufacturing opportunities. These possessed a different character than the dutiful imperial projects that had preceded them. As Elderkin put it in his closing remarks in a 1773 letter to Clement Biddle, a Philadelphia gentleman whom he had never met but who was involved in various public initiatives in Pennsylvania, 'the purpose of making silk in North America' was now assuming a different complexion, as once-separate colonies and colonists increasingly came together, and began to articulate homespun silken ambitions in new ways.[3] In short time, 'Colonel' Elderkin would be playing an instrumental role in the Revolutionary War, creating a foundry in Salisbury and a gunpowder manufactory in Willimantic. But he returned to his large plantation of mulberry trees in South Windham, and in his will in 1792 left to his wife Anne his 'mulberry lands near Auwebetuck' and 'the appurtenances belonging to my silk manufactory' near the fast-flowing Shetucket River. Elderkin's ending revealed another kind of convergence that straddled the end of the eighteenth and the early nineteenth century: the linkage of raw silk production to silk manufacturing on North American soil. Within a few years of his death, and a few miles upstream, driven by the waters of the Fenton River (which flows into the Shetucket via the Natchaug), Horace and Rodney Hanks would build the first water-powered silk mill in the United States in 1810.[4]

Historians have often separated and flattened these threads out, tending to impose a periodisation shaped exclusively by political events or industrial pioneering – both of which have tended to over-masculinise and over-mechanise developments. Perhaps the most fitting illustration of this was the lifting of the Hanks Mill in its entirety out of its physical and evolutionary context, under the order of Henry Ford in 1931. Relocated from Connecticut to Ford's museum at Greenfield Village in Michigan (see Plate 14), it was held to celebrate a sort of miraculous industrial conception, rather than being treated – as it ought to have been – as the product of a gradual evolution whose genesis lay in the situational foundations established by eighteenth-century silk-raising communities in New England. What we learn when we fully re-entangle silk in revolutionary contexts is that it offered a powerful means of bringing Americans together. Here was a Eurasian import that permeated

---

[3] Jedediah Elderkin to Clement Biddle, Windham, 22 January 1773, copied in Dyer W. Elderkin, *Genealogy of the Elderkin Family with Intermarriages* (Pittsburgh: Fisher, Stewart & Co, 1888), 16.

[4] Elderkin died 3 March 1793, and his will was proved on 27 March 1793, as recorded in Elderkin, 19. For the quotes and other details on his silk production, William J. Heller, *History of Northampton County Pennsylvania and the Grand Valley of the Lehigh*, 3 vols. (Boston: American Historical Society, 1920), 1: 157.

numerous Atlantic markets and symbolised European luxury (for good or ill). Here was an American raw product which had yet to deliver commercially but had repeatedly demonstrated promise all across the eastern seaboard. And here was a textile system often knotted up in the Old World by protectionism and industrial discontent, which manufacturers in the fledgling United States viewed as a potential coup for their markets. The convergence of these threads was not straightforward, as we shall see, and it was not so much a question of leaving aside 'the manufactures, the fashions and vices of Europe' as of rhetorically repatriating them to fit a new projective landscape. Pursuit of a conscientiously *American* sericulture connected silk raisers across regions, oriented their output away from British markets towards domestic manufactures, and ultimately offered a way to justify the revitalised consumption of silk following the hiatus imposed by revolutionary boycotts and war. As a consequence, even after independence movements brought a forceful end to the centuries-long ambitions of European empires to generate raw silk in the Americas, small-scale silk production continued.

Atlantic Tastes in Eighteenth-Century Silks

In the decades that preceded the American Revolution, Atlantic purchases of European-made silks and of Asian-made silks transported by European trading companies and merchants were reaching new heights. Silks constituted one of the most luxurious and visible slices of a larger pie chart of consumption that was growing to unprecedented size as the colonies increased in scale and refinement over the course of the eighteenth century. Its traces can be found in any number of historical sources – from flamboyant costume celebrated in portraiture, surviving fabrics, advertisements, and material culture, to unwitting references sprinkled across mercantile papers, probate inventories, criminal records and correspondence.[5] For a long time, the diffuse spread of American settler populations and their limited wealth (with no recognisable court or aristocracy) and minimal manufacturing capacity had meant that the most expensive and fashionable fabrics, particularly all-silk figured garments and larger furnishings, were difficult to access. Even where capital and inclination existed, the opportunity to display fine fabrics could be inhibited by the colonial cultural landscape, especially outside the larger seaport cities.[6] But whereas early consumption was concentrated amongst a handful of elites, typically brokered by colonial

---

[5] Berg, *Luxury and Pleasure*; Anishanslin, *Portrait of a Woman in Silk*.
[6] Robert S. DuPlessis, 'Cloth and the Emergence of the Atlantic Economy', in *The Atlantic Economy during the Seventeenth and Eighteenth Centuries: Organization, Operation, Practice, and Personnel*, ed. Peter A. Coclanis (Columbia, SC: University of South Carolina Press,

merchants as a by-product of their transatlantic commercial activity, by the late eighteenth century, this picture had changed. American consumers, so long enthralled to woollens and linens, could find a growing array of ever-cheaper cotton and silk goods available to order and to purchase in the port cities, with the first newspaper notices of their kind listing fine silks available in New York and Philadelphia in the 1730s.[7]

Textiles were the biggest category of consumer goods exported to the Americas, and constituted the second-largest household expenditure after foodstuffs, as well as being critical from the earliest encounters to trade relations with indigenous peoples. Distinctive regional textile preferences were perceptible to some extent, as colonies expressed their own tastes and trends according to their climates, cultural mix, distribution of wealth, and trading links. Between the 1680s and 1730s, chilly Montreal merchants had high proportions of woollens in their stock, whereas their temperate Philadelphia counterparts leaned towards linens, merchants in muggy New Orleans held larger proportions of lighter cottons, and Port Royal merchants (like others in the Caribbean) complained that 'no woollen cloths will do', showing especially high demand for silks. Textile distribution was affected by major regional variables such as the prevalence of unfree labour or slavery, which brought demand for cheap, durable, and uncomfortable fabrics such as osnaburgs (course unbleached linen or hempen cloth) and *étoffe à Nègre* (a woollen fabric). It depended also on the volume of onwards trade to colonial settlements or indigenous markets in the continental interior, or seaborne distribution along or across the Pacific. For all the site-specific variation in what Robert DuPlessis has helpfully termed Atlantic 'dress regimes' though, analysis of merchant stocks and inventories suggests that over the course of the eighteenth century there was something of a 'consumption convergence' across European empires, all sharing for example the growing inclination to replace woollens proportionately with cottons.[8]

Silk was amongst the lesser fibres ranked by volume, but it remained highly valued and an integral component of understandings of 'fashion',

2005), 76. Lazaro, 'Fashion and Frugality: English Patterned Silks in Connecticut River Valley Women's Dress, 1660–1800', 59.

[7] DuPlessis, 'Cloth and the Emergence of the Atlantic Economy', 72–94; Rothstein, 'The 18th-Century English Silk Industry'; Kate Haulman, *The Politics of Fashion in Eighteenth-Century America* (Chapel Hill, NC: University of North Carolina Press, 2011), 18–19.

[8] Carole Shammas, 'How Self-Sufficient Was Early America?', *Journal of Interdisciplinary History* 13, no. 2 (1982): 256–9; Linda Baumgarten, *What Clothes Reveal: The Language of Clothing in Colonial and Federal America* (Williamsburg, VA: Colonial Williamsburg Foundation in association with Yale University Press, 2002), 76; DuPlessis, *The Material Atlantic: Clothing, Commerce, and Colonization in the Atlantic World, 1650–1800*; DuPlessis, 'Cloth and the Emergence of the Atlantic Economy'; West Indian quote cited in Zahedieh, *The Capital and the Colonies*, 265.

a term specifically linked to silk, according to Richard Rolt, in his pioneering dictionary for Anglo-American merchants.[9] When it came to woven
silks, North American consumers in the eighteenth century rarely enjoyed
the concentration amongst many of their colonial free counterparts in
Central and South America (mostly supplied by non-Iberian merchants),
or the levels of silk saturation supported by metropolitan European
markets.[10] But though starting from a very low baseline, silk's proportional increase, particularly in American seaports, was nonetheless dramatic. And silk's lesser aggregate presence in wardrobes and inventories
on the western side of the Atlantic strengthened its appeal – as the fabric
that best articulated social status and carried connotations of European
refinement. More than other fibres, as we know particularly from altera-
tions made to surviving garments, silk was worth saving, updating, and
refashioning.[11] It drew increasing attention not just from smugglers and
criminals, but from indigenous peoples in the interior, where silk small-
ware (such as handkerchiefs) became more frequently used in diplomatic
exchanges.[12]

In different ways, then, but with increasing visibility, silk goods permeated the marketplaces and social sensibilities of Atlantic populations,
who used them to materialise notions of civility and cultural status. As
a dress fabric, silk was perhaps intrinsically less suited to warmer climates,
where heat and humidity compromised its wearability (in both senses of
the word). Other fibres were less vulnerable or cheaper to replace when
attacked by perspiration, or by armies of moth larvae, and some have
claimed that this rendered southern colonies 'less relevant' to silk imports
from Europe.[13] But such environmental challenges were offset by the

[9] Richard Rolt, *A New Dictionary of Trade and Commerce* (London: T. Osborne and J. Shipton, 1756), 290.
[10] Daniel Roche, *The Culture of Clothing: Dress and Fashion in the Ancien Regime* (Cambridge: Cambridge University Press, 1994), 127, 138; DuPlessis, 'Cloth and the Emergence of the Atlantic Economy', 74, 78, 81.
[11] See silken examples in Baumgarten, *What Clothes Reveal*, 193–9.
[12] On silk in Haudenosaunee (Iroquois) gifts and signals of safe conduct: Samuel Hazard, *Minutes of the Provincial Council of Pennsylvania from the Organization to the Termination of the Proprietary Government*, 10 vols. (Philadelphia: J. Severns, 1851), 2: 70, 3: 167–170, 5: 84, 7: 34 & 490, 9: 332; DuPlessis, *The Material Atlantic: Clothing, Commerce, and Colonization in the Atlantic World, 1650–1800*, 117. On instances of criminal gangs targeting silks: *Pennsylvania Gazette*, 14 and 21 November 1771; *New-York Journal; or, the General Advertiser*, 23 January 1769; *An Account of the Robberies Committed by John Morrison, and His Accomplices, in and near Philadelphia, 1750* (Philadelphia: Anthony Armbruster, 1751); Serena R. Zabin, *Dangerous Economies: Status and Commerce in Imperial New York* (Philadelphia: University of Pennsylvania Press, 2009), 67–71.
[13] Rothstein, 'The 18th-Century English Silk Industry', 13. See also R. Nash, 'Domestic Material Culture and Consumer Demand in the British-Atlantic World: Colonial South Carolina, 1670–1770', *Manchester Papers in Economic and Social History*, 2007, 29.

steep wealth disparity that tended to characterise plantation colonies, which generated grandiose creole elites with Atlantic sensibilities and capital to indulge in luxury consumption, as reflected in their need for specialist silk washers even in new colonies such as British Georgia.[14] Even allowing for a healthy degree of exaggeration, the residents of Spanish American cities (especially the viceregal capitals Mexico City and Lima) were distinctively elaborate in their silk habits, which owed in part to the continuation of a silk-weaving industry and in part to their commercial positioning.[15] In the Caribbean above all, where consumption of manufactures was skewed towards luxury products already by the start of the eighteenth century, elites seemed to value show over sweat. The fortunes that were fashioned out of African slave labour and staple-crop (particularly sugar) production facilitated silk consumption, while the vibrant exchanges amongst island populations, and strong metropolitan trade links, gave the emulation of European modes a distinctive creole piquancy – including amongst free people of colour.[16]

Put together, the scale of the eighteenth-century American market for silks or mixed-silk fabrics was therefore increasingly imposing. It was reflected in some way in almost all regions and amongst all populations – from the indigenous American interior, where silk ribbons now festooned women's hair, to the heartlands of Atlantic settler-colonial societies, where it touched all points of the life cycle, from the satin cream gowns worn by children being christened, through to the matte black mourning wear that followed death.[17] Silk consumers were everywhere, all wanting to be fashionable but with different tastes and purses, as revealed in the inventories of 350 houses and stores destroyed in a devastating Boston fire in March 1760: a free black, Pompey Blackman, registered just one silk handkerchief valued at eighteen shillings (old tenor), whereas retailer Sarah McNeal claimed over £18,900 worth of goods dominated by

---

[14] DuPlessis, 'Cloth and the Emergence of the Atlantic Economy', 76 (merchant stock in Charleston); Haulman, *The Politics of Fashion in Eighteenth-Century America*, 35–6; Nash, 'Domestic Material Culture and Consumer Demand in the British-Atlantic World: Colonial South Carolina, 1670–1770', 29. On silk washers, Savannah *Georgia Gazette*, 1 October 1766 (Mary Hughes), 12 January 1774 (Mary Martin).

[15] Phipps, 'The Iberian Globe: Textile Traditions and Trade in Latin America'; Aspe, 'Artes asiáticas y novohispañas'; Elena Phipps, Johanna Hecht, Esteras Martín et al., *The Colonial Andes*, 81–2; Gasch Tomás, 'Global Trade, Circulation and Consumption', 324; Arteaga, 'Vestido y desnudo', 199–200.

[16] Cooke, *A Voyage to the South Sea*, 2: x–xvi; Savary des Brûlons and Savary, *Dictionnaire*, 1: 506; Zahedieh, *The Capital and the Colonies*, 259–68; Paul Butel, 'Traditions and Changes in French Atlantic Trade between 1780 and 1830', *Culture Theory and Critique* 30, no. 1 (1986): 131; Walter Bodmer, 'Schweizer Tropenkaufleute und Plantagenbesitzer in Niederländisch-Westindien im 18. und zu Beginn des 19. Jh.,' *Acta Tropica*, 1946, 304.

[17] Bartram, *Travels*, 501.

a huge yardage of silk fabrics.[18] Export figures generated by economic historians from customs ledgers (recorded by British imperial officers from the 1690s) give a clear sense of the scale of Atlantic increase, though even these likely underestimate silk's worth, for they often exclude mixed silks (which get clustered with woollens).[19] As far as British exports to the Atlantic world were concerned, manufactured silks to the 'official' value (which were largely fixed by 1702) of £55,000 sterling per annum were dispatched between 1699 and 1701, dipping slightly to £46,000 in 1722–1724 before beginning a pronounced rise to £71,000 in 1752–4 and a dramatic hike to £164,000 in 1772–4.[20] The thirteen North American colonies which would go on to declare independence enjoyed by far the bulk of this British export trade by the 1760s, and constituted 81 per cent by value in 1772.[21] Since the actual market price of the commodities departed from the 'official' values, establishing the value of the trade in individual goods at any given point is more problematic, but by the end of the eighteenth century the value of British silk manufactures exported was roughly twice their 'official' value. We might therefore confidently estimate that British American consumers were spending more than a quarter of a million pounds sterling in peak years to buy a combination of 'India' silks (wrought silks from the East Indies trade) and those of English manufacture – let alone the additional sums they spent to smuggle in these and European-wrought silks, though contrary to the Navigation Acts.[22] It seemed, as Benjamin Franklin put it,

[18] Inventories listed in Boston, *Records Relating to Boston*, 29: 1–100. Sarah McNeal's losses (valued in old tenor and equating to around £1,900 sterling), 39–42. For contemporary accounts of the fire: *Boston Post Boy & Advertiser*, 24 March 1760; *Boston Evening-Post*, 24 March 1760; Thomas Hutchinson, *The History of the Province of Massachusetts Bay, from 1749 to 1774* (London: John Murray, 1828), 1: 80–1.

[19] One pioneering work, from whose data many others have drawn, listed silk and worsted stuffs and 'silk or cotton & grogram yarn' under 'woollens', meaning perhaps a quarter of the volume of silk exported may have been missed. Elizabeth Boody Schumpeter, *English Overseas Trade Statistics* (Oxford: Clarendon Press, 1960, 1961), 29–30, 35–38.

[20] The 'Atlantic world' here referred to has been created by aggregating the subsections 'America' and 'British Islands' in Ralph Davis's listings of overseas trade, which then comprises: North America, British and foreign West Indies, and Spanish America, Ireland, Channel Islands, West Africa. His listings are technically of 'English' trade, though see his discussion for the ways in which Scottish commerce was rolled into this via London. Ralph Davis, 'English Foreign Trade, 1700–1774', *Economic History Review* 15, no. 2 (1962): 285–303.

[21] S. D. Smith, 'Prices and the Value of English Exports in the Eighteenth Century: Evidence from the North American Colonial Trade', *Economic History Review* 48, no. 3 (1995): table 5, 586. Smith has, 'Silk' re-exports listed at £1,000, £1,900, and £1,800 respectively (dwarfed by the re-exports of calicoes and linens, whose figures were over a hundred times the value), which seems surprisingly low compared to others, though the category perhaps describes a subset of silk exports.

[22] For discussions of these difficulties, see S. D. Smith, 'The Market for Manufactures in the Thirteen Continental Colonies, 1698–1776', *Economic History Review* 51, no. 4 (1998):

'impossible to overstock the Market, as the Demand is continually increasing, Silk being more and more worn, and daily entering into the composition of more and a greater Variety of Manufactures'.[23]

Paying for all of this luxury consumption was a problem that troubled individual colonists, of course, and, as the debts incurred by buying British goods on credit increased, it became an issue that exercised political economists more generally. Linking silk to trade deficits was not new: as we have seen, reducing the cost of luxury expenditure had for centuries been one of the motivations for silk import substitution, spurring the pursuit of silk-manufacturing industries as well as raw silk production in new regions. For much of the eighteenth century, cultivating raw silk – including the diverse approaches taken in locales such as South Carolina, New England, and Georgia – had been held up, in essence, as a way of bankrolling colonials' continuing spending spree, with production aimed at offsetting consumption, such that 'every trader to Great-Britain will be desirous to purchase [raw silk] for remittance, in discharge of his debts there'.[24] Before the late 1760s, this fit snugly into a mercantilist framework of imperial specialisation: the colonists produced the raw material, the mother country manufactured it into finished products, and the merchant marine shipped it back and forth. The projected system had been recognised as prospectively mutually beneficial on both sides of the Atlantic – the American side anticipating in particular that raw silk exports could alleviate the growing 'debt' problem and help redeem a balance sheet that showed colonial entrapment to British credit.[25] But long-held sensibilities and systems were

676–708; John J. McCusker, 'The Current Value of English Exports, 1697 to 1800', *The William and Mary Quarterly*, 3rd Ser. 28, no. 4 (1971): 607–28; Phyllis Deane and W. A. Cole, *British Economic Growth, 1688–1959: Trends and Structure*, 2 vols. (London: Cambridge University Press, 1967), 2: 207. Sources for figures quoted here and elsewhere in this section: Davis, 'English Foreign Trade, 1700–1774'; Schumpeter, *English Overseas Trade Statistics*; Deane and Cole, *British Economic Growth*; Brian R. Mitchell and Phyllis Deane, *Abstract of British Historical Statistics* (Cambridge: Cambridge University Press, 1962); McCusker, 'The Current Value of English Exports, 1697 to 1800.' On the intermixture of wrought silk imports, Amelia Peck, '"India Chints" and "China Taffaty": East India Company Textiles for the North American Market', in *Interwoven Globe: The Worldwide Textile Trade, 1500–1800*, ed. Amelia Peck (London: Thames and Hudson, 2013), 104–19. For an example of authorities complaining of contraband purchases, Mr Comptroller Weare to the President of the Board of Trade, *c.*1769, Massachusetts, *Collections of MHS*, ser. 1, 1: 80.

[23] Letter from Ben Franklin to Cadwalader Evans, London, 4 July 1771, Samuel Hazard, *Hazard's Register of Pennsylvania, Devoted to the Preservation of Facts and Documents, and Every Kind of Useful Information Respecting the State of Pennsylvania*, 16 vols. (Philadelphia: W. F. Geddes, 1828), 5: 92.

[24] *Boston Evening-Post*, 8 August 1768, p. 2.

[25] For a discussion of the political economists and theories mobilised around this 'British system', see Lawrence A. Peskin, *Manufacturing Revolution: The Intellectual Origins of Early American Industry* (Baltimore, MD: Johns Hopkins University Press, 2003), 1–29.

about to be thrown into disarray by the enveloping imperial crisis, with which the rapidly increasing American outlay on finished silks coincided. In the heated debates about dependency, representation, and identity that followed, the place of silk in American life and the potential of raw silk in an American economy would both be repositioned.

Silk in an Imperial Crisis

Historians have comprehensively documented the dramatic changes in ideologies, consumer behaviours, fashions, and commercial trade in the period between mid-century and the creation of the new entity of the United States. Some have located the 1750s as being the source of new debates surrounding virtue and gendered consumption, rather than the crucible of revolution, which makes good sense in relation to the upsurge in Atlantic luxury trades and the spread of wider European ideological fashions. But beginning in late 1764, Americans' resistance to parliamentary acts clearly sharpened sartorial sensibilities and allowed them to cut open new political meanings, with clothing eventually becoming what Michael Zakim has neatly characterised as a mechanism of 'revolutionary agitation'. Over the course of the following two decades, the prior pattern of Atlantic silk consumption came under emphatic challenge as consumers, merchants, and manufacturers all navigated paths as best they could through waves of popular protest, commercial disruption, political upheaval, and war. To understand the changing nature of American attempts at silk cultivation – which were most evident in Pennsylvania – it is necessary to sketch out these developments in a little more detail.[26]

Particularly at the start of the eighteenth century, as the trappings of luxury and exotic stuffs were revolutionising the ways people behaved, consumed, and socialised, debates over luxury became more complicated. Plenty of theorists such as Nicholas Barbon and later David Hume devised justifications for the expansion of luxury trades such as silk: they heralded the march of civilisation, or the improvement of economic infrastructure. Newer thinkers across Europe were reconsidering people's 'Envy' and 'Vanity' not as sins but 'Ministers of Industry', as

---

[26] Anishanslin, *Portrait of a Woman in Silk*; Haulman, *The Politics of Fashion in Eighteenth-Century America*; T. H. Breen, *The Marketplace of Revolution: How Consumer Politics Shaped American Independence* (New York: Oxford University Press, 2004); Laurel Ulrich, *The Age of Homespun: Objects and Stories in the Creation of an American Myth* (New York: Knopf, 2001); Michael Zakim, *Ready-Made Democracy: A History of Men's Dress in the American Republic, 1760–1860* (Chicago: University of Chicago Press, 2003), (quote on 11); Baumgarten, *What Clothes Reveal*; Peskin, *Manufacturing Revolution*; Linda K. Kerber, *Women of the Republic: Intellect and Ideology in Revolutionary America* (Chapel Hill: University of North Carolina Press, 1980), 73–113.

Bernard de Mandeville satirically proposed.[27] Eventually many American theorists would come round to these sorts of claims and connections to justify a new place for silk in the New World. But at first, pressurised by the circumstances of political protest in the 1770s, they resorted to explosive repudiation of the commodity.

The novel arguments defending luxury trades had never hushed the shrill cries of reformers and purists, who continued to challenge the excess indulgence and social corrosion that they perceived around them – what one vexed English writer described in 1745 as 'the vast foolish Expence of so much Silk'.[28] Disapprobation could be stirred by European consumers' globalising horizons, and drew from deep reserves of classical thought, Christian virtue, traditionalism, and localism. British Americans, even before the need to repudiate 'superfluities' as part of the economics of protest in the 1760s, had found powerful inspiration in the classical tradition, to which they instinctively reached out. In his pro-republican *History of Rome* (written at the end of the first century BCE), Livy complained often of corrupting eastern extravagance, and warned that the lure of luxuries had preceded 'the destruction of every great empire'.[29] Livy lived through the genesis of the early Roman Empire, when sumptuary laws forbade men from wearing silk, and writers in subsequent generations such as Pliny the Elder, Suetonius, and Juvenal all disapproved of silks and characterised them as degenerate and foppish.[30] American colonists likewise found inspiration in Christian and specifically Protestant imperatives, with their emphasis on humility in dress, simplicity, and asceticism. The waves of transatlantic revivalism from the 1730s included sumptuary admonitions issued by preachers associated with the nascent Methodist movement and by Quaker reformers, and important attacks on luxury and opulence, as when James Davenport choreographed a bonfire of silk gowns and other lavish dress in New London, Connecticut, in 1743.[31] The self-

---

[27] Bernard Mandeville and F. B. Kaye, *The Fable of the Bees, or, Private Vices, Publick Benefits*, 2 vols. (Indianapolis: Liberty Classics, 1988), 1: 20.

[28] Maxine Berg and Elizabeth Eger, *Luxury in the Eighteenth Century: Debates, Desires and Delectable Goods* (Houndmills: Palgrave, 2003), 7. Quote from A. W., *The Enormous Abomination of the Hoop-Petticoat: As The Fashion Now Is …* (London: William Russel, 1745), 8. On British debates over dress, wealth and virtue, see John Styles, *The Dress of the People: Everyday Fashion in Eighteenth-Century England* (New Haven: Yale University Press, 2007), ch. 11.

[29] Titus Livius, *The History of Rome*, 4 vols., trans. D. Spillan and Cyrus R. Edmonds (London: Henry G. Bohn, 1850), book 34: 4.

[30] Aileen Ribeiro, *Dress and Morality* (New York: Holmes & Meier, 1986), 22.

[31] On Quaker and other sects' teachings on dressing plainly, see Styles, *The Dress of the People: Everyday Fashion in Eighteenth-Century England*, 203–6; David S. Lovejoy, *Religious Enthusiasm and the Great Awakening* (Englewood Cliffs: Prentice-Hall, 1969), 68.

same influences and authors who would help colonists to reconceptualise their understanding of political virtue, in other words, were typically condemning of excessive silks.[32]

Of powerful relevance to Americans in the 1760s were critiques of foreign silks by earlier British writers (then seeking to erect a platform for emergent British and Irish industries). Philosophers, economists, Anglican rectors, and novelists alike made hay out of the relationship between consumers' attitudes to silks and patriotism (and particularly anti-French sentiment). Through such authors as George Berkeley, Daniel Defoe, and Tobias Smollett, Americans had been assured that French silks and fashions were effeminising, wasteful, and trivial. Smollett warned that Britons (particularly women) were 'slaves' to French silk fashions, and Ames's popular American almanac for 1768 reprinted Smollett's indictment of luxurious fashions, repurposing it to encourage his readers to be a 'true Patriot and Friend' to their country by dressing appropriately.[33]

In the immediate aftermath of the Stamp Act in 1765–6, when colonial boycotts had first been proposed and attempted, there was little to suggest any enduring challenge to importing appetites, albeit a model of economic resistance and a language of marketing homemade virtue had been advanced.[34] Silk dyers and other specialist finishers such as Thomas Littlewood of London and Thomas Mewse of Norwich were opening businesses in seaports 'in the Silk & Woolen way'.[35] Existing retailers were also profiting well enough, as recorded in the diary of the prominent Boston merchant John Rowe, who fell victim to burglary when his store was broken into and stripped of many silks.[36] Benjamin Franklin's claim before Parliament that in 1766 Americans had stopped indulging in

---

[32] Charles de Secondat Baron de Montesquieu, Thomas Nugent, and Jean le Rond d'Alembert, *The Spirit of Laws*, 2 vols. (New York: The Colonial Press, 1899), 1: 98; Jean-Jacques Rousseau, *The Social Contract and Discourses by Jean-Jacques Rousseau*, trans. G. D. H. Cole (London: J. M. Dent & Sons, 1923), ch. 4.

[33] John Harris, *A Treatise Upon the Modes: Or, a Farewell to French Kicks* (London: J. Roberts, 1715); George Berkeley, *The Querist* (Dublin, 1735), 1: 1 50–5; Tobias Smollett, *Travels through France and Italy*, 2 vols. (London: R. Baldwin, 1766), 97–8 (letter six, dated 1763); Nathaniel Ames, *An Astronomical Diary; or, Almanack for the Year of Our Lord Christ 1768 . . .* (Boston: Draper et al., 1767), preface; Defoe, *A Plan of the English Commerce: Being a Compleat Prospect of the Trade of This Nation, as Well the Home Trade as the Foreign*, 181. Quote from poem accompanying satirical print, *Pantin a la Mode: or, Polite Conversation* (1748), attr. J. June, British Museum, AN434073001.

[34] Michele C. Busse, 'Got Silk? Buying, Selling, and Advertising British Luxury Imports during the Stamp Act *Crisis*' (University of North Texas, 2007), 11, 38–9.

[35] Boston, *Records Relating to Boston*, 20: 257, 311.

[36] Anne Rowe Cunningham, ed., *Letters and Diary of John Rowe, Boston Merchant, 1759–1762, 1764–1779* (Boston: W.B. Clarke Co., 1903), 5–6, 137 (theft), 139 (recovery), 140 (conviction).

British fashions and were now taking pride in 'wear[ing] their old clothes over again till they can make new ones' was premature at best.[37]

The virtues of silk were more roundly called into question with the renewal of non-consumption and non-importation movements in the wake of the Townshend Acts (1767–8). Subscribers to non-importation agreements gave highest priority to those items specifically enumerated in the acts, but most lists included a wider cross-section of manufactures, and silks assumed a dominant position whether it be in Boston (where John Rowe now chaired the city's committee to prevent luxury imports and encourage domestic manufactures), Annapolis, Williamsburg, or Charleston.[38] It was one thing for Theophilus Lillie of Boston to sell all manner of silks in the 1750s and early 1760s, but when he publicly advertised his wares again at the end of the decade, his shop was quickly listed as one that 'audaciously continues to counteract' the non-importation agreement. Targeted by townspeople, he was ultimately forced to close up and move away.[39] One contributor to a Boston newspaper urged readers to eschew 'foreign trifles' and instead 'recommend[ed] to every Farmer the growth of Hemp and Flax'.[40] A counterpart in South Carolina extolled ladies there to 'at least wear out your old silk gowns, purchase no new ones 'till this heavy storm is past (storms are apt to spoil new silks): this will please your economical husbands; it will certainly be a sacrifice worthy to them'.[41] A Connecticut female contributor mocked the hypocrisy of males now pulling the bandwagon of frugality, pointing out that until the crisis, homespun had been demeaned as the fabric of kitchen maids, and 'if one of us was loaded or even over-loaded with Silks, Ruffles and Lace, above the rest, she was your Phoenix'.[42]

As these differing viewpoints on gendered finery amongst Patriots implied, fashion could be both a site of conflict and a site of convergence within protest activities, and silk occupied a major ascriptive role. In the aftermath of the non-importation and non-consumption movements, in 1766 and 1770, there were bursts of commercial adrenalin, and silk imports

[37] Benjamin Franklin, *The Papers of Benjamin Franklin*, ed. Leonard W. Labaree et al., 43 vols. (New Haven: Yale University Press, 1959), 13: 159; Haulman, *The Politics of Fashion in Eighteenth-Century America*, 115.
[38] Breen, *The Marketplace of Revolution*, 237.
[39] See example of Lillie's extensive silk goods in *SUPPLEMENT to the Boston-Gazette*, 22 May 1758, p. 4; his argument in *Boston Chronicle*, 15 January 1770; and his identification as 'opposed to the united Sentiments of their Countrymen' in e.g. *Boston Evening-Post*, 29 January 1770, p. 2; *SUPPLEMENT to the Boston-Gazette, &c.*, 12 March 1770, p. 1.
[40] *The Boston Post-Boy & Advertiser*, 16 November 1767, p. 2.
[41] *South Carolina Gazette*, 13 July 1769, p. 1.
[42] *Connecticut Journal, and New-Haven Post-Boy*, 8 April 1768.

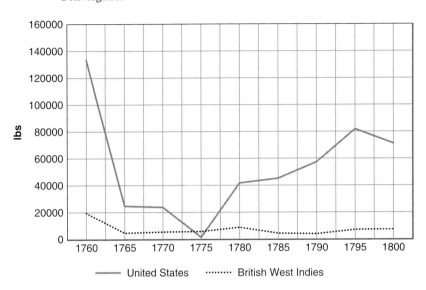

Figure 8.1 English exports of wrought silk to the Anglo-Atlantic (1760–1800). Compiled from figures in Customs 3 (1696–1780), National Archives tabulated by E. B. Schumpeter, *English Overseas Trade Statistics* (Oxford, 1961), table 35 ('Exports of Wrought Silk by Geographical Division, 1700–1800'), page 67. Figures effectively for exports from England and Wales, 1700–1790, and from Great Britain, 1795–1800

again flew into merchant storehouses, accompanied by extravagant fashions that made a mockery of the pursuit of rustic plainness. Customs export figures seem to bear this pattern out: American disruptions help account for why English silk exports (see Fig. 8.1) fell from a peak of £348,000 (official value) in 1760 to £164,000 in 1766 and £132,000 in 1770, with the thirteen colonies' share dropping from 67 per cent in 1760 to 44 per cent in 1770.[43] Once Parliament repealed the duties (except on tea) in 1770, even where colonial consumers had pronouncedly moved towards asceticism, they happily backtracked towards finery, amongst them Ezra and Elizabeth Stiles of course, eagerly awaiting the arrival of their Spitalfields fabric. Exports of silks bounced back to an average of £231,000 across 1771–2, some 57 per cent of which were sent to the thirteen disobedient colonies.[44] Readers of the Annapolis *Maryland Gazette* were exposed in the

[43] Market share calculated from Schumpeter, *English Overseas Trade Statistics*, 67.
[44] Breen, *The Marketplace of Revolution*, 238; Haulman, *The Politics of Fashion in Eighteenth-Century America*, 129; Mitchell and Deane, *Abstract of British Historical Statistics*, 468–70.

opening pages to colonial legislatures' strong recommendations 'to our countrymen' to eschew East India commodities, and encouraged to join the fray and the anti-importation and anti-consumption movements 'until the grievances of America are redressed', only to turn to the back pages (which had not caught up) to find advertisements under the title 'Just Imported' that offered extensive listings of silken goods – including striped lute-strings, tobined ducapes, and flowered brocades, alamode, Persian taffeta, and silk Persian and satin petticoats![45]

It is telling that even amongst those contemporaries who demeaned the efficacy of colonial economic resistance, silk was selected as a salient, bellwether commodity.[46] In effect, it was accruing incremental damage to its cultural cachet that would deepen with each step towards republicanism. The world of fabrics was being turned upside down, even if more on paper than on person: rich brocaded silk no longer occupied the highest but 'the lowest place' in Robert Livingston's portrayal of an America ruined by imperial vanity.[47] Satires such as the rather ponderous pamphlet *News from the Moon … Very Suitable to the Present Times*, printed in Boston in 1772, described a dystopia (borrowing again from an older British model first sketched out by Daniel Defoe in 1705) which ridiculed the 'silk gowns and scarlet cloaks' that were statements of pride and gluttony, and stood to damage the moral and material well-being of future generations.[48] True liberty was contrasted against being slaves 'rustling in silks and ribbons, or glittering with jewels'.[49]

The moral currency of silk depreciated with more rapidity with the creation of the 'Continental Association' in October 1774, a compact amongst the colonies that would generate a much more effective boycott on imports than those which preceded it, effective from 1 December. The Association took steps that went beyond commercial boycotts to sumptuary restraints, re-sharpening a tool that had long been blunted for European consumers. It explicitly gave pride of place to wool as the best republican material, and sought to 'discountenance and discourage every species of extravagance and dissipation' and to prevent expensive clothing being displayed at events or even in mourning dress. Wool and linen were the choice fibres of the revolution, and silk was left off the list of textiles to

[45] Annapolis *Maryland Gazette*, 2 June 1774.
[46] For instance, the claim of 'very little alteration in the demand for Tea, Silks, ribbons, Lace'. *Pennsylvania Gazette*, 25 May 1769.
[47] Robert R. Livingston, 'A Letter on the Ladies Wearing Homespun at the Time of the Stamp Act', n.d., Livingston Papers, NYHS. On impact in Williamsburg, Baumgarten, *What Clothes Reveal*, 95.
[48] *News from the Moon: Containing a Brief Account of the Manners and Customs of the Inhabitants* (Boston: Printing-Office near the Mill-Bridge, 1772).
[49] *New London Gazette*, 15 April 1768.

be pursued at the new radical 'American Manufactory' founded in 1775.[50] This repudiation was soon reflected in trade figures: in 1775, English exports of silk reached their lowest point in the second half of the eighteenth century, at £98,000 (official).[51] In that year, only 1,327 lb of wrought silks were recorded as sent to the thirteen colonies, which, put in chronological perspective, was a hundredth of the quantity exported there in 1760 and a sixtieth of the amount sent out in 1795 after trade relations were restored. Or, put in Atlantic geographical perspective, in 1775, for the first time in the British silk industry's eighteenth-century history, fewer wrought silks were exported to North America than to Africa or to Northern Europe, while the British West Indies restored an advantage it had not enjoyed since 1720. Or finally, put in textile perspective, the thirteen colonies' market share in the quantity of British silk exports dropped 64 percentage points between 1760 and 1775 (down to 3 per cent), compared to a drop of 44 in linens (down to 11 per cent), between 8 and 30 percentage points in a range of other fabrics, and a fall of around 20 points in beaver hats and men's worsted stockings.[52]

During the war that followed, silk remained a lowly commodity in the eyes of Patriots. John Adams argued that 'Silks and Velvets and Lace must be dispensed with' as 'Trifles in a Contest for Liberty'.[53] One former dry goods merchant, John Cadwalader, closed his business and transformed his ornate house into a muster point for a new company of Philadelphia soldiers, thereafter known ironically as the 'Silk Stocking Company' for its uncharacteristic origins and dress.[54] That the extravagant furnishings were

---

[50] Peter Force, *American Archives: Consisting of a Collection of Authentick Records, State Papers, Debates, and Letters and Other Notices of Publick Affairs ...*, (Washington, 1837), ser. 4, 1: 913 (Association); 1: 1256 (American Manufactory). For examples of wool and linen being upheld as the utmost patriotic fibres, see Zakim, *Ready-Made Democracy*, 11–14. On this period and radical manufacturing initiatives of woollens, cottons, and linens, Peskin, *Manufacturing Revolution*, 47–8, 57; Richard Alan Ryerson, *The Revolution Is Now Begun: The Radical Committees of Philadelphia, 1765–1776* (Philadelphia: University of Pennsylvania Press, 1978), 112–15.

[51] Mitchell and Deane, *Abstract of British Historical Statistics*, 468–70.

[52] Schumpeter, *English Overseas Trade Statistics*, 67 & 66. These included stout fustians, single and double bays (collectively), long and short cloths (collectively); printed cottons and linens were only tabulated from 1765, though do look to have shared a more similar fate to silk exports in market share terms in 1775.

[53] John Adams to James Warren, 20 October 1775; another example of his disdain for silk can be found in his comments on French luxury in his autobiography, 20 May 1778. C. James Taylor, ed., 'Founding Families: Digital Editions of the Papers of the Winthrops and the *Adamses*' (Boston: Massachusetts Historical Society, January 2007), www.masshist.org/digitaladams/hereinafter cited as *Adams Papers Online*.

[54] The company was known variously as the 3rd Battalion of Associators, The Greens, and formerly The City Troop. David Hayfield Conyngham and Horace Edwin Hayden, *The Reminiscences of David Hayfield Conyngham, 1750–1834, a Hero of the Revolution* (Wilkes-Barre, PA: Printed for the society, 1904), 18n9.

deemed antithetical to Patriot wartime sensibilities made Cadwalader's home on Second Street a logical choice for British General William Howe to lodge in after his successful occupation of the city in 1777. With a British boycott in place for the duration of the war, consumer silks were on the retreat commercially as well as ideologically, even if they were still mobilised on some public occasions.[55]

By the early 1780s, judging by the vexed diary of Loyalist Samuel Shoemaker, as a consequence of this interruption, American tastes in silk had rather frozen in time. Shoemaker was a Quaker merchant who had once signed non-importation agreements but thereafter become a pronounced Loyalist, and evacuated with the British army from New York in 1783. Shortly afterwards, looking to replenish his wardrobe, Shoemaker was informed that the sort of silk (black paduasoy) 'I want is entirely out of wear here and that none has been made or can be had.' After several days' haranguing a range of silk mercers and manufacturers, he compromised, accepting that 'that kind of silk is quite out of wear except among some particular people of our society'.[56] American silk consumption, so vibrant for so long, had temporarily stalled. As Sarah Franklin Bache put it, in noting that her silk petticoat had been worn out in Pennsylvania in 1778, 'I find I can go without many things I once thought absolutely necessary.'[57]

---

[55] Durand Echeverria, 'The American Character: A Frenchman Views the New Republic from Philadelphia', *William and Mary Quarterly* 16 (1959): 409. For a comparative view, Leora Auslander, *Cultural Revolutions: The Politics of Everyday Life in Britain, North America and France* (Oxford: Berg, 2009), 84–91.

[56] Samuel Shoemaker, 'A Pennsylvania Loyalist's Interview with George III. Extract from the MS. Diary of Samuel Shoemaker', *Pennsylvania Magazine of History and Biography* 2, no. 1 (1878): 35–9; Samuel Shoemaker, *Diary of Samuel Shoemaker of Philadelphia, from November 7, 1783 to October 5, 1785. Copied from the Original in the Possession of the Historical Society of Pennsylvania* (Philadelphia: Typescript, Historical Society of Pennsylvania, 1892), 23–5.

[57] Sarah Bache to Benjamin Franklin, Philadelphia, 22 October 1778, in The Packard Institute of Humanities: The Papers of Benjamin Franklin [www.franklinpapers.org], hereinafter cited as *Franklin Papers Online*.

These wider currents in the flow and ebb of foreign silk goods within the Atlantic economy naturally had a bearing on the American pursuit of silk production, though not always as simple an influence as one might suppose. Even as imported finished silks were being expressly targeted as a symptom of Old World decadence, and the very virtues of the fibre called into question by shifts in fashion and trade during the Age of Revolutions, the reality (or possibility) of American-raised raw silk could and did hold out promise. Non-importation was not necessarily synonymous with anti-consumption, and where domestic manufacturing could be encouraged or other supply routes could be found, the rhetoric of cultural repudiation could be toned down.[1] Had protesting Americans been able to grow all their silks, weave some of their silks, or buy all their silks through, say, St Eustatius, the likelihood is that the commodity would have been less victimised. We might take, by comparison, the protest movement in contemporary Ireland, where non-importation and non-consumption were also invoked against British textile manufactures, but without the same tone or commodity specificity: where the Irish objected, they rather targeted silk's place of weaving and later its colours.[2] So while plenty of commentators have assumed that the revolution definitively put paid to raw silk schemes, and are right to note that colonists had little capital or inclination to spare for projective experiments in the context of revolutionary political and economic upheavals, this interpretation needs to be nuanced in time and place. Some silk trials were discouraged by the evaporation of British commercial support, some undermined by the arrival of war, and others outmuscled by the new opportunities which arrived as the states and their economies were reconstituted from the 1780s, when budgetary constraints meant that the use of

---

[1] Zakim, *Ready-Made Democracy*, 17.
[2] See e.g. Dublin non-importation agreement, 5 September 1780, in David B. Horn and Mary Ransome, eds., *English Historical Documents, 1714–1783*, vol. 7 (repr.) (New York: Routledge, 2003), 694; Sarah Foster, 'Buying Irish: Consumer Nationalism in 18th-Century Dublin', *History Today* 47, no. 6 (1997).

bounties generally declined. Still others were not entirely uprooted, however, bending like reeds with the winds of revolution, and recovering their shape in the 1790s.[3]

The most damage to prospects occurred in the South. The impossibility of shipping produce to Britain undermined the remaining export-oriented silk raisers in Ebenezer, Georgia and in South Carolina, where a balance of £3,000 was still held by the public treasurers as a 'Bounty on silk manufactory'; provincial finances could not uphold this luxurious commitment once the cost of revolution began to bite. The arrival of full-blown war in the southern theatre in 1780 disrupted operations, and had a particularly devastating effect on one of the principal centres at Purrysburg, also claiming the life of one of its major proponents in New Bordeaux. In the war's aftermath, where good stocks of mulberries remained, some diminutive local production persisted.[4] But the very forces that had sustained experimental production of silk for so much of the colonial era in the Lower South were critically compromised with the severing of imperial connections, the withdrawal of British patronage, the destruction in the backcountry, the dispersal of enslaved people in the Lowcountry, and the weakening of planters' interest in the face of more pressing challenges and opportunities – amongst them the reconstitution of estates and the sudden viability of short-staple cotton in many southern environs thanks to technological advance and relentless manufacturing demand.

It is to one of the later regions pursuing sericulture, Pennsylvania, that we must turn to find the best illustration of how silken ambitions survived and were reshaped to fit new political and economic environments in the later eighteenth century. Pennsylvanian silk swung from being a dutiful imperial pursuit, albeit one with particular local characteristics, to being an objective very much in step with American independence. It constituted a unique kind of homespun that not only came to embody domestic elegance but also provided ammunition for broader debates over political economy and the future identity of American industrial development.

[3] For claims of termination and lack of revival until late 1820s: Albert Keller Hostetter, 'The Early Silk Industry of Lancaster County', *Historical Papers and Addresses of the Lancaster County Historical Society* 23, no. 2 (1919): 31; Charles Arthur Sheffeld, *Silk Its Origin, Culture, and Manufacture* (Florence, MA: The Corticelli silk mills, 1911), 8. Cf. case for revival or wartime enhancement: Richard Dobson Margrave, *The Emigration of Silk Workers from England to the United States in the Nineteenth Century, with Special Reference to Coventry, Macclesfield, Paterson, New Jersey, and South Manchester, Connecticut* (New York and London: Garland Publishing, Inc., 1986), 21; William C. Wyckoff, *American Silk Manufacture* (New York: John L. Murphy Publishing Co, 1887), 30.
[4] William Edwin Hemphill, Wylma Anne Wates, and R. Nicholas Olsberg, eds., *Journals of the General Assembly and House of Representatives, 1776–1780* (Columbia: University of South Carolina Press, 1970), 155; Migliazzo, *To Make This Land Our Own*, 238, 266–75; Pinney, *A History of Wine in America: From the Beginnings to Prohibition*, 100.

Philadelphia, situated in the heart of the North American colonies, was the first home of the Continental Congress, the city where the Declaration of Independence was signed in 1776, and the site of the federal capital for ten years between 1790 and 1800. Before all that, it was also the location of the mid-Atlantic's first silk filature, and in 1771 reeled the cocoons of approximately 700,000 American silkworms.

The Coming Together of a Silk Society

The presence of indigenous American mulberry trees in the mid-Atlantic (*M. rubra*, initially classified as *Morus nigra Americana*) had ensured that this zone enjoyed a small share of early silk projection, initially following the environmental logic articulated for seventeenth-century English Virginia, and emulating its patterns and problems.[5] Spoilage of silkworm eggs had cut short experimentation in New Netherlands in 1657, while English Quaker William Penn talked the talk upon being granted a vast tranche of lands by proprietary charter in 1681 – insisting his major landowners 'preserve oak and mulberries, for silk and shipping,' and naming one of Philadelphia's gridded streets 'Mulberry Street' – without doing much to ensure silkworm supplies or specialists were available to Pennsylvania's first settlers.[6] The first active top-down encouragement of sericulture occurred in 1726, in parallel with some of the developing efforts in the Lower South and New England, when Pennsylvania's new governor Patrick Gordon gave a speech to urge the general assembly to support attempts, accepting that '[a]s the Business is new, People will naturally be backward in falling into the Practice', but pointing out that

[5] This attribution in Peter Kalm and Esther Louise Larsen, 'Peter Kalm's Short Account of the Natural Position, Use, and Care of Some Plants, of Which the Seeds Were Recently Brought Home from North America for the Service of Those Who Take Pleasure in Experimenting with the Cultivation of the Same in Our Climate', *Agricultural History* 13, no. 1 (1939): 51–5. Kalm also claimed to have found an 'intermediate between the black and white mulberry tree' in New Bristol that he classified as *Morus Bristolensis*. Ibid., 56. Confusion over species by the eighteenth century likely reflected a high degree of hybridisation, which has since gradually placed *M. rubra* at a strong disadvantage to the point where it is now endangered in Canada. Burgess and Husband, 'Habitat Differentiation and the Ecological Costs of Hybridization: The Effects of Introduced Mulberry (Morus Alba) on a Native Congener (M. Rubra).'

[6] Hans Fantel, *William Penn; Apostle of Dissent* (New York: Morrow, 1974), 29, 54–5, 238; Albert Cook Myers, *Narratives of Early Pennsylvania, West New Jersey and Delaware, 1630–1707* (New York: C. Scribner's Sons, 1912), 207; Hazard, *Hazard's Register*, 1: 28. William Penn, *A Further Account of the Province of Pennsylvania and Its Improvements* (s.n., 1685), 3. Mulberry Street was thereafter named Arch Street, becoming the commercial heart of late colonial Philadelphia, but it continued to form the southern boundary line of 'Mulberry Ward'. Mulberry Ward was further divided into North and South Mulberry Wards in 1786.

'all Manufactures were so at first', including West Indian sugar (the commodity model so often idealised by Atlantic settlers).[7] What seems to have tipped Pennsylvania into a more sustained and active commitment to sericulture was the addition of extra variables from the 1760s: scientific interest, the rise of Enlightenment associations, and the changing view of silk as a consequence of the imperial crisis.

As a function of its dramatic commercial growth, religious toleration and the mixed populations in its hinterland, Philadelphia had developed a distinctive identity by the mid-eighteenth century – evolving a vibrant print culture and expansive public sphere and discursive society. This manifested itself in an array of Enlightenment associations that spanned natural science, commerce, agriculture, and the arts, including, most famously, the American Philosophical Society. In 1768, the year that non-importation campaigns were renewed against British goods in the colonies (though Philadelphian merchants dragged their heels), this Society heard Moses Bartram, one of a famous family of naturalists, read his entomological paper on 'the Native Silk Worms of North-America' (probably the univoltine *Hyalophora cecropia*). Bartram described his experiments and gave a firm recommendation to cultivate silkworms, though tellingly he had not yet attempted to unwind the cocoons he had raised. Nonetheless, they appeared to him 'much easier raised than the Italian or foreign silk worms', with less tendency to sicken or suffer from trauma from thunderstorms. Bartram's proud public characterisation of the native worms – in language similar to Stiles's private musings – offered a contribution to arguments that had long been raging about whether the Americas were inherently degenerative, challenging the notion that the New World was a site of comparative natural poverty, whose environment eroded Old World flora and fauna (as according to the influential Comte de Buffon).[8]

From the late 1760s, silk production was treated as a 'public-spirited' design which had the capacity to merge social, economic, and scientific progress in Pennsylvania with commercial and industrial development in Britain. Importantly though, compared to earlier imperial initiatives in pursuit of Atlantic sericulture, metropolitan incentives were downgraded to a secondary role. The vehicle for considerable uptake of silk raising in

---

[7] Hazard, 3: 265. *Pennsylvania Archives*, 138 vols. (Philadelphia: Published by the State, 1835), ser. 4, 1:476. Discussed in more depth in Ben Marsh, '"The Honour of the Thing": Silk Culture in Eighteenth-Century Pennsylvania', in *Threads of Global Desire: Silk in the Pre-Modern World*, ed. Dagmar Schäfer, Giorgio Riello, and Luca Mola (Woodbridge: Boydell and Brewer, 2018).

[8] Richard William Judd, *The Untilled Garden: Natural History and the Spirit of Conservation in America, 1740–1840* (New York: Cambridge University Press, 2009), 58, 70, 106–7. Stiles, 'Journal of Silkworms', 111–12, 113, 123, 249.

Pennsylvania was the Society for Promoting Useful Knowledge. Its president, Benjamin Franklin, did an impressive job of pulling the strings via correspondence, since he was based in London from 1764 to 1775, and at one point visited Thomas Lombe's famous silk-throwing mill at Derby.[9] Franklin began by sending over literature. French treatises arrived for Quaker physician Cadwalader Evans, and extracts were translated and shared amongst the Society's members. One was authored by Pierre-Augustin Boissier de Sauvages de Lacroix, one of two brother botanists from Languedoc (the other being François) born in the silk-raising centre of Alès – where Louis Pasteur would later undertake his groundbreaking research into silkworm diseases. They propounded theories on insect classification and technical development that reflected the region's advancing sericulture, driven by the opportunity silkworms presented to enrich the region, and perhaps to challenge the dominance of Paris in matters of natural science. Pierre-Augustin (later the Abbé de Sauvages) produced detailed work on the subject that introduced a rationalism and empirical aspect that was credited with improving silkworm practices in late eighteenth-century France, creating a workshop and research programme with royal support in the 1750s, and later undertaking multiple research trips to Italy. Another source circulated in Pennsylvania was the memoir of Henri de Goyon de La Plombanie, a philosophe and political economist from the Périgord who sought to modernise silk-raising techniques in Languedoc, and whose principal recommendation was not to mix the types of mulberry leaves fed to silkworms.[10] Armed with such information, Cadwalader Evans enlisted support from like-minded Pennsylvanians, quirkily proposing at first that a premium on cocoons might be defrayed by a tax upon dogs, 'whose great number is become

---

[9] Journal of Jonathan Williams, Jr., of 'His Tour with Franklin and Others through Northern England', 28 May 1771, in *Franklin Papers Online*.

[10] Franklin to Cadwalader Evans, London, 7 September 1769, 8 September 1769, 17 March 1770, in *Franklin Papers Online*; part-translation submitted by 'Pennsylvaniensis' to *Pennsylvania Chronicle*, 5 June 1769. See also extracts of silk literature in *Poor Richard's Almanack* in 1771, as advertised in, e.g., *Pennsylvania Gazette*, 20 September 1770. Principal works of the de Sauvages were: de Sauvages, *Mémoires sur l'éducation des vers à soie*; Francois de Sauvages, 'Sur les vers à soie et sur la maniere la plus sure de les élever', in *Histoire de La Société Royale Des Sciences Établie à Montpellier* (Montpellier: Jean Martel Ainé, 1778), 251–68; Pierre Augustin Boissier de Sauvages, *L'art d'élever les vers à soie* (Avignon: J. J. Niel, 1788). Goyon de la Plombanie, 'Mémoire sur la manière d'élever des vers à soye en france & dans tous les climats où les mûriers peuvent être cultivés', *Journal Économique* (1752), 43. On networks and Languedoc scientific and sericultural particularities, J. Livesey, 'London by the Light of Montpellier: Scientific Networks between British, Northern Europe and the Languedoc', *Studies on Voltaire and the Eighteenth Century* 4 (2010): 85–102; Stockland, 'Patriotic Natural History and Sericulture in the French Enlightenment', 9–12.

a nu[i]sance'.[11] Franklin proposed to Evans in a letter that: 'if some provision were made by the Assembly for promoting the growth of mulberry trees in all parts of the province, the culture of silk might afterwards follow easily', and advised of two potential models of silk production in the Mediterranean: in northern Italy, cocoons were bought up from farming households and processed centrally, while in Sicily, 'each Family winds its own Silk' which was then brought to market.[12]

The plans for Pennsylvania, unusually, sought to draw on lessons learnt previously in the colonies – there was something of a scientific method in evidence that depended upon the integration and convergence of information. Most agreed that the best course of action was to establish a public filature in Philadelphia and to promote the growth of sufficient mulberry trees – particularly of 'Italian' or 'French' mulberries (i.e. *M. alba*). The idea of offering premiums for mulberries themselves, however, was withdrawn precisely because of the 'experience of a neighbouring government'. Silkworm eggs were to be sought from existent stocks in Georgia and Carolina. But the Society's plans hit a roadblock upon discovering that the Assembly was unwilling to fund them. Undeterred, the Society restructured its ambitions and, confident of popular support amongst middling and wealthy Philadelphians, went about raising a public subscription and establishing a stock company – something which would have been hard to pull off anywhere else in the British colonies. As one Englishman observed to his brother about the new scheme: 'the people of this city are far beyond the inhabitants of any other part of the continent in public spirit: I mean in that proper useful spirit of improvement'.[13] In 1770, 'The Society for Encouraging the Culture of Silk in Pennsylvania' was formed, supported to the tune of £850 by private subscriptions of amounts ranging from £1 to £20, with the largest sum put forward by John Penn, of the proprietary family. The success of the private subscriptions relied on word of mouth and the energies of a number of prominent Philadelphians, as reflected in the diary of Jacob Hiltzheimer (a Rhineland émigré who had married a Quaker), which recorded that amidst his usual fare of cockfights and horse races, on 15 March 1770 'Edward Penington and Clement Biddle called on me with a subscription paper to encourage the manufacture of

---

[11] Cadwalader Evans to Benjamin Franklin, Philadelphia, 15 July 1769, 27 November 1769 in *Franklin Papers Online*.

[12] Benjamin Franklin to Cadwalader Evans, London, 7 September 1769, in *Franklin Papers Online*.

[13] Alexander Mackraby to Sir Philip Francis, Philadelphia, 4 May 1770, in A. Mackraby, 'Philadelphia Society before the Revolution (Concluded)', *The Pennsylvania Magazine of History and Biography* 11, no. 4 (1888): 494.

silk here. I subscribed 40 shillings.'[14] The movement was led by, as one historian has put it, the 'very men who were most anxious to use science to advance the material welfare of the colonies', and included a large proportion of Quakers (including Moses Bartram).[15]

The Philadelphia filature was opened in 1770, in a house on Seventh Street between Arch and High Streets. Though very much centred on Philadelphia, over the next years this institution drew within its orbit silk raisers from neighbouring counties including those across other colonies, offering a focal point for experimenters from New Jersey, Delaware, and beyond. In 1769, Sabina Blandenburgh Rumsey had determined to turn her hand to silk raising at her house on the Bohemia River in Cecil County, Maryland. She wrote to the Pennsylvania Silk Society a year later, in response to their call for local insights into silk raising, and explained that, 'having been presented with [Samuel] *Pullein* on the Culture of Silk, and some Eggs of the Georgian Worms, I deposited them in a Room on the South-East Part of our House, the second Floor, where the Frosts of March could not affect them, nor was the Place so warm, that they would hatch before Food from the Mulberry could be procured to nourish the Worms'. Rumsey recorded how until the point of reeling, 'the Business had been easy, indeed pleasing to me', finding it agreeable to have 2,000 silkworms 'engaged in one's immediate Interest, I the sole Proprietress, and Finery the intended Consequence'. The trial did not end so enjoyably, and Rumsey finished her letter explaining that she could not cope with the hot steam required to reel off the cocoons. However, she observed that should there emerge the incentive of an additional colonial premium in Pennsylvania, it 'may make me alter my Resolution, not from Avarice, believe me, Sir, but the Honour of the Thing'. In due course the Pennsylvania Society would take up many of the themes raised in Rumsey's short letter, which was published in the *Pennsylvania Gazette*, as the Society harnessed local interest and determination, globally sourced literature and resources, and the uncomfortable motivational trio of finery, avarice, and honour.[16]

---

[14] Jacob Hiltzheimer, 'Extracts from the Diary of Jacob Hiltzheimer, of Philadelphia, 1768–1798', *The Pennsylvania Magazine of History and Biography* 16, no. 1 (1892): 95.

[15] Brooke Hindle, *The Pursuit of Science in Revolutionary America, 1735–1789* (Chapel Hill: University of North Carolina Press, 1956), 201. The managers, as listed in *Pennsylvania Gazette*, 22 March 1770, were: Cadwalader Evans, Israel Pemberton, Benjamin Morgan, Moses Bartram, Dr Francis Alison, Dr William Smith, John Rhea, Samuel Rhoads, Thomas Fisher, Owen Biddle, Henry Drinker, and Robert Strettell Jones, and the treasurer was Edward Penington. For a full list of Quaker members of the Society, see Frederick Barnes Tolles, *Meeting House and Counting House: The Quaker Merchants of Colonial Philadelphia, 1682–1763* (Chapel Hill, NC: University of North Carolina Press, 1948), 98.

[16] *Pennsylvania Gazette*, 11 January 1770 (invitation for information); 29 March 1770 (letter from Rumsey to Charles Thomson).

The encouragement schemes constructed by the Silk Society were amongst the most complex and carefully orchestrated of all of those offered in the eighteenth century. They addressed issues of timing, quantity, and quality, and sought to offer rewards which broadened uptake of silkworm rearing and silk reeling, thereby generating increasing momentum and investment. Payments were generous, beginning in 1770 at four shillings per pound of 'sound and merchantable' cocoons of the 'Italian or foreign Silk-Worm' and twenty-five shillings per thousand 'of the Native, or American Worm', the quality of which Moses Bartram remained adamant about. Besides the regular payment and an additional bounty, special prizes were earmarked for those producing the largest number of 'sound Cocoons' exceeding 30,000, which were claimable in Pennsylvania, Delaware, New Jersey, or Maryland. The payments in later years were adjusted to take into account the dramatic difference in weight that existed between fresh cocoons (with the pupae still alive inside) and those which had become much lighter, having lost moisture but not quality over time, after the pupae had been terminated. The adjustment for 1773 meant the filature paid out the same sum for 24 oz of early-July cocoons as it did for 16 oz of mid-August cocoons, or even 13 oz of cocoons submitted later, provided they were 'extraordinary good, and very dry' and still from the first crop. By incentivising delayed submission, this had the added advantage of sustaining filature activity and preserving young mulberry leafing over the course of a season. Bivoltine yields were attempted in the second year, but the second crops were found to be much smaller and of poor quality. Prizes also changed somewhat in later years, growing to include not just rewards for larger quantities of cocoons, but also for the finest samples of reeled silk. By 1773 the winning cocoon contributors could expect to receive not only cash prizes (respectively of £15, £10, and £5) but also a silk-reeling machine and a copper kettle. Restrictions were placed on silk claimants; these insisted that their silk should be produced as one crop and by the claimant's family, and also that 5 per cent of the claimant's harvest be retained as eggs to create a decent stock for subsequent years.[17]

The *Pennsylvania Gazette* reported that sixty-four families had already 'made a Beginning' in 1769, even before the Silk Society was up and running, many of them raising between 10,000 and 20,000 silkworms, with one woman in Chester County having raised 'upwards of 30,000' silkworms. These experimenters were described as 'animated with Spirit and Resolution to prosecute the design', but

---

[17] Payments and prizes listed variously in: *Pennsylvania Gazette*, 14 June 1770, 3 October 1771, 31 January 1771, 25 June 1772, 29 July 1772, 7 April 1773.

were not very good at reeling: that year, an estimated 100,000 cocoons were spoiled, 'for Want of being reeled'.[18] Like iron filings to a magnet, such household producers were quick to respond to the pull of the filature: the Silk Society estimated that the quantity of cocoons purchased in 1771 was twenty times that in 1770, ranging in weight from as little as 4 oz to the 68 lb sold by Mary Thorn (probably the daughter of a New Jersey weaver). In total, some 2,300 lb were offered for sale, of which 1,754 lb were bought up and reeled, of which 150 lb raw silk worth 20–25 shillings per lb (exclusive of the parliamentary bounty) were eventually exported to London. More than half of the people who actually sold the cocoons were women, and most seem to have been operating at single-household level, though a handful of depositors, including 'John Etwine' (either Moravian leader Johann or his wife Johanetta Ettwein) probably submitted the output of larger communities – in their case producers at Bethlehem in Northampton County, Pennsylvania – even though magistrates were to ensure via certificates that 'all the Cocoons ... were actually raised with the Claimant's Family *only*'. The figures suggest that as many as twenty-eight of the producers were from outside Pennsylvania (mostly from New Jersey), and that, if they were reasonably prompt with the delivery of their cocoons, nearly half had completed their work by late June, a third in the first week of July, and the remainder later in the season.[19]

The Silk Society was just as careful and selective in its building and equipping of the Philadelphia filature, its quest for stocks of trees and worms, and its hiring of specialists as it was in its commissioning of publications, and its elaborate system of payments and prizes. Calls had gone out for experienced silk raisers in its earliest public statements, and by late August 1770 the Silk Society had tempted Piedmontese-born Joseph Ottolenghe up from his position in Savannah to Philadelphia, 'at great wages', where he would help to train 'any Persons, MEN, WOMEN, or GIRLS' in reeling.[20] This was not a move sanctioned by or funded by

---

[18] *Pennsylvania Gazette*, 15 March 1770.

[19] *Pennsylvania Gazette*, 3 October 1771; 'Letter on the Culture of Silk', *American Museum*, 3 (January 1788): 86–9; Hostetter, 'Early Silk Industry of Lancaster County', 30; John Fanning Watson, *Annals of Philadelphia* (Philadelphia, 1830), 618. Johann Ettwein was elsewhere credited with the introduction of 'the Persian mulberry' into Bethlehem, Pennsylvania, as in US Committee on Agriculture, John D'Homergue, and Peter S. Duponceau, *Report of the Committee on Agriculture on the Growth and Manufacture of Silk; to Which Is Annexed, Essays on American Silk, with Directions to Farmers for Raising Silk Worms, by John D'Homergue, Silk Manufacturer; and Peter Stephen Duponceau* (Washington: Duff Green, 1830), 76.

[20] *Pennsylvania Gazette*, 30 August 1770, 3 October 1771.

imperial or state authorities, but a function of the growing internal connectivity and conviction of American colonial networks. Had Ottolenghe not been persuadable, Franklin schemed to 'procure you such a Hand from Italy, a great Silk Merchant here having offered me his Assistance for that purpose if wanted'.[21] Expertise in America was again called for in June 1772, when the managers of the Silk Society advertised the position of 'Superintendant', requiring 'A PERSON, who understands the Quality of COCOONS, and of SILK when reeled'.[22] In light of the rapid progress in Philadelphia, a tone of cautious optimism was apparent: Humphry Marshall, a farmer in Chester County who would later become a fully-fledged nurseryman, noted 'Our people Seems to make a great Noise about raising Silk how it will turn out I Know not.'[23] Likewise, Thomas Gilphin stated in 1770 that 'The silk business is in a fair way and I am convinced will be of consequence if attended to.'[24] In fact, the take-up of production soon threatened to exhaust the company's capital, and in 1772 the Pennsylvania Assembly agreed to appropriate £1,000 on the condition that an equal sum were raised by popular subscription – though this had the damaging side-effect that out-of-state producers like Sabina Rumsey were no longer eligible for many premiums.[25]

The Silk Producers and Their Motives

Pennsylvania silk raisers appear to have been a heterogeneous bunch, reflecting the marked ethnic diversity of the middle colonies, where Philadelphia acted as a primary landing point for Europeans seeking new lives in British America. They included Quakers, Scots-Irish Presbyterians, and a large number of settlers of German origin, such as Johanetta Ettwein of Bethlehem who won the £10 prize in 1771; in the listings of cocoon sales it is possible to detect over time, as in Georgia, a greater labour effort and output amongst German communities in Pennsylvania.[26] Some indication of the status of these silk raisers can be found in extant county tax assessment records. By the 1770s, the

[21] Franklin to Cadwalader Evans, London, 27 August 1770; Cadwalader Evans to Franklin, Philadelphia, 4 May 1771, *Franklin Papers Online. Pennsylvania Gazette*, 3 October 1771.
[22] *Pennsylvania Gazette*, 11 June 1772.
[23] Humphry Marshall to Franklin, Chester County, 28 May 1770, *Franklin Papers Online. Humphry Marshall, Arbustrum Americanum: The American Grove* (Philadelphia: Printed by Joseph Crukshank, 1785), 93–4 on mulberries.
[24] Thomas Gilpin to Franklin, Philadelphia, 21 September 1770, in *Franklin Papers Online.*
[25] Some two-fifths of the premium payments went to New Jersey residents in 1771, for instance. *Pennsylvania Gazette*, 30 April 1772.
[26] Silk raising seems to have been pursued in Bethlehem since 1753 with the experimentation of Rev. Christian Bader, later the Moravian pastor at the Hebron church. John

Pennsylvania Assembly was levying an annual tax of eighteen pence per pound value of assessed wealth in real and personal property (or 7.5 per cent of assessed value), and a corresponding poll tax of fifteen shillings for unpropertied freemen – all of it collected by county tax commissioners. When cross-indexed against the Silk Society's prizes for cocoon production (see Fig. 9.1), it seems that many Pennsylvania silk raisers were of middling status, ranging from families headed by prominent locals down to the occasional freeman, and a disproportionately large number of widows and women.[27]

At one end of the spectrum stood Isaac Whitelock, a wealthy and prominent Yorkshire-born Quaker, who was a town burgess and later treasurer of the borough of Lancaster, Pennsylvania, where he had lived since before 1745; he would later serve once in the colonial assembly. His attention to sericulture seems to have reflected a long-standing willingness to pursue commercial and manufacturing ventures. Before raising silk he had built a brewery (on Prince Street, where there was a spring) and tannery, and also advertised for sale in 1769 'a lot of ground in the borough of Lancaster, whereon is erected a large house convenient for manufacturing pot ashes'.[28] Fellow Lancaster burgess William Henry (from 1766) also had a practical predisposition that might have encouraged interest in the theoretical and technical challenges of silk production. Henry was an engineer, mechanic, and gunsmith who had served in the Seven Years' War and later lent his experience to the Continental Army in an unenviable role as its commissary. Besides owning a workshop and business, his house was reputed as a salon for men of culture, and numbered amongst its lodgers the likes of Thomas Paine, Benjamin West, Robert Fulton, and David Rittenhouse. His wife Ann Wood Henry likely made an important contribution to his silk raising, and she was described in one biography as 'a thrifty, singularly clear-headed woman of affairs, with an aptitude for administration not often found in her sex', on the grounds that she became

---

W. Heisey, 'Extracts from the Diary of the Moravian Pastors of the Hebron Church, Lebanon, 1755–1814', *Pennsylvania History* 34, no. 1 (1967): 52n44.

[27] Taxation information from Alvin Rabushka, *Taxation in Colonial America* (Princeton: Princeton University Press, 2008), 810–14; William Pencak, *Pennsylvania's Revolution* (University Park, PA: Pennsylvania State University Press, 2010), 284–85. Six individuals from Lancaster County can be linked to silk production, whose assumed value ranges from one unpropertied freeman (Casper Forteny) up to £43, 6s, 8d (the property of Isaac Whitlock, which included 32 acres, 3 horses, and 1 cattle). 'Returns and Assessments for the Fourteenth Eighteen-Penny Tax for the County of Lancaster', PA Archives, Series 3, Volume 17.

[28] Quote from Philadelphia *Pennsylvania Chronicle*, 15 February 1769. Franklin Ellis and Samuel Evans, *History of Lancaster County, Pennsylvania* (Philadelphia: Everts & Peck, 1883), chapter 29; Francis Jordan, *The Life of William Henry, of Lancaster, Pennsylvania* (Lancaster, PA: New Era Printing Co., 1910).

The MANAGERS OF THE CONTRIBUTIONS FOR PRO-
MOTING THE CULTURE OF SILK, having finally determined
the PREMIUMS offered, for raifing the greateft Number of *Cocoons*,
and for REELING THE BEST SILK, for the Year 1772, hereby
inform the *Claimants* who have not yet applied, that on Application to the Managers, they may receive the Reward annexed to
their refpective Names, viz.

Widow Stoner, Lancafter County,	72,800 Cocoons,	£ 15	0	0
James Millhoufe, Chefter Co.	41,820	10	0	0
Richard Gorman, Ditto,	34,850	6	0	0
William Hill, Philadelphia Co.	31,330	3	0	0
Phœbe Trimble, Chefter County,	29,059	3	0	0
Lewis Valaret, Philadelphia Co.	25,000	3	0	0
Cafper Farkney, Lancafter Co.	22,845	3	0	0
Mary Parker, Chefter County,	22,700	3	0	0
Catherine Steimer, Lancafter Co.	21,800	3	0	0
Mary Bifhop, Chefter County,	21,479	a Silk Reel.		
Lucia Hinton, Bucks County,	20,000	Ditto.		
James Wright, Lancafter Co.	17,600	Ditto.		
Caleb Harrifon, Chefter County,	16,500	Ditto.		

Rebecca Park, Lancafter County, for the beft Sam-
ple of reeled Silk,   -   -   -   £ 3   0   0
Jofeph Ferree, Lancafter County, for 2d beft Ditto,   2   0   0
Phœbe Cornthwaite, Bucks Co. for 3d beft Ditto,   1   0   0
A Lift of Premiums, *with the* Prices *propofed to be given for* Co-
coons, *for the Year* 1773, *will fhortly be publifhed.*
N. B. Thofe Perfons who propofe raifing Silk-worms the en-
fuing Seafon, and want a Supply of Eggs, will be furnifhed
therewith gratis, by a fpeedy Application to JOHN KAIGHN, in
Second-ftreet.

Figure 9.1 Pennsylvania prizewinning cocoon producers in 1773.
Detail from page 3 of the *Pennsylvania Gazette* (17 March 1773)
containing a listing of the prizewinning cocoon harvesters in
Pennsylvania that year. The Library Company of Philadelphia

the first women to hold public office in Pennsylvania when she assumed
William's duties as treasurer of Lancaster County for four years after his
death in 1786.[29] Growing silk alongside such middling artisan/manufac-
turers in Lancaster County was Caleb Johnson, a Quaker schoolmaster
who remained a Loyalist during the Revolutionary war. But outperforming
them all in 1772 was the widow Stoner, whose estate was assessed at just

[29] Jordan, *The Life of William Henry, of Lancaster, Pennsylvania*, 20.

£2 but who won the Silk Society's top prize (worth £15) for raising 72,800 cocoons that year.[30]

The Silk Society eagerly shipped samples of these silk raisers' output from the first year to experts in London for their opinion on its quality. The responses again pay testament to how American bodies were now reaching beyond imperial middlemen – such as the Board of Trade or Premium Society – to link up directly with wider networks, a pattern that would persist into and beyond the revolution. When one Mr Walpole advised on some imperfections and promised to procure the best eggs from Valencia and reelers from Italy, the managers explained they had already 'hired a Languedocian to superintend the Filature next season', who was 'born and bred in the middle of a silk country ... and having been in the East Indies, has some knowledge of their method and management of it also'.[31] A Mr Patterson offered extraordinarily detailed feedback on the specimens, recommending for instance that the water be changed more frequently in the basins, and that they should stick with the Piedmontese reel and aim for an 'Italian' smell which he described as 'the natural smell of the Silk when prepared in perfection'. Dispute over the best technology persisted, and at the insistence of Samuel Pullein that 'his Reel, as lately improved, is better than what you reel with', Franklin had one made under his direction and shipped across so that the filature managers could 'judge of it'.[32] If global insights were being sought for American production and technology, so too do the experiments show the extension of American influences abroad, as when German writers such as Göttingen professor Gottfried Achenwall took up the subject, or Swedish botanist Pehr Kalm updated and republished his verdict on North American mulberry trees and their fitness for transplantation abroad.[33]

The various technical and specialist insights into Pennsylvanian silk clearly helped, for by 1773, a broker described it as much 'improv'd in the

---

[30] Kirkpatrick Sale, *The Fire of His Genius: Robert Fulton and the American Dream* (New York: Simon & Schuster, 2002), 43.

[31] Franklin to Cadwalader Evans, London, 10 February 1771; Cadwalader Evans to Franklin, Philadelphia, 4 May 1771, *Franklin Papers Online*.

[32] Franklin to Cadwalader Evans, London, 4 July 1771; Franklin to the 'Managers of the Philadelphia Silk Filature', London [Before 10 May 1772], *Franklin Papers Online*.

[33] Gottfried Achenwall, *Achenwall's Observations on North America, 1767*, trans. J. G. Rosengarten (Philadelphia: s.n., 1903), 12. Pehr Kalm, 'Beskrifning på Norr-Americanske Mulbärsträdet, Morus rubra Kalladt' (1776) transl. in Larsen, 'Pehr Kalm's Description of the North American Mulberry Tree.' See also Pehr Kalm and Adolph B. Benson, *Peter Kalm's Travels in North America; the America of 1750; the English Version of 1770, Rev. from the Original Swedish and Edited by Adolph B. Benson, with a Translation of New Material from Kalm's Diary Notes*, 2 vols. (New York: Dover Publications, 1966), 1: vii; Paula I. Robbins, *The Travels of Peter Kalm, Finnish-Swedish Naturalist, through Colonial North America, 1748–1751* (Fleischmanns, NY: Purple Mountain Press, 2007), 167.

Table 2 *Comparative raw silk prices in London (1773)*

Place of Origin	Highest price per lb in shillings/pence	Lowest Price
China	22/6 ('skain-silk')	[none]
Fossumbrun (Italy)	20/8	[none]
Pizarro (Spain)	20/0	19/8
Bengal	20/0	5/7½
Carolina & Georgia	19/6	9/2
Pennsylvania	19/2	10/0
Milan	19/0	17/0
Murcia	17/4	16/8
Rheggio (Italy)	17/4	16/8
Brutia (Turkey)	17/0	16/8
Calabria	16/4	14/0
Ghilan (Persia)	15/9	12/0

Sources: Benjamin Franklin to Cadwalader Evans, London, 6 April 1773 and Franklin to the 'Managers of the Philadelphia Silk Filature', London, 14 July 1773, Franklin Papers Online; 'Extract of a Letter from Leicester', *Pennsylvania Gazette*, 14 June 1771

Winding Part, and that some of it is equal to almost any brought to Market here'. Franklin noted 'our Silk is in high Credit; we may therefore hope for rising Prices, the Manufacturers being at first doubtful of a new Commodity, not knowing till Trial has been made how it will work'. After 1771 the top-end Pennsylvania raw silk (see Table 2) tended to be priced only a few pence beneath Piedmontese organzine, a remarkable achievement, and silk mercers were happy to dispose of it.[34] As one Leicester manufacturer put it, who was turning Pennsylvania silk into stockings, '[t]here wants no Improvement in it ... there wants only Quantity'.[35]

One reason for the small quantity exported to London was that, unlike many earlier Board of Trade initiatives, the Pennsylvania filature was not geared exclusively for export, but made provision to return reeled silk to the cocoon raisers for their own use. Indeed, in 1770 (the first year of operations) the silk reeled at the filature was offered for public sale within the colony instead of being exported. Even the leftover product, 'all the floss and refuse Cocoons', was to be auctioned, the waste silk to be processed in households

[34] For an example of one such mercer who did, see James Freeman to Franklin, Rotterdam, 20 May 1785, *Franklin Papers Online.*
[35] Franklin to Cadwalader Evans, London, 6 April 1773 and Franklin to the 'Managers of the Philadelphia Silk Filature', London, 14 July 1773, *Franklin Papers Online*; 'Extract of a Letter from Leicester', *Pennsylvania Gazette*, 14 June 1771.

(presumably by hand-combing and spinning).[36] In later years, provision was regularly made for reeling and returning local silk, with the price in 1773 quoted at sixpence per ounce, and discounted for larger amounts.[37] The home market was always a significant feature of Pennsylvanian production, as shown in Humphry Marshall's observation on Chester County in 1771: 'there is Numbers of people that raises Silk reels it them Selves and mixes it With Worsted Which makes Good Sort of Crape Which Some of our people have made themselves Cloathes of already'.[38] Albert Hostetter claimed that likewise in Lancaster County, 'many cocoons were also raised in private families'.[39] A growing awareness of American capacity for working silk up was even demonstrated by occasional English commentators, as when one London correspondent wrote of their hope, contrary to conventional wisdom about colonial manufacturing, that all manner of 'silks, which are now purchased from France, Italy, and the East Indies, might be bought of our fellow subjects' across the Atlantic.[40]

The growing appetite for homespun silk amongst Pennsylvanians owed much to two distinct but overlapping motivations of 'honour' by the 1770s. The first of these related to the heritage of Quaker beliefs and practices in the colony, and the second, more recent impulse, was powered by the growing clamour against British impositions and luxuries in the context of political protest. The pursuit of homespun fitted well with an era of reform as many Quakers lamented the pollution of the Society of Friends; this was a period marked by divisions within the Pennsylvania Quaker gentry, and many followed reformist impulses to eschew lavish imported finery and return to original principles. Dressing plainly (with rustic styles and colours) was both a socio-religious statement and a fashion statement with long roots.[41] In the 1740s, one visitor had perceptively noted how although cosmopolitan Quakers 'pretend not to have their clothes made after the latest fashion, or wear cuffs and be dressed as gaily as others, they strangely enough have their garments made of the finest and costliest material than can be produced'.[42] By the 1760s, the Quaker majority had become a minority, subject to growing animosity from other settlers, and many Quakers sought to counter

---

[36] *Pennsylvania Gazette*, 6 December 1770.   [37] *Pennsylvania Gazette*, 29 July 1772.
[38] Humphry Marshall to Franklin, Chester County, 27 November 1771, in *Franklin Papers Online*.
[39] Hostetter, 'The Early Silk Industry of Lancaster County', 30.
[40] London correspondent quoted in *Pennsylvania Gazette*, 21 November 1771.
[41] David Shi, 'Early American Simplicity: The Quaker Ethic', in *Voluntary Simplicity: Responding to Consumer Culture*, ed. Daniel Doherty and Amitai Etzioni (Oxford: Rowman & Littlefield, 2003), 107–8.
[42] Kalm and Benson, *Per Kalm's Travels*, 2: 651.

their own sense of moral pollution by more strenuously embracing cleansing practices that would encourage spiritual purity. Quaker reformers such as John Churchman dreamed of children dressed uniformly in dove-grey clothes, Samuel Fothergill of people dressed in white, while John Woolman and his followers wore undyed homespun clothes – partly because dyestuffs were a product associated with another corrupting evil, slavery.[43] Inspired or shamed by such figures, there was a greater recourse to sumptuary disciplinary action in Meeting Houses, particularly amongst rural traditionalists.[44]

Given this revitalised scrutiny, then, material produced or manufactured at home, including silk, was accruing its own distinctive value. Grace Fisher, a widely known Quaker preacher, was one who integrated silk raising with her reformism: in this period she 'made considerable silk stuff', and one of her pieces was later presented by Governor John Dickinson to Catharine Macauley as an instance of female initiative.[45] A fellow well-connected Quaker spinster and sometime poet from the rural district of Lancaster County (now Columbia, on the Susquehanna) was Susanna Wright, one of the first winners of the Silk Society prizes, who had long been active in silk-raising and generated 18,000 cocoons in 1773.[46] One diarist described Wright as, although very accomplished and refined, 'dressed very plain . . . her dress was of no consequence to her'.[47] But this was a misperception, for Wright's correspondence showed an intense interest in clothing.[48] The nineteenth-century antiquarian John Fanning Watson recorded that Wright had an extensive yardage of homespun fabric, including mantua, sewing silk, stockings, and mixed silk and cotton stuffs; he appended swatches (presented to him by her grand-niece) to his manuscript copy showing a suitably buff-coloured silk.[49]

---

[43] Jack D. Marietta, *The Reformation of American Quakerism, 1748–1783* (Philadelphia: University of Pennsylvania Press, 1984), 94–5, 109; John Woolman, *The Journal of John Woolman* (New York: P. F. Collier & Son, 1909), 319.

[44] Marietta, *The Reformation of American Quakerism*, 23.

[45] John Fanning Watson, *Annals of Philadelphia* (Philadelphia: E. L. Carey & A. Hart, 1830), 618.

[46] According to at least one source, in 1759 a pair of silk stockings made by Wright had been presented to Gen. Jeffrey Amherst, the British commander in America during the Seven Years' War. Charles Norris to Susanna Wright, 19 April 1759, cited in Willis L. Shirk Jr., 'Wright's Ferry: A Glimpse into the Susquehanna Backcountry', *Pennsylvania Magazine of History and Biography* 120 (1996): 78.

[47] Deborah Norris Logan, Diary, XI, appendix (HSP)

[48] Letter from Sally Armitt to Susanna Wright, Philadelphia, 1755. 'Notes and Queries', *The Pennsylvania Magazine of History and Biography* 38, no. 1 (1914): 122–23.

[49] 'List of Relics' appended to Library Company of Philadelphia copy of Watson, *Annals of Philadelphia*, 71, 165, 230. Also attached amongst what Watson described as a 'List of Relics' is a slightly larger matte silk, in dark grey, which was purportedly raised by Miss Catharine Haines at Germantown.

A manuscript account of Susanna Wright's sericultural method, discovered some decades after her death in 1784, substantiated many of Watson's claims, and was full of local tips – warning, for instance, that a small species of ants 'very common in Pennsylvania, is peculiarly destructive to the silk-worm'. Wright explained in careful terms how to work up the waste silk, including unreelable cocoons, in soap and water 'until they open, and become as soft as cotton; it may then be spun out of the hand upon a wheel, but can never be carded'.[50] Like others in the 1760s, then, Susanna Wright improvised a use for the waste silk that involved much extra labour but generated extra yarn or filling (see Plate 15).

Susanna Wright's authority on silk production and home manufacture led to her being sent silk samples by others to comment on – such as the package sent by her friend Milcah Martha Moore in 1771. Moore admitted hers was an 'imperfect production' but nonetheless was clearly proud to send 'a p[ai]r of silk garters rais'd, dyed & wove in our own House' and that she deemed acceptable enough for Wright to wear. Moore also mentioned a better loom, which Susanna's nephew Samuel Wright had promised to make her, that she hoped would improve her homespun. The correspondence between these women engaged in experimental production suggests that their ambitions were in parallel with, rather than fully in step with, the wider colonial political economy expressed by the British and Pennsylvanian authorities. Their output was oriented towards the immediate household economy, and a finished product that had been home-manufactured. Moore shared with Wright her recipes for silk dyes, sending phials made out of 'Barberry root' (yellow) and Brazil wood with pearl ash (purple) mixed with alum, though she could not 'promise that they will stand'. Moore's silk-dyeing experiments sought less to contribute to colonial economic health than to economise and avoid participation in the overpriced Atlantic marketplace.[51]

Silk production's second and more dominant motivation of 'honour' absorbed this Quaker activity from the late 1760s, aligning and adapting silk cultivation increasingly to revolutionary agendas.[52] Benjamin Franklin and other enthusiasts very early recognised the value of advances in the event

[50] Susanna Wright, 'Directions for the Management of Silk-Worms', *Philadelphia Medical and Physical Journal* 1 (1804): 103–7.
[51] Letter from M. Moore to Susanna Wright, Philadelphia, 20 February 1771. 'Notes and Queries', 1914.
[52] For a wider considering of this impulse across American manufacturing, see Peskin, *Manufacturing Revolution*, 30–44.

of a break with Britain. As Franklin wrote in 1769: 'When once you can raise plenty of Silk, you may have Manufactures enow from hence.'[53] The prospect of silk seemed to underscore what Hannah Griffitts promised in her anonymous poem in response to the Townshend Acts: 'Pennsylvania's gay Meadows can richly afford, To pamper our Fancy or furnish our Board.'[54] On several occasions silk filatures were described in terms suggestive of a covert first step towards wider manufactures, which were largely proscribed under colonial law, and explicitly so in relation to textile machinery in 1774, when the British legislated against 'the exportation to foreign parts of utensils made use of in the cotton, linen, woollen, and silk manufactures'.[55] Thus while Pennsylvanians publicly celebrated that 'the Article of Raw Silk may shortly become a valuable Remittance from hence to Great-Britain' in the summer of 1771, Franklin privately used telling expressions to describe his hopes for persevering 'in the silk Business till they have conquer'd all Difficulties. *By Diligence and Patience the Mouse ate in twain the Cable*'. In another sign of a convergence of ambition, John Adams likewise hinted that a Massachusetts plan for a society for encouraging manufactures 'may be of greater Extent and Duration than at first We may imagine', and that this plan could potentially draw on mulberry trees, which Pehr Kalm also anticipated that Americans would now 'pay more attention to'; meanwhile Silk Society manager Cadwalader Evans reported how folk were 'handsomely clad in their own manufactures'.[56] By 1773 Franklin was more explicit in his words and actions, recommending a Quaker Spitalfields silk-weaver, Joseph Clark, and his family to the Silk Society, noting 'I should think it not amiss to begin early the laying a Foundation for the future Manufacture of it, and perhaps this Person, if he finds Employment, may be a means of raising Hands for that purpose.'[57] As resistance turned to revolution, Pennsylvanians' patriotism found expression in their pointed celebration of silk homespun: Franklin promised to 'honour much every young Lady that I find on my Return dress'd in Silk of their own raising', while his daughter thanked him for having Pennsylvanian produce worked up in Spitalfields into a 'French Grey Ducape', declaring 'I never

---

[53] Benjamin Franklin to Cadwalader Evans, London, 7 September 1769, in *Franklin Papers Online*

[54] Hannah Griffitts, 'The Female Patriots', in Philadelphia *Pennsylvania Chronicle*, 25 December 1769.

[55] 14 Geo. III *c*.71

[56] John Adams Papers online, 8 February 1771, Docno: DJA02d002. Larsen, 'Pehr Kalm's Description of the North American Mulberry Tree', 225. Cadwalader Evans to Samuel Wharton, Philadelphia, 20 April 1770, MS 2001.8, John D. Rockefeller, Jr. Library, Colonial Williamsburg Foundation.

[57] Franklin to Cadwalader Evans, London, 4 July 1771; Franklin to the 'Managers of the Philadelphia Silk Filature', London, 15 March 1773, *Franklin Papers Online.*

knew what it was to be proud of a new Garment before. This I shall wear with pride and pleasure.[58]

Despite the widespread assault on silk's cultural reputation then, in parts of the country where sericulture had shown promise, including Massachusetts, defenders found new ways to justify its pursuit. In January 1771, the *Massachusetts Spy* prefaced a discussion of silk with the laden observation that 'the culture of Arts and Manufactures, &c. has the most direct tendency to make a community rich; and riches have a natural tendency to make them independent'. It went on to explain how Joseph Belknap, a Boston tanner and furrier, and his wife Sarah Byles Belknap, had successfully raised silkworms in their house on Ann Street, just a few doors down from the blocked-up privy in which lay the silk fragments discarded in the seventeenth century. The Belknaps were put forward as a model of how to turn silkworms to profit in such an urban setting, having made twenty yards of 'silk camblet' (a popular warp-faced striped textile, often made in Europe from goat's hair or, increasingly, other fibres mixed with silk).[59] Combining his long-standing experience in hides and furs with the new opportunities in silk, camlet literally and figuratively suited Belknap, and in the process made a statement about his independence.[60] Advocates of improvements in New England husbandry now described silk raising as part of the unfulfilled potential of the colonies under imperial rule: its pursuit promised a pathway to forms of greater independence.[61]

In Pennsylvania, silk was defended as 'the happiest of all Inventions for Cloathing' on the grounds that wool, flax, and hemp took up and impoverished larger quantities of acreage than mulberry trees, which 'may be planted in Hedge Rows, or Walks or Avenues … where nothing else is wanted to grow'. Besides the zero cost on arable land, proponents emphasised that vegetables or livestock feed could still be produced beneath the mulberries. Finally, relative to other fibres, defenders claimed that 'the Wear of Silken Garments continues so much longer, from the Strength of the Materials, as to give it greatly the Preference'. One 'Pennsylvanian

[58] Franklin to Deborah Franklin, London, 28 January 1772; Sarah Bache to Franklin, Philadelphia, 30 October 1773; see also Franklin to Rebecca Haydock, London, 5 February 1772 and her reply, 20 May 1773. *Franklin Papers Online*.

[59] Montgomery, *Textiles in America*, 188–9; Charlotte E. Jirousek, 'Rediscovering Camlet: Traditional Mohair Cloth Weaving in Southeastern Turkey', in *Textiles as Cultural Expressions; Textile Society of America Biennial Symposium*, 2008.

[60] The notice also advertised that mulberry trees were available from a Lieut. Johnson in Bridgewater, for one penny apiece. Boston *Massachusetts Spy*, 1 August 1771.

[61] Boston *Massachusetts Spy*, 2 January 1772. Boston *Royal American Magazine*, 1 April 1774, pp. 146–7. Bishop, Freedley, and Young, *History of American Manufactures*, 1: 362; Bagnall, *The Textile Industries of the United States*, 44.

Planter' cautioned readers that the Mother Country had intentionally crushed manufacturing to prevent creativity and development, and warned that Americans contributed to their own enslavement when they discouraged new pursuits 'because they are not quite so cheap, or not yet quite so good, as antient or foreign Ones', warning that 'if we do not encourage imperfect Works, we shall never get perfect Ones'.[62] Familiarity with the life cycle of the silkworms even made the creatures themselves a frame of reference: shortly after the opening volleys of the Revolutionary War, the American Congress of 'United Colonies' wrote a self-justifying public letter to the 'People of Ireland' to explain their actions, in which they explicitly likened their Irish brethren to silkworms, whose labours 'were of little moment to herself; but served only to give luxury to those who *neither toil nor spin*'.[63]

Perhaps the new-found links between silk production and patriotism were best encapsulated in the redirection of silk produce in response to political ruptures. During the revolution, with transatlantic processing impossible and rudimentary hand-thrown yarns the only option, silk raisers in both Pennsylvania and upcountry South Carolina concentrated on mixing silk with other fabrics as homespun, or generating sewing silk which could have a range of uses. Thomas McCall reported that the silk producers at New Bordeaux, in the Carolina Piedmont, apparently supplied 'much of the high country' with sewing silk during the early stages of the war.[64] It is unclear quite what became of the Silk Society during the actual conflict: no price or production lists survive, and it seems logical to conclude that the filature was not operational beyond 1774, perhaps reflecting that experts had left or that the funding base was inadequate to cover further outlay.[65] But it had galvanised productive capacity in mixed-stuff textile manufacture that included silk yarns, as in Lancaster County and Philadelphia, where John Watson emphasised how 'ladies in

[62] Benjamin Franklin to Cadwalader Evans, London, 7 September 1769, *Franklin Papers Online*; *Pennsylvania Gazette*, 1 August 1771, 30 March 1774.
[63] 'Address to the People of Ireland', 28 July 1775, printed in *Pennsylvania Evening Post*, 5 August 1775.
[64] United States, *Letter from the Secretary of the Treasury . . . on the Growth and Manufacture of Silk* (Washington: D. Green, 1828), 24.
[65] Benjamin Franklin to Abel James and Benjamin Morgan, London, 18 February 1774, American Philosophical Society, *The Record of the Celebration of the Two Hundredth Anniversary of the Birth of Benjamin Franklin*, ed. I. M. Hays, 6 vols. (Philadelphia: American Philosophical Society, 1906), 3: 494. That the organisation did not entirely fold but was rather suspended is apparent from a special meeting in June 1781 and an Act of Assembly of 15 April 1782. The remaining assets were transferred to the Philosophical Society, which undertook to 're-deliver the same, whenever a majority of the subscribers to the Silk Society shall request it, to revive their institution'. Henry D. Biddle, 'Owen Biddle', *Pennsylvania Magazine of History and Biography1* 16 (1892): 306.

particular gave much attention to the subject, and especially after the war had begun . . . to provide for their personal or family wants'; amongst these ladies were Deborah Norris Logan and Mary Johnson Hopkinson.[66]

Some of the Pennsylvania output was symbolically redirected. In 1772, the British Queen Charlotte received a choice sample from the Philadelphia filature, 'humbly offered as a Mark of the affectionate Respect of her Subjects there'; she agreed to have it woven and promised to wear it on the occasion of the king's birthday.[67] Franklin pulled off this publicity coup through his friend, travel companion, and chess opponent, Sir John Pringle (shortly afterwards appointed in the unenviable role of physician to King George III).[68] Just seven years later, in 1779, Pennsylvanian silk was on its way across the Atlantic to Britain's imperial nemesis, and the wardrobe of French Queen Marie-Antoinette, in a move intended to 'shew what can be sent from America to the Looms of France', now that the two countries were allied. Franklin wrote to his daughter, Sarah Franklin Bache, to commiserate with her on the fact that the silk had been spoiled traversing the Atlantic, and he chastened her, wondering how 'having yourself scarce Shoes to your Feet, it should come into your Head to give Cloathes to a Queen'. He would see if the stains made by salt water might be concealed by dyeing the silk, and proposed instead to 'make Summer Suits of it, for myself'. But Sarah Bache did not apparently receive this news, only learning much later from her nephew that the twenty-two yards of 'American spun silk' had been 'entirely spoilt'. This missed opportunity may indeed have been symbolic of the subsequent relationship between American and French silk ambitions in the revolutionary era.[69]

Overall, what was distinctive about Pennsylvanian attempts at silk raising and the Silk Society was that they were pioneered not before but after the flooding of American markets with consumer goods, and that they were encouraged by voluntary associations and public-minded local intellectual and commercial elites rather than by the machinery or agents

[66] *Pennsylvania Gazette*, 14 June 1770; Watson, *Annals of Philadelphia*, 618–19.

[67] Franklin letter published in *Pennsylvania Gazette*, 29 July 1772. Other recipients of gifts included female members of the proprietary family: Lady Juliana Fermor Penn (wife of Thomas Penn), Hannah Lardner Penn (widow of Richard Penn), Anne Allen Penn (wife of John Penn), as well as Franklin himself. Edward Pennington et al. to Drs Franklin and Fothergill, Philadelphia, 8 November 1771; Abel James and Benjamin Morgan to Franklin, Philadelphia, 17 November 1772, *Franklin Papers Online*.

[68] Franklin to Sir John Pringle, London, [before 10 May 1772], *Franklin Papers Online*.

[69] Sarah Bache to Benjamin Franklin, Philadelphia, 17 January and 14 September 1779 and to William Temple Franklin, 30 October and 26 December 1780; Franklin to Sarah Bache, Passy, 16 March 1780; William Temple Franklin to Sarah Bache, Passy, 19 February 1791, *Franklin Papers Online*.

of the state. They constituted a new kind of convergence: the managers of and subscribers to the Silk Society, as well as the numerous, middling silk producers, were deeply conscious of having their own agendas. Whether motivated by interests in natural history, technology, political economy, and colonial development (like Franklin) or the household economy, short-term gain, and the aesthetic (like the Widow Stoner or Susanna Wright), they showed a growing recognition of local identity and local priorities: home rule, homespun, home manufacturing. And their partly successful activity, undertaken at the very point of imperial partition, set down a marker that permitted American silk ambitions to survive outside their previous colonial 'niche ... within the British economic system'.[70] For all of the new ground being broken in Pennsylvania, however, the configuration of labour remained obstinately gendered: as in other American silk trials, most of those doing the actual handiwork at the worm-littered shelves and at the steaming reels were women, in households spread widely in terms of geography, ethnicity, and class, including the daughters of the likes of Benjamin Franklin and John Bartram.[71]

---

[70] Peskin, *Manufacturing Revolution*, 32, 33.
[71] John Bartram to Benjamin Franklin, Philadelphia, 29 April 1771, in *Franklin Papers Online*.

10   Silk Production in the Wake of Revolution

> It is my Judgement that the Silk business will be the first brought to perfection – But I could tell with more certainty if I knew the kinds of Silk the Country Produces … I think if they were to put the raisers of Silk into a Perfect Method of reeling it from the Worm – that would be a very great improvement. Neither the Assiatics nor many of the Europeans do that business as it ought to be, a very little extra, trouble and care would add near 10 per Cent to the Value of Raw silks.
>
> – Edmund Clegg (silk manufacturer) to Benjamin Franklin, Spitalfields (London), 10 May 1782

A New Political Economy of Silk in the United States

The independence of the United States blew apart the projected formula for silk production that had held sway for over 150 years in the British regions that had persisted with sericulture – namely, that raw silk might be produced on the western side of the Atlantic and then manufactured on the eastern side. Though not entirely separable, it is nonetheless ironic that this occurred at the point when more British Americans than ever had been engaged in attempts at silk raising, and when sericulture had gained real traction in new regions beyond the south. As a consumer good, silk continued to experience something of a tug of war, inhabiting a new homespun republican world that remained heavily influenced by old cultural, commercial, and sartorial practices. But really, as of 1776, people pursuing silk cultivation no longer needed to fixate upon exportation to Britain. Rather, either the goal of sericulture might itself fall away, discarded onto the same scrapheap as monarchy and an established church, or the goal of silk production now needed to be definitively repackaged for an American economy. In the final quarter of the eighteenth century, political economists and silk producers alike made important strides towards ensuring a future for silk production, and they largely did so by linking it to American manufacturing.

Before the war, muted ambitions to manufacture silk had been growing in volume for a few years, as we have seen, and were strengthened by the construction of institutions such as the reeling filatures in Philadelphia and Charleston. The arrival of full-blown war compromised such operations in the short term but also heralded new opportunities, most of them contingent upon foreign expertise. Over the next years, a handful of well-connected Americans reached out to potential experts to help stimulate a native industry that might build on colonial efforts, but now operate from silkworm rearing through to the finished fabric. In 1776 the American Manufactory in Philadelphia recommended an appropriation of £40 to encourage John Marshall, an English thread-maker, to construct a silk twisting and throwing mill, but the project and invention seem to have fallen victim to the arrival of war in Philadelphia.[1] In the years that followed, a number of European manufacturers, from Manchester to Turin, sought passports to migrate and set up new orchards, cocooneries, workshops, or weaving operations, motivated by a combination of ideological support for the revolution and (mostly) socio-economic self-interest. Two days before news of Cornwallis's surrender at Yorktown had reached Britain in November 1781, Stockport's Henry Royle proposed to settle in Pennsylvania and establish a silk and fustian (a pile face and twill-woven cotton) and a calico business – ambitiously requested a seven-year monopoly, state support, and other conditions of service for himself and four other weavers and their families![2] The next year, two gentlemen in Derby 'signified their determined Resolution, to go over to Virginia, and there fix Engins to cast [throw] silk by upon the same Model of those at Derby'.[3] Joseph Maroteau, a Belgian merchant, recommended a Catholic family from Tournay who were capable of all kinds of manufactures, including local specialties such as silk gauze for all manner of trimmings, for which they had perfected the processing of luxury silk sewing thread.[4] On the day that the Peace of Paris was signed, formally ending the American war in 1783, François Giordana of Turin offered his services 'to establish there the art of silk'.[5]

[1] Bishop, Freedley, and Young, *History of American Manufactures*, 1: 579; Wyckoff, *American Silk Manufacture*, 31.
[2] Henry Royle et al. to Franklin, [23 November 1781]; Franklin to Henry Royle, Passy, 4 January 1782, *Franklin Papers Online*. Judging by a subsequent unpublished note, from Henry Royle to Franklin, 23 September 1786, he did indeed later erect a calico works 'at Carby [Darby?] near the City of Philadelphia', though there is no mention of the silk aspect.
[3] Henry Wyld to Franklin, Hatherlow, 9 April 1782; Edmund Clegg to Franklin, Spitalfields, 10 May 1782, *Franklin Papers Online*.
[4] Joseph Maroteau to Franklin, Tournay, 22 August 1783, *Franklin Papers Online*.
[5] François Giordana to Franklin, Turin, 3 September and 22 October 1783. In this vaguer category, see also 'Proposals' of painter and porcelain manufacturer Jean-Jacques Bachelier to Franklin, Paris, 9 June 1777.

Other experts seem to have had less practical knowledge of silk culture but nonetheless sought to package themselves in such a way as to secure support. Shortly after the peace was announced, a Frenchman named Charvet wrote from Serrières, a manufacturing town powered by the Rhône river just south of Lyons, to take up the subject of silk culture. He recognised this was not an original idea, and was already well advanced in America (particularly 'in Carolina') if not yet a fixed commercial presence, but proposed to realise on a grand scale what he had thus far only managed on a small scale – namely an unprecedentedly high ratio of silkworm eggs to raw silk production. Though local practices in his native Vivarais were already successful to a point, he claimed that silk raisers there were blindly wedded to traditional techniques and unreceptive to new ideas and improvement. Charvet averred that his method integrated his own memorised observations and trials with the latest recommendations of celebrated writers (including the Abbé de Sauvages), and he was willing to make it available first to Americans, where he was confident the new ideas would have a better reception, even if silkworm harvests were initially smaller.[6]

Perhaps the most promising effort to jump-start silk manufactures, to be superimposed upon American raw silk production, came from a consortium led by Spitalfields weaver Edmund Clegg in 1782. Clegg dreamed of collapsing the long chain of British silk processing, which now linked various throwing, spinning, and dyeing operations located in the north-west to the broadloom weaving concentrated in London, into one manufactory in Philadelphia: 'Joining all the Manufactories of Spitalfields & Manchester together, in the most Perfect manner.' Clegg's party of around sixteen from Spitalfields had collected 'all kinds of Models' and were prepared to smuggle out 'that part of our Utencils called Reeds' which they doubted would be available in America. They intended to depart from Liverpool, taking some part-finished silks with them so that they would be immediately employed once set up across the Atlantic. 'If we get safe over', promised Clegg, who was also a Baptist preacher, 'we shall be able, without any material obstruction, to perform more than you can as yet Conceive and with respect to the silk Manufactory. If the Country can yeild [sic] a Sufficient quantity of Raw silks We can make it as independant upon Europe for those Goods.'

Henry Wyld of Hatherlow (near Stockport), a silk throwster, led the northern contingent, though he worried about whether America would be able to furnish the right kinds of small screws for 'putting Engins together'. Clegg wanted information about 'the dif[feren]t kinds of Silks

---

[6] [Jean-Gabriel?] Charvet to Franklin, 4 October 1783, *Franklin Papers Online*.

Produced in N. America & the Prices they are respectively worth in that Country', expecting they would be adequate at least for the weft (or 'shute') silk in many broadloom fabrics. In the event that American producers were not yet able to provide an adequate quantity of raw silks, he hoped that American merchants might open up direct trade to Italian and Far Eastern export markets. Clegg was convinced that with a little tweaking, an American silk industry could flourish, and the prospect of experienced throwsters offering on-hand guidance would help Americans to somersault 'the Assiatics' and 'many of the Europeans' whose reeling was deficient. Clegg actually arrived in Pennsylvania in early 1784, presumably with his two sons, with whom he intended to 'Perform the silk Manufactory thro' both in Plain & Figured Goods both broads and Narrow – but chiefly the former', admitting a limitation in his skill at dyeing 'of most fancy Colours – But can Perform properly all Common Col[ou]rs'. Unfortunately he did the wrong kind of dying, contracting a sudden illness on 20 July when, as the *Gazette* put it, 'just on the point of engaging in his favorite employ', and was buried in the Philadelphia Baptist Ground.[7]

As if the competition between Spitalfields and Lyons was not fierce enough in Europe throughout the eighteenth century, it appears that French specialists contested the prospect of being the first to manufacture silks in an independent America. A similar project to Clegg's came to light in January 1783 when Jean Penide, a French silk throwster from Chavaray near Lyons, announced his intention to migrate. Penide had heard of wonderful mulberry lands, and promised that he was capable of overseeing all stages from the raising of worms, through throwing and spinning, and finally to the creation of the finest silks. For companions he proposed two distinct experts, the first a dyer and mixed-stuff manufacturer (who possessed the best recipes for dyeing woollens as well as silks), who would willingly take American apprentices on. The second was a designer of silk fabrics and an accomplished engraver with a particular skill in 'Indiennes' (light printed or painted textiles, usually cotton, which had only in 1759 been permitted in France). Between them, these three therefore offered a complementary mixture of skills to bring on a new industry, though Penide cautioned that it would be several years before they had silk fabrics in production, due to the need for mulberry plantations to mature. Where Clegg and Wyld underlined their historic connection to English liberties, stressing that 'all the real Liberty now, or

[7] Henry Wyld to Franklin, Hatherlow, 2 January, 18 March, 9 and 12 April, and 12 August 1782; Edmund Clegg to Franklin, Spitalfields, London, 4 and 24 April, 10 May, and 16 June 1782; Franklin to Edmund Clegg, 26 April 1782, *Franklin Papers Online*. Philadelphia *Pennsylvania Gazette*, 28 July 1784.

hearafter enjoy'd in this Island may be with great Justice attributed to the Noble heroes of No[rth] America', Penide emphasised the French were motivated by a desire to make the most of new alliances.[8] Other French sericultural experts took advantage of the interest in America to try to secure greater support at home from royal patrons, warning pointedly that 'foreign powers cherish ambitions for this branch'.[9]

The commercial relationships between the new United States and Europe were also up for renegotiation as British ties became frayed and then momentarily severed. The British had been fairly effective at prohibiting French silks strictly from 1766, creating an apparent 'dearth' of fashionable French silks in the British colonies.[10] Colonists were already aware from February 1773, in their critiques of British trade policy, of how 'The Dutch, the Danes and French, took the Advantage thus offered them', and with 'Smuggling of course considered as Patriotism', old consumption patterns under challenge: 'the cheap French Silks, formerly rejected as not to the Taste of the Colonists, may have found their way with the Wares of India, and now established themselves in the popular Use and Opinion'.[11] Before the war's end, merchants and entrepreneurs sought to predict how patterns of Atlantic trade in silk might be tectonically shifting, to get a jump on the emerging market patterns. Scottish merchants in Glasgow such as John Woddrop sought information about 'the most sootible Merchandize' for 'the infant and new rising United States of America', wondering whether the 'silk gauze, manufactured in and about Glasgow will answer'.[12] Northern Italians such as the experienced François Gianolio offered exports 'in the way of silk cloth, thread, ribbons, etc.' He stressed that Turin was 'the center of the silk trade', and sought partners to ship 'what is manufactured locally'.[13] That the French were keenly aware of this market opportunity was reflected in the 1778 Treaty of Amity and Commerce between France and the 'United States of North America', which listed textiles as the first 'merchandize ... not [to] be reckoned among Contraband or prohibited goods' and to be freely traded – the first formalisation of an Atlantic free trade zone.[14]

---

[8] [Jean] Penide to Franklin, Lyons, 16 January 1783, *Franklin Papers Online*.

[9] Walsh de Valoit to Vergennes, 15 June 1785, F/12/1439, ANF.

[10] Baumgarten, *What Clothes Reveal*, 84; Rothstein, *Silk Designs of the Eighteenth Century*, 23–6.

[11] Benjamin Franklin, 'Preface to the Declaration of the Boston Town Meeting, February 1773', in Franklin, *The Papers of Benjamin Franklin*, 20: 82–7.

[12] John Woddrop to Franklin, Glasgow, 17 February 1783, *Franklin Papers Online*.

[13] François Gianolio to Franklin, Turin, 12 November 1777, in *Franklin Papers Online*.

[14] Allan Potofsky, 'The Political Economy of the French–American Debt Debate: The Ideological Uses of Atlantic Commerce, 1787 to 1800', *The William and Mary Quarterly*, 3rd Ser. 63, no. 3 (2006): 489. See also J. R. Harris, *Industrial Espionage and Technology Transfer: Britain and France in the Eighteenth Century* (London: Routledge, 1998), 161–9.

French hopes of capturing a new silk market were arguably far more realistic than most other manufactured goods (especially other textiles and hardware), where the British were rightly confident that superior quality and lower price would ensure commercial continuity even in a more open Atlantic market. And it was a signal of British apprehension about the Atlantic silk trade that, soon after the war, merchants advised that Parliament should continue to offer bounties on silk exports to the United States to lessen the danger of French rivalry. 'The Silk Manufacture has a claim to particular attention', they warned, 'as being one of the most valuable, as furnishing Employment for a very considerable number of our poor, and as being in great Danger from the Rivalship of France.' Such fears ensured that only silk was expressly excluded from the relaxing of Anglo-French trade in the Eden treaty of 1786, a measure that also reflected the political power of the Weavers' Company of London.[15] French writers and diplomats emphasised the potential for political stability and closer economic relations with the United States that would grow out of the blossoming interchange of luxurious French aristocratic manufactures (such as silks) and the rustic products of the American yeoman. Such ideas materialised prominently in the economically troubled 1780s, in the arguments of François Barbé-Marbois, the secretary of the French legation to the United States, and later in the political economy of Étienne Clavière and Jacques-Pierre Brissot de Warville, who founded the Société Gallo-Américaine in 1787. The designs were encouraged by such influential figures as George Washington, who epitomised the considerable American appetite for French goods, and took advantage of the new opportunity to buy French in the green silk furniture upholstery and matching green silk window curtains he purchased in 1790. French ideas and possibilities even survived the collapse of the monarchy for a time, as some proponents contemplated a republican Atlantic trade zone, until silk – and Lyons in particular – became a temporary victim of the French Revolution.[16]

---

[15] 'Observations of London Merchants on American Trade, 1783', *American Historical Review* 18, no. 4 (1913): 770, 778, 779; Dora Mae Clark, 'British Opinion of Franco-American Relations, 1775–1795', *The William and Mary Quarterly*, 3rd Ser. 4, no. 3 (1947): 308, 310.

[16] Paul Cheney, 'A False Dawn for Enlightenment Cosmopolitanism? Franco-American Trade during the American War of Independence', *The William and Mary Quarterly*, 3rd Ser. 63, no. 3 (2006): 463–88; Potofsky, 'Political Economy of the French-American Debt Debate'; Peter P. Hill, *French Perceptions of the Early American Republic, 1783–1793* (Philadelphia: American Philosophical Society, 1988); Carol Borchert Cadou, *The George Washington Collection: Fine and Decorative Arts at Mount Vernon* (Manchester: Hudson Hills Press, 2006), 130–1.

As Washington's outlay suggests, for their part, Americans were also initially proactive in attempts to reorganise the exchange of Atlantic silk. Even John Adams grudgingly proposed that 'a freer intercourse' with Spain might provide access to 'some Silks, some Linnens perhaps, and with any quantity of Wool, which is now exported to foreign Countries for Manufacture'.[17] Importers did indeed seek to find new sources of silk goods in France, for example Philadelphia's Abel James. He explained 'I am not much in Trade yet have been very attentive to the Goods imported here from France', and concluded that 'England to be sure has the Advantage in woollen & worsted as well as Iron & Steel Wares' but noted with pleasure that in regard to silks, 'the [French] spinning & weaving rather excel & the Dyes are equal'.[18] Abigail Adams, for one, ran a sideline in selling European silk handkerchiefs, in spite of her husband's fervent earlier wish to 'forever banish and exclude from America' silks and other luxuries.[19] And as early as 1781, Benjamin Franklin was assuring the Comte de Vergennes (the French foreign minister) that 'there are many Commodities much cheaper in France, such as Wines, Silks, Oil, Modes, &c which will be of great Consumption in America'. He urged patience, noting that 'It is difficult to change suddenly the whole Current, of Connections, Correspondencies & Confidences that subsist between Merchants.'[20]

Such difficulties, ultimately, proved nigh insurmountable. The Philadelphia house of Bache & Shee, for example, complained in November 1783 that 'unwilling as we are to renew our correspondence with England, we find almost insuperable difficulties, in our propos'd plans with other Countries,' including the forging of links with manufacturers of 'Silks, in the Kingdom of France.' They and other merchants, seeking to establish new networks, struggled and largely failed to overcome problems involving language, credit, and ignorance about the quality of materials and French systems of distribution and customs.[21] Jonathan Williams wrote from Nantes in 1782 to lament the hamstringing bureaucratic mechanisms which he described as an 'immense Detail of

[17] John Adams to President of Congress, 16 January 1780, *Adams Papers Online*.

[18] Letter from Abel James (unpublished) to Benjamin Franklin, n.d. [before 8 December 1782], *Franklin Papers Online*.

[19] John Adams to Abigail Adams, Passy (France), 3 June 1778, and Jean de Neufville & Son to Abigail Adams, Amsterdam, 25 May 1781, in *Adams Papers Online*. Woody Holton, *Abigail Adams* (New York: Free Press, 2009), 154.

[20] Benjamin Franklin to Vergennes (II), AL (draft): Library of Congress [on or before 6 July 1781], *Franklin Papers Online*.

[21] Bache & Shee to William Temple Franklin, Philadelphia, 1 November 1783, *Franklin Papers Online*. On the importance of networks: Pierre Gervais, 'Neither Imperial, nor Atlantic: A Merchant Perspective on International Trade in the Eighteenth Century', *History of European Ideas* 34 (2008): 465–73.

trifling things', particularly the confusing range of duties and exemptions. He explained:

> if I order a Trunck of Silks from Lyons, my Correspondent must enter into a bond under Penalties of four times the Duty to return in three Months a Certificate of its Reception at the Custom House in Nantes; in order to obtain this certificate, I must enter into a Bond of the same Kind, from which I cannot be released 'till after the Custom House Officer certifies having seen the Trunk in the hold of the Ship with all its Seals entire; so that to enjoy this Exemption each Kind of goods of the several Manufactories, should be for one Mark only, and packed by themselves, without having it in my Power to know whether they are well or ill put up 'till after they arrive in America.

Such merchants were deeply conscious of the limited window of opportunity: 'The French may think our Commerce worth preserving at a Peace; but if they do, they must begin to encourage it now, so as the mercantile Part of America may understand all the Advantages of trading with them before other Channels open.'[22] A range of French writers campaigned for greater state involvement in supporting Franco-American trade in the 1780s, many of them showing particular optimism in relation to luxury goods such as silks. But looking back from 1790, James Swan, an opportunistic Atlantic libertarian-cum-merchant, summarised the problems in a widely read French pamphlet. He blamed conservative American buying habits, French invasive customs bureaucracy and port delays, and the inflexibility of French manufacturers and exporters who, since the war, had sent inappropriate goods: 'badly chosen, alien both to our climate and our usage; the colours and designs were equally shocking and defective'. Swan anticipated that one day French silks, ribbons, and stockings would be preferred to all others in the United States (especially in the large cities), and advised his French readers to 'lengthen the independent Americans' taste for manufactured goods, above all luxuries', but warned that this would not happen overnight, and that the best prospects in the interim lay in 'their interloping commerce with the Spanish [in the Americas]' and the appetite for finery of plantation societies, whose 'masters and slaves hankered only for luxury, pomp, finery' and would eagerly snap up the lavish French silk fabrics, especially if the

---

[22] Jonathan Williams, Jr to Franklin, Nantes, 15 June 1782, in *Franklin Papers Online*. For a French memoir speaking to the same issues in the luxury textile trade, see 'Réflexions problématiques proposées à Philippe Mazzei par un Seigneur Français' (1784), Archives des Affaires Etrangères, Correspondance Politique, Etats-Unis, ANF, ser. 27, 229: 32.

French government would permit small consignments to be loaded directly on board ships and bypass delays.[23]

By contrast the British marketing system of silks, though elaborate, was less convoluted, with fewer or no internal customs and charges. As we have seen, Atlantic sales depended to some degree on trust and personal acquaintance, but also increasingly on order books in English with samples or patterns attached to invoices or mounted on cards.[24] This kind of marketing had in fact been pioneered by Lyonnais manufacturers in the first half of the eighteenth century, when they not only deployed traditional tactics at the prestigious fairs of Europe, but fostered a more modern commercialisation through mail-order style attachments of samples (or *cartes d'échantillons*) to correspondence. After the 1750s, many French silk manufacturers abandoned this practice because they deemed it pernicious to the industry – as it allowed competitors to acquire and copy previews of the latest designs and fashions. Though partly safeguarding the season's innovations from imitation, they therefore relinquished a powerful mechanism of marketing that others perhaps more freely exploited. Parisian shop windows and specialist travelling salesmen (*commissionnaires*) may have been more secure, but for obvious reasons they were less effective in engaging diffuse overseas markets.[25] By the end of the eighteenth century, both weavers and merchants in Lyons seem to have become remarkably conservative in their outlook.[26] The combination of all these elements meant that American and French merchants found it extraordinarily difficult to break pre-existent links. Instead, the virtues of low price and high quality in British manufactures (particularly textiles), alongside the swiftly restored networks and infrastructure of Atlantic trade, aided the resumption of American silk consumption, albeit now outside rather than within the formal empire.[27] In 1784, the year after the Peace of Paris had restored trade relations and recognised American independence, English silk exports reached £322,000, their second-highest value of the century.[28] But even as the flow of the

---

[23] James Swan, *Causes qui se sont opposées aux progrès du commerce* (Paris: L. Potier de Lille, 1790), 28, 67–74, 103, 126–31.

[24] Rothstein, 'The 18th-Century English Silk Industry', 12; Deborah E. Kraak, '"Just Imported from London"· English Silks in 18th-Century Philadelphia', in *18th-Century Silks: The Industries of England and Northern Europe*, ed. Regula Schorta (Riggisberg: Abegg-Stiftung, 2000), 111.

[25] Lesley Ellis Miller, 'Innovation and Industrial Espionage in Eighteenth-Century France: An Investigation of the Selling of Silks through Samples', *Journal of Design History* 12, no. 3 (1999): 271–92.

[26] David L. Longfellow, 'Silk Weavers and the Social Struggle in Lyons during the French Revolution, 1789–94', *French Historical Studies* 12, no. 1 (1981): 7.

[27] Davis, 'English Foreign Trade, 1700–1774', 297.

[28] Mitchell and Deane, *Abstract of British Historical Statistics*, 468–70.

Anglo-American textile trade returned to high levels, it manifested subtle changes, for instance in the decreasing position of London in preference of direct trade with manufacturing towns and ports in the north of England and in Ireland.[29]

As Edmund Clegg had hoped, American independence not only unleashed new possibilities in the Atlantic silk trade but also the prospect of direct trade with the great silk-producing and manufacturing regions of Asia. Opportunistic merchants opened a fledgling Asian trade within months of the Peace of Paris, when the *Empress of China* (fittingly a converted privateer) departed New York for Guangzhou in early 1784. Its supercargo Samuel Shaw, later an American consul to China, reported upon his return that Americans had now become 'more conspicuous' to the Qing Empire, a fact emphasised by their symbolic gift of two pieces of silk to US negotiators (which he relayed to John Jay).[30] Over subsequent decades, as the formative China trade found more of an established rhythm – albeit within a lopsided trading relationship that saw Americans scrabbling for influence and depending more on imports than their exports – US ships prioritised silk amongst their return cargos to ports including Philadelphia and Boston and later New York, Salem, and Baltimore. In time, as a slim market evolved alongside nascent American manufacturing, raw silk would also join the list of trade goods (including porcelain and tea) sought from the Far East, eventually via a Pacific route first opened in 1788.[31]

The earnest efforts by this array of merchants and entrepreneurs reveal, of course, that in spite of the challenge to silk posed by the republican turn and the upheaval of the war, there remained a lively appetite for silk goods amongst American consumers that soon re-emerged in the early 1780s. Self-denial had certainly been a means of revolution, but for a growing consumer population who still wanted to purchase and display silks, it was not an end. For one thing, one of the side effects of the revolution had been to set wealthy residents in Atlantic motion (including Loyalists), and these diasporic elites, many of whom ultimately returned home, sustained American links to European modes and materials. Brissot de Warville observed too

[29] Peter Maw, 'Anglo-American Trade during the Industrial Revolution: A Study of the Lancashire and Yorkshire Textile Industries, 1750–1825' (PhD thesis, University of Manchester, 2005); Dunlevy, *Pomp and Poverty: A History of Silk in Ireland.*
[30] Letter from Samuel Shaw to John Jay, New York, 19 May 1785, in Samuel Shaw, *The Journals of Major Samuel Shaw, the First American Consul at Canton,* ed. Josiah Quincy (Boston: Crosby & Nichols, 1847).
[31] Initial preferences were for black taffetas, satins, and an expansive variety of inexpensive ribbons, handkerchiefs, trimmings, and sewing silks. Jean Gordon Lee, *Philadelphians and the China Trade, 1784–1844* (Philadelphia: Philadelphia Museum of Art, 1984); Kariann Akemi Yokota, 'Transatlantic and Transpacific Connections in Early American History', *Pacific Historical Review* 83, no. 2 (May 2014): 204–19; Peck, '"India Chints" and "China Taffaty"'.

many silks for his liking in New York and Philadelphia in his 1788 tour of the United States. He noted that Americans' taste for luxury still seemed in thrall to 'the interested avarice of their old masters, the English', and lamented the 'great misfortune that, in republics, women should sacrifice so much time to trifles' – a viewpoint that anticipated the temporary French rejection of silk during their imminent violent lurch to republicanism.[32] Further north, Charles Storer described Bostonians 'flirting about in silk and satin' in 1786 while a year earlier John Quincy Adams felt that the best analogy for how fondness for dress in Boston had changed over the revolutionary era was *Bombyx mori* itself. He claimed that 'Not a few persons have been like the silk worm, first a mean insect, then a tawdry butterfly', and he anticipated that soon necessity and cost would force another reform, so that they became, 'at length again, a worm of the dust'.[33]

No less than the opportunistic manufacturers and merchants identified above (with whom they overlapped), American political economists were quick to take up the subject of silk, and to reposition it within post-revolutionary culture and society. In so doing, they presented a spectrum of proposals that ranged from outright prohibition to extensive state support, and characterised the commodity as everything from an evil and destructive superfluity to an essential foundation for social and economic development. The absence of consensus, of course, reflected the diverse regional economies and the varied sartorial cultures of the newly confederated states, in a period when former imperial subjects were deeply conscious of their problems of confederation, credit, economic sustainability, and ideological accord. Getting back in step with the latest European fashions may have preoccupied some Philadelphia and Charleston elites, but was not often high on the agenda for agitated western farming families and veterans overburdened with taxes, watching their currency depreciate during a biting depression.

Patterns in the setting of import tariffs perhaps hint at a gradual reconciliation of silks within the new polity: tariffs erected in the 1780s continued some of the moral and economic legwork of the earlier revolutionary period, with silks commonly enumerated amongst the categories paying the highest *ad valorem* duties, such as the 10 per cent rate levied on 'European or East Indian silks or china', in the Georgia legislation of 1786 or the 15 per cent in Massachusetts from 1785. But silks seem to have been less explicitly targeted over time, and in spite of his promise in the Federalist Papers to make the 'luxury of the rich tributary

---

[32] Brissot de Warville, *New Travels in the United States of America* (Bowling Green, OH: Historical Publications Co., 1919), 189–90.
[33] John Quincy Adams to Abigail Adams [Jr], Boston, 15 September 1785; Charles Storer to Abigail Adams Smith, Boston, 8 August 1786, *Adams Papers Online*.

to the public treasury', in Alexander Hamilton's federal Tariff Act of 1790, silks sat alongside other textiles again with a rate of 7.5 per cent for American-shipped goods.[34] The other discernible pattern in the political economy of the 1780s and 1790s was the way that ambitions of silk *manufacturing* continued to temper characterisations of silk as an ornamental luxury. Moral misgivings about finished goods could be diluted by staking a claim to the process of production. The means, in other words, could now go a long way towards justifying the ends.

Adjusting to Silk in a Revolutionary World

This dawning realisation was most apparent in the volte-face performed by one writer in particular: the Philadelphia businessman and theorist Pelatiah Webster, whose writings on public finances in the 1780s and 1790s were influential in debates over constitutional reform, credit, and banking. During the Revolutionary War, Webster published a series of essays 'on Free Trade and Finance', in which he was at pains to emphasise the relationship between republican morality and the operation of the market.[35] In his early writings, Webster was clearly hostile to silk as an anti-republican product. He proposed to hike import tariffs so that they were '*much heavier* on all articles of *luxury or mere ornament* . . . which are consumed principally by the *rich* or prodigal part of the community, such as *silks* of all sorts'. By overpricing this manifestation of Old World inequality, Webster anticipated that the American '*husbandman, the mechanic*, and the *poor*' would be eased. Putting silk out of reach would, he put it, 'have all the practical effects of a *sumptuary law*; would mend the economy, and increase the industry, of the community', as well as protecting the morals of the people.[36] Webster depicted silks and other luxuries as addictive poisons that ordinary American farmers and families needed help to resist.[37] Even in his use of metaphors, Webster maligned

---

[34] William Frank Zornow, 'Georgia Tariff Policies, 1775 to 1789', *Georgia Historical Quarterly* 38, no. 1 (1954): 5; M. E. Kelley, 'Tariff Acts under the Confederation', *Quarterly Journal of Economics* 2, no. 4 (1888): 474. The 1790 tariff rate was 12.5 per cent for non-American-shipped products direct from the Far East, which would have included many silks, and 17.5 per cent for non-American-shipped goods. Hamilton cited (as 'Publius') in Federalist Paper 36, in James Madison et al., *The Federalist Papers* (London: Penguin, 1987), 240.

[35] Pelatiah Webster, *Political Essays on the Nature and Operation of Money, Public Finances, and Other Subjects Published during the American War, and Continued up to the Present Year, 1791* (Philadelphia: Printed and sold by J. Crukshank, 1791), 14.

[36] From 'Dissertation on the Political Union and Constitution of the Thirteen United States of North America' (1783). Webster, *Political Essays*, 203.

[37] From 'Sixth Essay on Free Trade and Finance' (1783). Webster, *Political Essays*, 233, 241.

silk, contrasting the 'ingenious arguments, spun as fine as silk' of land speculators against the rights of the republican soldiers whose arguments were 'strong as iron'.[38] Webster's initial arguments were in chorus with a number of other writers who likewise drew attention to the threat to national political economy posed by love of luxury, as when a contributor to the popular *American Museum* urged American ladies to resume 'laying aside their richest silks, and superfluous decorations'.[39] Such appeals to republican virtue had only proved partly and temporarily effective in directing consumer demand away from British luxury, but they retained a considerable gravitational pull for American writers and social commentators, particularly amongst Anti-Federalists.[40]

But by 1790, writing anonymously as 'A Citizen of Philadelphia', Webster had changed his tune. He had apparently discovered that '[t]he climate of *our Union*, especially the middle states, is found to be very favorable both to the silk-worm and its food'. Gone were Webster's lambasting statements about corruption and excess, about sumptuary laws and textile wastage. In their stead were careful arguments about the natural bounty of the infant republic, and the distinctive ingenuity of its citizenry, for which a few lines can stand, fittingly, as representatives:

nature has furnished us with *abundant and perfect advantages* for carrying into execution the most extensive scale of this very lucrative and delicate manufacture . . . the genius of our people is capable of improving these advantages to the best effect; for it is well known that our mechanics make the most difficult fabrics in as high perfection as any that are imported from abroad, and commonly add great improvements . . . our people have genius enough, and numbers enough to work them up into fabrics of the best quality, and in the greatest quantity that can be wished . . . enlivening the country with *industry, riches, virtue, and peace*.

Webster was twisting his earlier language of luxury into a language of delicacy and excellence. Likewise, he was reorientating the notion of waste away from a critique of sumptuary extravagance (wasteful vanity) and towards the profitable market opportunity that would avert wasted labour. As charted in the epilogue below, the arguments put forward in Webster's rather obscure, anonymous essay would grow into a deafening

---

[38] From 'Seventh Essay on Free Trade and Finance' (1785). Webster, *Political Essays*, 281.
[39] *American Museum*, 2, no. 2 (August 1787): 165.
[40] Herbert J. Storing, *The Complete Anti-Federalist*, 7 vols. (Chicago: University of Chicago Press, 2008), 1: 21. For broader assessments of relationship between ideology and consumption: Haulman, *The Politics of Fashion in Eighteenth-Century America*, 181–2, 201–4; Zakim, *Ready-Made Democracy*, 22–32; Berg, *Luxury and Pleasure*, 300; Auslander, *Cultural Revolutions: The Politics of Everyday Life in Britain, North America and France*, 99–111.

national chorus by the 1830s, supported by a horde of experts and statistics.[41]

Others took up similar themes, as schemes for developing the political economy of the infant United States found space for the revival of hopes for silk cultivation, but with particular virtuous inflections. In 1785 an article published in many newspapers proposed the formation of a voluntary 'Silk Company' across New England that would involve 'patriotic and public spirited persons' planting out millions of mulberry trees across towns and counties – similar to Ezra Stiles's congregational plan. A 'systematical diffusion' of mulberry plants and silkworm eggs to the 'whole body of the people' would prompt 'merchants and others' to set up filatures to buy up and process the cocoons. The author emphasised that silk 'is proposed rather as a staple for exportation . . . for making remittances in commerce'. In this way, like Webster, they not only side-stepped the thorny issue of silk being a rather ostentatious and elitist product to aim for in a new republic, but were also able to link together constituencies, 'the husbandman *and* merchant', who were often arrayed against one another in contemporary political and economic debates.[42]

Arguments and evidence from beyond the British empire were naturally attractive to those looking to encourage the post-revolutionary pursuit of American sericulture. One essay on commercial improvement was translated from a French manuscript and printed in the *National Gazette*, whence it was recirculated by regional papers. It drew not only on French insights to stress how raw silk was imperative to ideas of 'a national manufacture', but looked specifically to the example of non-British European attempts such as those in contemporary Prussia – where the author celebrated the interventionist legislation, sumptuary laws, and industry encouragement offered by the king. They asserted that attention to the culture of white mulberry trees was a benchmark of development

---

[41] Pelatiah Webster, *An Essay on the Culture of Silk, and Raising White Mulberry Trees, the Leaves of Which Are the Only Proper Food of the Silk-Worm* (Philadelphia: Printed and sold by Joseph Crukshank, 1790). Quotes (in turn) from 3, 4, 6. Attribution of this essay to Webster is based on a close scrutiny of the writing style, the fact that he used the same printer and title for other publications, marginalia in the copies at the Library Company of Philadelphia and New York Public Library ('sent from Mr. Webster of Philadelphia'), all of which confirm an ascription made in Franklin Bowditch Dexter, *Biographical Sketches of Graduates of Yale: Yale College with Annals of the College History*, 6 vols. (New York, 1912), 2: 101. The work was subsequently serialised in newspapers such as *Burlington Advertiser*, 12 April 1791.

[42] Notice 'To the Public', *New-Haven Gazette*, 14 April 1785. Repeated e.g. in New Haven *Connecticut Journal*, 12 April 1786, p. 1; *The Plymouth Journal, and the Massachusetts Advertiser*, 31 May 1785, p. 4; Boston *Independent Ledger and the American Advertiser*, 2 May 1785, p. 1; Philadelphia *Pennsylvania Mercury and Universal Advertiser*, 19 May 1786, p. 1; Philadelphia *American Museum*, 1 October 1787.

amongst the other 'civilized' northern powers of Europe, including German and Scandinavian states, and warned that 'the enterprize and industry of the British nation will, if that is allowed, always find means to baffle America both in her manufactures and commerce'.[43] Best practices and environmental claims about sericulture from foreign-language treatises were also increasingly translated and excerpted.[44]

Such arguments were able to synthesise anti-British sentiment, the older critiques of foreign luxuries, and the new emphases on manufacturing and independence. 'Citizens of America', urged a contributor to the *American Museum*, 'Now you are gloriously emancipated from the political thraldom of England, disdain to be held by her in commercial chains. Revive the silk manufacture.' They proposed a homespun textile oath that should be sworn by all federal officers at the time they took office. Officers might pledge their honour 'that whenever I perform the functions of my office I will be dressed principally in the manufactures of the united states', and each transgression by wearing hats, coats, waistcoats, stockings, or shoes 'of foreign manufacture' should result in a fine of one silver dollar, payable to the federal clerk of assembly!'[45]

Whether George Washington read this article or not in January 1788, as Americans were furiously debating whether to accept the newly proposed Constitution, he and other 'Founding Fathers' were extremely careful with the image they projected in their dress and their uses of silk. For his first inauguration on 30 April 1789, Washington famously wore a suit of domestic superfine brown broadcloth from Hartford, Connecticut, though it is seldom remembered that his silk stockings, also, were made in America.[46] Given Washington's appreciation of fine silks and his preoccupation with ploughing an exemplary American furrow, it is perhaps not surprising that he also held a long-standing interest in the prospects of silk culture, and had twice experimented with mulberries on his own estates. According to his diary he was fascinated by the large numbers of white mulberries used to feed silkworms in the town of Wallingford, Connecticut, which he visited in October 1789. There, he 'saw samples of lustring (exceeding good) which had been manufactured from the

---

[43] 'A Political Enquiry into the Best Means of Improving the Commerce of the American States', dated 17 May 1791. Originally published in Philadelphia *National Gazette*, 24 November 1791 and subsequent issues. Recirculated in e.g. Boston *Independent Chronicle and Universal Advertiser*, 19 January 1792.

[44] See e.g. translation of *Observations sur la culture du mûrier & l'education des vers à soie*, in a short-lived periodical aimed at the French refugee readership in Pennsylvania, *The Level of Europe*, 1 October 1794.

[45] 'Letter on the Culture of Silk', *American Museum*, 3 (January 1788): 89.

[46] Cadou, *The George Washington Collection*, 230; Zakim, *Ready-Made Democracy*, 24–5.

Cocoon raised in this Town, and silk thread very fine'.[47] During his presidency in 1794, even though it confessedly broke his own 'established maxim', he accepted a gift of American-raised silk from fellow Virginian Mary Dabney Anderson (whose husband owned around a dozen bonds-people on the Pamunkey River in Gloucester County), promising that he would 'have it made up, and will wear it as a memento', evincing as it did 'what our climate, aided by industry, is capable of yielding', and this may not have been the first time he had received such a silken token.[48] Washington's moderated presidential use of silk was reflected in the eulogy penned for him by Louis-Marcelin de Fontanes in 1800 (commissioned by Napoleon in 1800 as a thinly veiled tribute to his own accomplishments), in which he described Washington as: 'an enemy of vain ostentation, [yet] he wished that republican customs be clad with dignity'.[49]

Like the Washingtons before him, Jefferson took stock of his wardrobe and appearance as a consequence of the revolution. According to the later testimony of one of his enslaved males, on returning from diplomatic duties in France in 1789, Jefferson 'brought a great many clothes from France with him', but according to contemporary Deborah Logan, his 'suit of silk, ruffles and an elegant topaz ring' gave way as he 'soon adopted a more republican garb, and was reproached with going to the other extreme'.[50] Jefferson seems not to have opted to attempt silk production on his own estates, preferring to invest in coarser cloth-manufacturing operations for his bondspeople, though he named the centre of his plantation 'Mulberry Row' after trees planted there from the 1770s. While he only passingly referenced the silkworm in his *Notes on the State of Virginia*, he did correspond closely on the subject with

[47] George Washington, Donald Jackson, and Dorothy Twohig, *The Diaries of George Washington*, 6 vols. (Charlottesville: University Press of Virginia, 1976), 6: 136.

[48] Washington, Jackson, and Twohig, 1: 335–6; 4: 96; 5: 467. George Washington to Mrs. Matthew Anderson, 20 July 1794, George Washington, *The Writings of George Washington from the Original Manuscript Sources, 1745–1799*, ed. John Clement Fitzpatrick, 39 vols. (Washington: U.S. Govt. Print. Off, 1931), 33: 433. Zalmon Storrs claimed that he remembered hearing Nathaniel Aspinwall say 'that he took two silk vest patterns to Philadelphia while Congress was in session there and made a present of one to General Washington and the other to Dr. Franklin'. Note from Zalmon Storrs to William Weaver, 18 December 1864, cited in Elderkin, *Genealogy of the Elderkin Family*, 15.

[49] Gilbert Chinard, *George Washington as the French Knew Him* (Princeton, NJ: Princeton University Press, 1940), 135.

[50] Isaac Granger Jefferson's memoir was originally published in 1847. Isaac Jefferson, *Memoirs of a Monticello Slave, As Dictated to Charles Campbell in the 1840's by Isaac, one of Thomas Jefferson's Slaves*, ed. Rayford W. Logan (Charlottesville: University of Virginia Press, 1951), 45, 11, 19–20; Deborah Norris Logan, *Memoir of Dr. George Logan of Stenton* (Philadelphia: The Historical Society of Pennsylvania, 1899), 50.

European experts such as the Italian Filippo Mazzei and the Dutch sericulturist Willem van Hasselt, and as a retired grandfather he oversaw the tending of silkworms in Monticello and linked them to the homespun agenda, jesting with his younger granddaughters that they might only get married 'as soon as they can get wedding gowns from this spinner'.[51]

Of all the major 'Founding Fathers' though, Benjamin Franklin most deliberately and most effectively refashioned himself during the revolutionary period, much of which he spent overseas. Where Washington and Jefferson were conscious of the use of silk in their own dress, invested in it as an agricultural product, and linked it to the symbolism of homespun, Franklin took this to another level. As shown in his correspondence and gifts to his wife and daughter, Franklin had long recognised both the value of silk and its sartorial dangers, and generally had two modes of engaging with luxuries: publicly scorning or privately spending.[52] Once established in France, he performed his own metamorphosis, significantly altering his earlier emulative dress style and instead – to the delight of his French hosts – donning a brown suit, famous spectacles, and a marten fur cap, describing himself as 'very plainly dress'd', in deliberate contraposition to 'the powder'd heads of Paris'.[53] Confident that his intellectual reputation went before him, Franklin wanted his apparel to symbolise honesty and directness, but without

[51] Thomas Jefferson and Merrill D. Peterson, *Writings* (New York, NY: Literary Classics of the US, 1984), 164. 'Plan of Philip Mazzei's Agricultural Company, 1774', Julian P. Boyd et al., eds., *The Papers of Thomas Jefferson*, 42 vols. (Princeton, NJ: Princeton University Press, 1950), 1: 156–9. Willem H. van Hasselt to Thomas Jefferson, Le Hague, 20 June 1802. Henricus F. J. M. van den Eerenbeemt, *Op zoek naar het zachte goud: Pogingen tot innovatie via een Zijdeteelt in Nederland 17e–20e eeuw* (Tilburg: Gianotten, 1993), 41. Thomas Jefferson to Cornelia J. Randolph, Monticello, 3 June 1811, in Thomas Jefferson, *The Papers of Thomas Jefferson: Retirement Series*, ed. J. Jefferson Looney, 8 vols. (Princeton, NJ: Princeton University Press, 2004), 3: 635. Silkworms returned to Monticello in considerable number after Jefferson's death, for the estate's 1831 purchaser, James Barclay, swiftly saturated the grounds with various species of mulberries in an ambitious scheme to launch Virginian sericulture, describing it as 'perhaps one of the most eligible situations in the world for the lucrative pursuit of the culture of Silk'. Marc Leepson, *Saving Monticello: The Levy Family's Epic Quest to Rescue the House That Jefferson Built* (New York: Free Press, 2001), 27–30, 40.

[52] Benjamin Franklin, *The Works of Benjamin Franklin, Containing Several Political and Historical Tracts Not Included in Any Former Edition*, ed. Jared Sparks, 10 vols. (Boston: Tappan & Whittemore, 1844), 2: 99. Peter Collinson to Franklin, London, 27 January 1753 and 26 January 1754; Franklin to Deborah Franklin, London, 19 February 1758, 6 April 1766, and 14 February 1773; in *Franklin Papers Online*.

[53] Franklin to Emma Thompson, Paris, 8 February 1777, in *Franklin Papers Online*. For a wider discussion of Franklin's combination of practicality and symbolism, see Baumgarten, *What Clothes Reveal*, 97–100 (quote on 99); Nian-Sheng Huang, *Benjamin Franklin in American Thought and Culture, 1790–1990* (American Philosophical Society, 1994), 129.

repudiating elegance and a certain nobility of carriage, and this contrivance was proved a winner.[54]

The adjustments made to their habits by these rising American celebrities between the 1770s and the 1790s, as they developed iconic positions within attentive political cultures, involved a downscaling of the exuberance of their silks. In this they were by no means exceptional, for Americans' embracing of a frugal homespun idyll was itself both a consequence and a cause of wider Atlantic fashionable trends towards simplicity in style and design in the later eighteenth century, coinciding with the rise of cottons, fashion magazines, and the exploding outcomes of industrial and political revolutions in Britain, America, and then France.[55] Queen Marie-Antoinette had earlier antagonised the French silk industry through her capricious and exhaustive orders for court dress, with new patterns and colours that challenged Lyonnais business practices.[56] In the 1780s, by embracing plainness (in her popularisation of light cotton and linen gowns), French writers xenophobically vilified the '*Autrichienne*' for now unpatriotically deserting and 'conspiring to ruin our manufacturers of beautiful silks', with the Abbé Jean-Louis Giraud-Soulavie claiming that her 'revolution in France in costumes and fashions' in the 1780s had devastated silkworm raisers in Provence and Languedoc and three-quarters of the Lyonnais manufacturing population.[57] Perhaps it was just as well she never received the Franklins' gift of Pennsylvanian raw silk, or she would have got it in the neck for that, too. By 1788, when other European courts and major aristocratic markets were likewise gravitating away from traditional dress silks, the city of Lyons informed the king that more than 15 million pieces of finished cloth were unsold in merchant warehouses.[58]

The French silk industry's prospects did not improve with the arrival of political revolution, and it is instructive briefly to compare the experiences in France with those across the Atlantic – not least because the former rebounded upon the Atlantic silk trade and Americans' view of it in the

---

[54] For examples of the portraits capturing dress 'à la Franklin' see the 1777 engraving by Charles-Nicolas Cochin (copied by Augustine de Saint Aubin) and the 1778 pastel and then oil painting, the latter in the Friedsam Collection, Metropolitan Museum of Art. Huang, *Benjamin Franklin in American Thought and Culture, 1790–1990*.
[55] On the way that both the American and French revolutions pulled inescapably towards the neoclassicism and natural lines that already featured in English country styles, Ribeiro, *Dress and Morality*, 111.
[56] Caroline Weber, *Queen of Fashion: What Marie Antoinette Wore to the Revolution* (New York: H. Holt, 2006), 156–63.
[57] Jean-Louis Soulavie, *Mémoires historiques et politiques du règne de Louis XVI, depuis son mariage jusqu'à sa mort*, 6 vols. (Paris: Treuttel et Würtz, 1801), 6: 39–45 (quote on 41).
[58] 'Memoire de la ville de Lyon au roi' (2 May 1788), cited in Longfellow, 'Silk Weavers and the Social Struggle in Lyon during the French Revolution, 1789–94', 10.

1790s. The prominent French fashion magazine, *Le Cabinet des modes*, might have been talking about either revolution when it summarised the zeitgeist on 21 September 1790: 'luxury went out, but is now within reach of all citizens'.[59] As in the thirteen rebellious British colonies, during the French Revolution silk quickly became typified as the trademark textile of aristocratic lassitude, while true republicans embraced wool, linen, and cotton, which were associated with nature, austerity, and classical virtue.[60] The very phrase 'sans-culottes' (i.e. without bourgeois silken knee-breeches) was appropriated by radicals as a way of distinguishing themselves from the moderate reformers and revolutionaries who invested in the fashionable legwear rather than the traditional *pantalons* (trousers) of the urban labourers. As the revolution spiralled in its scale and intensity, political imperatives converged more forcefully with dress in France, and after King Louis XVI's execution, silk was banned for its noble associations. All future cockades were to be made from 'patriotic' wool – echoing the Continental Association – and in France, to a greater degree, colour came to signify political affiliation. The uniform of the sans-culottes did not really take hold across the country, and was discarded with the Jacobins' collapse in July 1794, when the Convention sought to install a national costume, commissioning the artist Jacques-Louis David to create one, though it did not take on.[61] Looking back from the 1830s, the writer Honoré de Balzac neatly summarised that the French Revolution had boiled down to 'a contest between silk and cloth'.[62]

During the American Revolution, it was the distant British silk industry and its workers who suffered from the interruptions to consumption. But the same was not true in France, where the hardships of the city of Lyons were extreme, and extended well beyond its walls to secondary towns and rural areas of silk throwing and sericulture.[63] Already suffering from the cultural and economic crises of the late 1780s, which had seen production halved, the onset of revolution dealt a severe blow to the silk industry that had sustained a majority of the population in one way or another. Figured

---

[59] Nicole Pellegrin, *Les vêtements de la liberté: Abécédaire des pratiques vestimentaires en France de 1780 à 1800* (Aix: Alinéa, 1989).

[60] Roche, *The Culture of Clothing*, 148.

[61] Philip Mansel, *Dressed to Rule: Royal and Court Costume from Louis XIV to Elizabeth II* (New Haven: Yale University Press, 2005), 68, 71, 74–5; James Maxwell Anderson, *Daily Life during the French Revolution* (Westport, CT: Greenwood Press, 2007), 75.

[62] Honoré de Balzac, *Traité de la vie élégante: Suivi de la théorie de la démarche* (Paris: Editions Bossard, 1922), 60.

[63] For the traumatic impact on especially the auxiliary female labour force such as *dévideuses* and *ovalistes* involved in preparing silk yarn, see Daryl M. Hafter, *Women at Work in Preindustrial France* (University Park, PA: Pennsylvania State University, 2007), 258–89.

silks had been on the retreat for some time, and now the flight of French aristocrats removed Lyons' major domestic clientele, while the early abolition of the privileges of the Grande Fabrique undermined the efficacy of an organised response. Raw silk output collapsed, specialists fled to Spain and other regions, and one émigré, the Comte de Pousargues, even found a role advising British sericulturists about improving production.[64] To make matters worse, the French Revolution fostered factional disputes between merchants and weavers, whose bitter rivalry was no longer contained by their common trade.[65] As in Spitalfields (where disputes between master weavers and journeymen over piece-rate wages became violent and required legislative intervention in the 1760s and 1770s), the combination of an urban working class manufacturing luxury goods threw up particular political paradoxes: the poverty and unemployment of Lyons weavers forced them into an ultimately unsuccessful local alliance with the Jacobins, who as we have seen, outlawed their only outlet.

During the 1790s, some hopes remained of exporting French silks directly and in bulk to US markets, and efforts were made in particular by James Swan, the American trader who had become a purchasing agent for the French Republic. Swan's importance to the early French republic lay in his ability to marshal shipments of American foodstuffs, so vital to the Commission des Subsistances, the body which struggled to provision the French nation and its bedraggled army from 1793. To pay for these purchases from neutral polities, which besides the United States included Genoa, Switzerland, Hamburg, and Denmark, the Commission requisitioned silks, cloths, and wine and brandy. Swan struggled, however, to match French supply to American demand: he stressed that American consumers would buy 'Silk, taffetas, [and] satins', but he specified that the colours needed to be neutral such as 'brown, *ramoneur*, Quaker'. He noted that there was a demand for silk stockings, 'but few of de luxe quality'. However, the thousands of pounds of silks and satins that Swan was authorised to take as credit in 1794 comprised not goods-to-order, but the stocks of confiscated aristocratic luxury goods stored in the national warehouses. These were distributed at auctions through subagents at all principal American ports, but they did not sell well, partly, ironically, because some

---

[64] Etienne Mayet, *Mémoire sur les manufactures de Lyon* (London: Chez Moutard, 1786); Françoise Clavairolle, *Le Magnan et l'arbre d'or* (Paris: Éditions de la Maison des sciences de l'homme, 2003), 41. Letter from Le Comte de Pousarques, London (1 May 1793), RSA PR.MC/102/10/89.

[65] Longfellow, 'Silk Weavers and the Social Struggle in Lyon during the French Revolution, 1789–94', 18.

Francophile Americans, sporting their *tricolore* cockades, preferred the new dress *de la République*.[66]

By the summer of 1793, when 'federalist' revolt brought civil war and a bloody siege to Lyons, the number of looms had already plummeted to 5,000, and thereafter the French industry came precariously close to complete collapse. A heavy proportion of industry leaders were executed or migrated with their capital, demand had evaporated in the wider context of war and recession, skilled labour had been decimated and dispersed, and amidst the confiscations, there had been much destruction of fabrics, designs, and equipment. What silk production limped on largely catered for external markets such as the German cities (especially Leipzig, Frankfurt, and Hamburg) and Spanish and Russian courts, and was increasingly permeated by German and Swiss merchant houses. It would take the heavily targeted patronage and protectionism of Napoleon Bonaparte to once again revitalise silk production, slowly, in the early nineteenth century, much of it commissioned for his lavish satellite courts. Only with the end of the Napoleonic Wars in 1815 did the Lyonnais industry recover, helped by the pointed revitalisation of sericulture in southern France and the impact of Jacquard's revolutionary loom. Lost markets were soon retaken, and within the space of a decade, French silks had broken definitively into the major Atlantic markets in Britain and the growing United States.[67] Both major Atlantic revolutions had jeopardised the cultural and commercial place of silk goods in their respective societies, but radical early disruptions had been allayed, thanks in part to the rehabilitation of silkworms and their real or imagined potential.

[66] Howard C. Rice, 'James Swan: Agent of the French Republic 1794–1796', *The New England Quarterly* 10, no. 3 (1937): 464–86. Many might have actually been re-exported to Caribbean and Latin American markets – as occurred commonly in the US imports of Bordeaux wine, brandy, and dry goods analysed by Silvia Marzagalli, 'The Failure of a Transatlantic Alliance? Franco-American Trade, 1783–1815', *History of European Ideas* 34 (2008): 456–64.

[67] Justin Godart, *L'Ouvrier en soie: Monographie du tisseur lyonnais*, 2 vols. (Lyons: Bernoux & Cumin, 1899), volume 2; Maurice Garden, *Lyon et les lyonnais au xviiie siècle* (Paris: Flammarion, 1975), 180–2; Bernard Tassinari, *La soie à Lyon: De la grande fabrique aux textiles du xxie siècle* (Lyons: Editions lyonnaises d'art et d'histoire, 2005), 20; André Latreille, *Histoire de Lyon et du lyonnais* (Toulouse: Privat, 1975); P. Leon, *Papiers d'industriels et de commerçants lyonnais* (Lyons: Centre d'histoire économique et sociale de la région lyonnaise, 1976); Pierre Arizzoli-Clémentel and Chantal Gastinet-Coural, *Soieries de Lyon: Commandes royales au XVIIIe siècle, 1730–1800* (Lyons: Musée Historique des Tissus, 1998), 15–17; Pierre Cayez, 'Entreprises et entrepreneurs lyonnais sous la révolution et l'empire', *Histoire, Économie et Société* 12, no. 1 (1993): 17–27. The other important innovation that helped Lyons recover was the greater consistency produced in French sericulture by the application of steam to cocoon reeling, as pioneered by the invention of Joseph Ferdinand Gensoul, who constructed an expensive boiler apparatus, patented in 1805.

Perseverance in American Silk Raising

While all these international developments in silk fashions, political economy, trade, and production were swirling around the Atlantic in the
1780s and the 1790s, many silk raisers in the United States doggedly
persevered with their mulberry planting and leaf picking, silkworm feeding, cocoon reeling, and domestic manufacturing activities each springtime. Indeed, in his pamphlet of 1790, James Swan had acknowledged
some French concerns about competition from the continued progression of American sericulture and homespun. Swan downplayed the threat
of further American non-importation of European silks, and stressed that
'it is not to be feared that they make silk'.[68] But quietly, and as yet
unobtrusively, American silk raisers found themselves fortified in some
respects by the positive spin that Webster and others now put on the
moral prospects of silk manufacturing, and the place that seemed assured
for plain, low-grade homespun silk products and accessories in light of the
patronage of leaders such as Franklin and Washington.

In 1784 the Connecticut General Assembly had passed 'An Act to
promote the making of Raw-Silk within this State', which responded to
the continuing activity in sericulture and sought to shore it up with state
encouragement in the way that Webster and others advocated. The law
offered a payment of ten shillings for every 100 white mulberry trees
planted (of three or more years' growth), providing they were certified
to have been well maintained, with the bounty running for ten years.
Furthermore, a fifteen-year bounty was established for raw silk raised in
Connecticut, promising payments of three pence 'for each ounce of such
dry silk, which he, she, or they shall make' by 'properly winding the
same from the balls or cacoons'. The law stipulated that two Justices of
the Peace should examine and certify each claim, and that any fraud was
to be treated as forgery.[69]

Evidence of the widespread claiming of bounties for Connecticut silk
cultivation can be found in the extant fifty-odd slips of paper signed by
Justices of the Peace in the state between 1789 and 1791, which took the
following format:

These certify that Elias Chapman of Ashford in Windham County has manufactured the courant year from worms and mulberry trees of his own raising within
this state forty six ounces of well dried raw silk properly wound from the balls since

---

[68] Swan, *Causes qui se sont opposées aux progrès du commerce*, 128–9.
[69] The act was later amended to reduce the bounty from three pence to two pence per ounce
of dry reeled silk. Connecticut, *Acts and Laws of the State of Connecticut in America* (New
London: Printed by T. Green, Printer to the Governor and Company of the State of
Connecticut, 1784), 232, 282–3. Hartford *Connecticut Courant*, 9 March 1784.

the first day of July last for which he is intitled to a bounty from this State of seven shillings & eight pence L[a]wful money and collect[or]s of the State Tax in Ashford is hearby ordered to pay the same [to] said Chapman out of the Civil list Tax.[70]

Surviving receipts recorded a total of 151 lb being rewarded with 307 shillings, and claimants ranged from Dorothy Triscott's paltry seven ounces up to Jabez Barrows Jr.'s fifteen lb and two ounces, for which he received thirty shillings and four pence (which equated to the price of more than fifteen days' agricultural labour in the region or around eight bushels of corn).[71] Most slips listed the claimant's town, from which we can gauge that the heaviest concentration was in Mansfield, followed by Wallingford (where George Washington had admired the pursuit), Guilford, and Ashford, but in general they reflected a wide geographical uptake.[72]

Ezra Stiles, having successfully negotiated Yale through the American Revolution, proudly wore a gown made of Connecticut silk at the College's Commencement in 1789, the gesture proving that his interest in silk had not evaporated but been distilled by the political transformation across the continent.[73] Along with putting into action his rekindled ideas for the organisation of silk growers, Stiles purposefully became a sort of archivist of national progress in silk. In New Haven in June 1786 he wrote in his diary that '[t]he Spirit for Raising Silk Worms is great in this Town', and at one site he had visited an estimated 130,000 silk-worms spread over some 1,022 square feet of boards, housed in a 60 x 30 foot loft.[74] Four years later, he sent in an account to the New Haven paper, listing the 60 families who had raised an estimated 442,000 cocoons that season, ranging from Abraham Thomason's 60,000 down to Miss Lydia Griswold's 100, and including a sizeable number of single females (including spinsters and widows) and names suggestive of black heritage (such as 'Belfast' and 'Sue Cato').[75] He tabulated producers in New Haven and Northford in his notebook, estimating in the latter town they had made 1,200 'Runs' which would equate to '400

[70] 'Justices of the Peace Records, 1786–92', MS 69784, Connecticut Historical Society, Hartford CT, 1792.

[71] Values estimated from Carroll D. Wright, *Comparative Wages, Prices, and Cost of Living: From the Sixteenth Annual Report of the Massachusetts Bureau of Statistics of Labor, for 1885* (Boston: Wright & Potter, 1889), 41, 46.

[72] 'Justices of the Peace Records, 1786–92', MS 69784, Connecticut Historical Society, Hartford CT.

[73] Aspinwall, *The Aspinwall Genealogy*, 57.

[74] Stiles, *The Literary Diary of Ezra Stiles*, 3: 229.

[75] Stiles, 'Journal of Silkworms', 290–1. Philadelphia *American Museum, or, Universal Magazine*, 1 November 1790.

yds of silk cloth ¾ yd wide . . . But much was twist[ed] into sewing silk & so worth much more.'[76]

As this phrase suggests, increasingly, Stiles's post-revolutionary references to silk producers included attention to the later manufacturing processes required to turn raw silk into usable material: home boiling, twisting, spinning, and so forth – the improvised 'throwing' of American-reared silk to make it 'fit for weav[in]g'.[77] By 1790, he was impressed to note that 'Mans[field] Windsters acco[unt] 10 lbs Balls to 1 lb Raw Silk', one of the most impressive reeling ratios documented in the Americas. Newspapers attributed around 200 lb raw silk to this town alone in 1789 and 150 lb in 1790.[78] Stiles also mentioned a growing number of fabrics and apparel manufactured out of American-raised silk, including lustrings and satins of three-quarters of a yard wide, woven and dyed in New Haven and Guilford.[79] In 1791, white silk stockings were woven 'at Norwich in a Loom made there', and handkerchiefs at Northford, both out of silk raised in 'North Haven & Branford'.[80] Mrs Atwater of Branford was particularly prolific, '[m]uch to the Honour of her Ingenuity and Industry'. By the end of 1792, she had made herself a 'handsome genteel silk Cloke', and her husband, the Reverend Jason Atwater, a 'Jacket & Breeches', and, to Ezra Stiles's particular delight, a black gown, 'the first Clergyman's silk Gown raised and made in America'.[81] Notions of honour and home production, so important to the producers who had straddled colonial and revolutionary paradigms in Pennsyvlania, continued to resonate – with the fibre and the fabric now produced locally.

Outside of New England, Nathaniel Aspinwall expanded his campaign to prosper from sales of mulberry trees, offering 'White Italian' saplings in 1790 from nurseries planted out near the College of Princeton (New Jersey) and a mile and a half northwest out of Philadelphia on the Ridge Road, an 'almost impassable' waggon way, now Spring Garden neighbourhood.[82]

[76] Stiles, 'Journal of Silkworms', 291, 297.
[77] Stiles, 'Itineraries (6 vols.), Ezra Stiles Papers, Beinecke Library, Yale University', 5: 263.
[78] Stiles, 'Journal of Silkworms', 380. Elizabethtown (NJ) *Christian's, Scholar's, & Farmer's Magazine*, 1 December 1789; Worcester *Massachusetts Spy*, 28 March 1792, p. 1.
[79] Stiles, *The Literary Diary of Ezra Stiles*, 3: 320; Stiles, 'Journal of Silkworms', 296.
[80] Stiles, *The Literary Diary of Ezra Stiles*, 3: 409–10.
[81] Stiles, *Literary Diary*, 3: 495. Stiles listed the production as '10½ yards 24 inches wide 18 oz raw silk . . . 2½ yds black silk weaving 1/9 per yard'.
[82] Philadelphia *Independent Gazetteer*, 24 April 1790. The Philadelphia nursery was on the lands of Samuel Meredith, Treasurer of the United States. For the description of Ridge Road, François-Alexandre-Frédéric de La Rochefoucauld-Liancourt, *Travels through the United States of North America: The Country of the Iroquois, and Upper Canada, in the Years 1795, 1796, and 1797*, 4 vols., vol. 2 (London: R. Phillips, 1800), 1: 2–3. Aspinwall's 'laudable' ambitions in Pennsylvania were described earlier in a letter from William Barton to Franklin, Philadelphia, 2 May 1789, in *Franklin Papers Online*.

In 1791 with his partner Peter DeWitt (a Philadelphia merchant), Aspinwall targeted citizens of New York, who were well placed to take advantage of his Long Island stocks.[83] He threw in a few extra arguments in his newer advertisements to enhance the merits of his mulberries, stressing the suitability of their timber for shipbuilding, and the soil-enriching effect of their berries which made the grass taste better for cattle (though quite how he knew this is unclear).[84] In 1792 the trees were selling for twenty shillings per hundred, and Aspinwall based himself in Philadelphia, at an address between Market and Arch streets, where a growing range of samples 'of American made Silk both in Piece and Skain ... of a variety of colours and kinds, may be seen'.[85] Little wonder that the Society for Establishing Useful Manufactures which in 1791 founded an industrial town at Paterson, New Jersey, that was primarily aimed at cotton and grist mills (powered by the falls of the Passaic River) also initially pursued the possible manufacture of raw silk based upon local supplies.[86] Aspinwall died 'of a tedious and lingering disorder' in New Haven in 1800, and one short obituary prophesied that he would 'be remembered as a benefactor to his country' should silk manufactures ever be established. His initiatives and those documented in New England – supported by much investment of female household labour – acted as precarious footholds, allowing rudimentary yarn-processing and manufacturing operations to emerge that offered small returns for silk. These were not the great leaps forward promised by the likes of Edmund Clegg and other foreign experts during the revolutionary years, but they would offer a platform from which first American-born manufacturers and from the 1820s new waves of foreign experts could successfully operate.[87]

In Pennsylvania, there is good evidence of silk production persisting through the 1780s, though no longer co-ordinated by the Silk Society or its Philadelphia filature. The large household of James Thompson, at East Caln in Chester County, had by 1788 been breeding silkworms for several years, processing the silk, and 'manufacturing it into various articles of dress', including stockings, handkerchiefs, and gowns. An admiring writer explained their operations to the *Federal Gazette*: 'the girls attend the worms and dress the silk, the men weave it into cloth; and most of the

---

[83] Philadelphia *Independent Gazetteer*, 17 April 1790; Philadelphia *Mail; or, ClayPoole's Daily Advertiser*, 15 June 1791, p. 4; *New-York Journal, & Patriotic Register*, 9 April 1791, p. 109; Philadelphia *General Advertiser*, 24 March 1792, p. 4.
[84] *New-York Journal, & Patriotic Register*, 9 April 1791, p. 109.
[85] Philadelphia *General Advertiser*, 24 March 1792, p. 4.
[86] Margrave, Emigration of Silk Workers, 42; Marcia A. Dente, *Paterson Great Falls : From Local Landmark to National Historical Park* (Charleston: History Press, 2012), 87.
[87] Jacqueline Field, Marjorie Senechal, and Madelyn Shaw, *American Silk, 1830–1930: Entrepreneurs and Artifacts* (Lubbock, TX: Texas Tech University Press, 2007), 15; Margrave, *Emigration of Silk Workers*, 30–83.

business is done in intervals of other work of the farm'. Such efforts were linked to the ideal of 'a truly FEDERAL DRESS' that would 'see our country and town ladies dressed out in silks of their own manufacture'.[88] The existence of localised silk activity is also suggested by a number of items in the newspapers that gave indications of Pennsylvania production, such as advertisements for fishing tackle that included 'Best silkworm's gut'. This actually referred to the mature caterpillar's silk glands which were removed as translucent sinewy blobs, stretched, dried, and twisted into strands, and attached to fish hooks to make fly-fishing leaders.[89] Other evidence of domestic activity can be inferred from the advertisements of specialist silk ribbon dyers such as Frenchman Alexandre Morel in Philadelphia who offered blue and violet dyes, 'ready mixed' and 'easily made use of', to stain domestically manufactured ribbons.[90] Lastly, a handful of references crop up in comic or anecdotal material, as in the curious parable offered by a contributor to the *Federal Gazette* in 1791, which in a descriptive aside mentioned 'several *female freeholders* that have little cottages round that lady's estate, and make a scanty living by rearing silk-worms, and selling fruit'.[91]

In the southern states, though raw silk production on a centralised scale had been crippled by factors discussed above, eclectic producers across occasional plantations, farms, and cities continued to make use of supplies of mulberry trees and disposable labour to pursue small-scale production. Locally oriented production seems to have trickled on amongst private persons, though not at the community-wide level of more northern areas: Willem Van Hasselt was reportedly raising silk in the vicinity of Charleston in 1787, while the next year an Elizabeth Taverner advertised that she sold the 'curiosity of silk worms making silk' for two shillings per head, in her house at the upper end of King Street.[92] Ralph Izard, a planter in South Carolina's wealthy Goose Creek district, had invested in sericulture after spending some time in Europe in the 1770s, setting aside and manuring a part of his garden behind the stables at his The Elms plantation, and sowing 'a good quantity of white mulberry-seed' some of which he sourced in Italy. He reprised these efforts in the early 1790s, now entering into correspondence with Connecticut silk raisers – another

[88] Letter from 'I. M.', Philadelphia *Federal Gazette*, 10 October 1788.
[89] Silk was also commonly used for fishing lines. Examples: Pennsylvania Ledger, 18 February 1775; Philadelphia *General Advertiser*, 3 May 1791; *Dunlap's American Daily Advertiser*, 4 May 1793.
[90] Philadelphia *General Advertiser*, 19 April 1791.
[91] Philadelphia *Federal Gazette*, 27 December 1791.
[92] States, *Letter from Treasury Secretary on Growth of Silk*, 23–4; David Ramsay, *History of South Carolina: From Its First Settlement in 1670 to the Year 1808* (Spartanburg, SC: Reprint Co, 1959), 124. Charleston *City Gazette and Daily Advertiser*, 29 April 1788.

testament to converging American sensibilities.[93] Meanwhile in Georgia, over 200 lb of raw silk was brought to Savannah in 1790 for exportation, while Chatham County shopkeeper Edward Hart's inventory in 1794 listed 62 lb of raw silk in 1794. Further inland, the inhabitants of New Bordeaux were reportedly still manufacturing some silk in 1809.[94]

The post-revolutionary era also saw something of a transition in American publications on the subject of silk raising, as printed instructions and treatises became both more widely available and more targeted to an American citizenry. Ottolenghe's *Directions for Breeding Silk Worms* were republished in a newspaper in Worcester, Massachusetts, in 1791, and other instructions including Dr John Morgan's manuscript letters were circulated via popular collections such as the *Transactions of the American Philosophical Society* and the monthly literary magazine the *American Museum* – eventually being published in their entirety in Windham, under the title 'Some Modern Directions for the Culture of Silk'.[95] The New York Society for Promoting Useful Knowledge noted its particular thanks to a gentleman who 'favored them with his remarks on the propagation and management of the silk-worm in this country' in March 1787, and other sericultural insights were selectively relayed in the newspapers of the Early Republic, especially where they promised to help solve ongoing difficulties.[96] Readers learned of new technologies and new techniques, as when a botanist in Turin, Carlo Antonio Ludovico Bellardi, pioneered a method of feeding silkworms with dried leaves that promised to offset the damage of early hatching or late frosts.[97]

American silk raisers increasingly benefited from instructions printed in newspapers, which democratised tips on timing and technique. The first of June became widely reputed in Connecticut as the day the worms should be taken from storage to hatch. Warnings were issued that now embraced American soundscapes such as the

---

[93] Letter from Ralph Izard to Henry Laurens, Florence, 18 October 1774, in Ralph Izard, *Correspondence of Mr. Ralph Izard of South Carolina: From the Year 1774 to 1804, with a Short Memoir* (New York: AMS Press, 1976), 15–17, see also 31. Ralph Izard to Jeremiah Wadsworth, New York, 25 September 1791, Jeremiah Wadsworth Papers, Box 20 (folder 140), Connecticut Historical Society, Hartford CT.

[94] Shaw, 'Silk in Georgia, 1732–1840', 69; Stevens, 'A Brief History', 188; Ramsay, *History of South Carolina*, 11.

[95] 'Directions for Breeding Silk Worms', *Thomas's Massachusetts Spy: Or, the Worcester Gazette*, 23 June 1791, p. 1; advertisement by Robert Aitken, *Pennsylvania Packet*, 5 December 1786; *The American Museum*, 5 (1789), 166–9, 272–5, 355–8. A Friend to the Public, *Some Modern Directions for the Culture and Manufacture of Silk, Taken from a Manuscript as It Was Wrote by a Gentleman in Italy* (Windham, CN: Storrs and Eldredge of Mansfield, 1792).

[96] *Independent Gazetteer*, 7 April 1787.

[97] Philadelphia *Independent Gazetteer*, 21 August 1790.

noise of pealing bells, and the latest suggestion for reviving apathetic silkworms was to broil bacon in their chamber. Reeling also engaged an increasing proportion of column space, and it appears that various combinations were used to generate a skein of raw silk, attesting to the widening inventive technological environment, especially in the northeast. One writer described a 'reel or frame' machine constructed such that four skeins could be reeled in parallel, allowing variable numbers of filaments to be reeled, 'requisite for the work they are intended for', from eight for 'ribbands and velvets' upwards to as many as thirty. Two winders attended respectively to the tasks of managing the handle and skeins and of managing the cocoons and threads, and it was estimated that 3 lb of silk could be reeled in a day, leaving plenty of waste silk for processing too at a later date.[98] Day books and ledgers allow us to follow some of this silk as it made its way to subsequent manufacturing stages. Clothier James H. Boyd, for instance, dyed small amounts of coarse homespun silk yarn for a number of customers in 1798. It was probably not a coincidence that this yarn was dyed in late July and August, which fit with that season's silk raising. Cash, however, was not the only currency used: the wife of Joseph Cogdell of Woodstock paid with a mixture of cheese and cash for dyeing 10 oz 'New Silk Crow [black] colour' in October, while Jedediah Corbin settled with soap for his blue silk yarn, the most common colour requested.[99]

Overall, by the 1790s, silk production had retrenched into a seasonal pursuit which made a marginal but visible contribution to the domestic economy across parts of New England, with some regions such as Connecticut's Windham and Tolland counties soon to develop into the leading producers throughout the entire Americas.[100] One unnamed ten-year old reportedly cleared twenty dollars in one season for pocket money (enough to buy a silver watch), 'by his own industry, without being detailed from school more than one single week'.[101] Individuals and families planted, built, shared, and sold silk-related items, such as

---

[98] Worcester *Massachusetts Spy*, 28 March 1792, p. 1. For a fine discussion of regional concentration and the peculiarities of reeling techniques, see Janice E. Stockard, 'On Women's Work in Silk Reeling: Gender, Labor, and Technology in the Historical Silk Industries of Connecticut and South China', in *Silk Roads, Other Roads: Proceedings of the Textile Society of America Biennial Symposium* (Textile Society of America, 2002).

[99] James H. Boyd, 'Day Book & Ledger', 1797–1800, Gen. MSS vol. 188, Beinecke Library, Yale.

[100] The US census in 1810 recorded for the first time the production of 'sewing silk and raw silk', giving a figure of $28,503 for Connecticut, most of it produced in Windham county, and a value of $608 for Massachusetts.

[101] *New-York Journal, & Patriotic Register*, 9 April 1791, p. 109. Watch estimated from Wright, *Comparative Wages, Prices, and Cost of Living*, 151.

Ebenezer Willis's 'fine nursery of white mulberry trees' in New Bedford that was sold by the dozen or single trees in September 1795.[102] New England's durability provided an important influence in sustaining increasingly isolated mulberry and silkworm enterprises in other parts of the United States, as when stocks of silkworm from Newport were used in 1793 to replenish the degenerating cohorts at Nazareth, Pennsylvania – the former seeming 'much stronger' to David Zeisberger, who tended the worms, reeled the cocoons, and 'prepares the Silk for the needle' there.[103] Scanty and seasonal it may have been, but sericulture and these simple silk products encouraged the later stimulation of more advanced manufacturing in New England and East Coast cities.[104]

Between the 1760s and the 1790s, American silk had survived revolutions in politics, trade, and fashion, and though somewhat more confined regionally, was drawing sustenance from the prevailing cultural emphases on home manufacturing and independence, and a connective print culture. Silk apparel made in America drew particular comment and admiration from contemporaries, and it took only a small quantity of, say, home-produced sewing silk, to allow the individualisation of clothing or furnishings through embroidery – a little, in other words, could go a long way.[105] It was not only 'Founding Fathers' who carried this message in their habits: one Connecticut farmer's daughter was married in a silk gown 'that she had spun, wove, and made up, with her own hands; and which was the production of silk worms, which she had tended and fed with mulberry-leaves'.[106] Nor was this silk cultivation purely tokenistic or ceremonial, for there developed a robust market for raw silk and silk thread which was brokered by pedlars and small stores, and helped to diversify the resource base of many households, especially in parts of New England. By 1804, the town of Mansfield alone was raising nearly 1,300 lb of 'well dried raw silk; every pound of which when made into sewing silk, is worth about seven dollars, and finds a ready market at Boston, Providence, &c.'[107]

The local production of Connecticut women such as the stockings, handkerchiefs, vest patterns, and pieces of dress silk with which the

---

[102] *Medley or New Bedford Marine Journal*, 18 September 1795, p. 3.
[103] 'Notes and Queries', *The Pennsylvania Magazine of History and Biography* 39, no. 2 (1915): 220.
[104] Margrave, *Emigration of Silk Workers*, 20.
[105] On how objects and textile products could be transformed from the anonymity of the market place to signifiers of identity, Ulrich, *The Age of Homespun*; Anishanslin, *Portrait of a Woman in Silk*.
[106] New York *Mercantile Advertiser*, 3 September 1803, p. 3.
[107] Philadelphia *Evening Fire-side, or Weekly Intelligence in the Civil, Natural, Moral, Literary & Religious Worlds*, 22 June 1805.

daughters of Col. Jedediah Elderkin (whose family convergences began this section) 'adorned themselves' owed a great deal to developmental efforts in the colonial and revolutionary eras; they were the crackling embers of once great imperial ambitions.[108] One writer claimed that in 1792 'the experiments made in our own country have universally succeeded', and that silk's history in recent centuries of being 'slowly spread from place to place on the shores of the Mediterranean' could be accelerated across the Atlantic, given the 'attention of the governments and people of America'.[109] As the nineteenth century progressed and the United States grew into a world of increasing trade, consumption, and industrialisation, these burning cinders would help ignite one final grand explosion of national activity in silk culture. The rudimentary thread, silk, and mixed-silk products, worked up by American households, helped to stimulate manufacturing activity as American sericulture brought silk factories, silk experts, and silk technology in its wake.

Broken European Threads

The loss of the bulk of mainland British America, including the concession of East and West Florida to Spain as part of the peace settlement in 1783, had finally put an end to remaining British hopes of engineering new sites for the production of raw silk across the Atlantic. Forced to turn away from North America, British efforts continued in the late eighteenth and early nineteenth centuries to locate new imperial domains that were suitable for raw silk production. Those within the purview of the East India Company, as we have seen, were already thriving, and attention to both the quantity and the quality of raw silk coming from Bengal became even more pressing firstly as a consequence of the American Revolution, and again once the Napoleonic Wars foreclosed access to Italy and much of Europe, leading to more concerted centralisation of reeling, and economic exploitation of indigenous labour in the Indian subcontinent (both by the British and by opportunistic indigenous rulers such as Tipu Sultan in Mysore).[110] Between the 1790s and the 1850s, the average annual poundage of raw silk exported from Bengal increased

---

[108] Heller, *History of Northampton County*, 1: 157.

[109] Philadelphia *General Advertiser*, 19 March 1792.

[110] For a pointed claim about the ways that investing in Bengal raw silk could advance geopolitical positioning against France: George Williamson, *Mr. Williamson's Address to the Court of Directors, Together with His Proposals to Them for Improving and Increasing the Manufactures of Silk in Bengal, so as to Preclude the Necessity of Importing Raw Silk into England, from Italy, Turky, &c.* (London, 1775), 20.

fourfold to 1.7 million lb, a growing proportion of which was filature-reeled rather than 'country wound' in the traditional manner that European agents disdained.[111] Outwith Indian dominions, in spite of the nineteenth-century leaps forward in scientific understanding, technology, and the capacity to conquer limitations in transport and temperature, few if any of the British domestic or imperial projects in new locales offered as concerted or potent a package as those they had once supported in America. In 1783, the very year that – as George III lamented – America was 'lost!', the Royal Society of Arts sounded a tone of ironic triumph in reporting that in recent years its rewards had incentivised 11,575 lb of exported American raw silk. They persisted with bounties and medals for a few years at home, including a brief flurry of excitement around 1790, but would offer no premium on English-reared silk beyond 1800.[112]

The Cape Colony seized by the British and ceded in the Anglo-Dutch Treaty of 1814 presented a southern African possibility. It had earlier played host to brief silk-raising initiatives pursued by Dutch governors with silk trade connections, boosted by an influx of Huguenots in the 1720s. The street name in Rondebosch ('Spin Street') and a black mulberry tree remain as vestiges of these efforts which had sought to use enslaved children to tend silkworms in a bespoke three-storey cocoonery, but as with efforts on the other side of the Atlantic, the project fell foul of difficulties with silkworm transit, a dispersed mulberry base, fragile settler communities, and inclement conditions.[113] The convergence of British sovereignty and a more stable settler demography allowed some claims about North America – notably the environmental conclusions reached about wild mulberries – to be rearticulated for southern Africa in the 1820s, when a Cape committee with the support of Lt. Gov. Bourke

---

[111] Works on the Indian Ocean trade and production are extensive, but for selected overviews: Brenda M. King, *Silk and Empire* (Manchester: Manchester University Press, 2005); Prakash, *Bullion for Goods: European and Indian Merchants in the Indian Ocean Trade, 1500–1800*; Chandra Guha, *Silk Industry of Malda and Murshidabad*, figures on 48; Hutková, 'The British Silk Connection: The English East India Company's Silk Enterprise in Bengal, 1757–1812'; S. R. Charsley, *Culture and Sericulture: Social Anthropology and Development in a South Indian Livestock Industry* (London: Academic Press, 1982); Farrell, 'Silk and Globalisation in Eighteenth-Century London', 59–70.

[112] *Transactions of the Society, Instituted at London, for the Encouragement of Arts, Manufactures, and Commerce* (London: Royal Society of Arts, 1783), 1: 22; 8: 163; 18:51. George III, 'Essay on America and Future Colonial Policy' (1783/4), GEO/ADD/32/2010–1, Royal Archives, *Georgian Papers Online*.

[113] H. C. V. Leibbrandt, ed., *Precis of the Archives of the Cape of Good Hope*, 17 vols. (Cape Town: W. A. Richards, 1896), 1–2: 267; 17: 470; George McCall Theal, *Willem Adriaan Van Der Stel and Other Historical Sketches* (Cape Town: William Clowes and Sons, 1913), 204; Hermann Giliomee, *Historian: An Autobiography* (Charlottesville, VA: University of Virginia Press, 2017), 1–3.

dedicated itself to trials in sericulture.[114] Some 2,000 miles farther west, a few years after the exiled Napoleon Bonaparte expired on St Helena, the Longwood estate on which he had been confined was also planted out with mulberries, thanks to the ardent patronage of Governor Alexander Walker. In spite of the death of silkworms in transit from India in 1824, a second supply of seed from China allowed some poor-quality imperial produce to be reeled and sent on to London in 1829.[115] These sources reflected that it had become accepted wisdom that silkworm seed prospered best in its native half of the globe, and ought to be shipped from the southern hemisphere rather than dispatched from Europe.[116]

Just as American projectors would need to find a new way of packaging their ambitions after cutting the imperial cord, so new British settler initiatives in sericulture which limped on into the nineteenth century developed particularities of language, ethnicity, and identity in an effort to generate interest. In the British African colony of Sierra Leone in the 1790s, the naturalist Adam Afzelius developed a garden at Freetown in which he imported and planted out mulberry trees amongst other fruit trees from England, as part of abolitionists' larger quest for agricultural output that might become commercially viable, and thereby produce an economic breakthrough that progressively connected free African labour to British market demand.[117] Blunter racial and economic claims would follow in other parts of the world – John Lett in Australia, for instance, proposing sericulture as viable 'in this vast colony, if we go to work as *Saxons* do, when they are in *earnest*'.[118]

Sporadic efforts developed to plant out mulberries and sustain silkworms from Anglesey to Tasmania, British Guiana to Gravesend, Stellenbosch to Malta, and Ireland to Queensland, sometimes promising to address larger social issues such as the legacy of slave emancipation or the condition of the Irish peasantry – and oftentimes pinned to long-

---

[114] George McCall Theal, ed., *Records of the Cape Colony from February to April 1825* ([London]: Government of the Cape Colony, 1904), 95; 'Introduction of the Silkworm at the Cape of Good Hope', *The Asiatic Journal and Monthly Miscellany* 25 (January 1828): 144.

[115] Hudson Ralph Janisch, ed., *Extracts from the St. Helena Records* (St Helena: Benjamin Grant, 1885), 225, 226, 231.

[116] *The Journal of the Society of Arts*, 21 (1873): 849. Chinese eggs had earlier been transported to Bengal from the 1780s, and Bengalese eggs to Mauritius in the 1810s. Porter, *A Treatise on the Silk Manufacture*, 42–3.

[117] Adam Afzelius, *Sierra Leone Journal 1795–1796*, ed. Alexander Peter Kup (Uppsala: nst. för allm. och jämförande etnografi, 1967), 36; Suzanne Schwarz, 'A Just and Honourable Commerce': Abolitionist Experimentation in Sierra Leone in the Late Eighteenth and Early Nineteenth Centuries, Annual Lecture 2013 (London: The Hakluyt Society, 2014).

[118] John Lett, 'Letter on the Culture of Silk', *The Sydney Morning Herald* (New South Wales), 22 August 1849, p. 3.

standing notions about female and family labour. The imperial silk-worms, however, seem to have paid little heed to the imperious language, and continued to die, for none of these colonial or experimental environments fulfilled adequately the preconditions of successful transplantation. Lacking an authentic history of colonial silk, B. Francis Cobb in his 'Hints to Colonists' on 8 August 1873 proposed that it was not a fact but an opinion 'founded originally in error' that held 'that the English people can do nothing with silkworms, and that the worms cannot be reared at all, except in the recognised silk-producing countries'. His obduracy, however, was further proof that – as in so many of its earlier guises – post-American British sericulture simultaneously articulated empire's practical environmental limits and its unbounded cultural power.[119]

Beyond the British Atlantic, the changing contours of revolutionary geo-politics in the late eighteenth century had encouraged some Iberian and French reassessment of the feasibility of new imperial initiatives, but these were similarly short-lived. In New Spain, a revitalisation of interest in reshaping silk trade and manufacture in the 1780s prompted sporadic efforts to reintroduce Mexican sericulture, under the viceroy the Conde de Revillagigedo. The priest and soon-to-be-revolutionary Miguel Hidalgo y Costilla had absorbed some of this literature of encouragement – likely through French influences – and planted mulberries and sought to raise raw silk on his lands in the province of Guanajuato from 1803. This was probably the scheme north-west of Mexico City using Indian populations also described by Alexander von Humboldt, who lamented that such attempts had not received adequate support from viceroys who 'dread[ed] to infringe' on Spanish production. Conservative historian Lucas Alamán would later cruelly characterise Hidalgo's ineffective revolution in 1810 as 'like his silk-worm raising, and with similar results'.[120] Abortive attempts were likewise recorded in Brazil, perhaps stimulated by the temporary rejuvenation of

[119] *The Journal of the Society of Arts*, 5: 177; 18: 125, 914; 19: 623; 21: 7, 51, 742 (Cobb quote); 30: 281; *Transactions of the RSA*, 2: 153–80; 4: 147–70; 5: 63–75; 6: 171–9; 7: 121–39; 29: 20. On the well-capitalised company pushing production in Ireland, Dunlevy, *Pomp and Poverty: A History of Silk in Ireland*, 111–12. On the brief Malta investment: Lady Judith Montefiore, *Private Journal of a Visit to Egypt and Palestine, by Way of Italy and the Mediterranean* (London: Joseph Rickerby, 1836), 92–94.

[120] Elena Phipps, 'New Textiles in a New World: 18th Century Textile Samples from the Viceregal Americas', *Textile Society of America Symposium Proceedings*, 2014, 3–5; W. Dirk Raat, *Mexico, from Independence to Revolution, 1810–1910* (Lincoln: University of Nebraska Press, 1982), 22–5; Barbara H. Stein and Stanley J. Stein, *Edge of Crisis: War and Trade in the Spanish Atlantic, 1789–1808* (Baltimore, MD: Johns Hopkins University Press, 2009), 128–9, 156; Alexander von Humboldt, *Political Essay on the Kingdom of New Spain*, 3 vols. (London: Longman & Co., 1811), 3: 57–9; Lucas Alamán, *Historia de Mexico*, 5 vols. (Mexico: Victoriano Agueros & Co., 1883), 1: 315, 316, 320 (quote).

sericulture in Trás-os-Montes in Portugal (with the help of Piedmontese experts), before Napoleonic invasion and war devastated the region from 1807.[121] Only in the 1930s would sericulture gain a sustainable foothold in Brazil, bolstered by Japanese expertise and materials that could now be sustained through industrial transport and technology, leaving Brazil as raw silk's 'only producer in commercial-scale ... in the West' in the twenty-first century.[122] France introduced or reintroduced silkworms to the Mascarenes (in the Indian Ocean) in a bid to render them agriculturally productive, shortly before it lost possession of the islands to the British as a result of naval inferiority in 1810, which 'rendered these attempts abortive'.[123]

In contrast to the imperial regression in Atlantic domains, new expectations and new pressures developed amongst those regions of Europe that continued to fulfil sericulture's prerequisites in the early nineteenth century – particularly in the brief 'golden age' of Bourbon Restoration southern France, in northern Italy and the Tyrol, and eastern Spain – which would witness raw silk production deepen in intensity. As has been well documented, they assumed a more centralised character to fit to the needs of increasingly industrialised processing technologies, aided and abetted by new scientific literatures and methodologies. Asian silk regions drawn into northern European commercial orbits also deepened their production in the early nineteenth century, relying particularly on their superior density of labour and conducive environments for mulberry-silkworm symbiosis, and progressively inflecting their reeled raw product towards the demands of European markets, as global distances shrank and interdependencies hardened throughout the nineteenth century.[124]

---

[121] Marquis de Lavradio to Luiz de Vasconcellos e Souza, 19 June 1779, in John Armitage, *The History of Brazil: From the Period of the Arrival of the Braganza Family in 1808*, 2 vols. (London: Smith, Elder & Co., 1836), 2: 231. Brazilian attempts were unsuccessful 'either from the unfitness of the climate, the improper methods employed in the management of the insects, or from some other cause'. Andrew Grant, *History of Brazil* (London: Henry Colburn, 1809), 273, 277. De Sousa, 'Silk Industry in Trás-Os-Montes', 11–14.

[122] Federico, *An Economic History of the Silk Industry, 1830–1930*, 79; Alessandra Maria Giacomin et al., 'Brazilian Silk Production: Economic and Sustainability Aspects', *Procedia Engineering* 200 (2017): 90 (quote).

[123] R. T. Farquhar, 'Silk from the Isle of France', *Transactions of the RSA* 42 (1823): 168–75; Felix Pascalis Ouvrière, *Practical Instructions and Directions for Silkworm Nurseries, and for the Culture of the Mulberry Tree*, 2 vols. (New York: J. Seymour, Printer, 1829), 1: 15, 37; Porter, *A Treatise on the Silk Manufacture*, 42 (quote).

[124] On the French golden age, see esp. Clavairolle, *Le Magnan et l'arbre d'or*, 41–7; Junko T. Takeda, 'Global Insects: Silkworms, Sericulture, and Statecraft in Napoleonic France and Tokugawa Japan', *French History* 28, no. 2 (2014): 212–14. On wider developments and exchanges in the nineteenth century: Zanier, *Where the Roads Met. East and West in the Silk Production Processes (17th to 19th Centuries)*; Patrizia Sione, 'From Home to Factory: Women in the Nineteenth Century Italian Silk Industry', in

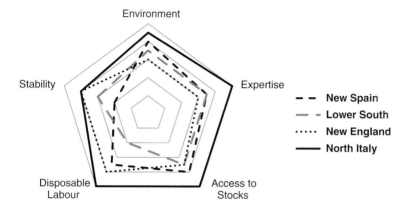

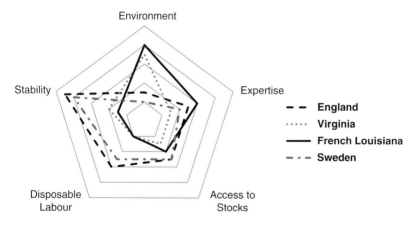

Figure 10.1 Diagrammatic visual summary of the comparative performance and reasons for failure in regions where major trials were documented. Each locale was ascribed a subjective score across five core criteria that influenced successful production, treating northern Italy as the benchmark for output

European Women and Pre-Industrial Craft, ed. Daryl M. Hafter (Bloomington, IN: 1995); Federico, *An Economic History of the Silk Industry, 1830–1930*. Two major new authorities somewhat normalised practices from the 1820s: Vincenzo Dandolo, *The Art of Rearing Silk-Worms* (London: J. Murray, 1825); Matthieu Bonafous, *De la culture des mûriers* (Lyons: J. M. Barret, 1822).

By the start of the nineteenth century, the attempted transplantation of *Bombyx* sericulture across the Atlantic by settlers under the auspices of European empires had reached a collective endpoint of sorts. Successive independence movements in Atlantic polities closed off any lingering prospect of colonists exporting American raw silk eastward. Imperial dreams of new productive zones persisted, carrying with them facets of the political economy and technical apparatus of Atlantic production, and drawing from a selective history that remembered some elements (such as flagship episodes of production) and forgot others (such as the utilisation of enslaved labour). But relative to what had gone before, these were marginal in scope, duration, and ambition. The Atlantic world had offered a profound and distinctive fractal space for projection, experimentation, and production, with mulberries planted from Cape Town to Lund and silkworms nurtured from Minas Gerais to Massachusetts. But for different reasons (simplified in Fig. 10.1), in different places, with different timescales, the complexities associated with sustained raw silk production had prevented the product from competing commercially amidst the impatient, extractive, labour-scarce economic systems that abounded in the Americas.

11 Epilogue

This country, to which Providence has been so bountiful, may avail
herself of the gifts she has received from the hands of her Creator, to
reach the end to which she appears destined, and become a rich silk-
growing and silk-manufacturing country.

> Jean D'Homergue, *Historical Review of the Rise
> of the Silk Culture* (1831), 18

It has been erroneously supposed that the manufacture of silk was
attended with extraordinary difficulties; that it required much complex
and expansive machinery, and a skill which Americans were incapable of
acquiring ... Silk is no longer considered a luxury, but an indispensable
article. So common has it become, that it forms a considerable part of
our wardrobes, and enters more or less into almost every garment, both
of male and female dress. However unnecessary and extravagant silk
may have anciently been considered, it cannot now be confined to the
wealthy ... Wealth and descent are no longer the thermometer of
respectability, but industry, frugality, and the practice of the moral and
social virtues. The poor as well as the rich must be clothed in silk: and
why should they not?

> Andrew T. Judson, Report to US Congress (1836)[1]

The Republic's New Clothes

In 1837, the year that Hans Christian Andersen first published his story
'The Emperor's New Clothes' about the collective denial of naked reality,
a substantial number of Americans were busy collaborating on their own
fairytale: the transformation of the United States into a mass silk-
producing country. They confidently anticipated that history would
'record to endless remembrance, the names of those illustrious individuals' who threw their weight behind American silk production.[2] They

---

[1] Andrew Judson, enquiry and report to Congress cited in *New England Farmer* 15 (1836–7)
no. 48 (7 June 1837), 379.
[2] William Kenrick, *The American Silk Grower's Guide or, The Art of Raising the Mulberry and
Silk, and the System of Successive Crops in Each Season*, 2nd ed. (Boston: Weeks, Jordan &
Co., 1839), vi.

were wrong. But the real fascination with Andersen's tale, of course, lay not in the empirical absence of fabric but in the way the illusion was created and perpetuated. Attempts at antebellum silk cultivation, like the Emperor's suit, would prove to be a temporary triumph of credibility over feasibility. They took to a new national level the powerful convergence that had occurred in prior decades to reconceptualise sericulture in a politically post-revolutionary but commercially imperial Atlantic world. To make American silk, proponents realised they first had to make silk American. In the process of definitively Americanising the commodity, they boldly re-confronted ideological objections, climactic imperfections, and significant shortcomings of appropriate experience.

Ultimately, the same matrix of formidable obstacles that had compromised many earlier sericultural starts in the New World again showed through in the nineteenth century: environmental deficiencies affecting trees or worms (or both!), labour costs, lack of expertise, and the existence of more reliable and remunerative alternative products to raw silk. But attempts at silk production also yielded stories of success that – as in the case of Connecticut in the 1790s – ought to moderate and complicate our sense of agricultural diversity, household agency, and regional sensibilities between the 1820s and 1840s. That raw silk secured the impressive uptake that it did was not purely down to boosterism or an investment bubble, but a reflection of new developments in the associational infrastructure of American agricultural life between the 1820s and 1840s. As a consequence of the empowerment of voluntarism through the press, the post, the agricultural society, and the political lobby, sericulture again flourished as a unique national platform for agricultural reformism for a brief window of time, a platform erected almost entirely from the bottom up. Silk promoters and cultivators created a far-flung, self-sustaining community of fellow enthusiasts who straddled status, party, and region. So whereas the observers of the Emperor's suit indulged in false articulation, pretending to see what they could not, for the vast majority of experimenters, raw silk remained an authentic ambition that often involved substantial amounts of time and labour, and for some of them ended in meaningful produce (see Plate 16).

The raising of raw silk in the United States at the start of the nineteenth century was a local phenomenon that was largely concentrated in areas that had a colonial legacy – notably in Connecticut and the hinterland of Philadelphia, regions that had been subject to very different schemes to plant large numbers of white mulberries. In the context of a fast-diversifying economy and the meteoric rise of cotton occurring in the South, it gave little hint of being a branch of agriculture that had the potential to reach across the expanding United States. American

sericulture appeared consigned to a marginal, perhaps diminishing position, largely ignored by farmers and manufacturers alike, who found
plenty of proven investments on which to stake their capital. Silk more
often than not made the papers in the form of quirky histories of the
commodity, or entertainment pieces recounting the fabric's peculiar
scientific or medical properties.[3] 'Why won't our farmers plant these
mulberry trees and busy themselves in the culture of this silk?' demanded
a contributor to the *Massachusetts Magazine* in 1792, concluding 'It is for
want of thought.'[4] Silk's advocates had found few answers to the question
that an exasperated Dutch pioneer William van Hasselt posed Thomas
Jefferson in 1802: 'how can one persuade such simple, ignorant people' to
'undertake a project they had never heard of?'[5]

Between 1820 and 1845, van Hasselt's question was definitively
answered. Pockets of cultivation (see Map 5) had developed across
the length and breadth of the United States, from Maine to
Louisiana, with almost a third of US counties in the 1840 census
(374 out of 1269) registering the raising of cocoons. Most of these
efforts raised small quantities which tended to be reeled locally and
inexpertly, and were twisted into sewing thread. This accounts for the
wide variation in values of the 15,745 lb of 'reeled, thrown, or other
silk made' in 130 counties listed in the census of 1840, which ranged
from $1 per lb for processed silk in Monongalia (western Virginia) to
the $25 per lb in Wabash (Illinois). Women and children were
employed in these manufacturing stages in over twice the numbers
of men, though only around half of the counties reported the break-
down of manufacturing labour. In 1843, one estimate placed the
value of American silk produced at $1.4 million (the equivalent to
about $50 million today).[6] By then, around fifty companies had been
formed with the intention of practising sericulture as part of their

---

[3] See, for an example of short histories, 'Amusement' section of *Boston Weekly Magazine*,
19 February 1803, 71. On scientific and medical properties, see for respective examples
'Spontaneous Decomposition of a Fabric of Silk', *Medical Repository*, 3 December 1802,
458–61; 'Efficacy of Silk', *Analectic Magazine*, 1 September 1818, 259–61.

[4] 'Expense and Profit of Raising Silk Worms', *Massachusetts Magazine, or, Monthly Museum
of Knowledge & Rational Entertainment*, 1 June 1792, 374–5.

[5] Letter from Willem H. van Hasselt to Thomas Jefferson, Le Hague, 20 June 1802.
Eerenbeemt, *Op Zoek Naar Het Zachte Goud: Pogingen Tot Innovatie via Een Zijdeteelt in
Nederland 17e–20e Eeuw*, 41. See also advocacy from Siena (Italy) of Robert K. Lowry,
'A Memoir on the Treatment of the Silk-Worm, Communicated to Mr. Jefferson', in
Barton's Medical & Physical Journal (Philadelphia, 1806), 97–8.

[6] L. P. Brockett, *The Silk Industry in America, a History: Prepared for the Centennial Exposition*
(New York: Silk Association of America, 1876), 198. See also estimate in Wyckoff,
American Silk Manufacture, 28. Comparative figure derived from historic CPI calculator
at: www.officialdata.org/us/inflation/1843.

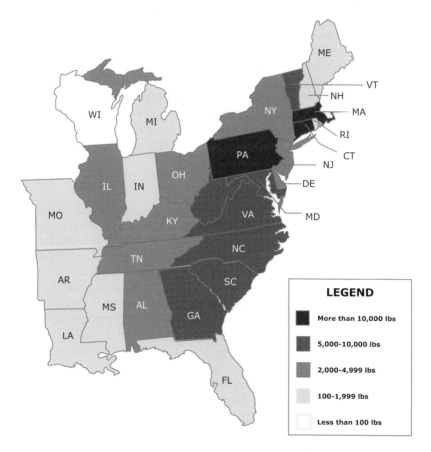

Map 5 US silk cocoon production (1842). Source: Henry Leavitt
Ellsworth, Henry Colman, and Willis Gaylord, *Improvements in
Agriculture, Arts, &c. of the United States* (New York: Greeley &
McElrath, 1843)

operations, over fifty new books – most of them manuals and treatises – had been published and widely disseminated, and the subject
of silk was now literally making the newspapers: more than a dozen
periodicals dedicated explicitly to silk raising had been founded, even
as the conventional agricultural press was widely colonised by articles
on silk and mulberry growing. Sericulture had received the sanction
of Congress, where in 1830 a US silk flag about 12 × 6 feet had been
draped over a statue of Lafayette; it had been woven in Philadelphia

out of cocoons raised all across the Union.[7] By 1841, all kinds of
specimens of American silk graced the table in the Executive
Chamber at the Capitol, and at the opposite end of the social spectrum, the inmates of the State Prison at Auburn, New York, manufactured some $12,762 worth of American sewing silk.[8] The sudden
proliferation of interest in silk from the 1820s, this step change, owed
much to the kaleidoscopic appeal of a new rhetoric, discussed below,
which awkwardly reconciled seemingly contradictory forces: nationalism and sectionalism, progress and nostalgia, farmer and industri-
alist. No longer fuelled by the political economy and networks of
Atlantic empires, the final and largest American pursuit of sericulture
in the antebellum era depended on the spectacular mobilisation of
popular associational power.

Most of the associational prerequisites required for the spread of sericulture were not unique to that field, and accompanied the wider amor-
phous market revolution in American society.[9] Three mutually
reinforcing vehicles in particular shaped the antebellum efforts at silk:
the agricultural press, the postal service, and the agricultural society.
Though inseparable, they each generated dynamism in different locales,
sending pulses respectively through a national readership, through networks of interested individuals, and through local communities.
Put together, this connective circuit had a public reach that far eclipsed
the private correspondence of late-colonial Enlightenment experimenters. Sericulture was to antebellum agriculture a variation of what the
'Second Great Awakening' was to religion, what 'Jacksonian Democracy'
was to political culture: a harnessing of the power of mass dissemination
to a national participatory ethos. Of course, it carried none of the transformative effects of those movements, and as a consequence has seldom
drawn the attention of historians. Even before production collapsed in the

[7] US *House Journal*, 1830. 21st Cong., 2nd sess., 21 December; United States Committee
on Agriculture, Jean D'Homergue, and Peter S. Duponceau, *Report of the Committee on
Agriculture on the Growth and Manufacture of Silk; to which is annexed, Essays on American
Silk, with Directions to Farmers for Raising Silk Worms* (Washington, DC: Duff Green,
1830), 8, 15 (hereinafter *Essays on American Silk*).
[8] Remarks attributed to a Mr. Ward, 'On the Bill to encourage the growth and manufacture
of Silk' in assembly, 13 April 1841. Quoted in in-sleeve cutting titled 'The Silk Culture'
from the Albany *Evening Journal*, glued to the Library Company of Philadelphia copy of
The Silk Culturist, Nos. 1–2 (New York: W.B. Gilley, 1829). Hereinafter cited as Ward's
remarks in LCP *Silk Culturist*. For figures on prison production: Wyckoff, *American Silk
Manufacture*, 30.
[9] On the much-contested phrase 'market revolution' and the rapid integration of the
economy in the half-century after 1790: Charles Grier Sellers, *The Market Revolution:
Jacksonian America, 1815–1846* (New York: Oxford University Press, 1991); John
Lauritz Larson, *The Market Revolution in America: Liberty, Ambition, and the Eclipse of the
Common Good* (Cambridge: Cambridge University Press, 2010).

1840s, the movement was being dismissed as a 'craze' or a 'mania': comfortably compartmentalised as a delusion that had overtaken gullible book-farmers (lacking practical experience) or greedy corporations. But closer examination of the three forces at play reveals that the silk movement was powered by ordinary people, people who did not see it as necessarily in the shadow of the relentless advance of cotton production, but potentially in its slipstream (see Fig. 11.1).[10]

The genre of the agricultural periodical originated in the 1790s, and grew markedly over subsequent decades. Farming journals spearheaded the circulation of new ideas, technologies, and information; their national readership had reached perhaps 100,000 subscribers by 1840, when papers such as the *Cultivator*, the *New England Farmer*, the *Farmers' Register*, and the *American Farmer* were common to many households, and they also intermixed with a small number of national newspapers such as *Niles' Weekly Register* and a large array of local and regional hybrids.[11] The major agricultural journals devoted increasing amounts of ink to silk culture from the late 1820s, and the keen interest shown by leading proprietors amongst the most respected farming journals, such as Jesse Buel and Luther Tucker, was of critical value to the extension of sericulture. In late 1836, a congressional report noted that even beyond the agricultural papers, 'most of the political, commercial, and literary publications of the day' now contained paragraphs on the subject.[12] By the mid-1830s, a veritable 'silk press' had evolved to cater for market interest, with around a dozen newspapers founded, many of them edited by experienced hands such as Gideon B. Smith and Thomas G. Fessenden, and some of them shrewdly combining reportage with commercial seed sales, most successfully achieved by William Kenrick and the Comstock family.[13] These journals, focusing extensively on

[10] Philip J. Pauly, *Fruits and Plains: The Horticultural Transformation of America* (Cambridge, MA: Harvard University Press, 2007), 102.
[11] Estimates can be found in Albert Lowther Demaree, *The American Agricultural Press, 1819–1860* (New York: Columbia University press, 1941), 18. For northern journals see Clarence H. Danhof, *Change in Agriculture: The Northern United States, 1820–1870* (Cambridge, MA: Harvard University Press, 1969), 56. For southern see John D. Majewski, *Modernizing a Slave Economy: The Economic Vision of the Confederate Nation* (Chapel Hill, NC: University of North Carolina Press, 2009), 58.
[12] Comment by Andrew T. Judson, member of the Committee of Manufactures tasked with gauging national interest in sericulture in late 1836. US *House Journal*. 1837, 24th Cong., 2nd sess., 25 February; quote from published report in *New England Farmer*, 15, no. 48 (7 June 1837): 377.
[13] The phrase 'silk press' is neatly coined by David Rossell, 'The Culture of Silk: Markets, Households, and the Meaning of an Antebellum Agricultural *Movement*' (PhD thesis, SUNY Buffalo, 2001), xv. Some of the most prominent were the *Silk Culturist and Farmers' Manual* (Hartford, 1835–9); *Fessenden's Silk Manual and Practical Farmer*,

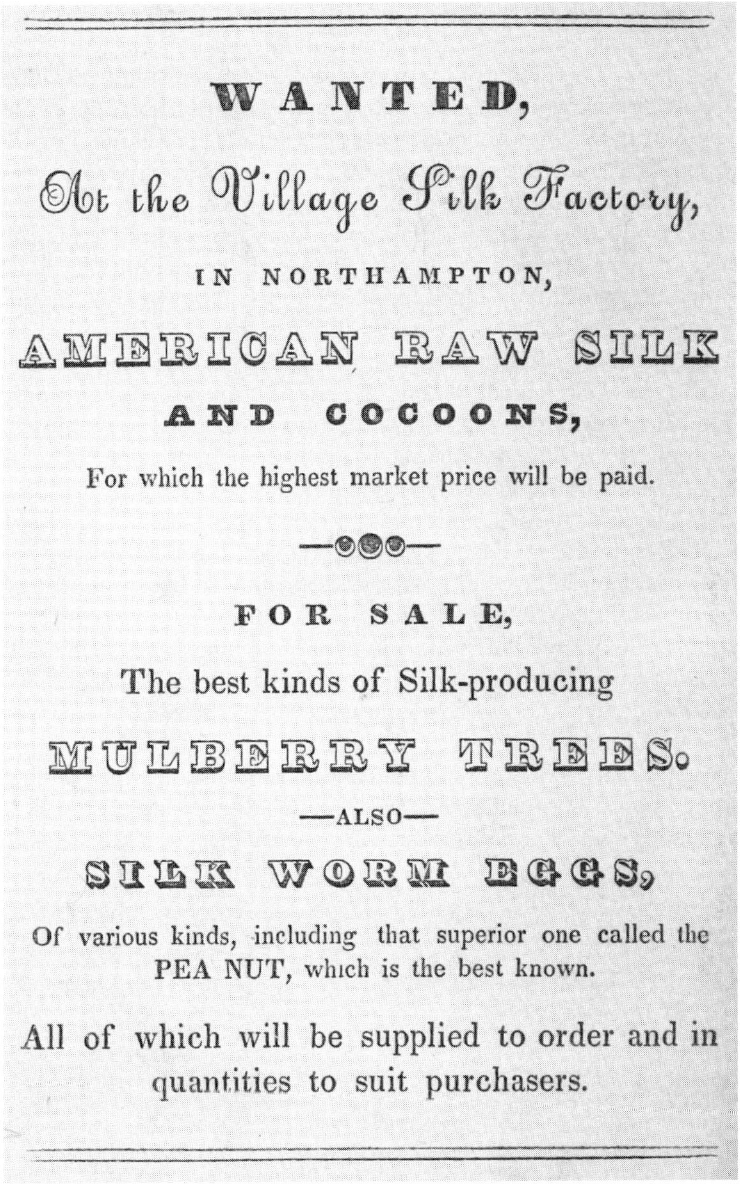

WANTED,

At the Village Silk Factory,

IN NORTHAMPTON,

AMERICAN RAW SILK

AND COCOONS,

For which the highest market price will be paid.

—◉◉◉—

FOR SALE,

The best kinds of Silk-producing

MULBERRY TREES.

—ALSO—

SILK WORM EGGS,

Of various kinds, including that superior one called the
PEA NUT, which is the best known.

All of which will be supplied to order and in
quantities to suit purchasers.

Figure 11.1 Demand for American raw silk for domestic manufacturing
(1839). Advertisement for 'American Raw Silk and Cocoons' in
Northampton, Massachusetts, in Samuel Whitmarsh, *Eight Years
Experience and Observation in the Culture of the Mulberry Tree*
(Northampton, MA: J. H. Butler, 1839). Getty Research Institute

'single-issue' agriculture, broke new ground in the degree to which they drew on geographic breadth in their content.[14]

The silk press provided a forum in which not only could ideas be planted, but also where planters of all regions and backgrounds could locate a supportive community replete with scientific, economic, technical, and practical information. Powered largely by correspondence, and the cross-posting of published letters, it lent cohesion and credibility to the pursuits of moriculture and sericulture. In all kinds of ways, the silk press, with its incessant self-referencing, imposed a certain order on the discussions and experiments taking place around the country. John James Dufour noted as early as 1825 that 'I could find the word cocoon in no English Dictionary, and I was advised to write cacoon, but the *Baltimore Patriot*, writes cocoon, so will I now.' Because at the whim of ordinary contributors, this imposed order was not always beneficial to the movement – it took a long time, for instance, to dispose of ill-founded notions about food substitution, which caused indigestion to many unfortunate silkworms placed on unpalatable diets of oak leaves, lettuce, or Osage orange. The readers of Franklin G. Comstock's *Silk Culturist*, for instance, came from a diverse social and geographical background that mirrored other broader trends in agricultural journals.[15] The dedicated silk manuals also revealed a wide socio-economic target spectrum, with works ranging from a few paragraphs long (emphasising ideas taking root 'in the field' and not 'in the closet') to hundreds of pages with complicated plates and technical theory.[16]

The reliance of the silk press on voluntarism for its content and funding explained not only its dramatic rise but also its journals' short lifespans, for once credibility began to evaporate, periodicals quickly became

---

Devoted to the Culture of Silk, Agriculture, and Rural Economy (Boston, 1835–7); *The Silk-Worm* (Albany, 1835–7); *American Silk Grower and Agriculturist* (Keene, 1836–9); *American Silk-Grower and Farmers' Manual* (Philadelphia, 1838–9); *Southern Silk Manual and Farmers' Magazine* (Baltimore, 1838–9); *Journal of the American Silk Society* (Baltimore, 1839–41).

[14] See Demaree, *The American Agricultural Press, 1819–1860*, 183; Majewski, *Modernizing a Slave Economy*, 76–80.

[15] Rossell, 'The Culture of Silk', 128. On the wider debate and patterns: Richard Bardolph, *Agricultural Education in Illinois to 1870* (Urbana, IL: University of Illinois Press, 1944); Demaree, *The American Agricultural Press, 1819–1860*; Paul Wallace Gates, *The Farmer's Age: Agriculture, 1815–1860* (New York: Holt, Rinehart and Winston, 1960).

[16] The contrast of field and closet is from the article on silk by Thomas Spalding in *Southern Agriculturalist and Register of Rural Affairs* 1, no.8 (August 1828): 339. For examples of either end of the spectrum, see, for instance, John Clarke, *Sericon* (Philadelphia: The author, 1841); Jonathan Dennis, *Dennis' Silk Manual* (New York: Press of Mahlon, Day & Co., 1839); Samuel Whitmarsh, *Eight Years Experience and Observation in the Culture of the Mulberry Tree, and in the Care of the Silk Worm; with Remarks Adapted to the American System of Producing Raw Silk for Exportation* (Northampton, MA: J. H. Butler, 1839).

unviable commercially. Tellingly, though reaching out to tens of thousands of subscribers, many of the silk journals lasted less than two years. When high hopes for a new imported type of mulberry, the *Morus alba* var. *multicaulis*, collapsed at the end of the 1830s, leaving investors and companies stranded and sceptical, few remaining journals dared to adopt the defiant tone that some silk conventions and advocates continued to express in the early 1840s. The new mulberry (see Plate 17), introduced to the United States from China via France, had been celebrated for its swift growth, purported hardiness, and luxuriant foliage, and according to a classic discussion of the topic by Arthur Cole, no class or section of the community was unaffected by the craze. But for reasons explained below, hopes that the new 'species' might resolve the long-standing difficulties with raw silk production would prove chimerical.[17] In its brief window of existence and influence, the silk press had nonetheless evidenced a wide periodical readership, and a yet wider filtration of information beyond subscribers into traditional community networks.

If evidence from silk publications suggests that the people who expended time on silk culture were not necessarily wealthy, it also shows that they were well connected. Postmasters played a critical role in advancing the reach of journalism generally in this era, benefiting as they did from postal subsidies (a franking privilege allowed them to send mail for free) which made them ideal nodes of information; many of them launched agricultural periodicals themselves.[18] They were especially important to the regional grounding of the silk movement, securing local anchors that prevented nationalistic idealism and technical advice from floating into insignificance. Daniel Bulkeley was the postmaster in Hampton, Connecticut, and his post 'office' was the business he did in his general merchandise store. Like his 29,955 colleagues around the nation in 1828, Bulkeley had to be well connected, for when a package arrived

---

[17] On the mulberry bubble, see: Wyckoff, *American Silk Manufacture*, 16–25; Arthur H. Cole, 'Agricultural Crazes: A Neglected Chapter in American Economic History', *The American Economic Review* 16, no. 4 (1926): 627–32; Robert Price, 'Morus Multicaulis, or, Silkworms Must Eat', *Ohio State Archaeological and Historical Quarterly* 45 (1936): 265–7?; Elizabeth Hawes Ryland, 'America's "Multicaulis Mania"', *The William and Mary Quarterly*, 2nd Ser. 19, no. 1 (1939): 25 33; Gates, *The Farmer's Age: Agriculture, 1815–1860*, 303–6; Nelson Klose, 'Sericulture in the United States', *Agricultural History* 37, no. 4 (1963): 225–7; Pauly, *Fruits and Plains*, 101–3. For examples of a continuing defiant tone, see *The Silk Question Settled: Report of the Proceedings of the National Convention ... Held in New York ...* (Boston: T. R. Marvin, 1844). Also, A. C. Van Epps, 'Silk and the Silk Culture', in *DeBow's Review*, 5, no. 6 (June 1848): 419.

[18] Richard R. John, *Spreading the News: The American Postal System from Franklin to Morse* (Cambridge, MA: Harvard University Press, 1995); Wayne Edison Fuller, *The American Mail: Enlarger of the Common Life*, The Chicago History of American Civilization (Chicago: University of Chicago Press, 1972).

from the mail agent or stagecoach, it was his job to get word to the addressees through friends, neighbours, or kin.[19] Bulkeley retailed garden seed, passed on newspapers to subscribers, and was the first point of information for inquiries about local projects and capital. Unsurprisingly, given his location and these activities, he soon became heavily involved in all facets of silk culture. Bulkeley advertised white mulberry trees in the *Windham County Advertiser*, transmitted seeds and silkworm eggs in 'papers', and bought up and sold thousands of skeins of silk to merchants in larger cities (especially New York, Philadelphia, and Providence). Besides these commercial operations, his voluminous correspondence shows him fielding all kinds of queries: to find a reeling woman to send to Philadelphia, to furnish information about fledgling silk-manufacturing mills in Massachusetts, to report on the success of mulberry plantations in upper New York state, and so on.[20] Some of Bulkeley's correspondents were clearly gentlemen, such as William Budd of Smyrna, Delaware, who reported how his experimentation had 'excited the attention of the farmers'.[21] But many others were farmers themselves, such as Godfrey Cady of Boston, whose inferior status was given away in his writing, 'I have been to the seed store & enquired Morris Multicurris Seed.'[22]

Evidence can be found in almost every page of the silk press of the cross-regional transmission of information about sericulture that was contingent upon the growing integration of the postal service and the interest of postmasters. One example illustrates the case well: in Edmund Ruffin's *Farmers' Register* of January 1837, he printed a letter that had been sent by a postmaster in Monongalia County, Virginia, not to Ruffin's editorial office in the same state but to the Hartford, Connecticut, publisher of *The Silk Culturist* (himself a former postmaster). The Monongalia postmaster spoke of having 'read many encouraging accounts' of silk prospects in 1835. Then, having agreed with his neighbours to attempt local production, they divided their efforts

---

[19] The number of post offices in the US grew from 75 in 1790 to 7,530 in 1828, with 29,956 postal employees (the largest employer in the executive branch); it would increase dramatically by the end of Jackson's presidency, by which time rail engines had been added to the steamboats that had carried the mail since 1815. Figures from *The United States Postal Service: An American History, 1775–2006* (Washington, DC: Government Relations, United States Postal Service, 2007), 10.

[20] *Windham County Advertiser*, 27 November 1832. Bulkeley's correspondence is in boxes 8–11 of the Taintor-Davis Family Papers, 1763–1917, MSS. Box 'T', American Antiquarian Society, Worcester MA.

[21] Letter from William A. Budd to Daniel Bulkeley, 29 January 1829, Philadelphia. Taintor-Davis Family Papers, AAS.

[22] Letter from Godfrey Cady to Daniel Bulkeley, 19 December 1834, Boston. Taintor-Davis Family Papers, AAS.

according to the different procedures outlined by manuals published respectively in Baltimore and Connecticut, and using silkworm eggs procured from Meadville, Pennsylvania to be fed on the indigenous red mulberry trees (*M. rubra*) that grew wild in the vicinity of their homes.[23]

Postmasters could be both beneficiaries and victims of high circulation – they were as vulnerable as anyone else to the hyperbole, but were exposed to it with much higher frequency, as the conduit points for journal editors and nurserymen. George Luther, a postmaster in Martha's Vineyard, North Carolina who found himself bankrupted with a wife and eight daughters to support, was sucked into experimenting after 'by chance [having] seen some . . . publications on the subject of the Silk Business', though he struggled to persuade counterparts in the Cape Fear river region that the silkworms did not bring 'infectious disorder' to households.[24] But regardless of the extent of their own involvement, postmasters helped silk culturists to improvise around market relations in a strange new world that hybridised the traditional model of local exchange and neighbourly obligation with the newer possibilities of distance transactions between customer and unseen merchant.[25] They shifted newspapers, linked correspondents, connected nurseries to farmers, and producers to merchants and manufacturers. As political appointees, and a major component of the Federal 'spoils system' implemented from 1828, postmasters would also amplify the relative political volume of sericulturists.

Silk promotion colonised agricultural periodicals and spilled over into new journals because it occupied a prominent position in the activities of the growing numbers of agricultural societies in the nation.[26] These were locally rooted associations, typically spearheaded by local elites, which sought to promote agricultural improvement in their regions and to encourage production by coordinating annual fairs, prizes, and medals, and the dissemination of information. As with the press, interest in sericulture soon prompted the founding of new bespoke voluntary associations that eclipsed other societies in scale because they drew in both

---

[23] *The Farmers' Register*, 4, no. 9 (January 1837): 536.
[24] Cited in Rossell, 'The Culture of Silk', 236. The suspicion that silkworms were unhealthy also appeared in other forms, especially in the South – see, for example, the comments of Thomas Spalding of Georgia asserting that 'in France, without careful ventilation, the very milk of the women who attend to the rearing of the Silk-Worm . . . carries death to the infant nourished by it'. *Southern Agriculturalist and Register of Rural Affairs*, 1, no. 3 (March 1828): 106.
[25] Rossell, 'The Culture of Silk', 155. For discussions of the transformations in market relations more generally, see Christopher Clark, *The Roots of Rural Capitalism: Western Massachusetts, 1780–1860* (Ithaca: Cornell University Press, 1990).
[26] Rossell, 'The Culture of Silk', 159–64.

manufacturers and farmers, besides the 'gentlemen amateurs, nursery-men, scientists, and government officials' that typically made up sister horticultural networks.[27] Citizenly association was loosely constructed, especially in the society speeches and reports that echoed through the silk press, to allow the fullest emphasis on participation: the chartering of well-capitalised manufacturing corporations in Philadelphia and the measuring of mulberry trees at a county fair in Tennessee could thus both be invoked as making contributions to the social capital of the movement.[28] Several of the silk societies grew far beyond their original geographical region and instituted a number of 'conventions' to which enthusiasts travelled from far and wide – including the American Silk Society of Baltimore and the United States Silk Society of Washington. Scientific and technological institutes in larger cities were also quick to respond to sericulture boosterism, and the earliest commercial nurseries branched out to meet demand, swiftly stocking up with multiple varieties of mulberry trees.[29] The harnessing of these associational forces behind one goal, raw silk, provided a lesson in how to drive forward national agricultural agendas using local voluntarism that would assume other shapes in years to come.[30]

Besides further illustrating the extension of networks, local agricultural or sericultural associations were important because they provided evidence that silk enthusiasm was not simply an exercise on paper. Silk's profile was enhanced by its visible presence at social, educational, and recreational events for the farming community.[31] Across county fairs and agricultural shows, on plantations in the South and across farmsteads in

---

[27] Pauly, *Fruits and Plains*, 265. On horticultural societies: Tamara P. Thornton, 'The Moral Dimensions of Horticulture in Antebellum America', *The New England Quarterly* 57, no. 1 (1984): 3–24. The membership of the Pennsylvania Silk Society, for instance, was socially mixed. See Pennsylvania Silk Convention, *Proceedings of the Pennsylvania Silk Convention, Held at Harrisburg on the Twenty-Second and Twenty-Third Days of February, 1839* (Harrisburg: Printed by E. Guyer, 1839).

[28] On one page of the *Silk Culturist and Farmer's Manual* in 1836 it was recorded that 'a number of the Citizens of Nantucket have recently associated', 'a number of gentlemen of Warren County, New Jersey, have given notice of their intention to apply to the Legislature of that State for a charter', and 'a company has lately been formed in Philadelphia ...' Silk Society Hartford County, *The Silk Culturist and Farmer's Manual*, ed. F. G. Comstock (Hartford, CN, 1836), 77.

[29] These included the American Institute of New York City of 1829 and the Franklin Institute of Philadelphia of 1824: for a discussion of these institutes in the context of silk promotion: Wyckoff, *American Silk Manufacture*, 22–3; on nurseries, Rossell, 'The Culture of Silk', 164–6.

[30] Sarah T. Phillips, 'Antebellum Agricultural Reform, Republican Ideology, and Sectional Tension', *Agricultural History* 74, no. 4 (2000): 824; Pauly, *Fruits and Plains*, 104–5.

[31] Linda J. Borish, '"A Fair, Without the Fair, Is No Fair at All": Women at the New England Agricultural Fair in the Mid-Nineteenth Century,' *Journal of Sport History* 24, no. 2 (1997): 155–76.

the north-east and Midwest, novice sericulturists proudly displayed their produce, sometimes in the form of cocoons, sometimes as raw silk, and on occasion as vaunted local manufactures. Innumerable bounties, certificates, and cash prizes were handed out for specimens of silk and mulberry orchards by agricultural bodies.[32] In Northampton, Massachusetts – whose town seal was proudly adorned with silk moths – women commonly displayed stockings knitted from their silkworms at the 'Hampshire-Franklin-Hampden Cattle Show and Fair'; in Hamilton County, Ohio, it was more usually silk handkerchiefs; in Wayne County, Indiana, silk shawls.[33] Attendees of the Worcester County Cattle Show in October 1829 agreed that Sarah Earle's knitted silk stockings (made from her own silkworms in Leicester, Massachusetts) were 'of a much more durable quality than those that are imported'.[34] Southern journals similarly trumpeted the fair and society awards given to worthy silk raisers at Charleston and Black Oak (SC), Sparta and Augusta (GA), Baton Rouge (LA), Henrico (VA), and elsewhere.[35]

Making Silk American

These new networks, forums, and mechanisms for agricultural socialisation – on paper and in person – help explain how the ambitions for American sericulture were able to grow beyond their late-colonial geographic and social confines. But they alone do not explain its reach and persistence. The tight grip that sericulture secured on America's agricultural imagination between 1825 and 1845 owed as much to the convincing arguments of silk's advocates as it did to the associational integration discussed above. Journals, societies, and postmasters could share empirical information and materials, and could create lobbying pressure, but in the absence of sustained successful production, credibility had to be

---

[32] See, for example, the list of winners (top prize fifteen dollars) judged by the New York Agricultural Society committee on silk in *Transactions of the New-York State Agricultural Society, Together with an Abstract of the Proceedings of the County Agricultural Societies, and of the American Institute, Vol. V – 1846* (Albany: E. Mack, 1846), 133. Premiums offered by Pennsylvania Society for Promoting the Culture of the Mulberry and the Raising of Silk Worms in Benjamin R. Morgan and Mathew Carey, *At a Meeting of the Subscribers to the Plan for Promoting the Culture of the Mulberry Tree* (Philadelphia, 1828), 599.

[33] Field, Senechal, and Shaw, *American Silk, 1830–1930*, 20; M. B. Bateham, ed., *The Ohio Cultivator. A Semi-Monthly Journal, Devoted to the Improvement of Agriculture and Horticulture, and the Promotion of Domestic Industry, The Ohio Cultivator* (Columbus, OH: M. B. Bateham, 1845), 161; Wyckoff, *American Silk Manufacture*, 31.

[34] Worcester *Massachusetts Spy*, 21 October 1829.

[35] *DeBow's Review*, 7, no. 4 (October 1849): 346–7; *Southern Cultivator* 1, no. 1 (1 March 1843): 8 and no. 13 (21 June 1843): 104; *Southern Planter* 2, no. 1 (January 1842): 16; *Southern Agriculturist* 6, no. 6 (June 1846): 236; *Soil of the South* 3 (February 1853): 432.

found elsewhere. How was this vital credibility achieved? How did proponents succeed in making silk American and stimulating so much experimental conviction?

The first trick was to explain away earlier transatlantic failures as functions of abusive European power. Americans sprinkled their new narratives of the world history of silk culture with revealing comments about their contemporary sensibilities: silk had supposedly collapsed in Spain because of Spanish colonialism, an evil which encouraged 'avarice' and discouraged 'industry'; commentators referred to 'the shackles of despotism' cramping silken efforts in other nations.[36] Likewise, British colonialism had struggled because of the 'monopolizing system' it permitted, and attempts in Virginia and the Lower South were overblown as simply the 'selfish desire of English kings to keep the colonies dependent'.[37] A certain retrospective freedom was also assumed about the Revolutionary War: one account claimed 'the British soldiery … destroyed the mulberry wherever it was found; determined if we gained our liberties, to deprive us of this source of national wealth and prosperity'.[38] In contrast, the absence of measurable progress in US silk cultivation outwith parts of New England between 1790 and 1825 was peremptorily dismissed for such specious reasons as: 'the *spirit of the country* and the general state of things, in those early times, were unpropitious'.[39]

Anti-European rhetoric seems to have been important to the democratisation of sericulture, with works aimed at common people most routinely indulging in attacks. Samuel Whitmarsh, a year before he declared bankruptcy, advocated an 'American system' of silk raising and claimed that in Northampton, Massachusetts, 'the petty details of foreign authors … are not necessary for us'.[40] American writers widely adapted foreign publications, considering their 'air of philosophical apparatus' unsuited to the 'cares of the husbandman'.[41] One congressional report

---

[36] Jean d'Homergue, *An Historical Review of the Rise, Progress, Present State, and Prospects, of the Silk Culture, Manufacture, and Trade, in Europe & America* (Philadelphia: Printed by L. R. Bailey, 1831), 6, 9. Ward's remarks in LCP *Silk Culturist*.

[37] Brockett, *The Silk Industry in America*, 26.

[38] Ward's remarks in LCP *Silk Culturist*. There is no evidence for this, and for a contrary viewpoint on silk culture and the effects of war, see Molà, *The Silk Industry of Renaissance Venice*, 219. Cf. Pascalis Ouvrière, *Practical Instructions and Directions*, 1:26.

[39] Homergue, *Historical Review of the Rise of the Silk Culture*, 24. See also in-sleeve cutting by J. R. Barbour, Esq., of Oxford Massachusetts, in Library Company of Philadelphia copy of *The Silk Culturist*.

[40] Whitmarsh, *Eight Years Experience and Observation*. This booklet is just 4 × 6.5 inches in dimension, and stretched to 156 pages, but is actually rather thin on detail, especially in regard to manufacturing. Whitmarsh was subsequently unsuccessful in similar projects in Jamaica. Field, Senechal, and Shaw, *American Silk, 1830–1930*, 28.

[41] *The Silk Culturist*, 29, 67.

noted that US experts had 'cautiously, and I think wisely, passed over the ingenious theories of foreign writers'.[42] Disdain for Old World sericulture tended to be the appetiser (which European-born authors usually skipped) to a lavish main course of American agro-environmental exceptionalism. Indeed, Manifest Destiny – complete with political and religious overtones – was harnessed to sericulture long before John O'Sullivan coined the phrase.[43] It is tempting to dismiss some of these sound bites as nationalised boosterism, as when one leading silk grower declared to large cheers that silk would succeed because 'our soil is virgin, our sky is blue, and our people are Protestant!' (a curious claim given the historic supremacy of non-Protestants in sericulture).[44] But these exceptionalist assumptions were based on supposedly hard evidence, and brought with them important consequences. Experimenters were convinced that cohorts of silkworm breeds improved over generations in the United States whereas they degenerated in Europe: 'Facts, proud facts', exclaimed Mr. Sharrod McCall, of Gadsden County, Florida, 'demonstrated ... the superiority of every American animal and vegetable, when compared with similar productions in the old world'.[45] The superiority of American silk was also contended through claims that had sounded many times before in sericultural projection, but rarely at this amplified volume: the idea that proportionally fewer cocoons were needed to reel 1 lb of raw silk, that silkworm eggs hatched in shorter time, that there was greater space for trees, or that the existence of indigenous red mulberries 'proved' a well-adapted soil.[46]

[42] *New England Farmer* 15, no. 48 (7 June 1837): 377.
[43] The New England Silk Convention, for example, declared that silk suitability was 'a manifest indication of Divine Providence'. Ronald Savoie, 'The Silk Industry in Northampton', *Historical Journal of Western Massachusetts* 5 (1977): 21–32.
[44] Comments of Rev. J. R. Barbour in *The Silk Question Settled*, 8. For comparable claims, see: Francis S. Wiggins, James Pedder, and Josiah Tatum, *The Farmers' Cabinet and American Herd-Book*, 12 vols. (Philadelphia: Moore & Waterhouse, 1837), 9: 217; American Institute of the City of New York, *Proceedings of the National Convention of Farmers, Gardeners and Silk Culturists Held at Mechanics' Hall, in the City of New York, on the 12th, 13th, and 16th Days of October, 1846.* (New York: J. H. Jennings, 1846), 4.
[45] US Treasury, *Letter from the Secretary*, 112–13. See also comments on degeneration by Mr. Samuel Alexander of Philadelphia on same pages and by Thomas Spalding in *Southern Agriculturalist and Register of Rural Affairs*, 1, no. 9 (September 1828): 389. On trope of American degeneration more broadly, Pauly, *Fruits and Plains*, 9–29.
[46] Homergue, *Historical Review of the Rise of the Silk Culture*, 19. D'Homergue elsewhere quantified this alleged superiority, alleging that 12 lb of cocoons were required in France and Italy compared to 8 lb in the United States. D'Homergue and Duponceau, *Essays on American Silk*, 5. For examples of claims on fibre strength: Kenrick, *American Silk Grower's Guide*, 150. On faster hatching: Peter Delabigarre in *Transactions of the Society Instituted in the State of New-York, for the Promotion of Agriculture, Arts, and Manufactures* (New York: Childs and Swaine, 1792), 178. On spatial advantages, *The Silk Culturist*, 29, 67. On *M. rubra*: Henry Leavitt Ellsworth, Henry Colman, and Willis Gaylord,

Part of the price of selling sericulture to a wide American audience, in other words, was a qualified repudiation of foreign experience. Yet this made it hard for American ambitions to fulfil a key condition of successful global transfers of sericulture into new regions – namely, its dependency upon migrant expertise at critical juncture points. Efforts to bring silk and mixed-silk textile *manufactures* to the antebellum United States did draw on migrant expertise and technology, increasingly young English skilled silk workers from depressed textile regions. But even where some Americans were willing to pursue it, the challenge of recruiting the right kind of worker for producing *raw* silk was complicated and did not line up well with emigration pathways. People with the critical cocoon-raising and -reeling expertise, who were often from the same Mediterranean areas from which Americans secured their mulberry cuttings and silk-worm seed, were found to be 'women, of the lowest class, who are very ignorant, and unwilling to leave their native villages', though attempts were made by US agents in Marseille and Normandy.[47]

The situation had changed somewhat by the 1840s and 1850s – after the mulberry fever had calmed and a credibility gap had been exposed. Remaining entrepreneurs willing to invest in silk, such as the Cheney brothers, now took more pains to engage with European experiences and to contract European labourers.[48] A. C. Van Epps, for one, celebrated that public attention in 1846 was now 'regulated by the experience of the past, and the information we are acquiring from the silk-producing countries of the Old World'.[49] Indeed, the collapse of the chain vertically linking American silk-growing and American silk-manufacturing interests had arguably weakened the capital of native entrepreneurs, and allowed immigrant-owned silk companies to direct the future growth of the industry from mid-century.[50]

Improvements in Agriculture, Arts, &c. of the United States (New York: Greeley & McElrath, 1843), 16.

[47] Homergue, *Historical Review of the Rise of the Silk Culture*, 28. For the attempt in Marseille, see letter from Mr. J. W. Morse, an American in Marseille, to a gentleman of Philadelphia, dated 21 March 1829, quoted in D'Homergue and Duponceau, *Essays on American Silk*, 56. On Normans in Florida, William Warren Rogers and Erica R. Clark, *The Croom Family and Goodwood Plantation: Land, Litigation, and Southern Lives* (Athens: University of Georgia Press, 2009), 34.

[48] For evidence of Old World workers playing key roles in American successes: Alfred Theodore Lilly, *The Silk Industry of the United States, from 1766 to 1874* (New York: Jenkins & Thomas, printers, 1882), 4; Brockett, *The Silk Industry in America*, 134; D'Homergue and Duponceau, *Essays on American Silk*, 11; Wiggins, Pedder, and Tatum, *The Farmers' Cabinet*, 216. 'Foreign workmen' were employed extensively at Lisbon, Connecticut, and other Spitalfields migrants are mentioned in Bishop, Freedley, and Young, *History of American Manufactures*, 2: 393.

[49] A. C. Van Epps, 'Silk and Silk Culture', *Debow's Review*, 5, no. 6 (June 1848): 419.

[50] Margrave, *Emigration of Silk Workers*, 29, 32, 39, 40.

Before then, the Americanisation of silk in the antebellum era reinforced people's willingness to experiment in sericulture in a myriad of ways. Advocates naturally reached for resonant themes in contemporary life, and their articles were replete with the language of republican virtue and especially independence, which sericulture would allegedly secure for individuals, families, and for a nation whose balance of trade showed worrisome spending on silk imports. One manual, for example, argued that sericulture promised to raise 'the moral character of its proprietors', and 'the dignity of our nation'.[51] As rehabilitated by Pelatiah Webster during the revolutionary era, writers now found virtue in luxury, by emphasising productive processes over lavish outcomes, by stressing commercial autonomy, and by foregrounding the qualities of the strong fabric and the industrious insect. Writers vaunted little silkworms as models of labour, industry, punctuality, and of course self-sacrifice, one going so far as to ascribe to them the capacity to 'soften the natural selfishness of the human heart'.[52] Juvenile literature embraced the silkworm and its developmental Protestant industriousness – its rags-to-riches momentum – as in 'Peter Parley's' *Story of the Unhappy Family* which described a world when 'few knew' the silkworm's 'nature or history', but in which a forlorn immigrant silk-weaver implausibly manages, through sheer honesty, to lead his children from starvation to salvation.[53] Even observations about the fussiness of the worms managed to emphasise their reforming credentials: according to one writer, amongst other things, they disliked people who smelled of wine, 'persons who pound rice in mortars', and 'dirty or slovenly persons to attend them, or enter their room'.[54] Perhaps most important to silk's uptake, and also its failure, was the fact that it could be all things to all people, a reforming salve par excellence. Amongst its adherents were slaveholders and abolitionists, and high-profile men who would not normally be found lined up together: Daniel Webster (elitist champion of modernisation), Andrew Jackson (populist democrat frontiersman), Henry Clay (proponent of economic nationalisation), and Edmund Ruffin (pro-slavery agronomist and states' rights adherent).[55]

---

[51] Clarke, *Sericon*, 8–9. On virtue, independence, and other central tenets of economic nationalism as it evolved within a classical republican framework, see Drew R. McCoy, *The Elusive Republic: Political Economy in Jeffersonian America* (New York: Norton, 1982).

[52] *The Silk Grower and Farmer's Manual* 1, no. 1 (1838): 77.

[53] Samuel G. Goodrich, *Peter Parley's Story of the Unhappy Family* (Boston: Carter & Hendee, 1830), 9; Matthew Wynn Sivils, *American Environmental Fiction, 1782–1847* (Farnham: Ashgate, 2016).

[54] *Debow's Review*, 5, no. 4 (April 1848): 338–9.

[55] On Webster, *New England Farmer*, 14, no. 37 (1 June 1836): 371. On Jackson, *Niles' Weekly Register*, 48 (2 May 1835): 154–5. On Clay, Field, Senechal, and Shaw, *American Silk, 1830–1930*, 8; J. H. Cobb, *A Manual Containing Information Respecting the Growth of*

When families in the north-east read about silk they found appeals built on the tensions between domestic familial labour and waged industrial labour – silk as a fresh option for people hoping to keep their daughters on the farm in a nation at the tipping point of industrialisation.[56] One New Hampshire broadside contrasted the 'pure country air' where 'the untiring silkworm' thrived (and, by association, his human helpers) with 'the stench and danger of Cotton Mills'.[57] The newspapers celebrated that Connecticut women earned over 100 dollars for just 90 days of work raising silk, compared with less than 20 in the factory.[58] Silk was held to be even more republican than other textiles, because it was 'entirely free from the monopolising effect of the large cotton and woollen establishments, and with as little danger to morals as any agricultural employment'.[59] In reality, the propagandists' 'homespun' was loosely defined and somewhat disingenuously invoked, for although most writers advocated silkworm rearing at home, a declining number approved of the quality of domestic cocoon reeling, and most recognised that a successful national industry required throwing and subsequent manufacturing processes to be centralised (see Plate 18).[60] But the potential egalitarianism of silk's originating across American households and farms – produced by ordinary citizens not colonial governors, plantocracies or industrialists – was used to lend the product patriotic credibility.

For residents of longer-settled regions on the eastern seaboard (including both North and South), encouragement to grow silk was dressed up in its purported suitability for exhausted soils and stagnated landscapes, for areas of high population density, and for the profitable employment of the urban poor.[61] In the South, sericulture was excitedly seized as a chance to

the *Mulberry Tree*, (Boston: Carter, Hendee and Co., 1833), 59. On Ruffin, *The Farmers' Register*, 4, no. 2 (June 1836): 126–7 or 4, no. 6 (August 1836): 251. For other national figures involved in sericulture: Nicholas B. Wainwright, 'Andalusia: Countryseat of the Craig Family and of Nicholas Biddle and His Descendants', *Pennsylvania Magazine of History and Biography* 101 (1977): 46–7. See also accounts of the intersection of abolitionism and sericulture at the 'Northampton Association of Education and Industry', in Christopher Clark, *The Communitarian Moment: The Radical Challenge of the Northampton Association* (Ithaca: Cornell University Press, 1995); Field, Senechal, and Shaw, *American Silk, 1830–1930*, ch. 3.

[56] Ulrich, *The Age of Homespun*, 377; Clark, *The Communitarian Moment: The Radical Challenge of the Northampton Association*, 142–43. On tensions between female labour and textile industrialisation in New England, Thomas Dublin, *Women at Work: The Transformation of Work and Community in Lowell, Massachusetts, 1826–1860*, vol. 2nd (New York: Columbia University Press, 1993), ch. 3.

[57] Undated broadside, Woodman Institute, Dover, New Hampshire, cited in Ulrich, *The Age of Homespun*, 395.

[58] 'An Enterprising Lady, or Another "Yankee Trick"', in *Niles' Weekly Register* 45, no. 8 (19 October 1835): 116.

[59] *The Silk Culturist*, 102.   [60] See for example *The Silk Question Settled*, 69–70.

[61] Edmund Ruffin, *Nature's Management: Writings on Landscape and Reform, 1822–1859*, ed. Jack Temple Kirby (Athens: University of Georgia Press, 2000), 256. On southern

counter outmigration, economic decline, and the market saturation of cotton. Some reservations were expressed about enslaved people's capacities to grow silk, as writers (as we have seen) deemed them to be lacking in the 'intelligence, delicacy, and unwearied attention required for little animals'.[62] Yet a growing challenge to this view emerged as experimentation spread: even Edmund Ruffin confessedly 'learned' in 1840 after having inspected a cocoonery operated by two black women in New Bern, North Carolina, 'to be much more confident than I had been as to trusting the details of the business to such ignorant as well as inexperienced operators as we must now find in our negroes'.[63] The compatibility of slavery with sericulture received a particular boost when the price of cotton dipped sharply in the 1840s. At one agricultural convention in 1845, Mr Hennen of New Orleans was convinced that 'the South could clothe its negroes cheaper in silk than with wool or cotton'.[64] Literature aimed at families in interior, mountainous, or Western regions appealed to raw silk's value by weight (easier to transport to market entrepôts than bulky commodities), its speed of growth, and its climatic suitability – especially in areas where red mulberries were to be found.[65]

Thanks to the integration of a national circuit of sericulturists, regional arguments found national iteration, and the reform literature evinced a remarkable degree of consensus. The agricultural press had always shown an anti-sectional sensibility, but the silk press took this further: a coalition of the willing, acting to mute dissonance and muffle scepticism.[66] Northern writers urged southerners to use their enslaved labourers in silk, largely evading ideological clash points, and

understandings of agricultural reformism and environmental conditions, see Majewski, *Modernizing a Slave Economy*. On silk operations attempted at poor houses, Rossell, 'The Culture of Silk', 95–97.

[62] *The Silk Culturist*, 30; Porter, *A Treatise on the Silk Manufacture*, 40. See also *Niles' Weekly Register*, 48 (2 May 1835): 157; United States, *Annual Report of the Commissioner of Patents, for the Year 1848* (Washington: Wendell and Van Benthuysen, 1849), 501.

[63] Ruffin, *Nature's Management*, 257.

[64] A Colonel Clark likewise believed that enslaved people could 'produce results far exceeding any present pursuit'. *Transactions of the NY State Agricultural Society*, 524–25. This changing emphasis also reflected a more aggressive southern defence of slavery in the 1840s and 1850s in agricultural reform circles.

[65] For an example from Louisiana, see accounts of Judge Henry Bry's efforts at Layton Castle in 'Miscellaneous' section, *Niles' Weekly Register*, 32, no. 21 (21 July 1827): 344, and *Debow's Review*, 4, no. 2 (Oct 1847): 226–9; for a clear (over)statement of the transport costs case, see: *Journal of the American Silk Society*, 3 vols. (Baltimore, MD: American Silk Society, 1839), 2: 53.

[66] Phillips, 'Antebellum Agricultural Reform', 810; Albert Lowther Demaree, 'The Farm Journals, Their Editors, and Their Public, 1830–1860', *Agricultural History* 15, no. 4 (1941): 185. Arthur Cole pointed out that scepticism did not appear about *M. multicaulis* until 1838, and then only in the form of a 'note'. Cole, 'Agricultural Crazes', 631.

New Yorkers wrote lengthy pieces on behalf of Louisianans.[67] Where consensus was challenged, the challenges rarely ran deep, but rather picked at superficial particularities. When Everest Maury pledged to 'expose the defects, inaccuracies, and false theories' in his promisingly titled 1832 work *The Silk Undertaking Abandoned*, he really meant he was going to take issue with a few statistics and lay claim to having personally been the instigator of congressional attention to the subject. Editors such as Franklin Comstock were quick to smooth over negative remarks: 'We hope our friends in Maine, will not be deterred ... by the remark of Mr. Gray. It must be remembered that he is a Virginian, enjoying a climate peculiarly mild.'[68] Ruffin and other southern reformers celebrated the 'hardiness of worms of southern stock' and attacked monopolistic northern nurserymen, but never to the point where they jeopardised their attachment to networks of publication and correspondence.[69] As one anonymous contributor to the *Farmers' Register* put it in 1836: 'in the numerous publications on the subject that I have looked over, I do not remember to have met with one word of discouragement'.[70]

Sheltered beneath this canopy of supportive rhetoric and literature in the public domain, we find silk enthusiasm and investment flourishing in the undergrowth of the historical record: private journals, letters, diaries, and material remnants. The material consequences of the push for sericulture have probably been under-acknowledged because the vast majority of American silk was made into sewing thread and distributed locally, or worked up into cherished garments and decorations. Virginian Martha Harness wore a tubular seven-foot silk net wedding veil, made from cocoons raised by her at her family's plantation, on the occasion of her marriage in 1817.[71] Henry Stark of Dunbarton, New Hampshire, recorded the rise of his mulberry plantation from the first 1,100 mulberry

---

[67] Philadelphia authors pointed to enslaved workers increasing their value to owners as a result: 'a female slave, skilled in the art of reeling silk, will command a price proportioned to the advantage which their knowledge will produce to their owners'. Homergue, *Historical Review of the Rise of the Silk Culture*, 31. For a good discussion of the awkward coexistence of different ideologies within the silk movement, see Rossell, 'The Culture of Silk', ch. 2. For the New York example, see A. C. Van Epps's article on 'Silk and the Silk Culture' serialised in: *Debow's Review* 5, no. 4 (April 1848): 324–6 and 5, no. 6 (June 1848): 411–45.

[68] Extract printed from the *Silk Culturist* in *The Farmers' Register* 4, no. 9 (January 1837): 549.

[69] 'Importance of Proper Selection of Silkworms' Eggs. Difference Between Northern and Southern Eggs', *The Farmers' Register* 7, no. 7 (30 July 1839): 444.

[70] Letter to Edmund Ruffin dated 16 December 1836 in *The Farmers' Register* 4, no. 9 (January 1837): 570.

[71] Emily Noyes Vanderpoel and Elizabeth C. B. Buel, *American Lace & Lace-Makers* (New Haven: Yale University Press, 1924), Plate 72.

trees planted in September 1828 to his 1,600 silkworms in 1830 to his 2 lb of sewing silk in 1831; five years later two females in the family were awarded national prizes for their successful use of a patented silk-reeling machine to make fine silk sewing thread.[72] That same year, widowed Mary Palmer Tyler of Brattleboro, Vermont, kept a miniature silk-skein memento to mark the first thread she had made with her son from their own silkworms in what proved to be his last summer, and her diaries and correspondence elsewhere document her planting of 450 mulberry trees and her home spinning, twisting, and dyeing of silk.[73] As the Starks and Tylers were embarking on their new projects, at the other end of the country, South Carolinian octogenarian Harriett Pinckney Horry was proudly dropping into a letter a sample of the colonial raw silk raised by her mother, Eliza Pinckney, in order to encourage the two adult daughters of Judge Thomas Waties to persist with sericulture; she wished them 'a more favorable Butterfly season than the last'.[74] These and other familial and material fragments leave an appropriate legacy to characterise the silk-growing movement as a whole: they were eclectically spread, experimental, optimistically couched, and often incomplete.[75]

Above all, production records emphasise that if much of the talking up of silk was done by men, most of the taking up of silk – the concentrated leaf picking, worm feeding, cocoon sorting, baking, intricate reeling, and home twisting and dyeing – was done by women. In some parts of the country, as first demonstrated in rural Connecticut in the 1800s, silk raising became a commonplace supplementary source of income, with skeins of silk used in local barter and exchange.[76] In 1882 Alfred Lilly recalled that after having 'dyed her silk with her own hands, the matron repaired to the country merchant to exchange it for dry goods or

---

[72] Stark Family Papers (1813–1832), MS 134, Milne Special Collections, University of New Hampshire, Durham NH. See especially oversize box 1, folders 1 & 2 containing deeds, correspondence, and record of activities of silk production; American Institute, 'No Title', *Journal of the American Institute* 1 (1836): 78.

[73] Mary Tyler's diary from 1821 to 1842, Royall Tyler Collection, 1753–1935, Doc. 45, Vermont Historical Society, Barre VT. The extant thread is discussed in Ulrich, *The Age of Homespun*, 380. Tyler's general efforts are summarised in Marilyn S. Blackwell, 'Love and Duty: Mary Palmer Tyler and Republican *Childrearing*' (MA thesis, University of Vermont, 1990), 166–7.

[74] Letter from Harriett Pinckney Horry to Mrs [Margaret Anne] Waties, *c.*1829 MS, South Caroliniana Library, University of South Carolina, Columbia.

[75] See also cocoon and raw silk in Witter Family Papers, MS 1075, box 1, folder 13, Manuscripts & Archives, Yale University Library, New Haven CT. Southern heirlooms are briefly mentioned in Klose, 'Sericulture in the United States', 227.

[76] This local silk exchange was estimated to be worth $18,000 per annum. States, *Letter from Treasury Secretary on Growth of Silk*, 25.

groceries'.[77] Another writer observed in 1876 that '[m]any persons now living have a vivid recollection of having seen small groves of white mulberries, and rude cocooneries built of rough boards or shingled, in which the women of the generation immediately following the Revolution used to feed silk-worms'.[78] Such accounts drip, of course, with the reverential syrup of the 'age of homespun' which was juxtaposed nostalgically against industrial modernity in late-nineteenth-century New England.[79] But contemporary sources such as bounty claimant records and store account ledgers reaffirm this as an accurate picture of a model – albeit fleeting – of production in some areas.

Between June 1827 and August 1832, Robert Barrows ran up debts of around eight dollars with local dealer Luther Kingsley at his store in Mansfield, for repairing pans, spectacles, wheel heads, and teapots. With the exception of one bushel of turnips (worth one quarter), Barrows settled this account entirely with silk produce, amongst them several hundred cocoons in 1827, 85 skeins of silk (valued at 3 cents a skein) in 1828, and 23,000 'silk eggs' in 1830. Dozens of other customers did likewise, and although the laws of coverture dictated there are few female-named accounts, women's participation does break through in Kingsley's absent-minded detail: 'rec[eive]d of Mrs. Lilly', 'By silk recd of Sarah', 'By 4 skeins silk, recd of Mrs. G[urley]'.[80] The depositing of such raw silk came at the end of a period of concentrated household labour for these women and their families that had left domestic spaces completely rearranged. Even for elites, such as Martha Ogle Forman, a wealthy plantation mistress in Cecil County Maryland, the reconfiguration could apparently be traumatic: she recorded in her diary, 'Cleaning and scouring the parlor after the silkworms but the floor will never be clean again.'[81] Luther Kingsley's accounts indicate he was not dealing with 'book-farmers' indulging their leisurely surpluses (indeed, a few of his customers worked off the debts they had accrued for his reading or writing documents on their behalf). Benjamin Keech partially paid by carrying wood, cutting straw, husking corn, delivering five skeins of silk, and mowing bushes – perhaps to clear access 'under mulberry trees' as did

[77] He estimated their annual output to be worth some $50,000. Lilly, *The Silk Industry of the United States, from 1766 to 1874*, 2–4, 271.
[78] Brockett, *The Silk Industry in America*, 31.
[79] For the definitive consideration of the meaning and material culture of homespun, including several silk items, see Ulrich, *The Age of Homespun*.
[80] Account Book of Luther Kingsley, 1827–1834, MS 69662, Connecticut Historical Society, Hartford CT.
[81] Martha Ogle Forman, *Plantation Life at Rose Hill: The Diaries of Martha Ogle Forman, 1814–1845*, ed. W. Emerson Wilson (Wilmington, DE: Historical Society of Delaware, 1976), 271.

Jeffery Sweet in 1833. Besides raw silk and basic silken manufactures such as thread, ribbons, stockings, and handkerchiefs, Kingsley's customers paid him in mutton, beef, linseed oil, sugar, brooms, buttons, and by pasturing his horse, or making him and his wife shoes. In turn, Kingsley and country traders others like him, committed this silk to pedlars or sold it on to larger merchants like Daniel Bulkeley, or clothiers and hat makers in return for wrought textiles and other domestic manufactures.[82] With the proliferation of water-powered textile mills from the first decades of the nineteenth century (and the first silk-manufacturing works from 1810), Kingsley's customers found a new set of buyers interested in raw silk.[83]

Sustained by the amalgamation of developments in print culture, communication, and agricultural reformism, antebellum sericulture strengthened as it moved back and forth from word of mouth through small-scale traders and postal networks to county fairs, regional associations, a dedicated national press, state support, and the sanction of congressional approval. Table 3 gives an indication of what was achieved, in the face of environmental constraints, by ordinary producers (most of them female). The method of regional extension varied from state to state: sometimes it reflected internal settlement patterns, as when northbound Connecticut migrants carried sericulture to western Massachusetts, or roaming New Englanders and western New Yorkers brought the enthusiasm to Ohio and even to Michigan.[84] Sometimes pivotal individuals or companies initiated the widespread planting of mulberries, seeking to take advantage of a perceived market opportunity, and were frequently spurred on by the arrival of new expertise or technology. They hailed from all over: prominent examples included Gideon B. Smith of Maryland; H. P. Byram of Meade County, Kentucky; Gertrude Rapp of Economy, Pennsylvania; John S. Pierce and Sally Fisher of Vermont; Dr Phillips of Natchez, Mississippi; John Gill of Mount Pleasant, Ohio; and Everest Maury of Delaware.[85] In other cases production was taken up as

---

[82] Skeins of silk were estimated as worth 4 dollars per lb in 1828. Homergue, *Historical Review of the Rise of the Silk Culture*, 23.

[83] For discussions of the earliest silk manufacturing works, see: Brockett, *The Silk Industry in America*, 50–79; Margrave, *Emigration of Silk Workers*, 30–83; Clark, *The Communitarian Moment: The Radical Challenge of the Northampton Association*, 162.

[84] Sidney Glazer, 'The Early Silk Industry in Michigan', *Agricultural History* 18, no. 2 (1944): 92.

[85] Byram wrote an award-winning essay about his efforts in *Transactions of the NY State Agricultural Society*, 133–52. For the impact of Pierce and Phillips, see *Transactions of the NY State Agricultural Society*, 524–5. On Rapp and the Harmonists, see: Karl J. Arndt, 'Three Hungarian Travelers Visit Economy', *Pennsylvania Magazine of History and Biography* 79 (1955): 203; Elizabeth Armstrong Hall, 'If Looms Could Speak: The Story of Pennsylvania's Silk Industry', *Pennsylvania Heritage* 32, no. 3 (2006): 26–7.

Table 3 Silk cocoon production in the United States by region (1840–1860)*

	1840		1842		1844		1850		1860	
	lb	%	lb	%	lb	%	lb	%	lb	%
Northeast	24,644	40	150,326	62	227,980	57	1,046	10	92	1
Mid-Atlantic	18,556	30	45,874	19	66,920	17	2,638	24	650	5
Southeast	8,211	13	17,053	7	23,150	6	1,171	11	430	4
Central	6,917	11	21,191	9	65,180	16	5,231	48	8,382	70
Southeast	2,095	3	6,566	3	9,020	2	258	2	357	3
Northeast	1,221	2	3,124	1	4,540	1	479	4	2,016	17
Total	61,643	100	244,134	100	396,790	100	10,823	100	11,927	100

* States comprising the regions listed are as follows: 'Northeast' = Connecticut, Maine, Massachusetts, New Hampshire, Rhode Island, Vermont; 'Mid-Atlantic' = DC, Delaware, Maryland, New Jersey, New York, Pennsylvania, Virginia; 'Southeast' = Florida, Georgia, North Carolina, South Carolina; 'Central' = Indiana, Kentucky, Michigan, Ohio, Tennessee; 'Southwest' = Alabama, Arkansas, Louisiana, Mississippi, Texas; 'Northwest' = Illinois, Iowa, Kansas, Minnesota, Missouri, Nebraska, Wisconsin. The sources for this data are combined from decadal census figures (with aggregates corrected where errors were apparent) and patent office annual reports: United States Census Office, *Compendium of the Enumeration of the Inhabitants and Statistics of the United States as Obtained from the Returns of the Sixth Census* (Washington: Thomas Allen, 1841); Henry Leavitt Ellsworth, Henry Colman, and Willis Gaylord, *Improvements in Agriculture, Arts, &c. of the United States* (New York: Greeley & McElrath, 1843); United States Patent Office and Edmund Burke, *Annual Report of the Commissioner of Patents: Report of the Commissioner of Patents for the Year 1845* (Washington, DC: GPO, 1846); United States Census Office and J. D. B. De Bow, *Statistical View of the United States, Embracing Its Territory, Population – White, Free Colored, and Slave – Moral and Social Condition, Industry, Property, and Revenue ... Being a Compendium of the Seventh Census* (Washington: A. O. P. Nicholson, public printer, 1854); United States Census Office and J. C. G. Kennedy, *Agriculture of the United States in 1860. . .Compiled from the Original Returns of the Eighth Census* (Washington, DC: GPO, 1864).

a wholesome exercise in the context of wider communalism: Shakers in Kentucky and Harmonists in Pennsylvania in particular made notable headway with sericulture, as would the later Mormons of Utah.[86] As is keenly apparent in even a brief survey of the specialist journals, these disparate individuals and groups often viewed one another not as potential competitors, but fellow devotees – a peculiarity of silk boosterism that was perhaps an indication of the fragility of their experiments.

Census records, showing silk return by county, suggest a pattern of regional bursts: few counties around the nation hung on to sustained production over the course of a decade, reflecting the part that would be played by environmental determinism sooner or later; but plenty recorded notable peaks. In 444 counties (out of 1269), silk production had either disappeared completely between 1840 and 1850, or had appeared in an area where it was previously absent. In contrast, only 90 counties showed sustained production. By the late 1840s, it seems clear however that there had been a distinct shift westwards in the limited remaining US production, as old centres in the east abandoned the pursuit, and left the Ohio Valley, Tennessee, and other western regions to ply more localised projects, using mainly white mulberries, and marketing to a regional consumer base. Naturally, the census and patent estimates should be considered very fragile figures – a US commissioner's report even abandoned trying to estimate silk in 1848, noting that '[t]he extreme difficulty of gaining anything like correct estimates of the amount of *silk* in cocoons, or manufactured into raw silk, has induced us to drop this article from the table this year'. Historians have differed in their readings, but it is probably fair to surmise that the drop-off in production was accurate even if the overall level of production of raw silk had been considerably under-reported.[87]

On Maury and Delaware, see: Charles M. Allmond III, 'The Great Silk Bubble', *Delaware History* 11 (1965): 208–28. Other individuals are highlighted in regional pieces, such as: Mabel Agnes Rice, *Trees and Shrubs of Nantucket: Descriptions, Identification Keys, List of Trees and Shrubs* (Ann Arbor, MI: Lithoprinted by Edwards Brothers, Inc., 1946), 20–1; Price, 'Morus Multicaulis, or, Silkworms Must Eat.' Examples of companies which sought to include silk raising among their operations were: Atlantic Silk Company (Nantucket, MA); Rhode Island Silk Company (Providence, RI); Concord Silk Company (Concord, NH); Massachusetts Silk Company (Boston, MA); Beaver Silk Culture and Manufacturing Company (Philadelphia, PA); summarised from various sources in Bishop, Freedley, and Young, *History of American Manufactures*, 2: 392–4; Wyckoff, *American Silk Manufacture*, 16–18.

[86] For a detailed consideration of the output and gifting practices of the Shakers of Pleasant Hill, Kentucky, see Donna Parker and Jonathan Jeffrey, 'Sericulture, Silk and South Union Shakers', *DLSC Faculty Publications Paper* 21 (1993): 1–17.

[87] States, *Annual Report of the Commissioner of Patents, for the Year 1848*, 158. For clashing views, Robert E. Gallman, 'A Note on the Patent Office Crop Estimates, 1841–1848',

A signal indication of the reach of silk networks and the force of their accompanying rhetoric was that advocates of sericulture were more successful in canvassing for city, state, and national support than many other agricultural schemes.[88] Most historians have followed contemporaries in ascribing to the federal government a foundational role in initiating interest through its actions in 1828, when the congressional Committee of Agriculture printed 6,000 copies of a manual on the culture and manufacture of silk, describing it 'of vast national advantage in many points of view', and claiming that the 'climate of every State in the Union is adapted to the culture of silk'.[89] But the relationship between centre and peripheries was multidirectional, for congressional interest was attracted in the first place by silk enthusiasts in early 1826. That proponents from both Pennsylvania (Charles Miner and Peter S. Duponceau) and New York (Stephen van Rensselaer and E. C. Genet) staked claims to have set the initiative afoot, and that the earliest congressional reports discussed silk being grown in Kentucky, New York, Georgia, Pennsylvania, and Connecticut, pointed to pressure arising from multiple regions simultaneously.[90] The development of congressional resolve depended upon the returns sent by the 'Several Governors of States and Territories' to Richard Rush following his circular letter sent out in 1826.[91] The whole exercise was a pyramidal feat of consultation that involved sericulturists across the nation, which would have been largely unworkable twenty years earlier, for it depended on a functionally integrated communication structure. In a short space of time, Rush had heard back from Oliver Wolcott, Governor of Connecticut, who himself heard back from, amongst others, Zalmon Storrs, the postmaster in Mansfield, where Jeffery Sweet mowed the mulberry bushes near Luther Kingsley's little store, in the neighbouring district to Daniel Bulkeley.[92] The existence of localised pockets of silk culture was thus able to influence

The Journal of Economic History 23, no. 2 (1963): 185n1; Rossell, 'The Culture of Silk', 207–8.

[88] For comparative discussions: Pauly, *Fruits and Plains*, 55–8; Majewski, *Modernizing a Slave Economy*, 56.

[89] The manual was presented to Congress on 11 February 1828. D'Homergue and Duponceau, *Essays on American Silk*, 6.

[90] For different verdicts on the relative case of these instigators: E. C. Genet, 'Notes on the Growth and Manufacture of Silk in the United States', *New England Farmer*, 4 (1826): 380; Cole, 'Agricultural Crazes', 628; Rossell, 'The Culture of Silk', 29–30; Pauly, *Fruits and Plains*, 103. U.S. *House Report* No. 182, 'Mulberry-Silk Worm.' 1826. 19th Cong., 1st sess., 2 May.

[91] Richard Rush, 'Circular Letter to the Several Governors of States and Territories', 29 July 1826, in *New England Farmer* 5 (1827): 69–70.

[92] Letter from Oliver Wolcott to Zalmon Storrs, Windham, 19 August 1826. Folder XXXVIII: 18, Oliver Wolcott, Jr. Papers, Connecticut Historical Society, Hartford. Storrs later ran a silk-thread-manufacturing company with his sons in Mansfield Hollow.

national authorities, whose attention, in turn, rebounded to further galvanise editors, postmasters, nurserymen, enthusiasts, and ordinary farmers.

Silk culture went on to receive a high degree of federal assistance and patronage, though never extending to the national bounty system or educational programmes that its advocates desired, or that had preceded it in British America. Congress paid to subsidise, translate and disseminate thousands of copies of treatises, and lent its seal of approval through the positive reports of numerous Committees of Agriculture and the Census and Patent Offices (which enumerated production and supported technological developments). Much of this success should be put down to the way in which the objective of silk culture straddled the deepening political divide as the United States moved towards the so-called Second Party System after 1828, with its divide between Democrats and Whigs.

A majority of silk advocates were proto-Whigs, men who viewed the nurturing of manufacturing capacity and commercial integration as objectives worthy of national intervention.[93] But growing trees and feeding worms also carried significant appeal for many Jacksonian Democrats with their paramount emphasis on empowering producers. South Carolina Democrat George McDuffie complained about Congress paying for one of the silk manuals in 1830, not on partisan grounds but because it was 'too complex for unlettered people ... Persons in his part of the country, who made many pounds of silk every year, could derive no benefit from this book'.[94] Some 28 Jacksonians voted for a motion in February 1833 to print and distribute another manual written by Jonathan H. Cobb of Boston, enough to carry the bill by a margin of 81 to 75 (67 of which opponents were fellow party members). Democrat acquiescence at the federal level, however, only went as far as supporting dissemination: more ambitious schemes, such as Peter S. Duponceau and Jean D'Homergue's proposal to create a national training filature in Philadelphia, were narrowly defeated, while petitions seeking preferential land grants and corporate patronage were quickly dismissed.[95]

Jean D'Homergue of Nîmes (France) had first offered his services to the Committee of Agriculture in 1829 in a very ambitious proposal.

[93] For the classic overview of this divide, Michael F. Holt, *The Rise and Fall of the American Whig Party: Jacksonian Politics and the Onset of the Civil War* (New York: Oxford University Press, 1999).

[94] US *House Journal*. 1830. 21st Cong., 1st sess., 3 May. Fellow Jacksonian James Wayne of Georgia disagreed, and 'referred to societies formed or forming in Georgia' that would benefit from circulating materials.

[95] For the congressional debates on this and other motions, see US *House Journal*: 21st Cong., 2nd sess., 21 December 1830; 21st Cong., 2nd sess., 11 February 1831; 22nd Cong., 1st sess., 20 January 1832 and 22 May 1832.

D'Homergue planned to train up sixty young men aged 18–25, selected by the President from across the United States in proportion to congressional representation. These trainee directors would learn filature management with D'Homergue, using a workforce of twenty-odd local women, and would then carry this expertise back to their states. Instead of waiting on Congress, D'Homergue erected a filature in Philadelphia with ten reeling machines, hired women, and purchased cocoons from all parts of the United States. It was their labour that culminated in the weaving of the two symbolic US flags mentioned earlier in the chapter. Samples of the silk were also sent to England, France, and a small amount sold in Mexico. But it was a signal warning that the fledgling American throwsters to whom D'Homergue sent his raw silk were unable to process it, having a backlog of too much China silk to work up.[96]

Still more impressive than congressional support were the results that the silk circuit secured at the state level. One by one, legislatures relented under pressure from associations, and passed supportive measures.[97] In Delaware, resolutions were passed between 1829 and 1845 to make lands tax-free for ten years if devoted to growing mulberry trees, to give bounties on cocoon production, and to increase criminal penalties for the wilful injury or destruction of mulberry trees or silk equipment.[98] The bounty paid in Pennsylvania was $4,418 in 1841, and Ohio paid out $6,700 the next year.[99] State legislatures and executives also initiated their own programmes of research and dissemination, as occurred in 1830 when the New Hampshire legislature dispatched a committee to Connecticut to observe and document the best practices in production.[100]

The shape of state support for sericulture reflected the heavier regional production in the north-east, yet belied any categorical sectional or class division: the Georgia bounty was higher than any of the New England states, while Kentucky deliberately skewed its bounty to offer greater

---

[96] D'Homergue and Duponceau, *Essays on American Silk*, 8, 15.

[97] Like the specialist publications, most of these bounties lasted only for a short time: Connecticut, 1832–9; Massachusetts, 1835–1848; Vermont, 1835–1845; Maine, 1836–1903; Delaware, 1829–1845; New Jersey & Georgia, 1838–9; Pennsylvania, 1838–1843; Illinois, 1839–1842; Ohio, 1839–1844; New York, 1841–1846. For a summary of measures see Fred W. Powell, 'Industrial Bounties and Rewards by American States', *The Quarterly Journal of Economics* 28, no. 1 (1913): 194–7; Rossell, 'The Culture of Silk', 188–90; Louis Hartz, *Economic Policy and Democratic Thought: Pennsylvania, 1776–1860*, Studies in Economic History (Cambridge, MA: Harvard University Press, 1948), 333.

[98] Allmond III, 'The Great Silk Bubble', 214–17.

[99] Ellsworth, Colman, and Gaylord, *Improvements in Agriculture*, 17.

[100] Joseph M. Harper, *Mr. Harper's Report to the Legislature of the State of New-Hampshire on the Culture of Silk* (Concord: Jacob Bailey Moore Pamphlet Collection (Library of Congress), 1830), 13–15.

encouragement to smaller producers. By 1839, the citizens of Somerset County were able to petition the Maryland legislature without even bothering to go into any depth, so assured were they that the General Assembly would already be familiar with 'what is known, and with what is anticipated'. Rather, they boldly warned their legislators to take action to emulate silk bounties in other states, or leave 'Maryland far in the rear of the enlightened policy of the age, and cause the cheeks of her sons to tingle with the blush of shame' and face the consequences of headlong emigration.[101] Occasional public and municipal initiatives also received state support: in New York, there was an innovative departure from the contract system that prevailed in penitentiary workshops, as prisons including Sing Sing and Auburn were marshalled towards undertaking and supporting sericulture. Convicts at both institutions planted mulberry trees, and set up silk-throwing works taking in cocoons from all over the nation, using not contractors but state-owned machinery and state marketing of their output. The penitential silk experiments were wound up in 1843, as they were not making an adequate profit, and had found the noise of the silkworms or silk-making machinery provided too much opportunity for prisoner communication, in contravention of the strict rule of silence.[102]

A Familiar Tail

In spite of such wide and innovative encouragement, the sustained problems which beset American sericulturists eventually overwhelmed the associational structures and arguments that they had doggedly built to support their efforts. Much had been proven to be possible, but rarely had it been proven to be profitable – either according to commercial returns or medium-term sustainability. Though largely absent from the mainstream silk press, depressing news had often punctuated private correspondence and company records when scrutinised closely: accounts of frozen mulberry roots, raw silk with knots in it that was impossible to work up, impossibly low returns, diseased trees and worms, and people abandoning mulberry trees and sericulture as fast as they took it up.[103] The

---

[101] *Memorial of a Committee of the Citizens of Somerset County, Asking a Bounty on the Domestic Production of Silk* (Annapolis: William M'Neir, 1839), 3, 5.

[102] *Laws of the State of New-York, Passed at the Fifty-Eighth Session of the Legislature, Begun and Held at the City of Albany, The Sixth Day of January, 1835* (Albany: E. Croswell, 1835), 341–44. W. David Lewis, *From Newgate to Dannemora: The Rise of the Penitentiary in New York, 1796–1848* (Ithaca, NY: Cornell University Press, 1965), 193–6.

[103] For Bulkeley [DB], see for example, letters from Justus Blanchard to DB, 25 June 1832, Catskill NY; Edmund Badger to DB, 2 August 1833, Philadelphia; John B. Chapman to DB, 12 December 1834, Warehouse Point [CT]; Thomas Gibson to DB, 1 June 1834,

fundamental reasons for the failure of attempts to produce raw silk in the antebellum United States were the same as those that had compromised late-colonial experimentation. Part-buried under the mulch of wishful agricultural nationalism, they would break through in turn to strangle personal, communal, and corporate aspirations.

In no region of the United States did the environmental requirements and the labour configuration fit well enough together to allow sericulture to endure effectively. Put crudely, moving on an axis from north-east to south-west, the temperatures got warmer, which allowed for stronger prospects of aligning the needs of mulberry trees and silkworms, but the demographics and configuration of the labour base became less service-able, with sparser populations as well as the formidable configuration of the cotton-slavery complex throughout much of the South.[104] Large, sedentary, and concentrated peasant populations able to incorporate a short burst of intensive domestic labour into their late springtime agricultural routines, typically operating within a compressed cash or wage nexus, was what raw silk ordinarily required. In the silk-producing areas of France, for example, with their high population densities in 1840, landlessness, underemployment, and low wages encouraged families to supplement income with work in sericulture and rural industries, a pattern matched in other high-density European regions such as north-ern Italy and Sicily. In contrast, neither the restless land-rich and labour-scarce free-farming populations in the United States (whose population density was less than ten people per square mile in 1840), nor the relent-lessly expanding numbers of enslaved workers whose worsening fates and increasing values were bound up with cotton expansionism, offered a conducive fit for such a fragile endeavour.[105]

Conneaut; A. B. Jones to DB, 25 July 1837, Bucklands Corner [MA]; S. & N. Richmond to DB, 23 November 1830, Providence RI; all in Taintor-Davis Family Papers, AAS. For Northampton Association see 'Northampton Association of Education and Industry Records, 1836–53', MSS Dept. Folio Vols 'N', Volume 4 (Correspondence), letters to David Hall, 3 February 1843; to C. T. Talbot & Co., 15 April 1844; to Messrs Bullard, Lee & Co., 31 May 1844; to John Miller, 30 December 1844; to Thomas Whitlemore, 28 January 1845.

[104] For a visual expression of this density, 'Population of the US by density (1830, 1840)', in Francis A. Walker, *Statistical Atlas of the United States Based on the Results of the Ninth Census 1870* (New York: Library of Congress, 1874), 66. On comparative population density and labour: Alexander B. Murphy, Douglas L. Johnson, and Viola Haarmann, *Cultural Encounters with the Environment: Enduring and Evolving Geographic Themes* (Oxford: Rowman & Littlefield, 2000), 99–101.

[105] David B. Grigg, *Population Growth and Agrarian Change: An Historical Perspective* (Cambridge: Cambridge University Press, 1980), 196–97; Norman John Greville. Pounds, *An Historical Geography of Europe, 1500–1840* (Cambridge: Cambridge University Press, 1979), 309–17.

In a handful of regions, and most notably Connecticut, a mix of textile heritage and comparatively high localised population density (over fifty per square mile) offered a genuine foothold for production. But environmental factors in most of these locales undermined sustainability sooner or later, usually through periods of cold weather. Despite claims of their hardiness, in the 1840s a string of cold winters tore through young mulberries (and especially *M. multicaulis* orchards in the east), culminating in a fungal blight in 1844 which devastated the weakened trees. Quite apart from the extra labour costs associated with locating adequate mulberry leaves and sustaining silkworms in colder climes (as Swedish authors had discovered in the eighteenth century), the volume and quality of the cocoons produced under adverse conditions were likely to be deficient. Variable cocoon-sorting practices and cocoon-reeling methods also undermined the quality and consistency of the product, especially where undertaken by novices, and in combination with inferior or partial harvests that encouraged a trend towards thicker and less workable raw silk skeins. The geographic spread of production and unreliable seasonal yields made centralised reeling operations (filatures) uneconomic, while the variability of domestic output frustrated manufacturers trying to work up the raw silk, who turned to imports of superior grade from China and Italy that could be more reliably acquired and could better tolerate mechanised processing. If producers managed to resolve issues of temperature, humidity, sourcing stock, ensuring attentive labour, avoiding silkworm disease, maintaining cocoon quality, and sorting and reeling effectively, they were doing extraordinarily well. But the point of take-off was always tantalisingly beyond reach, and the next year would throw up an unforeseen challenge, proving that silk was harder to naturalise than anticipated – harder than rival products or rival income-securing activities.[106]

The distinctive circuitry that gave cohesion to the antebellum silk movement also contributed to its downfall, with its unbridled boosterism and its insulation against learning from failure. The consensual literature on silk was not, as it often claimed, the result of a sober and empirically rooted dialectic moving towards progressive synthesis, but rather a house of cards. Omissions, exaggerations, false claims, and inflated 'scientific' data in the chorus of pro-silk propaganda all played their part in concealing the scale of the gap between rhetoric and reality. Some of it was undoubtedly benignly

---

[106] For discussions of the failure of sericulture, see Pauly, *Fruits and Plains*, 103–4; Allmond III, 'The Great Silk Bubble', 209; Klose, 'Sericulture in the United States', 226–7; Margrave, *Emigration of Silk Workers*, 22–7; Rossell, 'The Culture of Silk', 38–44; Howard S. Russell, *A Long, Deep Furrow: Three Centuries of Farming in New England* (Hanover, NH: University Press of New England, 1976), 382–3.

fuelled by the optimistic self-confidence so characteristic of the era.[107] Some also leaned towards the fraudulent: nurserymen and entrepreneurs stood to gain, of course, from offloading swiftly propagated *M. multicaulis* trees, millions of which were advertised and sold through the pages of the silk journals and general publications.[108] Editors had a vested interest – and, as they saw it, a responsibility to their subscribers – in trumpeting new culturists, ventures, inventions, and companies. But when the speculation in *M. multicaulis* trees collapsed, coinciding with an acute economic depression from 1837 to 1843, it carried away with it not only a huge amount of capital but also the long-term credibility of the larger silk movement.[109]

Many producers struggled on, motivated by conviction, pride, or desperation, and with some localised successes. But they did so in an environment increasingly characterised by scepticism (as other defects in sericulture were increasingly discussed and exposed), and marked by the abandonment of enterprises, journals, and orchards. By the late 1840s sericulture was consigned to the margins in established parts of the country – though some of the old plaudits would resurface in attempts in California, Utah, and Kansas in the second half of the century.[110] Writing in 1876, Linus Brockett mocked the rhetorical excesses of earlier generations: 'No one expects to see in the present generation, every citizen of the great Republic sitting under the shade of his own *multicaulis* trees ... Nor does any one believe, that in our time, every farmer will go to his work in silk attire, or that every milk-maid will attend to her duties, in a brocaded silk with a trail two yards in length.'[111] But although it

[107] Joyce Oldham Appleby, *Inheriting the Revolution: The First Generation of Americans* (Cambridge, MA: Belknap Press, 2000), 56–89.
[108] The most famous case of alleged commercial fraud involved Samuel Whitmarsh, on which see: *The Farmer's Register*, 4, No. 9 (January 1837): 558–9. Clark, *The Communitarian Moment: The Radical Challenge of the Northampton Association*, 32–3; Rossell, 'The Culture of Silk', 131–3.
[109] Nelson Klose suggests that many speculated with the *M. multicaulis* in an attempt to recoup fortunes reduced by the Panic of 1837. Klose, 'Sericulture in the United States', 227. Others have assumed that efforts at sericulture ended abruptly with the speculation (e.g. James Oliver Robertson and Janet C. Robertson, *All Our Yesterdays: A Century of Family Life in an American Small Town* (New York: HarperCollins Publishers, 1993), 159), whereas there is good evidence of continued attempts, not least in the census production figures.
[110] Clark S. Monson, 'Mulberry Trees: The Basis and Remnant of the Utah Silk Industry', *Economic Botany* 50, no. 1 (1996): 130–8; Nelson Klose, 'California's Experimentation in Sericulture', *Pacific Historical Review* 30 (1961): 213–27; L. O. Howard, 'The United States Department of Agriculture and Silk Culture', in *Yearbook of the United States Department of Agriculture, 1903*, ed. G. W. Hill (Washington, DC: Government Printing Office, 1904), 139.
[111] Brockett, *The Silk Industry in America*, 131.

quickly became easy to ridicule the 'new clothes' of the antebellum silk movement – and 'multicaulis' became an expression for absurd get-rich-quick schemes – its accomplishment was nonetheless profound.[112] Sericulturists were hamstrung by environmentally imposed constraints and often self-defeating in their posturing. Yet they advanced a unique and inclusive form of agricultural nationalism and sustained it for decades, by linking individual experimenters of all classes and regions together, behind a creative rhetoric that virtuously reconciled agriculture with manufacturing, production with consumption, and progress with nostalgia. If we look past their innumerable individual failures, we find not only occasional meaningful production but also a powerful lesson in imagined collectivism.

The challenge of making silk American had been accomplished, and had helped to bring new silk-related manufactories to the United States, especially in the north-east, where demand would grow for raw materials, and capacity and market share grow into the later nineteenth century. The challenge of making American raw silk had been embraced, particularly at the behest of female labourers. Sometimes it had turned into sporadic and fleeting successes, helping to generate a wide array of improvised silk ware which had limited economic value or circulation but was often laden with meaning for its participants. But the challenge of making American raw silk profitable remained a dream that had once again unravelled, some 300 years and 3,000 miles from where it had begun in earnest.

---

[112] The oral history of this expression is reported in Ryland, 'America's "Multicaulis Mania"', 26. This association can be overstated, however, and Arthur Cole was quite wrong to suggest that 'one finds little or no indication that high hopes ever centered upon' *M. alba*, and to be 'inclined to associate all immoderate statements about mulberry cultivation with the rapidly advancing morus multicaulis'. Cole, 'Agricultural Crazes', 629.

Select Bibliography

Anishanslin, Zara. *Portrait of a Woman in Silk: Hidden Histories of the British Atlantic World*. New Haven: Yale University Press, 2016.

Aram, Bethany, and Bartolomé Yun Casalilla. *Global Goods and the Spanish Empire, 1492–1824: Circulation, Resistance and Diversity*. London: Palgrave Macmillan, 2014.

Arteaga, Diego. 'Vestido y desnudo: La seda en Cuenca (Ecuador) durante los siglos XVI y XVII.' *Artesanías de América: Revista Del CIDAP* 58 (2005): 189–205.

Auslander, Leora. *Cultural Revolutions: The Politics of Everyday Life in Britain, North America and France*. Oxford: Berg, 2009.

Battistini, Francesco. *Gelsi, Bozzoli e Caldaie: L'industria della seta in Toscana Tra Citt ..., Borghi e Campagne (Sec. XVI–XVIII)*. L'officina Dello Storico. Florence: L. S. Olschki, 1998.

Berg, Maxine, and Elizabeth Eger. *Luxury in the Eighteenth Century: Debates, Desires and Delectable Goods*. Basingstoke: Palgrave Macmillan, 2003.

Bigelow, Allison M. 'Gendered Language and the Science of Colonial Silk.' *Early American Literature* 49, no. 2 (2014): 271–325.

Borah, Woodrow Wilson. *Silk Raising in Colonial Mexico*. Berkeley and Los Angeles: University of California Press, 1943.

Brockett, L. P. *The Silk Industry in America, a History: Prepared for the Centennial Exposition*. New York: Silk Association of America, 1876.

Campos, Teresa de, and Teresa Castelló Yturbide. *Historia y arte de la seda en México: siglos XVI–XX*. Mexico City: Banamex, 1990.

Chandra Guha, Sujit. *Silk Industry of Malda and Murshidabad from 1660 to 1833: A Study of Its Production Organisation, Production Relations, Market and the Effect of Decline on the Economy of the People*. Shivmandir: N. L. Publishers, 2003.

Chicco, Giuseppe. *La seta in Piemonte 1650–1800. Un sistema industriale d'ancien regime*. Milan: Angeli, 1995.

Ciriacono, Salvatore. 'Silk Manufacturing in France and Italy in the XVIIth Century: Two Models Compared.' *The Journal of European Economic History* 10, no. 1 (1981): 167–200.

Ciszuk, Martin. 'Silk-Weaving in Sweden during the 19th Century.' Licentiate thesis, Chalmers University of Technology, Gothenburg, 2012.

Cizakca, Murat. 'A Short History of the Bursa Silk Industry (1500–1900).' *Journal of the Economic and Social History of the Orient* 23, no. 1/2 (April 1980): 142–52.

Cobb, Matthew. 'Malpighi, Swammerdam and the Colourful Silkworm: Replication and Visual Representation in Early Modern Science.' *Annals of Science* 59, no. 2 (January 2002): 111–47.

Coles, Peter. *Mulberry*. London: Reaktion Books, 2019.

Comisión Española de la Ruta de la Seda, El. *España y Portugal en las rutas de la seda: Diez siglos de producción y comercio entre oriente y occidente*. Barcelona: Universitat de Barcelona Publicacions, 1996.

Davini, Roberto. 'Bengali Raw Silk, the East India Company and the European Global Market, 1770–1833.' *Journal of Global History* 4 (2009): 57–79.

Dunlevy, Mairead. *Pomp and Poverty: A History of Silk in Ireland*. New Haven: Yale University Press, 2011.

Eacott, Jonathan. *Selling Empire: India in the Making of Britain and America, 1600–1830*. Chapel Hill, NC: University of North Carolina Press, 2017.

Farrell, William. 'Smuggling Silks into Eighteenth-Century Britain: Geography, Perpetrators, and Consumers.' *Journal of British Studies* 55, no. 2 (11 April 2016): 268–94.

Federico, G. *An Economic History of the Silk Industry, 1830–1930*. Cambridge: Cambridge University Press, 1997.

Field, Jacqueline, Marjorie Senechal, and Madelyn Shaw. *American Silk, 1830–1930: Entrepreneurs and Artifacts*. Lubbock: Texas Tech University Press, 2007.

Flynn, Dennis O, and Arturo Giráldez. 'Silk for Silver: Manila-Macao Trade in the 17th Century.' *Philippine Studies* 44 (1996): 52–68.

Garzón Pareja, Manuel. *La industria sedera en España: El arte de la seda de Granada*. Granada: Archivo de la Real Chancillería, 1972.

Gasch Tomás, José Luis. 'Global Trade, Circulation and Consumption of Asian Goods in the Atlantic World: The Manila Galleons and the Social Elites of Mexico and Seville (1580–1640).' PhD thesis, European University Institute, Florence, 2012.

Good, I. L., J. M. Kenoyer, and R. H. Meadow. 'New Evidence for Early Silk in the Indus Civilization.' *Archaeometry* 51 (2009): 457–66.

Halde, J. B. Du, and Mario Bussagli. *Seta*. Milan: F. M. Ricci, 2001.

Hatch, Charles E. 'Mulberry Trees and Silkworms: Sericulture in Early Virginia.' *The Virginia Magazine of History and Biography* 65 (1957): 3–61.

Haulman, Kate. *The Politics of Fashion in Eighteenth-Century America*. Chapel Hill, NC: University of North Carolina Press, 2011.

Herzig, Edmund M. 'The Iranian Raw Silk Trade and European Manufacture.' In *Textiles: Production, Trade and Demand*, edited by Maureen Fennell Mazzaoui, 27–43. Aldershot: Ashgate, 1998.

Hodacs, Hanna. *Silk and Tea in the North: Scandinavian Trade and the Market for Asian Goods in Eighteenth-Century Europe*. London: Palgrave Macmillan, 2016.

Hutková, Karolina. 'The British Silk Connection: The English East India Company's Silk Enterprise in Bengal, 1757–1812.' PhD thesis, University of Warwick, 2015.

Istituto Internazionale di Storia Economica. *La seta in Europa sec. XII–XX*. Edited by Simonetta Cavaciocchi. Florence: Le Monnier, 1993.

Jacoby, David. 'Silk Production.' In *The Oxford Handbook of Byzantine Studies*, edited by Elizabeth Jeffreys, John F. Haldon, and Robin Cormack, 421–8. Oxford: Oxford University Press, 2008.

Jirousek, Charlotte E. 'The End of the Silk Road: Implications of the Decline of Turkish Sericulture.' *Textile History* 29, no. 2 (1998): 201–25.

Johansson Åbonde, Anders. 'Drömmen Om Svenskt Silke: Silkesodlingens Historia i Sverige 1735–1920.' Licentiate thesis, Swedish University of Agricultural Sciences, Alnarp, 2010.

Kerridge, Eric. *Textile Manufactures in Early Modern England*. Manchester: Manchester University Press, 1985.

King, Brenda M. *Silk and Empire*. Manchester: Manchester University Press, 2005.

Kisch, Herbert. 'Prussian Mercantilism and the Rise of the Krefeld Silk Industry: Variations upon an Eighteenth-Century Theme.' *Transactions of the American Philosophical Society* 58, no. 7 (1968): 3–50.

Klose, Nelson. 'Sericulture in the United States.' *Agricultural History* 37, no. 4 (1963): 225–34.

Kriger, Colleen E. *Cloth in West African History*. Lanham: AltaMira Press, 2006.

Kuhn, Dieter, ed. *Chinese Silks*. New Haven: Yale University Press, 2012.

Leibsohn, Dana. 'Made in China, Made in Mexico.' In *At the Crossroads: The Arts of Spanish America & Early Global Trade, 1492–1850*, edited by Donna Pierce and Ronald Y. Otsuka, 11–41. Denver Art Museum, 2012.

Lemire, Beverly, and Giorgio Riello. 'East & West: Textiles and Fashion in Early Modern Europe.' *Journal of Social History* 41, no. 4 (2008): 887–916.

Liu, Xinru. *Silk and Religion: An Exploration of Material Life and the Thought of People, AD 600–1200*. Delhi: Oxford University Press, 1996.

Luu, Lien Bich. 'French-Speaking Refugees and the Foundation of the London Silk Industry in the Sixteenth Century.' *Proceedings of the Huguenot Society* 26 (1997): 564–76.

Ma, Debin. 'The Great Silk Exchange: How the World Was Connected and Developed.' In *Pacific Centuries: Pacific and Pacific Rim History since the Sixteenth Century*, edited by Dennis Owen Flynn, Lionel Frost, and A. J. H. Latham, 38–65. London: Routledge, 1999.

Ed. *Textiles in the Pacific, 1500–1900*. The Pacific World. Aldershot: Ashgate/ Variorum, 2005.

Manchester, Herbert. *The Story of Silk & Cheney Silks*. South Manchester, CT: Cheney Brothers, 1916.

Margrave, Richard Dobson. *The Emigration of Silk Workers from England to the United States in the Nineteenth Century, with Special Reference to Coventry, Macclesfield, Paterson, New Jersey, and South Manchester, Connecticut*. New York and London: Garland Publishing, Inc, 1986.

Matthee, Rudolph P. *The Politics of Trade in Safavid Iran Silk for Silver, 1600–1730*. Cambridge: Cambridge University Press, 1999.

Maw, Peter. 'Anglo-American Trade during the Industrial Revolution: A Study of the Lancashire and Yorkshire Textile Industries, 1750–1825.' PhD thesis, University of Manchester, 2005.

McKinney, E., and J. B. Eicher. 'Unexpected Luxury: Wild Silk Textile Production among the Yoruba of Nigeria.' *Textile – the Journal of Cloth & Culture* 7, no. 1 (2009): 40–55.

Miller, Lesley Ellis. *Selling Silks: A Merchant's Sample Book 1764*. London: V&A Press, 2014.

Miralles Martínez, Pedro. 'Seda, trabajo y sociedad en la Murcia del siglo XVII.' PhD thesis, Universidad de Murcia, 2000.

Molà, Luca, Reinhold C. Mueller, Claudio Zanier, and Cini Giorgio, eds. *La seta in Italia dal medioevo al seicento: Dal baco al drappo*. Venice: Marsilio, 2000.

Molà, Luca. *The Silk Industry of Renaissance Venice*. Baltimore, MD: Johns Hopkins University Press, 2000.

Monson, Clark S. 'Mulberry Trees: The Basis and Remnant of the Utah Silk Industry.' *Economic Botany* 50, no. 1 (1996): 130–8.

Montgomery, Florence M. *Textiles in America, 1650–1870: A Dictionary Based on Original Documents, Prints and Paintings, Commercial Records, American Merchants' Papers, Shopkeepers' Advertisements, and Pattern Books with Original Swatches of Cloth*. 2 vols. New York: Norton, 1984.

Muthesius, Anna. 'The Byzantine Silk Industry: Lopez and Beyond.' *Journal of Medieval History* 19, no. 1–2 (January 1993): 1–67.

Olivares Galvañ, Pedro. *Historia de La Seda En Murcia*. 2nd ed. Murcia: Editora Regional de Murcia, 2005.

Phipps, Elena. 'The Iberian Globe: Textile Traditions and Trade in Latin America.' In *Interwoven Globe: The Worldwide Textile Trade, 1500–1800*, edited by Amelia Peck, 28–45. London: Thames and Hudson, 2013.

Prakash, Om. 'From Negotiation to Coercion: Textile Manufacturing in India in the Eighteenth Century.' *Modern Asian Studies* 41, no. 6 (2007): 1331–68.

Ransome, David R., and David C. Lees. 'The Virginian Silkworm: From Myth to Moth. Or: How a Businessman Turned into a Naturalist.' *Antenna* 41, no. 3 (2017): 120–7.

Roche, Daniel. *The Culture of Clothing: Dress and Fashion in the Ancien Regime*. Cambridge: Cambridge University Press, 1994.

Rosquillas Quilés, Hortensia. 'El sello de la seda en la Mixteca Alta.' *Restuara: Revista Electrónica de Conservación* 1 (2000): 1–10.

Rothstein, Natalie. 'Silk in the Early Modern Period, c.1500–1780.' In *The Cambridge History of Western Textiles*, edited by David Jenkins, 528–61. Cambridge: Cambridge University Press, 2003.

Ryland, Elizabeth Hawes. 'America's "Multicaulis Mania".' *The William and Mary Quarterly, 2nd Ser.* 19, no. 1 (1939): 25–33.

Savoie, Ronald. 'The Silk Industry in Northampton.' *Historical Journal of Western Massachusetts* 5 (1977): 21–32.

Schäfer, Dagmar, Giorgio Riello, and Luca Molà, eds. *Threads of Global Desire: Silk in the Pre-Modern World*. Woodbridge: Boydell and Brewer, 2018.

Schoeser, Mary, and Bruno Marcandalli. *Silk*. New Haven: Yale University Press, 2007.

Schorta, Regula, ed. *18th-Century Silks: The Industries of England and Northern Europe*. Riggisberg: Abegg-Stiftung, 2000.

Scott, Alison V. *Literature and the Idea of Luxury in Early Modern England*. Abingdon: Routledge, 2016.

Scott, Philippa. *The Book of Silk*. London: Thames and Hudson, 1993.

Shaw, Madelyn. 'Silk in Georgia, 1732–1840: From Sericulture to Status Symbol.' In *Decorative Arts in Georgia: Historic Sites, Historic Contents*, edited by Ashley Callahan, 59–78. Athens, GA: Georgia Museum of Art, 2008.

Sousa, Fernando de. 'The Silk Industry in Trás-Os-Montes during the Ancient Regime.' *Journal of Portuguese History* 3, no. 2 (2005): 1–14.

Stockard, Janice E. 'On Women's Work in Silk Reeling: Gender, Labor, and Technology in the Historical Silk Industries of Connecticut and South China.' In *Silk Roads, Other Roads: Proceedings of the Textile Society of America Biennial Symposium*. Northampton, MA: Textile Society of America, 2002. https://digitalcommons.unl.edu/tsaconf/419/

Stockland, E. 'Patriotic Natural History and Sericulture in the French Enlightenment.' *Archives of Natural History* 44, no. 1 (2017): 1–18.

Styles, John. *The Dress of the People: Everyday Fashion in Eighteenth-Century England*. New Haven: Yale University Press, 2007.

Takeda, Junko T. 'Global Insects: Silkworms, Sericulture, and Statecraft in Napoleonic France and Tokugawa Japan.' *French History* 28, no. 2 (2014): 207–25.

Tassinari, Bernard. *La soie à Lyon: De la grande fabrique aux textiles du XXIe siècle*. Lyons: Editions lyonnaises d'art et d'histoire, 2005.

Teisseyre-Sallmann, Line. *L'industrie de la soie en Bas-Languedoc: XVIIe–XVIIIe siècles*. Paris: École nationale des chartes, 1995.

Thornton, Peter. *Baroque and Rococo Silks*. London: Faber and Faber, 1965.

Tuskes, Paul M., James P. Tuttle, and Michael M. Collins. *The Wild Silk Moths of North America : A Natural History of the Saturniidae of the United States and Canada*. Ithaca, NY: Comstock Pub. Associates, 1996.

Vainker, Shelagh. *Chinese Silk: A Cultural History*. New Brunswick: Rutgers University Press, 2004.

Warner, Frank. *The Silk Industry of the United Kingdom: Its Origin and Development*. London: Drane's, 1921.

Wright, Louis B. *The Dream of Prosperity in Colonial America*. New York: New York University Press, 1965.

Wyckoff, William C. *American Silk Manufacture*. New York: John L. Murphy Publishing Co, 1887.

Zahedieh, Nuala. *The Capital and the Colonies: London and the Atlantic Economy, 1660–1700*. Cambridge: Cambridge University Press, 2010.

Zanier, Claudio. *Where the Roads Met. East and West in the Silk Production Processes (17th to 19th Centuries)*. Kyoto: Italian School of East Asian Studies, 1994.

Index